Steve Vogel was born in Berlin, where his father, a CIA case officer, served from 1957 to 1962, during some of the tensest years of the Cold War. As a reporter for the W wrote frequently about military af from the wars in Afghanistan and in Afghanistan was part of a pac selected as a finalist for the 2002 Pu in Iraq and the first Gulf War, as w ~~~perations in Rwanda, Somalia, and the Balkans, and the September 11, 2001, terrorist attack on the Pentagon.

Praise for *Betrayal in Berlin*

'This is a fascinating, fast-paced narrative, and Vogel is particularly well-suited to write it' *Washington Post*

'Swiftly moving, richly detailed . . . As well paced as a le Carré novel, with deep insight into the tangled world of Cold War espionage' *Kirkus*

'A fascinating commentary on the height of the Cold War with Eisenhower, Kennedy and Khrushchev intimately involved in the skulduggery in Berlin' Peter Snow

'A crackling Cold War espionage story, *Betrayal in Berlin* takes you to the peaks of spying ambition and the depths of betrayal' David E. Hoffman, author of *The Billion Dollar Spy*

'One of the most dramatic spy stories of the Cold War, superbly told by a real authority on the subject' Michael Dobbs, author of *One Minute to Midnight*

'Through fresh interviews with principal participants and extensive archival research, Steve Vogel has made the story of the Berlin Tunnel new again. I was riveted to the narrative from start to finish' Monte Reel, author of *A Brotherhood of Spies*

'Steve Vogel is a talented and gifted writer who brings the personalities and idiosyncrasies of every participant in this operation to life . . . truly one of those rare books you can't put down' Sandra "Sandy" Grimes, co-author of *Circle of Treason*

ALSO BY STEVE VOGEL

Through the Perilous Fight: Six Weeks That Saved the Nation

The Pentagon: A History

BETRAYAL

IN

BERLIN

George Blake, the Berlin Tunnel and the
Greatest Conspiracy of the Cold War

STEVE VOGEL

JOHN MURRAY

First published in Great Britain in 2019 by John Murray (Publishers)
An Hachette UK company

This paperback edition published in 2020

1

Front matter maps by Gene Thorp

A CIP catalogue record for this title is
available from the British Library

Paperback ISBN 978-1-473-64751-0
eBook ISBN 978-1-473-64750-3

Printed and bound in Great Britain Clays Ltd, Elcograf S.p.A.

John Murray policy is to use papers that are natural, renewable
and recyclable products and made from wood grown in sustainable forests.
The logging and manufacturing processes are expected to conform to
the environmental regulations of the country of origin.

John Murray (Publishers)
Carmelite House
50 Victoria Embankment
London EC4Y 0DZ

www.johnmurraypress.co.uk

To the undying friendship and devoted service of three happy warriors:
Don Vogel, Ben Pepper, and Gus Hathaway

Contents

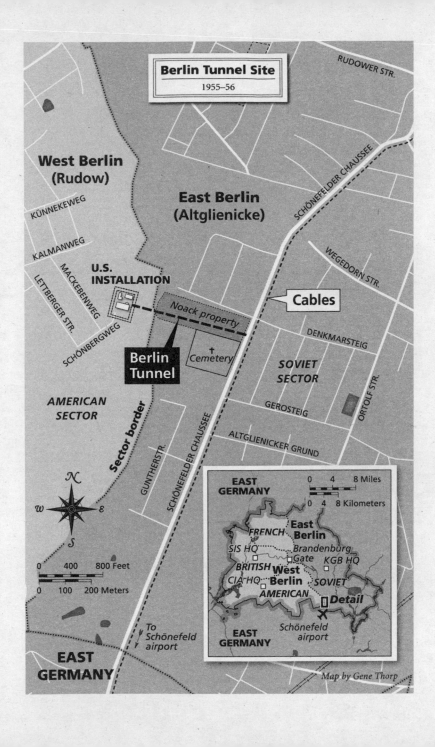

Berlin Tunnel Site
1955–56

West Berlin
(Rudow)

East Berlin
(Altglienicke)

RUDOWER STR.

SCHÖNEFELDER CHAUSSEE

KÜNNEKEWEG

KALMANWEG

U.S.
INSTALLATION

Noack property

Cables

WEGEDORN STR.

LETTBERGER STR.

MACKEBENWEG

Berlin
Tunnel

Cemetery

DENKMARSTEIG

SCHÖNBERGWEG

SOVIET
SECTOR

ORTOLF STR.

AMERICAN
SECTOR

Sector border

GEROSTEIG

ALTGLIENICKER GRUND

GUNTHERSTR.

SCHÖNEFELDER CHAUSSEE

0   400   800 Feet

0   100   200 Meters

To
Schönefeld
airport

EAST
GERMANY

EAST
GERMANY

0   4   8 Miles

0   4   8 Kilometers

FRENCH

SIS HQ

BRITISH

CIA HQ

East
Berlin

Brandenburg
Gate

West
Berlin

AMERICAN

KGB HQ

SOVIET

Detail

EAST
GERMANY

Schönefeld
airport

Map by Gene Thorp

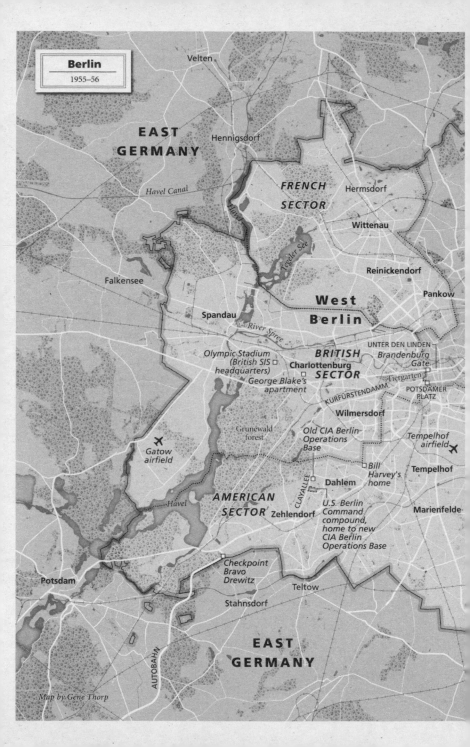

Copenhagen ★ **SWEDEN**
DENMARK Baltic Sea
North **USSR**
Sea
Hamburg ● Schwerin
UNITED **NETHERLANDS** *SOVIET*
KINGDOM Amsterdam ● *BRITISH* Berlin
The Hague ● Hanover ● Wünsdorf ● Warsaw ★
London ★ Rotterdam ● **EAST** **POLAND**
Portsmouth ★ Ostende ● Bonn ● **WEST** **GERMANY**
Brussels ★ **GERMANY** Dresden ●
English Channel **BELGIUM** *FRENCH* Prague ●
LUXEMBOURG Frankfurt ● **CZECHOSLOVAKIA**
Paris ★ Luxembourg *AMERICAN*
Munich ● Vienna ★ Budapest ★
FRENCH *(rock icon)* **HUNGARY**
FRANCE Bern ● **AUSTRIA**
Geneva ● **SWITZERLAND**
Lyon ● Venice ●
YUGOSLAVIA
ITALY
☐ NATO
▨ Neutral or
Non-aligned
▨ Warsaw
Pact
Irun ●
Pamplona ●
SPAIN *Mediterranean Sea*
0   100   200 Miles
0   100   200 Kilometers

Blankenfelde
SOVIET
SECTOR
Weissensee

East
Berlin *Wuhle*
Lichtenberg
Friedrichshain Friedrichsfelde Kaulsdorf **EAST**
KGB **GERMANY**
headquarters
Treptow Karlshorst
Neukölln *River Spree* Schöneiche
Köpenick
Adlershof *Grosser*
AMERICAN **Berlin Tunnel** *Müggelsee* Rahnsdorf
SECTOR *SOVIET*
Rudow Altglienicke *SECTOR*
SCHÖNEFELDER Müggelheim
CHAUSSEE *Langer*
Bohnsdorf *See* *Seddinsee*
Wassmannsdorf
✈ *Schönefeld* *N*
airport *W* ✦ *E*
Zeuthener *S*
See *Crossinsee*
0   2   4 Miles
0   2   4 Kilometers

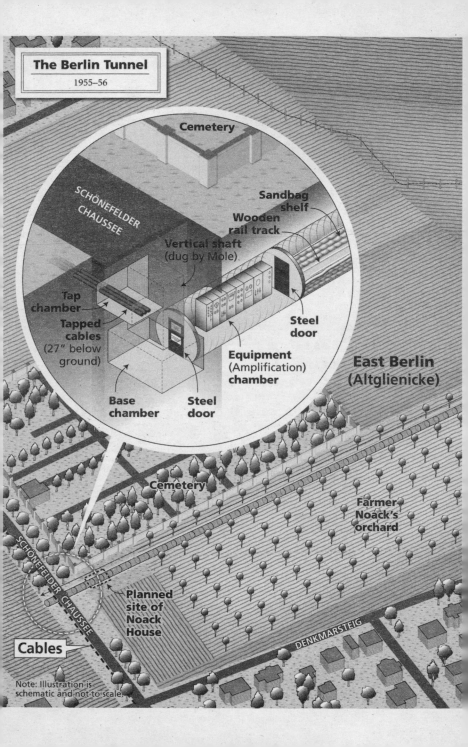

The Berlin Tunnel
1955–56

Cemetery

SCHÖNEFELDER CHAUSSEE

Sandbag shelf

Wooden rail track

Vertical shaft (dug by Mole)

Tap chamber

Tapped cables (27" below ground)

Steel door

Equipment (Amplification) chamber

Base chamber

Steel door

East Berlin (Altglienicke)

Cemetery

Farmer Noack's orchard

SCHÖNEFELDER CHAUSSEE

Planned site of Noack House

DENKMARSTEIG

Cables

Note: Illustration is schematic and not to scale.

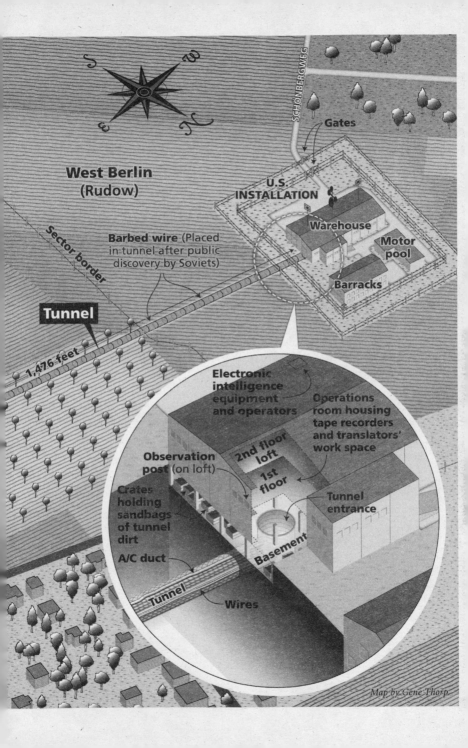

N

W

S

E

SCHÖNBERGWEG

Gates

West Berlin
(Rudow)

Barbed wire (Placed in tunnel after public discovery by Soviets)

Sector border

U.S. INSTALLATION

Warehouse

Motor pool

Barracks

Tunnel

1,476 feet

Electronic intelligence equipment and operators

Operations room housing tape recorders and translators' work space

Observation post (on loft)

2nd floor loft

1st floor

Crates holding sandbags of tunnel dirt

Tunnel entrance

A/C duct

Basement

Tunnel

Wires

Map by Gene Thorp

Prelude

At midnight, the British, American, and French prisoners were taken from the Seoul police headquarters and bundled into the back of a North Korean army truck, guarded by soldiers holding submachine guns and bayonet-tipped rifles. The captives, including diplomats, missionaries, and businessmen, had been rounded up when the North Korean army launched a surprise attack on the south a week earlier and swept into the South Korean capital. When the British diplomats had asked to bring clothes for the journey, they were told, rather ominously, that it would not be necessary.

The prisoners were taken through a landscape of burned villages and bomb craters, the air pungent from the smell of rotting corpses. As they drove, the North Korean officer escorting the captives practiced with his newly issued Russian weapon, firing blindly into the night and further fraying nerves. For an hour, the truck climbed a mountain road, and then continued down into a remote valley, where it came to a halt. George Blake, vice-consul for the British legation in Seoul, exchanged looks with his fellow prisoners. All had the same realization: They had been taken to this isolated spot to be summarily executed. Blake saw that the truck was carrying a spare barrel of gasoline and concluded that it would be used to burn their bodies afterwards. Herbert Lord, a British citizen who served as commissioner for the Salvation Army in Korea, thought it appropriate to lead the group in a short prayer.

Unbeknownst to his captors, as well as to almost all of his fellow prisoners, Blake's diplomatic title was cover for his true role as chief of station in South Korea for the British Secret Intelligence Service (SIS)—also known as MI6. The son of a Dutch woman and a Turkish subject who had fought for the British Empire, Blake had a cosmopolitan background, experience in hazardous situations, and a facility for languages—Russian, German, French, and Dutch, among others—that made him a natural for espionage. Just twenty-eight years old, he had already survived great dangers in Nazi-occupied Europe. After the German conquest of the Netherlands in 1940, Blake, then a schoolboy, served heroically, delivering messages for the Dutch resistance. In 1942, he made a daring escape through France and Spain before he made it to England. There, he joined the Royal Navy and was recruited by the SIS, and at war's end was dispatched to occupied Germany to gather intelligence on the Soviet Red Army. In 1949, he was sent to South Korea, tasked with trying to establish an intelligence network to spy on the Soviets in the Far East.

The North Korean invasion on June 25, 1950, had triggered the Cold War's first armed conflict. The United States, with the support of the United Nations, had rushed troops to defend South Korea, but the unprepared Americans were knocked back almost to the sea by overwhelming North Korean force. Westerners based in Korea were caught up in the chaos accompanying the brutal and dangerous first days of the war.

Now it had come to this. Sitting in the back of the truck awaiting execution, Blake was forcibly struck with a bitter realization of "how perfectly useless" his death would be. After an excruciating wait of twenty minutes, a jeep carrying two North Korean army officers arrived. But instead of overseeing an execution, the officers ordered the vehicles to resume driving north. The prisoners were alive, but their ordeal was only beginning.

———

Blake and his fellow captives were taken to the northern town of Manpo, nestled on the banks of the Yalu River on the frontier with

Manchuria. Over several months, their group grew to include Turkish and White Russian businessmen and their families who had been detained in Seoul. More Western clergy, including elderly French priests and nuns, were also rounded up from across Korea, as well as several journalists, among them Philip Deane, the dashing and cocky correspondent covering the war for the London *Observer*.

The civilian prisoners, now numbering about 70, were being held near a camp holding 777 American prisoners of war—soldiers from the 24th Infantry Division units overrun by the North Koreans at the start of the war. The POWs were in dreadful condition, still wearing the summer fatigues in which they had been captured during the initial weeks of the war, and many now without shoes. These were not battle-hardened veterans of World War II; most were poorly trained and badly equipped conscripts who had been on cushy occupation duty in Japan before being sent into the fight. "They had been taken out of this paradise and thrown into the hell of the Korean War," Blake observed. The civilian prisoners were shocked by the haggard and emaciated appearance of the POWs, many of them infested with lice. "These ragged, dirty, hollow-eyed men did not look like any American soldiers that I had ever seen," recalled Larry Zellers, a lanky Methodist missionary from Texas who had served as an airman in World War II.

But in mid-September, the prospects for all the Western captives suddenly soared. One morning while Zellers was drawing water at a well, a brave Korean schoolboy surreptitiously handed him a note reporting that General Douglas MacArthur, commander of UN forces, had turned the war around with a landing behind enemy lines at Inchon, triggering a massive North Korean retreat with American and UN troops in pursuit. Two weeks later, the prisoners were overjoyed by news that MacArthur had recaptured Seoul and was driving north.

Blake, like the others, believed liberation was at hand, and the captives debated how many days or weeks remained until they were freed. All were deflated when they learned in early October that they were being moved to more secure locations farther from the front. After two weeks at an interim camp, the prisoners marched up a mountain trail to Jui-am-nee, a derelict old mining town. But even at the new location, the sounds of approaching artillery and the disorderly bands of retreating North Korean soldiers who came over the hills pointed to a quick end to the war. "It became clear to us that the North Korean regime was collapsing and the army disintegrating," Blake recalled. The front remained near—American lines were reported to be only fifty miles away, and freedom was tantalizingly close.

———

Escape came naturally to Blake. During his thousand-mile journey across Europe in World War II, he had jumped off a moving train in Belgium to evade German soldiers and trekked across the snowy Pyrenees on a mule trail. So it was no surprise that he was among a band of eight prisoners who planned to make a break. The group persuaded two nervous North Korean guards to help them reach American lines, where they could organize a rescue attempt to free the rest of the prisoners. They set out south on the morning of October 25, taking narrow mountain paths to avoid villages, and slept that night in a small valley. The next day, they encountered three North Korean soldiers moving in the opposite direction who stopped to confer with the two guards accompanying the westerners. The soldiers had stunning news of another turn in the war—Chinese forces had intervened to aid North Korea and had pushed back the Americans. The prisoners concluded that "it was now too dangerous, indeed impossible, to get through to the American lines," Blake recalled. They returned to the camp.

But back at Jui-am-nee, Blake despaired. "I do not want to die in North Korea," he told Jean Meadmore, a French diplomat who had become a close friend. By October 30, he had resolved to make another break for freedom. "I'm going to try to escape tonight—do you come with me?" Blake asked.

Meadmore refused. "It's absolutely doomed to failure," he told Blake. "We haven't got a chance." Deane had agreed to join the escape, but at 11 p.m., when Blake crawled to the correspondent's hole, Deane had changed his mind, calling it too dangerous.

Alone, Blake crawled from the unfenced camp. When he had made it a safe distance, he moved quickly, climbing for two hours to reach the top of a mountain leading to the south. He had been descending in the dark for an hour when a North Korean soldier stepped from behind a bush and barred the path with his rifle. Blake was taken to a nearby farmhouse serving as a headquarters for a North Korean troop encampment. With his rudimentary Korean, he claimed to be a Russian who had lost his way, but the North Koreans were not fooled. In the morning, soldiers accused him of being an American spy and shouted that he would be shot.

Blake was then escorted back to the camp by a North Korean army major who was taking command of the detainees. In front of an assembly of prisoners, the officer berated him for twenty minutes before releasing him with a warning that he would be summarily shot if he again tried to escape.

That afternoon, October 31, the new commanding officer addressed the prisoners. The major was tall and lithe, wearing knee breeches and a tight-fitting jacket, and he moved nervously, his mouth in a perpetual grimace. He announced that the civilian detainees, together with the American POWs, were about to begin "a long march" to stay ahead of the advancing front line. No transport was available because of the critical situation in the field. Everyone—elderly missionaries, nuns, mothers with children, weak and sick POWs in bare feet—would have to walk.

"But they will die if they have to march," protested Herbert Lord, the Salvation Army commissioner, who spoke fluent Korean.

"Then let them march till they die," replied the major.

The prisoners were ordered to toss aside any item the major deemed a weapon, including walking sticks and even rolled-up sleeping mats. Father Paul Villemot, an eighty-two-year-old French priest, had to surrender his cane. The prisoners passed word among each other—the vicious new commander would be called the Tiger.

Late that afternoon, the long and wretched line of more than eight hundred prisoners began marching northeast along the Yalu River. The POWs were in front, divided into sections, each with a U.S. officer held responsible for their progress. North Korean guards trotted alongside, screaming in the prisoners' ears: "*Bali! Bali!* Quickly! Quickly!"

It was midnight before the column stopped to rest. After several sleepless hours on the cold, wet ground, the prisoners resumed the march. The brutal pace demanded by the Tiger was too much for many GIs, already weakened by their meager daily ration of half-cooked corn, and soon the columns were falling apart. Weaker prisoners unable to keep pace fell along the road. The Tiger assembled the group leaders and demanded that the commander of the section with the most stragglers identify himself.

Lieutenant Cordus H. Thornton of Longview, Texas, calmly stepped forward. The Tiger demanded to know why he had allowed his men to drop out. "Because, sir, they were dying," Thornton replied.

The Tiger called to some nearby North Korean soldiers: "What should be done to a man who disobeys the People's Army?"

"Shoot him," they shouted back.

The Tiger turned to Thornton. "There, you have had your trial," the major said.

"In Texas, sir, we would call that a lynching," Thornton replied.

Thornton was blindfolded and escorted to the top of a small knoll. The major placed his pistol to the back of Thornton's head, tipped up the back of the American's cap with the muzzle, and pulled the trigger. Stunned GIs carried Thornton's lifeless body to the side of the road, dug a shallow grave, and covered it with rocks.

Conditions worsened but the brutal pace continued. The weather had turned punishingly cold, leaving the prisoners exposed in their summer clothes. They covered twenty miles of rugged terrain before stopping for the night. While the civilian captives were allowed to sleep in a farmhouse, the GIs were left in a field. POWs who crawled to the guards' fires for warmth were beaten away. When the sun rose, the huddled forms of ten frozen American soldiers lay dead on the ground. Some men who managed to doze off awoke to find themselves hugging corpses. Another eight were too weak to continue and were left behind, to be shot by the guards.

The march continued northward, past destroyed villages into ever-wilder territory. It seemed to Blake that the whole country was a battlefield, with a level of destruction surpassing anything he had seen in Germany. Though he was younger and fitter than most of the civilians, he struggled as well. He gave his tunic to a nun and faced the cold in light flannels and a sports coat. Like many of the prisoners, he suffered from dysentery, "a most demoralizing illness," he said. He and Deane helped the more vulnerable civilians continue moving, including Sir Vyvyan Holt, the elderly British minister, who was fading.

That night, November 2, the civilians and some GIs were allowed to sleep in a schoolhouse, but it was far too small to accommodate them all. Many excluded soldiers tried to push their way in to escape the terrible cold. Those inside were crushed against walls and pressed against each other, unable to move, with dysentery adding to the misery. Some men passed out, while others screamed uncontrollably; those who wouldn't stop were thrown outside.

In the morning, several GIs were dead; some, it was said, died on their feet. Blake was oddly unsympathetic when it came to the Americans, appalled not at the deaths but at their lack of discipline. "They refused to obey their own officers and degenerated into a cursing, fighting group of rabble," he later said.

———

Each day brought new horrors. Mother Beatrix, a seventy-six-year-old nun who had dedicated her life to caring for Korean orphans, lost strength and was assisted by a younger nun, Sister Eugenie. But when Beatrix fell to the ground on November 3, the guards tore Eugenie away and forced her to continue; soon a shot rang out.

On November 4, the column crossed the Kosan Mountain pass in a blizzard. Despite the punishing cold, some prisoners tossed aside blankets and clothing they no longer had the strength to carry. More and more GIs dropped out and lay on the roadside, awaiting execution. Philip Crosbie, a thirty-five-year-old Catholic priest from Australia, walked by the soldiers as closely and slowly as he dared, and whispered words about "God's love and mercy." One GI, barely more than a boy, waited on the roadside, tears streaming down his face, singing "God Bless America" as loudly as his soft voice could muster, until a guard's bullet stilled the sound. Another begged to be hit in the head with a rock. Deane saw a redheaded GI sobbing, being kicked forward by a guard who forced him to abandon a dying friend. Another soldier carried a buddy as far as he could until the friend collapsed on the ground, unable to rise. Before leaving him, the stronger soldier took his friend's boots to put on his own bare feet.

The Tiger roamed at the back of the column, gripping a handgun. "He was just anxious to shoot somebody," Ed Sheffield, a soldier in Thornton's unit, recalled more than six decades later. Sheffield and other POWs carried sick and starved comrades as far as they could, but when they fell to the back of the column, the Tiger would motion for the soldiers to put down their comrades and move on. "Our buddies would beg us not to leave them but there was nothing we could do," said Sheffield. "As soon as we got thirty feet away, you'd hear the gun shoot. He would kick them over the side of the mountain road."

For men such as Sheffield, Zellers, and Crosbie, the death march would remain seared in their memories as the most painful and bitter days of their lives. Blake, though, saw it differently. Shooting stragglers, he would later say, was an "act of mercy," saving them from "a slow but certain death from cold and hunger." He also felt increasing contempt for the American soldiers. "I could not but be dismayed at the thought that the ultimate defence of the Western world was in the hands of a nation whose soldiers showed so little mental and physical resilience in the face of adversity," he later wrote.

———

On November 8, 1950, after nine excruciating days, the prisoner column reached its destination of Chunggangjin, and a week later marched another five miles to the deserted village of Hanjang-Ni, where they would spend the winter. They had walked some 110 miles through rugged terrain in the most bitter cold, leaving almost a hundred dead men and women behind.

Though the death march was over, the dying was not. Many of the approximately seven hundred who survived the march were so debilitated that the continued poor diet, lack of medicine, and extreme cold at the winter camp proved too much. The Gombert brothers, two French clerics in their mid-seventies who had ministered their entire adult lives in Korea, faded fast. Father Antoine died first, on the afternoon of November 12. "When you are with God, call me," his brother, Father Julien, told Antoine in his last moments. Julien died the next day. The ground was too frozen to bury the clerics, so Blake and the others covered their bodies with snow and stones.

Vyvyan Holt and Blake's deputy, Norman Owen, collapsed from pneumonia soon after arrival, delirious from fever and close to death. Blake and Deane gave their own food rations to the two men and nursed them back to health. But many others failed to recover, and within a few weeks, fourteen civilians had died.

Their losses were mild in comparison to the American POWs, who were dying at a terrible rate, six a day. By the time they were split off from the civilians on February 1, more than 60 percent of the 777 American prisoners were dead. Blake ascribed this to their "lack of an inner discipline."

Blake's harsh assessment ignored what his fellow captives recognized—the soldiers were given treatment "far grimmer" than that endured by the civilians, as Crosbie noted. The POWs had begun the death march already weakened by three months of poor treatment. While the civilians were sometimes allowed to briefly fall behind, Crosbie said, the POWs "were driven on without mercy . . . and none that fell were spared." At Hanjang-Ni, they were given fewer rations and had less adequate clothing. Unlike the civilians, they were denied rice-straw mats to sleep on, and given no heating stoves or chamber pots; even the sick had to relieve themselves outside in temperatures reaching seventy degrees below. The soldiers died of pneumonia, they died of dysentery, they died of cold, they died of malnutrition, they died of thirst, and they died of exhaustion. Some died because other soldiers stole their food. A flu epidemic wiped out many who would have survived had they been given decent treatment. Some lost the will to live and stopped eating. "They drifted away by degrees, the human body being no match for the evil of humankind," said Zellers.

———

Blake's own resilience in the face of the brutal treatment won him the admiration of his fellow captives. On December 5, he and Deane made three trips to the well to fill a water barrel, carrying buckets on a yoke over their shoulders, an arduous task in the icy cold that left Blake without feeling in his hands. When a guard told them to make another trip, Blake refused, saying there was enough water. The guard struck him violently and ordered the two men to their knees, kicking and beating them with the butt of his rifle. "George, who got the worst of it, smiled throughout the ordeal, his left eyebrow cocked ironically at the guard, his Elizabethan beard aggressively thrust forward," Deane later wrote. The other prisoners were called to watch as the two were forced to crouch in the snow for over an hour, their heads bowed and hands behind their backs.

Blake was "a good man to be interned with," Lord, the Salvation Army commissioner, later said. He cheerfully helped with cooking, cleaning, or any other chores assigned by the guards. His calm demeanor and what Deane called "his characteristic ability to shed worry" buoyed the spirits of others. As the weeks stretched into months, his stories of escaping the Nazis or his wondrous years in Cairo as a youth were always welcome. He possessed "a boyish charm," and was a good conversationalist as well as a listener, recalled Zellers. He was curious about America, particularly the history of the Old West.

But Zellers was occasionally disturbed by things Blake would say. Despite his status as a British diplomat, he made little effort to hide his disdain for the American government, blaming the captives' predicament on the U.S. intervention in Korea to prop up the corrupt government of South Korean Syngman Rhee. There were flashes of arrogance as well. Blake would often chat fluently with the French diplomats in their native language. After one conversation, Zellers asked what had been discussed. Blake was snide in his reply. "Larry, don't you know French?"

Decades later, Zellers mused about Blake, "I wonder if anyone really knew him."

———

MacArthur's pursuit of the enemy toward the Yalu River turned disastrously wrong in late November 1950 when the Chinese Red Army intervened on a massive scale across all fronts, contrary to American expectations. After having pushed the North Korean army to the far north, U.S. forces were thrown back south, and Seoul once again fell to the communists. But by February 1951, the front had settled more or less along the 38th parallel dividing the two Koreas. The stability brought much-improved conditions for the prisoners. The Tiger had been replaced as commandant by a more humane officer, and the captives were given better clothing and rations. Blake's group, including the diplomats and journalists, were separated from the rest of the prisoners and kept under improved conditions at a farmhouse in a valley north of Manpo. "Apart from the boredom, life became bearable again," Blake recalled.

For Blake, the quiet was a time of reflection. The wartime suffering, he later said, affected him profoundly. But it was not so much the cruel treatment his fellow captives received from the North Koreans that seemed to bother him, but rather the "equally merciless" bombing campaigns by the Americans and their allies. He had seen the devastation in Germany after the war, but believed it to be "absolutely nothing" compared to what he saw in North Korea. "When you saw these very heavy American Flying Fortresses flying very low over senseless Korean villages, I honestly did not feel very much pride being on the western side," he said.

In the spring, a parcel of books sent by the Soviet embassy in Pyongyang arrived at the camp. The only book in English was *Treasure Island,* which all the prisoners read several times over. The rest were political books in Russian, including *Das Kapital* by Karl Marx. Holt, the British minister, had lost his glasses during the march, and he asked Blake to read to him. As the weather warmed, Blake and Holt would wander down to the green mounds of a family graveyard behind the farmhouse, where they would read and discuss the books for hours.

Blake was somewhat in awe of the eccentric Holt, a tall bird-like man with skin the color and consistency of wrinkled brown leather from a lifetime of postings in the Arab world. Though from a conservative background, Holt held unorthodox views for a British diplomat, sympathizing with socialist principles, and, as the British Empire declined, coming to accept a continued rise of communism as inevitable. Holt's opinions had "a strong effect on my mind," Blake later confessed.

Blake, who as a young man considered becoming a priest, no

longer thought of himself as a believing Christian. "So there was a vacuum in my mind," he said. "I viewed communism as an attempt to create the kingdom of God in this world. The communists were trying to do by action what the church had tried to achieve by prayer and precept. And the upshot of that [is] . . . I came to the conclusion that I was no longer fighting on the right side."

Blake came to believe he was ideally positioned to make a difference in this struggle, and the idea appealed to him. "As an SIS officer it was my task to do everything in my power to undermine the communist system," he later explained. "And I felt that not only should it not be undermined, but on the contrary, it should be assisted."

One night in November 1951, after his fellow prisoners were asleep, Blake later related, he opened the door of the guardroom, where a North Korean officer and several soldiers were sitting. Putting his finger on his lips, he handed a note to the officer, who looked surprised but took the paper without saying a word. The note, written in Russian and addressed to the Soviet embassy in Pyongyang, requested a meeting with Soviet officials. Blake wrote that he had "something important to communicate which they might find of interest."

Part I

THE SINS INSIDE

CHAPTER 1

Black Friday

It was known in intelligence lore as "Black Friday."

Since 1943, the United States had been intercepting and de-crypting secret Soviet radio communications, compiling a surprisingly comprehensive view of the USSR's military capabilities and intentions. Painstaking work by codebreakers at the U.S. Army Security Agency headquarters at Arlington Hall in Virginia near the Pentagon was producing uniquely valuable intelligence. The secret program, code-named VENONA, would eventually help expose some of the Soviets' most dangerous spies, including the physicist Klaus Fuchs, who was passing American atomic secrets to Moscow, and the British diplomat Donald Maclean, the first member of the later notorious Cambridge spy ring to fall under suspicion.

But in late October 1948, almost overnight and without warning, the Soviets began changing their cryptographic systems, leaving the U.S. codebreakers in the cold. One by one, in rapid succession, each of the cipher systems went dark. At the same time, just as mysteriously, Soviet military, intelligence, and diplomatic headquarters in Germany and Austria stopped using ultrahigh frequency (UHF) radio to communicate with Moscow, shifting instead to landlines, depriving the West of a valuable stream of intercepts.

U.S. intelligence spent months trying to learn what had gone wrong. Navy investigators decided it was simply a routine systems upgrade by the Soviets, but others were not so sure. Only later would the Americans learn that VENONA had been betrayed by two Soviet spies. The first was William Weisband, a gregarious and well-liked Russian-language linguist at Arlington Hall. Born in Egypt to Russian parents, Weisband had emigrated to the United States in the 1920s and was recruited by the KGB in 1934. Making the office rounds and chatting with coworkers, he had learned of the Western success in breaking the codes. And Harold "Kim" Philby, the SIS liaison in Washington, had likewise been recruited by the KGB while a student at Cambridge in the 1930s. Conveniently for the Soviets, he'd been assigned to work with the Americans on VENONA. Based on the warnings of one or likely both spies, Moscow changed its ciphers and radio operating procedures.

By some estimates, Black Friday was the worst intelligence loss in U.S. history, leaving the West almost entirely in the dark about Moscow's military capabilities and intentions.

The United States paid the most immediate consequences in Korea. The North Korean invasion of the south in June 1950 had been an intelligence disaster, with the failure to pick up even a hint of a war launched with the approval of Soviet leader Joseph Stalin setting off alarms in Washington and London. And not only had the Central Intelligence Agency missed the start of the war, but it had been wrong about the possibility of Chinese intervention, and wrong about North Korean capabilities.

The communist aggression in Korea was seen in Western capitals as a possible prelude to a similar attack on Western Europe by the enormous Red Army force that had not been withdrawn at the conclusion of World War II and still occupied eastern Germany and Poland. The brutality of the fighting in Asia and the surprising power shown by communist forces during the first year of the conflict only added to the fear that the United States and its allies were unprepared. Unsurprisingly, with Cold War tensions escalating and Washington deprived of the flow of valuable intelligence, pressure on the CIA to supply early warning of a Soviet attack "skyrocketed," recalled Richard Helms, the future director of the agency, then serving as chief of operations for its clandestine service.

Thus far in its young history, the CIA was proving itself thoroughly outmatched by the formidable KGB. Since the creation of the Cheka during the Bolshevik Revolution in 1917, the Soviet secret police and intelligence organization had been known by many different names, but still relied on what founder Felix Dzerzhinsky called "organized terror" in pursuit of its aims.* The strengthening of the police state under Stalin made it next to impossible to recruit any spies in Russia. Getting an agent to report from inside the Kremlin "was as improbable as placing resident spies on the planet Mars," complained Helms, a razor-sharp former wire service reporter who had served in Germany with the Office of Strategic Services, the World War II military intelligence agency that was a forerunner to the CIA.

In 1949, the CIA began parachuting Russians who had fled the USSR back into the country with the idea of establishing a network of agents to spy on military installations and the like. Almost all of the agents were arrested as soon as they landed, and of the few who did not disappear, most if not all were forced to serve as double agents by Soviet intelligence, meaning any information they sent was compromised.

Western intelligence therefore had to rely on outdated World War II information, details garnered from the censored Soviet press, and reports from occasional defectors. A small amount of signals intelligence—the collection and analysis of communications and electronic emissions—was trickling in from the first U.S. intercept stations being constructed around the Soviet Union's perimeter. Other than rare overflights along the periphery of Soviet territory by U.S. and British military aircraft, there was none of the overhead imagery that the U-2 and satellites would later provide. "We were simply blind," said David Murphy, a CIA officer who would serve in Berlin.

WASHINGTON, LONDON, AND BERLIN, 1951

The Berlin tunnel was born of this desperation.

The CIA, created by the National Security Act of 1947 signed

---

* Among the abbreviations by which the Soviet state security agency was known during periods discussed in this book are NKVD and MGB. Though it did not become known as the KGB until 1954, the author uses this term throughout to avoid confusion.

by President Harry Truman, had been given the task of centralizing and coordinating American intelligence. But its true mission was even more simply stated: "I don't care what it does, all I want from them is twenty-four hours' notice of a Soviet attack," Secretary of State George C. Marshall famously declared. Given its performance, the chances of getting that warning did not seem promising.

Even before Korea, fear of Soviet aggression against the West had been escalating. Following the successful Soviet testing of atomic weapons in August 1949, a secret National Security Council report issued in April 1950, NSC-68, declared that the United States was "mortally challenged" by the Soviet Union and must intensify intelligence operations to get early warning of an attack.

If war came, Germany would be the main battleground and Berlin the likely flashpoint. The divided former German capital, deep in East German territory, was on the front line of the Cold War with the United States, Britain, France, and the Soviet Union each controlling their own zone in the city. It was the place where the Soviets and the Western Allies met most intimately—and uneasily.

Tensions in Berlin reached new heights in June 1948, when the Soviets blocked roads and rail lines leading to the Western sectors, expecting that they could force the United States and its allies to abandon the divided city. Instead, the West overcame the blockade with a magnificent airlift, flying in four thousand tons of coal, food, and other supplies daily for almost eleven months. Throughout the crisis, Washington feared that the Soviets might launch a war, but in the end, Stalin lifted the blockade in May 1949.

The North Korean invasion one year later was halfway around the globe, but it was seen by the CIA as an even more serious threat to Berlin than the blockade. "We considered it much more likely this time that the Soviets might move west," said Peter Sichel, then chief of the CIA's Berlin base.

Some three hundred thousand Red Army troops were positioned in eastern Germany. The United States, which had fewer than a hundred thousand troops in West Germany when the Korean War started, rushed over more forces and soon had a quarter million. But the Soviet bloc retained an overwhelming advantage among conventional forces. British intelligence calculated that the Soviets and their allies had 216 active divisions available for use in Europe, compared with 51 for NATO, the new Western alliance. Moreover, there was a danger that the Soviets would resort to a first nuclear strike because they assumed that the United States would use atomic weapons to stop the Red Army from overrunning Western Europe.

A CIA estimate in February 1951 concluded that the Soviets' "ultimate aim" was to gain control over all of Germany and eliminate the presence of the Western powers in Berlin. If they were unable to meet these goals with political pressure, the agency reported, the Soviets might risk starting another world war. Knowing what the Soviets were up to in Berlin was thus a matter of the utmost importance, with millions of lives potentially at stake.

———

Perhaps no one was more frustrated by the loss of Soviet radio traffic than a pipe-smoking and genteel Virginian named Frank Rowlett. Though unknown to the American public, Rowlett was an unsung hero of World War II and one of the nation's top codebreakers. Mild-mannered and unpretentious, with rimless glasses on his round face, he looked like the high school math teacher he had once been back home in southwest Virginia. He had arrived in Washington in 1930 as one of the original three cryptanalysts hired for the newly created Army Signal Intelligence Service by the father of modern American cryptology, William Friedman. Rowlett had confessed to his wife that he did not have the slightest idea what a cryptanalyst did. But he proved to be an inspired choice, rising to help lead the VENONA project and playing a key role in designing SIGABA, the cipher machine credited with saving thousands of American lives during World War II by protecting U.S. military communications. He also led the team trying to crack the Japanese diplomatic code, dubbed PURPLE by the Americans. With tensions in the Pacific rising sharply, Japan had in 1939 introduced a highly sophisticated cipher machine for cable traffic between Tokyo and its embassies around the world. In September 1940, after eighteen months and untold hours of analysis, Rowlett's team discovered a critical pattern of letters that led to breaking the code. "That's it! That's it!" the normally unflappable Rowlett cried, jumping up and down in excitement. He sent out for bottles of Coca-Cola for the whole team. Then they got back to work. Within two days, they were deciphering their first messages. It was a triumph of grinding work and true genius.

The intelligence derived from the decrypted Japanese cables was code-named MAGIC, and Rowlett and his team were considered magicians. The United States was able to read Tokyo's messages to and from the Japanese ambassador in Berlin, providing crucial intelligence on both Japanese and German intentions. But the United States failed to mount a big enough effort to break the codes used by the Japanese army and navy—at heavy cost.

On December 3, 1941, Rowlett walked into his office at the Munitions Building in Washington and found a single-page translation of a PURPLE intercept from Tokyo to the Japanese embassy in Washington waiting on his desk. He was stunned to read that Tokyo had ordered the embassy to destroy its codebooks and cipher machines. He and a colleague concluded that the order meant Japan was preparing to go to war with the United States, and they quickly reported this up the chain of command. But with no matching intelligence about any Japanese military preparations or movements, the U.S. government did not anticipate the attack on Pearl Harbor.

A decade later, Rowlett feared the United States could face a new Pearl Harbor—this one with nuclear weapons. In 1951, he was serving as technical director of operations at the Armed Forces Security Agency, predecessor to the National Security Agency. Since VENONA, he had worked closely with Bill Harvey, a former FBI G-man who was then chief of the counterintelligence staff at the CIA. On the surface, the gruff and profane Harvey was as different from the courtly, soft-spoken Rowlett as could be imagined. Harvey, who drank martinis by the quart, referred to the coffee-eschewing Rowlett behind his back as "Our Father." But the two quickly developed a mutual respect, as well as a shared sense of urgency on the need to fill in the gaps in American intelligence.

In early 1951, Rowlett and Harvey commiserated over the lost intelligence due to the Soviets' Black Friday shift from radio to landlines. Perhaps they could figure out a way and place to attack Soviet landlines on a scale not previously considered necessary, or even possible.

Two cities were obvious targets: Vienna and Berlin. Since Soviet and Western forces jointly occupied both cities, there might be locations where the CIA could reach landlines used by the Red Army. But when the CIA began investigating Vienna in 1951, they discovered they were late to the game: British intelligence had been tapping Soviet cables through a system of small tunnels in and around Vienna for two years. Informing the Americans of this, the Brits magnanimously offered to share the take. The CIA was duly impressed with the intelligence collected about Soviet military capabilities and intentions, and rather than pursue its own project, it agreed to join the SIS operation. "There was too much at stake to risk any overlapping effort in such a narrow field," recalled Helms. The British also suggested that "similar opportunities might be present in the Berlin area," according to a CIA history. That possibility intrigued Harvey and Rowlett.

Berlin held potential for an operation on a far grander scale than Vienna. It was the central circuit for communications in Eastern Europe, the hub for an enormous network of lines dating from pre–World War I imperial days, stretching to Moscow. That role had been interrupted by World War II, but long-distance telephone and telegraph lines connecting the city to the rest of Europe had been restored in 1946. Still, the Americans and British were uncertain about how much Soviet forces actually used the cables, and what the intelligence value might be.

———

In mid-1951, Staff D, the CIA's new, highly secret office responsible for clandestine electronic surveillance targeting foreign communications, held exploratory talks in Washington about mounting an attack on Soviet landlines in East Germany, in particular Berlin.

Based on those discussions, the CIA base in Berlin was assigned to penetrate the East Berlin office of the East German Post and Telecommunications Ministry, which operated the telephone lines in

Berlin. Neither Berlin base chief Peter Sichel nor his deputy Henry Hecksher were told anything about a tap or a tunnel—all they knew was that headquarters wanted information about the telephone cables.

Penetrating the ministry was not particularly difficult. Hecksher, a native German who had left Germany in the 1930s because of his Jewish background, had close contacts with Berlin authorities. It helped that the Berlin postal office had been one central entity before the occupation, so West Berlin postal officials had close working relationships with former colleagues on the other side, including some who supervised cables. Hecksher developed a network that brought in "reams" of material about the cable network, Sichel said.

The Soviets used two types of landlines in Germany: overhead lines strung on telephone poles, and buried cables. On the one hand, the overhead lines seemed an attractive target, as they carried the highest-level intelligence and military communications. But these special KGB-operated lines were guarded closely by roving patrols on the lookout for taps or other problems. The underground cables were likely a better target, since they were not visually inspected. If the CIA could place a tap, it might go undetected for some time.

The intelligence gathered from East German ministry sources showed that the underground cables in Berlin still followed the conduits created by the old German imperial system. Moreover, all Soviet telephone communications between Moscow, Warsaw, Budapest, Bucharest, and Vienna again went through Berlin. There was something else important, Sichel recalled: "Our intelligence brought to light the fact that these cables went close to the western border" in some locations.

Back at CIA headquarters in Washington, Helms was intrigued. The proximity of the cables in Berlin "suggested a long-shot possibility" of digging a tunnel to break into communications between Moscow and its military headquarters in Germany, Austria, Poland, and Hungary.

A long shot was more than enough for Harvey, who went to work laying the groundwork. He coordinated with Rowlett, who would soon join the CIA to take charge of Staff D. Discussion of the possible project was restricted to a very small group. Helms, despite his position high in the CIA's hierarchy, assisted with the planning to keep the circle small. "I was, in effect, the action officer, and at times dealt with routine matters which in other operations would be the lot of an officer with a year's experience under his belt," he recalled.

To learn more about the Berlin cables, Staff D stationed an officer in Germany. Alan Conway, a seasoned former Army signals intelligence officer, operated from the Frankfurt headquarters independently of the CIA base in Berlin, in order to keep knowledge tight.

Lacking any engineering expertise, the team in Washington asked Gerald Fellon, a civil engineer in the CIA's Office of Communications, to meet with Staff D to discuss a mysterious new project. Fellon, who had served with the Army during the war, was hardly an expert on tunnels—his entire experience was limited to several night shift visits to the Brooklyn–Battery Tunnel as a student civil engineer in 1948. But he knew more than anyone else at the agency.

It was a short meeting, Fellon recalled: "The only question they asked was whether a tunnel could be dug in secret." He was told nothing about where this tunnel might be built, or why. Fellon replied rather vaguely that a tunnel could be built anywhere, though building one in secret would depend on the size. It would also take more time, and cost more money, he added, but it was possible.

That was the right answer. After the meeting, Fellon was transferred to Staff D and put to work on the project. He recalled, "Thus began planning for the construction of the Berlin Tunnel."

CHAPTER 2

To Betray, You First Have to Belong

MANPO, NORTH KOREA

In the fall of 1951, three Russian visitors arrived in Manpo in a large black sedan, news that the Western captives held in the nearby prisoner camps quickly learned from Korean children they had befriended. It had been about six weeks since George Blake had handed his note to his North Korean captors requesting a meeting with the Soviets.

Vyvyan Holt, the senior British diplomat, was summoned to accompany the camp commandant into town. Holt returned hours later and reported that he had been questioned by a pleasant young Russian who asked him to sign a statement condemning the war. Holt had refused.

The next morning, it was Blake's turn to walk with the commandant into Manpo. The town, located at a point on the Yalu River where a railway bridge crossed into China, was a frequent target of U.S. Air Force bombs, and after more than a year of war, most of it was in ruins. Blake was escorted to one of the few buildings still standing.

One of the visitors was waiting in a bare room on the first floor that contained only a table and two chairs. Addressing Blake in Russian, the man invited him to sit at the table, and took the chair opposite him. Blake's note was on the table. In a friendly tone, the Russian gestured to the note and asked the British captive what he wished to talk about.

Blake, by his later account, said he was a British intelligence officer, and he had a proposition: "I want to offer my services to the Soviet authorities."

Blake said he told the Russian he would inform the KGB of any present or future SIS operations directed against the Soviet Union, other socialist countries, or the "world Communist movement." He said he was not seeking reward for his services and insisted he should not receive special treatment compared with the other captives.

The Russian showed "considerable interest" in the offer, according to Blake, occasionally interrupting him to clarify a point. The Russian then asked him to write down in English everything he had just said, leaving him alone in the room. When he returned, he peppered Blake with questions about his early life and his work for British intelligence.

The Russian was likely Nikolai Loenko, a KGB officer from the Vladivostok regional office, which had oversight of Manchuria and North Korea. Though only twenty-five years old, the suave and charming Loenko was already a rising star in the KGB, an effective officer with a skillful command of English and several more languages. He was so familiar with the intelligence landscape in the region that his colleagues later called him, perhaps with a touch of sarcasm, "Lawrence of the Far East."

Blake's claim that he had requested the meeting notwithstanding, Loenko already knew about the Western diplomats, journalists, and missionaries being held at various camps along the Yalu, and been granted clearance from the North Koreans and Chinese to interview the prisoners. Loenko later told a KGB colleague that he had spotted Blake among the captives and marked him as a potential recruit. In this version, Loenko eventually broke the ice with Blake with gifts of bread, tinned food, and chocolate, and over time built a rapport based on a shared sense of humor. "Word by word, we quietly moved forward to the serious conversations when the Englishman made his choice," Loenko reportedly said. But other KGB officers who worked with Blake, including his longtime handler, Sergei Kondrashev, corroborated Blake's version.

Whether it was Blake or Loenko who initiated the contact, there is little doubt that the British intelligence officer was a willing convert.

———

To divert suspicion from Blake's regular meetings with Loenko, the Russians also met with the other Western civilians. "Every person in turn was called up; there were discussions about the rights and wrongs of the Korean War . . . ," Blake later said. "They were just kept talking, as it were, to fill the day." Instead of Loenko, the captives usually met with a tall, fair-skinned Russian with aristocratic manners whom they nicknamed Blondie. He would extol the virtues of communism, though after a few sessions he gave up talking about Marxism and brought vodka.

Blake would frequently disappear for what his fellow prisoners assumed were similar sessions with Blondie. Blake made a point of being "more contemptuous" of the amateurish efforts than any of the captives, according to Herbert Lord. "Afterwards Blake would return to our room and tell us he was treating these conversations as a huge joke," Lord later said. "Mind you, Blake never talked a great deal about what went on when he was alone with 'Blondie.'"

After several sessions with Blake, Loenko believed he was genuine, but there were doubts at Moscow Center, as the KGB headquarters in the Soviet capital was known. Could Blake be a plant by British intelligence, meant to infiltrate the KGB? "At the beginning, a few people suspected Blake," recalled Viktor Malyavin, a senior KGB officer. "We wondered about his motives."

Vasily Dozhdalev, a thirty-year-old KGB officer based in London who spoke excellent English, was dispatched to North Korea by Moscow Center to help Loenko conduct an in-depth assessment of the prisoner. The KGB wanted to know: Exactly who was George Blake?

———

Already to this point, Blake had lived a remarkable, storybook life, part *Grimms' Fairy Tales,* part *One Thousand and One Nights,* and part

The Great Escape. He had been born George Behar in Rotterdam on Armistice Day in 1922, four years after the end of the Great War. His father, Albert Behar, a Turkish subject, was from an old Jewish family that found refuge in Constantinople after their expulsion from Spain at the end of the fifteenth century. Behar had served in World War I with the British Army and had been seriously wounded in France on the Western Front, and he gained British citizenship.

Stationed with the army in Holland helping to repatriate POWs after the armistice was signed, the dark and handsome Behar met Catherine Beijderwellen, a fair-haired twenty-six-year-old Dutch woman from a well-established Protestant family in Rotterdam. Albert passed himself off as a Lutheran to overcome objections from her family, and they wed in 1922. Feeling a "surge of patriotism" on his way to the birth registrar after their child was born, he named his son after the British monarch, King George V.

Behar, a charming if temperamentally difficult man, opened a small factory in Rotterdam that manufactured leather gloves for the port's many longshoremen. Blake remembered him as a "rather remote" father whose main influence was to make sure his son respected Britain and disliked Germany. George and his two sisters spoke Dutch at home, which Albert did not understand, making communication a challenge. "I suppose my father was always something of a stranger to me," Blake later said. By language and circumstance, young George was always closer to his mother. Albert worked long hours and was always too tired to accompany the family on Sunday walks, when George would listen to endless stories told by his mother and aunt. "I developed the habit of listening rather than talking," he recalled. He was raised in his mother's faith, the Remonstrant Church, attending services every Sunday, his imagination fired by Old Testament stories of Abraham, Joseph, and David.

Albert Behar's health had not been good since the war, when by family lore he was exposed to mustard gas. To escape the smoky air of Rotterdam, they moved in 1933 to the seaside town of Scheveningen. But Behar's health continued to worsen, and in late 1934 he was diagnosed with lung cancer. He spent the last three months of his life in a nearby hospital in The Hague, with George visiting at his bedside after school every day, struggling to understand his father's labored requests. One day his father asked him to close the curtain around the bed and grew angry when George could not make out what he was saying. "I felt desperate and was almost in tears," he recalled. Fortunately, the patient in the next bed explained the request, and his father calmed down. "But I shall never forget this experience, especially as he died shortly afterwards," Blake later said.

Behar's death was followed by hardship. His business went bankrupt, leaving the family in debt. George's mother took in boarders and cooked meals to make money. Before he died, Albert told his wife she should seek assistance in raising the children from his wealthy relatives in Cairo, the Curiel family, whom George and his mother had never met. When she contacted the Curiels, the family offered to take George into their home in Cairo and see to his education. His mother was reluctant, but recognized that the offer might provide her son with better prospects than staying in Holland. She left the final decision to him. George was frightened at the thought of leaving home, but after a few days told his mother he would go. "It was this thirst for adventure and the unknown which proved the stronger," he later said.

In September 1936, thirteen-year-old George sailed alone on a cargo ship to Egypt. The Curiel family, originally from Tuscany, was a wealthy, eccentric, and cosmopolitan group, some carrying Italian passports, and others French, Turkish, or Egyptian. Uncle Daniel, the patriarch, a wealthy banker and a collector of antiques, was blind, always wearing dark glasses that gave him a mysterious appearance. Aunt Zephirah, Albert Behar's sister, had been sent from Constantinople to Cairo at age sixteen for an arranged marriage with Daniel. She was a kindhearted and pious woman, "inclined to mysticism," Blake recalled. Uncle Max was a playboy who spent his evenings at nightclubs with his many mistresses. Cousin Raoul was a scholarly archaeologist, while Cousin Henri was a tall and thin law student who had embraced left-wing politics at Cairo University.

The family lived in an Italian palazzo, a hidden palace surrounded by palm trees on an island in the Nile, with seventeen rooms adorned by beautiful tapestries, oriental carpets, and rare paintings. Six-course lunches were served by Nubian servants wearing white gowns with red sashes. George attended a French lycée his first year, and the next an English school with British expatriate children preparing to attend university in England. There were summer holidays in Europe, when he traveled to Holland for reunions with his mother and other Dutch relatives and visited England for the first time. It was in some respects a dream life for a young teenager, Blake later said, but he also spoke of a sense of dislocation and confusion. "I lived through an identity crisis in those years," he said. "Where did I belong?"

George spent a good deal of time with Henri, his charismatic cousin eight years his elder. Henri brought George along on visits to a family estate fifty miles outside Cairo, where they walked among poor Egyptians living in miserable conditions, the younger boy's first exposure to the vast gulf in wealth between the haves and have-nots of the world. "It was a shock for George," said Sylvie Braibant, a cousin of Henri.

Henri Curiel—who was later a cofounder of the Egyptian Communist Party and would be murdered by right-wing extremists in Paris in 1978—had long political discussions about communism with his younger cousin. "They were a great influence on me, but I resisted them at that time because I was a very religious boy," Blake later said. "But, with hindsight, many of Henri's views acted as a time-bomb."

———

In the autumn of 1939, with the Nazi invasion of Poland and the outbreak of war in Europe, and given the U-boat threat to ships, the Dutch relatives thought it best that George, now sixteen, stay in Holland. He lived with his grandmother in Rotterdam so he could attend school in the city and joined his mother and sisters at their home in Scheveningen on the weekends. There was hope that the neutral Netherlands could escape the storm engulfing Europe. But in Rotterdam on the morning of May 10, 1940, George was awoken by the sound of explosions and machine-gun fire. The radio reported that German troops were attacking across the border.

At midday on May 14, waves of German bombers hit Rotterdam. George and his grandmother rode out the bombardment under the dining room table with kitchen pans on their heads, listening to the sickening whine of Stuka dive bombers and endless explosions. When the drone of the German planes finally disappeared, George and his grandmother emerged from the home to find much of the city destroyed. The attack had ignited a firestorm, and the entire old center of the city was in flames. "The streets were full of people fleeing from the burning hell," he recalled. He helped at a nearby church that had been set up as a hospital to treat the wounded.

The Netherlands surrendered the next day, but it was several days before George felt it was safe to ride his bicycle to Scheveningen to check on his mother and sisters, whom he had been unable to contact. He was stunned to find the home empty, with dirty teacups on the table, most unlike his neat mother. A neighbor reported that his mother and sisters, as British subjects, had been hurriedly evacuated to England aboard a Royal Navy ship, leaving behind all their belongings. His mother had been told George would be evacuated as well, but the boy had never received notice from the British consulate and it was now too late.

His remaining Dutch relatives thought the seventeen-year-old boy would be safer away from the city, so he was sent to live for the summer with his uncle, a grain merchant in the village of Warnsveld. But within two weeks, the village constable knocked on the door with orders to arrest George as a British citizen. He was taken by train to a camp north of Amsterdam for British and French internees. The skull and crossbones on the caps of the Waffen-SS troops guarding the camp "did nothing to reassure me," he later said. But after a month, he was among a small group of prisoners released because they were under eighteen or over sixty-five years old. Back at his grandmother's home, as the war in Europe broadened, there was little comfort. George faced a growing likelihood that he would again be arrested upon his eighteenth birthday. His uncle arranged for the boy to live with a farmer deep in the country in the hamlet of Hummelo. The boy was given false papers identifying him as a Dutch citizen. George Behar's clandestine life had begun.

———

In Hummelo, George worked as a farmhand and attended the Dutch Reformed church in a nearby town. He had decided to become a minister after the war, and attended confirmation classes led by Dominee Nicholas Padt, a minister who spoke out against the Nazis despite being jailed for six weeks for his sermons. As the occupation grew more oppressive, the boy gave thought to joining the burgeoning Dutch resistance. "I was a British subject; I was half Jewish, so there was every reason for me," he later said.

In the spring of 1941, he approached Padt, who was rumored to have connections with the Dutch underground, and asked him for help joining the resistance. A week later, the minister brought him to the town of Devanter, where they met with a local resistance leader known as Max. George was now eighteen, with experiences abroad that had given him unusual confidence and maturity, but he still looked like a lad of fourteen or fifteen. Max decided that George could be used as a courier.

For more than a year, George traveled all about Holland by bicycle and train, picking up and delivering parcels, messages, and intelligence about the German military. It was dangerous work, as travelers were regularly stopped for inspection, but his boyish looks worked in his favor. "When people saw me with my satchel, I don't think it occurred to them that I was anything else but a schoolboy on his way to or from school," he later said. Once, as he rushed to catch a tram, a stack of resistance newspapers fell from his coat and spilled to the ground. A German officer standing nearby helped him pick them up, handing them wordlessly to the boy. George thanked him profusely and jumped on the tram.

———

In the summer of 1942, following the death of his beloved grandmother, George decided to escape to England. He hoped to find his mother and sisters, with whom he had had no contact since their evacuation more than a year earlier.

George approached Max, who brought his courier to meet Piet de Bie, a resistance sympathizer in the village of Zundert in the southern Netherlands who regularly helped smuggle people across the nearby border into Belgium. After moving into the de Bie home for several weeks, George set out on a beautiful Sunday morning in mid-July with two of de Bie's younger sisters, who guided him along remote footpaths toward the frontier. They were walking along a pinewoods, a hundred yards from the border, when a young German soldier carrying a rifle emerged from behind a haystack and angrily blocked their path. Blake froze in fear, but the soldier relaxed when he recognized the girls. They had recently befriended him at a local Catholic church youth group meeting, and he let them pass.

In the afternoon, they reached Antwerp, where the girls left George at the home of their aunt and bade him farewell. "For the first time, I experienced a feeling which was often to recur in later life—a feeling of the inadequacy of words to express gratitude and admiration to people who, by assuming very considerable risks, had ensured my safety and freedom," he later said.

George was given the name of a Dominican monk in Paris who could help him further, and the next day he boarded a train headed to the French capital. He kept his British passport hidden in a loaf of bread and was told there would be no check crossing from Belgium into occupied France, as both were under German control. But approaching Mons, the last Belgian town before the border, he spotted two German military policemen methodically working their way up the crowded car, checking everyone's papers. As the train slowed to enter Mons, he leapt off and ran down the platform and out of the station, disappearing down narrow streets and hiding in an old church. He waited until he calmed down and felt it was safe.

Following directions given to him by a priest in the church, George headed south by tram and foot until he reached a hamlet along the border. Approaching the checkpoint cautiously, he saw two Belgian customs officers looking contemptuously at a German airman who was riding off on a bicycle. George had lived long enough in occupied territory to know that the men did not like Germans. "I decided to risk it," he later said.

He walked up to the barrier, where the customs officers asked for his identity card. "I haven't got one," he told them. "I am an Englishman on my way to France."

The two Belgians smiled. "Why didn't you say so at once?" one said. After examining George's British passport, one of the officers took him home for dinner with his family, pulling out a bottle of brandy for a toast to Allied victory. The next morning, the officer escorted George on foot across the border to the town of Maubeuge, turning him over to a friendly French official. By evening, traveling by bus and train, he had reached Paris.

He went to the home of the Dominican monk, who in turn brought him to a middle-aged couple who kept him in their apartment for several weeks. The couple arranged for him to meet with a tall, broad-shouldered resistance leader known as "the Belgian," who gave George a false French identity card and a house address in the village of Salies de Bearned, in southwestern France. There, he was told, he could connect with people able to help him escape across the nearby border into unoccupied France, under the collaborationist Vichy government, from where it would be easier to make it to Spain. Arriving in the village by train, George went to the house, and after giving the proper password to the man who answered the door, he was allowed in and told to be ready for a crossing that night. Three Jewish women fleeing Nazi persecution were also trying to escape.

Two tough-looking Basque men wearing black berets showed up at the house after dark, accompanied by a dog to alert them to any German patrols. The Basques guided the party through back alleys out of town and toward the border, scrambling across ditches and crawling through fields until they reached a farm that lay in unoccupied France. "An immense burden of fear and gloom was lifted from me," Blake said. "I was out of the hands of the enemy."

———

But his journey was far from over. He was sent east to Lyon, which, by virtue of its strategic location in the southeast and its labyrinth of secret passages known as *traboules,* had become a resistance stronghold in unoccupied France. Following instructions, he reported to the American consulate, where the British representative working from the office agreed to help. George would be issued a British travel document showing him to be sixteen—below military age—in the hope that Vichy authorities would issue him an exit visa allowing safe passage into Spain. After several weeks, George received the false British papers and applied for the visa. In November, while waiting in a village near Grenoble, south of Lyon, he learned

that Allied forces had landed in French North Africa and that in
response Hitler had ordered German forces into unoccupied France.

George realized he needed to reach the Spanish frontier quickly
before German troops sealed it off. A resistance contact urged him to
travel immediately to Toulouse in southern France, giving him the
name of a friend who might be able to help get him across the Pyrenees and into Spain. Emerging from the train station in Toulouse,
his heart sank when he saw a column of German armor moving into
the city. His contact there, a local journalist, connected him with a
passeur, as the guides who smuggled people across the border were
called. The *passeur,* an elegantly dressed man named Fernandez, accompanied George on a two-day bus trip to Seix, an ancient mountain village dominated by a castle commissioned by Charlemagne.

Fernandez turned George over to two French mountain guides
who would lead him across the Pyrenees on foot. They were joined
by a second traveler, a heavyset Portuguese businessman who had
been trapped in unoccupied France by the German invasion and was
trying to get back to his wife and children in Portugal. The four-man
party left the village after dark and began climbing a steep slope.
The guides urged them to move quickly, as it was critical to get far
from the village before their absence was noted. They climbed until
nearly dawn, finally reaching a mountain hut, and sleeping a few
hours before continuing. They hiked through the next day, passing
the snow line, but built no fire at a mountain hut that night for fear
of attracting attention from patrols. On the third day, they climbed
through deep snow to reach the Pic du Midi, the highest point on
the trail, and began descending on easier terrain.

Eventually, they reached a meadow where the guides stopped and
informed the travelers that they had reached Spain. All four celebrated with a deep drink of wine from a goatskin bota bag, and then
the guides headed back, directing the travelers to continue down a
mule trail to a nearby farmhouse. But the guides had deserted them
early. Blake and his partner found no farmhouse. The Portuguese
man was convinced they were lost and should retrace their steps.
George refused, insisting they were going the right way. "This was a
matter of life and death for both of us," he later said. "The one who
was wrong would be returning to German-occupied France." Soon

after they parted, George encountered a shepherd who told him he was going in the right direction, but was still in France. He ran to find his companion, and together they continued back toward the border.

Finally, they reached a hillcrest overlooking the farm in Spanish territory, but saw Spanish soldiers moving through the woods below. The travelers ducked behind a rock, but they had already been spotted. After a warning shot was fired over their heads, they surrendered and were surrounded by the soldiers. Said Blake, "We were in Spain, but no longer free."

———

The two men were taken to the border city of Irun, where other refugees were being held. Under the rule of the dictator Francisco Franco, Spain openly sympathized with Nazi Germany, though officially it was a non-belligerent. Rumors flew that they would be turned over to the German troops manning the French border fifty yards away. The refugees were taken to a prison in the provincial capital of Pamplona, where they had their heads shaved and were held in crowded, unheated cells. After three weeks, Guardia Civil wearing Napoleonic-era hats and wide capes marched the detainees in handcuffs to the train station. They were taken to Miranda del Ebro, a notorious prison camp established by Franco for Republican prisoners during the Spanish Civil War. Hundreds of detainees from twenty-six different nations were now being held there in squalid conditions. George had been in Spanish captivity for nearly two months when the Poles, the largest contingent at the camp, organized a weeklong hunger strike in January 1943. It succeeded in drawing international attention to the situation and putting pressure on the Spanish government to improve conditions and speed up releases.

A few days after the strike ended, Blake was among a group of about fifteen prisoners whose freedom was negotiated by the British and other governments. Within days, he was on a train to the British territory of Gibraltar and soon after aboard the ocean liner RMS *Empress of Australia,* traveling to England in a convoy to protect against German U-boats and aircraft.

After the ship docked at the Scottish port of Greenock, the detainees were taken to London for days of questioning by intelligence officers about their backgrounds and experiences in Nazi territory. Authorities located George's mother, who was working as a housekeeper in Northwood, a suburb of London. After several days of questioning, George was released and given train fare to Northwood. "It was dark and raining, but at the end of the platform I recognized at once the waiting figure of my mother," Blake later wrote. "I was home."

———

The teenage boy Catherine Behar had last seen three years before had grown into a "fine handsome young man." Yet it seemed that her son's remarkable experiences had changed him surprisingly little. He showed no outward scars from the hardships, although he had an "intense hatred of Nazis."

Around this time, Catherine decided to change the family name from Behar, apparently wanting a more English name. She considered Drake, the name of her employer, before settling on Blake, filing papers to make the change legal.

In the days after the grand family reunion, George Blake roamed about London. It was his first good look at his fellow countrymen, and he found himself impressed by the solidarity and "stern sense of duty" he saw everywhere in a nation at war. But once the excitement of his return and new surroundings wore off, he was bored and contemplated ways to get back in the action. "I began to miss the excitement and tension to which two years of illegal existence had accustomed me," he said.

He went to a recruiting station in Trafalgar Square and volunteered for service in the Royal Navy. After months of training, he was commissioned as a sub-lieutenant in April 1944. To his disappointment, he was assigned as a diver for the submarine service. But after he fell unconscious during a practice dive and had to be rescued, the Royal Navy reconsidered the posting.

Blake's commander, who had taken a liking to the young officer and recognized his linguistic skills, took a fateful step: He passed Blake's name on to the British Secret Intelligence Service as a possible recruit. Blake was told only that he was being considered for an assignment with the Royal Navy's fast boat service and reported as instructed to an office. After preliminaries, a Navy officer escorted him to a nearby building at 54 Broadway, which, though Blake did not realize it, was the SIS headquarters.

A week later, Blake was called back to the same building and brought into a large boardroom with a long polished table. He was directed to take a seat facing a half dozen men, some in military uniform, and others in civilian dress. For thirty minutes, they peppered him with questions about his background. By now, Blake suspected that the assignment involved something other than fast boats. But he was both shocked and ecstatic when he reported again several days later and was told he was now an officer with SIS. "That I would actually become an officer in the British Secret Service, this legendary centre of hidden power, commonly believed to have a decisive influence on the great events of this world, was something that far exceeded my wildest expectations," he wrote.

He was sent to the SIS Dutch section, which was a beehive of activity following the D-Day landings in June. With Allied forces pushing into the Netherlands, he was assigned as a conducting officer, preparing Dutch agents to be flown from England and dropped into occupied Holland to send critically needed information about German military positions.

Sometimes he would accompany an agent to the airfield on the night of a dropping operation, stopping off at a pub, trying to keep the atmosphere light. Just before takeoff, the agent would change into clothes of Dutch origin. "I had to check carefully that he had no English coins, letters, bus or cinema tickets, or anything else on his person, which might give him away," Blake recalled. "Then I gave him his false Dutch identity documents, his money, his codes and transmitting schedules and, if he wished, a lethal pill." Not all the agents survived. In April 1945, Blake saw off a fair-haired boy from Amsterdam who had just turned eighteen and was jumping into Holland to serve as a radio operator. Word came back two days later that he had drowned when he landed in a lake and had been unable to disconnect his parachute harness.

Germany's surrender came soon afterwards, and Blake was among a joyful throng at Buckingham Palace on May 8 for VE celebrations. A week later, he was sent to Holland to assist with postwar operations, an assignment that allowed for tearful reunions with his Dutch relatives. He also had the somber job of assisting the families of agents who had been killed. Nevertheless, with the exuberance of the war's end, the time in Holland was an "almost unbroken round of parties, drinking sessions and high living," he recalled.

Amid all this, Blake became smitten with Iris Peake, a lovely SIS secretary with whom he was serving in Holland. Most of the SIS secretaries came from good families, but Peake, a former debutante whose grandfather was the Earl of Essex, was particularly blue-blooded. In Holland, the two were inseparable, but once they were back in England, the romance petered out, an ending that acquaintances attributed to pressure from Peake's family. "He was in love with her, but could not possibly marry her because of his circumstances," Gillian Blake, who would be his first wife, later said. For Blake, it was a bitter lesson in the class system that ruled Britain.

———

With the demobilization at war's end, many of Blake's SIS colleagues were returning to civilian life. Blake, however, jumped at an offer to continue intelligence work. He was sent under Navy cover to the SIS station in Hamburg, in the northern German zone now occupied by British troops. In part, Blake's assignment was to keep tabs on German U-boat officers being held in a nearby prison camp to make sure no "fanatical elements" were contemplating attacks on the British occupation. But already the main target was shifting from the Nazis to the Red Army. Blake's real mission was to use the German naval officers to establish a network of agents to spy on Russian forces in the Soviet zone in eastern Germany.

Blake was enthusiastic about the assignment, a heady responsibility for a twenty-three-year-old officer. Still looking younger than his years, he hardly seemed ready to take on tough U-boat commanders, more than a few of whom were unrepentant Nazis. "George Blake, however, was a fair match for them . . . ," another intelligence officer in Hamburg recalled. "The sheer exuberance of his interviewing techniques came as a nasty surprise to his charges."

Blake churned out an "interminable flow of reports, minutes and memoranda," to the annoyance of colleagues, who derisively referred to him as "the mad Dutchman." Royal Marine captain Charles Wheeler, who turned over command of the intelligence unit to Blake, found his successor charming to the point of irritation. "He smiled a lot, smiled rather too much, smiled at breakfast, you know," Wheeler recalled. Blake's conspiratorial manner and his fascination with invisible ink and other tools of the espionage trade amused the officer. "He . . . obviously got an enormous kick out of playing around with these sort of toys," Wheeler said.

Though colleagues considered him a goody-two-shoes who did not join in the seedy fun readily available in Hamburg, Blake was plagued by guilt for enjoying the life of large villas, requisitioned cars, champagne, and beautiful women that surrounded the Navy headquarters. "All this gave me a feeling of importance and did nothing for my humility," he later said. "What I call my Calvinistic side . . . strongly disapproved and thought it all rather dissolute." One consequence, he said, was that he abandoned his onetime ambition for the priesthood because he felt he was "no longer worthy."

Regardless of what his colleagues thought, officials at SIS headquarters were impressed with Blake's performance in Hamburg. His dogged work had succeeded in establishing two agent networks of German former military officers who reported on Soviet forces in East Germany. Perhaps even more attractive was his ease with languages, including fluency in Dutch, German, and French, not to mention perfectly precise, though Dutch-accented, English.

Shortly before his assignment in Hamburg ended in March 1947, Blake had dinner with several visiting senior SIS officers, including Andrew King, who would soon oversee operations in Germany, Austria, and Switzerland. King was intrigued by Blake's "cosmopolitan background." Kenneth Cohen, director of production for SIS, summed up Blake's attraction succinctly: "A gallant past, numerous languages, and an ingenious mind."

In April, soon after Blake's return to London, SIS offered him a permanent post, which he immediately accepted. Taking into consideration Albert Behar's service in World War I, Cohen waived a rule requiring all SIS officers to have been born in the United

Kingdom or its territories abroad. A requirement that officers have a university degree was also waived. The four languages Blake already spoke were three more than most SIS recruits. Given his talent, SIS elected to send him straight away to a special Russian-language course at Cambridge University.

———

Bicycling along the narrow streets beneath the ancient spires of Cambridge, Blake reveled in the university life he had never had because of the war. He immersed himself in his studies, skipping the social life, and living a monkish existence in a boardinghouse five miles from town. Under the tutelage of Dr. Elizabeth Hill, who trained generations of Russian scholars at Cambridge, he was infused with an enthusiasm for the culture. He read Tolstoy's *Anna Karenina* in Russian, attended lectures on Russian history and literature, and accompanied Hill to services at a Russian Orthodox church in London. His dislike of Russians was replaced by what he called "a romantic admiration for everything Russian."

Cambridge, Blake later said, "was one of the decisive moments in my conversion, although I didn't realize that myself then." But he insisted it did not change his political views. Unlike the still undiscovered Cambridge Five espionage ring formed by students at the university in the 1930s, comprising Kim Philby, Donald Maclean, Guy Burgess, Anthony Blunt, and John Cairncross, Blake was not part of any radical social set. His mentor, Hill, was disdainful of the Soviet regime. By the time he left Cambridge, Blake said, "I was as firmly hostile to communism as before."

But his time in Cambridge was accompanied by a dramatic change to his religious beliefs. He would often sit quietly inside King's College Chapel, contemplating his concept of Christianity as he listened to organ music fill the soaring space inside the Gothic masterpiece. He believed in predestination, that all sin is preordained, and decided this meant there could be no sin in the sight of God, and hence no need for God to send a savior. By the time he departed Cambridge, he had concluded that Christ was therefore not divine. "I found I had argued myself out of the Christian religion and could no longer call myself a Christian," he later said. What remained was his strong sense of fatalism, a belief he would find rather convenient: "That is why I believe it is justified for someone to say, 'You cannot punish me for my sins because my sins were put inside me and are not my fault.'"

———

Back at SIS headquarters in the summer of 1948, Blake learned that he had been appointed head of a new station being established in Seoul. Having hoped for a posting in the Arab world, he was disappointed. But Korea was a burgeoning hot spot. The division of the Korean peninsula along the 38th parallel at the end of World War II, meant to be a temporary arrangement between the United States and the Soviet Union, was hardening into a new permanence. Elections held in August in the U.S.-controlled south installed strongman Syngman Rhee as president. The Soviets soon designated North Korean Communist Party leader Kim Il-sung as premier of the newly created Democratic People's Republic of Korea. Both client states were being armed to the teeth as relations worsened between the communist and Western worlds. "As it turned out," Blake later said, "I got more than I bargained for."

As part of his preparations, Blake was given a booklet entitled "Theory and Practice of Communism," written by an SIS scholar. It presented an evenhanded and lucid explanation of the philosophical, economic, and political basis of Marxist theory, meant to help SIS officers understand the attractions communism held to the dispossessed of the world. To the ever-impressionable Blake, stripped of his faith in Christianity and reading deeply about communism for the first time, the theory "sounded convincing," and its objective of helping the world's downtrodden seemed both "wholly desirable" and not much different from Christian ideals. "I began to ask myself whether Communism was really the terrible evil it was made out to be," he would later write.

———

In late October 1948, Blake flew to Seoul. He had a brief stopover in Cairo, allowing for a sad reunion with the Curiel family, whom he had not seen since before the war. Following the creation of the state of Israel in May, Jews in Cairo were subjected to harassment and restrictions, and Blake found Aunt Zephira and Uncle Daniel in poor health and living in reduced circumstances, fretting because their son Henri had been jailed for his communist activities. After a few hours' visit, Blake left at midnight to resume his flight. "With a heavy heart, I said goodbye to these . . . aged and lonely people who had done so much for me," he said.

He arrived in Seoul with the daunting job of establishing an intelligence network in the Soviet Maritime Province, with a focus on Vladivostok, the provincial capital and home to the Soviets' Pacific Fleet. The Russian city was almost five hundred miles away as the crow flies, either via North Korea or over the Sea of Japan. As Blake discovered, there were no communication, trade, or other links between Seoul and Vladivostok, and he soon concluded that he had been given "a very unrealistic task." Since he spoke little Korean, his attempts to penetrate North Korea were equally futile. He felt abandoned and disillusioned with SIS.

In the spring of 1950, Maurice Firth, the snobbish head of the SIS Singapore Station, who had oversight over Blake, visited Seoul for a briefing on his activities. Firth severely reprimanded Blake for his inability to establish any network in Vladivostok or North Korea. Known to dislike foreigners, Firth made clear his disdain for Blake. "He doesn't belong in the service," the officer told colleagues.

Blake grew attached to Korea despite his unhappiness. The British minister, Vyvyan Holt, took him under his wing, accompanying him on long walks through the narrow streets of old Seoul and to the orchards dotting the lower mountain slopes on the outskirts of the city. The two men shared a distaste for flashy Americans, and considered the Rhee regime to be loathsome and dictatorial.

In their view, widespread corruption had left an elite of greedy businessmen, speculators, and corrupt politicians milking the American aid pouring into the country. "The population benefitted very little or not at all, and the poverty remained appalling," Blake said. One cold night as he walked home well sated from a dinner party at the home of an American acquaintance, he heard a whimpering cry as he passed the doorway of a building and saw a figure huddled under a rice sack. "It was one of the many homeless young beggar boys who filled the streets of Seoul," he recalled. After a pause, he continued on his way home, "but that pitiful whimper remained on my conscience for a long time," he said.

———

Despite his lost Christian faith, George Blake regularly attended church services in Seoul, both from force of habit and with the hope of developing contacts in the missionary community who could help him penetrate North Korea. He was a bit groggy when he arrived on Sunday morning, June 25, 1950, for services at the Anglican Cathedral, which he preferred for its lack of incense and genuflection. Jean Meadmore, the French vice-consul with whom he lived, had hosted a party at their home the evening before, and some guests had not left until dawn.

Sitting in his pew alongside Captain Holt, Blake watched an American officer walk in and whisper in the ears of U.S. embassy and military personnel attending the service. One by one they tiptoed out, but Blake and Holt stayed put. When they emerged at the end of the service, they found clusters of people talking excitedly. North Korean troops had crossed the border early that morning, and heavy fighting was reported all along the 38th parallel.

With U.S. intervention looming, most Americans were soon evacuating the city. Blake had clear instructions from SIS headquarters to stay in place in the event of war and serve as a listening post, reporting on developments back to London. Holt likewise kept the British legation in place as non-belligerents.

But on the evening of June 28, Blake and the other British diplomats gathered at Holt's home were stunned to hear a BBC report that the British prime minister, Clement Attlee, was sending troops to aid the United States and United Nations in their defense of South Korea. The decision left the British quite vulnerable. "Instead of being neutrals, as we thought, we were now belligerents in enemy territory," Blake said. It was too late to flee the city. Blake and his colleagues spent the night burning codes and secret documents in the garden. The next morning, they poured the legation's ample liquor supplies down the bath, uneasy at the idea of a mob getting hold of the alcohol.

On the morning of Sunday, July 2, just after tea, a party of armed North Korean soldiers drove up to the gates of the British legation in three jeeps and demanded entry. Within minutes, the British diplomats had been put in the jeeps and were driven to the Seoul police headquarters for questioning. George Blake was again a prisoner.

———

In justifying his betrayal, Blake would point to a litany of motivations: his disgust with the Rhee regime of South Korea; his revulsion at witnessing the American bombing of North Korea and the shocking destruction across the country; his disenchantment with American leadership; the vacuum left in his mind by the loss of his Christian faith; and his growing infatuation with communism. The war, he later said, "acted as a catalyst" for his decision, which was made "in unusual circumstances of violence and destruction," and likely would not have been taken if he were living comfortably in a London apartment.

These explanations likely have some truth. While some have scoffed at the idea of someone as intelligent as Blake converting to communism, particularly at a time when Stalin's crimes had become known in the West, his conversion appears both genuine and voluntary, and it would last a lifetime.

Yet those reasons hardly tell the whole story. Other factors were at play, perhaps chief among them Blake's feeling of self-importance. "He had Walter Mitty dreams," Philip Deane, the correspondent Blake befriended in captivity, would observe. Being the deus ex machina that altered the course of the Cold War appealed to this sense. "I think George liked to be the power behind the scenes . . . ," his wife Gillian would later say. "He didn't want power for himself, for his own sake. . . . He wanted to manipulate the strings and know what was going on."

Declaring allegiance to communism was akin to a religious conversion for Blake, a construct that appealed to his ego. "I feel above nationality," he would later say. "I don't approve of national feelings. Loyalty to humanity, loyalty to a human cause, loyalty to religion is higher than loyalty to country."

Blake's sense of allegiance to Britain was not particularly strong to start with; in many respects, he had closer ties to the Netherlands and Egypt than to England, where he had lived for only three years. The decade-long adventure he had lived since even before he reached adulthood had left him enthralled with deception and espionage. From his days as a teenage courier for the Dutch resistance to his escape across Europe to his work in Hamburg establishing agent networks, he had lived many lies. "Illegal work was not new to me," he noted dryly.

He also harbored grievances against England, even though the country had given sanctuary to his family and made him an officer of the hallowed SIS. He deeply resented the class consciousness and snobbery he encountered. The realization that he would never have been allowed to marry Iris Peake "might have added to his restless state of mind" in Korea, said Gillian Blake. The disdainful treatment he had received from Firth, the SIS Singapore station chief, can only have added to his alienation and insecurity. "Blake was partially motivated by his feeling that he would never be accepted as a social equal by his British colleagues because he was foreign born," Dick White, who would come to lead SIS, later told Richard Helms.

"To betray, you first have to belong," Blake would say. "I never belonged."

———

Subsequently, some would accuse Blake of acting out of self-preservation, speculating that he cut a deal when he was captured by the North Koreans after his second attempt at escape. One story has him about to be shot by a firing squad when he announced that he was a British spy. "Maybe to save his life, he told them, 'You don't know who you're going to shoot. I'm really working for MI6,'" his fellow captive and onetime friend Jean Meadmore later suggested.

Yet in those chaotic few hours after Blake's capture, with control of the surrounding areas swinging wildly between the Americans and Chinese, there would scarcely have been an opportunity for his North Korean captors to negotiate an espionage arrangement. And if they had, it seems unlikely that the Soviets, Chinese, or North Koreans would have allowed him to suffer the hardships he endured—the death march immediately afterwards, the beating at the hands of a guard, the exposure to subfreezing temperatures, the dysentery and malnutrition. Moreover, while Blake's character flaws were many, they did not seem to include cowardice.

MANPO, NORTH KOREA

Blake's decision that he was fighting on the wrong side was for him perhaps easier than what came next: "Having reached this conclusion, for better or for worse, the question was, what I was going to do about it?"

The easiest route, he reflected, would have been to offer himself to his North Korean captors for anti-American propaganda, but he found the idea distasteful. "I could also have kept my thoughts to myself and after my release left government service and joined the communist party. That would perhaps have been the most honourable way to act," he later admitted. But given his self-image, the idea of peddling the *Daily Worker* on street corners in London was scarcely more palatable than being a propaganda prop.

He convinced himself there was a grander path. His work for SIS left him well positioned to make a difference in the Cold War. Undoubtedly, this appealed to his sense of self-worth. "To be in a position to render assistance to so great a cause and not to do so, would be an even greater wrong," he said. He would rather melodramatically describe it as a decision "to live no more for myself but only for this purpose."

In the end, he surprised himself at how readily he turned. "I didn't know I was capable of that sort of thing, but apparently I was," he said.

———

For weeks, the Soviet KGB officers, Loenko and Dozhdalev, quizzed Blake during their periodic meetings, testing his answers and probing his story. At one point, they suggested that his offer was a British provocation dreamed up by Captain Holt, which Blake heatedly denied. The KGB was particularly worried by his description of the agent network he had controlled in Hamburg to spy on the Soviet military, which as he later recalled was "so vague" that it furthered suspicions that his offer was a "ploy of the British intelligence service."

At another meeting, Loenko asked him to write down everything he knew about SIS's structure. Unknown to him, the information he supplied was compared to what the KGB had learned from another source: Kim Philby. Blake's information checked out.

Eventually, Dozhdalev was satisfied. He returned to Moscow Center and recommended follow-up with Blake. KGB headquarters finally agreed. "After three months, those doubts disappeared," recalled Malyavin, the KGB officer. "Afterwards we had no doubts at all."

Blake was given the code name Diomid, or, as translated to English, Diamond. The name reflected the enormous potential the KGB placed on him. A file on Diomid was opened at Moscow Center, with severely restricted access.

At a final meeting in Manpo, Loenko told Blake that his offer had been accepted, and that when the time came, the KGB would be in contact. Loenko, who would later be known in the KGB as "Blake's godfather," bade the English spy farewell with kisses on both cheeks.

Blake was enormously relieved. "My inward struggle was over," he said. "I had been accepted and was fully committed."

He realized something else: "There was no way back."

CHAPTER 3

Bill Harvey, of All People

On the surface, it seemed strange that Bill Harvey had been chosen to take over the Berlin Operations Base, one of the CIA's most important and prestigious installations. He spoke no German, or any other foreign language, and he had no service overseas—he had never even *been* overseas. Unlike so many of his CIA colleagues, Harvey had not served with the OSS during the war, and had no dashing stories of time behind enemy lines.

Harvey did not look the type either. The former FBI G-man from Indiana was nothing like his more refined colleagues, with their boarding school pedigrees, Ivy League connections, and easy grace. Some were amused and more than a few appalled by Harvey, a blue-collar gumshoe who did not even own a trench coat. In a CIA then dominated by the blue-blooded eastern establishment, Harvey was defiantly, almost gleefully midwestern.

Just under six feet, with a bullet-shaped head and bulbous, pear-shaped body that was big and getting bigger, Harvey looked like a flatfoot from a Raymond Chandler novel. His eyes bulged from his head owing to a toxic thyroid nodule, giving him a perpetually manic look. Yet the lips beneath his pencil-thin mustache were strangely delicate—"a glamour-girl's mouth in a toad's face," wrote Norman Mailer, who used Harvey as a character in *Harlot's Ghost,* his novel about the CIA. Harvey had a voice like an acetylene torch emanating from somewhere deep inside his gut. With little prompting, he could erupt with strings of obscenities that were as terrifying as they were creative.

Some suspected that his crude speech and "deliberately countrified manner" were calculated to shock his more genteel colleagues; indeed, the politer the company, the more he seemed to swear. Stories circulated of his rampant womanizing, though they were likely untrue and probably planted by Harvey himself to add to his persona.

What was not exaggerated was his drinking, which even by the prodigious CIA standards of the day was in a league of its own. Waiters at his favored lunch spots on Connecticut Avenue knew to have a pitcher of martinis waiting the moment they spotted his distinctive figure at the door, blocking light. Two generously poured martinis would be gulped down before the food even arrived, and another pair downed by the time Harvey ambled back to work with his distinctive "duck-like strut that was part waddle and part swagger." Back at the office, it was not unusual to see him snoring at his desk by early afternoon.

Generally, Harvey was enshrouded in clouds of smoke from the three-plus packs of Camels or Chesterfields he inhaled every day. He sat at meetings paring his nails with a hunting knife, or repeatedly flipping the lid of his Zippo lighter, or, even more disconcertingly, spinning the cylinder of his snub-nosed revolver. No one else at the CIA regularly carried weapons, but Harvey always did, with one gun in a shoulder holster and often a second tucked in the back of his pants. "If you ever know as many secrets as I do, then you'll know why I carry a gun," he growled at anyone who asked.

Harvey was having lunch in Georgetown with Bill Hood, a CIA officer who had served in the OSS, when they noticed another officer at a nearby table. "Fucking namby-pamby," Harvey growled. "Not worth shit."

Hood stopped him short. "Listen, Bill, that man was a radio operator who jumped into France with less protection on him than you're wearing right now."

Beyond what he carried on his person, Harvey kept a virtual armory in his office, usually including a gun sitting in plain view atop his desk, as if he were awaiting an ambush. When visitors dropped in, he would fiddle with the weapon, loading it and gently letting the hammer down. Some theorized that his fascination with guns reflected a subconscious need to compensate for his lack of military service in World War II; others ascribed it to a frontier mentality. "Maybe, amateur psychoanalysis aside, he just liked firearms," theorized David Murphy, a longtime colleague.

Regardless, there were good and obvious reasons to be sending Harvey to the world's hottest intelligence battleground. He was a warrior, for whom "the Cold War was as real as . . . hand-to-hand combat," one contemporary said. Harvey, it was said, had a nose for a spy. It had been Bill Harvey who had laid out the case in June 1951 that Kim Philby, the smooth and popular SIS liaison in Washington, was actually a KGB spy who had been draining Western intelligence of precious secrets for years. "He turned out to be right on Kim Philby and that counted for a lot," said Tom Polgar, a CIA colleague.

The Philby episode was more proof of what even his detractors had to concede was true: No one in the young CIA knew more about Soviet intelligence than Harvey.

———

Some CIA officers attributed Harvey's attitude to a sense of inferiority to the East Coast elite and envy that he was not part of the establishment. Others concluded that he simply did not like the "Yale boys," as he often called them. What is clear is that Harvey never tried to fit into the prevailing East Coast ethos, not that it would have been remotely possible.

William King Harvey believed he was smarter than the Ivy Leaguers, and he was usually right. He was born in 1915 in Danville, Indiana, where his father, an attorney, died ten months after his birth. His mother, Sara King Harvey, who had studied at Oxford and held a PhD in Elizabethan literature, taught at Indiana State University at a time when females in academia were unusual. Bill, an only child, had a close bond with his mother, an elegant woman who spoke perfectly inflected English without a trace of the local Hoosier twang; the two engaged in Shakespeare quotation duels throughout her life. An Eagle Scout who finished high school early,

Bill went to work at age fifteen as a reporter and printer at the newspaper owned by his grandfather.

In 1933, he entered Indiana State, where he excelled, completing the coursework at such a fast pace that he was admitted to the law school after only two years and graduated with a law degree in 1937. He also left Indiana a married man, having wed a fellow student, Libby McIntire. In March 1938, he opened a law practice in her hometown of Maysville, Kentucky, southeast of Cincinnati on the Ohio River. But his heart was never in it, nor did Harvey have anything close to the glad-handing demeanor helpful for a small-town lawyer.

Not long after Germany invaded Poland in September 1939, Harvey applied to the FBI, eager for some kind of action. A bureau special agent sent to investigate him found him to be self-confident and "very level-headed," as well as possessing a "good vocabulary." The applicant, he noted, "admits taking a social drink." Harvey was offered a job in November 1940.

Harvey was assigned to the prestigious New York field office and was soon in the thick of FBI attempts to penetrate German espionage rings in the United States. He was part of a team that recruited an agent inside the German consulate in New York, leading to the arrest of thirty-seven reputed spies working for German military intelligence, known as the Abwehr. After Pearl Harbor, he pleaded for an assignment overseas, but his superiors wanted to keep his skills close to home. He was sent to the German desk at FBI headquarters in Washington, where his enthusiasm and expertise in combatting the Abwehr throughout the war were rated as "particularly outstanding."

But Harvey had a streak of independence that drew the ire of the one person who mattered at the FBI—its powerful director, J. Edgar Hoover. In October 1945, shortly after the war's end, Harvey approved a bugging operation in New York City without higher approval. Hoover was irate, telling him that he had "exercised extremely bad judgment."

Despite this misstep, Harvey was soon thereafter among a trio of FBI agents who made up the first U.S. counterespionage team aimed at the Soviets. He was in the thick of a case that became one of the biggest spy stories of the time when it was made public several years later. In the fall of 1945, a woman named Elizabeth Bentley approached the FBI to confess that she had worked for years as a courier for a Soviet spy ring, exposing a shocking penetration of the U.S. government by Soviet intelligence. Eventually, she gave the names of more than a hundred people in the United States and Canada who were working for the Soviets, including twenty-seven people in government agencies, among them Alger Hiss, a senior State Department official.

For the next two years, Harvey was consumed with the investigation, working leads and gathering evidence, and in the process becoming an authority on Soviet espionage operations in the United States. Despite the tremendous volume of material collected, the FBI was unable to build enough of a case to prosecute anyone for espionage, although Hiss was later convicted of perjury. Harvey again drew high marks for his "vigorous, forceful and aggressive" work, and he was rated one of the best FBI supervisors in Washington in a 1947 efficiency report. "His grasp of the details of Russian espionage operations in this country was a revelation to most agents," according to an FBI evaluation.

But his FBI career came to a sudden end when he again displeased Hoover. On the night of July 11, 1947, Harvey played poker and drank some beers at a farewell party in Arlington for an FBI agent who was being transferred. He was driving through Rock Creek Park in Northwest Washington on his way home when his car stalled in a heavy downpour. Unable to get the engine restarted, he dozed off in the car. By the time he awoke, it was 10 a.m., and when he made his way home, he found that his worried wife had contacted his office. He immediately called to report that he was fine, but it was too late—an investigation had started. The FBI's head of domestic security, Mickey Ladd—who had been at the party—reported "no indication that Harvey was drinking any more or any less than anyone else." But beyond driving intoxicated, Harvey had violated one of Hoover's strict rules: Agents were required to either telephone the office every two hours or leave a phone number where they could be reached.

Harvey's supervisors recommended leniency, considering his talent and the long hours he put in on the job. Hoover saw it differently, directing that Harvey be transferred to the Indianapolis office, a humiliation for someone of his experience. Within weeks, Harvey resigned from the bureau.

———

The CIA was only too happy to have Harvey. Several weeks after his resignation, he was hired by the Central Intelligence Group, which soon thereafter became the CIA. The fledgling agency had almost no counterintelligence expertise. Harvey arrived with high prestige as an expert on Soviet espionage, which was exactly what the CIA needed. "No one cared that Harvey had run afoul of J. Edgar Hoover's chickenshit regulations," recalled Tom Polgar.

Harvey was soon assigned to be chief of the CIA's counterintelligence staff. He made waves from the start, gaining notice with his intense focus, hard work, and air of self-assurance. "He was a full speed ahead type of guy," Polgar said. Beyond that, Harvey had what colleagues called an "extraordinary counterintelligence mind." They were astonished by the encyclopedic recall he had of every detail of every case from every file he had ever looked at in his years studying Soviet intelligence at the FBI. "Here was a guy from Indiana, who had no foreign background and spoke no foreign languages," said Murphy. "It was strange to find a guy who was as well informed as he was on Soviet activity with no background on Soviet affairs."

Hoover was infuriated at Harvey's hire, particularly as he realized how much the CIA valued him. In July 1950, Hoover sent an emissary to Admiral Roscoe Hillenkoetter, the CIA director, to complain that Harvey was being "hostile" to the FBI in his liaison work with the bureau on counterintelligence issues. Hillenkoetter replied that "Harvey's sarcasm was merely the result of a forceful and ambitious personality," but he nonetheless ordered Harvey to "tone down" his language.

———

In January 1951, Kim Philby hosted the most ill-fated dinner party in the history of the nation's capital, or at least since the British captured Washington in 1814, found the White House dining room table set for dinner, and torched the building after eating the meal.

Philby, serving as the SIS liaison in Washington, invited all his FBI and CIA contacts and their wives to his home on Nebraska Avenue in Northwest Washington. The two dozen guests included the FBI mole hunter Robert Lamphere and the cadaver-like James Angleton, a rising force in the CIA who had been unwittingly spilling secrets to Philby for years during long, alcohol-infused lunches.

Also present were the Harveys. Bill Harvey was Philby's closest contact in the CIA, other than Angleton. Though Harvey had "a dim view of almost everything British," Helms recalled, he had been impressed when Philby arrived in Washington in 1949. "At last the Limeys have sent someone over here that I can talk business with," he told a colleague.

Philby, for his part, was privately dismissive of Harvey, considering him a hick and a drunk. The first time Bill and Libby attended a dinner party at his home, Philby later wrote, Bill Harvey "fell asleep over the coffee and sat snoring gently until midnight when his wife took him away, saying: 'Come now, Daddy, it's time you were in bed.'"

At the party on January 19, 1951, it was Libby Harvey—herself a heavy drinker, often ill at ease in the Washington social swirl, and unhappy in her marriage—who was in her cups even before arriving. "She'd already had a lot to drink and wanted to share her disgust at the entire array of dinner guests and the party itself with anyone who'd listen," recalled Lamphere. "Somehow she became my dinner partner, and I spent most of the meal attempting to quiet her." The tenseness at the dinner was not eased by the awkward discomfort of CIA and FBI guests who by and large did not like each other.

Into this combustible scene walked a drunken Guy Burgess, one of Philby's Cambridge classmates who had been recruited into the spy ring in the 1930s. Burgess's wildly excessive drinking and notorious ill behavior had hampered his usefulness as a Soviet spy. He had recently been assigned to the British embassy in Washington as a second secretary and was staying as a houseguest at Philby's home.

Burgess, a skilled sketch artist, began an inebriated conversation with Libby Harvey. "How extraordinary to see the face I've been doodling all my life," he slurred. Libby invited him to sketch her portrait. Burgess responded with a lewd sketch portraying Libby with her dress hiked above her waist. When Burgess showed the finished work to party guests, Libby burst into tears. Outraged, Bill Harvey took a wild swing at Burgess, missed, and then jumped on the British diplomat, throttling him with both hands around his neck. Philby and two guests managed to pull Harvey off. Angleton took Harvey on a walk around the block to cool him down. The Harveys departed in a huff, and the party wound down without further violence.

A distraught Philby sat in his kitchen afterwards with his head in his hands. Harvey was a bad enemy to have. "How could you?" Philby moaned repeatedly to the unabashed Burgess. He took Harvey to lunch the next day trying to make amends for the incident. "I had apologized handsomely for [Burgess's] behavior, and the apology had apparently been accepted," he later said.

But if Harvey forgave, he certainly did not forget.

———

On May 25, 1951, a rented Austin pulled up in a hurry shortly before midnight on a dock in Southampton, England. Out popped Guy Burgess, accompanied by Donald Maclean, another member of the Cambridge spy ring. Abandoning the car at the dock, the two scrambled up a gangplank and boarded a cross-Channel ferry bound for Saint-Malo, France, the start of a journey that would take them in short order to Switzerland, Prague, and then Moscow. They would never return.

Maclean had escaped in the nick of time. For a while, VENONA intercepts had raised suspicion that the Soviets had a highly placed spy, code-named Homer, in the British embassy in Washington. Not long after Philby's dinner party, an intercept decoded at Arlington Hall pointed to the likelihood that Homer was Maclean, who had been stationed in Washington from 1944 to 1948.

Getting wind that Maclean was in danger, Philby had sent Burgess to Britain with an urgent warning for Maclean that he needed to escape to Russia. But Philby had not expected that Burgess would run too—a development that left Philby dangerously exposed.

Maclean's disappearance raised grave alarms in London and Washington. It was not very long before Burgess's involvement with the escape led to curiosity about Philby's role in all this, particularly in the mind of Harvey. The dinner party incident earlier that year had "fixed the relationship of Philby and Burgess with outraged clarity in his mind," author David Martin wrote in *Wilderness of Mirrors*.

Harvey's opinion of Philby "had thoroughly eroded" by now, Helms said. Harvey pored over everything that was known about Philby's life and career, working through the facts in his analytic mind. As he sat stuck in traffic one morning on the way to work, the pieces suddenly clicked: Philby's embrace of left-wing ideology as a young student; a cryptic warning in 1940 from a Soviet defector about a British spy who matched Philby's biography; an aborted defection in Istanbul in 1945 of a KGB officer, whom Philby had been in a position to betray; and now the flight of Maclean and Burgess. Not only was Philby one of the few people in a position to know the suspicions about Maclean, but he was a close friend of Burgess. On June 13, 1951, Harvey sent his findings to the CIA director, Walter Bedell Smith. Harvey's memo was a tour de force laying out the case that Philby was a Soviet spy. Angleton submitted his own memo a few days later, with far more equivocation. Smith was persuaded, and soon afterwards sent a chilly letter to Stewart Menzies, or "C," as the head of SIS was known, presenting the memos and insisting that Philby be removed as liaison in Washington.

Philby had already been summoned back to London for questioning by MI5, the British domestic intelligence agency roughly equivalent to the FBI, which had its own growing suspicions. Given the case against him, Philby had little choice but to resign. But the evidence was not clear-cut enough to arrest him without a confession, leaving him on the periphery of SIS with a cloud of suspicion over his head.

Philby later learned that Smith's demand had been based largely on Harvey's memo, which, he fumed, was a "cheap trick" and a "retrospective exercise in spite" for the dinner party debacle. What annoyed Philby the most was the realization that his treachery, which had fooled the best minds of Western intelligence for more than a decade, had been discovered by Bill Harvey, "of all people!"

———

Now Bill Harvey, of all people, was headed to Berlin. Even at the highest levels of the CIA, very few people knew the real reason for the assignment: Harvey would oversee the development, construction, and operation of a long tunnel into East Berlin to tap into Soviet military communication lines.

In the late summer of 1952, as Harvey prepared for the assignment, he approached Peter Sichel, who had served as Berlin base chief until May. While in Berlin, Sichel had not been told of plans for a tunnel, despite overseeing the successful penetration of the East German postal ministry. He had nonetheless deduced that some kind of tapping operation was in the works. "I had no idea, however, that it involved us trying to put a major listening post into the Soviet sector," he later said.

Now that he had taken over the German desk at CIA headquarters, Sichel was read in to the tunnel project. A decidedly cosmopolitan and elegant man, he came from a family of winemakers who had fled from Germany because they were Jews. He had joined the OSS and was sent to Berlin at the end of the war, staying on and eventually transferring to the CIA, where he rose to head the Berlin base. While not an Ivy Leaguer, he was, even worse in Harvey's eyes, a cultivated foreigner. But Harvey was willing to overlook that to get Sichel's support for his Berlin venture. "I was about as strange an animal as he could ever think of, everything he disapproved of," Sichel recalled. "He was probably surprised I wasn't a homosexual. But somehow he made up his mind that I was going to be his best friend."

For his part, Sichel had heard about Harvey's eccentricities, and he was not disappointed. "I knew he was strange," Sichel recalled. "I knew he had four dry martinis at lunch and what have you." By sheer willpower, the two got along.

Harvey "immediately got me involved in the tunnel business," said Sichel, who recognized that Harvey was the ideal man to lead the project. "He from the start was the brain of it, and ultimately the executor of it," Sichel said.

———

While Harvey's preparations continued in Washington, his man in Germany—Alan Conway, the Staff D operative in Frankfurt given the code name "Fleetwood" by Harvey—was investigating where a tap on Soviet lines could be made. The news was all good.

Conway was a veteran signals intelligence officer who commanded an OSS communications unit in London and later an Army Security Agency unit in Germany. He had started his military career as an enlisted man, but by virtue of his quiet authority became an officer. Transferring to the CIA in spring 1951, Conway proved to be a taciturn soul, a nonconformist who did not suffer fools gladly, especially if they were from headquarters. He once responded to an annoying cable from Washington by sending back three paragraphs of gibberish. "Headquarters never again asked for a repeat or clarification," said Charlie Bray, who worked closely with Conway.

The one thing Fleetwood prized over anything else was secrecy, and the tunnel operation he set up, another CIA officer said, would show "how covert covert can be." Conway insisted on airtight compartmentalization, so officers working on the operation in Berlin had no idea what was being done in Frankfurt, and vice versa. "The man was obsessed with maintaining the security of his operation," said John Osborne, a CIA officer who assisted Conway on the project.

Conway had been assigned by Harvey to do a survey of the Berlin landlines to locate a spot from where they could be tapped, picking up on the work the Berlin base had done the previous year. He operated from the CIA's Germany station headquarters in the IG Farben building, the massive and iconic former home of the German chemical giant that had been taken over by the United States to house its occupation command structure. Conway needed help, and the first person he brought into the tunnel operation was Walter O'Brien, a tough-talking and capable CIA officer. O'Brien—universally known as Obie—had a varied career to that point, including one stint as a professional baseball player and another as a lawyer in Chicago. He served in Europe during the war as an Army infantry officer, moving into military intelligence and learning German so he could interrogate Nazi prisoners.

O'Brien was sent to Berlin in early 1952 to take over the job of recruiting agents in the East Berlin office of the East German Post and Telecommunications Ministry. Ostensibly, his job was to serve as chief of counterespionage in Berlin, a full-time job in itself. His real assignment was so secret that no one in Berlin knew about it. Even Lester Houck, filling in as Berlin base chief until Harvey's arrival, was in the dark.

Working under the close control of Conway in Frankfurt and Harvey in Washington, O'Brien used contacts in the West Berlin postal office to recruit more agents working on the East Berlin side. O'Brien knew little about communications, but he was a good talker. "It's a sales job, really," he later said. "My father was a sales manager and it wasn't much different." Many of the postal workers were nonpolitical technicians who deeply disliked the Soviet occupying forces, and it was not a tough sell.

O'Brien targeted much of his efforts at the telephone exchange in the Lichtenberg district of East Berlin, where the Soviets controlled all ninety-three telephone trunk lines running into East Germany. O'Brien recruited a long-distance worker in the Lichtenberg office who had access to books of circuit drawings showing who used what cables. The agent made many trips lugging the hefty volumes to a rendezvous point with O'Brien near the American sector border. Obie would drive the books to the Berlin base headquarters in the Dahlem district, photograph them, then hurry them back to the agent before they were discovered missing. Gradually, O'Brien and Conway built up a list with the precise location of the cables used by the Soviets.

A huge break soon followed when a senior postal official defected to West Berlin. The agent, code-named CANDARE 4, had been a high-level Reichspost technician during the war, and he had a photographic memory for circuits. Conway brought him to Frankfurt to help decipher the material O'Brien had collected.

Conway's German was minimal, and he needed someone who spoke the language impeccably to help with the debriefing. His sights soon set upon John Osborne, a twenty-five-year-old aspiring academic from Maryland. Osborne worked as a reports officer at the Frankfurt headquarters, where he recalled being "bored to tears but bilingual." He was the only linguist at the Frankfurt headquarters whose parents were not recent immigrants from Germany—and hence security risks in Conway's mind, because they might have relatives living in the East.

In the spring of 1952, Conway accosted Osborne in the hallway, escorted him to his office, closed the door, and told him he needed his help on an unspecified interpreting job. Osborne had little idea who Conway was. "I knew only that he was involved in the most sensitive operations, the 'read this and then burn yourself' sort of things," he recalled. When Osborne said he would need to get his boss's approval, Conway told him no: The work had already been cleared "higher up," and his boss had no need to know.

A day or so later, Osborne walked with Conway to a nearby apartment to meet the defector, an amiable if nervous man about fifty years old. The three huddled around a microfilm reader on which Osborne could make out a series of curious drawings of lines with numbers attached. Unknown to him, these were the circuit drawings that O'Brien had photographed in Berlin. Conway had specific questions about the circuits, and CANDARE 4 was able to explain the drawings in great detail. "None of it made a helluva lot of sense to me, but Fleetwood seemed satisfied," Osborne recalled.

In the weeks that followed, CANDARE 4 provided a mountain of detailed information about the cables. Though he knew better than to say anything to Conway, Osborne had gleaned that the operation dealt with telecommunications in Berlin. "I had the impression that Fleetwood knew exactly where the major landlines in the East were and was focused exclusively on determining which circuits would be carrying traffic of interest to him," Osborne said.

By July 1952, Conway had identified three long-distance cables—*Fernkabel*—that were of great interest. The trunk cables, laid in the nineteenth century by the German Imperial Postal Service, carried the designations FK 150, FK 151, and FK 152. Combined, they carried several hundred circuits dedicated for the Soviet military, among them a critical high-security link between Moscow and the new Soviet military headquarters south of Berlin in Wünsdorf. Moreover, the cables ran close enough to the border to be reached by tunnel.

Conway sent Osborne to Berlin with instructions to scour the city to find the most detailed maps possible. Osborne learned that German military surveyors had made maps in the 1930s that showed every street, highway, alley, byway, and building in Berlin. But how to find a set? Osborne called map stores all over town before finding a firm operating out of a partially burned-out building in the British sector that had an incomplete set. Osborne returned to Frankfurt with every map sheet they had.

Conway directed Osborne to have the ones showing the border between the Western and Soviet sectors enlarged as much as possible, handing him wads of German marks to pay for everything. "Don't ask for receipts," he told Osborne. Once the enlargements were ready, Osborne took them to a safe house where he assembled the pantographs into one "monster" map sheet showing a swath of Berlin along the border between the Western and Soviet sectors. Below the ground in the Soviet sector, tantalizingly close to the border in spots, ran FK 150, FK 151, and FK 152.

———

By the late fall of 1952, the man who would be Harvey's closest partner on the tunnel project had arrived at CIA headquarters. Frank Rowlett had grown unhappy at the Armed Forces Security Agency, which had overseen signals intelligence since 1947 and was undergoing a major reorganization, including reincarnation as the National Security Agency under a secret executive order signed by Truman in October 1952.

Rowlett's move came against the backdrop of a simmering turf war between the CIA and the AFSA, and now the NSA. Signals intelligence collected by the NSA was often not shared with the CIA. The result was that CIA assessments and reports "were regularly contradicted by closely held cryptologic information, damaging the Agency's credibility," according to a CIA journal. It was embarrassing for the CIA to present the White House with an intelligence assessment only to have it proven demonstrably wrong by signals intelligence the agency had never seen.

The CIA decided the thing to do was collect its own signals intelligence. CIA deputy director Allen Dulles, who with Dwight D.

Eisenhower's election as president in November 1952 would soon be named director, wanted Rowlett to take over the technical collection effort.

Rowlett was ripe for the plucking. General Ralph Canine, a hard-charging Army artillery officer who had served under George Patton, made sweeping changes after taking charge of AFSA in 1951 and was now in charge of the new NSA. Among the feathers Canine managed to ruffle were Rowlett's. The genteel Virginian, serving as the chief of signals intelligence, balked at Canine's attempt to move him to the code-making side of the NSA. "Canine didn't like me," Rowlett recalled. "I didn't move fast enough to suit him and I think he sensed I didn't have much respect for the way he was running the business because I was pretty outspoken." With the encouragement of Harvey, who knew the value he would bring to the tunnel, Rowlett accepted an offer to join the CIA as head of Staff D, overseeing the office responsible for clandestine electronic surveillance operations against foreign communications. The CIA badly needed Rowlett's expertise. "Most of the people at CIA had not come from the technical end of the business," he said. "They didn't quite understand what was required in terms of a cryptanalytic organization."

Dulles assured Rowlett that the CIA was not trying to usurp the NSA's mission. "Dulles put it flatly, we're not going into competition with NSA," Rowlett recalled. "We've got enough to do in CIA and we're not going to fragmentize our efforts." However, that was not the way Canine saw it. He was livid at the poaching of Rowlett and several other senior cryptologists, viewing it as an attempt by the CIA to establish a rival cryptologic organization. The result was even less cooperation between the two spy agencies. "NSA limited its assistance to CIA whenever and wherever it could, regardless of possible damage to operations and analysis," according to a later CIA account. That only furthered the CIA's determination to get its own signals intelligence, and made the idea of a tunnel tapping directly into sensitive Red Army communications in Berlin even more attractive.

The three top players in the CIA's tunnel team were now set and in position. Harvey would oversee the operation in Berlin. Rowlett, atop Staff D in Washington, would provide the headquarters support. Conway, the communications specialist in Frankfurt, was in charge of the technical aspects. They had "a complete free hand to do whatever they needed to do, and money was no object," said Hugh Montgomery, a CIA officer who would join the team.

In December 1952, Harvey departed Washington for Germany, arriving with two suitcases and a green light.

CHAPTER 4

Ground Zero

BERLIN, WINTER 1952-53

The Berlin Operations Base veterans were unsure what to make of their new chief. Bill Harvey was little known outside of counterintelligence circles in Washington. "To the case officers of Berlin Base he was a creature from another planet," according to David Murphy, who would serve as Harvey's deputy in Berlin.

The outgoing chief, Lester Houck, hosted a welcome party in January 1953 at the magnificent house on Lepsiusstrasse that Harvey was inheriting. The weather was unseasonably mild for winter, and the party was held outdoors around the swimming pool. Bayard "Bay" Stockton, a young CIA officer, stood with colleagues snickering at the "bulky bibulous" Harvey, who looked nothing like the swashbuckling figures they imagined themselves to be. Some gasped when they caught a glimpse of his size and shape—"round in the middle, but really round, like the halves of two avocados glued together," said Stockton. If Harvey realized he was the object of ridicule, he gave no inkling. "We eyed Harvey's ungainly figure skeptically as he circled the eerily lit pool, grasped each of us firmly by the hand, and took our measure in an instant of deep contact," Stockton recalled.

None of them had correctly gauged their new chief. "We had no inkling of the surging quality of the man, nor how he would affect our lives, let alone the impact he would have on the CIA," Stockton later wrote. "Nor did we have a clue about the plans Harvey had for the base, much less that he was in Berlin to mastermind a huge and most-delicate operation, the Berlin Tunnel."

———

The base Harvey was taking over still held a wartime aura from its OSS days, with an esprit that was forged even deeper during the airlift four years earlier, when the Allies kept West Berlin alive in the face of the Soviet blockade. The Berlin Operations Base, or BOB, as it was known, had a palpable swagger, fed by the moral certainty that had accompanied winning a world war and now standing up to the communist threat. "We were the good guys, rebuilding Europe and West Germany into successful democracies, and then there were the Soviets, anxious to expand their empire," recalled Peter Sichel, who had led BOB until May. "We had no doubt that we were defending the Western world."

The base was still headquartered in the same spot chosen by Allen Dulles when the OSS entered the city in July 1945. The high-gabled redbrick building at Föhrenweg 21, a quiet, tree-lined street in the lovely Dahlem district in the American sector, had been designed by Hitler's architect Albert Speer, and used during the war as a command post by Field Marshal Wilhelm Keitel, chief of the German High Command. It was consequently a small fortress with three stories below ground for air raid protection, all surrounded by a nice garden and a high fence.

Harvey inherited about twenty case officers, a half dozen reports officers, three communications officers, and other support personnel, a relatively small contingent but one that was quite active and rapidly growing. Berlin was "the point of the spear," said David Chavchavadze, one of Harvey's officers. "To be in Berlin at that time was perhaps the most prestigious and elite assignment anywhere."

In the years before the construction of the Berlin Wall, the divided city was the espionage capital of the world. Easy travel across the sectors made it ideal territory for recruiting agents, meeting with operatives, and passing along information. Tens of thousands of Berliners crossed the sector borders every day, many of them East

Berliners coming to jobs in the West, and others West Berliners visiting relatives in the East or buying fresh vegetables from East German farms. Residents could move freely across the sector borders by
riding the S–Bahn, the elevated railway, or the U–Bahn, the subway,
or they could simply walk or drive across with little restriction other
than checkpoints at main street crossings.

All four powers operated with multiple intelligence agencies, as
did some of their allies. The U.S. Army and Air Force each had
their own clandestine intelligence units operating in Berlin, as did
the Navy, despite the fact there was "no body of water large enough
to accommodate anything much larger than a river barge," recalled
John Osborne, who had finished his work with Alan Conway in
Frankfurt and was now stationed in Berlin.

"Berlin had so many intelligence officers, agents and goons in it
that they must have made up a measurable percentage of the population," said Chavchavadze. "I mean, there were in addition to ourselves and the other American services, at least two services each
from the British, French, West Germans, East Germans, Soviets,
Czechs, Poles and God knows who else." The East German government complained that at least eighty Western intelligence agencies
were operating in the city, but Western officials privately insisted
it was only around forty. The intelligence agencies operated with
countless front organizations meant to disguise the espionage, ranging from jam exporters to clothing shops to research institutes.

Certainly, there were more intelligence operatives per acre in
Berlin than anywhere else in the world. The war's aftermath had
left the capital fertile ground for recruiting desperate, dissolute, or
discontented individuals who might or might not have access to useful intelligence. Some operators would sell information of varying
quality to the highest bidder; others simply made it up. "There were
a lot of what we call intelligence mills," said Sichel. "People who did
not have intelligence, did not have agents, did not have access, but
who wrote intelligence reports and sold them. It was an industry."

Despite its aura, BOB to that point was outmatched in the battle
for intelligence in Berlin. The occupation of Berlin had barely started
before the KGB went to work, recruiting spies wholesale to spy on

Allied installations, and the CIA was struggling to catch up. Soviet and East German agents thoroughly penetrated many German and Allied government offices in Berlin and West Germany, including the U.S. military mission in Berlin. (Not long after Harvey's arrival, the KGB recruited an Army sergeant stationed in Berlin, Robert Lee Johnson, who would pass on secrets to the Soviets for a decade.) The police state created by the East German and Soviet authorities made it much more difficult for the West to plant its own spies.

When BOB secretly established and funded the Free Jurists Committee, an organization of Berlin lawyers opposed to the Soviet regime, the KGB, working with the equally ruthless East German Stasi, responded by kidnapping one of the leaders of the organization, Walter Linse, from outside his home in the American sector in July 1952. He died a year later in a Soviet prison. It was just one of dozens of kidnappings that took place in Berlin around that time.

The KGB was headquartered in the former St. Antonius Hospital in the Karlshorst district of East Berlin, with a staff of almost a thousand across East Germany, including hundreds of officers and technical personnel, the largest KGB operation outside the Soviet Union. Karlshorst was a self-contained, 160-acre compound, including the Kommandatura—the headquarters for the Red Army's Berlin garrison, and housing for troops and embassy personnel, all surrounded by a fence and patrolled by well-armed Stasi guards.

While Berlin was not as critical to the KGB as it was to Western intelligence, the city provided the Soviets with an important window into the U.S. and NATO military presence in Western Europe. Apart from countering Western intelligence operations, the overriding focus of the KGB in Berlin was to prevent the rise of a new German military threat, and to ensure that any unification of Germany would be on terms friendly to the Soviet Union.

———

Harvey was arriving in Berlin at a time of rising tension between the Soviets and the Western Allies. Joseph Stalin had made overtures for German unification in 1952, but the Allies viewed his proposals as a propaganda ploy to force the United States, Britain, and France out of Berlin and West Germany. The West insisted that unification be accompanied by free elections across the country, which the Soviets opposed, and no progress had been made.

An air of menace surrounded East-West relations in the divided city. In April 1952, two Soviet MiG-15 fighters attacked an Air France plane as it approached Berlin on a routine flight, wounding two passengers; and in October, Soviet aircraft fired on a U.S. military medical evacuation plane flying between Frankfurt and Berlin. Soon after Harvey's arrival, the Soviets shot down a British bomber on a routine training mission.

Berlin's isolation, surrounded by East German territory just fifty miles from the border with Poland, bred a close-knit sense of camaraderie among the BOBers. "We were in fact stuck on an island in a sea of red . . . and that island was damn small," recalled John Osborne. Two years earlier, Red Army troops in East Germany— known as the Group of Soviet Forces Germany (GSFG)—had numbered 300,000. The force now stood at 405,000, with a considerable increase in the number of tanks, and its formations were "virtually on a war footing," capable of spearheading a surprise attack into Western Europe without calling up reinforcements, according to a 1953 British military intelligence assessment. GSFG headquarters had moved in May 1952 from Potsdam just outside Berlin to Wünsdorf, a large military complex southeast of the city that had housed the Wehrmacht command during the war. The new headquarters, restored from bombing damage, provided more security for the Soviet command, with underground facilities and a location removed from close contact with the Western Allies.

Berlin in 1953 was still recovering from the war, especially in the East. Much of the city had been destroyed by two years of heavy bombing followed by its capture by the Red Army. Nearly eight years after the war, visitors to the East were stunned at the amount of rubble still spread around the city.

In the West, however, a renaissance was under way. The Kurfürstendamm, the main shopping boulevard known as "the Fifth Avenue of Berlin," had seen whole blocks destroyed by street fighting and aerial bombardment. But it had burst back to life and was now a maze of movie theaters, sidewalk restaurants, and shop windows, radiating come sundown with neon light. Berlin's thriving and of-tentimes seedy nightlife had been restored to its prewar heights.

To Bay Stockton, Berlin carried an atmosphere of "spine-tingling sleaziness . . . on the fringes of [a] titanic struggle." Nightclubs and cafés served as playgrounds and espionage meeting grounds, often at the same time. The famous Resi in Hasenheide was an enormous dance palace featuring an eighteen-piece orchestra and hundreds of tables connected by telephones and pneumatic tubes for delivering messages, allowing patrons to ask others for dances or pass along compliments. The Badewanne on Nürnbergerstrasse was "cheap and loud but bursting with Berlin vitality," in the words of one visitor, Ian Fleming.

In East Berlin, Café Warsaw served as a "stock exchange for se-crets," with many tables often occupied by agents purporting to be working for the Soviets, Czechs, Poles, British, Americans, French, and East and West Germans. But allegiances were fleeting. "A few dollars were enough to make many of the boys change sides between cups of coffee," one Western officer said.

"Berlin was like Dodge City and Casablanca rolled into one," recalled Charlie Bray. It was perfect for Harvey.

While Harvey had domain in Berlin, he was under the command of the German station headquarters in Frankfurt, overseen by the CIA senior representative in Germany, Lucian Truscott, the retired U.S. Army general. Truscott's leadership in Italy through some of the hardest fighting in the European theater at Sicily, Salerno, and Anzio had earned him the reputation as one of the Army's finest World War II combat commanders. He was one of the toughest, too, with a voice like a foghorn, reputedly from swallowing carbolic acid as a child in Texas, and a craggy face that looked as if it had been "hewn directly out of hard rock."

CIA director Walter Bedell Smith, the similarly cantankerous Army general who had served as Eisenhower's chief of staff during the war, had called his comrade-in-arms out of retirement to help bring order to the sprawling CIA operation in Germany, which in-cluded more than a thousand people in eight operations and liaison bases, plus countless sub-bases and support.

Smith was worried that the CIA station was undertaking too

many half-baked covert paramilitary operations instead of focusing on intelligence collection, and he directed Truscott to put a stop to anything he deemed questionable. Truscott was not the sort to be led down a garden path. "I'm going to go out there and find out what those weirdos are up to," he promised Smith.

Since arriving in the spring of 1951, Truscott had succeeded in bringing better coordination and reason to CIA operations in Germany. "He had a wonderful methodology to get agreement with him at meetings," recalled Sichel. "He wouldn't let anyone take a pee until they made sufficient progress. The urgency of that caused people to agree to things they may not have agreed to otherwise."

Harvey had a healthy respect for Truscott, but dealt with him at arm's length, going around the general straight back to Washington on operational issues whenever he could. But he needed Truscott's support for the tunnel, not only because of his position overseeing Germany, but because digging a tunnel in Berlin would depend on getting logistical help from the military. Truscott, a respected figure among his Army peers, could help ensure that.

Truscott had been briefed on the tunnel operation by Smith in Washington in the spring of 1952. Harvey and Truscott had likewise conferred in Washington, and the two were on the same wavelength. After Harvey's arrival in Germany, he and Truscott met one-on-one frequently to talk about the tunnel. Normally, Truscott's aide, Tom Polgar, would sit in on the general's operational meetings, but Truscott had Polgar leave the room for the meetings with Harvey. This was at the insistence of Harvey; Polgar, a native Hungarian who had served with the OSS during the war, had family behind the Iron Curtain in Budapest, and that was a security risk in Harvey's book— the KGB might try to get to him via his relatives. Between his curious exclusion from the meetings with Harvey and a big buildup of personnel in Berlin that he observed, Polgar said, "it was obvious to me that something [was] going on in Berlin." Indeed there was.

———

Harvey was beholden to Truscott on a second, perhaps even more important matter. Harvey had left Washington without his family, his troubled marriage crumbling. He and Libby were in the midst of a bitter divorce, and their young son, Jimmy, had been sent to live with Harvey's mother in Indiana.

Upon his arrival in Germany shortly before Christmas 1952, Harvey had spent several days in Frankfurt meeting with Truscott and other key officials at the station headquarters. The general was usually gruff and not particularly friendly to subordinates—Truscott's guiding leadership principle was "no sonofabitch, no commander"—but he had a sentimental streak a mile wide. The general concluded that Harvey was lonely.

"Take this guy in hand," he ordered Clara Grace "CG" Follick, his stocky and energetic administrative assistant.

The tough-minded Follick had been born in a log cabin on her father's tenant farm in White County, Ohio. He named her Clara Grace, after two former girlfriends, but her mother did not like either name, so the young girl was simply known as CG, with no periods. She earned a scholarship to Ohio State, and, following Pearl Harbor, volunteered for the Women's Army Auxiliary Corps. Upon graduating with the first training class in 1942, Follick was assigned as a military liaison to Eleanor Roosevelt, accompanying the First Lady on trips around the country to inspect training camps. After the war, she took a job with the CIA as a personnel officer and was sent to Frankfurt, where Truscott came to rely on her toughness and efficiency.

Now the general gave her the job of taking care of Harvey. "CG, I want you to see to it that he has a good holiday while he is over here," Truscott told her. Follick, who had worked with Harvey in the Washington headquarters and thought him a "pompous jackass," blanched at the instructions. "I thought, 'God, I couldn't stand him. . . . He's going to ruin my Christmas,'" she later said. "But of course, anything General Truscott told me to do, yes sir, I did it."

It turned out differently this time. Follick took Harvey along for a round of Christmas cocktail parties, dances, and dinners in Frankfurt. They kissed under the mistletoe at a party at Polgar's home. By the time Harvey went to Berlin after the holidays, a romance had blossomed.

———

Harvey wasted no time driving the tunnel project forward, from both Berlin and Frankfurt. He traveled regularly to the German station headquarters in the IG Farben building to confer with Truscott and Conway, timing his visits for Fridays, allowing him to see CG for the weekend. In Berlin, he pressed Walter O'Brien to find more sources and get more technical details about the Soviet landlines.

Once again, Obie struck gold. He recruited a lawyer from the East German Post and Telecommunications Ministry, who had detailed information about how the Soviets used the international telephone service, as well as the ministry's chief Russian interpreter, who was privy to high-level technical discussions with the Soviets.

But the biggest catch was a mere clerk—"one of these little old ladies in tennis shoes who kept everything on three-by-five cards," recalled Hugh Montgomery. CANDARE 4, the senior defector, put O'Brien in touch with her. The tunnel team knew her only as Nummer Mädchen, the Numbers Girl. She worked in a switching office, where long-distance cables were assigned and users were shifted from one cable to another.

Nummer Mädchen's index cards recorded which cables were used by senior Soviet and East German officials and would therefore carry the most sensitive intelligence. "It was a pretty elementary way of doing business," Montgomery said. "She would go right to the file of three-by-five cards and tell you who was using any given pair on that confounded cable. She had it all written out there."

With the information collected from CANDARE 4 and Nummer Mädchen, the tunnel team knew which cables to tap. But before moving ahead, they needed confirmation that the cables truly held what they suspected.

In January 1953, yet another of O'Brien's agents—working alone in the East Berlin telephone office in the midnight hours, when few people were about—covertly patched the targeted Soviet telephone traffic for a few minutes onto a cable connected to a West Berlin circuit. Across the sector border in a West Berlin telephone office, a German-speaking CIA technician posing as a telephone employee recorded the sample. This surreptitious patching continued sporadi-

cally for months. Usually, the patching lasted only two or three minutes, the longest the agent dared leave the patch in place, though one
time it was kept in place for nearly half an hour. After six months,
BOB had collected two hours of recordings. That was enough for
Harvey's team to conclude that the targeted cables carried "unique
material of high interest."

———

The nicknames Harvey liked to bestow on subordinates and superiors alike were rarely flattering, but he made exceptions for most of
the tunnel team. He dubbed O'Brien "Landsmann," a German term
of affection for a fellow countryman; O'Brien was a fellow midwest-
erner who traded as a tough Irishman from Chicago, a street fighter
of the Harvey mold. Likewise, Conway, with his easy professionalism, was Harvey's type of guy. "Fleetwood was Cadillac's top-of-
the-line brand, the American Rolls Royce," recalled Charlie Bray.
"Harvey thought it was a suitable nickname for his main partner on
the tunnel."

Harvey had names for those back in Washington, too. Rowlett,
born and reared in the town of Rose Hill on the southern tip of the
Blue Ridge in Virginia, was dubbed "Mountain Boy." The smooth
and urbane Helms was the "Boy Diplomat," while the conspiratorial
James Angleton, now head of counterintelligence, was the "Black
Prince." Truscott, with his pugilistic face and manner, was known
as "Jersey Joe."

It was not long before Harvey was awarded the nickname by
which he would always be remembered. As Stockton and Osborne
returned to work one afternoon after lunch at a French bistro where
the Beaujolais had flowed, they caught a glimpse of Harvey's silhou-
ette in a bay window at headquarters. "My God!" Osborne whispered. "He looks like a pear!" The two stifled their laughter and
slunk to their desks. The Pear moniker was soon in universal use
around the base, though not to Harvey's face.

Not long afterwards, Harvey and O'Brien were having a drink
when Harvey mused about Osborne's nickname, "John Bananas."
The sobriquet predated Harvey, and he didn't like it.

"No one should be nicknamed after a fruit," he declared.

O'Brien was puzzled: "But Bill, don't you know that they all call you the Pear?"

———

Even as he moved ahead with the tunnel project, Harvey was busy putting his stamp on BOB. He pushed an expansion that would continue for years, restructuring the base for an enduring, increasingly dangerous Cold War. He did not want to do away with the old BOB esprit de corps, but tried to co-opt it and remold in his own image. He gave seasoned officers slack to do things their way, but as the base grew, he began seeding it with his own people. Younger officers learned to do things the Harvey way. They soon learned to dread seeing the letters "PSM" scrawled on their reports. That was Harvey shorthand for "Please see me." Even worse was "OSOD." That meant "Oh shit, oh dear," generally reserved for statements of unspeakable inanity. The offender would hurry to Harvey's office, where he might be met with anything from an arch comment to a blistering tirade. Sometimes Harvey would say nothing at all, simply staring with his protruding, often bloodshot eyes until the offender blurted something stupid. Most unnerving of all was when Harvey sighted his gun on nearby objects, including whoever was sitting in his office.

Harvey did not let the fact he spoke no German and had a limited grasp of the nation's politics and history inhibit him in the least. When Paul Garbler, a former Navy fighter pilot who had joined the CIA at Harvey's urging, reported to BOB as a new officer, Harvey was outraged to learn that Garbler spoke no German. "Get your ass out of my office and don't come back until you can speak German," he roared.

"I left quickly, concerned he might shoot me," Garbler recalled.

As was the case in Washington, Harvey's obsession with guns caused a stir at BOB. Despite Berlin's Wild West atmosphere, it was still a shock when Harvey insisted that all new arrivals be issued weapons, and that case officers carry a gun anytime they met with an agent. The KGB and CIA had an unwritten agreement that neither service would kidnap or kill the officers of the other, but Harvey had little faith in such quaint arrangements.

John Hadden, a Berlin veteran who took a dim view of the new base chief, was working as the duty officer at BOB one night when Harvey returned from a visit to Frankfurt carrying a large briefcase. Placing it on a desk, Harvey unlocked the case and took out six loaded handguns. "That was bad enough, but when he dumped on the desk some six more from various pockets, shoulder holsters and the like, I burst out laughing, which he took very ill indeed," Hadden recalled.

Hadden asked Harvey if he had expected trouble in Frankfurt. No, that's my usual, Harvey replied coldly.

The most daunting test for new arrivals at BOB was a rite of passage that became known as the Harvey Martini Ritual, generally held in Harvey's living room, where he kept a butler's trolley stocked with Gilbey's gin, Noilly Prat vermouth, and an ice bucket. Harvey mixed the martinis himself, quickly and businesslike, with no fancy flourishes, using a healthy dose of gin and a whisper of vermouth. The drinks were poured into birdbath-sized glasses, perhaps garnished with an olive or a pearl onion, or sometimes a lemon twist. Harvey and his subject would sit in easy chairs facing each other in front of the fireplace. The first martini went down swiftly, recalled Stockton, a participant in the ritual; the second was slower, more reflective. After the third, it was back to work. Beyond lubrication, the martini ritual served another purpose, providing Harvey with a means of gauging who on his staff he could trust.

———

When it came to trust, Harvey could not extend a full measure to the British and their intelligence service. That was especially so since the flight of Donald Maclean and Guy Burgess, and Harvey's subsequent correct conclusion that Kim Philby was a spy. But there was no getting around the fact that the tunnel could not be built in Berlin without teaming up with the British. For one thing, there was little doubt that SIS was working on its own tunnel scheme.

During the Vienna tunnel operation, it had been the British who had first suggested to the CIA that Berlin might hold similar opportunities. And indeed, Peter Lunn, the veteran SIS officer who had masterminded the Vienna operation, would arrive in the summer of

1953 to take over the big British Berlin station, and he was eager to duplicate his success.

There would be later claims that the CIA dreamed up the tunnel project on its own, and that the British became involved only at the request of the Americans. Similarly, Blake would say that the tunnel was a British project from the start, and that the Americans were brought in to dig it and pay for it. Yet the evidence shows that both the CIA and SIS were independently investigating the project, and both agencies were well aware that the other was likely doing the same. After Vienna, that would have been no surprise.

Beyond that, an agreement to work together in Berlin was just a matter of time, as each agency held advantages that the other desperately needed. Tapping into the Soviet lines would be technically a very complex operation, and the fledgling CIA simply lacked people with the expertise to do it. "The British, of course, had the experience in Vienna and knew exactly how to attack this problem," said Hugh Montgomery.

Harvey recognized this, though he certainly retained his misgivings. "Bill probably was unhappy that the British were involved at all, but he had to live with it because we needed their experience," said Bray.

The British needed American help just as badly. The best place to launch a tunnel to reach the Soviet cables would likely be from the American sector. Moreover, Berlin would be a far more ambitious and expensive proposition than Vienna. With postwar Britain in financially dire straits, SIS had nowhere near the resources and manpower on its own needed to support what promised to be a very costly operation.

Peter Montagnon, an SIS officer who would play a critical role in the tunnel, saw parallels with the classical world, when the older Greek civilization held the reservoir of knowledge and the Romans were the wealthy, upstart empire. The Americans, he said, "saw us as Greeks to their Romans."

He added, "Coming out of our successes in Vienna, we had more practical knowledge of what to do and how to do it, but we needed the Americans because the job of digging the tunnel was sort of a typical American operation in terms of expertise. I suppose we could have done it, but they were pretty good at it."

With the circuit diagrams from CANDARE 4, the cable occupancy provided by Nummer Mädchen, and the patching operation in the first months of 1953 confirming that the targeted cables carried valuable intelligence, it was time for the Americans to confer with the British. "We had everything about the East German cable system, and we guessed they'd be doing something of the sort," recalled O'Brien.

In Washington, Helms and Rowlett agreed that the British should be approached. Alan Conway and O'Brien flew to London to brief SIS on what they learned thus far. Soon there was agreement that the tunnel would be a joint American-British operation. As with the Vienna tap, Helms believed the potential value of the intercept from Berlin was too great to risk overlapping efforts. "The British agreed, and we each cooperated to the hilt at all times," Helms said.

The CIA called the project PBJOINTLY—PB being the CIA's prefix for operations in Germany in the 1950s, JOINTLY being perhaps a nod to the joint operation with the British, but more likely just a random word. The SIS called the project Stopwatch. Both also used the name Operation Gold. The Vienna tunnel operation, which had produced valuable information, had been known as Silver. Berlin, with its potential for even greater intelligence riches, would be an ore of a higher value.

CHAPTER 5

A Hero's Return

MANPO, NORTH KOREA, MARCH 1953

The schoolchildren in the town of Manpo were warned not to tell the prisoners in the nearby camp, but they did not keep the news secret for long. George Blake and his fellow captives learned in mid-March that Soviet leader Joseph Stalin had died. The next day, the picture of the dictator that had adorned the walls of the guardroom disappeared. "This must have been the first and most rapid de-Stalinisation measure in the whole of the socialist commonwealth," Blake later quipped.

It was also the first sign of big changes for the prisoners. On March 20, a week after the news arrived, they were in the midst of their usual morning walk in the farmyard when the British nationals were told to gather their belongings. Fifteen minutes later, they were riding in the back of an open truck to Pyongyang.

It was an abrupt but welcome end to their long captivity. The prisoners' despair had grown as the war dragged on into its third year with little progress reported in peace talks. Their treatment had been mostly decent, though Philip Deane, the British correspondent, had organized occasional hunger strikes out of boredom as much as anything. Their other diversion had been caring for the three-year-old daughter of a camp cook. While the mother worked, the prisoners made the child clothes, soothed her, and played games with her, especially Blake, "who was the most patient and whom she regarded as her father," Deane said.

Stalin's death removed the last impediment for a prisoner release long sought by British diplomats. Perhaps it was a goodwill gesture by Moscow, or perhaps the Soviets were as eager as the British to see Blake free.

Arriving in Pyongyang after a two-day journey, Blake and his companions found themselves pampered by North Korean officials anxious to demonstrate that the captives had been well treated throughout their captivity, as if the death march could somehow be forgotten. They were given lavish meals, luxurious shaves from a barber, and tailor-made suits for their journey home. In early April, the delegation was taken by truck across the frontier to the Chinese border town of Antung, where the former captives reveled in the wonder of a huge communal bath, scrubbing themselves with scented soap and joyfully singing nursery rhymes. They were carried through China aboard the Trans-Manchurian Express in a special club car and served chicken and caviar by attentive waiters. On April 13, they reached the Soviet frontier town of Otpor, where they were to board the Trans-Siberian Express train for Moscow.

If Blake had any thoughts that his agreement to spy for the Soviet Union had been cast aside in the intervening year and a half, they were quickly dispelled. One by one, members of the British delegation were brought to meet with Soviet officials in the customs office and fill out forms. When it was Blake's turn, he was taken to the customs office, but then led through an inner door to a small room in the back, where a thickset man of around fifty waited. There was no introduction; the man simply told Blake they would be working together. As Blake would later learn, his new KGB contact was Nikolai Borisovich Rodin, alias Korovin, a veteran intelligence officer who was serving as the KGB *rezident* at the Soviet embassy in London. Rodin had a reputation as a cold-blooded and highly skilled professional, arrogant enough to put himself above the tight security provisions he insisted his subordinates follow.

Rodin was not one for small talk. He immediately launched into plans for their first clandestine meeting after Blake's arrival home.

Blake had asked that these first meetings take place in Holland. "I
felt more on my own ground there and imagined that I would sense
more quickly if anything was amiss," he said. They agreed to meet at
a city park in The Hague, setting a date in July, with several backup
dates. They would each carry a copy of the *Nieuwe Rotterdamsche
Courant* newspaper from the previous day as a sign that all was well.
With that, Rodin ended the meeting. Even though the KGB officer
rode aboard the train in a separate compartment for the weeklong,
sixty-five-hundred-mile journey across Russia, he and Blake never
spoke or gave a sign of recognition when they passed each other in
corridors and at station stops.

Aboard the express, caviar and vodka were "pressed upon us in
great quantities," Blake said, and the travelers were "overfed, rested,
and comatose" by the time they reached Moscow on April 20. The
freed captives were greeted by the British ambassador and treated to
yet another extravagant dinner. A Royal Air Force hospital plane
flew them the next morning to West Berlin, the last stop before their
final leg to England. Despite the pounds they had added on their
monthlong journey home, they still looked haggard and wan.

Charles Wheeler, the former Royal Marine captain who had
worked with Blake in Hamburg, was now stationed in Berlin as a
BBC correspondent. At the Berlin airfield, when Wheeler tapped
his former intelligence colleague on the shoulder to say hello, Blake
jumped in the air and turned pale. To Wheeler, Blake seemed
strangely nervous for a newly free man.

———

Stalin's death on March 5 set in motion events that would mark
1953 as one of the most pivotal years of the Cold War. Inside the
Kremlin, members of the Soviet Presidium, among them Nikita
Khrushchev, Georgy Malenkov, Vyacheslav Molotov, and Lavrentiy
Beria, were wrestling for power. The freeing of the prisoners in
Korea was taken as one indication of a more conciliatory attitude in
Moscow, but no one truly knew what direction the Kremlin would
take, including the Soviet leaders themselves.

The turmoil in Moscow was only part of the leadership changes involving the major powers. Six weeks before Stalin's death, Dwight D.

Eisenhower took the oath of office as president of the United States. The ascendancy of the former Allied commander had brought a reunion with another of the grand men of World War II; after being ousted from power near the end of the war, Winston Churchill had returned in 1951 to 10 Downing Street as prime minister.

Churchill, eager to reestablish personal ties with Ike, had sailed across the Atlantic to meet with Eisenhower in New York City in January 1953, several weeks before his inauguration. World War II comradeship aside, Churchill and Eisenhower privately held major reservations about the other that the meeting did nothing to assuage. Churchill, now seventy-eight, was not in good health; he had suffered an arterial spasm in 1952, and members of his own Conservative Party were suggesting that he turn power over to Foreign Secretary Anthony Eden, pressure Churchill stoutly resisted.

After dinner with the prime minister, Eisenhower found himself in agreement with Churchill's critics. "Churchill is as charming as ever, but he is quite definitely showing the effects of the passing years," Eisenhower wrote in his diary. He found Churchill imagining that he could once again direct world affairs from "some rather Olympian platform," just as he had at the World War II summits with Roosevelt and Stalin. In particular, Churchill expected that Britain—by which he meant himself—would resume "the special place of partnership" seen in the war, a notion Eisenhower tried to tone down. "He has developed an almost child-like faith that all of the answers are to be found merely in British-American partnership," Eisenhower complained.

Churchill had his own reservations about Eisenhower. He considered Ike "a real man of limited stature," a fine military commander but perhaps not the right man with the vision to lead the free world. He had been disappointed at the general's election in November, fearing that Eisenhower would be reluctant to talk to the Soviets. "I am greatly disturbed," he told Jock Colville, his private secretary. "I think this makes war much more probable." It made Churchill all the more determined to use his standing to broker a reconciliation between the United States and the Soviet Union, and he saw Stalin's death as an opening.

Eisenhower in fact had cautious hopes of making peace with the

Soviets, and he, too, saw Stalin's death as the opportunity for "at least a start toward the birth of mutual trust." Over the objections of his hard-line secretary of state, John Foster Dulles, Eisenhower on April 16 delivered what became known as "The Chance for Peace" speech, an eloquent plea for disarmament. "Every gun that is made, every warship launched, every rocket fired signifies, in the final sense, a theft from those who hunger and are not fed, those who are cold and are not clothed," he told an audience of newspaper editors in Washington. Despite the lofty words, Eisenhower was on the whole heeding Dulles's counsel, and he remained extremely wary of the new Soviet leadership. Churchill urged the president to meet with them, but Eisenhower refused, telling the prime minister he feared the Soviets would use a summit as "another propaganda mill."

One subject about which Churchill and Eisenhower agreed was the need for better intelligence. Eisenhower was angered upon Stalin's death to learn just how little American spy services knew about Soviet intentions or the machinations inside the Kremlin. "We are not even sure what difference his death makes," he complained. Even more disturbingly, Allen Dulles informed the president that at present the CIA could not provide him "any prior warning through intelligence channels of a Soviet sneak attack."

Churchill, who was also dismayed at the lack of good information about the Soviet military, had demanded a British intelligence offensive after taking office. Like Eisenhower, he was haunted by the fear that Soviet actions over Berlin might provoke a nuclear war in Europe—with apocalyptic consequences. Something must be done.

ABINGDON, ENGLAND, WEDNESDAY, APRIL 22, 1953

Cheers and songs greeted the Royal Air Force ambulance plane that touched down at Abingdon airfield in Great Britain, carrying six British civilians released from North Korean captivity, among them George Blake. Government officials and church dignitaries, including the archbishop of Canterbury, were on hand on the beautiful spring afternoon to welcome the first British prisoners to be released by North Korea.

When the plane stopped in front of the main building, a Salvation Army choir sang "Now Thank We All Our God," and the hymn was taken up by the waiting crowd of relatives and friends as the freed captives appeared on the gangway. Blake spotted the tearstained and happy face of his mother in the first row and hurried down the steps to embrace her. Catherine Blake was welcoming her son back from a harrowing wartime experience for the second time in his thirty-one-year-old life. Once again, George Blake looked no worse for the wear, with a neatly trimmed beard and a winning smile.

The freed prisoners were besieged by journalists. Blake, wearing a blazer over a sweater vest and dark tie, with a handkerchief poking out of his pocket, grinned awkwardly for a camera crew as he described the "adequate but very monotonous" diet of rice and turnips three times a day. With his arm around his mother, he told a reporter that he was "looking forward most of all to a few days rest at home."

One other person was waiting to greet Blake, an elegantly dressed elderly man who introduced himself as the personal representative of "C," the chief of the Secret Intelligence Service. Blake was asked to report to SIS the following week.

A car took Blake and his mother to her home in the town of Reigate, south of London, where waiting neighbors greeted the hero's arrival with applause. Hanging proudly from the window of his mother's home was the Union Jack.

LONDON, WEDNESDAY, APRIL 29, 1953

A week after his return, Blake reported as instructed at the War Office to Room 070, an office that was set aside for use by SIS to meet people who had not yet been cleared to enter the intelligence headquarters. He was welcomed by two "extremely friendly" SIS officers, who quizzed him sympathetically about his arrest in Seoul, the conditions of his captivity, and his interrogations by the North Koreans. Blake assured them he had not been subjected to any torture or duress. It was a relaxed atmosphere, interrupted by attractive secretaries bringing coffee. The gentle queries continued into a second day, when he was asked about any intelligence he had collected during his captivity and journey home. The one disappointment was that he had not thought to scoop up a sample of Siberian soil that could have been tested for any traces of radioactivity indicating a Soviet nuclear test.

After the two days of mild questioning, Blake was welcomed back to the SIS fold. Despite the uproar two years earlier surrounding Maclean, Burgess, and Philby, and the resulting pressure from the United States for the British to tighten up its vetting, SIS procedures remained astonishingly lax. Sir James Easton, the deputy chief of the service, signed papers restoring Blake's clearance. "We used to regard North Korea as a bit primitive and unsophisticated," Easton later said. "We really wouldn't have suspected them of doing anything in the way of turning him." The possibility that the KGB might have reached Blake during his captivity did not occur to anyone, he admitted.

The following Monday, Blake reported to work at the SIS Head Office—"the Holy of Holies," as he called it—in the Broadway buildings near St. James's Park. He was asked to meet with the chief, John Sinclair, and taken to the legendary inner sanctum office of "C," behind a soundproof door on the fourth floor. Sinclair, a tall, angular Scot with austere features who reminded Blake of a Presbyterian minister, solicitously got up from behind his desk to shake hands.

"Pleased to see you back with us, Blake," Sinclair said. "I have read the report on your experiences, but I wanted to have a talk with you myself. How have things been?"

"Well, sir," Blake replied, "only in the first year were conditions really bad." After some sympathetic chat, Sinclair suggested that Blake take a few months' leave while they searched for a suitable new assignment for him at headquarters.

Before taking his leave, Blake found himself to be "a bit of a celebrity" within the corridors of SIS. There was some talk of his being knighted, but the idea did not advance because of his sensitive intelligence position. On June 2, 1953, he was invited to join a select group of senior SIS officials at Carlton Gardens to watch the coronation of the new British monarch, Queen Elizabeth II. Stands had been erected in a narrow front garden overlooking the Mall to watch the coronation procession on its way to Westminster Abbey. As a special mark of favor, Blake was invited to join the champagne party held afterwards in the downstairs reception rooms. The celebration included a toast to his safe return.

BERLIN, TUESDAY, JUNE 16, 1953

Working the reports desk at the Berlin base, John "Bananas" Osborne had been picking up signs of trouble in the Soviet sector all week. Laborers in the East were angry about wage cuts, higher food prices, and increased work quotas announced in late May by the East German regime, which was desperate to prop up the country's forlorn economy. The worker rage was on top of growing discontent over the scarcity of food, fuel, and other goods that had become a fact of life in East Germany.

Already that week, there had been work stoppages at several construction projects. But the information coming in from agents and press reports on Tuesday, June 16, showed that the protests were growing to a new level. "By noon we began to get unbelievable reports," Osborne recalled. About five thousand workers were said to be marching down Stalin-Allee in the heart of East Berlin, initially in orderly fashion. But as the day wore on, the protesters, emboldened by the government's timid response and by news of other demonstrations across East Germany, began calling for free elections and the overthrow of the communist regime. A cabinet officer tried to address the crowd, but he was pushed aside by a worker declaring, "This is a people's revolt!"

"By this time we were taking this thing much more seriously and doing everything we could to find out what in hell was going on over there," recalled Osborne. "There were so many rumors and possibly unfounded allegations that our heads were swimming."

The East German uprising was the first major challenge to communist rule in Soviet-dominated Eastern Europe. But the anger on the streets was directed not so much at the Soviets as at the East German government, in particular Walter Ulbricht, its much-hated leader. Ulbricht, a lifelong communist who had fled the Nazi regime in 1934 and ended up in Moscow, had been chosen by Stalin to lead the East German Communist Party installed after the war. Shrill-voiced and condescending, with a goatee modeled after Lenin's, Ulbricht was a hard-line Stalinist who had defied hopes that the dictator's death would loosen the chains in the East. Shortly before his death, Stalin had approved Ulbricht's request to tighten access between East and West Berlin to stanch the flow of refugees leaving the East. But Stalin's successors reversed the decision, instead urging the East German regime to moderate its policies so that its citizens would want to stay rather than flee. Khrushchev warned Ulbricht that his population was growing more disgruntled, but the East German leader dismissed the notion.

Despite the signs of unrest, the protests had caught the CIA by complete surprise. General Truscott, head of the Germany station, learned of it from newsboys selling extras on the train platform in Würzburg.

But Soviet and East German government intelligence had not fared any better. The KGB in Berlin had not received any signs that trouble was expected. It certainly did not help that in the weeks before the uprising, Lavrentiy Beria, the ruthless head of Soviet state security who was maneuvering for power in the wake of Stalin's death, had initiated a major shake-up of Soviet intelligence, installing allies to strengthen his control. Beria had launched a massive overhaul of the KGB's German operations, creating chaos at Karlshorst at a critical time.

The East German state security, the Stasi, was likewise caught asleep. Markus Wolf, the new East German chief of foreign intelligence, was vacationing on the Baltic coast reading Hemingway novels when the trouble erupted. When he tried to drive back to Berlin, he was detained for hours by Soviet troops at a roadblock. "There I had a few hours to ruminate on who really ran things in our part of Germany!" he later mused.

The American radio station in Berlin, known as RIAS, had for years served as a "spiritual and psychological center of resistance" for East Germans, with some 70 percent listening regularly, according to U.S. intelligence. While it had not sparked the uprising, RIAS was playing a key role in spreading word about worker meetings and demonstrations. One unintended consequence was that many East Berliners believed they could count on U.S. support in the uprising. But while American propaganda had regularly encouraged dissatisfaction with the East German regime, the United States had no plans in place to exploit or assist an uprising.

President Eisenhower was certainly unwilling to instigate a further uprising. "Trouble was always afoot" in Berlin, he griped. The president had long been exasperated by the Western vulnerability in Berlin, going back to World War II when, as Allied commander, he had recommended to President Franklin D. Roosevelt that a cantonment capital be built at the junction of the American, British, and Soviet zones dividing Germany. Instead, Berlin, one hundred miles inside the Soviet zone, had been chosen. Now the division of the city had hardened into a permanence and it was a tinderbox. Any armed conflict involving the surrounded Allied garrisons in Berlin "would likely mean the initiation of World War III," Eisenhower believed.

———

At BOB the night of June 16, the lights were blazing late. Case officers had been sent out in full force to gather information. While base rules prohibited them from straying into the Soviet sector, they rendezvoused with agents crossing over from the East, and then hurried back to the office with the latest updates. Bill Harvey was out conferring with his SIS counterpart, Peter Lunn, who had recently arrived in Berlin.

Word arrived that Harvey was on his way back to the base and wanted an update on the demonstrations. Bay Stockton and John Osborne, who as reports officers were responsible for compiling intelligence into summaries to be sent to Frankfurt and Washington, sat on a battered couch in Harvey's office, preparing to brief the base chief on the latest news. Stockton, who had been recruited straight from Williams College into intelligence work, was at twenty-three the youngest officer in Berlin, and Osborne was not much older, but Harvey appreciated their ground knowledge about Berlin, everything from knowing where the most important factories were located to understanding the labyrinth of U-Bahn, S-Bahn, and bus lines used for meetings with agents. "The Pear . . . gave you his complete trust and support, once he had determined that you were OK at your job and would always level with him," Osborne said.

A klaxon-like buzzer signaled Harvey's arrival. He burst through the door and barged down the hallway, passing the base registry holding heavy metal safes, each with an incendiary canister on top to be used to destroy the sensitive files inside to keep them from falling into enemy hands. The base's plywood gun cabinet, which was normally locked, had been opened as a precaution, revealing rifles, carbines, grenades, and several World War II–vintage submachine guns. Harvey reached his office and swung his girth around his desk, awash in pale blue memoranda awaiting his initials. He glanced at Stockton and Osborne. "Well?" he rumbled. "Whatyagot?"

As Stockton began briefing, Harvey pulled a .38 revolver from his shoulder holster and dropped it into his right-hand desk drawer. Then, reaching back under his gabardine jacket, he retrieved a snub-nosed .32. Harvey saw the two officers staring "bug-eyed" at him. "I was meeting with the Brits," he growled. "Don't think I trust the bastards, do you?"

Once disarmed, Harvey sank heavily in his chair, and Stockton resumed his summary of the day's events. Before long, Harvey appeared to have dozed off. A smirking Osborne nudged Stockton and pointed his finger at the base chief. Just then, Harvey's eyes popped open and Osborne froze in fear. If he had spotted Osborne and his "shit-eating grin," Harvey gave no sign, and instead let out a loud phlegmatic rumble: "Please continue, Bay."

Stockton resumed his report, and Harvey settled down. "His eyes again closed, and unfailing signs of slumber recurred," recalled Osborne. Nonetheless, perhaps by osmosis, Harvey appeared to absorb every piece of the briefing.

The big news was that the workers were planning a general strike at dawn. The big question was what the Soviet response would be.

———

At 4:30 a.m. on June 17, 1953, West Berlin police spotted a dozen Soviet tanks rumbling on the southern edge of Berlin, not far from the American sector. Shortly afterwards, another twenty Russian tanks were seen moving toward the center of East Berlin.

Early that morning, Marshal Andrei A. Grechko, commander of the Group of Soviet Forces Germany, issued orders committing all twenty-two Soviet divisions across East Germany to move into positions to combat any revolt. In Berlin alone, some six hundred armored vehicles from the 2nd Mechanized Guard Army were taking up positions. For now, their orders were to stand ready.

It seemed they might be needed. As the workday began, it became clear that demonstrations were escalating far beyond anyone's expectations. Already at 8:30 a.m., a crowd of seventeen thousand was reported marching in central East Berlin, their numbers quickly swelling. Workers from railroads, steel mills, and textile factories occupied the government district, overturning kiosks and police shelters and tearing down communist flags and posters.

BOB was abuzz with activity. Osborne had arrived early and set up an impromptu East Berlin Demonstration Desk to handle the latest reports. Harvey sent Stockton to the Berlin Command headquarters to coordinate with military intelligence. Commanders were worried that the Soviets might move into West Berlin or even West Germany. "We've lost track of the 22 Soviet divisions in the zone, and we need anything you guys can give us," the Army colonel in charge of military intelligence in Berlin told Stockton.

A team from BOB commandeered the closest telephone kiosk to the Soviet sector they could find and dictated reports they were receiving from agents racing over from East Berlin. "We soon reported Soviet tanks were moving toward the center of Berlin in such haste they were simply pushing broken down, badly maintained vehicles of all descriptions off the roads to permit their columns to plow ahead," Stockton recalled.

BOB officer Si Rees strayed across the ill-marked sector border and was accidentally hit on the head by a brick thrown by a demonstrator. Harvey chewed him out for crossing the sector, then sent him back onto the streets to dig for more information.

By noon, estimates put the crowd at anywhere from fifty thousand to several hundred thousand. Demonstrators scaled the Brandenburg Gate and tore down the communist flag. At Potsdamer

Platz, the swelling crowd had massed outside the government's main headquarters. Columns of smoke began rising from the building. Police inside opened fire on the crowd, wounding some. But the gunfire and fire hoses failed to disperse the gathering.

Word of the uprising in Berlin traveled around the country, spread by sympathetic railroad workers and telephone operators, and demonstrations broke out in two hundred cities and towns across East Germany. The wrath of the workers everywhere was largely directed at the East German government, not the Soviets.

Ulbricht and other East German leaders were holed up in the Soviet compound at Karlshorst, paralyzed with fear, asking about having their families evacuated to Moscow. Vladimir Semyonov, a senior Soviet Foreign Ministry official at Karlshorst, looked with disgust at the East Germans and told them that RIAS was reporting there was no longer any government in East Germany. "Well, that is just about true," Semyonov added with disdain.

Ulbricht was despondent. "It's all over," he said at one point.

———

But it was not all over—the Soviets were not about to allow the collapse of the communist government in its most important satellite. Shortly after noon, Red Army commanders issued orders and dozens of Soviet tanks and armored cars accompanied by truckloads of machine gunners began firing automatic weapons and small arms at the demonstrators. Tanks drove into the crowd in front of the government headquarters, crushing some demonstrators; others were shot by Soviet troops.

Senior American diplomats and military commanders in Berlin, in consultation with their British and French counterparts, concluded that the Allies could do nothing to stop the Soviet crackdown or help the demonstrators. An Allied intervention in the Soviet sector could easily lead to war. The West could do little more than watch.

BOB officer David Chavchavadze had gone to Potsdamer Platz at the sector border, unwisely accompanied by his pregnant wife, Nell, who wanted to witness the demonstrations. Chavchavadze's family was part of the Romanov dynasty that ruled Russia for three hundred years, and both of his grandfathers had been shot by the

Bolsheviks. The Chavchavadzes were close to the border, milling about in an enormous crowd, when Soviet tanks appeared on the eastern side and opened fire. Chavchavadze hit the ground with his wife, landing in a puddle of oil, ruining their clothes but leaving the couple and their unborn child unhurt. "How strange it was to be under fire in anger . . . by my family's old nemesis, the Soviets!" he recalled.

Some demonstrators threw rocks and iron bars at the tanks, bravely but futilely. Heinz Homuth, an East Berlin construction worker, saw fellow demonstrators dropping to the ground, some dead or wounded. Most of the rest fled. "For us, the dream of freedom was over," he later said.

As Soviet forces took control, East German radio at 2:20 p.m. announced a state of emergency, with demonstrations and gatherings of more than three people banned. A curfew was imposed from 8 p.m. to 4 a.m. Soviet tanks massed near the border, with their guns pointed not at strikers, who had mostly scattered, but toward the Western sector. "There was considerable concern the Soviets might come across into West Berlin to put a stop to the subversion, as they put it," said Hugh Montgomery.

East German Volkspolizei, known as Vopos, were rounding up workers who had participated in the demonstrations, eventually arresting about sixteen thousand. Suspected provocateurs were summarily tried and some twenty of them shot under martial law, including several West Berliners. About seventy-five cities were ringed with Soviet and East German guards. Across East Germany, at least a hundred civilians had been killed.

The first major uprising against communist rule had been brutally suppressed. By 11 p.m. on June 17, the streets were quiet.

———

At midnight, Harvey, frustrated at the American inaction, burst into BOB headquarters after hours of meetings at the U.S. mission headquarters on Clayallee with military and State Department officials. "I've been up to my ass in midgets all day," he declared.

Harvey immediately convened a meeting with all officers to debate what advice to send to CIA headquarters in Washington. At the end of the dark and exhausting day, the mood was despondent and helpless. "A few minutes into the meeting . . . some of us realized that our coffee was just not stimulating enough to keep us going, and someone suggested breaking out the operational liquor," Osborne recalled. A bottle of Rémy Martin was duly opened and soon nearly emptied.

But the cognac did nothing to soften the grim news, and the realization that the CIA, like the State Department and the military, had no viable options to recommend for helping the East German workers. "The decision, after three hours, was that there was essentially nothing we could do but follow the advice we were giving our agents—lie low and hope for the best," said Osborne.

After the meeting broke up at 3 a.m., Harvey called Stockton into his office and, pacing like a "caged lion," dictated a memo to send to headquarters recommending that the U.S. Army Berlin infantry regiment be mobilized and forces in West Germany be put on alert. In Harvey's view, between RIAS broadcasts, the psychological warfare operations undertaken by the CIA, and the language of liberation espoused by John Foster Dulles, the U.S. government bore no small responsibility for the uprising. Harvey believed the United States should "stand up to its responsibilities, even if it meant risking a showdown with the Russians," said Stockton.

Harvey was going far out of his lane—it was not his job to propose military responses or government policy. The memo received a cool reception at headquarters.

———

At a National Security Council meeting in Washington on June 18, Eisenhower and Allen Dulles rejected suggestions that the demonstrators be given arms—such a step would be "just inviting a slaughter of these people." In any event, with the Red Army in firm control of East Germany, it was far too late—any intervention would be doomed.

———

In Moscow, the Berlin uprising provided a good pretext to oust state security chief Beria, who was much despised by his rivals struggling for control after Stalin's death. Beria's shake-up of Soviet intelligence was blamed for the failure to nip the uprising in the bud. This was added to a laundry list of grievances his colleagues had, the biggest boiling down to fear of Beria, a scheming and cruel man known as Stalin's bloody right hand for his role in some of the worst acts of terror committed under the dictator's rule. "He was a butcher and an assassin," said Khrushchev, who knew something of the subject.

At a special meeting of the Presidium on June 26, Beria was startled when Khrushchev announced that the only item on the agenda was "the anti-Party, divisive activity of imperialist agent Beria."

"What's going on, Nikita?" Beria asked.

"Just pay attention," said Khrushchev, who had come prepared with a gun in his pocket. "You'll find out soon enough." Khrushchev and the others took turns accusing Beria of traitorous behavior. Then a button was pressed, and an armed group of Red Army officers entered the room and took Beria away. He would be executed before the end of the year.

Despite retaining control of East Germany, the Kremlin was deeply unsettled by the Berlin uprising. Khrushchev saw it as a grave warning about the precarious Soviet position in Eastern Europe, in particular East Germany. The uprising had probably "increased the Soviets' basic incentive to rid themselves of the Western presence in Berlin," a National Security Council report presented to Eisenhower that summer accurately predicted.

Ulbricht was summoned to Moscow. Despite unhappiness with his performance, the Kremlin opted to keep him in power, apparently not wishing to risk further turmoil in East Germany. Ironically, back in Berlin, the uprising allowed Ulbricht to consolidate his power, giving him the excuse to force out rivals who favored reform. But long-term damage had been done to the legitimacy of the East German regime in the eyes of its people.

To keep better control in Berlin, Moscow Center chose Lieutenant General Yevgeny Pitovranov, a wily and highly experienced KGB professional in his mid-forties, to take over Karlshorst. Pitovranov had run deception operations using captured German spies to plant false intelligence with the Nazis during the war. He had been appointed chief of counterintelligence in 1949 and served ably, but in Beria's eyes he was suspect because he was the brother-in-law of Georgy Malenkov, one of Beria's rivals for power. Beria abruptly jailed him in October 1951, falsely accusing him of neglecting his duty. He was freed several weeks later by Stalin, who valued his skills and appointed him chief of foreign intelligence. Through all the turmoil, the bespectacled and well-educated Pitovranov had managed to stay on an even keel.

Within weeks of the uprising, Pitovranov learned he was being sent to Berlin. "Things need fixing," he was told. After a short time at Karlshorst, Pitovranov came to the same conclusion, reporting that the uprising had been "a complete surprise" to both the KGB and the Stasi. Moscow agreed to his request to increase the strength of the Karlshorst apparat.

Pitovranov was one of the KGB's best officers, and his assignment to Karlshorst was a sign that the Soviets were stepping up the intelligence battle in Berlin.

———

By early July, the CIA reported that conditions in East Germany were returning to normal. Some of the Soviet forces sent into Berlin had been withdrawn, though Red Army patrols continued around the country.

Soon after the uprising, Harvey, accompanied by Osborne, went to the U.S. mission headquarters to attend a briefing for James Conant, the former Harvard University president and Manhattan Project administrator who had recently been appointed as the U.S. high commissioner for Germany, the senior American representative in the country. Conant had traveled from Bonn, the West German capital, for the meeting with his retinue, and all the top military commanders and State Department representatives in Berlin were in attendance. The briefing had the atmosphere of a church service, the sort of setting Harvey hated. The gathering was uneventful until one of the briefers reported that truck traffic between West Berlin and West Germany had not been interdicted and was flowing normally, a key barometer of whether the Soviets would cut off access to West Berlin, as they had during the 1948–49 blockade. Conant interrupted to ask why the information was important.

"This question was so utterly stupid that the briefer gulped and stood there with mouth agape and everyone else in the room sat in stunned silence—except the Pear, who turned to me and muttered sotto voce, 'Good God, Bananas, did you hear that?'" Osborne recalled. "Unfortunately the voce wasn't sotto enough and everyone in the room must've heard it, including Conant, who turned around to see who the blasphemer was."

Harvey was unconcerned by the attention. Said Osborne, "I braced myself, because I knew what was coming next, and it did: the Pear's sotto voce groan, followed by an almost whispered 'Oshitodear.'"

Such moxie played well with BOB. The uprising had been Harvey's Berlin baptism, one that could have been a stumble, but was instead a stepping-stone. In Stockton's view, BOB had certainly not covered itself in glory, but then, none of the intelligence agencies had, including the KGB. What did draw notice, particularly among the base officers, was Harvey's command performance during the tense days of the uprising—his smarts, his ferocious capacity for work, his loyalty to and ability to inspire his troops, and the way he thumbed his nose at headquarters. "It was when he showed his mettle," said Osborne. The "snickering amusement" with which BOB officers viewed Harvey upon his arrival six months earlier had turned to a deep respect, Stockton recalled. More than that, a bond had been forged—a belief that Harvey had their backs.

"From then on," Stockton added, "Harvey was indisputably CIA Berlin."

CHAPTER 6

The Big Prize Was Going to Be Berlin

BERLIN, SUMMER 1953

With the dust from the East German uprising settling, Bill Harvey turned his attention back to the big job he faced: the Berlin tunnel. Critical decisions had to be made quickly. Perhaps the biggest were where to dig it, and how to disguise it.

Harvey's team inspected sites in the American and British zones from where it might be possible to tunnel to the three targeted cables. The farther from the border the tunnel started, the less curiosity would be aroused on the part of the Soviets or East Germans. But the longer the tunnel, the more soil would need to be excavated and disposed of, and the more difficult the project became.

Based on this, the team narrowed the choice for a launching point to two spots: one in the British sector, and one in the American. The British site would aim to reach the cables near the Anhalter train station in East Berlin. But the location in the center of the city, under heavy traffic and heavy observation, could create many problems.

The team soon focused on the second location, a remote corner of Berlin in the far southeast of the American sector, across from the East Berlin community of Altglienicke. Dating to medieval times, Altglienicke was a pleasant if run-down village that had been incorporated within the expansive boundaries of Berlin in 1920. It had a more country than city feel, a place where, according to one visitor, "self-important ducks and chickens strut like commissars" in the cobblestone streets. Nearby, the blades of Berlin's only working windmill swung lazily in the wind. It was where the three targeted cables came closest to the Western sector, and was soon deemed to be the more practical site.

The three target cables lay beneath the Schönefelder Chaussee, a highway on the edge of the village that ran parallel to the sector border. In stretches, it was little more than a two-lane country road. But because it connected the city to East Berlin's main airfield at Schönefeld, it was an important and heavily traveled artery. The highway ran so close to the border in Altglienicke that the site became "the obvious choice for such an undertaking," recalled Hugh Montgomery.

Across the boundary in the American sector lay Rudow, a sparsely populated community even more rural than Altglienicke, sitting on ground that jutted into the Soviet sector, close to the highway. Farm fields mingled with the beginnings of suburban settlement, though some homes were little more than shacks constructed from war rubble. The open fields were part of the attraction for the CIA—there was plenty of land available to build an installation that could cover the tunnel construction.

The ground in that area held another important advantage. Generally, the water table in Berlin was high, which meant one could not dig very deep before hitting water—a major problem for a tunnel. But around Rudow, the team estimated the water table to be thirty-two feet below the surface. That left enough room to dig and obviated the need for compressed air and watertight locks to keep the tunnel dry.

Thanks to the CANDARE agents BOB had recruited, the team had detailed information about the area, including the targeted cable diagrams and plans showing all the utilities. That "clinched the selection of the Rudow site," said Montgomery.

———

Whatever the Americans were thinking, SIS station chief Peter Lunn was going to make his own assessment about where and how to dig a tunnel in Berlin. As the mastermind of Operation Silver in Vienna, he certainly did not need coaching from the CIA on a tunnel project. Berlin's would be a much longer and much riskier tunnel than anything done in Vienna, but Lunn believed it held the potential of an unparalleled treasure trove of intelligence. "We could see that the big prize was going to be Berlin," said Peter Montagnon, who had worked with Lunn in Vienna.

At thirty-eight, Lunn was a rising star within SIS. He was held in the highest regard by the top leadership for what he had accomplished in Vienna, which even after his arrival in Berlin was still producing extremely useful intelligence. His value was reflected in his assignment to Berlin, the most important SIS operational station. Economic woes had left Britain in a losing battle to maintain its position on the world stage, and the CIA was already overshadowing SIS in importance and the scale of its operations around the globe, but Germany was one place where SIS could hold its own. Under the terms of the Allied occupation, two-thirds of SIS costs in the country were paid by the German government. The British took full advantage, and the Berlin SIS station, based at the Olympic Stadium, was the largest such facility in the world, with about a hundred officers and countless support staff.

Lunn was small and slightly built, with fast-receding, prematurely gray hair, and he was soft-spoken, with a noticeable lisp. But those who took his appearance as a sign he was timid or ineffective were making a serious misjudgment. "On the contrary, he was a zealot by nature, as he proved by everything he tackled," said an SIS officer who admired him—George Blake. A devout Roman Catholic, Lunn saw communism as a menace and tackled his work with gusto. He was decidedly upper class and a little reserved, but nonetheless friendly and not a bit stuffy.

The KGB would come to admire Lunn for his calm and self-assured professionalism. He was known to be demanding and exacting with his agents, giving them clearly defined tasks and paying for information only when necessary. He was cautious and adhered to strict security in his dealings with agents. His chief weakness—and it was significant—was a relaxed attitude toward station security, placing complete trust in his staff.

Lunn had been born into English Alpine royalty as the son of Sir Arnold Lunn, a pioneer of downhill skiing. Peter was raised in the Swiss Alps in Mürren, a village high in the Bernese Oberland that the Lunn family developed into the center of the British skiing world, amid the towering peaks of Schilthorn, Jungfrau, and Eiger. Peter was going down the mountains by the time he was two and never stopped. "I felt ashamed if I spent a day without falling," he later said. "It meant I hadn't been trying hard enough."

Lunn was admired for his fearlessness and speed on the slopes, and at age twenty-one he captained the British skiing team at the 1936 Winter Olympics in Garmisch in the Bavarian Alps. He skipped the opening parade of athletes, where Hitler was feted. Lunn would later be commended for his refusal to celebrate the Nazi dictator, but he called the praise "totally undeserved. I happen not to like marching about." He was disappointed at finishing fifteenth, blaming it on skiing too carefully, a mistake he vowed never to repeat.

When war broke out, he joined the armed forces and in 1941 was recruited into SIS, which sent him to Malta and Italy. He rose rapidly in the service, driven by his formidable willpower, intelligence, and ingenuity, and in 1947, he was given the prestigious job of heading the Hamburg station.

The following year, Menzies, the legendary spy chief, chose Lunn for an even more important assignment as head of the Vienna station. Like Berlin, the Austrian capital had suffered great destruction during the war and was divided among the four occupying powers. And like Berlin, Vienna was an intelligence battlefield with an aura of intrigue and danger, notorious for KGB abductions of anti-Soviet activists and spies. Red Army troops occupied the eastern half of Austria, meaning intelligence collected in Vienna could be critical to detecting a surprise Soviet attack on Western Europe.

Lunn brought to espionage the same aggressive style he deployed on the slopes. Reviewing reports provided by a source in the Austrian telephone office, he was intrigued to see that the Soviet command headquartered at the Imperial Hotel in central Vienna communicated with its subordinate units via Austrian trunk telephone and telegraph lines that ran beneath the British and French sectors in the

city. Lunn wasted no time getting to work. He brought in communications and mining experts who confirmed that the cables could
be reached by tunnel and tapped, and he quickly received approval
and funding for the project from London.

It was relatively simple to reach the cables, since they ran below
streets controlled by the West and could be easily reached by digging
tunnels from adjacent buildings. The tunnels were short, ranging
from a scant six feet to seventy feet long. One ran from the basement
of a police station, another from the basement of a villa the British
purchased in the suburb of Schwechat. Others were launched from
shops, including an imitation jewelry store and a Harris Tweed import shop.

Tapes of recorded conversations were flown from Vienna three
times a week aboard RAF aircraft and taken to SIS headquarters
in London, where they were transcribed with the help of Russian
émigrés. Eventually, the volume of material became so great that
SIS established a new office, Section Y, to handle the information.

A great deal of military intelligence was being captured, revealing the capabilities and intentions of Soviet forces. Perhaps the most
important was a conversation between two Russian sergeants discussing plans for demobilizing troops. "That was clear proof that
the Soviets had no intention of launching an attack," Lunn later
said. The information was of critical value to the United States in
determining the disposition of troops in Korea—if there was confidence that the Soviets were not planning an attack in the near term,
the United States had a freer hand to deploy forces in Asia.

The tunnel work was not glamorous. Soldiers from the British
Army Field Security sat in cramped and dank basements, listening
to the taps with earphones and turning on recorders to tape relevant
conversations. "So now you're in Vienna you think it's going to be
all wine, women and song," Lunn told a new arrival. "Well, let me
tell you, old boy, it's all beer, bitches and broadcasting."

———

Bill Harvey did not ski. His dislike for the British was well known.
In appearance and personality, Lunn was completely opposite from
Harvey. "The thing about Peter was he only spoke in a sort of whis-

per, quiet voice and appeared to be very, very gentle," recalled Montagnon. "As opposed to Bill Harvey, who was the bull in the china shop."

But the American took a shine toward his new British counterpart in Berlin. "He liked Peter Lunn, because Peter was very lowkey, didn't get upset, didn't have any airs or anything, didn't wear a monocle," said Hugh Montgomery. Beyond that, Harvey trusted Lunn.

Lunn was initially put off by Harvey's brash persona and his habit of going about with a pistol jammed into his trousers. During a welllubricated party hosted by the British station chief, Lunn turned to Harvey while addressing his guests. "I respect you as a professional intelligence officer, but as a man, I hate your guts," he said. When the British officer telephoned the next day to apologize, Harvey waved it off. "We both had too much to drink," he told him.

But Lunn soon liked Harvey as much as he respected him. "Once one had come to like and trust him, you couldn't have had a better friend," Lunn later said. "He held you closely in his heart, as I did him in mine." Harvey, he added, "was certainly a tough character, who would tell the truth as he saw it and damn the consequences. But as a friend he was very relaxed and easy going."

Philby was a hot topic of debate between the two; Lunn was not convinced of his guilt, but Harvey assured him otherwise. "I stake my reputation on a prophecy that you will come to me one day and say, 'Kim Philby was one of them,'" Harvey told Lunn.

Personal styles aside, both Lunn and Harvey realized they needed each other to pull off a tunnel on the scale necessary in Berlin. Both men felt intense pressure to succeed with the project, even if they disagreed on how to do it. Said Montagnon, "Peter Lunn knew that if it were to happen at all, he had to build some rapprochement with Bill Harvey."

———

One of Lunn's first steps in Berlin was to set up a special technical section to study intelligence from sources in the East German telephone office to find where a tap could be made. Lunn found two locations in the British sector that might work. One would target a cable running not far from the Brandenburg Gate that could be reached from the British sector. The second site was about a mile south, targeting cables near the Anhalter train station—the same spot considered by the Americans. But the location of both sites in the center of the city made them less than ideal.

That left the third possibility—the Rudow site in the American sector targeting Altglienicke, which Lunn recognized was the best. "After an awful lot of looking at it, we decided the best place to do it was where we did it in the end," said Montagnon. "That meant that Bill Harvey and Peter Lunn had to work in cahoots."

———

A Berlin project would be infinitely more complicated than anything attempted in Vienna, given the distance that would need to be tunneled, the enormous amount of communications traffic on the cables, and the fact that they were located not in the Western sector but on ground controlled by the Soviets. It would take a tunnel stretching a quarter mile in length—almost twenty times longer than the longest of the Vienna tunnels. "Our tunnels in Vienna had been rather small," said Montagnon. "This was an amazing scale."

Moreover, it would have to be dug literally underneath the eyes of Soviet MPs and East German Volkspolizei who patrolled the area heavily around the clock. Politically, it was far more dangerous, given the high tensions over Berlin and the fact that the tunnel amounted to an incursion into Eastern territory. "At the time, this was the most elaborate and costly secret operation ever undertaken within Soviet-occupied territory," recalled Richard Helms.

Telephone tapping by police and security forces was nothing new, but mostly involved single lines and was directed at individuals. Tapping of whole cables used by foreign armed forces was a novel concept with intriguing possibilities.

Berlin was known for its sandy soil, deposited by glaciers during the Pleistocene Ice Age 2.6 million years ago. For a tunnel, the sand was both a blessing and a curse. It would make for easy digging—an important consideration since the tunnel would have to be excavated by hand to avoid making noise. But sand was prone to collapse, which would be a problem, particularly when the team dug up to reach the cables.

Geological maps indicated that the area around Altglienicke and Rudow was mostly this type of soft soil. But analysis of aerial photographs showed possible disparities in how well the soil drained. Darker areas were probably wet, which could greatly complicate the digging and also damage electronic equipment in the tunnel. The lighter areas likely held well-drained deposits of sandy loam, ideal for a tunnel. One area looked uniformly light, but there was a troublesome complication: It included a cemetery. Digging under it did not seem wise. There was, however, room north of the graveyard wall for a tunnel.

Constructing a quarter-mile tunnel into enemy territory and tapping into Soviet lines would be a major feat of engineering beyond the capabilities of either the CIA or SIS. For that, they would need the help of both the U.S. Army Corps of Engineers and the British Royal Engineers. Discreet inquiries were needed at the highest level to secure the military's cooperation.

LONDON, SUMMER 1953

As the joint planning continued, Harvey and Alan Conway traveled to London in the summer of 1953 to meet with representatives of Section Y, the new SIS department overseeing the tapping operations. They were joined by Gerald Fellon, the young civil engineer working for Frank Rowlett at Staff D in Washington who had been charged with figuring out how to dig a secret tunnel.

Fellon had been busy inspecting tunnels around Washington, poking his head into utility bores, pedestrian walkways, storm drains, and railroad maintenance tunnels, looking for ideas on what size and structure was right for Berlin. Based on this, he figured that a tunnel six feet in diameter was big enough to allow comfortable working room for the excavation crew with space for all the necessary eavesdropping equipment. He combed through catalogs at the Library of Congress and found literature dealing with earth pressures on tunnels. He produced some preliminary calculations, which he proudly brought to the meeting in London.

But no one at the meeting wanted to hear engineering calculations. When Fellon began by describing his mathematical analysis of the tunnel structure, Harvey and the others looked at him blankly. "Clearly the attendees were not interested in mathematics," Fellon recalled.

Everyone was far more interested in debating the nuts and bolts of actually building the tunnel. The British suggested using heavy concrete blocks to line it, a method commonly used in the London Underground. The Americans were appalled at the idea. "Oh God, what a pain in the tail that would have been," one of the U.S. engineers later said. The blocks would have had to be moved into place by hand and then sealed together with grout.

Fellon proposed that they instead use steel liner plates, which would be easier to assemble and better for keeping out the sand as they dug. The idea gained quick approval from both sides. Given how sandy the soil was, they would probably also need to use an overhead shield to protect the roof of the tunnel from collapsing as they dug forward.

Harvey wanted quick action and recoiled at Fellon's suggestion that they wait to discuss the matter with the Army Corps of Engineers. "Bill Harvey got the impression that I did not know the difference between a shield and a coat of arms," Fellon recalled. He was directed to get to work immediately drawing up plans for the shield.

———

Other major questions remained. Most important was what to do with the mountain of earth from a six-foot-diameter tunnel stretching a quarter mile. Some three thousand tons of soil would have to be removed, and none of it could be transported from the site. Dump trucks driving away loaded with soil would give away the tunnel in no time to Soviet or East German observers. The dilemma stumped the team for weeks, and various solutions were proposed but rejected. Finally, someone sarcastically suggested that they dig a hole to hide the dirt.

"This in effect was the solution," a CIA history stated. They would have the Army build a big two-story warehouse, ostensibly for use by the Quartermaster Corps for storing equipment. Construction crews would excavate an area for a large basement, and then build a warehouse on top of the hole. Once the building was up, the basement would serve as the launching site for the tunnel. The soil excavated from the tunnel would be stored in the basement.

The idea that the Army would build warehouses in remote Rudow was perhaps unusual, but still "reasonable," the tunnel team argued in a report. "Although such constructions will attract attention, the fact remains that what transpires within these buildings is a matter not beyond control. In actuality, therefore, the problem is not so much the establishment of a perfect cover, but more a matter of maintaining absolute internal security within a physically enclosed area housing the operation."

The secret below should be safe, the CIA reasoned.

THE HAGUE, SATURDAY, JULY 11, 1953

George Blake made fine use of his time off from that summer, driving to Spain for a three-week holiday with his mother, his younger sister, and her husband in the Ford Anglia he bought with salary accumulated during his captivity. Then he and his mother continued up to Holland for a monthlong reunion with his Dutch relatives. And he had plans to rendezvous later in the summer in Paris with Jean Meadmore, his fellow former captive.

But there was an important piece of business to attend to on the morning of Saturday, July 11. Blake excused himself from his aunt's home in Rotterdam and drove a half hour to The Hague. He parked the Ford some distance away from his destination, a square at the end of the Laan van Meerdervoort, the longest avenue in the city. He walked slowly to the square, checking that he had not been followed. At that early hour, not many people were about, other than two mothers watching their children play in the fine weather. Blake immediately spotted Nikolai Rodin sitting alone on a bench, holding a copy of the *Nieuwe Rotterdamsche Courant,* as arranged.

Blake sat next to Rodin. As usual, the KGB officer eschewed

pleasantries and got down to business: What kind of reception had Blake received at SIS? Blake told Rodin of his warm welcome and mild vetting, and his quick acceptance back into the SIS fold. He said that he was "almost certain that I was not under any suspicion."

Blake also had intriguing news. SIS was putting a new emphasis on tapping telephone landlines in Soviet-controlled territory, and had created a new department, known as Section Y, to oversee the effort. Moreover, he had been told he would be posted to Section Y when he returned from leave. Rodin was pleased.

The two made plans for their next meeting. Despite Blake's comfort with Holland, Rodin insisted that it would be easier to meet in London, rather than having both men travel to the continent. Blake agreed, feeling more confident, and the two fixed the next meeting for the beginning of October near the Belsize Park Underground station.

It was hard for Blake to muster any warm feelings about Rodin. "There was too much of the iron fist in the velvet glove about him for that," he later said. Before departing, Blake could not resist mischievously pointing to the banner headline in the newspaper each carried with news that had just reached the West—Beria had been deposed as head of state security in Moscow and denounced as a British agent. Rodin "looked somewhat embarrassed and had obviously hoped that I would not refer to this painful event," Blake recalled. The KGB man hastily assured him that he had nothing to fear from this development.

After parting, Blake took a roundabout walk back to his car, watching for surveillance, and then drove along back roads to rejoin his relatives in Rotterdam. Though neither man knew it, it had been a narrow escape for Blake. As the KGB *rezident* in London, Rodin was known to British intelligence. He had been followed by an MI5 surveillance team when he departed London and taken a ferry to Holland. There, his surveillance had been picked up by the Dutch Security Service, but at some point before his arrival in The Hague, the Dutch team lost track of him, and did not pick up his trail again until he boarded the ferry back to England. The British and Dutch security services spent weeks afterwards speculating about the purpose of Rodin's mysterious trip to Holland, but came up with no answers.

———

By August 1953, Harvey and his team were completing detailed plans for the tunnel. Frank Rowlett flew to Frankfurt to help prepare a formal proposal for Allen Dulles. General Truscott, the Germany station chief, gained preliminary support on August 28 from Dulles, who "agreed that the intelligence potential of the . . . project justified its inherent risk and financial cost."

But Dulles held off on granting formal approval until he saw the details. Helms, helping shepherd the project in Washington, told Rowlett to see Dulles about it as soon as he returned from Germany. "He is anxious to go over this with you, particularly as to feasibility, amount of money required, and number of personnel that would have to be made available," Helms wrote.

Rowlett soon presented Dulles with the formal report. "The technical and engineering difficulties of this undertaking cannot be minimized," the report conceded. The price of the project was estimated to be "in the neighborhood of $500,000," not including the cost of the warehouse—a guess that was to prove woefully inadequate. The goal was to have the tunnel dug by the late summer of 1954, allowing the tapping to take place in a dry season.

Not everyone at headquarters was enamored of the project. "There were a lot of naysayers, particularly since it literally meant an invasion of Soviet territory," recalled Charlie Bray. Harvey traveled to Washington to meet with Dulles and stifle any opposition. "Without Harvey there would have been no tunnel," another officer said. "The easy thing was to say 'No,' and be on the safe side and not take a chance, but Harvey would keep badgering the chiefs, stripping away their objections."

———

Allen Dulles had appeared on the cover of *Time* magazine in August, a briar pipe clenched in his mouth beneath a full gray mustache and a somewhat forced jovial look on his face. The story inside described the new CIA director's "cheery manly manner," with a hearty laugh and bouncy enthusiasm "uncannily reminiscent of Teddy Roosevelt."

Most considered him decidedly more relaxed than his dour and moralistic older brother, Foster, the secretary of state. Still, there was something a bit unsettling about the enforced jollity. "The eyes are perhaps a bit too penetrating to go with the big booming laugh," noted Russell Baker of the *New York Times.*

Dulles, who had read Rudyard Kipling's *Kim* as a young man, held a romantic view of the "Great Game" of espionage. The grandson and nephew of secretaries of state, he joined the State Department as a foreign service officer in 1916 and, during postings to Vienna, Bern, Paris, and Berlin, was in the midst of the great events that reshaped the world during the final years of World War I and its aftermath. He proved himself skilled at collecting political intelligence, but was a bit of a bon vivant. In Bern one afternoon in 1917, he kept a tennis date with an attractive young lady rather than agree to an urgent request to meet with a visiting Bolshevik, who he later found out was Vladimir Lenin.

After leaving the Foreign Service in 1926, Dulles spent the rest of the interwar years as a Wall Street lawyer, work he found dull if lucrative. But he would get a second stint in Bern during World War II, when he was recruited to run OSS operations in Switzerland. He proved to be in his element, managing networks of spies that successfully penetrated Nazi-controlled Europe. He reveled in his reputation as a spymaster.

It was no surprise when Dulles joined the CIA in early 1951 to serve as deputy director of operations. But Walter Bedell Smith, the no-nonsense CIA director who had been a private in the Indiana National Guard while Dulles was a Princeton undergraduate, grew irritated at his deputy's clubby style. ("Allen, can't I ever mention a name that you haven't played tennis with?" he once asked Dulles.) Smith was not pleased when Eisenhower chose Dulles in 1953 to be the next director, arguing that while his subordinate was good at running clandestine operations, he was no administrator. Once ensconced as director, Dulles relished dipping his fingers into operations, earning the sardonic nickname within the agency as the "Great White Case Officer."

Peter Sichel, the former Berlin base chief now overseeing the German desk, accompanied Harvey at his request to a meeting with Dulles at the director's office, then housed in a red-stone building in Foggy Bottom. "We just came in case he had any questions and to get his approval," Sichel recalled.

Sichel had known Dulles since OSS days, when both were stationed in Berlin at the end of the war, and Harvey hoped that familiarity might smooth the way. As usual, Sichel found Dulles charming and exuding bonhomie, though he privately thought Dulles lacked the executive skills to be director. "He would have made a very good headmaster of an elite private school," Sichel concluded.

Dulles seemed bemused by Harvey, a creature so unlike the establishment crowd he preferred, with their good schools and good clubs. "That fellow Harvey is a conspiratorial cop," he once declared. "The only trouble is I can't tell if he's more conspiratorial or cop."

Harvey and Sichel came equipped with all the tunnel details as well as some of the diagrams collected from the CANDARE agents. "We had all these wonderful drawings from the postal authorities of where the wires were," recalled Sichel.

With his love of the clandestine, Dulles did not need much persuasion to back the tunnel. "He was gung-ho," said Sichel. "That was just up his alley." Though Dulles had trouble operating the telephone on his desk, he had no problem grasping the potential for technology to revolutionize intelligence work. Given the anxiety in Washington about a surprise Soviet attack, and uncertainty about what was happening in the Kremlin since Stalin's death six months earlier, the risks were well worth it, he believed. "When the fate of a nation and the lives of its soldiers are at stake, gentlemen do read each other's mail—if they can get their hands on it," he later said. The tunnel promised to deliver the mail—in the form of hundreds of thousands of telephone and teletype communications.

The CIA director informed a handful of top officials about the project, including his brother at the State Department, and Secretary of Defense Charles E. Wilson. Dulles personally secured agreement from the Army chief of staff, General Matthew Ridgway, to have the Corps of Engineers build the tunnel.

Dulles also briefed President Eisenhower and gained his ready approval. As much as any president since George Washington, Eisenhower did not need on-the-job training to understand the value of good intelligence. In June 1942, Churchill had invited the American commander to Chequers, the country home of British prime ministers, and after dinner let Eisenhower in on the greatest secret of the war: Ultra, the British codebreaking operation at Bletchley Park that allowed the Allies to read encrypted German communications. At the war's conclusion, Eisenhower told SIS chief Menzies, who had overseen the program, that Ultra had been "of priceless value to me." If war came again, the Berlin tunnel, a direct tap into the Red Army's communications back to Moscow, would be no less a treasure.

As president, Eisenhower pushed for aggressive intelligence gathering—within limits. "In general we should be as unprovocative as possible but he was willing to take some risks," recalled General Andrew Goodpaster, then an Army colonel serving as Eisenhower's staff secretary in the White House. Still, Ike felt the whole business was somehow unclean. "Espionage was distasteful but vital," he later said. In that vein, Eisenhower refrained from asking too many questions about exactly what the CIA was up to. "He insisted that he have access to everything, and I think we did," said Goodpaster. "But there were things that he deliberately did not inform himself about." Eisenhower liked having plausible deniability, to guard against having to lie to the press or Congress about what he had known.

"President Eisenhower did not feel that he wanted to know the specifics of all these activities," echoed Dillon Anderson, who served as Eisenhower's national security advisor. This included the Berlin tunnel. "I don't think he particularly wanted to know" the elaborate details of how the CIA intended to tunnel into Soviet-held territory to tap into their communications, Anderson said. But the president was keenly interested in the end product.

On August 12, 1953, the Soviet Union successfully detonated its first hydrogen bomb, a development that left Khrushchev "bursting" with excitement, his son Sergei recalled. It was an unpleasant surprise for Eisenhower—Western intelligence had no inkling that the Soviets would achieve such destructive capability so quickly.

Briefing the president weeks later, Allen Dulles warned that "the Russians could launch an atomic attack on the United States tomorrow." The grim news left Eisenhower wondering whether he would soon need to consider launching a first strike to preempt the Soviets. "As of now, the world is racing toward catastrophe," he wrote gloomily in his diary. For the president, early warning from a tunnel in Berlin could make all the difference.

Similar calculations were under way in London, where Winston Churchill was impatiently demanding better intelligence about the capabilities and intentions of Soviet forces in Eastern Europe. John Sinclair, the SIS chief, briefed Churchill on the success of the Vienna tunnels, and gained the prime minister's approval to pursue the new project in Berlin. SIS also consulted with top officials in the Foreign Office and military services. The consensus was that the tremendous amount of intelligence that could be captured was well worth the risk.

———

Lucian Truscott urged Dulles to allow work on the tunnel project to start as soon as possible. The general did not feel much need to show deference to Dulles; just the previous year, when then deputy director Dulles was visiting Germany and tried to laugh his way prematurely out of a meeting, Truscott barked, "Sit down!" In a note on September 16, Truscott informed the director that many preparations were needed before the first shovelful of dirt could be turned, and they needed to get cracking. "Considering the tremendous amount of time-consuming work that lies ahead of us in this undertaking, it is of the utmost importance that we begin as soon as possible," Truscott said.

Collaboration with U.S. and British army engineers needed to be established, and an officer with tunneling experience chosen to head the project. Teams to dig the tunnel and perform the tap had to be recruited and trained. A classified contract needed to be negotiated with a private U.S. company to manufacture the liner plates and shield for the tunnel. Land for the warehouse had to be leased in Berlin. Specialized electronic and recording equipment had to be procured and assembled. Units to transcribe and translate the recordings needed to be organized. The list went on and on.

Truscott also emphasized that the project required "the highest possible degree of security" to succeed. "For this reason I am most anxious to confine knowledge of the plan to an absolute minimum," he wrote. "In fact, it is my conviction that only those individuals who can make a specific contribution to the success of this operation should be made aware of its existence."

Given the stakes and scale, the operation required extraordinary security, far more than the usual CIA secrecy. The agency's own officers in Berlin, Frankfurt, and Washington, including senior officials, would be given false explanations about what was happening. "Cover stories within cover stories had to be invented to explain the presence of the specialists and the various closed doors to their fellow officers," recalled Helms. Accordingly, Dulles ordered that "as little as possible concerning the project would be reduced to writing," according to a later CIA history.

"It is probable," the account added, "that few orders have been so conscientiously obeyed."

CHAPTER 7

Agent Diomid

LONDON, SEPTEMBER 1953

On September 1, 1953, George Blake began work in Section Y, the secret new SIS office, housed near St. James's Park in a gracious Georgian mansion at 2 Carlton Gardens.

Section Y had been established to exploit the promising potential of penetrating the Soviet Union by tapping its telephone landlines. Much of the material it received came from the Vienna tunnels, but there was also a hefty take from the bugging of Soviet and East European embassies, residencies, and offices across Europe.

Section Y needed a deputy who spoke good Russian, and Blake fit the bill. It was a marvelous opportunity, the SIS personnel chief told him, as Section Y was "receiving much attention from the senior members of the service." Indeed, it was marvelous for Blake—his job would put him at the heart of many top-secret operations under way in Europe.

Section Y reflected the new importance Western spy services were giving to intelligence gathered by technical means such as electronic intercepts. SIS was investing more money in bugging and tapping operations, often working with the CIA. In the senior ranks of the service, Blake later said, there were "many who believed that the future of spying lay in the technical field and that in time the human element would become less and less important." To some extent, Blake agreed. The remarkable output of the Vienna tunnels was testament to that. But he was confident there would always be a need for critical intelligence that could "only be obtained by the man who sits in the inner councils."

———

Section Y's location—even its existence—was a tightly held secret within SIS, to avoid tipping off the Soviets as to the vulnerability of their communications and to prevent anyone from setting up photographic surveillance of those entering the heavy green double doors at Carlton Gardens. The mansion, once home to Lord Kitchener, the British imperial military commander and colonial administrator, had a somewhat faded elegance, with its chandeliered marble entrance hall and a magnificent curving staircase with wrought-iron gilded banisters. "Nobody . . . would have guessed the skullduggery, including my own, that went on and the passions that flared up behind the stately façade of this aristocratic London town house," Blake later said.

Section Y chief Tom Gimson, a retired Army colonel who had commanded the Irish Guards, a storied British Army regiment, was a ramrod-straight gentleman, always impeccably dressed in discreet dark pinstripes. He was known for his role at the British evacuation at Dunkirk in 1940, when he brought order to a mob of officers and men milling aimlessly on a beach under attack by German planes. With quiet authority, Gimson had commanded the men to get into parade formation and had run drills, allowing for an orderly retreat.

Now Gimson needed his skills to bring order to Section Y's unruly band of foreign-language transcribers, which included many Russian aristocrats who had fled after the 1917 revolution as well as a contingent of former army officers from Poland—a dashing if stiff bunch. All the émigrés were prickly about their respective social rank, and any violation of etiquette could be explosive. "It was really rather wonderful to watch these old princes and princesses in action," recalled signals officer Peter Montagnon, one of Blake's colleagues at Section Y. "Tom was very good at keeping them soothed."

In an office full of eccentrics, Blake fit in well. He was still suffering from the effects of his three-year captivity in Korea, and padded about the office in his socks, finding shoes too confining. Collars were similarly uncomfortable. After years of cabbage and turnips, the rich food he enjoyed during long lunches in nearby Soho restaurants made it difficult to stay awake. Back in the office, Blake would doze in a storeroom, using stationery as a pillow. The accommodating Section Y secretaries awoke him from his naps when needed and presented him with a pair of slippers.

Blake was "an amusing character" with a droll sense of humor, said Montagnon, a frequent lunch companion. "Everybody went a bit easy on George because he'd had a rough ride when he was a prisoner of war, so he didn't do an awful lot, really," he recalled. "But everybody liked him." They knew about his history with the Dutch resistance and as a North Korean captive, and it put him "in good stead," Montagnon added.

Blake was "in a quite wild and wooly state," recalled Gillian Allan, a tall and attractive Section Y secretary. Allan, twenty, sweet-natured, and possessing a mocking wit, found him charming and darkly handsome, with his hazel-brown eyes. "I was attracted to him because he was more mature [and] interesting than any man I had met," she later said. Blake was surprisingly carefree for someone who had endured three years of captivity in North Korea. "He took life very easily," she said.

He made friends easily, though rarely did anyone become very close. Allan was an exception, and it was not long before their relationship bloomed into a romance. Blake became a frequent visitor at her family home in Weybridge, southwest of London, gaining the approval of Gillian's father, Colonel Arthur Allan, an SIS Soviet expert impressed with Blake's knowledge of Russian.

As the Section Y liaison with the military, Blake was responsible for sending reports with intelligence of interest to the War Office and the Air Ministry. His colleagues considered him very intelligent, with a bright future ahead at SIS, though they realized he had little head for the nuts and bolts of communications and intercepts. "The technical stuff wasn't his forte at all," said Montagon.

Blake had been at Section Y less than two weeks when he received an urgent call from the SIS counterespionage office. Melinda Maclean, the wife of Donald Maclean, the KGB spy who had fled to Moscow with Guy Burgess two years earlier, had just disappeared herself while on a visit to Switzerland. It was suspected that she had gone to Russia to join her husband. Blake was asked to look for any suspicious conversations indicating that the Soviet military had flown her to Moscow.

To Blake's discomfort, the Burgess and Maclean affair became a frequent topic of conversation in the office. The talk of treason chilled him, he said: "It was too near the bone."

———

As Blake settled into Section Y, a new face appeared at the Soviet embassy in London. Sergei Aleksandrovich Kondrashev seemed a natural for the job as first secretary for cultural relations. Unusually jovial for a Soviet diplomat, Kondrashev hobnobbed with prominent figures in the British cultural world, moving easily in diplomatic circles and attending events at prestigious clubs along with his wife, Rosa. Since arriving in London in September, Kondrashev had been busy arranging visits to England by Russian academics, scientists, ballet troupes, and musicians. When important Soviets were visiting London, he hustled about getting tickets for them to attend sporting events, concerts, and the like.

But his real assignment was something entirely different. Kondrashev was a KGB officer, sent to London to take over a promising new spy. Moscow Center had decided it was too risky to have Nikolai Rodin continue meeting with Agent Diomid, given that he had handled Maclean and Burgess and was known to MI5. It was a wise decision, considering how narrowly Blake escaped exposure when he'd met with Rodin at The Hague.

Kondrashev proved to be a good choice. The child of two clerks, he grew up in modest circumstances in Moscow. Life grew harsher after his father, serving with the Red Army in the trenches outside the capital after the Nazi invasion, died of pneumonia in 1942, when Sergei was nineteen. He showed an early affinity for foreign languages, nurtured by German-speaking neighbors in the Moscow apartment building where he lived with his mother and grandmother. His excellent German, French, and English earned him a job in 1944 with the Soviet ministry responsible for overseas cultural relations, a position that exposed him to a new world of the arts. His talent for foreign languages soon came to the attention of the KGB. Kondrashev prudently agreed to keep the service informed about his encounters with foreigners.

The KGB was so impressed with his reports that in 1947 Kondrashev was recruited to serve in the counterintelligence directorate. He was part of a team that targeted the American embassy in Moscow, and he scored a major success by recruiting a U.S. military code clerk in Moscow, allowing the Soviets to read U.S. embassy cable traffic.

But Kondrashev's initial pride in his service turned into discomfort when he found that much of his work involved repressing Soviet writers, musicians, and artists the regime deemed unsuitable. Then, in 1949, respected colleagues and close friends began being arrested on spurious charges, part of a series of purges encouraged by Stalin to create a culture of fear and intimidation. Kondrashev was shocked when counterintelligence chief Yevgeny Pitovranov was arrested on Beria's orders in October 1951. A few nights later, KGB security officers burst into Kondrashev's office and arrested the chief of his section, Major General Georgy Utekhin, on bogus criminal charges. A shaken Kondrashev feared he could easily be next. "I thought at that very moment that the time has come for me to quit the service altogether," he later said.

Kondrashev submitted a request in March 1952 to leave the service to pursue academic studies, but he was curtly turned down—the KGB was not about to let someone with his language skills out the door. Instead, he was transferred to foreign intelligence, known as the First Chief Directorate, where he continued to excel.

In the early summer of 1953, Kondrashev was summoned to his chief's office in Moscow. "I was called in and told I would soon be posted to London to work with a very important source," he recalled. "That's all I was told." Moscow needed someone who spoke good English and was entirely unknown to British intelligence. On top of that, Kondrashev was expert in counterintelligence. It was a rare combination.

————

Kondrashev was given several months to prepare. He had never been to London and carefully studied maps of the city. He examined KGB files describing British methods of surveillance, which the Soviets considered formidable. These included establishing fixed observation posts around the city as well as using cabdrivers and traffic policemen as observers. If Kondrashev found himself under routine MI5 surveillance, the worst thing he could do would be to try to evade the watchers. Even if he succeeded in shaking the tail, his expertise would mark him as an espionage professional, and would ensure that he would find himself under permanent MI5 surveillance—possibly leading straight into a trap.

Eventually, he was given the Diomid file, which he studied carefully. He reviewed the history of Blake's recruitment in North Korea, trying to get a grasp of the spy's motivation and personality. He was disturbed to learn about Rodin's recent meeting with Blake in Holland, which struck him—correctly—as risky, since MI5 could be following Rodin. He also figured that British intelligence might be keeping a special watch on Blake given his imprisonment in North Korea. Certainly, the KGB would do that with any Soviet official held in Western captivity. But in this case, Kondrashev was giving the British too much credit.

After arriving in London, Kondrashev spent weeks establishing a normal diplomatic pattern, and learning how to navigate the city's confounding jumble of streets. The pompous and bombastic Rodin was of little help, resenting Kondrashev's selection to handle Blake and offering no guidance on how to operate locally. Rodin's departure for Moscow soon afterwards left Kondrashev as the sole KGB man in London with knowledge of Blake.

Moscow Center made it clear that he had no other task more important than the proper handling of Agent Diomid. "The pressure from Moscow was enormous, and I was pretty tense," Kondrashev recalled. "There was no room for mistakes."

———

One evening in late October, George Blake left his office shortly after 6 p.m. as usual, ambling through Soho to Oxford Street. His leisurely pace masked tight nerves. He checked constantly to see if he was being followed, and reached into the inside pocket of his jacket for reassurance that it still held a folded piece of paper. He stopped in a café for tea and cake, though he had little appetite, and he scanned his surroundings for signs of trouble. Seeing none, he entered the London Underground at Charing Cross, hopping onto a subway car just before the doors closed, then at the next station jumping off at the last second. He rode a subsequent train several stops to the Belsize Park station and exited, still watching for surveillance.

Through a gloomy mist, Blake walked away from the station in the direction of Hampstead, carrying a newspaper in his left hand as a recognition signal. "The further I went, the quieter it became," he recalled. Before long, a figure emerged from the fog, walking slowly toward him, also with a newspaper in his left hand. "In his grey, soft felt hat and smart grey raincoat he seemed almost part of the fog," Blake said. It was Kondrashev.

The two walked together along the nearly deserted street, and Blake handed the Russian the paper he was carrying. Without waiting for questions, Blake explained that it held details about a highly prized and top-secret SIS telephone tapping operation: the Vienna tunnels, Operation Silver, until that moment utterly unknown to the Soviets. The document also listed various bugging operations targeting Soviet buildings around Europe. As Kondrashev recognized the value of the information, Blake felt the Russian's suspicions vanishing and an "almost physical change towards me."

Before ending the brief meeting, they arranged to rendezvous a month later in another London suburb, setting alternative dates and sites in the event of problems. Blake headed to the flat he shared with his mother near the Barons Court station, where she had a nice home-cooked meal waiting. After the clandestine meeting on the damp London streets, he felt "particularly cosy and secure" as he enjoyed his dinner with a glass of wine.

Back at the Soviet embassy, Kondrashev was exhilarated as he reviewed the material he had received from Blake, all hugely damaging to SIS operations. Agent Diomid was living up to his name already.

———

At their second meeting, Kondrashev brought Blake a small Minox camera, a model that was commercially available and not at all unusual for an intelligence officer to own. That would be safer than giving him a smaller and more sophisticated spy camera the KGB had developed, which would be difficult to explain away if discovered.

Blake was disappointed not to get a fancier camera, but as Kondrashev correctly gauged, he was better off with a simple model, given his limited technical skills. Even so, his first efforts were largely useless, and Kondrashev had to patiently explain the fine points of how to handle and focus the Minox. With a little practice, Blake's photography skills improved. He took to carrying the camera to work every day in the back pocket of his trousers, ready to snap photos of any interesting documents that landed on his desk. Many did.

He would wait until the secretaries next door to his office were at lunch, or he would stay late. He would leave the door of his office open, so he could hear at once if anyone entered the outer room, giving him time to hide his camera before anyone walked into his office. He concentrated on little but getting the lighting and focus right. It was not long before he felt robotic: "I was reduced, as it were, to nothing, having become only the eye which looked through the viewfinder and the hand which pressed the button."

Occasionally, with larger reports, Blake found it easier to simply take away the document. Smuggling material out of Carlton Gardens was scarcely any more difficult than bringing in a camera, as the elderly watchman at the door never checked anyone's briefcase. Without fail, Blake reassembled a copy of the latest monthly Section Y bulletin on Soviet armed forces in Austria, which he pulled together from carbon copies that were supposed to be burned. The highly secret report was meant only for the highest levels of the British military and Foreign Office in London and the CIA in Washington, with each recipient listed. "I always wrote in the document for my Soviet comrades, 'One copy for Moscow,'" Blake said.

He rendezvoused with Kondrashev now and then for quick brush passes, wordlessly handing over undeveloped film or documents as they passed each other on narrow streets. Every three or four weeks, the two would meet to talk, always after office hours at a different location, usually outdoors near an Underground station in northern London. Kondrashev was far warmer than Rodin, and he and Blake bonded.

Kondrashev was protective of Blake. When the agent passed along information about which Soviet installations abroad had been bugged by Section Y, Kondrashev made sure it was handled cautiously. "We were in no rush to uncover it, because we were worried that analysis by the British or American side would lead to the exposure of George Blake," he said. The KGB would wait weeks or months before sending in a work crew to do routine maintenance that would uncover the bug.

At the Soviet embassy, Kondrashev alone handled Diomid's material. Even Rodin's successor as KGB *rezident* in London, Sergei Tikhvinsky, knew nothing about Blake and had been told only that Kondrashev was handling a source of special value and should be given all needed support. Kondrashev wrote the relevant reports, enciphered them, and sent them to Moscow, where they were seen only by top foreign intelligence officials. Based on the information Blake was providing about the Vienna tunnel, Kondrashev warned that the West was intercepting "first-class" intelligence.

BERMUDA, DECEMBER 1953

On December 2, 1953, Winston Churchill landed in Bermuda after a seventeen-hour flight, a long and difficult trip for the now seventy-nine-year-old prime minister. But Churchill had been determined to make the journey for a summit with President Dwight Eisenhower and French prime minister Joseph Laniel.

The conference, originally set for July, was shelved after Churchill suffered a serious stroke shortly beforehand. During his months of arduous recovery, Churchill impatiently waved off pointed suggestions—from his wife, Clementine, among others—that he retire. After regaining strength, he insisted that the summit be rescheduled.

Churchill was on a mission to broker a rapprochement between the Western powers and the Soviet Union, still convinced that Stalin's departure had created an opportunity that must be taken. But Eisenhower remained wary. Churchill complained privately during his recuperation that the president was "both weak and stupid."

Upon Eisenhower's arrival in Bermuda, it was clear that the former World War II comrades remained on a tense footing. Ike found speaking with Churchill so frustrating that he directed most of his comments to Foreign Minister Anthony Eden. "It has gotten to be almost impossible to explain anything to Mr. Churchill, who seems deliberately to use his deafness to avoid hearing anything he does not want to hear," Eisenhower griped in his diary.

After raising the possibility of outreach to Moscow during the first plenary session, Churchill was disappointed when Eisenhower dismissed any changes in the Kremlin since Stalin's death as cosmetic: "Despite bath, perfume or lace, it was the same old girl."

Perhaps more alarming, the president blithely confided to Churchill during a private talk that the United States was adapting its view on the use of nuclear weapons. "We have come to the conclusion that the atom bomb has to be treated as just another weapon in the arsenal," Eisenhower wrote in a diary entry while in Bermuda. Now that the Soviets had a growing arsenal of nuclear weapons, delaying their use for too long in the event of war could be fatal, Eisenhower told Churchill, leaving America vulnerable "to such widespread and devastating attack that retaliation would be next to impossible."

Eisenhower seemed surprised by Churchill's distraught reaction. "This awakened in Winston many fears which he voiced again and again," Eisenhower wrote. "Winston is a curious mixture of belligerence and of caution, sometimes amounting almost to hysterical fear."

Churchill made no apologies. It was a disappointed prime minister who departed Bermuda December 10 at the conclusion of the summit. It was clear to him that absent better intelligence about Soviet intentions, any confrontation between Washington and Moscow might trigger nuclear war.

LONDON, DECEMBER 1953

Five days later, on December 15, 1953, key American and British intelligence officers came together at Carlton Gardens to plan the Berlin tunnel, an operation that held promise of providing that early warning.

The meeting participants were mostly headquarters officers with technical expertise from Washington and London. Bill Harvey and Peter Lunn, who had attended previous tunnel meetings in London, stayed in Berlin, overseeing their respective bases.

Frank Rowlett flew in from Washington to head the CIA team, joined by Carl Nelson, the chief communications officer in Germany, Vyrl Leichliter, who would oversee the technical setup at the tunnel site, and several other experts. The SIS side was led by George Young, a flamboyant Scot and onetime journalist who had served as a military intelligence officer during the war. Section Y chief Tom Gimson sat in, bringing his expertise on processing recorded conversations, as did Peter Montagnon, who had played a key role in Vienna.

Another participant, also brought in because of his familiarity with the Vienna project, had been asked to keep the minutes of the meeting. George Blake diligently made notes, finding the topic illuminating. He had known nothing about the plans to dig an enormous spy tunnel in Berlin. "I realized, of course, how important this was," he later said. Despite his lack of technical knowledge, Blake took good notes. "He got the gist of it, all right," Montagnon later said.

The broad outlines of cooperation between the CIA and SIS were already set and approved earlier in December by Allen Dulles and John Sinclair. The Americans would pay for and dig the tunnel; the British would construct a vertical shaft to reach the cables and make the taps. The London meeting was to work out the many technical fine points and questions about how to process the material captured by the taps. "It was very painstaking stuff," recalled Montagnon. "There were a hell of a lot of details to get through."

The talks were cordial, if businesslike. "The Americans were clearly anxious to get down to brass tacks," recalled Blake. After breaking for lunch in "one of the smarter West End restaurants," they resumed talks in the afternoon. There was easy consensus to exploit the three targeted trunk cables to the maximum degree possible. "We are all agreed that we should plan to attack all circuits which are likely to appear off the three cables," Blake's minutes read.

Based on the survey work collected from the CANDARE agents, the team expected to collect an enormous volume of material—at least four hundred hours of conversations would be taped each day. Using the much smaller Vienna operation as a guide, the team calculated they would need a small army to process the voice traffic alone—a staff of at least 158, they reckoned, including 81 transcribers, 30 collators, 10 signals officers, and dozens of clerks and Russian-language typists. On top of that would be the intercepted telegraph traffic, which would require a separate large force to process.

It would be easier to move tapes to London and Washington than move so many transcribers to Berlin, but they delayed making a final decision until Harvey and Lunn were consulted. Some of the material would be too urgent to send to London or Washington— any intelligence that might provide early warning of a Soviet attack would need to be spotted and analyzed at once—so the team agreed that "the first priority" was to set up a small joint Anglo-American team, including signals officers and linguists, at the tunnel site in Berlin to scan the incoming traffic and flag any urgent information.

Flocks of transcribers fluent in Russian, German, and other languages would have to be vetted and trained. The CIA was wary about using anyone with relatives behind the Iron Curtain, fearing they could be security risks. To increase the pool of linguists, the two sides agreed that transcribers need not be native Russian speakers. Hours more were spent debating what type of technical equipment to purchase for the tap. Blake piped up in favor of using British tape recorders, but the CIA, which was footing the bill, insisted on American-made Ampex recorders.

On December 18, the three-day meeting ended amid growing excitement about the tunnel's prospects. Plans were made to meet again in February "to come to firm conclusions on the future conduct of the operation," according to Blake's notes. That afternoon, Rowlett flew to Frankfurt, where he briefed Truscott and Harvey about the London discussions.

Back at Section Y, George Blake typed up seven pages of detailed minutes of the meeting, keeping a yellow-green carbon copy for himself.

CHAPTER 8

This Was Explosive Material

LONDON, MONDAY, JANUARY 18, 1954
—

Sergei Kondrashev, the versatile cultural attaché at the Soviet embassy in London, escorted three Russian chess grandmasters to Heathrow Airport for their flight home to Moscow on January 18, 1954. The Soviets had suffered some embarrassing defeats to their British counterparts during their tour of England, but that was of little import to Kondrashev. He was happy with the timing of the departure, as it provided him with a legitimate diplomatic assignment to cover his real mission for the day—an important meeting with Agent Diomid.

After seeing off the disgraced chess delegation, Kondrashev returned to the city, where he shopped and watched a movie. Afterwards he went for a long stroll, taking a pre-plotted course that took him past a countersurveillance checkpoint, where a waiting KGB officer watched to make sure Kondrashev was not being tailed. If the officer spotted anything suspicious, he was to signal a colleague farther along the route, who would alert Kondrashev to abort the meeting. But there was nothing. Kondrashev continued to a nearby bus stop, boarding a double-decker scheduled to depart shortly.

A few blocks away, George Blake was walking to a street corner where he would catch the same double-decker several stops from where Kondrashev had boarded. But as he approached, he spotted a police car and several suspicious-looking people standing around. Blake feared he had walked into a trap. "What to do?" he recalled. "Turn back? Drop the meeting?" But he steeled his nerves and continued to the bus stop. The police, it turned out, were investigating some routine crime. When the bus arrived, Blake boarded, climbed to the top deck, and found Kondrashev waiting for him as arranged.

Blake hurriedly told Kondrashev the news: The CIA and SIS were planning to dig a quarter-mile-long tunnel from the American sector to the Soviet sector to tap highly sensitive Red Army communication lines. He handed him the carbon copy of the minutes he had taken at the meeting, along with a simple sketch he had drawn. It showed the targeted site along Schönefelder Chaussee in Altglienicke with the cables running parallel to the road, and the path of a tunnel running from a facility in the American sector, underneath the border, alongside the cemetery, and ending under the cables.

Kondrashev, stunned by the audacity of the Western scheme, slipped the material into the inside pocket of his jacket. "I was very tense," he later said. "I knew how important this thing was and I felt it was burning into my chest."

Blake was one of only a handful of people with knowledge of the plans. If the KGB took any steps to block the tunnel, he would come under instant suspicion. But he felt no need to request that Kondrashev exercise caution. "I didn't have to ask that," he said more than six decades later. "That was understood."

Kondrashev told Blake they would need to meet again soon to discuss the news in more detail and to follow any developments. After a few stops, Kondrashev left Blake and climbed off the bus, walking to a nearby alley where a waiting KGB car whisked him to the Soviet embassy.

Reading Blake's minutes, Kondrashev was even more astonished. "This was explosive material," he recalled. "I could not believe my eyes." That night, he sent a coded cable to Moscow Center reporting only that he had successfully met with Agent Diomid. The material from Blake was sealed in a steel case and sent via a diplomatic courier to be delivered to the KGB's chief of foreign intelligence. Normally,

Kondrashev would have photographed the papers and sent undeveloped film, but Blake's carbon copy was so barely legible that he
decided to send the document itself. If the courier was stopped, he
would activate a self-destruct device rather than take any chances.

WASHINGTON AND BERLIN, JANUARY 1954

Two days later, on January 20, 1954, CIA director Allen Dulles
gave formal approval to the project, oblivious that the plans for this
most precious secret had already been delivered to the KGB.

At the same time, foreign ministers from the Soviet Union, the
United States, France, and Great Britain were gathering in Berlin
for a landmark conference to discuss German unification. Across the
West, there was a sense that the meeting was a final chance to ease
Cold War tensions before they spiraled out of control. In European
capitals, some shared Churchill's optimism that Stalin's death might
end Soviet intractability on questions such as Germany. But Washington remained skeptical, and Dulles warned Eisenhower that the
Soviets might use the conference to divide the Western alliance.

Following up on Eisenhower's comments to Churchill in Bermuda, John Foster Dulles had publicly declared on January 11 that
U.S. defense policy was now based on the doctrine of "massive retaliation." The frightening prospect of a confrontation with the Soviets quickly escalating to nuclear war amplified the stakes of the
Berlin conference. "The fate of Europe hangs in the balance and our
fate is closely related," Dulles wrote Eisenhower before departing
for Germany. "At no time in our history have the stakes of successful diplomacy been as high as they are today. Never before has war
carried so devastating a threat and never before has the United States
been the principal target of so great and malignant a power as exists
in the world today."

Arriving in Berlin, Dulles was eager to embarrass the Soviet delegation and its formidable chief, V. M. Molotov, the poker-faced
Soviet foreign minister known for both his iron will and his iron
backside. With that in mind, Dulles and his aides suggested that
the CIA organize a demonstration of East Germans in front of the

Soviet embassy in East Berlin as a way to undercut Soviet claims of solidarity. Bill Harvey was appalled at the proposal, coming barely six months after the killings during the June 1953 uprising; even were it possible to gather demonstrators, they would be left at the mercy of Soviet and East German military and security. Germany station chief Lucian Truscott likewise called the idea absurd, and Dulles dropped it.

For the most part, Harvey remained in the shadows during the conference. Truscott excluded him from a meeting with Foster Dulles, figuring Harvey's personality might not mesh well with the upstanding secretary of state.

In any event, Harvey had other matters on his mind. After a discreet long-distance courtship over the past year with Truscott's aide, CG Follick, Harvey was looking to settle down. His marriage to Libby had ended badly. She was back in Kentucky, mired in heavy drinking, which her friends blamed on Harvey's treatment of her, and she had accused him of physical violence. A Kentucky court granted the divorce on January 26, 1954, awarding Harvey custody of their five-year-old son, Jimmy, who had been sent to live with his father in Berlin. But Harvey, consumed with tunnel preparations on top of running the Berlin base, had little time for the boy. Perhaps CG could help.

Harvey's proposal to CG was not particularly romantic. "Bill asked if I would consider leaving General Truscott and coming to Berlin and working for him and then we would be married," she recalled. She was a somewhat reluctant bride. Follick had grown accustomed to a life of privilege that came with serving as Truscott's aide, which gave her carte blanche for low-cost military travel across Western Europe. "It was like you owned Europe and I wanted to see all of it," she said. "I wasn't too interested in getting tied down to be a mommy." But in the end, her bond with Jimmy sold her on the idea. "He was adorable, and the poor little kid needed a mother," she said.

Whether out of old-fashioned gallantry or plain fear, Harvey asked Truscott for CG's hand in marriage. "Well, I'm not sure you deserve her, but I'll give you my blessing," the general growled. The couple was married in a quiet civil ceremony on February 4 in the American sector in Berlin, and took off for a honeymoon in Majorca.

BERLIN, FEBRUARY 1954

Day in and day out back at the Berlin conference, Molotov and Dulles parried and thrust, neither conceding an inch. After four weeks of "polemics and arguments," as Eisenhower put it, the Berlin foreign ministers conference ended without accomplishment, and with it the last major attempt to reunite Germany to be seen until the end of the Cold War. A permanence settled on the division of Europe, and, as if on cue, a Siberian freeze swept across the continent, driving temperatures in Berlin to twenty-two degrees below zero. "The news from Berlin is very bleak," Harold Macmillan, then a minister in Churchill's government, wrote in his diary. An "icy wind from Russia" had the continent in its grip.

MOSCOW, FEBRUARY 1954

On February 12, Sergei Kondrashev—using his code name, Rostov—sent a full report to Moscow Center with his analysis of the material Blake had delivered during their bus rendezvous. "The information on a planned intercept operation against internal telephone lines on [East German] territory is of interest," Kondrashev noted. That was putting it mildly.

Kondrashev's report was so sensitive that it was brought to Ivan Aleksandrovich Serov, who was taking over the KGB in the wake of deposed state security chief Lavrentiy Beria's execution in December.

In the pantheon of ruthless figures in Soviet intelligence history dating back to Felix Dzerzhinsky, Serov was "one of the most brutal," Dulles believed. Known for the cold-blooded competence with which he had crushed opposition to communist rule in the Soviet Union and Eastern Europe during and after the war, Serov had been responsible for the deportation of 134,000 "class enemies" from the

Baltic states alone to slave labor camps. Khrushchev had worked closely with Serov in Ukraine during the war and conceded that while there might be "a few dubious things" about his intelligence chief, Serov was someone he could trust.

Reviewing Kondrashev's report, the KGB leadership was shocked, both at the amount of resources the CIA and SIS were devoting to the project, and the huge volume of intelligence they expected to collect. Moscow had not realized how vulnerable its overseas installations were and had underestimated how much information could be captured by a large-scale penetration.

But there was another, more immediate concern. Agent Diomid had already proven himself far too important to risk exposure. To the KGB's great regret, Kim Philby was through as a spy. Though he still had not been charged with any crime, Philby's remarkable run of betrayal had largely ended, leaving the Soviets without such a highly placed mole. In his short time as an agent, George Blake was showing great promise. Given the highly sensitive position he had been given upon his release from Korea, the KGB had every reason to believe that he would go onward and upward.

The KGB leadership was faced with a dilemma: If they did anything to protect their communications in Berlin, much less block the tunnel, Western intelligence would immediately suspect a betrayal. Blake's position in Section Y would make him an obvious candidate. "It would have taken about 20 minutes to get a list of suspects and begin to work them over," said David Murphy, later Harvey's deputy in Berlin. So Serov and his subordinates made a calculation: "We weighed up in the balance what was important for us: to preserve George Blake in British intelligence and his important position, or to take a risk," said Kondrashev.

They decided not to take the risk. No one outside the tight KGB leadership circle would be informed of Blake's intelligence. Their own people would be left in the dark. Plans for the tunnel would be kept secret from the Soviet military leadership and even the KGB's own Berlin headquarters at Karlshorst. The KGB would do nothing that might signal it knew—or even suspected—that Soviet communications were not secure.

Arseny Vasilievich Tishkov, the foreign intelligence service deputy chief, was made personally responsible for ensuring that "not a bit of information from George Blake would be used in such a way to compromise his identity," Kondrashev recalled.

In London, Kondrashev reported the decision to Blake. The spy was not particularly surprised. "The safeguarding of my position was considered of paramount importance," Blake later said.

Nothing would be done to stop the tunnel. Left unanswered was what would happen when Soviet secrets began spilling across the lines.

Part II

THE WAREHOUSE

A Special Assignment

ALBUQUERQUE, NEW MEXICO, 1954

The call came out of the blue for Captain Keith Comstock one day in early 1954 at his office at the Albuquerque district Army Corps of Engineers, where he worked on several classified projects, including a rocket-powered sled and track being built for the nation's nascent space program to test how many g-forces a pilot could handle. On the telephone from Washington was his former commanding officer in Korea, Lieutenant Colonel Leslie M. Gross, saying he wanted to visit the young officer in New Mexico.

"I couldn't imagine why in the world he would want to come out and talk to me," recalled Comstock, who had been wary of Gross in Korea. "The only time it seemed he ever wanted to talk to me was when I did something wrong." Seared into Comstock's mind was the time in the spring of 1951 when his platoon was clearing a road of explosives as the Army advanced north. They blew up a five-hundred-pound bomb and a small piece sailed several hundred yards, landing in the 10th Engineers Headquarters mess tent, right next to Gross. The commanding officer summoned Comstock to the tent and chewed him out in front of all the other officers.

Gross's visit to Albuquerque several weeks after the phone call only heightened the mystery. Lumbering into the Corps of Engineers office, the burly colonel lowered his voice to a whisper: "Is there somewhere we can talk, just you and I?" Another officer vacated his private office to allow Gross and Comstock to speak.

Once they were alone, Gross lit his bent-stem meerschaum pipe, the same type he had smoked everywhere in Korea. "How would you like to volunteer for a special assignment?" he asked between puffs. "I can only tell you it will be dangerous and I can't tell you anything else. Are you interested?"

Comstock had already seen his share of danger in Korea, where he had been awarded two Bronze Stars. He had a wife and two young children to worry about. Nevertheless, he did not hesitate to accept. After some cursory chitchat about Korea days, Gross departed. Ten days later, Comstock received orders to report to the Pentagon.

———

Allen Dulles's request for help with the tunnel project had been well received by senior Army commanders, particularly the new chief of Army intelligence, Major General Arthur Trudeau, an engineer by training. Trudeau had been impressed by the intelligence collected by the Vienna tunnel, and was an enthusiastic supporter from the moment he learned about the Berlin project.

Les Gross was the Army's choice as engineer to oversee the tunnel construction. The forty-one-year-old New York City native was an expert in civil engineering, and he had done well commanding the 10th Engineers in Korea. Most important, he was the only available Corps of Engineers officer with tunneling experience.

Gross viewed himself as cut out for espionage work. "He was the kind of guy who really enjoyed this kind of hush-hush secret intrigue stuff," Comstock said. The pipe Gross perpetually puffed, which always reminded Comstock of something Sherlock Holmes would carry, only added to the effect.

Once assigned to the tunnel project, Gross worked out of a CIA office in a shabby building near the Lincoln Memorial, one of a number that had been built to temporarily house War Department workers during World War II but were still in use. He was often on the road, looking at military installations out west for a remote site to dig a practice tunnel. He also needed to find three Corps of Engineers officers to oversee the tunneling. Gross killed two birds with one stone during his visit to New Mexico, settling on Sandia Base near Albuquerque as the tunnel training site and successfully luring Comstock to the team.

Comstock, a graduate of the Colorado School of Mines, had mining and surveying experience. Along with his combat experience and the secret clearance he had for his classified work in New Mexico, he was a natural choice for the tunnel project. Gross also chose Army captain Jack E. McDonald, an easygoing Texan with an engineering degree from Texas A&M who, like Comstock, had served with a combat engineer battalion in Korea.

Gross's third choice was Captain Robert G. Williamson, a West Point graduate with a "super-colossal" mind who had done military intelligence work in Germany and had studied German and Russian. Williamson had been assigned to the Counterintelligence Corps in Washington when he received his own mysterious call. "They said they had a job for me, they wouldn't tell me what it was or where it was," recalled Williamson. "I said, 'I'll take it.'"

Following his orders, Williamson reported to a Pentagon office run by Army intelligence. "It was a very small, obscure little office off in a tiny corner of the Pentagon where the average person wouldn't go," he said. He was given the job of recruiting a crew of about twenty enlisted men. All he was told was that he needed people with the variety of skills required to dig a long tunnel. "Where or why wasn't known," Williamson said. "There was no discussion of that."

In early spring, Williamson scoured Army Corps of Engineers installations on the East Coast, from Virginia to New Jersey. "I'm looking for a top-class electrician, I'm looking for a sheet metal worker, I'm looking for this," he would tell personnel officers. He needed welders and he needed electrical mechanics. He needed an expert in hydraulics and an air-conditioning specialist. The search was complicated by the fact that anyone selected had to have an existing secret clearance; there was no time to wait on a process that could take months. But after a few weeks, Williamson had assembled a team.

THE PENTAGON, SPRING 1954

Comstock also reported to the Pentagon on the day designated by his orders and followed directions to a small conference room. Gross was there, as were two Corps of Engineers officers he did not yet know, Williamson and McDonald, and a couple of Army intelligence officers. To Comstock's surprise, several CIA officers were running the show. Comstock and the others were given no written material and told not to take notes. A CIA officer—possibly Frank Rowlett—gave a redacted rundown on their mission to dig a tunnel.

There was no mention of Berlin or tapping Soviet lines, but it was clear this would be no ordinary tunnel. It needed to be built in secret, as silently as possible, which meant by hand. It would be dug a quarter mile through soil prone to collapse and run beneath a major highway that carried tanks. A special shield to protect against collapse was being built. In a few weeks, the team of engineers would travel to New Mexico to test and train with the equipment. Then they would move to Virginia to pack everything up and ship out to their ultimate, unknown destination.

Comstock stared straight ahead as the briefing continued, doing mental calculations about the task ahead, including the amount of soil that would have to be removed. "I was shocked, like all the other guys who were there," he said. "I was so surprised at what we were going to do, I was overwhelmed."

Comstock stole glances at Williamson and McDonald. They looked as flabbergasted as he felt.

BERLIN, SPRING 1954

West Berlin farmer Hermann Massante was only too happy to oblige when four Americans representing the U.S. Berlin Command met with him to ask about renting an empty field he owned at the end of Schönbergweg, a little gravel road in Rudow. In twenty-four hours, the Americans had signed a ten-year lease for his nine-acre plot of land, which ran up to the Soviet sector border. The Americans

moved quickly to get construction started on a warehouse compound. To avoid drawing attention, it was important that the warehouse be built as any normal American military project in Berlin
would be, using local German contractors and materials.

The contract for the warehouse camp soon landed on the desk of
Walter Schaaf, an American civilian who was chief of engineering
and construction for the Army Corps of Engineers in Berlin. Schaaf
routinely handled contractual matters with German firms who were
hired to build schools, commissaries, hospitals, and the like for the
large American community in Berlin. But this contract seemed a bit
odd. "I knew something was screwy with it, but I didn't know what
it was, and I didn't ask," Schaaf recalled. "See, we had a thing there
that the less you knew about certain things, the better off you were."

Nonetheless, Schaaf made the mistake of discussing the contract
on the telephone with a colleague. He soon received a visit at his
home. "My doorbell rang, I opened the door, and I'm staring at
the belt buckle of a huge military police officer," he said. He was
brought before the Army colonel in charge of military intelligence
for the Berlin Command.

"You were discussing highly sensitive matters on the telephone,"
the colonel told him.

When Schaaf expressed bafflement, the colonel elaborated: "The
warehouse camp."

"I knew it was hush-hush," Schaaf protested. "I didn't know it
was classified."

Indeed, the warehouse contract had not been classified, likely to
avoid drawing attention to it. But Schaaf now knew enough not to
say another word about the project. "I had to sign the papers, which
I wasn't happy with because I didn't know what the hell was going
on," he said.

———

Schaaf was not the only one puzzled by the project. The CIA's proposed design called for the warehouse to have a deep basement to
store the tons of soil that would be excavated in order to dig such a
long tunnel.

This was a source of consternation for Army civilian engineers with the Berlin Command, who were supposed to oversee the project but were in the dark about the CIA involvement. It was odd to build a warehouse with a basement twelve feet deep. "Why build a cellar big enough to drive through with a dump truck?" asked one of the engineers. He was so disgusted he quit the project.

Nor was he "the only one to raise an eyebrow," recalled Gerald Fellon, the CIA civil engineer. A story needed to be put out. Subsequently, the engineers were told "it had been decided to experiment with a new type of warehouse, one which would be half above the ground and half below with a ramp suitable for running fork lift trucks from the basement to the first floor," according to a CIA account. Berlin had been chosen for this supposed experiment because labor was cheap and the project would benefit the local economy, it was further explained. Plus, the space was needed to store supplies in the event of another Soviet blockade.

When the grousing continued, orders came from the Army chief of engineers in Washington to shut up and build the warehouse as designed, including the huge basement. That did the trick, and the German contractors got to work building the compound.

LONDON, APRIL 1954

Sergei Kondrashev was sick with worry. After months of regular meetings and a stream of valuable intelligence, George Blake was missing. He had not shown up for a scheduled meeting with Kondrashev and then skipped an alternative meeting date.

Kondrashev proposed to Moscow Center that he try to intercept Blake on his commute to the office. "I knew his movements from home to work, and I thought that I could turn up and try to renew the contact," he recalled. But an order came back from Moscow: "Don't take any measures. Continue the meetings in accordance with the plan." A third scheduled meeting came and went with no sign of Blake.

A final alternative meeting had been arranged for inside a movie theater. Kondrashev arrived at the scheduled time, took a seat in a prearranged spot, and nervously scanned the audience. His heart jumped when he spotted Blake entering. "We had agreed that he would come in, and even if he saw me sitting in the hall, he would walk past me and sit down somewhere else," Kondrashev said.

Following the plan, Blake sat away from Kondrashev, and after a while he got up and left the theater. Kondrashev watched to make sure no one in the theater followed him. When Kondrashev saw no sign of trouble, he met him in front of the theater.

"Why didn't you come to the meetings?" the KGB officer asked.

The answer was connected to events around the world. Vladimir Petrov, the KGB *rezident* in Australia, had defected to Australian intelligence in April. When his wife attempted to join him, two KGB officers in Sydney roughly forced her onto a plane bound for Moscow. But Australian officials intercepted the abduction during a refueling stop in Darwin and freed her.

The story had made headlines around the world. Blake was alarmed by the news, aware that Petrov had previously worked in Moscow Center. He feared the defector might tip off British intelligence about the mole in Section Y. Blake had decided to lie low. "I thought that Petrov might know about me," he told Kondrashev.

"No, George, you shouldn't worry about this," Kondrashev told him. "Nobody knows about you."

Indeed, Moscow Center continued to take extraordinary measures to protect Agent Diomid. Only a handful of senior KGB officials were even allowed to see the material he was collecting, and no one was told the identity of the source. Even using the intelligence was strictly regulated by Tishkov, the deputy foreign intelligence service chief, who was one of the KGB's most experienced field officers. He spelled out the restrictions in a directive to department chiefs on April 9: "Proposals for dealing with this material are to be reported to me, and all measures on this question will be implemented only with my permission."

Blake was placated, but far from sanguine. "I trusted them in that respect, but one never knows in life," he later said. "Mistakes can easily be made."

SANDIA, NEW MEXICO, MAY–JULY 1954

On May 15, 1954, the men of the U.S. Army tunnel team—now designated the 8598th Engineer Support Team—reported to their new home at Sandia Base, located in beautiful high desert on the southeastern edge of Albuquerque. Following the end of World War II, the top-secret Defense Department installation had been given a primary role in the U.S. military's nuclear program. In addition to its remote sections and high security, Gross had chosen Sandia because its sandy soil was believed to be similar to that of Berlin.

The team's three officers and roughly fifteen enlisted men were taken to their assigned location, a secluded spot in the midst of a vast storage area with hundreds of widely scattered weapons storage bunkers known as igloos. "Thousands of acres of nothing except igloos storing nuclear weapons, and ammunition and stuff like that," recalled Comstock. The team's site was in a swale, a bit lower than the surrounding land, so it could not be easily seen, despite Sandia's wide-open vistas. Here they were to dig a practice tunnel using the shield and steel liner specially cast for the project.

The team began by excavating a sixteen-foot-wide hole about thirty feet into the ground, roughly the same dimensions they would need in Berlin, and then assembling the shield at the bottom. Next, they used short shovels to dig through the hard-packed sandy soil, working beneath the shield at their front to guard against collapse. As they moved forward, they installed curved sections of steel liner, each six feet long and three inches thick. "The shield would push against the installed liner until you got enough room to put in another length of liner," said Comstock. "Then we'd pull the shield forward and put in the liner and bolt it together. . . . Once enough soil had been removed, the crew would force the shield forward." They dug for weeks, trying "to get a feel for all the things that were going to happen," Comstock said. Gross and Fellon came to Sandia to observe the practice and were satisfied.

The training built camaraderie among the team members, who would be working in extremely close quarters. "These guys needed some time to get acquainted and know each other and develop rapport," said Comstock. "I was always amazed how well everybody got along." There were occasional nights of carousing in Albuquerque's wilder country-and-western bars, and one day several soldiers commandeered some horses for a ride. The men, all easterners, quickly found themselves over their heads as the horses took them barreling across Route 66, which bisected Sandia but was fortunately empty at the time. "The ponies had more brains than we did," recalled Corporal Floyd Hope, a Pennsylvanian. The horse carrying one of his friends "saw a barbed wire fence and put on the brakes," he said. "My buddy went over the fence. That was enough of that fun."

Back home, spouses grew increasingly disgruntled at the mysterious absence of their husbands. Captain Williamson wrote a letter on June 10 to the miffed wife of Sergeant First Class Marlin D. Keen at her home in Virginia to "express my appreciation for the sacrifices you must make and the difficulties and loneliness resulting from your husband's enforced absence." Williamson explained that Keen and the other men "are working together on an extremely important and difficult job," and that national security prevented them from disclosing any details.

"I fully realize that all the kind words in the world will not replace your absent husband," Williamson concluded, "but I ask you to be patient and tolerant."

LONGMOOR CAMP

Behind the gates of a locked military compound in rural Hampshire, fifty miles southwest of London, a team of British Royal Engineers was conducting its own tunnel experiments within the confines of a demolition pit at Longmoor Camp. The unit, designated No. 1 Specialist Team, had been assembled under the guidance of Major John Wyke, an SIS officer who had worked on the Vienna tunnel project.

While the Americans would dig the tunnel to a point below the Soviet cables, it would be up to the Royal Engineers to dig a vertical shaft from the tunnel's terminus up through the sandy soil and to build a chamber that would expose the cables, allowing them to be tapped. Like the Americans, the British engineers had been culled for skills needed for the specialized assignment, and likewise they were utterly clueless about their true mission. Nor were they a perfect match for the task. The only available Royal Engineers miners came from a unit based in Gibraltar, where they normally blew up solid rock with explosives and heavy drills. "Their expertise was of little value for a clandestine operation in soft soil," Major Robert Merrell, the Royal Engineers officer leading the team, noted dryly. Their main guide was an old military pamphlet from the 1920s describing tunneling techniques used on the Western Front in World War I.

Longmoor's demolition pit, normally used for explosives training, was an ideal tunnel testing ground, providing a near-vertical face into which the team could burrow. For weeks the team tried different techniques to excavate upwards through soft soil to within two feet of the top without collapsing the surface. Every attempt ended in frustrating failure.

Eventually, the team's sheet metal workers and carpenters assembled a hollow steel box with lateral cutters at the top interspersed with closable vanes. The odd contraption looked like a cross between a barbecue grill and a venetian blind. "Inevitably," Merrell recalled, "[it] became known as The Mole." Working from inside the box, the British engineers could scrape away the soil above an inch or two at a time without a collapse, jack up the Mole, and then painstakingly repeat the process.

Pleased with the progress, Merrell and Wyke traveled to Sandia to see how the Americans were getting along with their shield. "They in turn sent people over to see if we could really do what we said we could," Merrell said.

———

Among the few visitors to Longmoor were Bill Harvey and Gerald Fellon, who motored down from London to witness the Mole in action. During the trip, Harvey and Fellon talked about the need for a new cover story for the American warehouse at Rudow, which was nearing completion.

The "experimental warehouse" explanation seemed to be working for the construction, but it was not a good enough cover to carry the project once the tunneling began. They needed an excuse for the extraordinarily tight physical security that would be exercised at the site, which would be readily apparent to the Soviets and East Germans.

Fellon suggested putting a military communications station at the site as a cover. "This idea was met by icy stares," Fellon recalled. But before long, Harvey and Peter Lunn, the SIS station chief, warmed up to a variation of the idea—building a radar intercept station at the site.

Such stations were fairly common in Germany, operated by both sides to monitor the opposing military. Furthermore, there was a legitimate reason to have a radar intercept station at the site. Rudow was close to the main East Berlin airport, Schönefeld, which was used by the Soviet air force, and it was natural that the Americans would want to monitor the area. Putting a station in Rudow would draw attention from across the border, but that could be good. "It was argued that presenting the opposition with a reason for the site's existence would make it a less prominent target than leaving it a 'mysterious something,'" said a CIA report.

Radar intercept stations required tight security. It would be a classified operation, covering for the real secret below.

———

By early July, the conclusion in both the American and British camps was that they could really do what they said they could do. The Army engineers at Sandia had constructed a fifty-foot tunnel, long enough to be confident that their equipment worked and they knew how to handle it. The team celebrated with a barbecue. One of the men, a sergeant from Texas, commandeered a heavy-duty chain-link fence to slow-cook a hunk of beef over an enormous bed of coals, tending it for twenty-four hours. "He stayed with it the whole time," Comstock recalled. "The goddamn meat was so good. We had some beer, and all the other things, and sat around for an afternoon."

Then it was back to work. Inside the tunnel, the engineers disassembled the shield and pulled out all the steel liner they had bolted into place. Everything was loaded onto railcars and sent to Virginia

for the next phase of the operation. On July 7, the last contingent of
men from the 8598th Engineer Support Team, including Williamson and Comstock, boarded a train in Albuquerque for the journey
east.

FORT LEE, VIRGINIA, JULY 1954

Les Gross had long planned to use the boxing plant at the Army
Quartermaster Corps depot at Fort Lee, south of Richmond, to
pack the tunnel equipment for shipment to Germany. But he was
aghast to learn at the last minute that the Army was about to close
the facility. With the backing of the highest levels of the Pentagon,
Gross hurriedly negotiated a thirty-day extension.

Gross just needed the plant, not the soldiers who normally operated it. Nobody but the tunnel team was allowed to see the equipment, much less pack it up. "They sent all the quartermaster people
away from the building we were in, and we did it ourselves," said
Comstock.

Absolutely everything required to build the tunnel had been
shipped to Fort Lee to be packed in wooden crates: the shield, conveyor belts, air-conditioning, blowers, hydraulic systems, even a
small battery-powered forklift. Mostly, though, it was steel liner—
some 125 tons. All the metal pieces were sprayed with a rubberized
compound to keep them from clanking. "We wanted to avoid any
kind of cowbell chorus deep in the tunnel," Fellon recalled.

The team packed the curved steel liner in heavy wooden crates—
some holding four pieces, others six or eight—so they would not
look like they all held the same thing. To get to Berlin, all the material would have to be loaded on trains that would travel 110 miles
through East Germany to reach the city. It was vital to package it in
a way that was secure and deflected suspicion. The liner was double-crated for added security and held together with heavy metal bands,
and the crates given severe drop tests. "It was made pretty tight,"
said Williamson. "You needed heavy tools to crack it open."

When everything was ready, they had packaged more than two
hundred tons of equipment. All the crates were loaded onto railcars

and run to Norfolk to be loaded onto a large Navy Military Sea Transportation Service cargo ship bound for the West German port of Bremerhaven. The men were given leave to visit their families while their equipment sailed to Germany.

The 8598th Engineer Support Team was dissolved, as if it had never existed. All the paperwork from the short-lived Corps of Engineers outfit—mostly requisition forms and receipts—was taken to CIA headquarters and locked in a safe. When the men regrouped, they would form the new 9539th Technical Service Unit, part of the Army Signal Corps, in keeping with the deception plan to build a radar intercept station in Rudow. On August 10, Williamson, Comstock, and McDonald took the Corps of Engineers castle insignia off their uniforms and replaced it with the crossed-flags insignia worn by the Signal Corps.

By now, the men had learned their destination. "They left off telling us until it was no longer practical," recalled Williamson. It was not a huge surprise to learn that their tunnel would target the Soviet Union and that it would be dug in Berlin, focal point of the Cold War.

CHAPTER 10

It Was Getting So Complicated

BREMERHAVEN, WEST GERMANY, AUGUST 1954
—

Captain Keith Comstock nervously watched as West German longshoremen offloaded hundreds of crates filled with tunnel equipment from the military cargo ship docked in Bremerhaven. He had been sent in advance of the rest of the tunnel team to oversee the operation in the West German port, and had been warned by American MPs guarding the port that the longshoremen would try to pilfer anything of value to sell on the black market. It was also likely that Soviet and East German intelligence had agents at the port monitoring what was arriving on the American ships.

The first day had been uneventful, but by the second day, Comstock noted mounting frustration among the longshoremen, apparently because the crates were too tightly packed to crack open. Suddenly a cargo net holding several crates fell from a crane and the contents smashed on the dock.

"I see these longshoremen scoot over there like they were going to fix the net but they were really looking to see if there was anything there to take," Comstock said. He dashed down to the dock and to his relief saw that the dropped crates had not broken open. "You could probably drop it from the moon and it wasn't breaking," said Comstock. "I grabbed the MPs and caused a big fuss and scared the hell out of the longshoremen, so that was the end of that monkey business."

But the most dangerous part of the journey lay ahead. The equipment would have to be shipped to Berlin aboard the nightly U.S. military train that the postwar agreement required the Soviets to allow to pass along a rail corridor through East Germany to the city. The two hundred tons of equipment were loaded into boxcars in Bremerhaven. Comstock carried the paperwork for the shipment, "all phony stuff about radar equipment," he recalled.

It was after midnight when the train reached the border with the Soviet zone at Marienborn. "I was scared spitless because we had all these phony shipping documents, and I could just see it if the Russians decided they were going to look in one of those packages," Comstock said. "I just thought, 'Oh God, there goes me to the gulag.'"

A young Russian lieutenant walked on the platform alongside the train and approached Comstock. The Soviet officer "shuffled through the papers and looked at me and scowled, and that was that," said Comstock. "We went on through, and I breathed a big sigh of relief."

But after the train arrived in Berlin, the tunnel team discovered that an entire boxcar loaded with steel liner plate had gone missing somewhere between Bremerhaven and Berlin. "There was a hell of a scramble, as you can imagine," recalled Charlie Bray, who was monitoring the movement along with Alan Conway in Frankfurt. After frantic checks, the wayward car was located and sent along to Berlin. The boxcar had not been purloined—apparently, a railyard worker somewhere had neglected to attach it to the train.

It was a close call. Losing even one crate "could have blown the project," a CIA history noted.

BERLIN, AUGUST 1954

With the boxcars secure at the American military rail depot in Berlin, Comstock reported to the Corps of Engineers section at the Berlin Command headquarters to arrange for unloading the equipment and trucking it to the warehouse compound in Rudow, which had been completed by the German contractors earlier in the month and turned over to the U.S. government.

As an Army engineer, Comstock felt funny walking into the office wearing Signal Corps insignia. His uneasiness was well founded. The first person he ran into was Master Sergeant Crox, his former platoon sergeant from Korea. Crox, a coolheaded World War II veteran, had taken Comstock under his wing when the green lieutenant arrived in country and was immediately thrown into combat in the chaotic days after the Chinese intervention. Crox was now stationed in Berlin, and his jaw dropped when he saw Comstock's uniform. "What the hell are you doing in the Signal Corps?" the sergeant demanded.

Comstock did not have a good answer. "Well, it's just a trial run," the captain stammered. Recalled Comstock: "I really felt like hell because I couldn't tell him what was going on. He and I had shared some pretty tight things."

The problem worsened when Comstock was spotted the next day by his former company commander from Korea, again raising eyebrows. Comstock decided to make no more visits to the Berlin engineers section.

But he was not the only engineer so noticed by their brethren. Les Gross had arrived in Berlin and had also been seen wearing Signal Corps insignia. "So that made it even worse," Comstock said. "Two guys from our battalion in Korea, and both of them in the Signal Corps—what's going on?"

RUDOW, AUGUST 1954

As the equipment was loaded onto trucks for delivery to the warehouse site, Bob Williamson and the rest of the Army tunnel team arrived from the United States via a military flight to Frankfurt and train to Berlin. On August 28, the detachment was taken by Army truck to the Rudow site. The compound at Schönbergweg 11 sat in the middle of an open field, around one hundred yards from any other buildings. It was surrounded by two eight-foot-high chain-link fences, each topped by barbed wire. A large warehouse dominated the installation, with a smaller barracks building to its north, a motor pool behind that housing three large diesel generators, and guard shacks on the corners.

The Army installation commander, Lieutenant Colonel James E. Helgestad, welcomed the team to their new home. With his Scandinavian good looks, silver hair, and impressive bearing, the seasoned forty-three-year-old signals officer looked like a figure out of central casting—and in a sense he was. While Helgestad would oversee the military administration at Rudow, an unobtrusive dark-haired man in civilian clothes walking around the site was really in charge. CIA officer Vyrl Leichliter, a veteran of several major tapping operations and expert in telephone communications, had been recruited by Bill Harvey to serve as the tunnel's on-site case manager.

The same day the engineers arrived, Army trucks began delivering the tunnel equipment, bringing the material into the warehouse via a ramp on the west side of the building, out of sight from the east. By any measure, two hundred tons was a lot of equipment for a radar station. "I'm sure there were eyebrows raised," said Comstock. "If anybody was a radar specialist, they could say, 'This is way out of line, they don't need this much stuff for a radar station.' But it was done, and nobody said anything."

The deliveries continued through the night and the following day. There was no problem fitting everything in the big warehouse. "There was oodles of room," said Williamson. By the end of the day on August 29, everything had been stowed inside.

East German Volkspolizei across the sector border in Altglienicke trained their high-powered binoculars on the odd new warehouse compound, intently watching the buzz of activity. Harvey seemed pleased with the attention. "A considerable amount of interest, curiosity and observation of the installation has been noted," he told Lucian Truscott.

The Americans, in turn, intently watched the East Germans. Harvey directed a twenty-four-hour watch of the entire area between the warehouse and the target, a quarter mile away in the Soviet sector.

———

The Rudow compound was only part of Harvey's growing empire in Berlin. Even as the Army tunnel team set up shop inside the warehouse, the Berlin base was moving into new headquarters to accommodate its rapidly increasing size. A wave of new arrivals starting in late 1953 had crowded the old Berlin Operations Base headquarters in the redbrick villa on Föhrenweg. Harvey got money from the Berlin Command to add space by renovating the top floor of the building, assuring the commanding general it was the last such request he would make. But the paint had scarcely dried in the spring of 1954 when Harvey, with Truscott's backing, proposed moving the CIA base into a larger building in the nearby Berlin Command headquarters on Clayallee. The imposing nineteen-acre compound, a former Luftwaffe Air Defense Command headquarters, was now an American enclave, with ten major buildings housing the military command, State Department, American consulate, and other U.S. agencies. The three-story building assigned to BOB had its own gated entry on Saargemünder Strasse, away from the bustle at the main ceremonial gate on Clayallee.

The Berlin base move in August—with the detritus from a decade's worth of operations at Föhrenweg carried under guard on Army trucks—was only a half mile, but it marked the end of an era, the severance of the last ties to OSS days. Berlin was now the CIA's largest base, grander even than the agency's stations in most major capitals. With the new space, Harvey created separate sections overseeing operations—Soviet, East German, Satellite (including Czechoslovakia and Poland), and Counterespionage—each with its own chief and deputy.

Harvey's feeling of independence from higher headquarters was expanding in equally grand proportion. He chose his own people for Berlin, not who Washington told him to take. His second-floor office, which faced away from Saargemünder Strasse and into the compound, took on the feel of a bunker. "A master of the art of cable combat," as David Murphy called him, Harvey regularly challenged instructions from Washington, dictating his responses in a haze of cigarette smoke, pausing occasionally to allow suggestions from the circle of section chiefs and case officers sitting in his office.

Harvey treated Berlin as its own show rather than a base under the control of the station headquarters in Frankfurt. Truscott reprimanded him for going around Frankfurt and dealing directly with his allies in Washington, but Harvey kept doing it. "Harvey does not respond always easily to direction," the general complained. "He is sure that Berlin views are superior and almost any suggestion from Washington or Frankfurt invariably calls for extensive argument, even though he accepts the decision in the long run."

But when it came to the tunnel, Harvey, together with Rowlett in Washington, had carte blanche. "Everything that came into Berlin for this period was just written off," recalled Hugh Montgomery. "There was no bureaucracy at all, and nobody else knew what was going on. That was the day when we could spend a million dollars, whatever it took, and Harvey would order anything he felt he needed for the purpose—and he got it."

Anyone outside his immediate circle was suspect, even his ostensible partners. Harvey stopped going to the regular coordination meetings with the Berlin military command and instead sent the base support officer, Jack Corris, to represent BOB. "Don't you make any promises to those people and don't let them know what the hell we're doing," Harvey instructed. "But you report back to me if you find out what they're doing."

When visitors came to his office, Harvey expertly warded off prying questions. He launched into long monologues, his bullfrog voice dropping to a low monotone, using "strangled bureaucratic syntax" to further ensure that no one could make sense of anything he said. The listener would have no time or desire to probe further.

Still, high-level delegations needed succor. Corris would suggest that Harvey remove the revolvers from his desk, advice the base chief generally ignored. Once the visitors were seated, Harvey "gave them a rousing version of his signature speech, 'We're here to protect the United States against its enemies,'" recalled Murphy. "That done, the group would proceed in convoy to Bill's house for lunch, where the martinis were dry and plentiful." By the end, the visitors were usually more well-disposed to BOB than when they arrived.

The Harvey home at Lepsiusstrasse 16 served as a second home to base officers and their families, hosting meetings, briefings, and picnics, often well lubricated with spirits. "He considered alcohol a tool of the trade—necessary to relax people to get them talking," said CG.

It was not just Harvey. The BOB social circuit was incessant and incestuous, with constant rounds of get-togethers, often with the same people. "It was a frequent thing, even on weekday nights, to go to a cocktail party, a dinner party, an after-dinner party and end up at the Orient or the Mazurka [nightclubs], where we could sing Russian songs with the orchestra," said David Chavchavadze.

Harvey's drinking remained prodigious, but in those days generally seemed under control, not affecting his performance on the job. "He could put any of us under the table—and frequently did—but that was in his spare time," recalled Paul Garbler. John Osborne was with Harvey one night at a Zehlendorf bar bidding farewell to a departing BOB secretary, and they stayed "until the wee hours," drinking and warbling Irish songs. When Osborne slunk into the office the next morning, he was astonished to learn that Harvey had been at his desk for hours.

"In Berlin, he just poured the martinis down, with absolutely no visible effect," said Hugh Montgomery. If it was visible, Harvey maintained decorum in his own fashion. At one BOB party, he had consumed his usual martinis when he reached out to put his glass down on a massive dark oak German credenza. He missed and the glass smashed on the floor. "Without batting an eyelash, he just looked around with a straight face and said, 'Goddammit, who moved that credenza?'" recalled Montgomery. "It would have taken six men just to budge the thing."

Harvey regularly dozed off in public, including an embarrassing incident at a dinner party where he left his head slumped on the shoulder of a BOB wife sitting next to him. CG rarely said anything in public, but privately badgered him to drink less, particularly given how the junior officers at BOB "adulated" him. "You're setting a terrible example for these young guys," she told him.

Since her arrival in Berlin, CG had become a force to be reckoned with at BOB. Harvey got a waiver from agency nepotism rules and put her in charge of managing the base's large supply of safe houses, used for meetings with agents. She found the houses, assigned them to case officers, kept them supplied, and hired housekeepers.

Beyond that, CG had assumed an informal role as den mother for the burgeoning Berlin base. Fiercely loyal to Harvey, she soon knew more about what was going on with base families than her husband did, serving as his eyes and ears. She could be generous and warmhearted, but often with an undercurrent of fear and intimidation. CG "was really a mother hen for the whole base, and she ran things with an iron fist," said Montgomery. "If you crossed her, your name was mud, with a capital M."

CG was often heavy-handed with base spouses. After arriving in Berlin with her husband, Ben, Perky Pepper failed to promptly pay a call on the base chief's wife. "You were supposed to see her first, and I didn't know this," Pepper recalled. She apologized to CG, "but she never forgot it," Pepper said. Another spouse who skipped a base social event to rush to the hospital with a child who had swallowed a coin likewise earned CG's enmity.

BOB officers grew to dread her visits to the office, when everyone was expected to join in her loud enthusiasm. "We maintained happy face in her effervescent presence and then ducked into our fusty nooks and crannies for relief from all that enforced good cheer," said Bay Stockton.

———

Whatever his officers thought, Harvey was delighted to have CG riding herd, as it freed him from some of the administrative work he hated. There was no shortage of paperwork with a staff of 150, and Corris would hover outside Harvey's office, trying to gauge when the chief was in a good enough humor to sign some papers, generally never. Harvey would usually only get through a few before losing patience. "Goddamn it," he'd yell. "I have a lot of things on my mind, Jack." He did not bother to check if the monthly finance reports he signed added up or not. "The hell with it. He would not do it," Corris recalled. "But he'd say, 'If you don't spend the money right, I'll kill you.'"

Harvey was routinely working sixteen hours a day, a source of wonder at the base. What virtually no one at BOB knew was that he was not only managing the Berlin base, but he was also overseeing the Berlin tunnel, the largest covert operation the CIA had ever undertaken, out of his hip pocket. He strictly adhered to the need-to-know principle, and as far as he was concerned, no one needed to know. The tunnel remained a secret to everyone at the Berlin base, apart from Walter O'Brien, the CIA officer who had been handling the CANDARE agents, and John Osborne, who had learned of the tunnel through his work in Frankfurt assisting Fleetwood. Vyrl Leichliter, managing the Rudow site, was operating with a handful of assistants independently of BOB, and virtually no one at the base knew the men even existed, much less were preparing for a secret tunnel. Even Harvey's deputy, David Murphy, knew nothing of the tunnel when he arrived in Berlin in the summer of 1954, and he would only gradually be let in on the secret. Ted Shackley, who arrived in June 1954 and would soon be Harvey's chief of satellite operations, was told nothing. Apart from O'Brien and Leichliter, Harvey dealt almost exclusively on tunnel matters with Frank Rowlett in Washington and Alan Conway in Frankfurt.

But Harvey decided he needed one more Berlin officer in the fold, and he chose Hugh Montgomery, a relatively recent arrival at BOB. The thirty-year-old Montgomery, at the start of what would be a long and accomplished career with the CIA, was an exceptionally useful sort, a Harvard PhD who could handle himself in a bar fight.

The tall and bespectacled Montgomery had a cherubic face and an academic air that belied the dangers and horror he had seen in World War II. The Connecticut native had early on shown a remarkable affinity for linguistics picked up from his mother, a language teacher, and was studying modern languages at Harvard when the war broke out. Commissioned as an Army officer, he parachuted into France on D-Day with the 82nd Airborne, and was wounded during heavy fighting six weeks later at the Falaise Pocket during the breakout from Normandy.

By the time he recovered, Montgomery's language skills had come to the attention of Army intelligence and he was assigned to the OSS Counterintelligence Branch (X-2), an outfit so secret that he was never informed exactly who he was working for. For the next year, Montgomery led a team carrying out a series of daring missions behind enemy lines: They searched for German atomic physicists across Europe, arrested a key Nazi supporter in Munich, blew a bank vault in Cologne to get a microfilmed list of Abwehr sources, and captured a radio station in the Carinthian Alps used by German intelligence. The last mission included a brief but life-changing courtship of a young Austrian woman, Annemarie Janak, whose family had taken refuge in the mountains.

In April 1945, Montgomery's four-man team was sent to apprehend a German nuclear physicist in Weimar, in eastern Germany. They had taken a side road through the woods in the hopes of avoiding German forces when they noticed a ghastly smell coming from a clearing. "We slowed our pace and crept forward to a point in the clearing where we could see a large barbed wire enclosure with a few pathetic figures moving about," Montgomery recalled. Piles of corpses could be seen behind the fence.

Montgomery's team had stumbled on the Buchenwald concentration camp, one of the largest Nazi death camps, where fifty-six thousand people had perished. A group of survivors had just taken control of the camp from the few remaining Nazi guards, and they showed Montgomery and his team a litany of horrors. The team needed to continue on its mission to capture the scientist, but before leaving Montgomery broke secrecy protocol to radio a request that the Army send medical assistance to the camp. The survivors made a final request of him: "'Please give the guards to us, and we'll take care of them,'" he recalled them saying. "And I'm sure they did."

Several months later, Montgomery was one of the first Americans into Berlin, finding a city that "had been bombed back to the Stone Age." He worked closely with the OSS base chief, Richard Helms, who tried to persuade the impressive young officer to stay in Berlin to pursue intelligence work.

Instead, Montgomery returned to Harvard to resume his language studies, earning his doctorate and settling down with his new bride, Annemarie, whom he had tracked down in Austria and brought home to Connecticut. But Helms, now with the CIA, persisted in his efforts to recruit him, and Montgomery joined the agency in 1951. He was sent to Berlin with Annemarie in the summer of 1953.

It did not take Harvey long to recognize Montgomery's potential. The young BOB officer could speak eight languages fluently, including German and Russian, and get by in another half dozen. On top of that, he had a tremendously analytical mind, was supremely discreet, and quite collegial to boot. "He was a marvelous tool for Bill Harvey because he could supply Bill with things he couldn't do himself," said Dick Montague, a Berlin base officer.

———

Harvey brought Montgomery into his office in the fall of 1953 and briefed him on the tunnel. "He needed help," Montgomery recalled. "It was getting so complicated."

Part of the complication involved Walter O'Brien, who was carrying on an affair with the wife of an officer who worked for him. Harvey was unhappy with the discord this had created at BOB, and, worse for "Obie," CG also disapproved. "Bill thought it was best to break all that up because it was getting to be a real problem at the base," she said.

Harvey shipped O'Brien out of Berlin, directing him to hand the CANDARE cases over to Montgomery. "Bill Harvey knew he had a problem so he turned to this young kid, Hugh, and he gave him these key cases on which the tunnel's success or failure depended," said Murphy.

The tunnel team was still getting updates from various CANDAREs, including Nummer Mädchen, the redoubtable little old lady in tennis shoes, who tracked which cables served which users. "So when a change was made, she would get it to keep her records up to date, and as fast as she got it, we got it," said Montgomery. But Harvey pressed Montgomery to develop new sources at the East German Post and Telecommunications Ministry. He wanted assurances that no one suspected the planned tap.

Montgomery recruited from the flood of refugees coming to West Berlin, thousands of whom were arriving every week in 1954. They came from across East Germany, fed up with Soviet repression and the inanities of the communist regime, and seeking a better life in the West. Since the closing of the inter-German border in May 1952, Berlin had become virtually the only exit from the East, and three hundred thousand had sought refuge in 1953 alone. All the refugees came through the Marienfelde reception center in southeastern Berlin to be processed, which included screening by Army counterintelligence watching for plants sent by the KGB or Stasi to penetrate the West. Montgomery put out word among the screeners that he wanted to know about anybody who came through with connections to the East German ministry.

He soon had a steady stream of potential agents—men and women who worked for the ministry or had relatives or friends who did. Some agreed to go straight back east, before their absence was noted, so they could begin reporting, or recruit others who could help. Motivation was not a problem. Partly it was the extra spending cash the CIA paid for information, though the sums were not extravagant. "We were very careful not to give them a lot of money that would make them conspicuous," Montgomery said. More important, he said, was widespread "hatred of the East German regime— Walter Ulbricht and his thugs."

It was relatively simple to meet with the agents, who would simply ride to West Berlin on the S-Bahn or U-Bahn and rendezvous with Montgomery at a designated safe house at an agreed date and time. With tens of thousands of people crossing the border daily, there was little likelihood that the agents would be followed by the KGB or Stasi. Yet it was hardly risk-free work. "These people were pretty shrewd operators and they knew better than we what was at stake if they were caught," Montgomery said.

Certainly, the CANDAREs took no chances with the information they carried. A middle-aged ministry official, who worked in an important communications hub in the East German city of Magdeburg, regularly showed up at his meetings with Montgomery carrying cards listing cable users smuggled inside his underwear. "He would excuse himself and go into the bathroom and remove all the cards from his drawers, which were a little on the smelly side," Montgomery recalled.

Whatever the odor, Montgomery compiled a wealth of fresh

material. Before long, he had about twenty CANDAREs reporting from the ministry. "So anytime anyone sneezed over there, we
knew about it," he said. "If anything bubbled up, someone on our
payroll would have known."

Harvey could feel confident that no one had an inkling about the
planned tunnel—at least no one at the East German ministry.

LONDON, AUGUST 1954

For close to a year, George Blake had drained Section Y of its secrets, reporting on every operation of consequence to the KGB.
There was little more he could do from his position in London, he
believed. In any event, Section Y was being reorganized, and his
spot would be taken by an American.

Blake made it known he was interested in a posting abroad, telling his SIS superiors he wanted field experience at the heart of
the intelligence war. In August, he learned that his wish would be
granted with an assignment to Berlin.

It was a sensible move, given his experience in Germany, his fluent German and Russian, and the importance of Berlin. He thought
this would "suit everybody." The SIS expected the benefit of having
one of its most promising young officers working in a critical position. And the KGB would have a mole working in the largest and
most important SIS station.

But the assignment set off alarms with Sergei Kondrashev and his
superiors in Moscow, who preferred that Blake stay in London near
SIS headquarters. The news "made us very suspicious, because we
thought, 'Why was he transferred to Berlin where of course his potential for us is much less than, say, in Great Britain?'" said Kondrashev. The KGB feared that the transfer could mean Blake was under
suspicion. Perhaps SIS had discovered that intelligence was being
leaked from Section Y, and Blake would be put under surveillance
in Berlin to see if anyone made contact with him.

It all added up to exercising even more caution with Agent Diomid. "This was an argument not to take any measures against the
tunnel," Kondrashev recalled. Even with work on the tunnel set to

begin, KGB and Red Army headquarters in Berlin remained in the dark.

———

The pending assignment to Berlin was forcing a major life decision for Blake. For much of the time since joining Section Y, he had been seeing Gillian Allan, and they began talking about getting married and going overseas together. "He seemed rather surprised to find that I wanted to and surprised to find himself getting married," she recalled.

Blake had considerable misgivings, perhaps not surprising, given the double life he was living. "I should never have allowed things to develop to this point in the first place," he later said. "How to get out of it now?"

Gillian was politically conservative and came from what Blake considered a "conventional English family." She would be "absolutely horrified" to learn he was a Soviet spy, Blake said, and forced to choose between betraying her country or the man she loved. But if he broke off the relationship without giving her a good reason, she would be "terribly hurt." He told her about his Jewish background, half hoping her old-school father would find this off-putting enough to object to the wedding. Gillian assured him that did not matter; her family had grown quite fond of him. In the end, said Blake, "there was no reason why we should not get married except one, which I could not tell her."

They announced their engagement on September 3 and moved forward with their wedding plans in a tremendous rush, expecting to move to Berlin in November. Their SIS superiors approved of these sorts of in-house marriages. "It kept everything nicely in the family," Blake observed.

They were married in an Anglican service at St. Peter's Church in Marylebone on October 23, 1954, with many SIS colleagues in attendance. Blake had few close friends, so Gillian's brother was pressed into service as best man. Gillian looked beautiful in her white wedding gown, while Blake appeared uncomfortable wearing a traditional morning coat.

Hurrying the wedding proved in the end to be unnecessary; their posting to Berlin was delayed until the spring. After honeymooning in the South of France, the couple settled into married life in a flat at Barons Court in West London, awaiting their move to Berlin. "I put my conscience at rest by saying to myself that I was like a soldier in a war who might be killed but that did not prevent soldiers from marrying," Blake later wrote.

The analogy was not perfect, he conceded. "In this case my wife did not know there was a war on and that I was in it, nor, had she known, would we have been on the same side."

CHAPTER 11

The Dig

RUDOW, THURSDAY, SEPTEMBER 2, 1954

With no pomp and little circumstance, the U.S. Army engineers launched the tunnel construction on September 2, 1954, jackhammering through the warehouse's concrete floor. Tearing up a brand-new floor was a pain, but it would not have been wise to have the German crews build the warehouse with a big hole in the basement. "You didn't want to cause people to start talking," recalled Captain Keith Comstock.

The basement floor was already eight feet below ground level. The plan was to dig to about a dozen feet deeper, so that when the team began tunneling toward the Soviet sector, they would be at least twenty feet below the surface. "We intended to go reasonably deep, so when we were going horizontally, we'd have a real comfortable pile of dirt on top of us," said Captain Bob Williamson, overseeing one of the digging crews. After breaking through the floor, the team had dug only a few feet when disaster struck: They hit water. This was alarming. The water table was supposed to be thirty-two feet deep, but they found it at half that depth.

Work came to a halt. It was not an auspicious start. Water would not only greatly complicate the construction of a tunnel, but it would also pose a serious threat to the tapping equipment. "There

was much head-scratching and concern about how to handle it," said
Williamson. The engineers immediately brought in water pumps,
but more water kept flowing in, four hundred gallons a day. They
pumped for days, hoping there was a finite amount of water trapped
in the ground. But after a week, there was no sign of letup.

Digging a little deeper, the engineers found a layer of heavy clay,
impervious to water. This was another unpleasant surprise—based
on geologic data, they had expected nothing but sand. A test bore
dug from the bottom of the hole found that the layer of clay underneath was six feet thick. Below that, the ground was dry.

Had this been almost any other tunnel, the engineers could bore
test holes along the planned route to see if more water and clay lay
ahead. But this was hardly an option with East German guards and
Soviet MPs peering through binoculars at the installation. To at
least get an idea of the nearby ground, they bored a test hole behind
the warehouse, shielded from the view of the guards, and the news
was not good: They hit water and then clay again at roughly the
same depth. "The damn water table was out there," said Williamson.

The verdict was that the site held a perched water table—a pool of
water of unknown size held up from below by a layer of impervious
clay of unknown length. The perched water table probably did not
extend the entire length of the planned tunnel, but no one could say
for sure.

"This development was completely unanticipated," Bill Harvey
reported to Lucian Truscott. The discovery, he added, "raised a serious question as to exactly what construction approach should be
used."

Harvey and Peter Lunn, the SIS Berlin chief, held long discussions with the American and British military engineers. They had
two options, neither ideal. If the engineers dug through the clay
and tunneled beneath the perched water table, they ran a serious
risk of collapse. The clay might dip down farther along the route,
leaving the ground dangerously saturated with water. Moreover, if
the perched water table ran all the way to the target area, the British
sappers would have to dig straight up through water to reach the
cables, likely dooming the project.

The other option was to tunnel above the clay and perched water table. This meant the construction would be much closer to the surface and easier to detect, both because of noise and because it was more likely to disturb the soil at the ground level. But Harvey told Truscott this option could still succeed "if carefully done."

Regardless of the odds, Harvey was determined to proceed. "He wouldn't have allowed a little thing like that to stop him," recalled Hugh Montgomery.

After another round of inspections and consultations, on October 6 all parties agreed to move forward with construction right above the perched water table. They would keep a minimum overhead cover of eight to nine feet—any less would be too risky. If the clay lens and water rose closer to the surface, they would have no choice but to dig through the clay, with all the problems that would bring.

"We said we'd give it the old try," said Williamson.

———

The long delay had at least given the engineers plenty of time to make sure the tunnel would be dug straight to the target, a quarter mile away. It would be up to Comstock, the team member with the most surveying experience, to establish the tunnel alignment and keep it on course.

Lacking the electronic or satellite tools that would eventually make such an assignment much simpler, Comstock set up the tunnel alignment the old-fashioned way, using a transit and trigonometry. The transit—a small telescope mounted on a tripod for measuring angles—was set up in the warehouse observation post, which had been established in a second-floor loft with a window overlooking the field where the tunnel was to be dug. Comstock sighted it on the targeted point on the Schönefelder Chaussee. Flipping the transit over, he and his team ran the sighted line to the back of the building, and put a mark there. Then they set the transit over that mark and transferred that alignment down to the hole in the warehouse floor, and from there to the tunnel face.

Setting and keeping the alignment was relatively easy, as far as Comstock was concerned. "In surveying, it's not difficult at all when you've got good instruments, and we had the best there was," he said. What would be much trickier was figuring out exactly how far to dig the tunnel—extremely challenging to gauge from underground. If they dug even a few feet short or a few feet long, the British would miss the cables when they excavated up.

The engineers needed a reference point of a known size along the tunnel's path to get readings on the exact distance from the warehouse to the cables. They came up with a plan of having the soldiers play baseball and "accidentally" hit a ball deep into the Soviet zone. The ball would serve as the reference point. "You know exactly the size of the ball, and then you measure the angle of it with a transit, and with trigonometry, you get what the distance is based on that angle," said Comstock. It might have worked but for an unexpected snag: "This scheme was frustrated by the friendliness of the East German guards who kept returning the baseball," reported Vyrl Leichliter, the CIA site manager.

Another scheme was more successful. The CIA arranged for a CANDARE agent working for the East German Post and Telecommunications Ministry to drive a van along Schönefelder Chaussee. "They had somebody there park next to the position on the street where the junction box was directly below," said Comstock. While the van sat at the spot, the engineers at the warehouse measured the angle with a transit, allowing them to calculate the distance to the highway—1,476 feet, to be precise.

Even now, there was skepticism in some quarters in Washington and London that the operation could succeed. "No one had ever tunneled 1,476 feet under clandestine conditions with the expectation of hitting a target two inches in diameter and 27 inches below a main German/Soviet highway," a CIA history later noted. "There were those who manifested certain reservations on the feasibility of so doing."

————

On October 11, a month after striking water, the engineers finally resumed tunnel construction at a depth of sixteen and a half feet. Allowing for the six-foot diameter of the tunnel, they would have only about ten feet of cover above them, half of what had been expected. "Shallower than we would have liked, but we went ahead and kept our fingers crossed," said Williamson.

The engineers assembled the heavy steel shield at the bottom of the hole. After several days of adjustments, crews with shovels slowly dug forward, working under the protection of the shield, and on October 17 broke through the concrete foundation below the warehouse wall. Water pumps ran continually to keep everything dry, and as they moved forward the engineers did regular test borings to determine the depth of the clay below. If the level of the clay sank, as expected, the tunnel would follow it down.

The team had made it only about ten feet when a new crisis erupted: They hit sewage. "We were almost up to our knees in the stuff," recalled Hugh Montgomery, who regularly checked on the progress. "It stank and almost gassed the engineers."

It soon emerged that they had tunneled into the septic field for the warehouse compound's own sanitary system. During the installation's construction, the lay of the land had dictated that the cesspool for the barracks be placed on ground near the tunnel path, and the effluent had leaked farther than anticipated. "This was quite unfortunate because working conditions in the sector were, to say the least, highly unpleasant," Leichliter reported. The engineers used a pump to get rid of the sewage, though the odor remained a bad memory.

———

With the water and sewage behind them, the engineers soon developed a rhythm. The team had set up three six-man crews, each under the command of one of the captains. They were digging around the clock, each crew taking an eight-hour shift. They used Army entrenching tools—short-handled shovels normally used for digging foxholes and the like—which were easy to handle in the tight, six-foot diameter space at the face of the tunnel. "You'd have two people digging side by side, one digging, one holding the sandbag, so those tools were perfect," Comstock explained. The soldiers generally did not wear helmets, which got in the way in the cramped confines, and often stripped their shirts to keep cool as they labored. Everyone wore leather gloves as they dug to avoid blisters. Once enough soil had been removed, one of the men would operate the hydraulic jacks to force the shield forward about eighteen inches, the width of each section of steel liner. A new section would be bolted into place. Then the men would start digging again and the whole process would be repeated.

The soil turned out to be much looser than what they had trained with in Sandia, which made for easier digging, but raised the danger of collapse. One time, the men did not move the shield forward fast enough and suffered a minor cave-in, and after that, they took no chances. They were soon advancing a little over eleven feet a day, on average. "You just had to pace yourself and keep going," said Comstock. "After a couple of weeks, it got old hat. Your muscles got tuned up, and it went on smooth as silk." To keep a ten-foot cover overhead, the tunnel had a downward slope as they continued toward the Soviet border, following the sinking ground level. Periodically, the team unscrewed plugs that had been put in the liner and pumped in a grouting compound under high pressure, filling any gaps to keep the soil above the tunnel from settling. That would be a dangerous giveaway to anyone on the surface.

———

As they advanced, the engineers constructed a makeshift railroad, using wood from the shipping crates to lay a track with guide rails on the floor of the tunnel. An electric forklift pulled a string of little rubber-tired wooden boxcars that carried steel liner and other equipment to the tunnel face, and carried back countless sandbags loaded with fill. An electric lift raised the sandbags to the warehouse basement, where they were stored in the continuous supply of crates emptied of their steel liner. Thousands more sandbags were stacked on both sides of the tunnel as they progressed. They were secured in place with steel cables, creating a bench on each side of the tunnel that could support the miles of power cables, air-conditioning ducts, and communication lines that would eventually be needed. Additional sandbags, placed beneath the rail tracks, muffled the sound in the steel tunnel, making it less likely that the work could be heard from above.

The crews had jelled well; the officers worked alongside the men, adding to the esprit de corps. There was a bit of competition, particularly with the crew led by Williamson, who constantly pushed his engineers to dig a few more inches than the others. His men nicknamed him Whip Williamson—"He was the whip that kept us going," recalled Corporal Floyd Hope. "He was always right in the front, digging along with the boys."

Gross allowed the engineers occasional nights on the town in Berlin, contingent on following security restrictions and admonitions not to drink too much beer. "We were never allowed to go anywhere alone, always had to be a pair," said Hope. "Theoretically, if one of us started to blab, the other one was allowed to kill him. If you do, you get a carton of cigarettes and a transfer to another outfit. Which was probably true."

Gross gave the three captains wide discretion in handling the excavation, visiting Rudow only occasionally to check on progress. "He kind of laid back and let things happen," said Comstock. "We didn't even have a phone number to call him."

———

Bill Harvey liked to see things at Rudow for himself, though only at night. First, he would rid himself of the usual high-ranking out-of-town visitors, plying them with cocktails and wine at dinner and then ditching them at their quarters. "Guests out of the way, Harvey then departed for the tunnel," recalled Neill Prew, a BOB support officer. "Bill even handled General Truscott the same way." Harvey took circuitous routes to Rudow and changed cars to make sure he wasn't followed.

The Army engineers were not quite sure who he was. "The CIA guy from headquarters—he was always called Bill—would come out once in a while to take a look," said Comstock. "At the time I don't think any of us knew his last name."

With his chunky frame, Harvey had a bit of difficulty maneuvering in the tight tunnel quarters. "I probably wouldn't have met him if I hadn't tried to knock him down in the tunnel," said Comstock. "He was going down to the face, and I was coming back, and there wasn't hardly any room to pass, that's where we met. . . . He was really low-key, just came in, looked around, and didn't say much to anybody."

One thing Harvey noticed was how filthy the engineers looked.

"The Army lads who were doing the digging . . . had such dirty clothes," recalled CG Harvey. It wouldn't do to have the men seen walking around in muddy uniforms, since they were supposed to be Signal Corps. Sending dirty Signal uniforms to the Army laundry might likewise raise suspicions, so Harvey ordered a washer and dryer installed in the warehouse. "They were being so careful about every single detail," said CG.

Mostly, Harvey relied on Vyrl Leichliter, the CIA on-site case officer, to keep tabs on the excavation. The thirty-five-year-old Leichliter, who had served as a naval aviator in World War II and later joined the FBI, hailed from the tiny town of Clayton on the High Plains of Kansas. Leichliter had western charm and wavy dark hair, as well as a roughshod but genuine manner that made him easy to trust. "He was enormously American-looking, and he spoke with a wonderful, drawling accent—a great character," recalled Peter Montagnon, the British communications expert, who worked closely with him.

Harvey, dubious of easterners, bonded with the Kansan. "He was Bill's link with the site, the warehouse, the radar, and he ran the technical aspects of it, and was totally up to speed on all of that," said David Murphy. "Since Bill obviously couldn't be there 24 hours a day, he couldn't have done it without Vyrl." To preserve his anonymity, Leichliter never went to BOB headquarters and instead made regular nocturnal visits to Harvey's home. "Vyrl came to our house every night and they would sit there and drink and talk till practically morning," recalled CG.

Despite his easygoing nature, Leichliter ran a tight ship at Rudow, even censoring the engineers' mail. When one of the soldiers mentioned he was in Berlin in a letter to his girlfriend back home, Leichliter alerted Staff D in Washington. At their behest, Army counterintelligence sent an agent to befriend the woman and make sure she knew nothing about any tunnel.

———

Leichliter was assisted by Eddie Kindell, a CIA expert in electronic intelligence who served as chief communications engineer at the site.

Kindell, from Morton, Ohio, served during the war with the Army Signal Corps, and his electronics skills soon earned him a transfer to the OSS. Before he knew it, he was sent to India and then flying over "the Hump" to support OSS operations in Indochina. By war's end, he was running wiretapping operations targeting Germans in Shanghai. He earned an engineering degree on the GI Bill and was offered jobs with telephone and oil companies, but he turned them down to join the fledgling CIA and fight in the Cold War. "I didn't want to be on the mud end of a drill bit," he recalled. With his expertise, Kindell was a natural selection for the Berlin assignment, and he was so eager to do it that he postponed his wedding. "I had a reputation of being able to do whatever they wanted," he said.

While the engineers dug below, Kindell was up in the warehouse, preparing for the eventual tap. A large operations room, set up in a walled-off interior section on the first floor, would be the heart of the operation. Approximately 150 Ampex tape recorders were mounted two-high on a U-shaped wall, and the room painstakingly dustproofed to protect the electronics. Kindell and a team of technicians installed power ducts, electrical panels, and racks for the machines. They put air-conditioning in the warehouse and ran ducts to the tunnel face. In the short term, this would be a relief for the engineers, though the more important goal was to cool the electronics to be installed in the tunnel.

But the job Kindell really got into was making the warehouse appear to be a radar intercept station. The best way to make it look authentic was simple: Make it a real radar intercept station, with working antennas and equipment operated by genuine Signal Corps soldiers who would be brought in later. Kindell wanted to make the station look like a particularly sophisticated, classified operation, so he included a lot of strange-looking equipment that was strictly for the benefit of any Soviets or East Germans watching. "Just to keep 'em busy, figuring out what the hell was going on," Kindell said.

One large dish on the roof was pointed straight up at the sky, with cables running into the building through an L-shaped vent on the roof, but these did not connect to anything inside. Kindell and his technicians constantly fiddled with them nonetheless. "If we just put an antenna up there and just left it, didn't rotate it, they'd soon decide it wasn't being used," he said. "So we made sure somebody went up and adjusted things."

Aircraft periodically flew over the warehouse, presumably sent from the East to photograph the equipment. A delegation of locals— it was unclear if they were from the East or the West—came to the gate to complain that the American antennas were creating interference in the area. "Of course, we knew we weren't interfering with anything, because we didn't have anything on it," said Kindell. He got rid of them by telling them to complain to the Berlin Command.

Kindell spent so much time perfecting the radar look that Leichliter had to remind him that the tunnel was the important thing. "I kept getting pressure from Vyrl to forget the cover up there, and get down here and get the electronics thing going," he recalled.

As far as most Altglienicke residents were concerned, the problem with the American camp was not the strange antenna dishes, but rather the infernal noise from the three diesel generators that ran twenty-four hours a day, providing independent power for all the electronic equipment at the installation. Neighbors complained the noise rattled their windows and could be heard from a mile away, disrupting sleep.

Harvey, for one, was delighted with the racket. Not only did it make it nearly impossible for the KGB or Stasi to effectively bug the installation, but the noise and vibration "assist greatly in concealing construction noise below the ground," he told Truscott.

———

Paul Noack, a farmer in Altglienicke, had no choice but to get used to the noise. Through the late summer and into the fall of 1954, Noack planted an orchard with more than a thousand trees on the nine-acre plot of land his family owned directly across from the American radar installation in Rudow. The East Berlin farmer was methodical in his work, carefully planting nineteen rows each with fifty-four trees, including apples, cherries, plums, and pears.

Noack worked uncomplainingly despite the crutch he needed to move around, the result of a broken leg in his childhood that had not healed properly because his father had been unable to pay for a doctor. The leg at least had spared him from going to war and had given him a chance to raise a family.

The planting of the trees was a big step toward fulfilling a dream the forty-two-year-old Noack had long held to live on the plot of land. He would move the family from their tiny home on Grünauer Strasse in Altglienicke, and they would make a living selling fruits from the orchard, vegetables from the field, and flowers from a garden he would plant. Noack had already applied for permission from local authorities to build a house on the site and planned to get started in the coming months.

In the meantime, he spent long hours tending his field of potatoes, which were planted between the rows of trees. His twelve-year-old daughter, Dagmar, would help her father pick the bugs off the potato plants; Paul Noack, who did not hold much of a candle for communism, chortled at reports in the East Berlin newspaper that the bugs had been sent over from the West.

For months, Noack had watched with interest as the warehouse rose on the farmland across the border, and then the bustle of activity with the arrival of the Americans and all the antennas they put on the roof. Sometimes as he worked the land, he could hear something over the racket of the generators, a faint noise that sounded to him like a water pump. "He wasn't suspicious," said Dagmar. "He thought it was part of the radar station."

There was one odd thing, though: "What was funny was that in certain spots, the trees did not develop well," she recalled. Farmer Noack went back to work and replanted those trees.

———

In a small, dark room on the second-floor loft in the warehouse that served as the installation observation post, GIs peered out a rectangular window. They kept their binoculars trained on Farmer Noack and anyone else who strayed close to the tunnel's path, be it Soviet MPs or East German Volkspolizei who regularly patrolled the border, or civilians wandering by on foot or bicycles.

The observation post was connected by an Army field telephone strung close to the front of the tunnel. If the observer spotted any danger, he flipped a switch, which triggered red lights strung along the tunnel's ceiling. The engineers would cease their digging and wait until the lights turned off, signaling the all clear. "Everything stopped until they moved away, and then everything would start up again," said Kindell.

The observation post, manned around the clock, had black walls and was entered via a series of curtains, keeping it dark inside and difficult to see from outside. The guards had a clear view of the entire targeted area: over the double fence surrounding the installation, past a smaller wire fence marking the border, across Farmer Noack's fields to the Schönefelder Chaussee a quarter mile away. A tall wall to the right of the fields marked the border with the Altglienicke cemetery. To the left was a quiet wooded neighborhood with a few scattered homes. Straight ahead on the far side of the highway the guards could see a few nondescript buildings and a bus stop.

The observers kept a daily log of all pedestrian and vehicle movements, including the military convoys that regularly rolled down the highway, looking for any changes of patterns. Farmer Noack appeared most days, and whenever he approached the tunnel path, the guards flashed the red light, though no one was overly concerned; the GIs, some of them farm boys themselves, chuckled at his primitive equipment.

A bigger concern was when the East German and Soviet guards stopped directly across from the warehouse to scrutinize the American operation. But they always looked up, not down. "The sight of the Soviets and East Germans standing on top of the tunnel with binoculars focused . . . on the roof of the installation provided considerable amusement to personnel at the site," Leichliter said.

The radar station cover seemed to be fooling not only the Germans and Soviets, but also the U.S. military staff in Berlin, Harvey reported to Truscott. "We have every indication that the cover story used has been effective," he added. It was "even better than we had hoped."

MOSCOW, SEPTEMBER 20, 1954

KGB chief Ivan Serov was not one to feel guilty about much of anything. Still, it did seem that it might be time to warn the top Soviet military command—in general terms—about the danger to some of their sensitive communication lines.

The progress the Americans and British were making on the tunnel was worrisome. "When we understood that the tunnel was being built, of course we had a big task ahead of us," Sergei Kondrashev later said. "What should we do? Who should we inform about the existence of the tunnel?"

The answers, the KGB leadership decided, were almost nothing and virtually no one. Western intelligence had not yet succeeded in tapping the Soviet lines. Perhaps the outlandish project would fail. The hope was that Blake could continue to keep them informed about the tunnel's progress.

Now that excavation had started, the risk to Blake if the KGB blocked the tunnel was lower. "To be sure they would have blown him sky-high if they had shut the operation down before the digging started," CIA officer John Osborne later said. "But once the digging began, there were any number of ways the Sovs could have become aware of what was going on." They could have attributed the discovery to a talkative GI, for example, or to Vopos observing suspicious activities at Rudow.

But the KGB leadership did not want to take that chance. The tunnel had been carried off so secretly that the KGB at Karlshorst had not picked up any clues that it was being dug, Blake later said, and neither had the East Germans. Taking action against the tunnel could still lead to Blake—particularly given his pending assignment to Berlin. Even telling the Red Army to stop using telephone lines in Berlin for sensitive communications would likely raise a red flag to Western intelligence; indeed, the CANDARE agents almost certainly would have learned of this and warned their CIA handlers.

Rather than say anything about Berlin, Serov decided it would be permissible to warn Defense Minister Nikolai Bulganin that the Red Army's communication lines in Vienna had been tapped. A full year had passed since George Blake had informed the KGB about the Vienna taps, but only now that Operation Silver had ended was the top Soviet military leadership informed about the penetration.

On September 20, 1954, Serov sent Bulganin a memo reporting of "an English intelligence document . . . obtained clandestinely" with detailed information on the activities of Soviet occupation forces. He included the Russian translation of the ninety-page SIS document from the fall of 1953 purloined by Blake. Serov told Bulganin that it had been compiled by British intelligence from "monitored telephone conversations of Soviet officers and enlisted personnel stationed in Austria and Hungary."

The hope was the report would shock Red Army commanders into improving telephone security everywhere. Bulganin and the senior Soviet military leadership were indeed surprised by the amount and the quality of the information that Western intelligence had compiled. Serov asked Bulganin "to take measures to ensure that the officers talked less about state secrets on the communication lines," Kondrashev said. Accordingly, Bulganin issued a general order for officers across the force to exercise caution when using telephones.

But Serov gave the Red Army no hint that another operation, much larger than Vienna, was under way. It was nothing personal— the KGB in Berlin, which also used the lines, was still told nothing. Even Pitovranov, the KGB chief at Karlshorst and himself a former head of counterintelligence, was not yet informed.

Markus Wolf, head of East German foreign intelligence, was also in the dark, as was the entire East German government. "They never told us anything, leaving us unguarded and exposed," Wolf later complained. "This was lamentably not out of character for the Soviets: For them, intelligence generally flowed in one direction only."

The KGB likely saw some benefits to allowing the tunnel to continue. The operation would tie up CIA and SIS manpower and assets and cost a fortune. And the KGB stood to learn a great deal about the capabilities of Western intelligence. "The Soviets wanted to let the Americans finish their masterwork so as to evaluate their technological expertise," Wolf said. Indeed, Kondrashev later acknowledged, "certain KGB operations in later years had their roots in our knowledge of the tunnel."

WASHINGTON, DC, NOVEMBER 18, 1954

With the excavation approaching the Soviet border, it was time for Bill Harvey to get approval for emergency procedures if the tunnel was discovered—to include blowing it up if need be. Harvey traveled to Washington and together with Frank Rowlett went to the CIA director's office to brief the top leadership, including Allen Dulles, Richard Helms, and Frank Wisner.

The fear was that Soviet or East German troops could rush down the tunnel and take control of the U.S. installation, capturing sensitive equipment, not to mention the tunnel team. Harvey reported that a forty-foot-long stretch of the tunnel directly below the border would be mined with enough C-3 plastic explosive to collapse the passage, hopefully "without causing a major surface explosion."

When the tunnel was completed, two heavy, torchproof steel doors would be installed and kept shut with locks and bar. Helgestad, the Rudow installation commander, had authority to resist any attempt to enter the compound "with all means at his disposal."

They also needed a plan of what to say in the event the Soviets publicly protested the tunnel. That was simple—they would lie. "The official American reaction is to be flat, indignant denial ascribing any such protest to a baseless enemy provocation," according to the meeting summary prepared by Harvey.

Someone raised the issue of whether James Conant, the U.S. high commissioner for Germany, should be briefed on the plans. Dulles thought this over carefully. What if Conant protested to his brother, Secretary of State John Foster Dulles, or even President Eisenhower, both of whom had already blessed the tunnel? After considerable discussion, the CIA director ruled that Conant should not be briefed. Dulles "did not see any reason to re-raise this issue with the highest policy levels with whom it had been previously discussed."

Eisenhower, still desperate for better intelligence, certainly had not reconsidered his support for the tunnel. The same month that Dulles received the tunnel briefing, the CIA director went to the president seeking authorization for a program to develop a special high-altitude reconnaissance aircraft—what would become known as the U-2. Eisenhower did not hesitate to approve. "Our relative position in intelligence, compared to the Soviets, could scarcely have been worse," he later said. Bigger and better fleets of bombers and improved guided missile capability had given the Soviets an "ever-growing capacity for launching surprise attacks against the United States," Eisenhower believed. He admitted to being "haunted" by the threat of a nuclear Pearl Harbor, and he created two commissions in 1954 to examine the ability of U.S. intelligence to protect the nation against such an attack. On October 19, the president received the first report, a review of CIA covert operations from Lieutenant General James Doolittle, hero of the raid on Tokyo, who described the United States as losing an intelligence battle that could have apocalyptic consequences. "If the United States is to survive, long-standing American concepts of 'fair play' must be reconsidered," Doolittle wrote. "We must develop effective espionage and counterespionage services and must learn to subvert, sabotage and destroy our enemies by more clever, more sophisticated and more effective methods than those used against us."

The report of the second commission, headed by MIT president James Killian, was more sober-minded but equally chilling in its conclusions. "The advantage of surprise attack has never been so great as now," the Killian report said. The lack of human intelligence sources inside the Soviet Union demanded that the United States develop new scientific and technical means of espionage. "In order to find out what the USSR is planning, we must depend almost entirely on physical manifestations of activity," the report added.

This was precisely the intelligence the tunnel would have the capacity to deliver. Any Soviet attack would almost certainly involve the Group of Soviet Forces Germany. Readying the forces to strike would require communications on the landlines to be monitored through the tunnel—not just from higher levels of command, but from low levels making the logistical preparations. "The surest indicators were expected to emerge from chatter about the transfer of landline service from stationary GSFG barracks throughout East Germany to temporary locations closer to the West German border," Joe Evans, an officer on Rowlett's staff assigned to the project, later said.

Other breakthroughs were in the works, including the U-2 and satellite reconnaissance programs under consideration. But for now, it would just be the tunnel.

It could not come too soon, as far as Eisenhower was concerned. "Our old conceptions of the time that would be available to governments for making of decisions in the event of attack are no longer tenable," the president wrote Churchill in January 1955. "I think it possible that the very life of a nation, perhaps even of Western civilization, could . . . hang upon minutes and seconds used decisively at top speed or tragically wasted in indecision."

WASHINGTON AND LONDON, WINTER 1954–55

For months, CIA linguist Bill Romey reported to work at an agency building near the Reflecting Pool in Washington to prepare for a mysterious assignment he knew little about, other than the tantalizing prediction that "the project involved what was potentially one of the richest sources of important strategic and technical information that had ever been available to the United States." Romey and four other junior officers were supplied with stacks of German and Russian tapes, which they listened to for hours every day, perfecting their translation skills.

Romey was an Indiana native who had spent his junior year at college in France studying French and Russian. After seeing Paris, he was not interested in settling in Indiana and returned to France for graduate study in Russian. Given his language skills, a friend of his father's who worked at the CIA suggested that he could be a good candidate for the agency. Romey was hired when it was discovered that he spoke better Russian than the people who interviewed him.

Romey and his colleagues were part of a small vanguard being assembled from scratch to man the tunnel processing units in London, Washington, and Berlin. The number of translators and amount of equipment thus far assigned to the project would in retrospect be far short of what was needed, but this reflected the skepticism the project still had at senior levels at the CIA and SIS, despite the support at the very top from Allen Dulles and John Sinclair.

After months of practice, with no real guidance from higher-ups, Romey and his colleagues wondered if they had been forgotten. But in early January 1955, orders arrived for immediate travel to London. There, the CIA linguists were taken to an SIS office near Regent Square, where a joint British-American team was gearing up for the operation.

Romey and the others learned more details about their assignment: A major tapping operation was under way of Soviet telephone cables in Berlin. Because of his fluent Russian and German, Romey would be assigned to a small team at the site of the tap, listening to conversations as soon as they were recorded for any signs of trouble. "We learned that there would be many German-speaking operators and telephone repair personnel we would need to understand as well as our Soviet targets," Romey said. "Any trouble on the lines, possibly resulting from the tap, would probably be discussed in German. We would have to be ready to react immediately and give the alarm. People at the site of the tap—ourselves included—could be in imminent danger."

The British let the Americans listen to tapes from previous taps such as the Vienna operation, giving them good practice with recordings with varying voice quality, accents, slang, and the peculiarities of telephone talk, including the nuances of operator jargon in both Russian and German.

When not training, Romey adjusted to life in a London winter, which was dank and murky with the smoke of hundreds of thousands of coal fires. He and a second linguist took a flat in a rooming house in Dorset Square. They had to pump shillings into a gas meter to get a little heat, but the location was convenient, just across Regent's Park from the office.

Once again, they waited.

RUDOW, FEBRUARY 1955

For half a year, the Corps of Engineers team had been digging nonstop, save for a week's leave each crew was given at a U.S. Army resort in Garmisch in the Bavarian Alps, where the men mostly drank and slept. After the early problems with water and sewage, progress on the tunnel had continued unabated. On February 28, the engineers reached the point that they calculated was directly below the targeted cables underneath Schönefelder Chaussee. The 1,476 feet they had tunneled was 20 feet longer than the Empire State Building was tall.

Comstock was confident they were on target, but there was no way of knowing for sure until a vertical shaft was dug up to reach the cables. How that was to be done was a mystery to the American crews; to keep the British role quiet, Gross never informed them that a team of Royal Engineers was on standby to take over the operation. "They never told us that the British were even involved," said Comstock.

The end was abrupt. There was no ceremony or elaborate farewell, or even a chance to take leave in Europe. "They shipped us home," said Corporal Hope. "We couldn't even stay in Germany. Pissed me off. Sent us right back."

Still, said Williamson, the team departed with "a pretty solid sense of satisfaction," along with the gratitude of Harvey and Leichliter. The Corps of Engineers had done "what can only be described as a magnificent job in all respects," the CIA concluded.

The engineers signed statements prohibiting them from discussing the activities of the 9539th Technical Service Unit "to any person whatsoever," subject to prosecution under espionage laws, and were given orders restricting any travel outside the United States for two years for fear they could be captured and interrogated. On March 3, 1955, they departed Berlin at night via the military duty train for the flight home.

Said CIA officer Charlie Bray, the engineers "came to Berlin in the dark, so to speak, and left the same way."

LONDON, FRIDAY, MARCH 4, 1955
––––

With the tapping operation soon to get under way, Bill Harvey traveled to Section Y headquarters in London to iron out final details with SIS officials, including section chief Tom Gimson and George Young, the garrulous director of requirements.

George Blake was in his final weeks at Section Y, preparing for his move to Berlin in April. Blake had a special disdain for Bill Harvey, viewing him almost as a comic book figure. The CIA Berlin base chief's mannerisms confirmed his view of Americans as brash, uncouth amateurs when it came to espionage. Harvey "had rather a Wild West approach to intelligence and, as if wishing to deliberately draw attention to this, always carried a six-shooter in an arm holster with him," Blake sniffed. "Its unseemly bulge under his too-tight jacket looked somewhat incongruous in the quiet elegance of Tom Gimson's office in Carlton Gardens."

The atmosphere at the meeting was both ebullient and tense. The next few weeks would be crucial, determining whether the years of planning and construction would pay off. Tapping the cables was the most delicate part of the operation, the most technically difficult and fraught with peril.

When it was Harvey's turn to speak, he began as usual by emphasizing the need for secrecy. The suspected betrayal by Kim Philby and his ring of British traitors was on everyone's mind. It didn't need saying, but Harvey said it anyway—he hoped there were no Philbys present.

In his Scottish brogue, George Young emphatically agreed. "We don't want to be caught with our kilts up, Bill."

Part III

ACE IN THE HOLE

CHAPTER 12

The Baby Was Born

RUDOW, EARLY MARCH 1955

It was the dead of night when several U.S. Army trucks arrived at the American installation, which was a foreboding sight, lit up in the darkness and surrounded by two chain-link fences topped by barbed wire. Armed MPs let the trucks through the first gate—into a no-man's-land patrolled by German shepherds—and then onto the compound. Without pausing, the trucks drove behind the big warehouse, out of East German view, and continued up a ramp into the building, where a sliding door shut behind them.

Out from the enclosed rear of the trucks popped the men of the Royal Engineers No. 1 Specialist Team. They went to work offloading an odd-looking contraption strapped in one of the vehicles. It was the Mole, the vertical excavator they had designed at Longmoor.

The Royal Engineers team had been secluded for several months at the British airfield at Gatow in southwest Berlin, housed in an out-of-the-way hangar and practicing with the Mole at the bottom of a deep bunker. After almost a year of preparation, the men learned only shortly before boarding the trucks to Rudow the purpose of their mission—an excavation from inside the Soviet sector to reach Red Army communication lines.

It was imperative that the Soviets and East Germans watching the installation see no sign that a British unit was operating from Rudow. The Royal Engineers could not be seen outside in British uniform. They were given GI-style crew cuts, and even the food and beer were American. But there was no mistaking that the flavor of the operation, almost exclusively American to this point, had changed. The Brits had arrived.

Running the British operation at Rudow was Major John Edward Wyke of SIS, a cool and debonair expert in the art of both ballroom dancing and phone tapping. Wyke had been Peter Lunn's indispensable man during the Vienna operation and had been brought to Berlin to reprise the role. Tall and handsome, Wyke was a versatile officer, as comfortable with a swagger stick under one arm and a beautiful woman on the other as he was scaling a telephone pole in the dead of night to place a tap.

Wyke had served during World War II with the legendary Special Operations Executive, the British force created by Churchill, reputedly with instructions to "set Europe ablaze" with acts of sabotage behind enemy lines in Nazi-occupied territory. Wyke, who spoke fluent German and Dutch, had excelled in this role during dangerous operations in occupied Holland and the Balkans.

After the war, he joined SIS, where his phone tapping experience led to his assignment to Vienna to help Lunn launch Operation Silver. He embraced life in Vienna and was famous for the decadent parties he threw at his villa in the fashionable suburb of Schwechat. All the revelry served as a useful cover for digging a tunnel from the villa's basement to tap into a Soviet phone line. The Schwechat tunnel, the largest and most successful of the Vienna tunnels, was dubbed Operation Lord by SIS, a nod to Wyke's lifestyle.

As much for his experience and technical ability, Wyke was valued for his enthusiasm and creativity, both of which would be in high demand for Berlin. "It was due a lot to his cleverness and inspiration," said Peter Montagnon. "A lot of it had to be invented because it had never been done before."

Montagnon, a witty and lighthearted twenty-nine-year-old from Croydon, south of London, had served at war's end with the Royal Corps of Signals in Malaya, and his skill at bugging the cells of insurgent guerrilla leaders earned him a position at SIS. Montagnon was a bit of a Renaissance man—he would go on to an accomplished career as a documentary maker, coproducing and directing Kenneth Clark's landmark series *Civilisation* for the BBC. With useful expertise in both the Russian language and underground cables, Montagnon had been sent to Berlin to help Wyke supervise the tapping and analyze the cable traffic. The two had worked closely on the Vienna operation, which Montagnon said "was a great training ground for what was going to happen in Berlin."

But the challenge they faced now, he added, "dwarfed" what they had accomplished in Vienna.

———

The Royal Engineers started by constructing a watertight rectangular base chamber at the end of the tunnel to serve as a launching pad for the Mole. That was simple enough; much trickier was figuring out exactly where to position the Mole for excavation. The shaft needed to be dug slightly short of the cables, to allow space to construct a tap chamber that would give the telephone specialists room to work with the cables. The idea was to dig up about eight feet to the same height as the cables, and then gingerly forward in the hopes of finding them. "If we got it wrong and came up under the cables we were sunk," wrote Major Robert Merrell, leader of the Royal Engineer team. "If we got it wrong and came up with the cables behind us we were also sunk but would not even realize it." They played it safe by positioning the Mole a foot or two short of what they believed to be the exact point.

On March 10, 1955, the British sappers launched the Mole through the roof of the base chamber and began digging a shaft straight up through the soft and sandy soil. It was a painstaking operation. There was room for two men at a time to sit in the Mole; they would open a vane at the top, scrape away at the soil, and then close the vane and open the next, a process that would be repeated over and over. The Mole looked comically eccentric to Montagnon, especially compared with most of the high-tech wizardry the tunnel employed. "It was a strange thing, rather like a bit of kitchen equipment," he recalled. "You had to waggle bars and let the sand come through very carefully, and very slowly." Once a few inches of soil had been removed, the engineers raised the Mole in the vertical shaft with a decidedly Wyke-like means of improvisation. Since hammering and drilling it into place would make too much of a racket, the team's driver, Taffy Lewis, had suggested using the jack from the trunk of a car. Indeed, car jacks—eight of them in all, to support the Mole from all sides—proved to be just the thing.

For a few days everything worked "unnervingly to plan," Merrell said, but then came "moments of acute anxiety." One of the most worrisome was deciding when to stop digging up. The engineers had no way of precisely checking their position in relation to the cables, or how many inches they were below the road. The plans provided by the CANDAREs showed that the cables were buried twenty-seven inches deep along the far side of the highway. The top of the tap chamber would need to be even closer to the surface, only twelve to fourteen inches below the road, in order to give the intruders room to work with the cables.

By the last week of March, the Royal Engineers calculated that they were barely a foot below the road. It was time to put away the Mole and dig forward. This was the "most uneasy" stretch of all, Merrell said. "We scraped our way forward, hoping with every inch gained to see some evidence of cable laying." As they moved forward, they constructed a concrete chamber to house the tapping operation. The engineers were so close to the surface that the sound of pedestrians walking above them in hobnailed boots rattled their heads, and when someone wheeled a handcart overhead, it sounded like a railway car rolling on a bad track. They added insulation to the chamber hoping to stop the drumming. "In spite of the insulation, it was a weird sensation to be in the chamber when an iron-shod horse trotted across it," Vyrl Leichliter recalled. The real concern was whether the tap chamber could support the weight of heavy trucks and even tanks that ran down the highway. The chamber had a reinforced concrete roof, but it was still tense. "We had to be very careful," recalled Montagnon. "We were terribly worried that the whole lot was going to collapse."

The GIs in the observation post were on high alert, ready to switch on the red lights in the tunnel whenever anyone on the Eastern side approached the targeted area, signaling the team below Schönefelder

Chaussee to freeze. No one minded the breaks too much, as it afforded an opportunity to retreat down the tunnel for tea and biscuits or a smoke.

As they got closer and closer to the target, even the normally gregarious Wyke was tense. "It was hard to get anything out of him," said Eddie Kindell. "I didn't try, because he knew what he was doing. We didn't want any chit-chat going on when everybody was trying to get it done right now." For three days, the Royal Engineers inched their way forward, on their bellies or on their backs. Finally, on March 28, they brushed away some soil and spotted the cables, at the expected depth and location.

"Well," Merrell whispered, a note of satisfaction in his voice, "this is it."

———

In the days that followed, the Royal Engineers finished excavating the soil around the cables, trying to create enough space in the chamber to allow the tapping. Then their job was done. Before they even packed up, another British team had arrived at Rudow—a crack team of technicians from a secret outfit within the British General Post Office known as the Special Investigations Unit.

Special Investigations was based at Dollis Hill, a foreboding Victorian building in North London, where they ran technical research for British intelligence in a dark and overcrowded basement experimental laboratory. Peter Lunn had brought them in to do the taps for the Vienna tunnels, and now their unmatched expertise was needed for an even more complicated operation. The unit was led by John Taylor, who had served in North Africa as a communications officer with General Bernard Montgomery's Eighth Army. Taylor, who sported a pencil-thin mustache, was "an absolutely tiny man with a great brain," said Montagnon. "Rather extraordinary to look at." His size aside, Taylor carried himself with an abrupt military bearing and competency that demanded respect, reflected in the code name SIS assigned him: MAG I, short for Magician I.

Taylor's planning meetings with Bill Harvey for the Berlin operation were always entertaining to watch, "like a bit of Viennese opera." Montagnon recalled. "Harvey had a rumbling voice that seemed to come out of his boots. And Taylor had this very squeaky, high voice. So they made a very strange duet."

The postal team had been preparing for the Berlin mission for close to a year, under the guidance of one of Taylor's most experienced telecommunications engineers—Terence Harding, or MAG II—a smartly dressed, hands-on technical expert. Harding, a Royal Signals officer during the war trained in espionage and sabotage, had overseen the reconstruction of telephone networks destroyed by the Nazis as they retreated from Greece, and was a veteran of the Vienna tunnels and various tricky operations placing bugs behind the Iron Curtain. He and his team painstakingly designed amplifiers, oscillators, and other equipment in their laboratory that would fit into the tight quarters needed for Berlin. The Americans helped by delivering sections of steel tunnel liner to Dollis Hill inside large, sealed diplomatic pouches. The liner was assembled inside the laboratory, allowing Harding's men to build just the right size racks to hold the equipment. Once the work was done, there was no room to keep the tunnel sections in the cramped lab, but it did not seem wise to have the scrap man haul them away in public view. So over the course of several weekends, Harding squeezed the sections into his Morris Minor automobile, drove to his home in Rickmansworth, northwest of London, and dragged them into his garden at night, successfully hiding them in the tall grass.

Upon arrival in Berlin, the first mission of the Dollis Hill team was constructing an equipment chamber—sometimes referred to as an amplification chamber. The signals intercepted from the cables would, by necessity, be extremely weak to prevent the Soviets from noticing the tap. In order to be intelligible, they would have to be greatly amplified. That amplification had to take place as close to the tap as possible—the farther away, the more that outside interference from other electrical devices and loss of signal would damage the sound quality. It meant that the chamber, which would hold hundreds of large pieces of state-of-the-art electronic equipment, would have to be built at the far end of the tunnel, below the Schönefelder Chaussee.

Descending into the tunnel, the team found the area for the

equipment chamber to be a muddy mess. They spent a week putting down a solid floor, hauling in concrete from a mixer in the warehouse. Then they lined the chamber with plywood and fluorescent lighting and installed racks to hold a long bank of amplifiers. All the heavy electronic equipment was carried on the tunnel railway, installed on the racks, and connected with wires. Gauges monitored oxygen, temperature, and humidity levels.

Meanwhile, a cable was laid to serve as a branch line, connecting the tap chamber to the equipment chamber. When the time came, each of the three targeted Soviet cables would be attached to the branch line via a T-junction, feeding the tapped lines onto a cable leading to the American warehouse. All the electrical components had to be of the highest quality and were rigorously tested. It would be beyond embarrassing if, after all the work, the tap failed because of faulty Western equipment.

Harding, expert at placing microphones where they could not be found, installed a hidden microphone in the tap chamber that would allow those in the warehouse to monitor anything that happened at the other end of the tunnel. Harding had worked across Western and Eastern Europe as well as in the Middle East and North Africa, but the delicate job in the tap chamber was particularly nerve-racking. "There was a concern that if the tunnel was discovered that the Soviets might find some way to storm it and that anyone inside the tunnel would have nowhere to go if they fired machine guns straight down it," recalled his grandson, Phil Harding.

The job of laying cables to connect the equipment chamber with the warehouse was scarcely more relaxing. The Dollis Hill team was startled to learn that the CIA had already lined the area below the border with a garden hose packed with explosives; team members drew lots to decide who worked in that section.

Back at the warehouse, Eddie Kindell, assisted by U.S. Army Security Agency technicians, used "jillions of miles of wire" to connect the feed from the tunnel through more amplifiers and voltage stabilizers in the warehouse basement. From there, each line was routed via a patch panel into the big operations room on the first floor and connected to each of the recorders mounted on the walls.

Every connection was tested and retested. "With the recorders roll-ing at all times, we had to make sure they were all on good chan-nels," said Kindell.

When the equipment chamber was finished, the once-muddy section below the East German highway had been transformed and looked like a gleaming, ultra-modern command center. On one side, the electronic equipment was stacked in racks from floor to ceiling running the length of the chamber. A tabletop running along the other side held gauges and fans, with chairs where technicians could work and monitor the equipment. A heavy steel door to block entry by Soviet or East German forces was sunk in a concrete slab at the far end of the chamber, just before the vertical shaft. It was wired with an alarm system and kept locked to prevent any nasty surprises. As a final touch, Harvey ordered two official-looking signs put on the side of the door facing the Soviet sector. In Cyrillic and German, they read, in all capital letters, ENTRY IS FORBIDDEN BY ORDER OF THE COMMANDING GENERAL. Harvey's theory was that Soviet and East German soldiers were so conditioned to follow orders that the signs would buy some time for the Western team to evacuate the tunnel in an emergency.

———

All that remained was the tap itself.

Though the tap chamber was complete and the targeted cables fully exposed by April, the Dollis Hill team was not ready. It was es-sential to wait for an extended period of dry weather before starting; any moisture that got into the open cables could short-circuit not only the telephone lines but the entire operation.

To finish the job, Dollis Hill sent two of its best jointers, Les Sparks and Arthur Loomes, on a military flight to Berlin. John Wyke met them at Gatow and put them in the back of a U.S. Army truck for the usual surreptitious ride to Rudow. Once there, they were kept strictly at the installation—it was too risky to have telephone specialists spotted anywhere in Berlin.

Both men were used to working under pressure. During the war, Sparks was with the British Army on the beach at Normandy one day after D-Day, installing overhead telephone lines, a task he continued all the way to Berlin. He and Loomes had worked together on several SIS jobs, including Vienna.

Blake Rymer, a stoic Scotsman who spoke with a decided burr in his voice, would oversee the tapping operation. Rymer, "an enormously phlegmatic guy," in Montagnon's words, had worked with underground cables all his career. Despite his senior position at Dollis Hill, he was still considered the best jointer they had. "Everybody knew that if it came to actually putting hands on the cable, Blake Rymer was the man," said Montagnon.

The job they faced was "extraordinarily tricky," he added. "The great problem was how to put a cut into the cables without putting a fault in the line, which would make all the alarm bells go off in Hades."

BRITISH SECTOR, BERLIN, APRIL 1955

A new officer assigned to the British SIS station in Berlin had more than a passing interest in progress on the tunnel. George Blake arrived in Berlin for his new posting on April 14, 1955. He had driven to Berlin several weeks ahead of Gillian, giving him time to settle in to his new job and to find a place for them to live.

He chose a spacious top-floor apartment in a building reserved for British officials on Platanenallee, a pleasant street lined with sycamore trees in the Charlottenburg district, an area that had been spared heavy bombing damage during the war. Blake particularly liked that it was within walking distance to the SIS station headquarters at the Olympic Stadium complex.

Peter Lunn, presiding over the hundred officers and staff members at the station, was quite pleased to add Blake to his staff, having worked with him at Section Y. Blake's assignment, ironically, was to penetrate the KGB headquarters in Berlin. He was attached to a section responsible for collecting political intelligence on the Soviet Union, and given the job of making contact with Russians in East Berlin—in particular Soviet intelligence officers—with the goal of recruiting them as agents.

There was a second irony. Even though he was in Berlin and just a half-hour drive from Rudow, Blake had less information now about the tunnel progress than when he was in London. His duties no longer had anything to do with Stopwatch/Gold. Back in London, he had sat with Lunn on tunnel planning meetings, but it would raise a red flag to ask anything about it now. Lunn was as secretive as Harvey when it came to sharing knowledge of the tunnel outside of the team at Rudow.

Nor did Blake have much chance to pick up information from two SIS colleagues in Berlin playing key roles in the tunnel. He was close with Peter Montagnon from their time at Section Y. He was also well acquainted with John Wyke, whom he had met during the war, when both worked on SIS operations involving Holland. Wyke, partly of Dutch origin, admired Blake as a "man who had survived real horrors" in Korea. But Lunn had Wyke and Montagnon stay away from the Olympic Stadium to keep their presence quiet from his staff, and Blake had little or no interaction with them. It meant the KGB was now cut off from any up-to-date information about the tunnel. "They had no continuing detailed knowledge of the progress," Harvey's deputy, David Murphy, later said. "Blake didn't have the total access to predict or report what stage we were in."

In any event, Blake's KGB handlers were also keeping their distance from him. Moscow Center remained wary about his transfer to Berlin and reasoned that the best strategy was to watch if SIS gave any signs that Blake was under suspicion. "They would have to show it at their end," said Kondrashev. "So we believed that we should wait during that period of time and not take any measures." That especially meant the tunnel.

After a reasonable interval with no sign that Blake was being followed, the KGB felt it safe to reestablish contact. Nikolai Rodin, who had first met Blake on his return trip from Korea and was now head of the British department at Moscow Center, traveled to Berlin for the first meeting. He gave him a warning: Blake should not discuss the tunnel with anyone—including the KGB in Berlin.

Yevgeny Pitovranov, chief of the KGB station at Karlshorst, was finally informed about the tunnel, but likewise instructed to do nothing. He was told a KGB source had reported that cables were being tapped, but he was given no information about Blake. Pitovranov was powerless to do anything other than keep the American installation under observation and conduct some discreet background checks on residents living nearby. The Karlshorst chief could not inform his subordinates, take any actions against the tunnel, or even protect his own station against the Western intrusion below his feet.

RUDOW, MAY 1955

By the end of the first week of May, the ground around the tunnel was dry, the forecast good, and all the equipment ready. With approval from Washington and London, the night of May 11 was chosen to tap the first of the three cables.

In London, Bill Romey and a second CIA linguist were ordered to fly immediately to Berlin. Harvey and Lunn wanted the forward processing unit on hand at Rudow to listen in the moment the tap was placed in order to monitor for signs of trouble and quickly assess the value of the lines.

Arriving in Berlin on May 10, Romey and the second CIA officer were picked up by a nondescript military sedan with the windows muddied up. Approaching Rudow, they were told to lie on the floor. Once inside the warehouse, they were issued U.S. Army Signal Corps uniforms. Romey found the installation to be a curious hodgepodge of British telephone specialists and American signal soldiers. Everyone kept to themselves, exchanging only first names, and even those were of dubious provenance.

Vyrl Leichliter, the CIA site manager, gave them a tour of the warehouse, including the operations room, located behind two sets of double doors. The outer doors had to be closed before they were allowed into the inner sanctum. When the second set of doors opened, Romey was stunned. He counted well over a hundred Ampex tape recorders lining the walls, wired and ready to go.

It was only now that he understood the scale of the operation.

RUDOW, WEDNESDAY, MAY 11, 1955

The waiting on May 11 was agonizing. John Taylor had flown in from London to witness his Dollis Hill team try the biggest tapping operation ever attempted, and Peter Lunn was on hand as well. Everyone was edgy as the hours crawled by. The tap needed to be done late at night, when there was less telephone traffic and less chance that minor changes in voltage would be noticed.

Rymer, Sparks, and Loomes waited in the warehouse with little to do other than trudge over to the mess hall for meals. Most of their gear had already been placed in the tap chamber, which had been sealed off. Finally, late that night, they received final approval to place the tap. Leichliter patted the three specialists on their shoulders. "Go men," he told them.

The tap team made its way down the tunnel, through the equipment chamber, and up a built-in wooden ladder leading to the tap chamber. They set up their tools and began working with careful precision, an outward calm masking their high intensity. Wyke, Montagnon, and members of the Dollis Hill team were on hand to support the jointers, climbing in and out of the tap chamber as needed. But no one, not even Wyke, was allowed to watch the techniques they would use—those were secret.

The jointers' first task was cutting into the trunk cable, which was protected by an outer lead casing about one-tenth of an inch thick that had to be sliced and stripped away. "All these cables had constant surveillance electronically by the Russians and the Germans," said Montagnon. "So any minor fault you put on it by cutting it even for a microsecond would ring their alarms. We were all absolutely dead frightened."

After delicately making the cut on the cable, Rymer's team painstakingly attached it to the Western spur cable using a T-junction. "If [Rymer] had trembled once when he was doing the joining, then bingo! We'd have had half the Russian Army down on us," said Montagnon.

The cable held ninety-eight core pairs—two strands of wire twisted together, carrying telephone speech and telegraph circuits used by the Red Army. Each was protected by a lead sleeve and several layers of paper that needed to be removed in order to place the tap, a job requiring extraordinary delicacy. There was barely room to tug each core out from the bundle even a fraction of an inch. Once it was pulled as far as possible, the jointer gingerly stripped off the insulation and, working with surgical exactness, connected it to a matching wire in the cable leading to the amplifiers so there was no loss of signal.

The amount of current flowing on the Western wires had to be delicately balanced so that it did not draw away or add current to the East German cable. The tappers might not even know that they had triggered an alarm. In the observation post, sentries watched for any sign of trouble, fearing the arrival of an East German telephone repair van at any time—or, worse, a truckload of Soviet troops.

Conditions inside the dark and cramped tap chamber were claustrophobic. "A hellish place to work," recalled Montagnon. "It enormously stunk of unwashed men." Several times, the perspiration and breathing of the technicians raised the moisture level in the chamber to dangerous levels, forcing the tapping operation to be suspended until air-conditioning could dehumidify the space to safe levels.

Montagnon found himself praying that this would not be the moment a Soviet battle tank came rolling across the tap chamber. It was terrifying, unpleasant, and exhilarating, all at the same time. "All good Boy Scout stuff," he reflected sixty years later.

———

Back at the warehouse, where most of the American and British members of the tunnel team were waiting, the tension was scarcely lower. Occasionally, they received a progress report whispered into the tap chamber microphone, which was connected to a loudspeaker in the warehouse. They held their breath, not wanting to miss a sound coming from the other end.

Once the tapping team connected the first core pairs to the cable leading to the warehouse, Bill Romey and three other translators took their position at switching panels and put on earphones. They listened for any sign that the tapping had succeeded. But the lines were all silent. "It was bite your fingernails time," recalled Romey.

For a long time there was nothing. It was the middle of the night. Perhaps no calls were being made. Or perhaps the tap had failed. Suddenly Romey heard a click on his line. A voice came on.

"*Da?*" the voice asked, speaking Russian.

"*Tovarishch Polkovnik?*" a second voice replied—"Comrade Colonel?"

"*Da, eta ya,*" the first voice said—"Yes, it's I."

Romey let out a whoop and people gathered around. "I had caught the first call and we had a full-blooded colonel on the line," he recalled.

The rank of the callers was a good sign that they had hit the type of lines they were hoping for—headquarters for Soviet forces in Germany. It was a moment of euphoria for the gathered team.

More calls began popping up. Peter Montagnon listened to a conversation between two Soviet officers. "The Russians were just like any two squatters you could pick, and so they were talking about their lousy officers, and the German girls, et cetera, the usual desultory conversation," he recalled. The topic hardly mattered. "We knew we were on to it, and it was there, and we were all totally elated," Montagnon said.

Word was passed to the team in the tap chamber that they had already hit at least one good line. The jointers could only celebrate in silence and continue their work.

Sparks and Loomes needed to seal the joint with melted metal, but their blowtorches would make too much noise in the tap chamber, so other team members used torches farther down in the tunnel, and then hurried the melt up to the tap chamber before it hardened.

After four hours, they were done. The exhausted team members trudged back to the warehouse to congratulations.

There was joy at BOB headquarters when word arrived that the first cable had been safely tapped and the warehouse was receiving clear signals. A message was sent to Washington: "The baby was born."

CHAPTER 13

Striking Gold

RUDOW, BERLIN

A vast amount of information was soon flowing through the lines underneath the border and into the American warehouse. Some 150 Ampex recorders in the operations room were spitting out magnetic tape at fifteen inches per second—sometimes, it seemed, all at the same time. The tunnel team was like a gang of wildcatters who had struck oil. The challenge now was to tame the flow without drowning.

Bill Romey and the rest of the forward processing team monitored the conversations as they came in, listening for any hints that a tap was suspected, or for any other intelligence demanding immediate attention.

They scanned every line, trying to get an idea of what kind of traffic each carried. As soon as a conversation ended and the recorder clicked off, a team member grabbed the big reel-to-reel tape off the recorder, replaced it with a fresh tape to catch the next call, and then rushed to the workspace, located in a small room to the side.

The translator slapped the reel onto a tape player at his desk and connected the tape to a take-up reel, plugged in with earphones, and played the recording, using state-of-the-art, high-speed push-button controls to stop and rewind as needed. The room was soundproof and windowless—about the only place for a mile not disturbed by the noise of the generators—allowing the team members to hear the tapes in peace. As they listened, they grabbed paper from big stacks on the desks and typed brief summaries on sturdy Triumph typewriters.

The first priority was to identify the telephone service lines used by the Soviet and East German operators and technicians. They listened to those conversations immediately, in case they revealed any emergency connected with the tap.

Next in importance was to get a fix on the lines serving high-level Soviet offices, particularly those that might carry the most sensitive conversations about military movements or operations—these would be the ones they spent the most time monitoring. The rest of the lines, once identified as carrying low-level or domestic traffic, were spot-checked on a regular rotation to make sure they were not missing anything important. Even the domestic lines could have good intelligence—an officer calling a friend or family member might let something important slip.

Within a few days, the team had a general fix on most of the lines, and they kept detailed logs for each circuit. Some were very busy, others often quiet. Sometimes, to Romey's surprise, there was not much traffic at all. It could be startling when a recorder suddenly clicked on, automatically activated by a call, and then just as abruptly clicked off.

But usually the calls poured in, and team members were often working up to sixteen hours a day. When traffic was heavy, everyone would wade in to help log each tape. They hit fast forward if the chat sounded routine, knowing that the Main Processing Unit in London would transcribe each word. To speed the process, several Army signal soldiers cleared to participate in the operation took care of changing tapes, while another did nothing but maintain the recorders.

It was nerve-racking work. As the first line of defense, the forward team felt pressure not to miss anything important. When Romey saw traffic indicating that the Soviets and East Germans feared a major uprising to mark the second anniversary of the June

1953 riots, he flagged it, and a rush message made it all the way to President Eisenhower's desk. But nothing happened.

Romey was particularly anxious when the connection was bad and the conversation hard to hear. At times, he felt like shouting into the line: "Would you please stop mumbling and speak up!"

———

On May 21, the Dollis Hill team tapped the second of the three cables, another delicate operation that once again raised fears of setting off alarms. Peter Montagnon sat in the equipment chamber, plugging his earphones into a patch panel and monitoring conversations. "When we listened in, we found no hint of trouble and they were doing as usual, largely talking about sex and the incompetence of their officers," he recalled.

Nonetheless, Bill Harvey and Peter Lunn agreed with recommendations from the worried specialists to delay tapping the third cable, FK 150, which was in terrible condition, its insulation cracking. Tinkering with the brittle cable risked triggering an alarm through an inadvertent short circuit.

In any event, the team already had their hands full with two cables together capable of carrying close to a thousand communication channels. Nearly 150 reel-to-reel tapes were being made each day, and they needed to be sent out as quickly as possible—the voice traffic to London and the teletype to Washington—to be transcribed, fully translated, and analyzed.

Soldiers at Rudow ran the tapes holding the voice recordings to the Gatow airfield in the British sector for a Royal Air Force flight to London. Sometimes they rode in an Opel sedan, though often there were so many tapes that they took a two-and-a-half-ton Army truck, with a driver and officer riding shotgun and a guard in the back, all carrying loaded .45s.

It fell to Hugh Montgomery, Harvey's go-to officer for the tunnel, to get the tapes holding the teletype recordings on their way to Washington. Every night, Montgomery would drive out from the gated American compound housing the Berlin Operations Base headquarters as if departing the office on his way home. Somewhere along the way, he would find a discreet spot to park, take the official

U.S. license plates off his car, and switch to German plates. It was a speedy operation, thanks to special bolts that allowed him to make the change with a quick quarter turn. Then it was on to another out-of-the way spot—a prearranged location every night, and never the same place. Often he ended up on an empty stretch of road in the Grunewald, the big forest in western Berlin.

Vyrl Leichliter in his black Opel or Eddie Kindell in his Volkswagen would show up with the car packed with that day's tapes from Rudow, stacked on spindles inside sealed cardboard boxes. They would hurriedly transfer the boxes into the trunk of Montgomery's car. If anybody was watching, the hope was it would look like just another furtive Berlin black market deal, maybe someone selling cigarettes.

Montgomery would then drive the teletype tapes to the Berlin base—stopping along the way at some "hell and gone" spot to put his American plates back on. Then he lugged the boxes into the building, always a chore. "Those damn things weighed a ton," he recalled.

Every day, there were anywhere from six to twelve new boxes, which became an object of curiosity at the base, where almost no one knew about the tunnel. Norm Glasser, the BOB registry chief responsible for shipping items, griped about all the mysterious cartons he needed to send to Washington. "We had to have a cover story, of course, as to why I would appear every night lugging these big heavy boxes to the base," Montgomery said.

Montgomery brought the matter up with Harvey, who chuckled darkly. "These are going to be uranium samples," he told Montgomery. Word was accordingly put out that the boxes were loaded with processed uranium ore that had been smuggled out of an East German mine supplying the Soviet nuclear program; they were being sent on to Washington for analysis to help estimate the size of the Soviet atomic arsenal. It was a plausible explanation—BOB did have agents at the Wismut mine in southern East Germany, a vital supplier of uranium for the Soviets.

"We said, 'Be very careful, the boxes are lined with lead to protect any radioactivity from getting out,' so everybody just stayed away," Montgomery recalled. "Certainly the boxes were heavy enough to bear it out."

Glasser was duly impressed. "I better not be radiated by this stuff," he grumbled. No more questions were asked.

———

Harvey's deputy at BOB, David Murphy, had never been formally briefed on the tunnel, but Harvey indoctrinated him in bits and pieces as problems arose. Murphy was big and brash, a tough-minded, hands-on operator; his attempt to recruit a KGB officer in a Vienna café had ended with a beer being thrown in his face and a tussle with Soviet security. Murphy rubbed some colleagues the wrong way, but Harvey liked his aggressive style.

Murphy reviewed the intelligence summaries from Rudow, looking for any danger signals or perishable information that might have been missed by the team at the site. Harvey cabled anything particularly hot on his personal, highly secure communications line directly to Frank Rowlett in Washington or Alan Conway—Fleetwood—in Frankfurt.

"The tunnel was so secure, so compartmented, that we did not want the people in the communications department to even know what we were saying," recalled Charlie Bray, Conway's assistant. "So we super enciphered all the messages." In Frankfurt, only Fleetwood, Bray, and a handful of others were able to decode Harvey's cables. "If it was operational immediate or urgent or something like that, they'd call me in the middle of the night," said Bray. He would hurry to the station headquarters, take the cable to his office, pull down the shutters, take out his cipher machine, and break the code. If needed, he would call the new chief of station in Germany, Tracy Barnes, who had taken over from Lucian Truscott.

The late-night calls, disturbing Bray's wife and their two infant children, became more and more frequent, but that was unavoidable. "The take was enormous," said Bray.

WASHINGTON

At CIA headquarters, there was astonishment at "the torrent" of information flowing from the tunnel, recalled Richard Helms. "Our most optimistic estimates were fulfilled twenty times over," he said. At the highest levels of the agency, Bill Harvey was the toast of the town. He had "pushed the operation through its innumerable, and sometimes apparently unsolvable, problems," Helms later said.

The tunnel intelligence, given the code name REGAL, was extremely tightly held, with no indication given of its source. The first "TOP SECRET REGAL" report was issued on June 6. "I know that Allen Dulles was awfully glad to get a copy of anything with this cover name on it," Frank Rowlett later said.

After the disaster of Black Friday nearly seven years earlier, it was like finding an oasis in the desert, particularly since the United States still had virtually no overhead reconnaissance and few human sources. "We had no other way to obtain this information except what was coming through this tunnel," Murphy later said. "It was invaluable." It included detailed information on the Soviet army and air force, weapons, equipment, plans, combat readiness, personnel, and military administration. "The REGAL operation provided the United States and the British with a unique source of current intelligence on the Soviet Orbit of a kind and quality which had not been available since 1948," a CIA history concluded.

President Eisenhower, briefed by Dulles, was encouraged by the early reports, but tried not to get his hopes too high. "The telephone tap in Berlin, when that was found to be possible, was regarded [by Eisenhower] almost as a windfall that probably wouldn't last for too long," Andrew Goodpaster, Eisenhower's staff secretary, later said. "It would give very interesting and useful insight as to what [Soviet] policy was and how far they would push it. Berlin was a very dangerous trigger-point."

Dulles considered it "a highly valuable flow of raw intelligence." Now all they had to do was process it. For the teams assembled in London and Washington, that was proving far more of a challenge than anyone had dreamed.

CHESTER TERRACE, LONDON

The elegant Regency façade of the house on Chester Terrace near Regent's Park gave no hint of the chaos within. The offices inside—

disappointingly dingy compared to the handsome exterior—housed the tunnel's Main Processing Unit. Several dozen transcribers, translators, and analysts had been waiting for weeks—some for months— for material to arrive from Berlin, and had been getting restless. Now that tapes were arriving almost every day on flights from Gatow, they were soon overwhelmed.

Many of the team members were veterans of Vienna, including a large contingent from Section Y and some CIA officers who worked on Operation Silver. But the scale of the Berlin project was in a different realm than Vienna. On the average day at Chester Terrace, close to thirteen hundred phone conversations needed to be transcribed.

It was clear that many more linguists and transcribers were needed. SIS desperately pored over rosters of retired Army officers, bringing in some ancient Russian speakers whose service dated back as far as the Boer War. More linguists were culled from the Russian émigré community, which was eager as ever to strike back against the Soviets. The British signals intelligence organization, the Government Communications Headquarters (GCHQ), sent over everyone they could spare. SIS took over several adjoining Chester Terrace houses from the Agriculture Ministry to accommodate the burgeoning force, which eventually reached 317 persons.

It was an industrial-scale operation. One group would make precise, word-for-word transcriptions from the tapes, monitored by supervisors who would check for accuracy. A second group would translate the transcripts into English. The translations, together with the Russian transcript, were then studied by a third set of groups— one team looking for order of battle intelligence, others for political or economic intelligence, and another for strategic matters. Having the translation together with the Russian transcript for reference allowed the analysts to drill down, looking for second meanings to words, or different contexts for conversations.

"If you listen to any military's telephone lines, it's not chock-full of exciting stuff," said Peter Montagnon, who flew back from Berlin to take charge of Section Y's analysis of the cable traffic. "It's usually dreary as hell. The difference is how you put it together."

Montagnon's focus was "to see what exactly we'd caught." The

intelligence was of limited value until they could figure out which
Soviet military units or intelligence offices were using which circuits and, in particular, which commanders were on what lines.
"You couldn't do much until we'd identified the characters, and
who were the leading players, so to speak, to sort out who was what
and who was worth tagging out as being special," said Montagnon.
It was a tricky business, because the Soviets usually used code names.

A special section at Chester Terrace was devoted solely to monitoring the service lines, including those used by the Soviet and
East German telephone operators and technicians. "We got a huge
amount of incidental information which was worth its weight in
gold off these service lines," said Montagnon.

Operator chatter could be invaluable; one operator might explain
to another how to use new call signs and enciphering procedures.
Best of all was whenever high-ranking Soviet officers experienced
problems with their telephones. The service lines would light up
with "infuriated Russians, demanding that they sort it out," Montagnon recalled.

"All the normal caution—saying things in a code—would break
down, and they'd just discuss what was going on in plain, straightforward Russian," he added. "We'd hear more swear words than
anything else. You'd then get a good idea of what was going on and
who was talking."

One of the challenges the non–native Russian speakers faced was
coping with the astonishingly prolific and creative profanity. When
one of the Americans asked an elderly Russian émigré the meaning
of a word he kept hearing, the Russian blushed so hard that his entire bald pate turned red. He refused to say what it meant, but finally
agreed to write it on a piece of paper. A glossary was created for
reference and labeled TOP SECRET OBSCENE.

Joe Evans, part of the CIA cadre helping the British sort through
the voice traffic, pored over the transcribed material, looking for
any evidence that the Soviets were preparing a surprise attack. Evans,
a chain-smoking former newspaper reporter from Pennsylvania,
was floored at the intelligence provided about the Red Army. "We
were obtaining information on tactics, maneuvers, material, equipment, supplies, disposition of troops, order of battle, and personali-

ties," he said. "We were learning a great deal of basic information of lasting value about Soviet strengths and weaknesses." In the event of war, he said, knowing the disposition and preparedness of the four hundred thousand troops stationed in East Germany would be the West's "ace in the hole."

BUILDING T-32, WASHINGTON, SUMMER 1955

In contrast to the dignified appearance of Chester Terrace in London, Building T-32 was just another one of the ugly World War II temporary barracks–style buildings scarring the Mall in Washington. But the scene inside was just as frenetic as in London. The building, located just down from the Lincoln Memorial along the Potomac River, housed the tunnel's Technical Processing Unit, under the command of Frank Rowlett. It was responsible for processing the miles of teletype traffic being intercepted in Berlin.

The heart of the Washington operation was the machine room on the first floor, where a marvelous electronic apparatus known as the Bumblebee took the Soviet and East German transmissions recorded on magnetic tape and converted them into readable images that were printed on paper tape for translation by linguists. The Soviet circuits carried multiple teletype channels, meaning that the potential take on each six-hour teletype reel arriving in Washington was 216 hours of messages. The Bumblebee, developed by one of Rowlett's communications engineers, was a demodulator that broke the circuit apart onto single channels, each of which was tied into a teletype machine that printed the text onto reels the width of a cloth measuring tape.

No one was quite sure why it was nicknamed the Bumblebee. Some claimed it was because it made a buzzing sound as it operated; others said it was because it looked like it would never fly. But it worked like a charm, taking in and spitting out thousands of feet of text.

The entire room was shrouded in steel mesh to keep any electronic emissions from escaping the building, where they might be picked up by Soviet intelligence. No one was allowed in except the equipment operators and a few others with special clearance.

The finished product was carried upstairs to the second floor of T-32, holding offices crammed with Russian and German linguists, reports processors, and analysts. Supervisors fretted that Soviet agents in Washington might learn about the unusual operation taking place in the building. "All they would have to know is that we have this many Russian and German speakers together," one warned the staff.

All the teletype and reports had to be placed in safes when they were not being used, and as more and more material arrived, the number of safes multiplied. Before long, the second floor began to sag. The safes were repositioned atop load-bearing beams, but the place looked like it might collapse at any moment. So many cables and wires were strung through the building that workers took to calling it the hosiery mill.

The windows were barred and the glass painted over to keep anyone from snooping. The offices grew so rank and murky from cigarette smoke that supervisors grudgingly allowed the windows to be opened a crack to let in some fresh air.

"For a long time I never knew if it was day or night," said Alice Ojala, then a twenty-three-year-old CIA linguist. She had been studying Russian at Boston University the previous year when the agency came hunting for linguists and hired her. Ojala, assigned to a traffic analysis section, was equally in the dark about exactly where the information was coming from, but it was obvious from the rolls of classified Red Army traffic that Western intelligence had hit a mother lode. Whenever she found anything interesting, she would notify a supervisor, who would flag it for further analysis.

As in London, it was soon clear that more linguists were needed in Washington, and the CIA scrambled to find them. Lieutenant Bob Browne, twenty-two, a self-described "unsophisticated lad from Texas," was one of a dozen Army officers studying Russian at the Army Language School in Monterey, California, summoned to the commandant's office. "We had no idea why . . . and wondered if we had done something wrong," he recalled. "One by one we went into a meeting with a man in civilian clothes." The man told Browne he was being considered for an assignment with the CIA, but could tell him nothing else. "The program sounded weird to me, but I agreed to give it a shot," said Browne.

Browne and a half dozen others soon had orders to report to Washington with nothing but a phone number to call for further instructions. After a polygraph test and psychological screening, they were issued CIA badges and told to report to T-32.

Browne, assigned to the same section as Ojala, focused on building an intelligence database on some of the premier Soviet forces, including the 1st Guards Tank Army, headquartered in Dresden. He combed through the intercepts, looking for details on the locations of subordinate units, their armaments, their readiness levels, and the names of commanders. Any references to movement of units drew special attention, as such repositioning might be a precursor to blocking Western access to Berlin or a preparation for war. Even if just for training, as it usually was, the information was valuable. The routes that the Soviets used, readiness evaluations, and indications of training successes or failures all helped to gauge the warfighting capabilities of Soviet forces in Germany and to prepare Western defenses.

The ubiquitous Peter Montagnon, having helped launch the Berlin and London processing operations, was now sent to Washington to serve as the British liaison with the American operation. He found the fresh-faced American linguists in Washington quite a contrast to the worldly Russian aristocrats and ancient British Army colonels working in London. "They were innocent little creatures just out of college, and they didn't understand what the world was about, let alone the Russians," he said.

Nonetheless, those Washington innocents, whose numbers eventually reached 350, rose to the occasion, going through every day an average of four thousand feet of teletype packed with technical and obscure Russian. The work was "mentally exhausting and it was hard to be sharp," Browne recalled. The crew decompressed with weekend trips to Rehoboth Beach on the Delaware shore, as well as office romances that resulted in at least one marriage. Browne coached their recreational league basketball team, the T-32 Turtles, which compiled an undistinguished record. But it was hard to escape the pressure inside the building.

Sometimes, to Ojala's amusement, Browne would stick his head as far as he could through a window opening. "Hello world," he called. "I'm getting off."

———

Much of the teletype traffic arriving in Washington was encoded, and to crack it open, the CIA needed the assistance of the National Security Agency, its rival in the battle over signals intelligence. This was not a surprise to the CIA tunnel planners, who had early on realized that they needed help. But it came as a shock to NSA leaders, including the agency's fearsome director, General Ralph Canine, who had known nothing about the tunnel. The tap had been flowing for close to a month before the CIA even informed the NSA about the operation.

The CIA's reasoning was that PBJOINTLY was not a communications intelligence operation, but a clandestine operation, and therefore there had been no need to inform the NSA. The tunnel was, of course, both—in fact, it was simultaneously the largest signals intelligence and covert operation in Soviet-occupied ground the CIA had ever conducted.

Canine, who had built the NSA into a force to be reckoned with, did not see the irony or the humor. To add insult to injury, Allen Dulles initially denied the NSA director clearance to even see the intelligence. A bitter Canine never forgave the CIA, worsening already bad relations between the two agencies. Dulles regretted the general's anger, though he could not help but bask in victory; the NSA was largely dependent on intercepted radio communications, while the CIA had struck gold with a blockbuster landline operation.

Despite the tension, the two intelligence agencies had little choice but to cooperate. The CIA lacked the manpower, analytic skills, and equipment needed to speedily decrypt the material, while the less established NSA was eager to prove its worth and desperate for access to this intelligence trove.

Rowlett, who had left the NSA because of ill treatment from Canine, made arrangements for delivering the encrypted material to the NSA. He was too much of a professional to allow his resentment to affect the coordination, and he met regularly with two former NSA colleagues, Lou Tordella and Ollie Kirby, to "go over what was happening, to see if we needed to make any changes." Few people at the NSA were even aware of what was happening. "The project was very tightly held, even within NSA," Rowlett said.

The NSA had plenty of tools at its disposal. It was important to read the police traffic in and out of Altglienicke for any signs of trouble around the tap site. The Volkspolizei in East Berlin—whose lines were among those tapped—transmitted sensitive communications via old Enigma machines, the encrypting device used by Nazi Germany to send telegraph traffic in what was thought to be unbreakable code. Fortunately, the United States had held on to a few Bombe machines, the electromechanical device that successfully decrypted Enigma messages during World War II. Analysts in the NSA's East German cryptanalytic section at Arlington Hall could not understand why there was suddenly a top priority being placed on decoding seemingly mundane reports about police arrests, but they did as they were told.

Beyond police reports, the decryption of the encoded teletype traffic from Berlin was producing "high-quality intelligence," in the NSA's judgment. And the NSA did get some measure of revenge for being left in the dark about the tunnel, refusing to share its decryptions directly with the CIA on the grounds of operational security.

———

Richard Bissell, the CIA special programs manager who was overseeing the U-2 and would become head of clandestine services, considered the tunnel "a brilliant success," but eventually worried about the huge amount of product inundating the agency. "I was tempted to issue a ration to the German station of the number of words they could transmit a month, because I was convinced this flow of words into Washington was probably counter-productive," he later said. But he met resistance from senior CIA analysts, who did not want any intelligence filtered before it was sent from Berlin on the grounds that "you never knew when a little piece will just fit in and complete a puzzle," Bissell said. "We never did cut down."

Bit by bit, a mosaic was being painstakingly painted of the Soviet order of battle—its organization, deployment of forces, strength and weaknesses, training, tactics, weaponry and other equipment, radio and telephone networks, and system of passwords.

"We weren't after the great secrets—well, everybody was, I suppose—but above all, we wanted to know the Russian order of battle," said Montagnon. "It was all stuff that would have been absolutely vital if we'd been fighting them."

A warning of war was less likely to come from a conversation between commanders than it was from multiple conversations between supply clerks. "We could follow movements of matériel," said Eddie Kindell. "People can't invade if they can't move matériel. You put all these bits together, and you can tell whether somebody's preparing. That's one of the big things we got out of Berlin."

But the clerks were not the only ones spilling secrets.

CHAPTER 14

The Penetration of the CIA into Our Midst

Marshal Andrei Grechko, the tall and barrel-chested commander of all Soviet forces in East Germany, had a surprisingly high-pitched voice for such a fearsome figure. So thought the members of the forward processing team listening to his conversations in the Rudow warehouse.

Grechko had assumed command of the Group of Soviet Forces Germany in May 1953, and quickly proven his worth to the Kremlin by ruthlessly crushing the June uprising. In recognition of his heroic service in Ukraine during the war, he was one of a half dozen illustrious World War II commanders who had been recently elevated to the lofty rank of Marshal of the Soviet Union.

But all that power did not protect Grechko from having his telephone tapped. He, along with the entire Soviet Red Army headquarters at Wünsdorf south of Berlin, remained oblivious that hundreds of conversations and transmissions were being recorded and monitored every day by Western spies.

While lower-level functionaries might be useful for learning about troop movements and military preparations, generals were among the favorite chatterboxes for the teams processing conversations. "You could say the more senior the rank, the less security conscious they were," said Peter Montagnon. The senior Soviet officers "were convinced that they were far too intelligent and disciplined

ever to disclose anything of possible interest to any potential eaves-
dropper," Richard Helms later said of the Berlin and Vienna tunnels. "Little did they know. Their unvarnished comments on the
quality of Soviet military equipment, the intellectual capacity of
fellow officers, and the wisdom of Moscow's military policies were
in more than one sense priceless. SILVER and GOLD proved to be
apt cryptonyms."

———

George Blake's assignment to Berlin had left the Soviet Union—
including the Red Army, the Kremlin, and the KGB itself—
vulnerable to damaging exposure from the tunnel. Had he still been
at Section Y in London, Blake could have warned the KGB about
both the volume and the quality of the information being intercepted. Instead, he could do little more than speculate.

By the summer of 1955, Blake was reasonably certain the tunnel
was operating. At his office at the Olympic Stadium, he could see
that there were certain people who were somehow busy with something unexplained. Mysterious shipments were being flown regularly from the Gatow airfield to London. "I was aware of all that,
yes," he recalled, and he "of course" passed on this information to
the KGB.

Moscow Center's decision was the same as before: Nothing
should be done. The Soviet military, along with everyone else outside a tight leadership circle, would remain in the dark. The instructions from Arseny Tishkov, the deputy intelligence service chief
responsible for protecting Blake's identity, were clear. "The decision
was taken that we would not allow anyone to use the tunnel for any
purposes, disinformation or other purposes, so as to not endanger
George Blake," said Sergei Kondrashev. "He was too important
to us."

But with Blake unable to report in any detail on the tunnel, the
KGB did not understand how much was being lost. "The penetration of the CIA into our midst . . . was very deep, much deeper than
I anticipated," Kondrashev later admitted. "We were certainly aware
that enormous material was going to the other side," he added. But
no one had envisioned how enormous.

"How could anyone have known how much was going over those communication lines?" Hugh Montgomery asked. "I'm sure they had no idea of the volume of information that was being processed." After all, the CIA and SIS had also been blindsided by the amount.

In later years, after Blake's betrayal was known, the common assumption was that Moscow must have doctored the information. Yet the reality strongly suggests otherwise. Moscow Center was unwilling to plant false information because it presented too high a risk to Blake. Even if the KGB wanted to, very little could have been done without being detected.

"It was impossible for us to use the tunnel tapping for disinformation," Kondrashev said. "Why? . . . There was this large quantity of real information going through so many different phone lines. . . . To insert two or three pages of misinformation into this tremendous amount of material would have meant that a simple analysis with basic methods would have shown that this is information contradicting that huge amount of true information."

The deception would have stuck out like a sore thumb, as Blake realized. "American and British intelligence would get information which contradicted that false information, and immediately that would cause suspicion that the Soviets knew that we were tapping their telephone lines," Blake said. Montgomery's assessment was the same. "It would have given it away immediately, that something had leaked somewhere," he said. "It would have been clear to both the Americans and the British that there had been a leak, and the number of people with that knowledge was so limited that Blake would have been exposed in a fairly short time."

Any significant disinformation campaign would have required bringing hundreds and perhaps thousands of callers into the deception, each prepped to deliver bad information—not only logistically impossible, but even more guaranteed to reveal a leak. Even a more conservative step such as diverting the more sensitive traffic to untapped lines would have been a tip-off. "That would become very apparent if all of a sudden lots of Soviet circuits had disappeared," said Montgomery. The CANDAREs would have quickly reported the changes.

If they wanted to protect Blake, the KGB's hands were tied. "They couldn't do anything about it," David Murphy recalled gleefully sixty years later. "What could they have done about it?" So the taps flowed on, undisturbed.

———

The KGB's subtle warning to Defense Minister Nikolai Bulganin the previous fall had done little good. Lamented Kondrashev, "When two close friends wanted to exchange opinions on the situation in Berlin and Moscow, then it was often difficult to stop them."

Grechko was given additional warning that he and his generals in Germany should improve telephone security, according to Kondrashev. But the marshal was still told nothing about the tunnel or that his own communications had been targeted. In any event, it was hard to tell the generals anything. "The Soviet officers and our diplomats were terribly talkative," Kondrashev complained.

Certainly, the message did not reach Grechko's wife, Klavdiya, who kept busy on the telephone dealing in the black market. "They were stealing rugs from every house they could get into and shipping them back to Moscow," recalled Montgomery.

With her incessant complaints and demands, Klavdiya Grechkova was heartily disliked by the headquarters staff at Wünsdorf. One of the clerks at Grechko's headquarters blabbed about the general and his wife on such a regular basis that the American and British listeners fondly dubbed him the Town Crier. Many a late afternoon, after his superiors had departed for the day, he would call another clerk at a division headquarters with the latest tale of "Comrade Grechkova's foraging for another fur coat or grand piano."

———

Such stories were all very amusing and provided a window into the corrupt mind-set and influence peddling prevalent among the Soviet command in East Germany. What was more important was learning about what the CIA termed "a close and much-prized friendship" the Grechkos had with Nikita Khrushchev and his family.

Khrushchev remained a mysterious figure to the West in the summer of 1955. Georgy Malenkov, once seen as having the inside track among the collective leadership vying to succeed Stalin, had been outmaneuvered by Khrushchev and his allies and ousted as premier in February. Bulganin had taken over as Soviet premier, but some suspected that Khrushchev, the party first secretary, was the real power behind the throne.

The relationship between Khrushchev and Grechko dated to years of service together during the war, when Grechko was a top commander in Ukraine under the supervision of Khrushchev. After Stalin's death, Grechko and Khrushchev had rekindled their friendship, with benefits for both.

Grechko was a powerful figure in the Red Army, so his warm relationship with the party first secretary was viewed as a significant card in Khrushchev's favor. "Because Grechko was a Khrushchev loyalist, the CIA guys on site were betting that Khrushchev would rise to the top of the post-Stalin . . . leadership," one of the U.S. Army linguists at Rudow later said. CIA analysts prepared a top-secret report on "The GRECHKO FAMILY and their friends," which went into great detail about their relationship with the Khrushchevs. In the summer of 1955, the Grechko household was abuzz with preparations for a visit to Berlin by Khrushchev's wife, Nina. Klavdiya Grechko, who saw herself in competition with other high-ranking Soviet wives "for the favors" of Nina, was eager to cater to her every need, in particular lining up the best hairdresser. For the analysts, even such trivial details held clues about who was up and who was down in the byzantine Soviet hierarchy.

The Grechkos did manage a modicum of discretion in their discussions. "On no occasion was the name KHRUSHCHEV ever mentioned by them, nor did his first names—Nikita Sergeevich— ever pass their lips," the report noted. "However, frequent references to a cryptic personage, described, amongst other things, as 'he, himself' and 'Nina's husband' have left no doubt."

Not everyone at CIA headquarters in Washington was impressed with such reports. Gordon Stewart, chief of the foreign intelligence staff and a rather proper former academic known as the Bishop, took a dim view of Harvey. He dismissed the tunnel intelligence as useless gossip, calling it "stuff about Army wives, discussions of social arrangements, idiotic stuff." But Allen Dulles and Dick Helms felt differently, as did those working closely with the intelligence. "Nobody really knew these people," said Murphy. "Being able to listen to conversations between people in Berlin and people in Kiev and in Moscow, who were part of the Khrushchev household, gave us an enormously effective insight into what this new leadership was like." The gossip was "a very rich lode," said Montgomery. It was the glue that the analysts used to stick their mosaic together.

Still, knowing too much gossip was not without its risks. A U.S. Army general in Berlin had seen a tunnel report in which a Soviet general in Berlin mentioned his wife's pregnancy. Several weeks later, at a vodka-infused ceremonial event, the American general spotted the Soviet and sidled up to him, with a U.S. Army lieutenant on hand to serve as an interpreter. "I hear you're going to be a father," the American general said. "I hope it's going to be a boy and will grow up to be a great soldier like you!" Before the remark could be translated, the American realized his mistake; he swung wildly with his vodka glass and knocked the lieutenant to the ground. While the interpreter was still down, the general whispered urgently in his ear, "Don't translate that! Give him a bromide about Russo-American friendship."

The Russian seemed unfazed by the commotion and drank a toast. But the much-abashed American general reported his gaffe to BOB that evening. It was not until urgent queries established that the Russian spoke no English that anyone could relax.

———

Beyond the gossip, countless hard facts were being mined—often just small details, comments, or nuggets of information—that when assembled and analyzed allowed the West to make a much more precise assessment of the Soviet threat than previously possible.

A new Soviet battle tank was plagued by frequent mechanical breakdowns, illustrated by the near-daily complaints of a frustrated Soviet mechanic about a pin holding the tank track together that kept fracturing. The military struggled with equipment shortages and budget problems. East German railroad tracks and equipment—needed to move Soviet equipment in event of an attack—were in disrepair. So many examples of the Red Army's incompetence and poor morale were heard that some senior intelligence officials in Washington and London spoke of a "danger of overestimating the Soviets."

But other information gleaned from the intercepts was troubling. The Soviet air force in East Germany had improved its nuclear delivery capability and was armed with new bombers and jet interceptors with airborne radar. The number of Soviet bombers in Poland had doubled, protected by a new division of fighters. Analysts learned the location of about a hundred Soviet air force installations in East Germany, Poland, and the USSR, as well as previously unidentified Red Army units. They picked up field post numbers the Soviets used to conceal the real designations of military units, giving clues to their actual designation and location. They learned of a reorganization of the Soviet Defense Ministry, and compiled biographical data on thousands of Soviet officers. Some of the most crucial tunnel intelligence provided a window into the Soviet nuclear program, allowing the West to pinpoint the locations of Soviet nuclear facilities in the USSR as well as identify hundreds of people associated with the program. Beginning in March 1955, hundreds of German scientists who had been taken to Russia after the war to work on the Soviet nuclear program were released and returned to East Germany. Many of them were enticed by the CIA and SIS with offers of housing and jobs to leave for the West and reveal what they knew. The tunnel information allowed the West to cross-check reports from the newly released scientists. Based on all the new intelligence, the CIA quadrupled its estimate of Soviet production of uranium-235, and concluded that the Soviets had the capability to build higher-megaton nuclear weapons.

REGAL also gave the United States and Britain insight into momentous and conflicting developments that were sweeping across the Cold War landscape in 1955, some hardening the lines of division in Europe, and others offering hope for a more peaceful coexistence. On May 5, the Western Allies formally ended their occupation of West Germany, allowing its rearmament and admission into NATO, a major blow to the Soviets, who had sought to prevent the alliance of any part of Germany with the West and were deeply concerned about the prospect of rearming the Germans. In response, on May 14, just three days after the tap was placed, the USSR established the Warsaw Pact with its Eastern European satellites, creating a counter to NATO and expanding Soviet control over the East.

While many viewed the Warsaw Pact's creation as window dressing, tunnel intercepts showed the Red Army's plans for increased coordination with the Eastern European militaries, and the Soviet decision to establish an East German army. Some in the West feared that the Soviets would give the East German government control of East Berlin as a way of propping up Walter Ulbricht's regime and putting pressure on the Western powers to abandon the city, possibly leading to another blockade. But REGAL showed that the Soviets "did not intend to relinquish their prerogatives" as to control, according to a CIA report. Intercepts captured the growing tension between the Soviets and East Germans as to who was in charge in East Berlin. "REGAL provided a clear picture of the unpreparedness, confusion and indecision among Soviet and East German officials" whenever there was an international incident, the report said.

——

In essence, the KGB foreign intelligence directorate was sacrificing Soviet military, political, and scientific secrets to protect its own secret—George Blake. But those were not the only secrets the KGB was putting at risk. It was exposing its own intelligence partners—not only East German intelligence, but the GRU, the Soviet military intelligence branch, revealing that the KGB's relationship with the GRU was perhaps more dysfunctional than that between the CIA and NSA.

The tapped circuits included twenty-five lines carrying military intelligence traffic, mostly to GRU offices and units of the Red Army intelligence directorate. Many conversations between the intelligence directorate in East Germany and GRU headquarters in Moscow were intercepted, giving the CIA and SIS a window into the GRU and its officers. The intelligence siphoned from the lines allowed the West to identify more than 350 GRU and Red Army intelligence officers in East Germany. It revealed that the Red Army counterintelligence directorate in Potsdam was operating a large scattergun network of agents in West Berlin and West Germany. The secrets of Soviet military counterintelligence were "something we never expected to get," said Murphy. For the sake of Blake, the KGB allowed the secrets out.

More astonishing, even other KGB offices in East Germany were hung out to dry. The KGB's own military counterintelligence directorate in Potsdam, which worked closely with Red Army intelligence, was victimized. To their delight, the CIA listeners found that KGB officers in Potsdam were careless about details such as agents' identities and pseudonyms. "They were definitely not as close-lipped as their brothers at the KGB Residentura, or even perhaps as the military intelligence personnel," a CIA analysis said. "About the best that can be said is that they certainly were better than the [East German intelligence officers]." From these calls, the CIA and SIS learned details about KGB tradecraft, cases, safe houses, dead drops, and their procedures for handling papers. They were also getting information about KGB radio intercept capabilities, and the locations and telephone numbers for intelligence units across East Germany. REGAL was used to confirm the bona fides of East Germans and Soviets recruited for spying, guarding against KGB or Stasi plants, and it was invaluable for corroborating the reports they sent from the field.

"It was unique," said Joe Evans, the CIA officer reviewing reports at Chester Terrace in London. "KGB officers talking to KGB officers about their missions, operations and agents. About their organizations and their headquarters staffs, about their colleagues, about their superiors."

Added Murphy, "We were at that point totally on top—we thought—of the counterintelligence picture in Berlin and in the East."

———

To a certain extent, Yevgeny Pitovranov, chief of the KGB station at Karlshorst, could be confident that his apparat was safe from the phone taps. After all, his office used the special overhead lines operated by the KGB, reserved for the highest-level Soviet traffic—

including the First Chief Directorate, the KGB's foreign intelligence service—to communicate with Moscow.

But there was a problem: the Karlshorst headquarters communicated regularly with countless Soviet and East German intelligence units across the country, coordinating activities and discussing operations on landlines that were intercepted by the tunnel. "Everybody else, from the GRU, from the KGB military counterintelligence, from East German intelligence, would keep calling in," recalled Murphy. "It was a freebie, really, but it was very, very useful."

From these intercepted calls, BOB was learning many details on KGB operations in East Berlin. Eventually, REGAL intelligence identified three hundred KGB officers operating in East Germany and the Soviet Union.

Though Pitovranov may have realized that some KGB calls would be intercepted, he was helpless to stop the CIA and SIS from listening delightedly to his own conversations with other offices, as well as with his "rather listless and apathetic" wife, as the eavesdroppers described her. Even Pitovranov's plans to hunt wild boar at night in Berlin with high-powered rifles equipped with infrared telescopic sights were not safe. (Major General Pavel Dibrova, commandant of the Soviet garrison in Berlin, told a colleague he was "concerned over the danger of some of the local population getting killed in the process.")

Beyond the boar hunts, BOB was able to track Pitovranov's movements around East Germany and his travel to Moscow, as well as visits to Berlin by senior intelligence officials. The KGB's security detachment at the vital Wismut uranium mine supplying the Soviet nuclear program reported directly to Pitovranov, and their intercepted calls provided a wealth of information about the operation and the pace of the mining.

The intercepts also gave insight into Pitovranov's character and leadership style. He was well regarded, both by subordinates at Karlshorst and his counterparts at other intelligence offices across East Germany. A Red Army intelligence officer praised him for acting "as quick as lightning" in support of an operation. "He is a fighter and stands up for his people," M. I. Marchenko, a senior apparat officer, told a friend. But, Marchenko added, the apparat was under high pressure. Things were so hot at Karlshorst it was "like sitting on a powder barrel."

Only Pitovranov knew how explosive the barrel was.

GENEVA, SWITZERLAND, JULY 1955

No American president had met with a Soviet leader since the end of World War II, when Harry Truman sat down with Stalin in 1945. But on July 14, the presidential airplane, *Columbine III,* landed in Geneva carrying Dwight Eisenhower to attend the first Big Four summit since the Potsdam Conference.

Winston Churchill, who had for so long vainly pressed Eisenhower to meet with the new Soviet leaders, was not there. With his advancing age and declining health, he had finally given in to pressure from his own party to resign as prime minister. He stepped down on April 6, and his successor, Anthony Eden, the longtime foreign minister, was attending the gathering in his place.

A path had been cleared for the summit when the Soviets had signed a treaty on May 15 ending the occupation of Austria and establishing the nation as neutral. The step, taken over the objections of the hard-line foreign minister, V. M. Molotov, was meant as a goodwill gesture by the new Kremlin leadership. It was enough for Eisenhower to drop his long-standing opposition to a summit. "A new dawn may be coming," he said before departing Washington. Geneva would give Eisenhower and much of the West their first view of the new Soviet leadership, and hopes were high for a change from the Stalin era.

Soviet premier Nikolai Bulganin, as head of state, received the ceremonial welcome at the airport from the Swiss Guard. With his cowlick hair and white goatee, and wearing a light beige summer coat that dragged on the ground, Bulganin looked "for all the world like an old-time opera star," a reporter at the summit later wrote. Bulganin, a "consummate *apparatchik*" with a benign manner, had been chosen as premier because he was unthreatening to all factions in the Kremlin.

But there were hints that Khrushchev was driving the train. He had been infuriated upon arrival when a Swiss protocol official blocked his way to ensure that the party first secretary did not join in inspecting the honor guard. At a dinner hosted by the Americans, Khrushchev joked about what a heavy drinker Bulganin was. It did not escape notice that Khrushchev was "able with impunity to humiliate the premier of his country," said Charles Bohlen, the U.S. ambassador to Moscow, one of the attendees. The Western delegates were taken aback, as much by Khrushchev's appearance as by his behavior. "How can this fat, vulgar man with his pig eyes and ceaseless flow of talk, really be the head—the aspirant Tsar—of all those millions of people of this vast country," wondered Harold Macmillan, the British chancellor of the exchequer.

Khrushchev struck Eisenhower as "rather crude, quite shrewd, quick-as-a-flash, a man who obviously had the strength to battle his way to the top and stay there," according to Andrew Goodpaster. Khrushchev, for his part, judged the former Supreme Allied commander to be a "soft" man under the control of Secretary of State John Foster Dulles, who was viewed with great hostility in the Kremlin. "That vicious cur Dulles was always prowling around Eisenhower, snapping at him if he got out of line," Khrushchev later wrote. During meetings in Geneva, Khrushchev was scornful of how the president would take handwritten notes Dulles slipped to him and follow them "like a dutiful schoolboy taking his lead from his teacher."

With his roots in the peasantry and a passion for social justice, Khrushchev was the last "true believer" in the Bolshevik Revolution among the post-Stalin Soviet leadership. The onetime metal fitter working the coal pits in the Donbass region of Ukraine had become a labor organizer and after the revolution risen through the ranks to become Stalin's viceroy in Ukraine.

He was volatile and reckless, headstrong and given to extremes, and quite willing to rattle sabers in a nuclear age. When Malenkov had warned of the insanity of nuclear war, Khrushchev had attacked this as a sign of weakness and used it as a pretext for forcing out his rival. Yet now Khrushchev himself was moving toward a policy of peaceful coexistence with the West.

Certainly, Khrushchev had few illusions of winning a nuclear war. When Grechko, during a visit to Khrushchev's dacha, described his dream for conquering Western Europe, confidently outlining a scenario where Paris would be captured by day six, Khrushchev exploded: "Haven't you ever heard of nuclear weapons? What do you mean, Paris? You think you're Napoleon? On the first day there would be nothing left of you but a wet spot."

After two days of meetings at the marble Palais des Nations overlooking Lake Geneva, Eisenhower was frustrated at the lack of progress on any major issue, including arms control. He had come to Geneva "hoping to see if we could not penetrate the veil of Soviet intentions," he told his national security advisers. The Soviets, he added, likely had the same goal.

Eisenhower had been mulling an idea that he hoped would ease the mutual suspicion that was hindering progress—an "Open Skies" agreement that would give both sides the right to unlimited aerial reconnaissance. The unfinished proposal had bounced around within the administration for some time, and Eisenhower had come to the summit unsure whether he would introduce it. Determined to try to break the logjam at Geneva, he decided the time was right.

Before the third session on July 20, Eisenhower and his aides hastily put together the proposal, but it was still unfinished when the meeting began. Halfway through his remarks, Eisenhower took off his glasses, laid them on the table, and, looking directly at Bulganin and Khrushchev, delivered the proposal from memory. "Our two great countries admittedly possess new and terrible weapons in quantities which do give rise . . . to the fears and dangers of surprise attack," Eisenhower told them. He outlined the details, giving each side unlimited authority to fly over the other's country, take aerial photographs, and conduct ground inspections on anything suspicious.

The dramatic offer was punctuated by a bolt of lightning that flashed across Lake Geneva, visible through the high windows behind Eisenhower, temporarily knocking out power to the Palais. "I didn't mean to turn the lights out," the president joked.

Bulganin greeted the proposal politely. "I assure you we'll study it," he replied.

But shortly afterwards, when the delegations retired to the cocktail room, Khrushchev approached the president. "I don't agree with
our chairman," he told Eisenhower. "It's nothing but a spy thing, an
intelligence mission, and we'll have none of it." The prospects for
Open Skies were clearly dim. Nor was there much doubt anymore
about Khrushchev's position relative to Bulganin. "We knew who
the hell was boss, right then," Eisenhower later said.

The conference ended with no agreement and instead a tepid
mutual communiqué about holding further discussions. There was
enough goodwill for Eden to extend an invitation for the Soviets to
visit Britain.

Khrushchev did not see Geneva as a waste of time. "We hadn't
achieved any concrete results," he admitted. "But we were encouraged, realizing now that our enemies probably feared us as much as
we feared them."

For Eisenhower, there was also consolation. The secret U-2 project was getting closer to fruition, which would give the United
States the capability for aerial reconnaissance, whether the Soviets
liked it or not. Allen Dulles redoubled efforts to get the plane flying. And meanwhile, the tunnel intercepting Soviet communication
lines in Berlin continued its enormous flow of information to the
West.

"To betray you have to belong. I never belonged." George Blake at Manpo prison camp in North Korea in 1951, two years before his return to England to a hero's welcome.
Courtesy of the Blake family

Bill Harvey in Berlin. Officers at the CIA's Berlin Operations Base were unsure what to make of their new chief, who seemed to be "a creature from another planet."
© *Garston Wallace Driver*

Dwight Eisenhower and Winston Churchill in December 1953, at the end of a summit in Bermuda where Eisenhower professed willingness to use atomic weapons to stop Soviet aggression. It was clear to Churchill that absent better intelligence about Soviet intentions, any confrontation between Washington and Moscow might trigger nuclear war. *Library of Congress*

LEFT: Frank Rowlett. The courtly Virginian, one of America's greatest codebreakers, teamed with Bill Harvey to lead the tunnel project from Washington. *National Cryptologic Museum/NSA*

RIGHT: CIA director Allen Dulles. With his love of the clandestine, Dulles did not take much persuasion to back a tunnel into East Berlin. *National Archives*

Calls came out of the blue for Army Corps of Engineers captains Keith Comstock (*left*) and Bob Williamson (*right*), asking them to volunteer for a secret project: digging a tunnel into East Berlin. *Courtesy Keith G. Comstock and Chris Williamson*

Members of the U.S. Army Corps of Engineers team chosen to dig the tunnel, including Comstock (*front row, second from right*). They "came to Berlin in the dark, so to speak, and left the same way." *Courtesy Keith G. Comstock*

A 1959 aerial photo shows the American installation in the foreground, with the route of the tunnel marked running through Farmer Noack's orchard past the cemetery on the right to Schönefelder Chaussee and the cables below. *Allied Museum/W. Chodan*

The American compound in Rudow sat directly across from Farmer Noack's newly planted orchard. The warehouse, on the left, included sophisticated antennas on the roof for a radar intercept station—cover for the tunnel being dug from the basement. The motor pool is in the center and the barracks on the right. *Courtesy Altglienicke Museum*

East Berlin farmer Paul Noack planted an orchard with more than a thousand fruit trees as the tunnel was dug beneath his feet. "What was funny was that in certain spots the trees did not develop well," recalled his daughter. *Bundesarchiv, Bild 183-37896-0003 / Sturm, Horst / CC-BY-SA*

A sixteen-foot-wide hole jackhammered through the concrete floor in the warehouse basement served as the entrance to the tunnel. *CIA*

Working with short-handled shovels under the protection of a shield at the tunnel face, crews of Army engineers dug around the clock for six months to reach the targeted cables one-quarter mile away. *CIA*

The Royal Engineers No. 1 Specialist Team, with Robert Merrell and John Wyke (*front row, second and third from left*), had the task of digging straight up through sandy soil to reach the Soviet cables. *Courtesy Soraya Wyke*

The British team at work in the tunnel. The British had tapping skills and experience the Americans lacked. *Courtesy Soraya Wyke*

Major Robert Merrell, the Royal Engineers officer team leader, and Major John Wyke of SIS take a cigarette break. *Courtesy Soraya Wyke*

The three trunk cables carrying Soviet communications tapped by the British team. Branch lines are visible on the right leading to the equipment chamber and onto the American warehouse. *Bundesarchiv, Bild 183-37695-0004 / Junge, Peter Heinz / CC-BY-SA 3.0*

When the equipment chamber was finished, the once-muddy section below the East German highway had been transformed and looked like a gleaming, ultra-modern command center, with electronic equipment stacked in racks running the length of the chamber. *Bundesarchiv, Bild 183-37695-0005 / Junge, Peter Heinz / CC-BY-SA 3.0*

As a final touch, Harvey had signs placed on the steel door guarding the entrance of the tunnel. ENTRY IS FORBIDDEN BY ORDER OF THE COMMANDING GENERAL, they read in Russian and German. *Bundesarchiv, Bild 183-37695-0015 / Junge, Peter Heinz / CC-BY-SA 3.0*

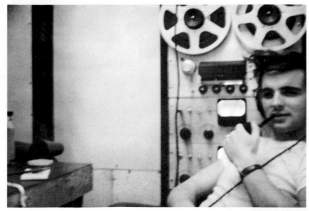

Some 150 Ampex recorders lined the wall in the warehouse operations center, recording hundreds of conversations and teletype communications every day. *Allied Museum*

Eugene Kregg was living the easy life in California as the lead bass soloist for the U.S. Army Language School's renowned Russian choir when he received a mysterious summons to Berlin. The Russian linguist found himself in the middle of "the hottest intelligence operation on the face of the planet." *Nick Kregg (aka Nick Kovalenko)*

Peter Montagnon, a witty and lighthearted SIS officer who was a bit of a Renaissance man, played a key role in Berlin, London, and Washington managing the enormous volume of captured communications. *Steve Vogel*

Marshal Andrei Grechko, the fearsome commander of all Red Army forces in Germany, was oblivious to the fact that hundreds of conversations involving him, his subordinates, and his wife were being recorded. *Mil.ru*

Soviet GRU officer Pyotr Popov, the CIA's first high-quality clandestine Soviet military source. Between the tunnel and Popov, the Berlin base in 1956 enjoyed an intelligence bonanza. *CIA*

The jovial KGB officer Sergei Kondrashev (*right*), shown in 1997 with former CIA Berlin base officer David Murphy, was ostensibly a cultural affairs secretary at the Soviet embassy in London but his real job was handling Agent Diomid. *Courtesy Steven Murphy*

CIA officer Hugh Montgomery, pictured with his Austrian bride, Annemarie, was an exceptionally useful sort, a Harvard PhD who could handle himself in a bar fight.
Personal collection of the Montgomery family

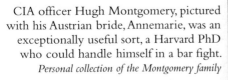

The view from the warehouse observation post, looking over the route of the tunnel. *Eugene Bialas*

The atmosphere at the Rudow installation was decidedly relaxed, including for Harris the guard dog, who spent more time playing with soldiers than patrolling the compound. *Eugene Bialas*

Soldiers took turns pulling guard duty from four posts set at the installation's corners. *Eugene Bialas*

"You know, we were young guys." Eugene Bialas, a nineteen-year-old Army private, in the barracks. *Courtesy Eugene Bialas*

Soviet Premier Nikolai Bulganin (*left*) and Party First Secretary Nikita Khrushchev (*right*) during their marathon visit to Great Britain in April 1956, as the tunnel was being discovered. © *PA Images*

Colonel Ivan Kotsyuba (*left*), the Soviet acting commandant for the Berlin garrison, brought the press to the site of the tunnel on the night of April 23, 1956, and with great umbrage pointed out the exposed tapped cables. *Bundesarchiv, Bild 183-37695-008 / Junge, Peter Heinz*

The Soviets promised "a sensational story about American espionage," and they delivered. *Bundesarchiv, Bild 183-37695-0020 / Junge, Peter Heinz / CC-BY-SA 3.0*

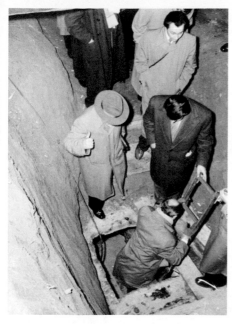

The reporters followed Kotsyuba down the ladder to the bottom of the shaft. "Come along, gentlemen," the colonel called from below. *Bundesarchiv, Bild 183-37695-0018 / Junge, Peter Heinz / CC-BY-SA 3.0*

Journalists explored down the tunnel, including a photographer not deterred by the barbed wire and sandbags placed at the American sector border. *Bundesarchiv, Bild 183-37695-0059 / CC-BY-SA 3.0*

Soviet officers admired the state-of-the art communications equipment. *Bundesarchiv, Bild 183-37695-0003 / Junge, Peter Heinz / CC-BY-SA 3.0*

Closer to the warehouse, reporters were stopped by a snarl of barbed wire and a sign warning in Russian and German: "Property of the United States of America. No Entry." *Bundesarchiv, Bild 183-37695-0032 / Junge, Peter Heinz / CC-BY-SA 3.0*

Reporters and officials congregated for days around the tap scene on Schönefelder Chaussee, the normally busy road connecting the East Berlin airport with the city. *Bundesarchiv, Bild 183-37695-0029 / CC-BY-SA 3.0*

The tunnel quickly became one of the top tourist attractions in town, drawing thousands of visitors who descended into the ground for a firsthand look at the invisible war. *Bundesarchiv, Bild 183-37896-0001 / Sturm, Horst / CC-BY-SA*

A souvenir booklet entitled *Tunnel Spione* (Tunnel Spies), available for ten pfennigs, was full of photographs and diagrams about the tunnel, which it termed the "Museum of U$A Villainy." *Courtesy Altglienicke Museum*

George Blake with wife Gillian and sons Anthony and James in England, 1960. Blake hoped a pending assignment to language school in Lebanon would allow escape from "the whole business of deceiving everyone around me and leading a double life." *Courtesy of the Blake family*

George Blake at his 1961 arrest. Gillian Blake was stunned, yet had no trouble believing the news: "I didn't think for a moment they'd made a mistake." © *PA Images*

Wormwood Scrubs, D Hall. On the rainy evening of October 22, 1966, Blake slipped out of a gap in the hall's large Gothic window and waited in the building shadows for Sean Bourke to toss a rope ladder over the prison wall. *National Archives of the United Kingdom*

"My life has fallen on pleasant lines, perhaps more so than many would say I deserve." George Blake in the kitchen of his dacha in Kratovo outside Moscow. © *George Carey*

Crews constructing an autobahn on the land between Rudow and Altglienicke were surprised in 2005 to find the remains of the largely forgotten tunnel. *Ronald Seiffert*

CHAPTER 15

The One-Man Tunnel

But the West was not the only side reaping an intelligence bonanza in Berlin. The KGB's man in Berlin was producing staggering amounts of information about Western intelligence operations. George Blake was one of an estimated ten thousand intelligence operatives working in Berlin in 1955, from many countries and sides, ranging from CIA, KGB, and SIS professionals to freelancers peddling secrets in cafés. Few, if any, were as productive as Blake. He was in effect a one-man tunnel.

Even Blake, with his long experience, was astonished at the scale of spying he found in Berlin. It was "one vast espionage web, with wires crossing in all directions," he later said. "One had the impression that at least every second adult Berliner was working for some intelligence organization or other and many for several at the same time."

Blake's office in the Berlin SIS station at the Olympic Stadium complex was in the former House of German Sport, a handsome four-story brick and granite building that served as the administrative headquarters of the German sporting world when the Nazis were in power. Two gold Reich eagles guarded the entrance from atop tall pillars, visible from Blake's space on the second floor.

Once the KGB was satisfied that Blake's move to Berlin did not mean he was under suspicion, he resumed his espionage work on their behalf. Much of that consisted of gathering every secret in the station he could safely get his hands on, a considerable quantity, even though he was discreet in what he took. "I wouldn't steal it off another man's desk, because that would be too dangerous, unless the circumstances were such that I realized I could do it in safety," he said. "But anything to which I had legitimate access, I would."

Blake was careful not to draw attention to himself in the station—and that included not poking around the tunnel operation. "I made it a point never to ask questions, and never to concern myself with what was not my business," he said.

Since he shared his office with a colleague, Blake had to wait until he was alone before he could use his trusty Minox to photograph the sensitive documents crossing his desk. Given the irregular schedule his officemate kept, he had to work quickly. "I could never be quite sure when my colleague . . . might return," he recalled. "If he had come back and found the door locked, this would certainly have caused eyebrows to be raised."

But once every six weeks, when Blake served as the station's duty officer, he was given astonishing access to the entire station. Despite the warning signals the Philby case should have sent, SIS still treated its officers as if they were above suspicion. Blake was left alone for the night, with keys to every room and combinations to every safe. No one could enter the building without his knowledge—he had free rein.

Every three weeks or so, he would take the U-Bahn into the Soviet sector to rendezvous with his KGB handlers and deliver his latest stash. He always marveled at how simple it was—if anything, it was safer than London. "Although the sector boundary was in fact a frontier separating not just two countries but two worlds . . . it was as easy to travel from West to East Berlin and back as from Hammersmith to Piccadilly." He would ride several stops into the Soviet sector, often exiting at the Spittelmarkt station. Much of East Berlin's center was still in ruins, and the streets were deserted at that late hour. He would walk a few blocks past the empty shells of houses. A large black car with drawn curtains would pull up next to him, and the door would be thrown open. Blake would dart in and the car would speed off to deliver him to a KGB safe house near Karlshorst.

Usually, he was greeted by his main handler in Berlin, Nikolai Sergeevich Miakotnykh, a thickset man of about fifty. Miakotnykh was a seasoned KGB officer who specialized in operations targeting British intelligence, and his low-key and fatherly manner appealed to his visitor. "He always listened attentively and his opinions when he gave them were well-considered," Blake said. Sometimes a familiar face with piercing dark eyes was also present: Vasily Dozhdalev, the KGB officer who had been sent to North Korea in 1951 to help assess whether Blake was a genuine defector, was now assigned to Berlin under diplomatic cover.

Blake would give the handlers his rolls of film, and over dinner and a glass of Hungarian wine he would explain what documents they held, identify SIS colleagues, relate the latest he had learned about British operations, and answer questions the KGB had.

Dozhdalev was astonished both at the volume and quality of the material delivered by Blake. He needed no direction. "He understood his work perfectly," Dozhdalev recalled. "We depended upon his judgement to choose what to send us. At headquarters, we never knew what we could get." It was impossible to measure how many documents he was turning over to the Soviets, Blake later said, "because it's so much."

Occasionally the KGB handlers asked if he needed money, but Blake rather piously insisted he rejected every offer. "This always annoyed me and I politely refused as my only excuse for this work, which in practice was most distasteful to me, was that I did it for a cause and not for personal gain or advantage of any kind," he later said.

"We never paid him a penny," Dozhdalev said. "I offered him money. I said, 'Perhaps you need something.' He always replied, 'No thanks, but if something happens to me, support my family.'"

After about an hour, Blake would be driven back to the center of East Berlin and let off near a U-Bahn station. He would be back in West Berlin within ten minutes, and soon be home.

———

For the KGB, Blake's documents were a trove of information about Western intelligence in general and the SIS in particular. Blake said he passed along "a great deal of information" on virtually every aspect of the Berlin station—its personnel, structure, agent networks, operations, reports, and policy directives. "They got a good inside view of how it operated," he said. Of particular interest to the KGB was knowing what intelligence—political, military, or economic— the SIS station was targeting in East Germany: "That was very important information for them, so they could protect these targets," Blake said. He provided "comprehensive knowledge of the working method, structure and employees of the British secret service," according to a later assessment by the Stasi, the East German security agency.

It was not just documents that George Blake was turning over to the KGB. It was names as well—the identities of agents working for SIS. Most of them were East Germans, though they included Soviets and other nationalities. As with the documents, Blake could not put a number on how many agents he betrayed. "I can't say, but it must have been maybe five hundred, six hundred," he later said.

The numbers are believable, given how many people were being arrested for espionage in those years by the Stasi. An operation in the spring of 1955, code-named Blitz, resulted in the arrest of 521 East Germans working for state agencies, the railway, and in factories. They were accused of spying for American, British, and West German intelligence, based on information supplied by the KGB, including intelligence from Blake. In September, the Stasi launched another operation, code-named Wespennest (Wasp's Nest), arresting 42 people accused of working on behalf of the CIA to induce East German scientists, engineers, and technicians to defect to the West.

Blake professed to finding this aspect of his betrayal unpleasant. "I was very reluctant to do this but . . . I had no good excuse for not passing the names to the Russians," he said. "I was by then so involved with the Russian Intelligence Service that I could not avoid this." He insisted that he stipulated to his handlers "every time I passed a name" that no action should be taken against the agent, and that the KGB merely take steps to limit access the agent had to classified material. The KGB agreed, according to Blake, but told him there was nothing they could do if the Stasi learned about the agent on its own. "I had every reason to believe the sincerity of the Russians in this matter, bearing in mind the attitude they adopted in the matter of the tunnelling operation in East Berlin which they allowed to start and continue," he said.

The KGB had to be careful with the names that Blake passed along, particularly Soviet names, for the same reason it did not stop the tunnel. "We might start watching that Soviet citizen, but . . . it was forbidden to take measures that would suddenly look suspicious to that Soviet citizen," Sergei Kondrashev said. "British intelligence would start analyzing how the Soviet side had found out about his cooperation, and then it would have led to George Blake." In some cases, he said, the KGB would hold on to the information for years before acting, or until they or the Stasi could get information from another source that would not lead to Blake.

Independently or not, the Stasi was sure getting a lot of names. And it is scarcely believable that some of them did not come from the KGB via Blake. Indeed, a later KGB report concluded that intelligence from three key spies—George Blake, Kim Philby, and Heinz Felfe, a Soviet agent in the West German intelligence service—made possible "the elimination of the adversary's agent network in East Germany" during the years 1953 to 1955.

Blake's treachery was undoing years of skillful SIS work in East Germany—and he was far from done.

———

For the KGB, Blake's performance in Berlin validated the decision to ignore the tunnel. By now he had established himself as by far their most important agent—and Moscow Center thought he might become even more important. "He was continuing to be of great value to us," said Kondrashev. "Perhaps, after Berlin, he would be *rezident* in Washington, Moscow or somewhere else, where his importance would be many times greater than the loss we had incurred as a result of the chatter of our officers down the communication lines."

Russian intelligence always placed value on protecting agents in place, Dick Helms later noted, but this was another level. "If they did all this to preserve the possibility that Blake was going to stay in place a long time, then he must have been an extraordinarily valuable agent to them," he said.

"You only need one spy to be effective," Oleg Gordievsky, who would serve as KGB chief in Britain before defecting, once said. He was speaking about George Blake.

———

The KGB was not the only agency pleased with Blake's performance. Even as he spied for the Soviets, he managed to delight SIS with his work supposedly on their behalf.

Blake was considered "an intelligence officer of above average competence," according to an SIS report. Montgomery Hyde, a member of parliament from Northern Ireland who had served with SIS during the war, made a courtesy call on station chief Peter Lunn while visiting Berlin in the summer of 1955. Lunn introduced him to Blake. "After Blake had left, Peter Lunn remarked what a good agent he was turning out to be," Hyde recalled. Lunn thought Blake was better at running agents than any other officer in Berlin.

To keep up his good standing with his superiors—and to continue his rise in SIS—it was important that Blake do well in Berlin. He had inherited a network of agents in East Germany, but he needed to find more, particularly Russians. "This was something much easier said than done," he noted. Russians stationed in East Berlin were discouraged by Soviet authorities from visiting the West, but it was impossible to stop them altogether. Blake thought the best strategies "all boiled down to exploiting common human weaknesses."

One scheme concocted by Blake and his colleagues was to set a fake shop close to the border, filled with luxury items such as silk stockings, underwear, jewelry, and other goods coveted by Russians. They recruited "beautiful girls" to work the restaurants around Karlshorst, trying to befriend Russians, in the hopes of luring them to the shop, he said. If they succeeded, the supposed shop owner, an agent known as Trautmann, would do anything possible to entice the Russian into returning, with promises of low prices and favorable exchange rates. Trautmann would then call Blake, who would come to the shop at the appropriate time, posing as a Russian-speaking businessman with black market connections. The scheme failed to lure any Russians of importance to the shop, and it collapsed altogether when Trautmann disappeared and showed up days later in East Berlin. It turned out he had been working for the East Germans the whole time.

But Blake had other irons in the fire. He immersed himself in Berlin's seedy world of double-dealing agents, who were always willing to sell out for a better offer. One of those assigned to him was Horst Eitner, an East German who had earned the nickname Mickey—with his bandy legs, small size, and big ears, he bore a startling resemblance to the cartoon mouse. "If the expression on his face had been less cheerful, it might have been called ratlike," Blake recalled.

Mickey knew Blake as "Max de Vries," a cover name Blake had used during his days as a courier for the Dutch underground. Mickey was a chain-smoking, heavy-drinking, and boisterous man—some called him vulgar—given to ribald stories. Max was reserved and low-key, drinking only in moderation. Yet somehow they hit it off.

Max was a frequent visitor to Mickey's home in a boardinghouse on Grolmanstrasse, where he lived with his wife, Brigitte, a dark-haired and petite native Pole in her mid-twenties. She had been in the business herself, having spied for the Americans in East Berlin as a teenager, and she served several years in a Russian labor camp after she was caught.

Max was a charming guest, telling amusing stories about his days in the Royal Navy. When the Eitners fretted about the health of their baby, who was born with a malformed hip and had to spend months in a cast, Max would bring small gifts to cheer them up. He was usually "pleasant and light-hearted and I would never have guessed he had a care in the world," Brigitte later said.

But sometimes Max seemed frustrated with the quality of Mickey's work. "Max could be moody too, you know," Brigitte said. "One minute he was gay and laughing and suddenly he would turn very serious and dry up." When it was time for Max and Mickey to talk business, Brigitte would go to the other room, or if they needed extra privacy, the two men would walk to an apartment Blake kept near the Berlin zoo for meeting with his agents.

The intelligence Mickey came up with was not exactly high-grade. "He had contacts in East Germany who gave him snippets

of political and economic information which he hotted up and
presented to us as reports from his agents," Blake recalled. "It was
mostly of little value." Nor was Blake impressed with Eitner's agents.
The couple worried that Mickey might be cut off from his British
stipend.

But Blake had a job in mind for Mickey that could make him
worthwhile.

———

To boost Agent Diomid's standing with his SIS superiors, the KGB
wanted to plant a genuine Soviet official on Blake whom he could
recruit as an agent. "This would be a feather in my cap and at the
same time provide an extra link with the KGB which could be used
in case of an emergency," he said.

The KGB chose a Soviet economist named "Boris" to be Blake's
"recruit." Boris worked in East Berlin for Comecon, a Soviet-led
organization that coordinated Eastern Bloc economies, and his duties included interpreting at high-level negotiations between the
Soviets and East Germans.

Mickey would be the vessel to bring Boris and Max together. In
keeping with the common SIS tactic, Mickey worked as a part-time
assistant at a clothing store in West Berlin's Wedding district that
was close to the sector border and drew occasional Russian custom-
ers. Boris was instructed to go to the shop in search of luxury goods,
and to "cooperate" with whatever transpired. He was given no hint
that he would be put in contact with a British spy working for the
KGB. Mickey, for his part, knew nothing of the plan. In this way,
the scheme would better stand up to any Western scrutiny.

It worked like a charm. When Boris stopped by the store looking
for a fur-lined jacket, Mickey sensed that the Russian could be a
target for recruitment and alerted Max. During a subsequent visit
to the shop, when Boris asked for a Swiss watch to give his wife,
Mickey told him that his friend Max would be willing to trade such
a watch for some pots of caviar.

Everyone met at Mickey's apartment one evening to make the
trade. Blake introduced himself to Boris as Max de Vries, a Dutch

newspaper journalist based in Berlin. After a convivial evening drinking wine and brandy, Max offered to show Boris the notorious local nightlife the next time he visited West Berlin. Boris was agreeable. His work brought him to West Berlin every three weeks, and he met with Max almost every time. Ostensibly, they got together to exchange luxury items for caviar, but, Blake said, "it was well understood between us that what I was really interested in was the information he was in a position to deliver." Boris always obliged with the latest political and economic intelligence, which Max supposedly wanted as background material for newspaper articles. To make Blake look good, the KGB fed Boris a considerable amount of information to pass along, some of it quite valuable for SIS.

Blake's superiors were over the moon at his accomplishment. "It was a great coup for me," he recalled. "I was the only SIS officer who had a real live Russian." He was bombarded with questions from London to put to Boris, and Boris almost always came up with the answers. "They thought he represented a source of great promise and should be carefully cultivated," Blake said. "Though he was not 'our man in the Kremlin' yet, there was a good prospect he might become one."

Everyone was happy. Blake's stock with his superiors rose. The SIS had a stream of valuable intelligence. Boris enjoyed inexpensive luxury goods and nights on the town in West Berlin. And Mickey got a five-hundred-mark bonus.

———

All the while, Blake and Gillian lived the sweet life of the victors in postwar Berlin, enjoying the inexpensive restaurants, the thriving nightlife, and travel across Europe. They were an attractive couple: Blake, the dashing and handsome war hero, with a wry humor and an ever-ready smile; Gillian, tall and attractive, with a sharp wit. Berlin was a "very happy" time, Gillian later said. "Life was easy."

They had favorite restaurants, like Maison de France, the Ritz for Middle Eastern cuisine, or Rollenhagen for German food. Sometimes they would visit one of the many nightclubs, "where you can spend an evening for the price of a bottle of wine dancing and watching the floor shows," Gillian said. "Then there are the cafes lining the streets of the Kurfürstendamm where you can have your drinks or meals outside and watch everyone pass by."

But Blake also loved quiet evenings at home, reading his books and listening to classical music records, mostly Bach, Beethoven, Mozart, and Schubert. Their spacious top-floor flat in Charlottenburg was, like those of other British officials, furnished with "recognizably army furniture," as Gillian called it, but they personalized it with belongings from home and prints they bought from galleries in Berlin. Blake had lost most of his books in Korea, but he was quickly rebuilding his library, including with gifts from his Russian contacts, a form of compensation he did not mind accepting. "He was often immersed in some great tome," Gillian recalled. He preferred to read in the original language, be it Russian, French, German, Dutch, or English. He usually read works of history, theology, or philosophy—Sartre and Spinoza were favorites—but did not have much time for novels, other than Dostoevsky. He read the British papers, mostly the *Guardian,* but turned his nose up at the tabloids.

Though West Berlin was effectively an island, they never felt isolated in the city, with its forests and lakes and outdoor recreation for escape. They bought a small boat and taught themselves to sail on the waters of the Havel, and they rode horses from the British Army riding stables through the vast Grunewald. Blake was not particularly sporty but would often go for a swim in the Olympic pool.

The Blakes hosted a steady procession of visitors—his mother, her mother, other relatives, and friends—who often stayed for weeks at a time. Blake delighted in showing the out-of-towners around Berlin, which he was getting to know well from walking about and driving around in the office Volkswagen.

The couple mostly socialized with other SIS officers and their wives from the Berlin station, along with British Army officers and "the odd Frenchman," Gillian recalled. "We would meet at the endless cocktail parties and what have you. The chat at these parties was like cocktail chat anywhere and it did get a bit pointless sometimes going to parties and meeting all the same people." Occasionally the Blakes threw their own party. "We weren't mad party goers or party givers, we were terribly normal," Gillian said. Colleagues thought of Blake as "a normal chap who could be met with his wife at the tennis parties of the British Commandant in Berlin."

Despite his friendliness, Blake avoided getting "terribly close to people," Gillian said. "George didn't attach very much importance to people, somehow. He liked people very much and got on with them very well, but he hadn't a lot of really great friends."

Blake was quite fond of many of his SIS colleagues, including Peter Lunn, later professing "the greatest admiration" for him. But it never stopped him from betraying them, and passing on their names to the KGB. "I thought about it later, of course," he admitted.

He embraced the role of an outsider; he liked having those he met guess his nationality. "It didn't occur to people that he was Dutch, because he was dark," said Gillian. "They would guess French quite often." In groups he would often play devil's advocate. "Because he hadn't any particular country of his own he took a much more objective interest in everything," she said. "He loved to hear everybody else's views and would really listen to it and would then argue against it or for it or anything."

———

Gillian remained utterly unaware of her husband's betrayal. Blake worked normal hours during the day, often coming home for lunch, but on many evenings and weekends there was "quite a lot of rushing off," Gillian said. She never worried when he was out late, given his line of work. "It didn't seem strange a bit that he had to be out," she said. "They're all doing that kind of work and there was no reason to suppose anything."

In retrospect, though, there were some hints. Sometimes they would argue about communism. He would defend it to be contrarian, she thought. After all, Blake certainly "didn't hate the capitalist world we lived in," Gillian said. But gradually it became clear that his attraction to communism was real. "He liked that idea. I knew that very well indeed," she said. "But I never dreamt he would put that into practice."

Occasionally Blake would speak admiringly of Khrushchev's diplomatic gambits. "How clever of him to put the West into such a position," he told Gillian.

"He would say this to me, not to anybody," she said. It would inevitably annoy Gillian, who thought Khrushchev a boor. Blake seemed to be gauging her reaction.

In the late summer of 1955, the Blakes drove their Ford Anglia to Lake Garda in northern Italy. It was their first real holiday since arriving in Berlin, and they basked in the sun and explored the lovely landscape surrounding the enormous alpine lake.

Sitting in an outdoor café overlooking the lake, Blake showed Gillian an article in a London newspaper reporting on a government investigation into the 1953 flight of Donald Maclean's wife, Melinda, to join her husband in Russia, where he had fled with fellow spy Guy Burgess two years earlier.

Seemingly jesting, Blake posed a question to his wife. "How would you feel, darling, if I went to Russia?" he asked. "What would you do?"

CHAPTER 16

The Hottest Intelligence Operation
on the Face of the Planet

RUDOW, FALL 1955

Corporal Eugene Kregg was enjoying life as the lead bass soloist for the renowned Russian choir at the U.S. Army Language School in Monterey, California, singing Russian opera and folk songs, when a mysterious order arrived to report to Fort Monmouth, New Jersey, and from there on to Germany.

Kregg flew from Frankfurt to Berlin in the back of an unheated and unpressurized DC-3 cargo plane, along with some sacks of mail. Arriving at Tempelhof, he was picked up by two scruffy soldiers in a jeep and taken to the lighted Rudow compound. His eyes got big when he spotted the large antenna dishes on the roof. "This is science fiction stuff," he thought.

He was told he would have to wait to be briefed on his mission until the installation commander, Lieutenant Colonel James Helgestad, returned. In the meantime, he was told to stay away from the warehouse. "Nobody was talking to me about what this unit did," he said. "Nobody said anything. That went on for several days."

The men he saw in the mess hall were a motley crew, including one group of older men sitting in the corner who did not even look like soldiers. "I didn't go near them," he said. "They looked a little weird and they were behaving differently." Lying in his bunk in the barracks at night, his head was spinning. "What the hell is all this and what am I doing here?" he thought.

After several days, Kregg was told that the colonel had returned and wanted to see him immediately. Captain Stanley E. Livingston, the crisp executive officer, escorted him to the back of the warehouse and took him inside through a large sliding door. As soon as the door closed behind them, Livingston addressed Kregg in a low, conspiratorial tone. "Corporal, this is not an Army unit," he said. "This is a CIA operation."

That meant nothing to Kregg. He was a twenty-one-year-old from Phoenix, Arizona, who had enlisted in the Army to attend its language school to avoid being drafted and sent to Korea. He had a predisposition for learning Russian. His father, born and raised in Ukraine, had fought for the White Army against the Bolsheviks. When the war ended, he fled Russia and found work as a sailor, eventually jumping ship in Boston and changing his name from Kovalenko to Kregg to hide his Russian roots. Inspired by the Zane Gray novels he read to learn English, he made his way out west to Arizona and married the daughter of Mormon pioneers. Their son Eugene had both musical talent and a gift for Russian. But he knew nothing about the CIA and the world of intelligence. He was starting to regret turning down the language school commandant's offer to keep him in Monterey.

Livingston took Kregg to an office inside the warehouse where Helgestad, an imposing figure with his silver hair and a chest full of ribbons, stood waiting for them. The officer looked Kregg over. "Corporal, you're standing on the hottest intelligence operation on the face of the planet, and you're the bottom of the barrel," he said. "We don't know if you're going to make it."

Recalled Kregg, "I didn't say anything. What the hell am I going to say to this guy?"

Helgestad explained that U.S. intelligence needed more linguists, and Kregg was "a last resort." The language school had recommended him "as someone with potential," the colonel added. "We will soon see."

Helgestad directed Kregg to follow him. They walked into the operations room, with the banks of whirring and clicking recorders lining the walls. The colonel took Kregg to one of the recorders, put a pair of earphones on him, and plugged it in. "As soon as one clicked on, I could recognize it as Russian, but it was going so fast, I didn't understand a thing," he said. "My heart sank."

Helgestad brought Kregg to a smaller room, where the forward processing team members were listening to tapes. It was the same group of strange men he had seen in the mess hall. After brief introductions, the colonel left. Kregg looked at the assembled group. "Fellas, I'm sorry to say this, but I think this is going to be a big bust for me," he said. "When the colonel put those earphones on me, I didn't understand a damn thing."

One of the men, a friendly U.S. Navy officer named Bill Cockell, spoke up. "Relax, Gene," he said. "We've all been through it."

———

The British postal team had tapped the third and final Soviet cable under Schönefelder Chaussee on August 2, again without incident. While it was not as productive as the first two, the tunnel team now had 273 core pairs tapped, together capable of transmitting 1,200 communication channels at the same time. The increased daily output was putting even more strain on the already overstretched processing teams in Berlin, London, and Washington. The original linguists in Berlin, who had been under the most pressure for months, were being rotated out and new ones brought in, including Kregg.

Despite Helgestad's concerns, Kregg turned out to be up to the task. He had a natural ear for the language, and the controls allowed him to quickly rewind conversations and listen a second or third time. Like the others, he had to learn Russian profanity in order to understand what the Soviet operators, clerks, and officers were saying. "They would swear and cuss and moan and piss," he said. "Their profanity is incredible—it's so colorful. We are so pathetic here in this country, we just can't compare."

Working eighteen to twenty hours a day, seven days a week, Kregg was soon up to speed. He was a fast typist, his fingers spitting out page after page of reports. Before long, he could identify Red Army officers by their voices or manners of speaking—sometimes just by how they breathed, or even how they picked up the phone.

There was General Markov, "a Don Giovanni type," who would buy nylons for mistresses back in Moscow. "This was stuff the agency could use to turn him," said Kregg. He would draw pictures in his mind of the speakers he heard and eventually sketched them on paper. He drew Markov as "a handsome rogue with a rose in his teeth." He also sketched Grechko, but based on his high voice, he drew the marshal much thinner than he was in real life.

Compared with the Soviet army officers, Kregg found the KGB officers far more disciplined on the phone. "They never completed a conversation on a particular line," he said, instead hanging up and calling back on a different line to continue. "But since we had them all tapped, it wasn't hard to piece them together to get the complete conversation," he added.

Kregg's fellow linguists in the forward processing unit were an eclectic but talented bunch. CIA linguist Bob Maguire was a light-hearted jokester who would eventually become a professor emeritus in the Department of Slavic Languages at Columbia University and an authority on early Soviet literature and the writings of Niko-lai Gogol. Bill Cockell, the big and jovial son of an admiral from Oswego, New York, and a graduate of the Russian Institute at Co-lumbia, was like an older brother to Kregg, taking him under his wing, bonding over long conversations at night about religion and philosophy. Cockell would become a rear admiral and deputy na-tional security advisor in the Reagan administration.

Kregg was less fond of the SIS linguist, Charlie Ebert, an aloof and bookish man who made no secret of his disdain for the young American soldier. "Charlie kept to himself and was averse to tak-ing a shower, thinking water was not good for his skin," Kregg recalled.

Kregg, younger and less experienced than the others, felt the weight of the world on his shoulders as he listened to the conversa-tions of Russian military and KGB officers, on the alert for any hint that the Soviets were mobilizing forces.

The tunnel was not the only part of the Rudow installation now producing at full blast. Atop the warehouse, the antennas had been hooked up, and Rudow was a fully operating U.S. Army electronic intelligence (ELINT) site.

Inside a station that had been set up on a second-floor loft directly below the antennas on the warehouse roof, Signal Corps soldiers sat in swivel chairs before consoles with radio receivers, listening with earphones for Russian radar, trying to get the frequency the Soviets were using. "When you found the frequency, if push came to shove, we could jam the Russian radar in case there was an all-out confrontation," recalled Larry Plapler, one of the signal soldiers.

The countermeasures station was scanning for radar and radio emissions around the clock seven days a week, "with recordings and analysis sent forward just as any other ELINT site in the world," according to Russ Knapp, a young electronic intelligence operator from Uxbridge, Massachusetts, who joined the Army out of high school and was sent straight from training to Rudow. Given the heavy Soviet military use of the nearby Schönefeld airport, Rudow was soon one of the more productive sites in Europe. Though the radar station had been included almost as an afterthought, it was "picking up useful information," said Hugh Montgomery.

At first, the unit kept the Army Signal Corps 9539th Technical Service Unit designation that had served as the cover for the Corps of Engineers team that built the tunnel. But now that the Rudow site was producing, it was transferred to the secretive Army Security Agency, which was taking over the Army's electronic intelligence mission. The 9539th disappeared as mysteriously as it was created and became the 22nd ASA Detachment, 7222nd Defense Unit.

John Quirk and Gene Bialas, nineteen-year-old Army privates from Chicago, arrived at Rudow in the summer of 1955 to help operate the electronic equipment. Quirk and Bialas were high school friends who had sung together in a pop quartet and, with job prospects bleak, joined the Army together soon after graduation. The Army buddy system guaranteed that they could stay together after enlistment—another incentive. They went through basic training and then the Army Signal School at Fort Monmouth, New Jersey, and after completing the course spent three months playing cards and waiting for an assignment. Unbeknownst to them, the Army was conducting extensive background checks on both. Bialas's mother called one day from Chicago. "Did you do something wrong?" she asked her son. "There's people asking questions about you all around here."

Finally, Quirk, Bialas, and several other soldiers from Fort Monmouth were flown to Germany in July 1955. When they arrived in Berlin, no one at headquarters knew where to send them. "Nobody knew what the outfit was, who we were, where we were," said Bialas.

After several hours of head-scratching, a sergeant had an idea. "I'll bet it's that spook outfit out in Rudow," he said. The soldiers were put in a military sedan and driven to the warehouse installation. When they showed up at the gate, Helgestad came out to inspect their orders. "We have been expecting you for weeks," the colonel told them.

Once the men were processed, the commander sat the men in an office and explained the rules. The unit was operating on two levels, Helgestad told them. The electronic intelligence operation was the "cover," he told them. The other operation was top secret, and known simply as "the project," he said. Some of the men would be assigned to the cover, and others to the project.

Helgestad revealed nothing more and warned the men not to be nosy. "Don't ask any questions about the project if you're not working in the project, because it's top secret, and if you're not working in there, you don't have to know about it," he said. Helgestad added that if they ever thought they had figured it out, they should come see him. "If you're right, I'll tell you you're right," he said.

Quirk and Bialas were given electronic intercept duties and spent hours every day listening for signals, determining where they came from, and measuring their strength. "You would write down everything you could figure out in the log," said Bialas. "That was the nature of the job. It was very dull." But after several weeks, Quirk was left plotting radar while Bialas and several others from Monmouth were pulled into the project. "They took us into the inner sanctum," said Bialas.

Helgestad himself led the tour of the warehouse. "After you were chosen and cleared, he would bring you in," Bialas recalled. "The first thing you saw was the room with the tape recorders." After a bit of gawking, the neophytes were taken down the hole in the warehouse basement.

They boarded the railcar, and the battery-powered forklift pulled them through the dimly lit steel tube, like a tunnel-of-love ride at an amusement park. After a two-minute excursion, they reached the end and stood before the sealed entrance to the equipment chamber. "They opened the door, we went inside and, wow, it was perfect. It was clean as an operating room," Bialas recalled. They marveled at the shiny state-of-the-art electronics.

Bialas worked mostly in the operations room with the recorders, keeping them supplied with new tapes. "When they had to be replaced, you'd run over and change them real quick," he said. He also spent many hours as a lookout in the observation post, watching the ground, flipping on the red light to warn people in the tunnel if someone was overhead. Sometimes, he would escort the voice tapes on a high-speed run to Gatow airfield for shipment to London.

For Quirk, a gung-ho kid itching for action, it was a bitter pill to be excluded while Bialas got to work on the project. "I always felt cheated," Quirk said. "He got the plum assignment, and I got the grape." What made it even worse was not knowing what the project was. The mystery drove him crazy. "That's the part that kept digging at you," he said. "I want to know what they're doing over there, but I can't ask anybody." His buddy Bialas wouldn't tell him a thing. "He was scared to death he'd go to jail," said Quirk.

———

To preserve anonymity, the four dozen men at the Rudow installation were kept entirely separate from the Army's Berlin Brigade, with their own mess hall, motor pool, and security. The support personnel, including the cooks, guards, and mechanics, were in the dark about the tunnel and not allowed in the warehouse.

Rudow also had a very different military culture. Helgestad was a taciturn but good-natured commander, something of a father figure to the young soldiers. He put little emphasis on regulations and

allowed a relaxed atmosphere, which proved to be the right touch
for the mix of Army, CIA, and SIS personnel. "Guys wore flannel
shirts and jeans," said Bialas. "That was the uniform of the day for
them. The colonel didn't care." The barracks, with bunks for three
dozen enlisted men, "looked more like a sloppy men's college dorm
than an army barracks," said Knapp. "Everyday operations were run
like it was a summer camp." Reveille was nonexistent.

Not coincidentally, morale was high. It helped that the mess hall
was supplied with far more rations than needed for such a small installation, along with cooks serious about their food. Even more important, the dayroom had a huge, well-stocked refrigerator loaded
with beer. At first it was a nickel for American beer and a dime for
German, but eventually it was free for the taking. "This just didn't
happen in the military," said Knapp. "We all took advantage of it,
some more than others." One of the motor pool guys, known as
Red, was "continually half-bagged," he added.

In the evenings, most of those not on duty congregated in the
dayroom wearing various odds and ends of uniforms to play chess
and penny ante poker. Movies were shown every night, though the
volume had to be turned up full blast so the soundtrack could be
heard over the din of the generators. To cope with the noise, the
soldiers got in the habit of shouting at each other like they were deaf.
Everyone became so used to sleeping with the generators that when
they suddenly stopped one night, the slumbering men all woke up.

To burn off pent-up energy, they played basketball on an outdoor
hoop and pitched horseshoes. The CIA linguists used a punching
bag as a surrogate to take out their frustration with an administrative officer in Washington who failed to send needed supplies. Soldiers fired their .45s in the warehouse basement, which, thanks to all
the sandbags filled with tunnel soil, made a perfect shooting range.
They built a big box kite and tried to fly it from the warehouse roof.
It soared over the border into the Soviet sector, but crashed into the
cemetery.

———

Perhaps the biggest diversion came from the two guard dogs, Aldo
and Harris. The German shepherds were supposed to bite anyone

who came in between the double fences, though most of the soldiers befriended the dogs and played fetch with them. Aldo could be a bit surly, but Harris, a handsome tan-and-black dog, had such a sunny disposition that "his value as a guard dog was probably moot," Quirk recalled.

All was well until Harris went AWOL. Early one morning a week later, as Quirk was finishing overnight guard duty in one of the shacks, he heard a bark in the distance. "For whatever reason, I was certain it was Harris," he said. Quirk trained his field glasses on an East German Volkspolizei truck that had pulled up across the border and saw a German shepherd jump out and back into the truck.

Quirk grabbed another soldier, Al Douglas, and the two purposefully walked up to the border, bent their way under the feeble strand of wire that marked the boundary, and strode up to the truck. Quirk, still carrying his M1 carbine from guard duty, declared in broken German that the dog was his. When the Vopos tried to wave him off, Quirk called for the dog. "In a flash, Harris cleared the tailgate of the truck and ran to Al and me, wagging his tail like mad and licking our hands," Quirk recalled. Mouths agape, the Vopos watched the Americans recross the border with their dog.

First Sergeant Charles McCullar, who had watched the incident in disbelief, chewed them out as soon as they got back. "You two might have started World War III," he told them. But the men were hailed as heroes by their comrades, and Harris stayed put after that.

———

Occasionally the soldiers were allowed to go downtown for the evening, subject to certain restrictions. They could not go to the East zone under any circumstances, and were forbidden to ride the S-Bahn or U-Bahn, for fear they might accidentally cross the border. An Army truck would drop them off downtown at 6 p.m. and pick them up at 10 p.m. sharp. "We always managed to cram a lot of fun into those few free hours," Quirk said. Some would go to the theater or sporting events, but mostly the soldiers would hit nightclubs. At the Mazurka one night, Kregg sang the "Song of the Volga Boatmen" to wild applause, accompanied by the club's balalaika orchestra.

If they had extra money in their pockets, they would go to the

Resi on Hasenheide, with its tabletop telephones and pneumatic tubes. "It didn't take long for the phone to ring or the message tube to make the swoosh sound of an incoming message," recalled Quirk. Girls were plentiful, but it was unthinkable to miss the truck ride back to Rudow.

The Army infantrymen stationed in the city with the Berlin Brigade did not think much of the Rudow interlopers, who hardly looked or acted like polished soldiers. "We were known as the spook outfit, because not much could be said to anybody outside the compound," said Knapp. One night, some of the Rudow crew were judged to be getting too friendly with the barmaids at an establishment favored by brigade troops. Afterwards, a posse of soldiers waited outside to jump the Rudow boys when they came out. "I remember getting smacked around by a couple of infantrymen," said Knapp.

The MPs who patrolled around nightspots where GIs congregated didn't like them either. All soldiers were supposed to wear ties when they went into town, but the Rudow contingent tried to get away with bolos. More than once, MPs in jeeps chased the Rudow truck all the way back to the warehouse. The guards opened the gate to let the truck zip in and then slammed it shut on the MPs. "That used to aggravate them," said Bialas.

While no one ever violated curfew, there was a huge security scare when one of the cooks went missing. He had been given permission to drive from Berlin to Frankfurt am Main, the big city in West Germany. But he mistakenly followed signs for Frankfurt an der Oder, an East German city on the border with Poland. "The sign said Frankfurt ahead, so he kept driving," said Eddie Kindell. "And he ended up in Frankfurt an der Oder." The hapless cook was taken into custody by East German border police.

Alarm bells sounded at Rudow when the cook was reported overdue in West Germany. Fortunately, the East German border police lines were among those tapped, and the tunnel team quickly learned that the cook was in their custody. "We were on the police channel, so we kept track of it every day, what was happening to him," said Kindell.

The cook knew nothing about the tunnel and had never even set foot in the warehouse. "They let him go, because he didn't know anything anyway," said Kindell. Once back in Rudow, the wayward cook was confined to quarters and soon shipped home.

Kregg managed to trigger his own alarms one day when Captain Livingston informed him he had a telephone call in the office. When Kregg picked up the phone, he heard a familiar voice speaking in Russian. It was Richard Smith, a buddy from the Army Language School. He had recently arrived in Berlin on a classified assignment and was trying to get together with Kregg, and thought it would be clever to speak in Russian. Kregg instinctively answered in that language.

"When Captain Livingston heard me speak Russian, he went white," Kregg said. "There wasn't supposed to be any hint of anybody knowing anything about Russian on this post." Livingston frantically drew his finger across his throat, signaling Kregg to get off the line. When Kregg stammered on, Livingston launched himself over the desk, grabbed the phone from the corporal's hands, and hung up. "That was a huge security breach," Kregg recalled.

Livingston nonetheless allowed Kregg to accompany Smith on a double date with two German women. That did not go well either. Kregg warned Smith not to let the Germans know he spoke Russian. As the foursome toured Berlin, the women tried to teach Kregg some German words, and he would repeat what they said. "The girls started getting really nervous," he said. "They were elbowing each other." It turns out he was speaking German with a Russian accent, and they were saying "Ivan, Ivan"—slang for a Russian.

"That ended my outings," Kregg recalled.

———

The first snow of the season came to Berlin early that year, starting with a predawn dusting on a mid-October morning. As dawn broke, the GI on duty in the warehouse observation post dropped his binoculars in shock and pushed the alarm button.

Eugene Kregg had shown up early for his shift monitoring recordings and was just settling down when he heard screams and shouts coming from the eastern part of the warehouse. Several soldiers stood at a window, pointing outside hysterically.

Kregg looked. "Oh my God!" he yelled. He could see it, too—a bare strip in the snow, running along the exact course of the tunnel, all the way from the warehouse to the tap. The snow was not sticking to the ground above the tunnel. "It was like somebody painted a big arrow—'Look at this!'" Kregg said. "It was just astonishing. Everybody's running around like a chicken with their heads cut off."

Eddie Kindell, the CIA's communications site chief, rushed to the scene. It was a moment of panic. Obviously the ground above the tunnel was warmer than the surrounding land. "It was melting as it hit the ground," said Kindell.

The equipment chamber underneath Schönefelder Chaussee was jammed with amplifiers, transformers, and tuners, all using vacuum tubes that generated a lot of heat in the closed room. "We knew it was going to be hot," said Kindell. That's why the designers had put an air-conditioning system in the warehouse to pump plenty of cool air via ducts to the chamber. What they had not anticipated was that excess heat from the chamber would travel down the length of the tunnel, warming the ground above it. While the air-conditioning kept the chamber relatively cool, said Kindell, "I guess it just wasn't enough."

But the tunnel team was in luck. It was an overcast, dark day, with limited visibility, and the snow kept falling, soon covering the bare strip. There was little to do in the short term except crank up the AC and hope nobody on the other side had noticed. "We had to make sure the [equipment chamber] was kept cool," said Kindell. Everybody held their breath. Kregg and his colleagues returned to their posts and resumed their work, nervously expecting the project to be exposed at any moment. But nothing happened.

Something had to be done before there was another frost or snow. At CIA headquarters in Washington, tunnel designer Gerald Fellon was put on the case. "Emergency action was needed," he recalled. Clearly, the air-conditioning had to be souped up, but there was no room to put extra air ducts on the already crowded sandbag benches running along both sides of the tunnel. A chilled-water system, which was much more compact, was the only solution. Fellon hastily ordered fifteen hundred feet of three-quarter-inch plastic irrigation tubing from Sears, Roebuck and rushed it to Berlin. Army heating and air-conditioning specialists quickly installed the system, nestling the tubing neatly alongside the existing air ducts.

Fellon then flew to Berlin to supervise the installation of state-of-the-art temperature sensors above the tunnel. The team unscrewed some of the grout plugs in the steel liner, drilled holes into the soil above the tunnel, and inserted the sensors into the soil above the tap chamber, the equipment room, and along the length of the tunnel. The sensors, connected via cables to the warehouse, confirmed that the soil above the equipment room was indeed decidedly warmer than the surrounding ground. But as the new air-conditioning kicked in, the temperature in the tunnel lowered considerably, to the point that it got "a bit chilly down there," said Montgomery.

Everyone sighed in relief, including Allen Dulles. "In all the complex and detailed planning that had gone into the design of this tunnel, this was something no one had anticipated," he later wrote. "It was a near mishap in one of the most valuable and daring projects ever undertaken."

The snow fiasco did at least provide an important clue to John Quirk, still working over in his mind what the project could conceivably be. Something was funny about one of the Army heating and cooling specialists who suddenly showed up at Rudow. "Several times I noticed he's wearing pants with wet sand on the bottom," Quirk recalled.

Another clue was the presence of Kregg, whose military skill, apart from singing, was speaking Russian. "What could a Russian linguist do except, of course, interpret Russian?" Quirk asked.

It was coming together for Quirk. "You can't live right on top of something and not be able to piece things together as clues are popping out at you," he said. And he wasn't alone. "I think everybody in the unit eventually woke up to what was going on, or at least the feeling of what was going on," he said.

Quirk felt smug about his detective work, but he and the others excluded from the project never took Helgestad up on his offer to bring him their conclusions. Said Quirk, "None of us had the nerve to go up and say, 'You're running a tunnel.'"

_____

After months of inaction, the KGB was finally getting up the nerve to do something about the tunnel. There was growing concern about how much was being lost. KGB chief Ivan Serov was among those worried, recalled Sergei Kondrashev, who had returned to Moscow following George Blake's departure from London and was now head of the German Department. "We discussed at top levels the questions of leakages from our channel," he said.

Blake had been gone from Section Y long enough that the risk of taking action would be much lower. "He had no direct connection to the tunnel at the time," said Kondrashev. In Berlin, Blake was kept apprised. "They said, 'This is enough, we have to put an end to this,'" Blake recalled.

By late 1955, Moscow Center had a working plan for discovering the tunnel while protecting Agent Diomid. The mission was given to Vadim Fyodorovich Goncharov, at thirty-four one of the KGB's most accomplished and savvy telephone tapping experts. Goncharov would be sent to Berlin with a team of technical experts from Moscow to hunt for possible breaches in the communication lines. To lend authenticity to the search and keep the West from suspecting a betrayal, Goncharov was given only general information about intercepted communications and told nothing about Agent Diomid.

After arriving in Berlin in the late fall of 1955, Goncharov's first step was to review telephone security at the Soviet military communications center in Karlshorst. To his alarm, Goncharov found "violations of the most elementary norms of security," he later said. Red Army officers and others routinely failed to use codes while discussing classified material, allowing "leaks of secret information." Goncharov reported his findings to the KGB *rezident,* Yevgeny Pitovranov.

One afternoon soon afterwards, Grechko was relaxing in his tracksuit and felt slippers at his family quarters, a magnificent villa he had appropriated, with a beautiful garden and nearby woods filled with wildlife, close to the Red Army headquarters at Wünsdorf. His reveries were interrupted by a call from his office reporting that Pitovranov was coming to Wünsdorf to meet him on an important matter.

Pitovranov, accompanied by Goncharov, showed Grechko the results of the KGB security check of Red Army phone lines. Grechko "initially couldn't believe that so much could be gleaned from telephone chatter," recalled Goncharov. Then the KGB officers played some of the conversations from Wünsdorf that Goncharov had taped. After listening to the sample, an abashed Grechko was convinced and ordered his commanders to crack down on telephone security.

But the tunnel remained the KGB's secret.

RUDOW, SATURDAY, DECEMBER 31, 1955

Despite the disagreement over Harris the guard dog and occasional exchanges of obscene gestures, relations between the Rudow GIs and the East German Vopos guarding the border were reasonably good. To mark the New Year, a group of Americans traipsed down with some scotch to the strand of wire dividing the sectors. "We took a bottle of booze over to the border and gave it to them," said Gene Bialas. "They shared it with us. You know, we were all young guys."

Inside the warehouse, however, it was business as usual. The tapped lines kept flowing with intelligence, and the tunnel continued producing valuable information. The CIA and SIS had picked up no signs that information was being diverted. The forward processing team members were listening in on one of their favorite targets—Grechko and his wife. The couple had flown to Moscow on December 25 for the sessions of the Supreme Soviet and then remained for the New Year. Despite the warnings from Goncharov, Grechko's family was as chatty as ever.

Klavdiya Grechko telephoned her adult daughter, Tatyana, at the Wünsdorf villa several times a day with updates on their interactions with Khrushchev. "He himself kissed me yesterday," she told her daughter.

"Who?" Tatyana asked.

"He himself."

Moreover, she related, Khrushchev had just telephoned to speak to the marshal. "Grechko was already reclining in his underpants but had hastily to pull on his trousers and go to the telephone," a CIA report said. Khrushchev, "full of bonhomie," invited the Grechkos for a New Year's Eve party at the Kremlin and then to spend the following day with the Khrushchevs at their dacha.

Klavdiya Grechko planned to wear her full mink coat, long rose brocade dress, and python-skin sandals for the occasion. She was proud of her husband for scoring the invitation. "He's so cunning!" she told Tatyana. "As usual with his nose to the wind."

CHAPTER 17

Berlin Was on the Top of the World

EAST BERLIN, JANUARY 1956

Vadim Goncharov did not have a lot of information to go on in his hunt for a breach in Soviet communications in Berlin. But for a man of his expertise, a tunnel near the sector border to tap into Soviet cables seemed an obvious possibility.

As Goncharov was well aware, the KGB had tapped an underground American phone cable near Potsdam. Why wouldn't the CIA or SIS try the same, perhaps even on a much larger scale in Berlin? (Goncharov was, however, puzzled that the Americans had stopped using the tapped cable. Only later would he learn that the CIA had discovered the Potsdam tap because the KGB intercept unit at Karlshorst that was running the operation had its own conversations intercepted by the Berlin tunnel.)

Goncharov's team began searching for Allied taps anywhere Soviet cables could be reached along the Berlin sector border. There was an enormous amount of ground to cover—more than thirty miles. Searches at night with heat-seeking equipment failed to locate any signs of a tap or a tunnel anywhere they checked, including around Altglienicke. Apparently the air-conditioning was working well.

But Goncharov was only getting started. Early in 1956, the team began zeroing in on smaller segments of the cables, operating from local telephone exchanges where the cables could be more closely studied. When they began working from a telephone office in the Altglienicke neighborhood, their equipment detected a tap on the nearby cables. From this, Goncharov concluded that the West must have a tunnel tapping into the main Soviet line running beneath the Schönefelder Chaussee.

Goncharov proudly informed Yevgeny Pitovranov of the discovery, not knowing that the Berlin KGB chief was well aware of the tunnel. But now Pitovranov could take action without jeopardizing Agent Diomid as the real source. His first step was to once again meet with Grechko.

At long last, the Soviet commander learned that the Group of Soviet Forces Germany headquarters' communications had been breached, and that the KGB technical team suspected Western intelligence had dug a tunnel tapping into Red Army lines. Presumably, Pitovranov kept a straight face and did not mention the awkward fact that the KGB had known about the tunnel from the start—even before it was built—but had done nothing to protect Red Army communications.

Nor was the charade anywhere near completion. It was vital that the discovery appear to be the result of a routine check by the Red Army of its communication lines, and not anything involving the KGB. Pitovranov suggested that Grechko create a special military signals company unit to physically "discover" the tunnel. The officers and enlisted personnel would be Soviet signal troops handpicked by commanders and screened by the KGB. Once assembled, the KGB would train and equip the signal unit with detection devices. But it would be a Red Army unit. Grechko agreed to the proposal.

The elaborate scheme would take some time to set up. And before taking action against the tunnel, Pitovranov needed approval from Moscow, so the tunnel's lease on life continued.

———

PBJOINTLY was firing on all cylinders, despite changes in early 1956. Vyrl Leichliter, the CIA site manager who had played such an integral part in the creation and operation of the Rudow site, suffered a personal tragedy. His wife, Vera, stationed in the Azores on special assignment with the Navy, died suddenly of a tropical disease in February, and shortly afterwards, Vyrl suffered a heart attack and was shipped back to the United States. To replace him, Bill Harvey brought in a veteran of the Vienna operation, Charlie Arnold, a CIA officer so laconic that Harvey's nickname for him was "the Great Stoneface." With Arnold at the helm in Rudow, Harvey was confident that the tunnel remained in good hands.

These were heady days for Harvey. Not only was the tunnel collecting a mountain of intelligence, but in January one of the most important spies in the CIA's history had fallen into his lap.

STRALSUND, EAST GERMANY, TUESDAY, JANUARY 10, 1956

A British military mission officer was making a routine tour of East Germany in early January, under the terms of an agreement that allowed each of the four powers to send military inspection teams into the other occupied zones. He was staying the night of January 10 in Stralsund, a port on the Baltic coast, and was reading in bed in his room at the Hotel Baltic when there was a knock at his door around 10:30 p.m. A short and stocky man with sallow skin and thinning hair wearing civilian clothes peeked in.

"He apologised, asked if I was English and if he might come in, to which I agreed," the officer wrote in a subsequent report. "He then asked if I would help him, to which I replied that I would be delighted."

The man explained that he was a lieutenant colonel assigned to the Red Army military intelligence headquarters in the nearby city of Schwerin, and was anxious to make contact with the Americans. He had come to Stralsund with his chief and, after spotting the British mission car parked outside, had entered the hotel without the knowledge of his superior officer.

The story reeked of a KGB trap. But there was something about the man's demeanor and appearance that struck the British officer as genuine. Despite the risk, he agreed to take a notebook from the Russian that contained information about Soviet nuclear weapons doctrine, along with a letter addressed to the CIA. He also set a follow-up meeting for January 24, where the Russian officer could meet with the Americans in a Stralsund café.

———

The mysterious visitor was Lieutenant Colonel Pyotr Semyonovich Popov, forty-two, the CIA's first high-quality clandestine Soviet military source. Popov had been born into peasantry in 1923 in Solnechnaya, a dirt-poor village far northeast of Moscow near the Volga River. Growing up, he saw his and other poor families suffer grave injustices during Stalin's forced collectivization of farms in the 1930s. But Popov was given an education and commissioned as an army officer, and then served honorably in World War II. He was selected near the end of the war to attend a prestigious military academy, and by virtue of his clean security record and dependable service, earned an assignment to the GRU, the Soviet military intelligence agency. Even as he rose through the ranks of the GRU, Popov became quietly enraged at the privileges enjoyed by the Communist Party elite and disaffected with the Soviet suppression of individual freedoms. He had never forgotten the treatment of the peasant families in Solnechnaya.

Popov took action after he was assigned to Austria in 1952 as a military intelligence officer with the Soviet occupation forces. On a Vienna street on New Year's Day 1953, he handed a letter offering his services to an American diplomat who was getting into a car. Despite fears that he might be a KGB plant, the CIA gingerly opened communications with him.

Popov was assigned to George Kisevalter, a legendary CIA case officer born in St. Petersburg, the son of a Czarist munitions expert who settled in America after the 1917 revolution. With his language skills, Kisevalter served with the U.S. Army in World War II in Alaska as a liaison with Soviet forces, and after the war was recruited into the CIA. He had a beautiful fluency and a deep understanding of Russian history. Equally important, he had a Russian soul and a strong sense of empathy, and quickly forged a deep bond with Popov, usually over vodka and Viennese sweets.

For more than two years, Popov delivered an array of important information to Kisevalter, including the identity of Soviet intelligence officers in Vienna, information on Warsaw Pact military forces, and, most valuably, a copy of the Soviet field service manual on battlefield tactics in a nuclear war. Popov was due to be sent back to Moscow in August 1955 following the withdrawal of Soviet forces from Austria. At their last meeting before his departure, Popov and Kisevalter drank a farewell vodka together. "This is what I like about your organization. You can find time to drink and relax," Popov told Kisevalter. "You have respect and regard for an individual. . . . With us, of course, the individual is nothing and the government interest is everything."

But the CIA had lost contact with Popov when a CIA officer assigned to reestablish contact in Moscow botched the job. Unknown to the agency, Popov was transferred in September 1955 to the Red Army's intelligence directorate in Schwerin. He had tried to signal his transfer to the CIA, but it was missed. He had arrived in East Germany with no set means of reestablishing contact with the agency, and had seized on the opportunity when he spotted the British liaison car.

Ironically, Popov's transfer to Schwerin had been intercepted by the tunnel. A telephone call from a personnel officer at Wünsdorf relayed information of his pending arrival in Schwerin, but the traffic had not yet been analyzed by the CIA.

The British liaison officer brought the material he had been given to the SIS station in Berlin, briefing Peter Lunn on the meeting with the mysterious Russian. Lunn naturally wanted to know the contents of the material and gave it to his staff for translation.

It is possible, but by no means certain, that George Blake learned of the letter. "It looks as though Bill Harvey's got a good GRU case, somewhere out in the zone," the translator mentioned casually to Blake, according to an account about Popov written by the CIA's Bill Hood, who served in Vienna and Berlin. Blake, backed by Kondrashev, denied knowing anything about Popov or giving any information about him to the KGB. But he was certainly in a position to learn about it, and his habit of vacuuming up everything that came his way is well established. Regardless, while any information Blake might have passed along would have alerted the KGB that the GRU had been penetrated, it was likely not enough to directly compromise Popov.

Once Lunn was finished with the material, Popov's letter and material were hand-delivered to Harvey at BOB headquarters. Harvey reviewed it with David Murphy, his deputy. "The liaison officer's description of Popov and the contents of the letter and notebook left no doubt that Popov had arrived and was again seeking contact," according to Murphy. Harvey immediately cabled CIA headquarters with the news. Kisevalter, then in Washington, rushed to Berlin.

Harvey arranged for the U.S. military liaison to meet Popov on the appointed day at a café in Stralsund, where the GRU officer passed along more intelligence documents and a plan for subsequent meetings. Popov was soon rendezvousing regularly with an elderly East Berlin pensioner—a CIA courier code-named the Old Man—who would take the train to Schwerin to deliver and pick up packages. Occasionally Popov would travel to East Berlin and take the S-Bahn to the Western sector to rendezvous with Kisevalter, meetings complicated by the Russian's habit of forgetting addresses of meeting places and his inability to master the Berlin public transportation system.

In his new position in East Germany, Popov was again privy to sensitive Soviet intelligence, including the code name and description of every agent being run in Western Europe by Red Army intelligence. He also passed along information about nuclear warfare tactics, strategic air operations, and missiles and guidance systems. The West first learned of the new Soviet T-10 heavy tank and PT-76 amphibious light tank from him. Popov "single-handedly supplied the most valuable intelligence on Soviet military matters of any human source available to the United States" during that time, Dick Helms later said.

Kisevalter, a big, disheveled man, was dubbed "Teddy Bear" by Harvey, who appreciated his irreverence toward headquarters and protected him from complaints by higher-ups that he was too garrulous for such a sensitive assignment. Kisevalter worked with the Popov material in a shielded room at BOB headquarters from which no sounds or electrical emissions could escape and where no one else other than a specially cleared secretary to assist him was allowed. He commandeered several unused high-speed tape recorders from the tunnel for transcribing tapes of his conversations with Popov and making copies for the "predilection of the curious muttonheads back home" who insisted on having their own.

Harvey cleared Kisevalter for PBJOINTLY. The dual flow of high-grade intelligence from the tunnel and Popov thus had a symbiotic relationship, providing an understanding that was greater than the sum of the parts. Tunnel intercepts were of "vital importance" in guiding Kisevalter, according to Murphy, corroborating and providing context to Popov's reports, adding invaluable details about Red Army intelligence officers and their activities, and supplying crucial detail to round out information about the Soviet military. Kisevalter likewise used Popov's reports to clarify or flesh out tunnel intercepts.

As a bonus, Kisevalter corrected garbled or misunderstood tunnel intercepts with his own matchless understanding of Russian, both the language and the mind-set. Harvey was concerned by a flurry of cryptic tunnel intercepts back and forth between Karlshorst and KGB officers in Stralsund, an area where they would not normally operate. He was not satisfied with the translations provided by the processing team in London and was convinced they were missing a major operation. "I think that they are screwing up in London with their translations," he complained to Kisevalter. "We have a whole battery of people there who don't know what the hell they are doing or listening to."

Kisevalter studied the traffic and soon divined its coded meaning. The KGB officers were on a duck hunting vacation on the Baltic coast, but it was unseasonably warm. "It's not duck weather," Kisevalter explained to Harvey. "Their allowable leave has expired and they are begging for some more time so that they can bring home some ducks." Harvey was disappointed not to have discovered a major KGB operation, but he could at least relax.

———

Between the tunnel and Popov—at the time the CIA's "only two productive clandestine sources of Soviet military information," according to a later agency historical analysis—the West's intelligence needs were finally being met. "In February of 1956, Berlin was on the top of the world," Murphy later said.

That month, Harvey sent a special "Eyes Only" cable to Helms and James Angleton, head of counterintelligence. He proposed that due to "the unique circumstances in Berlin," BOB should be made jointly responsible with Washington for handling Soviet counterintelligence involving Europe. Since Berlin had by far the largest concentration of reporting on Soviet intelligence in Western Europe, BOB should serve as the "clearing house" for counterintelligence cases. "We were all very excited about the prospect," said Murphy.

Harvey's proposal got an ice-cold reception in Washington. Angleton, who was creating a counterintelligence fiefdom, was not about to give up any control. Harvey never even received a reply from headquarters.

MOSCOW, FEBRUARY 1956

Klavdiya Grechkova was exultant about the star treatment she was receiving from party functionaries at the 20th Congress of the Communist Party of the Soviet Union. Marshal Grechko and his wife had flown from Berlin to attend the big party gathering, which opened on February 14 and continued for twelve days. Grechkova was particularly gratified at the favors showered on her in comparison to a Communist Party official's wife whom she viewed as a rival. "I am getting absolutely colossal attention, but she gets nothing, not even a telephone call," she gloated in a call on February 24 to her daughter, Tatyana, at the Grechko home in Wünsdorf. "They send me milk. They take me to the dressmakers. All the time."

It was the usual self-absorbed prattle from the marshal's wife. Far more consequential were her conversations about what happened the next day.

———

There had been no indications beforehand, in Western and Eastern capitals alike, or even in Moscow itself, that anything extraordinary would take place at the conclusion of the party congress. But on February 25, at an unscheduled session behind the locked doors of the Kremlin's Great Hall, party first secretary Nikita Khrushchev delivered his "secret speech" to the congress delegates, a sweeping denunciation of Stalin that laid bare the dictator's crimes, the terror he had unleashed that led to countless deaths of innocents in the 1930s, and his catastrophic failure to heed warnings of the Nazi invasion in 1941. Khrushchev called on the party to eradicate "the cult of personality" Stalin had created to protect his rule.

The shocked audience listened mostly in stony silence, though some cried and others shouted angrily. Among those stunned by the speech was Marshal Grechko, who soon shared the news with his wife. In no time she was on the telephone to her daughter to report what the marshal had told her.

"How did Father react?" Tatyana asked.

"He shat on the floor," Grechkova replied.

As usual, the tunnel caught the Grechko family conversations, and they were soon being translated, along with other intercepted phone calls made in the aftermath of the speech.

CIA analyst Joe Evans was among those in London trying to put together what exactly had happened at the party congress. "It was all in bits and pieces and wasn't extracted from a single 'piece of intelligence,'" he wrote. "Rather the story emerged as we translated and collated relevant items from a substantial number of conversations. At one end were influential Soviets in East Germany. At the other were their relatives and friends, who either attended or gossiped with those who did."

A highlight cable was sent to Washington with the astonishing headline "Khrushchev denigrates Stalin," according to Evans. "We were the very first to report news of the speech to Western intelligence," he said. In the days that followed, the tunnel captured more insight about the address, including reverberations in high levels of the Soviet military. Popov also heard about the speech and relayed to Kisevalter what he had learned from official briefings and the muted response of his fellow officers.

The speech had been an enormous risk for Khrushchev, rocking the communist world and unleashing unpredictable forces within the Soviet Union, Eastern Europe, and the Kremlin itself. Protests erupted in Georgia, where Stalin was born. The East German leadership was shocked at the anti-Stalinist broadside and upset at not having been warned in advance, giving it such a cold reception that Pitovranov did not even report the reaction to Moscow. In China, the speech so angered Communist Party chairman Mao Zedong that it helped plant the seeds for the Sino-Soviet split.

It was in no small part a power play by Khrushchev, allowing him to downplay his own responsibility for Stalin's crimes while painting rivals such as Molotov and Malenkov as more complicit. But it was by no means clear that the gambit would succeed. His denunciation of Stalin left Khrushchev vulnerable to criticism from Politburo rivals that he had gone soft on the West. Khrushchev needed to protect his flank from hard-liners in the Kremlin, and he needed to reassure the Stalinist governments in Eastern Europe, in particular Walter Ulbricht and the East German regime.

———

The Berlin tunnel presented Nikita Khrushchev with an opportunity.

Khrushchev had another big moment coming shortly—his first visit to a nation of the Western alliance. Following the invitation Prime Minister Anthony Eden had extended at the Geneva conference the previous July, Khrushchev and Bulganin would travel to Great Britain in early April. The two Soviet leaders, with unorthodox styles and publicity flourishes that were quite a contrast from the dour Stalin era, had become something of an international road show as they traveled about courting global sympathy. In addition to Geneva, they had made recent trips to India, Yugoslavia, and China, each of them a sensation. "Khrushchev—foremost of the Soviet leaders—has spared no effort in door-to-door campaign to sell Russian friendship to the Indian people," the CIA reported to the White House during the Soviets' visit to India in November 1955, adding, "B and K have clocked 3,000 miles by air, auto and elephant, visited 11 points, an intensive tour which has reduced them to near-exhaustion." The *New York Times* dubbed them "the wandering troubadours."

The visit to Britain would be their biggest trip yet. Khrushchev was disgruntled that the Soviet Union was still being painted as an aggressor by the West, despite having agreed the previous year both to the treaty withdrawing forces from Austria and to grant Soviet diplomatic recognition to West Germany. Khrushchev was insulted that Eisenhower and Eden issued a joint warning in February that any attack on West Berlin would be regarded as an attack on Britain or the United States. As the trip approached, recalled his son Sergei, "Father was nervous. He was particularly worried about making a fool of himself. . . . He expected all kinds of underhanded tricks from the imperialists."

There were urgent issues to discuss. Britain and the USSR were on a collision course in the Middle East, where Gamal Abdel Nasser, the nationalist president of Egypt, was taking steps that would lead to the seizure of the Suez Canal that summer. Eden was infuriated at the challenge to long-established British interests, and determined to put a stop to it. At the same time, the Soviets were eager to stake a claim in the Middle East, wooing Nasser with agreements to sell arms to Egypt.

Beyond the tensions in Egypt, the forthcoming trip to Britain was widely seen in the West as an attempt to foster divisions between the United States and Britain. The *New York Times*'s influential correspondent in London, Drew Middleton, labeled it "the Soviet Union's carefully planned attack on western unity." Indeed, Khrushchev saw the visit as an opportunity to divide the West, in keeping with the long-standing Soviet goal "to take apart this trans-Atlantic alliance that is under the control of the United States," said Sergei Khrushchev.

To clear the way, the KGB on February 11 staged a bizarre press conference in Moscow where Donald Maclean and Guy Burgess unexpectedly resurfaced, the first sight of the spies since their disappearance at the dock at Saint-Malo, France, five years earlier. For all that time, the Soviets had claimed they knew nothing of their whereabouts, and just two weeks earlier Khrushchev had said that the two were not in the Soviet Union. In a statement given to reporters at the press conference, Burgess and Maclean denied being spies, and said they had come to Russia to further peace, a goal they said the United States in particular was working against. The two

men declared that their absence was being "exploited by the op-
ponents of Anglo-Soviet understanding." Khrushchev likely hoped
the performance would deflect awkward questions about the pair's
whereabouts during his visit to Britain, and also advance the Soviet
line that Britain was being unwillingly dragged into Cold War confrontation by the Americans.

Khrushchev also asked Ivan Serov, the KGB chief, for ideas to
improve his bargaining position in London, seeking something
that would make a big propaganda splash. Serov referred the matter
to his foreign intelligence chief, Aleksandr Sakharovsky, who consulted with Sergei Kondrashev, now head of the German desk.

Kondrashev's polish and resourcefulness—and most of all, his
adroit handling of Agent Diomid—had earned him the respect of
his superiors. His star was rising at Moscow Center. Serov wanted
Kondrashev to accompany him to London ahead of the state visit to
make security arrangements. "You know our problems there better
than anyone else," Serov told him. There were those who considered
Kondrashev "a power-hungry courtier," while others thought he
had gone native during his stint in London. (One Soviet agent in
Britain had flatly refused to work with him after he showed up for a
meeting wearing flannel trousers and a blue blazer and walking a pet
poodle; the agent considered Kondrashev "too bourgeois.")

Kondrashev had a ready suggestion to Khrushchev's demand for
a PR coup: If possible, why not time the discovery of the Berlin
tunnel to coincide with the Soviet visit to London? In Berlin, the
special military signals company created by Pitovranov and Grechko
was ready to go. If the Soviets exposed the tunnel to the world before or during the visit, they could denounce the Western espionage
with great umbrage and gain needed leverage.

Sakharovsky and Serov liked the idea, but first the KGB needed
to consult with George Blake. "We had a discussion with him and
he didn't oppose the uncovering of the tunnel," Kondrashev said.

Blake was not queried for his opinion, however. "I wasn't asked
about whether it should be discovered or not discovered, but I was
told that it would be discovered within the near future," he said.
While he raised no objections, he was worried. "I was apprehensive,

naturally," he said. "Because the first question when the tunnel is discovered will be, 'How did the Soviets discover it? Why?'"

————

Serov brought the proposal to Khrushchev. News of the tunnel did not come as a surprise to the first secretary, according to Kondrashev and Blake. At some unknown point, the KGB, likely Serov himself, briefed Khrushchev about the tunnel. "I have no doubt that he was informed," said Sergei Khrushchev—the matter was simply too important for the KGB not to share with the Soviet leadership. Ironically, Khrushchev had even driven directly atop the tunnel when he and Bulganin stopped in Berlin on their way back from Geneva. The route to and from the East Berlin airport at Schönefeld went along the Schönefelder Chaussee, atop the tunnel, though what the Soviet leaders knew at the time is unclear.

Khrushchev understood that knowledge of the tunnel had to be kept quiet to avoid revealing the KGB's high-level source. With no plans to launch a surprise attack on the West, he did not see the harm in letting the tunnel continue for a while, his son said. "He didn't look at this information as very important," explained Sergei Khrushchev. "He thought, if they want to listen, let them listen." But Khrushchev, like the KGB, had little idea how much intelligence was actually being lost.

————

Depicting West Berlin as a nest of spies fit Khrushchev's needs perfectly. It would weaken the West's claims to be protecting the enclave as a bastion of democracy. It would deflect criticism over the Maclean and Burgess affair. The Soviets and East Germans would be seen as victims. How could the West accuse the Soviets of being aggressors when it was the West that had penetrated the Soviet sector and violated East German territory?

But Khrushchev wanted blame for the tunnel to be pinned solely on the Americans, seeing it as an opportunity to drive a wedge between the United States and Britain. It would support the Soviet narrative of the United States being the real obstacle to peace. "They wanted to leave the Americans in an embarrassing position," said Blake.

Besides, Khrushchev was eager for a diplomatic breakthrough with the British on his trip. The looming standoff in the Middle East was of particular concern to Khrushchev. "It was very important at the time to have propaganda cards in our hands, because the situation around the Suez Canal was getting quite tense," Kondrashev said. Perhaps leaving the British out of the line of fire when the tunnel was discovered would encourage Eden to cooperate. Observed Sergei Khrushchev, "You are just starting negotiations, and you go to talk with the British leadership, and then at the same time you're accusing them of spying, of course it affects the spirit of the negotiations."

Khrushchev approved the discovery of the tunnel. The decision made, Moscow sent instructions to Karlshorst and the Soviet embassy in Berlin in preparation. "These show very clearly that the decisions, how the diplomatic and political steps were to be taken, were made on the highest level," said Kondrashev. "That means with Khrushchev himself, and Serov, and other members of the Politburo. All those were informed of what had happened there, and what steps were going to be taken."

The tunnel had served American and British purposes long enough. It was time for it to serve Soviet purposes.

CHAPTER 18

There's a Fast One Coming

**ABOARD THE *ORDZHONIKIDZE* IN THE BALTIC SEA,
SUNDAY, APRIL 15, 1956**

E scorted by two Soviet destroyers, the cruiser *Ordzhonikidze* sailed
from the Baltic port of Kaliningrad on April 15, carrying Nikita
Khrushchev and Nikolai Bulganin for their state visit to Great Britain. The *Ordzhonikidze* was the most advanced of its class of Soviet
cruisers, able to sail faster than its counterparts through the rough waters of the North Atlantic thanks to a new hull shape and propellers.

But coming by ship was a consolation prize for Khrushchev, who
had wanted to fly to London aboard an experimental aircraft, the
Tupolev TU-104, the first Soviet passenger turbojet. "Father couldn't
wait to surprise the English," recalled his son Sergei Khrushchev,
then a university student accompanying the delegation. But Soviet
security had been aghast, arguing that Khrushchev would be risking
his life flying on a jet that had not been fully tested.

As a compromise, the TU-104 flew to London on March 22 with
the advance party, including KGB chief Ivan Serov and Sergei Kondrashev, who were to inspect security prior to the visit. The plane
was well received, but Serov was not. His presence caused an uproar
in Britain, where his role in the mass deportations in the Baltics,
Poland, and Crimea was well remembered by Eastern European and

other refugees who had resettled in England. The British newspapers dubbed him "Ivan the Terrible" and described him as "a butcher" and an "odious thug." The outcry was so loud that Serov departed London early, and Khrushchev ordered him to remain in Moscow to avoid a repeat.

It was a harbinger of what was shaping up to be a tense trip. The British public was "rather upset" about the pending visit, Chancellor of the Exchequer Harold Macmillan wrote in his diary, and he fretted about a detailed schedule for the Soviet visit published by the newspapers. "This is a gift to the would-be assassin!" he fumed.

The Soviet ships refueled while sailing through the Danish straits rather than waiting until they reached England. "No consideration was given to refueling at our destination—not because we begrudged the foreign currency, but because we were wary," recalled Sergei Khrushchev. "After all, we were not visiting friends and had to expect the worst."

BERLIN, MONDAY, APRIL 16

It had been an unusually wet spring in Berlin. Heavy rains soaked the city for days in April. The ground was saturated, and all around the city, water was seeping into cable channels, causing short circuits on the long-distance cables.

For the Soviets, the weather was perfectly timed. The KGB had been waiting for actual electrical faults to develop in the tunnel cables as cover for discovering the tap, and the problems were coinciding with the Soviet visit to Britain. At Karlshorst, KGB *rezident* Yevgeny Pitovranov gained permission to seize the opportunity. The special Red Army signals unit created to find the tunnel was mobilized. "Probably Khrushchev himself gave the last signal," said Kondrashev, who remained in London despite Serov's departure. "Our group of technical officers had started searching for leaking cables in various places all around Berlin."

The repair activity did not raise any alarms at the Rudow site, or at BOB and SIS headquarters in Berlin. "We knew from our sources in the East German Ministry of Telecommunications, and we knew from the tunnel itself, from the engineering circuits, that there were faults in the lines caused by seepage of water affecting the cables," said David Murphy.

In the meantime, the stream of intelligence from the tunnel showed no signs of diminishing. The tapped lines were abuzz in April with conversations about several inspections of KGB and GRU intelligence in East Germany by senior officials visiting from Moscow. Colonel Mikhail Smirnov, chief of a commission from the Red Army intelligence directorate, was full of interesting news from Moscow, including that bureaucrats at headquarters planned "an orgy of reductions" in the directorate. A concurrent inspection of KGB counterintelligence operations was causing much angst. "This shake-up is finished and my mood is frightful," Lieutenant Colonel A. I. Akimov, the officer in charge of the cadre office at the Wünsdorf headquarters, told his wife on April 14.

Reviewing the conversations in retrospect, there was still no indication that any of the senior intelligence officials suspected their lines were tapped.

———

Initially, the three tapped cables—FK 150, FK 151, and FK 152—were spared the problems caused by the rain. But on the night of April 16, a strong and steady downpour, accompanied by thunder and lightning, soaked Altglienicke and the surrounding neighborhoods of southeast Berlin. A number of telephone and telegraph cables were flooded and began to fault between Karlshorst and Schönefeld and points beyond.

On April 17, a major fault was discovered on FK 151 at Wassmannsdorf, about four miles southwest of the tap site. Crews cut out a ten-thousand-foot defective stretch and replaced it with a temporary cable, restoring service. But they were getting uncomfortably close to the tunnel.

PORTSMOUTH, ENGLAND, WEDNESDAY, APRIL 18

The seafaring books that Sergei Khrushchev remembered reading as a child always said the sight of birds was a sure sign of approaching land. As the *Ordzhonikidze* neared Portsmouth, he did not see any birds, but a squadron of small airplanes rented by the British press circled overhead, seeking pictures and footage of the Soviet leaders—or "Bulge and Krush," as newspapers dubbed the two.

Heads aboard the ship were a bit foggy. The previous evening, the Soviet delegation had celebrated Khrushchev's sixty-second birthday with dinner and plenty of champagne and vodka. They had included the British military attaché who was accompanying them on the journey, despite suspicions that he was a spy. "Naturally there was some drinking, and the Englishman showed that he had a well-developed taste for spirits," Nikita Khrushchev recalled. "In fact, he drank so much that he was barely able to get back to his cabin, much less go snooping around the ship looking for military secrets."

As the cruiser glided up Spithead on the sunny day toward the Royal Navy dockyard in Portsmouth, it was met with a regulation salute fired from ship and shore batteries. But the reception was cool and formal. Not a ship or boat in the crowded harbor whistled a greeting, and the small crowd was silent as Bulganin and Khrushchev descended the red-carpeted gangplank to the dockyard jetty.

Aboard a special train that carried them to London, the Soviets picked suspiciously at the turtle soup they were served for lunch in the salon car. At Victoria Station, they were greeted politely by Anthony Eden, but the atmosphere was again chilly. The prime minister pointedly commented on the "many events" that had taken place since their July meeting at Geneva. Though they were not mentioned, the growing tensions in the Middle East, the failure to make any progress on German unity or nuclear disarmament, and the reappearance of Burgess and Maclean hung in the air.

A cavalcade of cars took the delegation around London for a brief tour of Westminster Abbey, St. Paul's Cathedral, and the Tower of London. But the Soviets were more interested in the everyday prosperity they saw on the streets of the city. "It was like the discovery of the New World," Sergei Khrushchev recalled. "We lived in a closed world. Stalin's propaganda presented this very different image of the West. Then you came here and find they're not starving. The level of life was much higher than I expected. I was shocked by the windows of the shops in London." Nikita Khrushchev was less impressed, though no less curious than his son. "All this was very new to us," he later wrote. "We had never had much contact with foreigners before."

The Soviet delegation was staying at Claridge's, the finest hotel in London. Khrushchev, his senses on high alert for any slight, had demanded to know why they were not staying at a special government residence, as was the Soviet custom. Assured that all guests of the British government stayed in hotels, "Father was pacified," recalled Sergei. Even Nikita Khrushchev was impressed by the "superb" service at the hotel.

But Khrushchev had no illusions about how far the hospitality extended. When Sergei visited his father's room and began discussing sensitive material, the elder Khrushchev cut him off. "He grimaced and pointed to the ceiling," said Sergei. "He had no doubt that his room was bugged."

He was right. John Taylor and the Dollis Hill crew had wired Khrushchev's suite with a new, high-tech listening device that was virtually undetectable, but to their disappointment, they picked up no real intelligence. "Khrushchev was far too canny a bird to discuss anything of value in a hotel room," recalled Peter Wright, principal scientist for MI5.

BERLIN, THURSDAY, APRIL 19

Red Army communications were in crisis. No sooner was FK 151 repaired than more major faults appeared on other cables, including FK 150, another of the tunnel taps. The faults were creating major problems for the Soviets, leaving them vulnerable. The ones on FK 150 put the main Soviet signal center and the Soviet air warning control center in East Germany out of communication with Moscow. "During this period Soviet signal troops and East German Post and Telegraph technicians worked frantically to reestablish and maintain communications," according to a CIA history. On the other hand, Pitovranov now had all the cover he could possibly want to discover the tunnel.

On the morning of April 19, Rudow team members went down

the tunnel to check on the tapped cables and found them to be in good working order with no faults present. Harvey passed on word to Peter Lunn.

BOB cabled the update to Washington, adding, "Available precautions taken including primary one of crossing fingers."

PORTSMOUTH, THURSDAY, APRIL 19

In the early-morning light, Lionel "Buster" Crabb, a retired Royal Navy commander, boarded a dinghy in Portsmouth harbor, wearing a diving suit and an air tank on his back. Crabb, a veteran frogman who had been decorated for his work in the war removing German mines from merchant ships, had been hired by British intelligence to take photographs of the propeller, keel, and rudder of the *Ordzhonikidze*.

The Admiralty, desperate to find out why the Soviet cruiser was able to move so unexpectedly fast, wanted a close look at the ship's hull. Such inspections were not unprecedented—Soviet frogmen had recently examined British warships during a visit to Leningrad. And SIS had already unsuccessfully tried to investigate the *Ordzhonikidze* when it was at port in the Soviet Union.

But it was nonetheless astonishing that this mission was being attempted. When the Admiralty had raised the possibility of such an undertaking, Prime Minister Eden had expressly forbidden the intelligence services from making any attempt to spy on the Soviet warships during the visit, not wanting anything to disrupt the diplomacy. But at the behest of the Naval Intelligence Directorate, the chief of the SIS London station, Nicholas Elliott, approved the mission, dubbed Operation Claret, anyway.

Crabb was rowed about eighty yards offshore, still a long distance from the anchored Soviet cruiser. After adjusting his diving mask and grabbing an experimental Navy camera, he tipped backwards over the gunwale and slipped into the water. He resurfaced once, asking for some additional weight to put on his diving belt, and then disappeared again into the cold, dark water.

He never came back.

LONDON, THURSDAY, APRIL 19

Sergei Kondrashev was breakfasting at Claridge's when he received an urgent message to report to Khrushchev's suite. Khrushchev and Bulganin, preparing for their first day of meetings with the British, looked grim. The captain of the *Ordzhonikidze* had reported a problem at the ship. Kondrashev rushed to Portsmouth, where the ship's executive officer told him that sailors had spotted a frogman near the cruiser.

Yet the Soviets were apparently not taken by surprise by Crabb's mission. By Kondrashev's later account, the KGB had been given a detailed warning about the British plan from a source he did not identify. At the very least, the Soviets had expected the possibility and were prepared. "We had told the captain to take the necessary security precautions," Khrushchev later wrote. "Suddenly we got a report that our sailors had noticed someone swimming underwater around our cruiser, but apparently he evaded our men before they could do anything; that was the last that was seen of him."

Khrushchev certainly knew more about what had happened than Eden. No one had gotten up the nerve yet to inform the prime minister that not only had the mission been launched against his wishes, but a British frogman was missing.

Khrushchev now held two secrets.

ALTGLIENICKE, SATURDAY EVENING, APRIL 21

Lieutenant Colonel Vyunik, chief of the Red Army signal center at Wünsdorf, was getting worried. The early warning link between Moscow and Wünsdorf had failed again. Vyunik telephoned Major Alpatov, the chief of the Karlshorst signal center, at his home to report the failed circuit. The two officers, who had a regular and relaxed working relationship, agreed that it needed to be fixed before morning. Alpatov left immediately to report to his duty station.

Testing and rerouting of circuits was accordingly stepped up on the night of April 21. Listening in at Rudow, the warehouse team heard a Karlshorst technician tell a colleague at Wünsdorf that they would need another two days of work to clear up the problem on the troublesome FK 150 cable.

This was getting close to home. Lunn sent an urgent message to SIS headquarters in London: The tunnel was in jeopardy.

CHEQUERS, SATURDAY EVENING, APRIL 21

The Bulge and Krush road show arrived hours earlier than anticipated at Chequers, the country residence of the prime minister forty miles northwest of London.

A visit to the ancient university city of Oxford by the two Soviet leaders had been cut short. Khrushchev and Bulganin "were booed long and lustily" by students while touring the old town, and they were greeted by a banner hung from a building proclaiming "Big Brother is watching you." At one point, onlookers burst through a police cordon as the Soviet entourage passed, and shortly after Khrushchev and Bulganin entered Founder's Library in New College, a large firecracker exploded in a nearby passageway. Soon afterwards, a planned visit to Christ Church College was canceled and the procession of cars hastily departed for Chequers.

The Soviet leaders, expecting a sympathetic response from the English proletariat, were puzzled by the generally hostile reception they were receiving from the British public. "Bulganin occasionally mimicked the ruder gestures he had seen—tongues out, nose-thumbing, etc.—and, like Khrushchev, asked what the gestures meant," according to a CIA report delivered to Eisenhower. When Bulganin nodded politely at a crowd in the financial district, a London worker shouted at him, "We're not cheering you, Bulgy!"

In British ruling circles, Khrushchev's manners were causing a bit of a stir. He "lacks polish; his speech is often crude; he delights in telling simple and somewhat off-color jokes," the CIA report said. "He even told several anti-Soviet jokes to Prime Minister Eden and other British officials—which might have been amusing if all those present had not heard them before."

Khrushchev had sat next to Churchill at a dinner on April 19 hosted by Eden at Downing Street, a two-and-a-half-hour-long affair complete with brandy and cigars, but the two had not gotten along. "He was very old and fat and doddering," Khrushchev complained. The next evening, the Soviet had ruffled feathers at the Royal Naval College at Greenwich when he declared, "Great Britain was mistress of the seas, but that is all in the past." Without mentioning the frogman incident, he tweaked the Royal Navy for its fascination with the *Ordzhonikidze,* calling such cruisers "obsolete" in comparison with nuclear missiles and submarines that could deliver devastating attacks from afar.

At Chequers, Eden hosted a dinner for the Soviets, but the ambiance was not improved when Clarissa Eden, the prime minister's wife, asked Khrushchev "what sort of missiles" the Soviets had.

"They have a very long range," Khrushchev told her. "They could easily reach your island and quite a bit farther."

But Khrushchev managed to be more discreet about the espionage adventures playing out during their visit. Not only did the Soviet leaders remain coy about the frogman incident; they gave no hint of what was taking place in Berlin that night.

RUDOW, 12:50 A.M., SUNDAY, APRIL 22

Gazing through night vision glasses, the watchers in the warehouse observation post had no problem spotting the Red Army signal team when it showed up on the east side of Schönefelder Chaussee shortly before 1 a.m. Some forty or fifty men spread out over the entire length of the highway that the Americans could see from the warehouse. The Soviet troops began digging at three- to five-foot intervals along the highway—including atop the tap chamber.

The Rudow team sent a coded message to BOB headquarters: Problem at the site.

Bill and CG Harvey were having dinner at Dave Murphy's home, the usual late night with plenty of food and drink, when the phone rang. The duty officer at BOB, following emergency procedure to immediately notify Harvey of anything involving the site, relayed word that a message had arrived from Rudow. Harvey abruptly departed, leaving even Murphy in the dark about what was up.

Harvey went to BOB headquarters, read the coded message from the site, and grabbed the telephone, rousting Hugh Montgomery from slumber. "I got a call from Harvey at home saying, 'Get your ass in here,' in his usual subtle way," Montgomery recalled.

Harvey likewise called Charlie Bray at his home in Frankfurt. Alan Conway had departed the Frankfurt station, leaving Bray to oversee tunnel support. "Blackie, you'd better get down there," Harvey told him. "There's a fast one coming." Bray left immediately for the office. (Bray, an Oklahoman, was Black Charlie, or Blackie for short.)

Unshaven and unkempt, Montgomery hurriedly rendezvoused with Harvey at BOB, and they drove together to Rudow. Both feared the worst. They went straight to the warehouse, where Montgomery put on earphones to assist the forward processing team listening to live conversations on the engineering circuits. The exertions of the crews digging atop the tunnel were also audible via the microphone hidden in the tap chamber.

Harvey stood by impatiently, demanding translations. He was looking for any hint that the Soviets knew there was a tunnel below—any sign of betrayal.

While the Red Army team members were unaware that they were supposed to uncover a tunnel, they were getting some guidance from above. "From advance information by our friend [Blake], we determined the shortest possible route to the Schönefeld highway from the American cover installation," Pitovranov later said. "And we concentrated on that point." Blake confirmed this in an interview. "I knew exactly where the tunnel was," he said. "And they knew." The hand-drawn map he had given to Sergei Kondrashev more than two years earlier was quite accurate, showing the tunnel near the Altglienicke cemetery.

At 2 a.m., one of the Russian crews discovered a reinforced concrete roof—the top of the tap chamber.

Back at the warehouse, Montgomery and the other listeners could hear the first fragments of conversation picked up by the tap chamber microphone. It was clear that the Russians had no inkling what they had uncovered. "The discovery of the tap chamber aroused no suspicion among those present," according to a CIA account of the discovery. But Harvey knew it was only a matter of time before both the tap and the tunnel were discovered.

In keeping with the emergency protocol approved by Allen Dulles in case of discovery, team members largely stayed in the warehouse and did not stray far down the tunnel. The situation would become far worse if any of the Americans or British were caught inside the tunnel within the Soviet sector, and in any event, there was no time to remove the massive amount of electronics in the equipment room.

After a while, the Soviet team broke a small hole in the roof of the tap chamber big enough to peer inside. Captain Bartash, a signals officer overseeing the digging, walked over to take a look. After some discussion, Bartash and the others decided that the chamber probably housed an East German repeater point, an electronic device that received signals and retransmitted them at a higher strength, the sort of equipment routinely used in the system. No alarms were raised.

The crew began enlarging the hole. After about forty-five minutes, it was big enough to see cables below and a trapdoor on the floor of the chamber. "Those present began to speculate vaguely about its exact nature and the time of its construction," according to the CIA account.

A Soviet officer suggested that the chamber might be something left over from World War II. An East German long-distance line specialist who had arrived at the scene thought that it might be part of the sewage system. But one of the Soviets replied that they had already checked the sewer plans and the line was more than a hundred yards away.

Around 2:50 a.m., an unidentified Soviet colonel arrived at the scene, possibly Vadim Goncharov, leader of the KGB technical team, wearing a Red Army uniform to disguise the KGB involvement from the crews at the site, not to mention the observers in the warehouse. In any event, the casual and unconcerned tone at the dig soon changed. One of the Russians gave instructions that nothing in the chamber was to be touched. They must wait "until morning" for a decision on what to do next.

Barricades were put up around the excavation to keep people away. Shortly after 3:30 a.m., observers in the warehouse watched the Soviets drive off, leaving East German Volkspolizei to guard the location. For the next hour and a half, the team back at the warehouse could hear no sounds or voices.

RUDOW, EARLY SUNDAY MORNING, APRIL 22

The Army installation went on high alert. Soldiers were roused in the barracks in the middle of the night and told to report to duty. Somebody shook Gene Bialas awake. "Get up—they found it!"

Some of the troops had little or no idea what "it" was, as they had never been briefed on the project. They quickly learned. "I remember a staff sergeant coming around and saying what had happened and what the tunnel was," said Russ Knapp, one of the radar station ELINT operators, who had been kept out of the project but had guessed some kind of tunnel was involved.

The compound roiled with tension and excitement. "All hell broke loose in the warehouse," according to Bill Romey, the CIA linguist. "Guns were brought out in case any attempts were made to cross the border to our station."

"Rumors abounded, some of which were absurd, but nonetheless, just barely believable," recalled Knapp. One was that MPs at the site "were assigned the task of ending human evidence of the tunnel enterprise by shooting all of the enlisted men that had been directly involved."

Bialas got his gear on and rushed down to the tunnel. Soldiers built a makeshift barrier below the sector border, using sandbags removed from the side of the tunnel, along with a few strands of barbed wire. A second, more formidable coil was put up closer to the warehouse.

Warnings were hurriedly scribbled in German and Russian in black ink on cardboard signs and hung on the barbed wire. YOU ARE ENTERING THE AMERICAN SECTOR, read the one at the barrier. PROPERTY OF THE UNITED STATES OF AMERICA, read the second sign. NO ENTRY.

FRANKFURT, EARLY SUNDAY MORNING, APRIL 22

Charlie Bray was deciphering the increasingly grim cable traffic from Berlin: The Soviets had broken into the tap chamber. "I vividly recall feeling like I had been hit in the belly by an arrow as I started reading," he said.

Bray sent a message at 3 a.m. to Tracy Barnes, the Frankfurt station chief, who was on a visit to Switzerland with his wife, Janet, and Jim Critchfield, one of his senior officers. Barnes pounded on Critchfield's hotel room door. "Jesus Christ, it's been blown!" he told Critchfield.

"Tracy was wild," his wife later said. "He woke me and said, 'This is serious' and roared off to Bonn to tell the ambassador." Barnes raced his Mercedes at a hundred miles per hour up the autobahn in the middle of the night all the way to the West German capital. James Conant—whose title had changed to ambassador from high commissioner when the Western occupation of West Germany ended the previous year—was surprised on several scores. He had not known about the tunnel, at Dulles's insistence.

"I like cops and robbers, but I don't like getting caught," Conant told Barnes.

At Wünsdorf and Karlshorst, senior Soviet communications officers were being awoken in the middle of the night and told that their cables were tapped. After hearing from his superior officer, Lieutenant Colonel Vyunik telephoned Major Alpatov at Karlshorst. The normally chatty Soviet officers sounded strained. "When we speak we must do so carefully," Vyunik said.

Around 5 a.m., Soviet officials began returning to the site, including the unnamed Soviet colonel; Lieutenant Colonel Zolochko, deputy chief of the lines department at Wünsdorf; and Captain Bartash, leading the Red Army signal crew. The Soviets had circuit diagrams for the cables below.

Yevgeny Pitovranov had been standing by at the airfield at Schönefeld since 2:30 a.m. to be nearby once the discovery was made. It was now safe to go to Altglienicke, and sometime before 6 a.m., the KGB *rezident* arrived at the scene.

"We've found it," the colonel told Pitovranov. The KGB chief warned him to watch for booby traps.

Around 6:30 a.m., a member of the crew entered the chamber and examined the trunk lines. "The cable is tapped," someone announced.

An East German technician at the scene looked at the cables and could not understand how no one had detected the tap when it was made. "Everyone must have been quite drunk," he said.

———

Markus Wolf, the East German chief of foreign intelligence, was awoken around dawn by his housekeeper. "The minister is waiting for you at the garden gate," she told him. Puzzled, Wolf peered through a gap in the curtains and saw an aging Volkswagen Beetle parked below. Wolf was on edge. That was not the way members of the East German Politburo typically traveled. Perhaps a purge was under way.

Wolf grabbed the loaded pistol he kept on his bedside table and stuck it in his bathrobe pocket. At the front door he found his superior, Ernst Wollweber, the minister for state security, waiting impatiently with a cigar in his mouth. "Get a move on, Mischa," he told Wolf. "You won't believe what they found."

Wollweber explained that he had been roused from sleep by an emergency call from the Soviets. No one in the East German government—not even Walter Ulbricht—had been given advance warning of what was happening. Rather than wait for his guards and limousine to show up, Wollweber had borrowed his neighbor's car. Wolf and Wollweber rattled their way through the empty East Berlin streets in the VW until they reached Altglienicke.

In the gray dawn light, near the wall of the Altglienicke cemetery, Wolf could see Russian soldiers energetically digging as senior Soviet military intelligence officers looked on. Wolf walked to the edge of the trench and peered down into the chamber, watching with fascination as soldiers worked to see what lay below.

———

The tap was still functioning, but it was in its death throes. Some-time after 8 a.m., an agitated general on Grechko's staff called the Berlin garrison headquarters from the marshal's apartment. Grechko urgently needed to discuss the situation with Colonel Ivan Kotsyuba, the acting commandant for the Berlin garrison, but Kotsyuba could not be located. Soon after that, operators refused to place more calls. "I won't put you through to anyone," a Karlshorst operator told a frustrated caller. "Don't ring, that's all. I won't answer you anymore. It's in the order."

Those were the last calls of any interest made on the tapped lines.

CHEQUERS, SUNDAY MORNING, APRIL 22

Nikita Khrushchev, up bright and early Sunday morning, wandered down the second-floor hallway looking for Bulganin's room to wake him up. He knocked on a door, thinking it was the Soviet premier's.

"A woman's voice rang out; she was obviously surprised and frightened," Khrushchev recalled. "I realized that I had almost walked in on Eden's wife. I turned around and hurried back to my room without apologizing or identifying myself. Bulganin and I had a good laugh over this incident, but we decided not to mention it to our hosts."

Like a pair of errant schoolboys, Khrushchev and Bulganin man-aged to compose themselves in time for morning meetings with Eden and other British leaders. Then it was off to Windsor Castle, outside London, for an audience with Queen Elizabeth. Khrushchev had rather crankily insisted beforehand that they would not "get all dressed up in tails and top hats or anything else" indicating defer-ence to royalty.

But to their surprise, Khrushchev and Bulganin found themselves charmed by the gracious reception they received from the twenty-nine-year-old queen, nearing her third year on the throne. "She looked like the sort of young woman you'd be likely to meet walk-ing along Gorky Street on a balmy summer afternoon. . . . She was completely unpretentious, completely without the haughtiness that you'd expect of royalty," Khrushchev marveled.

"Bulganin apparently felt some throwback to the courtly days of the Czar," said the CIA report sent to Eisenhower. "He bowed deeply from the waist, and for a moment looked as though he would kiss the Queen's hand."

BERLIN, SUNDAY MORNING, APRIL 22

The comity at Windsor Castle was absent in the Rudow warehouse. Despite the initially benign chatter of the work crews, all the Soviets showing up across the border in Altglienicke were making Harvey suspicious. Their presence "made it unlikely that the discovery was an accident," Montgomery recalled.

Harvey decided it might be time to implement the destruction plan. The C-3 plastic explosive lining the tunnel underneath the border was connected to a plunger and ready to blow. Harvey ordered Montgomery to find Major General Charles Dasher, the Army officer commanding U.S. forces in Berlin. "Tell him that I'm seriously considering blowing up the tunnel to prevent the Soviets from coming through," Harvey told Montgomery.

Montgomery, ill-dressed and looking the worse for wear after a night with little sleep, made his way midmorning to the Wannsee Yacht Club, where Dasher was playing golf with the visiting Army chief of staff, General Maxwell Taylor. Montgomery found Dasher's aide, an Army captain, in the clubhouse.

"I have to talk to the general," Montgomery said.

"He's playing golf and I can't interrupt him," the aide replied.

"Well, I tell you, if you don't, and there's a loud explosion, you're going to have to explain why he wasn't aware of what's happening," Montgomery said.

The aide immediately left to get Dasher. The general did not conceal his displeasure at the interruption when he arrived in the clubhouse and saw a disheveled young CIA officer waiting for him. He was even less pleased when Montgomery quietly described what

was happening at Rudow, and told him that Harvey wanted to det-
onate the tunnel.

"Oh my God," Dasher said.

Dasher, a West Point graduate, was no shrinking violet, having
commanded a field artillery brigade in Europe during World War II
and the 24th Infantry Division in Korea. But the thought of an
explosion in Berlin made him blanch. "Is there any possibility that
Russians could be killed?" he asked.

Montgomery said it was a distinct possibility. "If they're in that
tunnel, they'll get blown up too," he said.

Dasher conferred with Taylor, then gave Montgomery a message
for Harvey. "Tell him he just can't do that," he said. Taylor nodded
in agreement.

Just to be clear, Dasher added, "I will not approve an action which
could be the start of World War III."

Montgomery reported the decision to Harvey back at the warehouse.

Harvey's reply was succinct: "Chicken shit."

ALTGLIENICKE, SUNDAY MORNING, APRIL 22

Further exploration of the tap chamber by the Soviets and East Germans was delayed for several hours by fears that the trapdoor on
the floor might be booby-trapped. Lieutenant Colonel Zolochko
suggested attaching a grappling hook to tear it off. "If there is no explosion then we can calmly go ahead and deal with it," he suggested.

No one took him up on the idea. Instead, a team of East German
workers was assigned to knock a hole through the floor next to
the trapdoor using pickaxes. By 11:45 a.m., it was big enough for a
worker to stick his head through and take a look. He called out in
excitement: There was a shaft, leading deeper into the ground.

With a little more work, they took the hinges off the bottom of
the trapdoor and pulled it off, exposing the rectangular shaft. Someone noted that the lock that had kept the trapdoor shut from below was British-made. The workers climbed down the ladder steps

lining the shaft around 12:30 p.m. Reaching the bottom sixteen and a half feet down, the team found yet another obstacle: a big, locked steel door. On it was the foreboding sign Harvey had ordered, written in German and Russian: ENTRY IS FORBIDDEN BY ORDER OF THE COMMANDING GENERAL.

Once again, progress screeched to a halt. "They didn't know quite what to make of that," said Montgomery, listening to the conversations picked up by the microphone. "There was much stewing about it and speculating and talking."

Finally, after consultations with superiors, they left the door alone and instead began breaking through the wall next to it. Back in the warehouse, the monitoring team heard a cacophony of noise picked up by the microphone—pickaxes pounding, debris falling, workers shoveling, men grunting, dogs barking, and roosters crowing.

When the workers broke through the wall, their astonishment was genuine. They could see a large, pristine chamber, loaded with state-of-the-art communications equipment. Beyond that, a passageway led to points unknown.

Somebody let out a long whistle.

"*Donnerwetter,*" said one. "I'll be damned."

"Look at that! It goes all the way under the highway!"

"It's fantastic!"

"I am speechless, man, I am speechless."

"What a filthy trick!"

———

Markus Wolf was one of the first to climb into the hole. Wolf would earn a reputation in coming years as the Cold War's most legendary and elusive spymaster, known as "the man without a face" because of the inability of Western intelligence to photograph him. But on this day, it was Wolf's turn to be dumbfounded. He was amazed as he examined the row of amplifiers and neat bundles of cables in the equipment room. "It was a perfectly designed underground listening post," he said. ". . . It takes no imagination to realize this was an intelligence man's dream."

Wolf and several others went exploring down the tunnel. "We groped our way along the tunnel in the darkness and silence, with only a weak flashlight beam to help us," he recalled. After a while, Wolf caught a glimpse of something light-colored ahead, and he shone the flashlight on it. "There, underground on the subterranean line dividing two systems and ideologies, some intelligence man with a well-developed sense of humor had placed a tiny roll of barbed wire and a piece of cardboard bearing the message in black pen, 'You are entering the American sector,'" he said.

Wolf could not help smiling. "Here I was, one of the prime enemies of the CIA, sharing this private joke of American intelligence workers!" he said. "For the first time during an extraordinary morning, I pinched myself to make sure I was not dreaming."

ALTGLIENICKE, SUNDAY, APRIL 22

The telephone rang Sunday morning at Paul Noack's home. It was one of the farmer's friends, with an odd message. "You're a fine one, Paul," the friend said. "Letting the army dig up your cellar." Noack had no idea what the man was talking about. An excavation was under way, his friend explained, right about the spot where Noack was planning to build his new family home.

Noack thought it was a bad joke, but nonetheless hurriedly dressed and hopped on his moped to drive to his farm plot. His family would not see him again for quite a while. Schönefelder Chaussee was blocked off, confounding residents trying to get to town and wreaking havoc on Berliners heading out for Sunday outings in the countryside. Noack continued on foot but found the area around his farm to be a military security zone. The Volkspolizei were turning people back, but Noack was not deterred. "He wasn't afraid, he wasn't going to wait," recalled his daughter, Dagmar Feick. "He insisted on going in, and was allowed in."

Noack saw the huge excavation that had ripped up Schönefelder Chaussee. A second, smaller hole was being dug on his property. "The cellar for our house was supposed to be built on precisely that spot, which was what made our friend's phone call so appropriate," said his daughter. Noack stood in front of the hole and demanded to know what was going on. It took a while, but he finally found out.

"They told him that a tunnel had been discovered" running below his property, Feick said.

Suddenly it was clear to Farmer Noack why some of the fruit trees he had planted were doing so poorly.

SOVIET EMBASSY, EAST BERLIN, SUNDAY, APRIL 22

A message arrived Sunday for Soviet ambassador Georgy Pushkin via secure telephone from Moscow. It was from Vladimir Semyonov, the senior Foreign Ministry official overseeing German affairs, directing the Soviet military commandant in Berlin to protest the tunnel to his American counterpart, General Dasher.

"Additional instructions concerning journalists and others will be given tomorrow," Semyonov added.

RUDOW, SUNDAY AFTERNOON, APRIL 22

Though his hopes of blowing up the tunnel had been foiled, Harvey had another line of defense prepared. At his behest, Lieutenant Colonel Helgestad, the installation commander, had placed a .50 caliber machine gun at the American end of the tunnel, pointing toward the Soviet sector.

Harvey and Montgomery went into the tunnel and took a position at the gun. The East German and Soviet forays down the tunnel were getting bolder. "We could hear them more than see them, tramping and stumbling around," said Montgomery. Around 3 p.m., he and Harvey heard footsteps approaching the American sector border.

They still could not see anyone—the dip that the tunnel took on its way east kept whoever was approaching out of view. But as they got closer, Montgomery and Harvey spotted several Soviet steel helmets—easily recognized a big red star on the front—bobbing into view as the soldiers cautiously advanced up the tunnel.

"That's what I was waiting for," Harvey grunted. "I think it's time to show these fellows they are not welcome in this part of Berlin."

He pulled the bolt of the machine gun back and let it go with a loud clang that reverberated down the tunnel. "That's a very sobering sound, if you've ever heard it, the bolt of a .50 caliber machine gun," recalled Montgomery. "Boy, those helmets disappeared so fast."

Harvey opted not to push the matter further. "Well, I guess that's the end of it," he told Montgomery. "We better get out of here."

The two departed, leaving the machine gun to be manned by Army soldiers. Harvey exited the tunnel for the last time.

Before leaving Rudow, Harvey gave instructions for the tunnel entry to be blocked. An Army crew led by Captain Stanley Livingston, the installation executive officer, got to work constructing a wall.

Harvey went back to BOB headquarters, where he sent an urgent cable to CIA headquarters appealing the decision not to blow the tunnel. The answer was again no, to Harvey's disappointment. "He would have loved to have buried some Soviets in the demolition of the site," said Bay Stockton.

ALTGLIENICKE, SUNDAY AFTERNOON, APRIL 22

Around 3:15 p.m., an East German telecommunications team inside the tap chamber began disabling the taps on the three cables. "Cut everything," one worker instructed. "Very, very, very, very cleanly." The painstaking work of the Dollis Hill team was snipped away in a matter of minutes. By 3:30, the last of the tap wires had been cut.

A few minutes later, several East Germans focused on a black circular object in the tap chamber wall. "Is that a microphone?" one asked.

"It probably is," another answered.

In the warehouse, the team could hear someone tapping on the microphone. "I need a big screwdriver," said a German worker.

The Rudow team listened in resignation. "They're taking the last one away from us now," someone said.

At 3:50 p.m., the microphone went dead. "It's gone, John," the unnamed Rudow team member said to a colleague.

"After 11 months and 11 days," a CIA report concluded, "the operational phase of PBJOINTLY was completed."

Part IV

A NEST OF SPIES

CHAPTER 19

A Sensational Story About American Espionage

WASHINGTON, MONDAY MORNING, APRIL 23, 1956

CIA director Allen Dulles was relaxed when he conferred on the telephone first thing Monday with his brother about how to handle the tunnel's discovery. The CIA director told John Foster Dulles that he planned to brief the president that afternoon.

Allen Dulles, exuberant over all the tunnel had produced, was disappointed but philosophical about its demise. "Most intelligence operations have a limited span of usefulness—a tunnel, a U-2 and the like," he later said. "This is assumed when the project starts." He was not particularly concerned about any repercussions. Both Harvey and his superiors in Washington were quite confident that once the tunnel was discovered, the Soviets "would probably suppress knowledge of the tunnel rather than admit to the world that Free World intelligence organs had the capability of successfully mounting an operation of this magnitude," according to a later CIA account.

But there was a surprise coming.

RUDOW, MONDAY MORNING, APRIL 23

Inside the tunnel, the Rudow soldiers kept the .50 caliber machine gun pointing toward the Soviet sector, with Corporal Noel Stegmeyer's finger on the trigger and PFC Gene Bialas holding the ammunition belt. Helgestad stood next to them, keeping his eyes peeled down the tunnel. Every now and then, a group from the Eastern side would come poking around with a flashlight, and the colonel would roar, "Don't come any closer, you're entering the American sector."

Behind the machine-gun position, a crew of soldiers was shoveling debris and pouring concrete in preparation for blocking the tunnel. "They were in a hurry to close that up," Bialas recalled.

Captain Livingston, muddied and coated in mortar dust, was overseeing the construction of two walls, each about a foot and a half thick, using both bricks and concrete. Russ Knapp's first visit into the tunnel was to assist Livingston in building the walls. They hastily rigged wire hangers from the barracks closet to use as rebar.

Everyone was on edge, uncertain what might happen. "Will the Russians actually come rampaging down the tunnel guns ablazing?" Knapp recalled thinking. He also spent time above ground on guard duty and was instructed by superiors to be especially alert. "As if I needed any urging in this area," Knapp said. "This seventeen-year-old kid was convinced that World War III had started and I was on the front lines!"

ALTGLIENICKE, MONDAY MORNING, APRIL 23

Across the border, Edmund Hohe, a nineteen-year-old Volkspolizei watch commander, was just as nervous. When the alarm for his unit sounded, everyone swung on their overcoats. Hohe thought it was a drill, but when they arrived at the site, he found himself eye to eye with U.S. soldiers guarding the compound. "We were only ten meters apart from each other," he said. Hohe feared a shooting war might break out any minute.

For now, the war was limited to comical insults. As Soviet officers trained their field glasses on the installation, some of the American soldiers stuck out their tongues at the Russians. Others flipped them the bird. A black pirate flag waved from one of the barracks windows, to the great amusement of the Russians.

BERLIN, MONDAY EVENING, APRIL 23

It was early evening when an office secretary left the Soviet embassy on Unter den Linden in the heart of Berlin, her purse filled with ten-pfennig coins. She went through the Brandenburg Gate, a five-minute walk away, and stopped at the first telephone booth she came to in West Berlin. Her assignment was to call every Western reporter and editor based in Berlin she could reach in the next half hour.

"Come immediately to the Karlshorst military headquarters," she told them. "We're offering a sensational story about American espionage."

To say the invitation was unusual was an understatement. It would be the first press conference Soviet military authorities in East Berlin had held with Western journalists since 1948. From across West Berlin, reporters raced to Karlshorst.

The Soviets had been rushing all day to prepare the tunnel for its public debut. They constructed a wooden shed over the entrance and installed slender ladders in the shaft to make it easier to climb down. Following the instructions from Moscow, Colonel Ivan Kotsyuba, the acting commandant of the Soviet Berlin garrison, met with General Dasher, the American commander, to protest the tunnel. "Dasher became extremely irritable," Kotsyuba reported to Moscow.

"We did not construct the underground tunnel," Dasher told Kotsyuba. "Only ordinary military communications installations are located in this district."

"Kotsyuba disputed the veracity of this version," according to the Soviet summary of the meeting. Dasher's mood was doubtlessly not improved by having to stick to an obvious lie.

After the meeting, Soviet officials in Berlin sent a joint message to

Moscow outlining a five-step plan of action, all of which had been worked out in advance:

1. File a formal protest with U.S. Army headquarters in Europe and release it to the press.

2. Invite correspondents from East and West Berlin "to inspect the object" uncovered in Altglienicke.

3. "Give permission to our German friends to speak out on this question" once it was made public.

4. "Dispatch a group of our specialists to study the equipment."

5. "Despite the fact that the tunnel contains English equipment, direct all accusations in the press against the Americans only."

The message was signed by the three most senior Soviet officials in East Germany: Marshal Andrei Grechko, Soviet ambassador Georgy Pushkin, and KGB *rezident* Yevgeny Pitovranov.

ALTGLIENICKE, MONDAY EVENING, APRIL 23

Despite having only a half-hour notice, about a hundred journalists made it to Karlshorst by 7 p.m. and were brought to the movie theater inside the Red Army officers' club. Colonel Kotsyuba, the short and plump acting commandant, stood behind a plush red lectern, with two Red Army lieutenants at his side to translate his remarks into English and German. Kotsyuba was filling in for the commandant of the Soviet garrison, who was out of Berlin, and he stepped into the role with relish.

With great umbrage, Kotsyuba announced that he had proof about the "wheeling and dealings of American spies." The previous day, he said, Soviet signal troops had discovered an "American spy tunnel" underneath Schönefelder Chaussee in the Soviet sector, running five hundred yards from a "mock radar station" in the American sector.

"The tunnel and equipment give clear evidence they were built with criminal and espionage intentions," Kotsyuba declared. The colonel appeared particularly perturbed about the DO NOT ENTER sign on the door to the equipment chamber, complaining that the Americans had "affixed misleading notices in the Russian and German languages."

The Soviets gave reporters copies of an official letter of protest sent that day to the American military authorities by the chief of staff of Soviet forces in Germany, Major General I. L. Zarenko, decrying the tunnel as an "illegal and intolerable action." It demanded a joint Russian-American investigation and insisted that "those responsible be brought to justice."

It was stunning news. But the show was only starting. Kotsyuba invited the journalists to come see the tunnel for themselves. A convoy of cars and buses carried the reporters at breakneck speed down a lonely stretch of road leading six miles from Karlshorst to Altglienicke, escorted by Soviet soldiers in jeeps and motorcycles.

It was dark by the time they reached the site, but the scene was brightly lit by Red Army floodlights powered by humming mobile generators. A contingent of Soviet officers and soldiers awaited. Kotsyuba, clad in a greatcoat and black leather gloves on the cold night, stood atop the tap chamber. He pointed accusingly at the tap attached to the three exposed cables.

At his direction, the reporters followed him in groups of ten down the ladder to the bottom of the shaft. "Come along, gentlemen," Kotsyuba called from below. "Come closer. Climb down to me."

Walter Sullivan of the *New York Times* was one of the first down. Entering the equipment chamber, which was brightly lit with neon tubes, he and his colleagues marveled at the rows of amplifiers and gadgets, including an oscillograph, recording devices, and a vacuum cleaner to keep out dust. "The chamber near the Soviet sector end of the tunnel looked like the communications center of a battleship," Sullivan wrote.

A helpful Red Army signal officer in the chamber described the equipment and tapping operation, calling it "expert work" and hinting that the circuits linked Soviet forces in Germany with Moscow. "This tunnel was built to last years," the officer said with a note of admiration. "The party responsible must have had a lot of money."

Sullivan observed that "much of the electronic equipment appeared to be English–made," though the tunnel was kept dry by pumps bearing the insignia of the Gould Pump Company in Seneca Falls, New York.

Reporters explored down the tunnel, taking note that the power cables and air–conditioning ducts running along the sides led to the American sector. They reached the sandbag barrier with barbed wire and cardboard sign marking the border. "There the lighting went out and newsmen could go no farther," wrote Nathan Margolin, a reporter for the U.S. military *Stars and Stripes* newspaper.

An East German reporter who accompanied a group of American, British, and French journalists recalled that his Western counterparts looked dazed as they toured the tunnel. "They didn't say a word," he wrote.

Emerging from the tunnel, the newsmen rushed back to West Berlin to file their stories. Asked for comment, a U.S. Berlin Command spokesman told reporters he had no information about the tunnel. Speaking on background, one American official called the Soviet accusations "ridiculous."

WASHINGTON, MONDAY EVENING, APRIL 23

At 6:01 p.m. Washington time, the Dulles brothers conferred again. Allen Dulles reported that he had briefed President Eisenhower about the tunnel's discovery. "He was relaxed and understanding about it," he told Foster.

But there had been an unexpected development. "The Soviets went to the press," Allen told Foster. The CIA director read some of the wire service stories coming over the ticker, which would soon make headlines around the world. It was the first time a major peacetime American espionage operation had been exposed to the world. The brothers fretted that the publicity might erode the moral authority that the United States liked to lord over the Soviets. Foster Dulles suggested to his brother that they prepare a counteroffensive against Soviet espionage by "looking up evidence of what they have done."

The secretary of state further suggested that the government effectively throw the CIA operators who had led the project under the bus. U.S. officials might paint the tunnel as a bit of a rogue operation, something not sanctioned from the top. This version could be given on background chats with favored reporters, an attempt to keep the Eisenhower administration's hands clean of the whole dirty business.

"Say maybe some of our people overstepped a bit," Foster Dulles suggested. "But the record of the Soviets' activities is such we are quite willing to have our record matched against theirs."

Allen Dulles agreed to "get on to it." He called his brother again the next morning at 9 a.m. with the further suggestion that they obfuscate, in time-honored Washington fashion. "We ought to tell [Ambassador James] Conant and the military to say they are referring everything to Washington—leave it fuzzed between Defense and State," Allen said. "This will give time for a better counteroffensive."

BOB HEADQUARTERS, TUESDAY MORNING, APRIL 24

The tunnel story that broke during the night was news to almost everyone at the Berlin base headquarters, save the handful in the know. John Osborne, hearing news reports on East German radio early Tuesday morning, rushed to the office and found Harvey already in his office. The base chief, "icy-cold furious" at the tunnel's demise according to Dave Murphy, was focused on finding out what had happened and "handholding the military on how to respond to Soviet pressure."

Harvey and Osborne discussed what, if anything, Harvey should say to the BOB staff. "The whole base would soon be buzzing with conjecture, and perhaps even some minor boasting or posturing by youngsters eager to appear to be in the know," recalled Osborne. Harvey agreed that "the sooner the lid was put on this the better."

Harvey called an all-hands meeting that morning and issued a simple order: Keep your mouths shut. "The tunnel was none of our affair, and no one was to discuss it or even mention it, not even in the office, not even to each other," said Osborne. "Amazingly, it worked."

Still, it was impossible to quash all the talk, which, apart from astonishment, reflected a palpable sense of pride. "They were rather pleased with it all," said Hugh Montgomery. BOB's collective sense of mystique puffed up several times over.

Among those who had worked on the tunnel, said Murphy, "there was a feeling of great unhappiness. On the other hand, you just sort of shrugged your shoulders and said, 'Well, we were lucky that it lasted that long.'"

Somebody—identity unknown—hung a black wreath on Harvey's door.

ALTGLIENICKE, TUESDAY MORNING, APRIL 24

Any Western hope that the tunnel discovery would be a one-day press sensation quickly dissipated. The Soviets were only getting started with their full-scale propaganda show. Streams of important visitors were taken to Altglienicke on buses Tuesday to share in the spectacle and public outrage. First to be brought into the tunnel were a group of Eastern Bloc diplomats, followed by a contingent of East German Communist Party leaders, and later a group of high-ranking Soviet army officers.

Even as they tut-tutted, the visitors could not help but admire the Western equipment, according to a high-ranking East German CANDARE agent on the tour who reported to BOB. The DO NOT ENTER sign in German and Russian drew smiles. Some visitors "considered the posting of this sign as one of the most audacious aspects of the entire undertaking," according to a CIA history.

In the afternoon, the Soviets hosted a second press tour. Some two hundred journalists showed up, twice as many as the day before, including a number who came back for a closer look. "The Russians appear eager to exploit the situation," Walter Sullivan reported in the *New York Times*. "They phoned every correspondent in West Berlin who might have been overlooked yesterday." Hordes of reporters crowded around the hole, bundled in raincoats and scarves against the raw weather. Cameramen jockeyed with microphone-wielding radio reporters for position atop piles of dirt. The roadside scene "resembled an archaeological site after exciting new finds, with benevolent Russian officers acting as guides to the curious," wrote Charles Hargrove, the *Times* of London correspondent.

This time, the reporters saw the site in daylight, including the American radar installation, which Colonel Kotsyuba helpfully pointed out. "This disclosed that the tunnel led directly toward a United States installation 550 yards away on the other side of the border," Sullivan wrote. Whatever skepticism remained among reporters of American involvement disappeared.

The correspondents crossed the border into West Berlin, where they approached the two fences surrounding the American installation. "A United States sentry with automatic rifle was on guard and a dozen or so G.I.s were watching from the windows of what appeared to be a barracks," Sullivan reported. No one was allowed to enter the compound.

But on the Eastern side, they were allowed to enter the tunnel. A reporter for the *Berliner Zeitung,* an Eastern daily newspaper, went down with several Western journalists and a Soviet officer. As soon as they left the equipment chamber and continued into the tunnel proper, the commotion from the hundreds of reporters milling above disappeared. As they walked between the tracks, they could hear nothing but the hollow sound of their footsteps, along with a quiet rush of air flowing through the ducts.

Reaching the first cardboard sign marking the American sector, the reporters noted that the German-language grammar was incorrect. "The Soviet officer assures us that the Russian is just as flawed as the German," the East German reporter wrote.

The officer would go no farther than the border, but the journalists stepped over the sandbags and continued. It was dark ahead, but by the flash of the photographer's camera, they spotted the second sign, warning against entry. The snarl of barbed wire in any event made it impossible to advance farther. Beyond it, another hundred yards away, they could see two glowing points in the distance that periodically brightened, then faded, and finally disappeared. Eventually, they realized it was two American observers standing on the other side, watching them and smoking cigarettes.

The group called out several times in German and English that they were journalists, but there was no response. It was unnerving. "The whole thing is like something from a bad crime novel," the reporter concluded. The journalists beat a hasty retreat.

"The Rats in the Tunnel are silent," an East Berlin newspaper headlined.

Reporters who called the Berlin Command were told by an Army spokesman that the American installation was "an experimental radar station for the passive defense of West Berlin."

———

Each side had its own fictions. The Eastern version, concocted by the KGB and distributed by the East German government news agency, ADN, claimed that the Americans had been caught red-handed inside the tunnel. Eavesdroppers wearing earphones below Schönefelder Chaussee were so absorbed in their work that they had not heard the excavation until the Soviets burst into the equipment room. The terrified Americans fled, including one Army sergeant who "nearly swallowed his chewing gum." Coffee was left brewing on a burner. A cartoon in the East German newspaper *Freies Wort* depicted the Americans as rats wearing Army caps, scurrying from the underground communications center when the Russians surprised them.

Another fiction was being industriously peddled: The Soviets continued to assert that the tunnel was solely an American enterprise, and leveled no accusations at the British, a version amplified by the East German press. "The East Berlin press has given great prominence to the affair, advancing it as proof that West Berlin is a nest of American spies and saboteurs and demanding that these activities be ended," a British diplomat reported to the Foreign Office in London. But not a word was directed against the British, he added. The Communist Party newspaper *Neues Deutschland* was particularly vituperative about the Americans, denouncing them as no better than "gangsters" or "Chicago bank robbers."

Hargrove, the *Times* of London correspondent, noted something odd. "Fluorescent lighting, fire extinguishers and other equipment in the switchboard section all bear familiar British trademarks," he wrote on Tuesday. "But the Russians have not yet accused the British authorities of complicity and maintain that the whole tunnel is recognizably American work."

The *Berliner Zeitung* explained the British equipment as "probably an attempt by the Americans to conceal their own responsibility."

LONDON, TUESDAY EVENING, APRIL 24

The Eastern version was a fiction Prime Minister Anthony Eden was happy to embrace. As the Soviet visit to Britain entered its second week, he instructed SIS to maintain a tight lid on British involvement with the tunnel, not wanting the affair to disrupt the delicate talks in London. The Soviet leaders also studiously avoided any mention of the spectacle unfolding in Altglienicke, letting surrogates in Berlin and Moscow do the talking.

The Soviets were likewise quiet about the British frogman, even though their security detail worried that a mine might have been attached to the hull of the *Ordzhonikidze* and could explode on their way home. Khrushchev erupted in anger at the suggestion, declaring that "such an act of piracy would mean war" with Britain, Sergei Khrushchev recalled. "He didn't fail to mention how many missiles would be required to wipe the island off the face of the earth."

Predictions were already widespread that the visit would end in failure. The day before, Khrushchev had set off a furor during a visit to the city of Birmingham when he declared that the Soviet Union planned to build a guided missile with a hydrogen bomb warhead capable of hitting targets "anywhere in the world." He also called Eisenhower's "Open Skies" proposal for aerial inspection "fantasy," dashing hopes for progress on arms control.

Back in London Monday night, a dinner with opposition Labour leaders had turned ugly when Khrushchev refused to accept a list of socialist politicians being held prisoner by communist regimes in

Eastern Europe. "The atmosphere surrounding the British-Russian talks has deteriorated swiftly in the last 48 hours," the *New York Times*'s Drew Middleton reported Tuesday.

On Tuesday evening, a bit of civility returned. Bulganin and Khrushchev joined Eden to watch Dame Margot Fonteyn of the Royal Ballet perform *Swan Lake* at the venerable Covent Garden Opera. Privately, Khrushchev was tired of *Swan Lake*. Adopted by the Soviet regime as a quasi-official emblem of the state, the Tchaikovsky composition was performed so often in the USSR that Khrushchev once complained that "I start to get sick to my stomach" at the thought of seeing it again.

But Dame Margot's performance succeeded in restoring a veneer of goodwill to the visit. "When Marshal Bulganin and Mr. Khrushchev visited the ballerina after the performance they burst in with a stream of praise that forced the interpreter to plead for time and a deep breath," the *New York Times* reported.

ALTGLIENICKE, TUESDAY EVENING, APRIL 24

From babes in arms to the town's eldest resident, ninety-one-year-old Frau Feistel, the people of Altglienicke packed the auditorium of Primary School 14 to denounce the "tunnel criminals" and protest the American espionage discovered beneath their feet. It was an "unspeakably mean trick," Paul Huhn, caretaker for the Altglienicke cemetery, told the audience.

The meeting was just part of an elaborate series of protests organized by authorities. Earlier in the day, Altglienicke schoolchildren marched through the streets carrying banners denouncing the tunnel moles. Franz Fischer, a local Communist Party representative, announced at the meeting Tuesday evening that public tours of the tunnel would soon begin, and that all Berliners, from East and West, were invited "to look at this American crime."

At one point a group of local young toughs—known as *Halbstarke*—advanced angrily on the Rudow installation. "They surrounded the compound and were throwing rocks at us and what have you," said John Vacca, then an eighteen-year-old private first class from

Brooklyn. "Finally the Berlin police came running down and ran after them and they ran across the border."

———

The onslaught in the press continued, both in Germany and around the world. The discovery hit the big screen in East Berlin on April 27, with forty theaters showing *Stop It!*, a hastily produced government film scolding the Americans. Photos and newspaper accounts of the tunnel were posted on bulletin boards in Chinese factories and shops. "The tunnel was undoubtedly the most highly publicized peacetime espionage enterprise in modern times prior to the 'U-2 incident,'" a CIA history later observed.

The continued U.S. silence in the face of the protests spoke volumes, taken widely as a winking admission of responsibility. "Our own talks with American officials here suggest so far they do not find the business too embarrassing, and indeed that the Administration may be glad to play it up as an example of Cold War toughness," a British diplomat in Bonn, C. P. Hope, informed London. "At the moment they are laughing it off as a good joke on the Soviet."

As requested by the Dulles brothers, the U.S. Army headquarters in Europe informed the Soviets that the issue was being referred to Washington. "I consider further discussions between military commanders here to be unnecessary and undesirable," Major General John F. Uncles, chief of staff for the U.S. Army in Europe, wrote his Soviet counterpart. "I have therefore reported the matter to Washington."

The Soviets were left to fume about the American "evasion."

———

Indeed, the reaction in the West was not what Khrushchev or the East Germans had hoped. Most of the coverage, especially in the United States and West Germany, was laudatory, with much admiration for the Americans' pluck. After years of Soviet intelligence coups, including the theft of atomic secrets by Manhattan Project spy Klaus Fuchs, the tunnel was celebrated. "The non-Communist world reacted with surprise and unconcealed delight to this indication that the U.S., almost universally regarded as a stumbling neophyte in espionage matters, was capable of a coup against the Soviet Union, which had long been the acknowledged master in such matters," a CIA history concluded.

There were some exceptions. The right-leaning *Frankfurter Allgemeine Zeitung* ran an angry editorial demanding that the German public "no longer tolerate the waging of a Russian-American cold war on German soil." But by and large, the Western press and public were applauding. The *Frankfurter Neue Presse* expressed surprise that the Americans "were capable of so much cleverness."

"We cannot help thinking the Communists have made a grievous mistake to raise so much fuss about their discovery," the *Washington Post* editorialized. "The Tunnel of Love," as the paper dubbed it, had been greeted in West Germany "with astonishment and delight as an evidence that the tradition of Yankee resourcefulness and ingenuity is not a myth after all." It had restored American prestige severely damaged by the tepid U.S. response to the workers' uprising three years earlier, the paper added.

The tunnel was "a venture of extraordinary audacity—the stuff of which thriller films are made," the *New York Herald Tribune* enthused. "If it was dug by American Intelligence forces, and that is the general assumption, it is a striking example of their capacity for daring undertakings."

SIS HEADQUARTERS, OLYMPIC STADIUM, BERLIN

For Peter Lunn, the proud SIS station chief, all the adulation thrown at the Americans was irritating. Even worse was the total silence about any British role, apart from a few brief mentions of English equipment. "This was too much for Peter Lunn," recalled George Blake.

Lunn pressed London to allow the British involvement to be publicly known. He was backed by senior SIS officials at the Broadway headquarters. But the Foreign Office strenuously objected, reflecting Eden's wishes.

Lunn settled for assembling his entire Berlin staff, from the lowest-ranking secretaries to the most senior officers, to tell them of the British role in the tunnel. It was a surprise to virtually all, Blake excepted, of course. Lunn "told the whole story from its inception to its untimely end," recalled Blake. "He made it quite clear that this had been essentially an SIS idea and his own to boot."

But there was a part of the story Lunn did not yet know.

LONDON, FRIDAY, APRIL 27

The epic Soviet visit to Britain was finally coming to an end. "These were the ten days that shook the Russians," the *New York Times* declared. Bulge and Krush were exhausted, and not just by the uproar that surrounded the visit. "The pace was grueling, and I began to let my dissatisfaction be known," Khrushchev recalled. He and Bulganin tried to scratch a planned visit to Scotland, but relented at Eden's pleading. Bulganin nearly choked when he tried to down a glass of scotch in Edinburgh.

Despite all the incidents, the visit was ending on a more positive note than the bleak assessments a few days earlier. The Soviets invited Eden to make a reciprocal visit to Russia and agreed to restrain their arms sales to the Middle East, a relief to the prime minister. Reassured that the British were eager to keep the peace, the Soviet leaders were privately planning to move forward with reductions in the Soviet armed forces.

Still unspoken were the two espionage capers that had unfolded during their visit. The tunnel remained a major international story, but with no mention of British involvement. Reports had appeared in the press about the mysterious disappearance of a British frogman off Portsmouth, but Eden and his ministers had still not been briefed on the incident.

Speaking to reporters Friday at Westminster before the Soviets boarded a train for the return trip to Portsmouth, Bulganin made a curious comment: "Without any risk of revealing a great secret, we can inform you—confident that our respected hosts also hold this opinion—that the course of the discussions met on their way underwater rocks."

This seemingly innocuous remark would be later puzzled over— was it a reference to the tunnel, or the frogman, or both?

———

In the weeks that followed, the CIA and SIS conducted an inquiry trying to determine whether the demise of the tunnel was truly a chance discovery, or whether the operation had been betrayed.

For Blake, it was a tense time. He anxiously followed the tunnel's exposure and its aftermath, looking for any sign that the CIA or SIS suspected the tunnel had been revealed by a mole. "I was rather on tenterhooks, as you can imagine, what the outcome would be," he later said.

Despite disappointment, few at CIA and SIS headquarters had been shocked by the tunnel's demise. "I wasn't terribly surprised," recalled Dick Helms. "I didn't think a thing like that could go on for very long, undiscovered, undetected, unsuspected, if you like. Naturally, I wondered what had caused this."

President Eisenhower felt the same way. "You had to anticipate that it was coming to an end," recalled Andrew Goodpaster, his staff secretary. Ever the general, Ike figured somebody on the American or British side had screwed up. "I think he felt that there had been carelessness that drew the attention of the East Germans," said Goodpaster.

The Dulles brothers' efforts to deflect responsibility for the tunnel away from the administration appeared to have worked. At his next press conference, Eisenhower was not asked a single question about the tunnel, despite the headlines around the world. Nonetheless, given the international flap, the president insisted that all future CIA operations that impinged on another nation's sovereignty be reported to the Special Group, a committee of senior advisers including representatives of State, Defense, and the White House that had been recently created to oversee covert operations.

Bill Harvey's fury at the tunnel's demise evolved into a depression. He traveled to Washington for part of the review. "He was very concerned to know why it blew," CG Harvey recalled. As Harvey saw it, the most persuasive evidence in favor of an accidental discovery was the obvious confusion and lack of awareness of the Soviet troops and East German telecommunications workers who had uncovered the tunnel. "They are never going to convince me that they knew where they were and what they were doing when they came in," he told CG. He was correct—the troops and workmen had not known what they were looking for. But the KGB had.

In Washington, analysts examined recent telephone traffic, listened to the conversations recorded by the tap chamber microphone, and went over the reports from observers in the warehouse. They found nothing pointing to any prior knowledge of the tap. According to David Murphy, Harvey grudgingly agreed with the conclusion that the tunnel's discovery had been a matter of chance. "Like all of us in Berlin at the time, Bill believed the Soviets found the tunnel in their search for cable faults caused by the heavy rains," Murphy said.

But two of the CIA officers who worked most closely with Harvey on the tunnel—Hugh Montgomery and Charlie Bray—say he always harbored some doubts. Harvey's suspicions were raised by the number of Soviets at the site as dawn broke, according to Montgomery. "Harvey never really accepted the proposition that the discovery was accidental," Bray added. "I never heard he had specific suspicions, but he was not satisfied blaming it on luck."

Likewise, in Washington, Frank Rowlett's gut feeling was someone had betrayed the tunnel. But there was no hard evidence. Rowlett later said that the Soviets "very clumsily put on an act of discovery."

However, in the view of the man who perhaps had the most at stake, the KGB had covered its tracks well. "I must say that it was done extremely skillfully," said George Blake.

There was one curious slip. Within several days of its discovery, the Soviets told Western reporters that the tunnel had been in operation since May 1955. Possibly they made this conclusion based on dates tagged to electronic equipment in the tunnel. But it would have been difficult to know with certainty without an inside source. Yet the CIA and SIS seem to have missed this clue.

———

Blake had kept a low profile during the investigation, worried that if there were suspicions, he would be placed under observation. "I passed some anxious weeks until the results of the inquiry became known and I could heave a sigh of relief," he later said.

The mole at the heart of Western intelligence in Berlin remained undiscovered.

CHAPTER 20

The Invisible War

In late April 1956, just a week after the Berlin tunnel's public discovery, a U.S. Air Force cargo plane landed at RAF Lakenheath northeast of London and taxied to an isolated hangar to be unloaded. Away from prying eyes, a team of technicians assembled the contents. When finished, they had put together an unusual aircraft, black and extremely lightweight, with long, tapered wings and no identification markings.

Ostensibly the aircraft was assigned to the "1st Provisional Weather Reconnaissance Squadron," which was tasked with studying meteorological conditions around the Baltic Sea. In truth, the aircraft was the first U-2 to arrive in Europe, one of several of the secret CIA spy planes that were ready to begin reconnaissance flights over the Soviet Union.

In most respects, the timing was excellent, almost like handing off a baton. For nearly a year, the tunnel had provided the early warning the United States and its allies needed. Now the U-2, with high-resolution cameras able to cover vast amounts of territory from an altitude of more than seventy thousand feet, would be able to track the movement of Soviet military equipment, weaponry, troops, and other logistical signs that might signal plans for an attack.

Unlike the tunnel, however, U-2 photographs could not capture conversations or orders with the most important intelligence of all: Soviet intent to attack. Still, the CIA's spy inside Soviet military intelligence, Lieutenant Colonel Pyotr Popov, remained in a position to pass along warning signals, and this, together with the U-2's arrival, eased the blow of the tunnel's discovery.

In one crucial respect, however, the timing was inconvenient. Prime Minister Anthony Eden had given permission to the CIA to fly the first U-2 missions from Lakenheath. But days after the aircraft's secret arrival, the mystery of missing frogman Buster Crabb blew up into a major diplomatic and political crisis.

With Soviet leaders Nikita Khrushchev and Nikolai Bulganin safely back in the USSR, Moscow sent a protest note to the British government on May 4 demanding an explanation for the frogman spotted near their ships in Portsmouth.

British intelligence had briefed Eden about the botched operation only the day before. The prime minister erupted in anger, not only that his explicit directions against it were disobeyed, but also that he had been kept in the dark once it happened. The diplomatic success he had engineered during the Soviet visit had now been consumed by the frogman affair.

For Eden, it was humiliating to learn that the Soviets had known far more about his own government's actions than he had. "Anthony wondered why Khrushchev kept on making jokes about cruisers being so obsolete," Lady Eden wrote in her diary. "They must think us perfect fools."

Eden addressed an angry Parliament and faced a barrage of criticism from the opposition Labour Party and the British press. He forced John Sinclair, head of SIS, to move up his planned retirement. Crabb's headless body, still in his diving suit, would be found near Portsmouth harbor a year later. His cause of death—whether he died in a diving accident, or was killed by Soviet frogmen protecting the ships, or by something else—remains a mystery.

Coming on the heels of the tunnel spectacle, the frogman affair put espionage front and center in the public eye. "The news reads these days like the script of a Hitchcock thriller," the *New York Times* columnist James Reston noted. The tunnel and the frogman sagas, he added, "are merely a few of the visible evidences of the invisible war that is now proceeding wherever Western and Communist interests meet, which is almost everywhere."

Adding a spy plane to the mix was too much for Eden, who asked

Eisenhower to move the U-2 program out of England. The president was sympathetic. While the tunnel had received nothing but plaudits in the West, Eden was being pummeled over the frogman fiasco. "Our boys forget what we might be thinking and doing if this were happening to us," Eisenhower told John Foster Dulles. He suggested "we ought to move out of there and try somewhere else."

That somewhere else was West Germany, where Chancellor Konrad Adenauer, perhaps impressed by the positive reception the tunnel had received, agreed to host the operation. The U-2 aircraft, pilots, and support teams moved to the air base in Wiesbaden, West Germany, and awaited permission from Eisenhower to begin the flights.

ALTGLIENICKE, APRIL AND MAY 1956

Farmer Noack and his family were among the first East Berliners given a tour of the tunnel. It was the least local authorities could do. Preparations for opening the tunnel to the public had left their property in disarray. The fields were a mess, covered by mounds of soil. Volkspolizei guarding the tunnel set up a semipermanent camp on the land, pitching tents by the cemetery wall. Crews helped themselves to a large pile of quality old bricks Noack had set aside for the house he planned to construct, using them instead to build a flight of steps for a tunnel entrance. It was a grand entry, wide and gradual enough to allow lines of tourists four abreast to easily walk down into the tunnel. An exit was built about two hundred yards down the tunnel, toward the American border. Crews uncovered a stretch of the tunnel, sliced open a six-foot hole in the steel liner, and constructed an exit with wooden boards and Noack's bricks. He had reluctantly concluded that his house project would be delayed.

Early on the morning of April 30, buses began rolling up to the site with loads of workers from the J. W. Stalin Elektro-Apparate-Werke, a state-owned electrical manufacturer. More buses followed with brake plant employees, postal clerks, and other workers on company outings.

Big crowds showed up when the tunnel opened to the general public on Thursday, May 3, with visitors from fifteen countries, including China, Romania, France, Britain, and Sweden. In the days that followed, there were classes of schoolchildren, military groups, American college students, geologists, a delegation of electrical mechanics from Stuttgart, and Sudanese dignitaries, among others.

The tunnel soon became a favorite outing for East and West Berliners alike eager to see the invisible war firsthand. It was open from 9 a.m. to 5 p.m. seven days a week, with a free thirty-minute guided tour. Visitors were offered binoculars to examine the American installation across the border. A large illustrated information board erected near the entrance described the tunnel design and equipment. Vopos escorted tourists through the tunnel, explaining the electronics and denouncing the Americans. "They told us what to say," recalled Günther Kuinke, then a twenty-two-year-old Volkspolizei officer. "We used the vocabulary of the Cold War."

After exiting the tunnel, visitors stopped at a table to sign a guestbook. A souvenir booklet entitled *Tunnel Spione* (Tunnel Spies), available for ten pfennigs, was chock-full of photographs and diagrams about the tunnel, which it termed the "Museum of U$A Villainy." It included a photo of Farmer Noack plowing his field, with a caption quoting him expressing the requisite outrage: "I worked cluelessly in my field while our security was being threatened by these horrific actions. I want to pursue my work in peace and quiet, therefore they should close the spy organizations."

Visitors often waited in long lines, particularly on weekends when as many as twenty-six hundred people a day toured the tunnel. By May 20, the tunnel had logged fifteen thousand visitors; by June 10, the number had reached thirty-one thousand. "It has been turned into a major tourist attraction and scarcely a day passes without delegations of one sort or another being conducted through it," a British diplomat reported. The crush was so great that a state trade organization opened a mobile sausage and beer stand. It did a thriving business, though *Neues Deutschland,* the official communist newspaper, complained that "the sausage is cold, and the buffet doesn't open early enough."

Most visitors were appropriately impressed by the wondrous

technology and the sheer spectacle, though despite the official outrage, many had trouble hiding their amusement at how the Soviets
had apparently been tricked by American intelligence.

Noting all the sightseers, NBC Radio Network news commen-
tator Alex Dreier made a suggestion to the U.S. government: "Why
don't we open a tourist entrance at our end of the tunnel and cash
in on the publicity?"

———

The favorable reviews the tunnel was receiving in the West only
further infuriated the East German and Soviet governments. The
annual May Day celebration on Marx-Engels-Platz in East Berlin
was given over to exhortations to throw the "American gangsters"
out of West Berlin.

Allen and John Foster Dulles, both favorite targets of the East
German regime, were vilified in the press. For good measure, the
official East German government news agency, ADN, claimed that
the tunnel was built "on the initiative and with the active support"
of their sister Eleanor, the special assistant in the State Department's
office of German affairs. This made headlines in the United States:
"Dulles' Sister the 'Brain' of Tunnel Spies, Say Reds," the *Chicago
Tribune* reported. John Foster Dulles called his sister to tease her
about the stories. Eleanor replied that she "thought it was all [Allen's]
fault."

The CIA director was quite happy to bask in the praise, at least
in closed circles. Soon after the tunnel's discovery, Dulles came by
the ramshackle T-32 building in Washington to thank the teams
processing the teletype. Bob Browne, Alice Ojala, and numerous
colleagues assembled in the machine room on the ground floor. For
many, including Browne, it was the first time they had even set foot
in the classified room holding the "Bumblebee" teletype demodulator. Many had not known that the intelligence they were examining
came from a tunnel until they read the news.

It was a triumphant moment for Dulles. The wave of good publicity would likely silence critics and garner support for the CIA in
Congress. "He was all smiles," said Ojala. "He said we had done a
good job and shook everybody's hands."

Then it was back to work for Browne, Ojala, and their colleagues. PBJOINTLY had not ended, despite the tunnel's discovery. An enormous backlog of tapes awaiting transcription and analysis had built up, and the work would continue for more than two years. While some team members in the Washington and London processing centers returned to their prior jobs or started new assignments, many others continued the work.

CIA linguist Bill Romey, who had been plugged in for the first tapped conversations in Berlin, stayed with the team in London. "The materials remained top secret and had continuing strategic and tactical importance of the highest order," he said. "But they would no longer give us insights into current intentions and plans that might be afoot."

It was impossible to maintain the manic intensity that had fueled the teams when the tunnel was live. Now they took frequent breaks for coffee or tea and enjoyed two-hour pub lunches. "For us, the drudges, the magic was gone," said Romey.

RUDOW

The magic was gone at Rudow as well. Soon after the discovery, Lieutenant Colonel Helgestad, the installation commander, assembled everyone at the site, had them stand and raise their right hands, and administered an oath of secrecy. "They had to swear they would never talk about what happened," said Russ Knapp.

It was a vow the soldiers kept, in most cases for decades. When Knapp left Germany and went to his parents' home in Rhode Island, he didn't say a word about what he'd done. He left a copy of *Life* magazine open to a photo spread about the tunnel on his parents' bed, hoping they might make the connection, but he heard "not a peep" from them.

The U.S. Army engineers who dug the tunnel were quietly recognized. The enlisted men earned Army Commendation Medals, while the officers were awarded the Legion of Merit for what was described as a "special project" on the citation. "I haven't the slightest idea of what you've done, but you must have done it pretty good," the general who presented Keith Comstock his decoration at Fort Belvoir, Virginia, told him.

Despite the tunnel's demise, the Army saw no reason to shut down the perfectly good ELINT station at Rudow, which continued capturing valuable electronic intelligence from Soviet operations at the Schönefeld airfield for years. Several dozen soldiers remained to operate the equipment, adding a new antenna atop a large black pole on the roof. "A Russian helicopter came over to see what the heck we were doing, and we brought it down, and they went back to Schönefeld, and we brought it back up," said John Vacca, who remained at the ELINT station until 1958. "We used to play cat and mouse."

Given the scrutiny on Rudow, the soldiers were confined to the installation and had to get used to life in the spotlight. "We were sort of like captives there, like in prison," said Vacca. "We couldn't go anywhere." Even their pickup basketball games were an object of fascination for tourists watching with binoculars from across the border.

After six months, when they were finally allowed to hit the town, scarcely a soldier remained sober.

———

On July 4, 1956, a U-2 took off from Wiesbaden, West Germany, flying over East Germany and Poland before crossing the border into the USSR and making the first overflight of Soviet territory. Among the first targets for aerial reconnaissance were Soviet atomic installations that had been identified by tunnel intelligence. The flight was picked up by Soviet radar, but MiG fighters were unable to intercept the high-flying aircraft.

Khrushchev, who had attended an Independence Day reception at the U.S. ambassador's residence in Moscow, was infuriated, considered it a "slap in the face" from Eisenhower. "Father thirsted for revenge," recalled his son Sergei Khrushchev.

That fall, two volatile crises exploded. On October 29, Israel invaded the Egyptian Sinai, soon joined by Britain and France, eager to regain control of the Suez Canal, which had been seized in the summer by Nasser. When the Soviets threatened to attack Britain and France with missiles, Eisenhower warned that the United States would respond with nuclear weapons. But the president also pressured Britain and France to withdraw their troops, defusing the crisis. A badly weakened Eden resigned two months later.

Even as fighting was under way in Egypt, the Kremlin sent Soviet tanks and troops to intervene in Hungary, where an October revolution had overthrown communist rule. Despite the hopes of Hungarian freedom fighters, Eisenhower believed it futile to intervene, and the revolt was crushed after four days of heavy fighting.

The hopes for peaceful coexistence raised by the meetings in Geneva and London appeared similarly doomed. The Cold War had fallen into a new, exceptionally dangerous period.

———

With tensions so high, it was perhaps natural that some at BOB and SIS headquarters in Berlin wistfully considered another tunnel. Even before PBJOINTLY blew, Bill Harvey and Peter Lunn were considering a new tunnel project, both to have a second source of intercepts and a backup if something happened to the first tunnel.

John Wyke, the redoubtable SIS officer who had played key roles in the Vienna and Berlin tunnels, was the prime instigator. He explored possible sites and came up with a junkyard in the British sector just across the border from Potsdamer Platz, where targeted cables serving East German ministers could be reached with a short tunnel. The proposed operation, given the code name Bronze, did not get far, with little support in Washington or London.

"It never really got beyond the talking stage," said Hugh Montgomery. "Everyone agreed, we'd pushed our luck, we'd had a good run, let's not spoil it all by having another one that blows up in our faces." After the very public exposure of the first tunnel, no one doubted the Soviets would be watching very closely for any copycat efforts, especially in Berlin.

With no tunnel, Lunn lost interest in Berlin, and departed in the summer of 1956 to head the station in Bonn, the West German capital, a position with important liaison duties. For his work on the tunnel, he was awarded the Most Distinguished Order of Saint Michael and Saint George, the highest decoration that could then be given to any SIS officer, save the chief.

ALTGLIENICKE, FALL 1956

By October, some ninety thousand visitors had toured the tunnel, and the city's most unusual tourist attraction finally closed. East German authorities decided that rather than allow the tunnel to continue to defile their soil, they would excavate and remove the section running in the Eastern sector.

This was easier said than done. Excavators, dump trucks, and other heavy equipment rumbled over Farmer Noack's field, digging an enormous ditch to get to the tunnel and wantonly destroying fruit trees; nearly half of the orchard disappeared. The earth where his house was supposed to be built was so churned up that it could not support a foundation. "When the tunnel was dug up, it looked as if a bomb had exploded," recalled Dagmar Feick, Noack's daughter. Even worse, trucks carted away the fertile topsoil. The clay from the perched water table that had caused so many headaches during the tunnel construction was now at the surface.

The American troops across the way at Rudow watched the progress as crews used cranes to lift out tunnel sections, reaching the border after several weeks. "One day we were all sitting there in the dayroom and there was a huge explosion, dirt and rocks and everything came flying down, and broke the outer windows," recalled Vacca. "It scared the hell out of us. We thought they were firing on us until we figured out what exactly they did." As a final act of purging, the East Germans had triggered explosives to collapse the ground where the tunnel had been.

Though removing the tunnel caused far more damage to the land than building it in the first place, the East German government refused responsibility. Instead, East Berlin authorities demanded that the West Berlin government pay $25,000 in compensation, claiming it had known about the tunnel in advance. The West Berlin Senate rejected the demand.

The East German government could not bring suit in the West Berlin courts, but East German citizens could, so authorities pressured Noack to file a case. "The trick was they needed a private person to sue the West Berlin government, but they wanted to add their own expenses to make money for themselves," Feick recalled.

Noack went along on the condition that the East German government finance the replanting of his field by paying him $1,600 as an advance on whatever sum was won in court. The government agreed and provided him with a top East Berlin attorney to handle the case. There was virtually no chance a suit could be successfully brought against the American government, so the West Berlin government was targeted. The suit, filed in December 1956, charged that the tunnel had "seriously endangered" Noack's livelihood as a farmer and noted that the trees he planted "were stunted for puzzling reasons."

But even as the suit began its long journey through the courts, Farmer Noack suffered a grave setback. His bad leg, which had left him disabled since his youth, had to be amputated due to infection. The loss seemed to drain much of his spirit, already battered by the tunnel travails. His dream of a family farm was dying. Said his daughter, "When he lost his leg, he didn't care."

BERLIN, MARCH 1957

In late March 1957, Lieutenant Colonel Pyotr Popov met with George Kisevalter, his CIA handler, in West Berlin and delivered his biggest intelligence coup since his arrival in East Germany a year earlier.

Marshal Georgy Zhukov, the Soviet war hero who led the Red Army's drive to capture Berlin and who was now serving as defense minister, had completed a four-day trip to East Germany on March 16 observing Red Army training exercises. During his visit, Zhukov addressed senior Group of Soviet Forces Germany commanders. Popov had managed to get access to notes of Zhukov's comments, which were loaded with sensitive intelligence.

Popov gave Kisevalter a summary of Zhukov's talk with details on the Soviet military intervention in Hungary the previous fall, as well as information about new Soviet weapons under development, including a heavy tank for use in atomic warfare and more accurate tactical guided missiles.

But the most jolting revelation was about Soviet contingency plans in the event war was expected, including striking first with a massive armored attack into Western Europe. "Operations must now be planned so that Soviet forces will reach the English Channel on the second day of war," Zhukov told the commanders.

"Zhukov emphasized the fact that the Soviets will definitely be the ones to start the war, in order to take advantage of the factor of surprise," according to Popov. "As soon as it is apparent that western forces are preparing to unleash a war, the Soviets must beat them to the punch."

In that regard, the hard-charging Zhukov was thoroughly displeased with the performance of the GSFG armored units he watched train during his visit—their tempo had been far too slow. When Grechko, the GSFG commander, tried to explain that the pace had been slowed for training purposes, Zhukov cut him off. "Tanks must force ahead and set the pace for the entire offensive," he declared.

Back at BOB headquarters, Kisevalter sent word to Washington. Popov had delivered "an intelligence bombshell," according to David Murphy, the deputy base chief.

On March 29, CIA headquarters distributed a report about Zhukov's remarks to a very limited audience in Washington under tight controls. The CIA also sent a copy to SIS headquarters in London, which was regularly apprised of intelligence gathered by Popov. Because of the important information about Soviet forces in Germany, London sent a copy to the SIS station in Berlin.

There, the report was likely seen by George Blake, who was still assigned to the Soviet section. In any event, the KGB soon had its own copy of the CIA report. It rocked KGB headquarters in Moscow, as it revealed that the CIA had a high-level penetration inside Soviet military headquarters in East Germany. It did not take long for KGB investigators to put together a list of the officers who had access to the speech. Among the names: Pyotr Popov.

WEST BERLIN, APRIL 1957

A week after Popov's stunning report, Gillian Blake gave birth to the couple's first child, Anthony, at the British Military Hospital Berlin at Spandau on April 4. "George was very pleased to have a son and a very proud father," Gillian recalled. The couple adapted easily from their weekends of riding and sailing in Berlin's parks to "pushing the pram along the roads of Charlottenburg."

But Blake's joy in fatherhood was not unreserved. He had been anxious when Gillian had informed him late in the previous summer that she was pregnant. "On the one hand I was delighted with the thought of becoming a father, and on the other, I was deeply aware of the fact that, in my position, I should not have any children," he recalled. "But how could I explain this to my wife without telling her the truth?"

Gillian detected that something was bothering her husband beneath his poised surface. "He was never completely relaxed and, I used to think, under a strain," she said. Later, she would understand why. "He is living, so to speak, a lie, and living it rather ruthlessly."

The Blakes traveled to London to have Anthony christened at St. Michael's Chester Square, a well-known Anglican church not far from where her parents lived. For Blake, the visit back to England and reunions with family highlighted the growing divide in his life. "Here I was, building with one hand a happy family life with its roots firmly attached to this country," he later said, "and with the other hand I was pulling the foundations from underneath it so that it might crumble any moment."

Blake's time to act, he recognized, was running short.

Part V

AMONG FRIENDS

CHAPTER 21

Exit Berlin

WEST BERLIN, NOVEMBER 17, 1958

Pyotr Popov arrived at an emergency meeting he had called with his CIA handlers ready with a joke about Nikita Khrushchev's earth-shaking declaration a week earlier.

On November 10, 1958, Khrushchev had fired the opening salvo of what would become known as the Berlin Crisis, a gambit meant to force the Western powers to pull their troops out of the city. Khrushchev, who had ousted Bulganin as premier in March 1958 and returned the Soviet Union to one-man rule, promised that Soviet forces would withdraw from the city, pressuring the Americans, British, and French to follow suit. In effect, it was a demand that the Western powers relinquish their right of access to Berlin that had been agreed to at the end of World War II. Doing so would mean abandoning West Berlin. In one fell swoop, Dwight Eisenhower later said, Khrushchev had turned Berlin "into a tinderbox."

"Well, are you preparing to leave Berlin?" Popov asked impishly when he arrived at the safe house where case officer George Kisevalter and Berlin deputy chief David Murphy waited.

"Are you chasing us out?" Kisevalter shot back.

Turning serious, Popov told the CIA officers that he believed

Khrushchev's threat was genuine and that it had been under consideration for some time.

Since the tunnel's discovery more than two years earlier, Popov, in Murphy's estimation, had been Western intelligence's best guarantee of early warning. The Russian also continued to provide sensitive intelligence on Soviet weapons, including missiles and guidance systems, and with his assignment to Karlshorst in June 1957, Popov hit the jackpot. He was now handling GRU "illegals"—Soviet intelligence agents who were given false identities, papers, and biographies, and planted as sleeper spies in the United States and other Western countries. By sharing such information, Popov was giving the West an unprecedented window into one of the most effective Soviet means of espionage.

Now Popov filled in the CIA officers on what he knew about Khrushchev's declaration. The Kremlin was anxious to learn the Western reaction, and Popov's office had instructions from Moscow to find out anything it could. "We are sending in daily reports concerning the popular reactions among the Germans in West Berlin and among the people of the occupation forces to Khrushchev's statement," Popov told them. The KGB, which disguised many of its officers in military positions, was already putting more intelligence officers undercover at the Soviet embassy and other nonmilitary offices where they could stay in Berlin if the Red Army was withdrawn.

The situation was fraught with danger, Popov warned. Already, just four days after Khrushchev's announcement, the Soviets detained a U.S. military convoy at a checkpoint outside West Berlin along the autobahn transit route to West Germany. When the Americans, following standard procedure giving troops of all four powers free access, declined to produce documents, the Soviets refused to allow them to continue or to return to West Berlin. The U.S. commander in Berlin ordered that tanks be prepared to free the convoy by force if necessary. After eight hours of negotiations with the Soviets, the convoy was released.

Popov warned that Khrushchev could use any American use of force to protect its convoys as a pretext for an overwhelming Soviet response. "And in that case, watch your step because, as he has often said, we have sufficient military strength here and may seize West Germany in one day," he told them.

Popov's discussion of Khrushchev's ultimatum was rushed, as there was another pressing matter. A cable from GRU headquarters had arrived at Popov's office the previous morning, summoning him to Moscow to hand-deliver a file about a case he was working.

There were reasons to be alarmed about whether this was the real reason Popov was being called to Moscow. There had been a dustup the previous year when an illegal agent he handled, Margarita Tairova, was sent to the United States to join her husband, another illegal running an important spy ring in New York. Popov had informed Kisevalter, who consulted with Bill Harvey. They had to report Tairova to CIA headquarters, though they knew that Allen Dulles would be obligated to alert Harvey's old nemesis, J. Edgar Hoover, the director of the FBI, which was responsible for combatting Soviet intelligence in the United States. They feared that heavy-handed FBI surveillance would alert Tairova. Harvey later said he was given assurances that this would not happen, but Hoover sent his agents out in force to follow Tairova, who detected the surveillance. She and her husband fled back to Russia, where she reported that she had been compromised. This had caused problems for Popov.

More recently, Popov's superiors had discovered that he had a Yugoslav girlfriend with anticommunist sympathies, and he had been sternly counseled for the security violation. And there were reasons for concern that BOB did not know—including the report on Zhukov's speech that Popov had delivered the previous year and that subsequently made its way to the KGB, perhaps thanks to Blake.

Still, as Kisevalter and Murphy discussed the summons to Moscow with Popov, no alarm bells went off. Popov was not concerned. Nor did the two CIA officers think "it particularly odd that Popov had been called to Moscow to discuss an ongoing case," Murphy later said.

Popov promised to try to find out more about what the fallout from Khrushchev's speech was back in Moscow, but he was mostly concerned about what presents to bring back to friends at home.

A generous soul "with a heart of gold," in Kisevalter's estimation, Popov often used the modest sums he received from the CIA to give gifts such as shirts and fur-lined boots to family and friends. Once he bought a calf so his brother and sister could have milk at their collective farm. "We laughingly claimed to have a CIA calf in the Soviet Union," Kisevalter later said.

As the BOB officers put on their coats at the end of the meeting and prepared to drop the agent off for a train ride back to East Berlin, Popov was still musing about what to bring home.

———

George Blake was eager to make his exit from Berlin. Gillian was pregnant with their second child, and he was feeling increasingly out of sorts about what he called "the whole business of deceiving everyone around me and leading a double life."

"He had acquired what the Communists call bourgeois trappings, a happy home life and family," Gillian later said. "And those were important to him. Of that I'm absolutely certain. But by that time he was so enmeshed that he couldn't get out."

Blake wanted to end his espionage career, but fleeing to Russia did not seem to him a good option. Not only would it mean abandoning his family, he later said, but he considered it "cowardly" to leave without being in any imminent danger of arrest.

But in the fall of 1958, a lifeline appeared. SIS headquarters suggested that he leave Berlin the following spring, return to London for a short stint, and then go to Lebanon to learn Arabic at a language school for diplomats and intelligence officers in the mountain village of Shemlan. After the Suez debacle, SIS needed smart officers with a better understanding of the modern Arab world. Blake, having spent part of his youth in Egypt, had made known his interest in the Middle East. He seemed a natural candidate.

Blake leapt at the offer. "I saw in this an opportunity to bring the work to an early end, and it would give me the opportunity to think of a permanent way out, possibly by trying to get, through my knowledge of Arabic, a good job in an oil company," he said. He seemed unbothered by any contradiction in pursuing work in such a capitalist field.

Gillian, eager to be free from the constraints of embassy life, was keen to go. "I thought a year with George in the mountains learning would be a jolly good idea," she said. Shortly after Christmas, the posting to London came through, and the Blakes prepared to leave Berlin in the spring.

———

Some 90,000 translated messages and conversations and 1,750 reports later, the processing of the Berlin tunnel material finally ended on September 30, 1958. Even more than two years after the taps were shut down, Harvey and his officers were still using tunnel reports in their analysis of Soviet and East German intelligence operations in Berlin. "Bill remained fascinated by this aspect of tunnel production," Murphy recalled. In Washington, CIA analysts continued to crank REGAL material into their assessments of the Soviet threat, including Khrushchev's ultimatum. "We were still getting information from the tunnel operation in 1958 and finding it useful," said Raymond Garthoff, who was then helping draft reports for the CIA's Office of National Estimates.

That would stay the case for years to come. "Because the bulk of the data was fundamental to any assessment of the Soviet military establishment, it remained valuable for a decade and more," Richard Helms later wrote.

The CIA put the total cost of PBJOINTLY at $6.7 million, much more than the $500,000 Harvey and Truscott had estimated it would cost, not including the warehouse construction. Considering all the support the operation required, the true cost was likely considerably more—by some estimates $25 to $30 million. More than one thousand Americans—translators, analysts, clerks, case officers, security guards, and users of the intelligence, among others—participated in some aspect of the operation, even though very few of them knew about the tunnel. The number of British was similarly large.

For many departing the project, it was as if neither the tunnel nor their work on behalf of the operation ever existed. After leaving the Washington processing center, Captain Bob Browne was given an Army assignment that required a sensitive compartmentalized intelligence clearance, something the CIA had conducted before he could work on the tunnel. "The agency would not even verify my clearance to the Army," he recalled. Doing so would mean acknowledging, however obliquely, that there had been a secret operation involving Russian speakers. The clearance had to be redone, a process that took months.

Corporal Eugene Kregg, the choir singer turned tunnel translator, had departed Berlin with his Army enlistment due to end soon. At the recommendation of CIA site manager Vyrl Leichliter and his successor Charlie Arnold, Kregg filled out extensive paperwork to apply to the agency. After being discharged from the Army at Fort Hamilton, New York, he called a telephone number he had been given and reported to CIA headquarters in Washington. Once there, he was directed to an intercom telephone on the wall outside a glass-enclosed receptionist desk.

A male voice was on the line: "I'm sorry, we have nothing for you."

MOSCOW, WINTER 1958-59

On Christmas Day 1958, Popov signaled for a meeting with Russell Langelle, the CIA officer assigned to his case in Moscow. Nine days later, on January 4, 1959, Popov brushed by Langelle on a Moscow street and handed off a written message with alarming news: He had been dismissed from the GRU, supposedly over concerns about his relationship with the Yugoslav woman. He had been told to await a new assignment with the army.

Back in Berlin, Kisevalter was already worried. A BOB source had reported that Popov's wife had prepared their baggage to return to the USSR.

But the news was worse than either Popov or the CIA realized. He was under surveillance by the KGB, which soon intercepted and deciphered a coded letter the CIA sent him with operational instructions. On February 18, 1959, he was arrested and taken to Moscow's Lefortovo prison, long infamous for torture, and the interrogations began.

BERLIN, WINTER 1958-59
—

Khrushchev's formal ultimatum calling for the withdrawal of the four powers from Berlin, delivered in Moscow on November 27, 1958, set a six-month deadline. Otherwise, he warned, the Soviet Union would sign a separate peace treaty with East Germany and cede control of access to the city to the Ulbricht regime, steps that could effectively end West Berlin's status as a free city. Berlin is a "malignant tumor," Khrushchev declared in his speech at the Moscow Sports Palace. "We have decided to do some surgery."

On New Year's Eve, the Allies officially rejected the Soviet demand, setting the stage for a dangerous confrontation. "Fear of a 'Russian invasion' was very real to those who were in Berlin following the ultimatum," according to Murphy. Both SIS and BOB prepared to operate without West Berlin as an espionage base. They distributed invisible ink and trained agents how to write coded messages, and established safe locations to send them. They gave shortwave radios to some agents and set dead drop locations so they could communicate if the city was closed off.

Among the biggest priorities was figuring out how to destroy the mountains of classified files BOB had accumulated for over a decade. Harvey still kept thermite grenades on top of his office safes, but a bigger and quicker method was needed. The agency Technical Services people demonstrated how to use incendiary devices placed on the headquarters roof.

Even as the preparations were made, BOB continued an urgent mission to monitor the Soviet military in East Berlin for any signs they were actually preparing to abandon the city—a critical indication of whether Khrushchev was bluffing. The two best sources for that type of intelligence—the tunnel and Popov—were gone. But other BOB sources sent a stream of information.

On January 16, 1959, BOB sent a cable to headquarters reporting "definite planning for evacuation" of all Soviet military units at Karlshorst. Repair budgets for Soviet military installations at Karlshorst were "drastically cut" in preparation for moving out of

Berlin. But Harvey and his officers suspected that at least some of the intelligence they picked up was being planted by the Soviets to send a false signal. Despite continuing indications in the following weeks that the Soviets were preparing for evacuation, BOB sent a cable to headquarters on February 11 expressing "doubt" that this would happen.

At CIA headquarters, the Office of National Estimates predicted that Khrushchev would back down. Eisenhower was increasingly confident in his determination to stand up to the Soviet leader's demands. He told congressional leaders in March that he had made it clear to the Soviets that "we will not be threatened or pushed out of Berlin," but that he was willing to discuss a peace treaty. Khrushchev, for his part, signaled that he would not go to war over Berlin. Foreign ministers from the four powers began talks in May in Geneva to defuse the crisis. John Foster Dulles, fatally ill with cancer, had resigned as secretary of state in April, and his seat in Geneva was filled by Christian Herter.

On May 27, Eisenhower and Winston Churchill attended the funeral service for Dulles at Washington National Cathedral, joined by many other world statesmen, including the Soviet, U.S., British, and French foreign ministers, who flew in from Geneva. The day also marked the six-month deadline set by Khrushchev, but it passed virtually unnoticed. "It was the ultimatum that, only a few months before, many had feared would bring up the curtain of World War III," Eisenhower later said. "The day came and went—a day lost in history."

But as Eisenhower well knew, the Berlin problem was hardly solved.

———

Popov's arrest had sounded alarms at Moscow Center, proving that the CIA had successfully penetrated Soviet military intelligence. It made clear to the KGB that the CIA's Berlin base remained a major security threat that needed to be neutralized.

"This unit [is] headed by the American Bill Harvey, known by the nickname 'Big Bill,'" a KGB memorandum said. ". . . The available material provides a basis for assuming that 'Big Bill' and his coworkers carry out active intelligence work against the countries of the Socialist camp, for which they have a large agent network."

KGB chairman Ivan Serov was abruptly transferred to take charge of the GRU, ostensibly to strengthen security in the military intelligence agency following the exposure of Popov's betrayal, but more likely because he had fallen out of favor with Khrushchev. Serov was replaced by Aleksandr Shelepin, head of the Communist Youth League.

Disinformation—*dezinformatsiya*—had long been a staple of Soviet intelligence. But in January 1959, Shelepin established a new organization, Department D, to create and coordinate disinformation programs. Department D's first priority was West Berlin. Resuming the drumbeat that followed the discovery of the tunnel, the KGB launched a new campaign portraying West Berlin as an espionage swamp and center of subversive activities.

The State Department feared that the Soviet propaganda might undercut Western solidarity about Berlin at the Geneva talks. BOB prepared a counterattack listing a long catalog of Soviet and East German espionage and covert operations run from East Berlin, many of them discovered by the tunnel. "Now that the tunnel was no longer running, we could use it all, and we did," said Murphy.

In Geneva on June 5, Herter confronted Soviet foreign minister Andrei Gromyko with the evidence, charging that East Berlin was "one of the heaviest concentrations of subversive and spying activities in the world." Gromyko "sat stony-faced through the recital," according to an official U.S. account. Finally, he responded that the Soviet file on Western spying in Berlin was "much more comprehensive" than the American list, but he needed to give only one example: "the matter of the tunnel dug from West to East Berlin."

Nonetheless, the American counterattack, widely reported by the press, blunted the Soviet campaign. "We may hear very little more about it," Herter predicted to Eisenhower.

BERLIN, SPRING 1959

Before leaving Berlin in mid-April, George Blake bade farewell to his long-standing agent, Horst Eitner, a.k.a. Mickey, along with his wife, Brigitte. They dined at a nice restaurant, and then Blake took them to Remde's St. Pauli, a Berlin nightclub well known for its striptease routines.

Max, as they knew him, was unusually exuberant, in good spirits about his pending departure. "He danced with me a number of times and took part with me in a jolly 'follow-your-leader' act for the guests at the club," recalled Brigitte. He even spilled some champagne on her dress in all the excitement.

Blake knew an interesting secret about the Eitners, one that he, of course, did not mention as they celebrated. Ostensibly agents for SIS, the Eitners had betrayed the British and had been working since late 1956 for the GRU. The Soviet military intelligence branch had offered better pay.

When the KGB learned this, they warned Blake, but did not tell the GRU that Blake was their man. Mickey had no idea that Blake was also working for the Soviets. Blake thought the recruiting of Mickey was "pretty pointless," but nothing could be done without explaining to the GRU that Blake was a mole. "On the other hand, it did not seem to matter very much and so it was left at that," he recalled.

That was Berlin in a nutshell. Blake and the Eitners, ostensibly all working for the British, were really working for the Soviets, but no one could talk about it.

———

Despite the stress over his split life, Blake's final years in Berlin had been exceptionally productive. Time and again, he frustrated intricate espionage operations launched by the Berlin CIA and SIS bases, leaving the Americans and British mystified.

In the late 1950s, the CIA learned that the Polish military mission in West Berlin was looking for a residence for its next head of mission. In coordination with the British, BOB deployed agents to work with Berlin real estate brokers, trying to ensure that the Poles would be shown only select properties, with the clear best choice being a nice villa in Wilmersdorf in the American sector. "We spent thousands of hours maneuvering . . . the Poles into signing a long-term lease on this residence," said Ted Shackley, the Berlin base chief of satellite operations. Before the Poles moved in, BOB sent a team of technicians to wire the house "up the kazoo." Base officers Paul Mott and Don Vogel took turns trying to keep the enthusiastic technicians quiet as they bugged every space in the house. "They were making such a racket we were afraid they would wake up the entire neighborhood," Mott recalled. The team placed state-of-the-art miniature microphones throughout the house, some linked to tiny radio transmitters. Others were connected to wires running inside pipes down to the basement, through the backyard, and then continuing via a trench to the next street, where the Americans had rented a safe house and equipped it with banks of tape recorders. When the head of the Polish mission, Wladyslaw Tykocinski, moved in, the CIA was delighted to find him frequently discussing sensitive military and political matters with his staff and foreign visitors. "The initial take was so rewarding," said Shackley. "We could finally see the fruit of our goddamned labors."

But then the Poles abruptly sent in a sweep team. The Americans, confident that the bugs would not be detected by a routine sweep, could hear the search continue for days without success. But then there were signs it was not routine. "We've got to keep looking, we know it's here," the sweep team leader told the others. In the end, the Poles gutted the building's interior and found everything.

The CIA suspected a breach and conducted an extensive counterintelligence review, examining all the agents who worked with the real estate brokers and every American and British officer involved with any aspect of the case. They found nothing, no sign of a leak or even an indiscreet comment.

It was only years later that they learned the reason. Blake had been walking the corridors of SIS headquarters at the Olympic Stadium and overhead two colleagues chatting about the operation, gleaning just enough to report to the Soviets that an unidentified Polish installation in Berlin was being bugged.

Blake also continued his devastation of British agent networks in East Germany. Beginning in 1958, after SIS penetrated East German army offices and government ministries, he helped identify about a hundred spies in East Germany, according to a 1976 Stasi memorandum. His intelligence enabled "the liquidation of the

British secret service agent networks on East German territory,"
the report said.

Those betrayed included high-grade "dangerous agents," among
them Otto Georgi, a senior stenographer assigned to the East German chancellery and parliament who had been reporting to the
British since 1948. He was arrested in March 1958 and sentenced to
life in prison, but released in 1964. Hans Möhring, a State Planning
Commission official arrested in 1959, was sentenced to life imprisonment and released in 1976. The records do not show the fate of an
East German army colonel betrayed by Blake, a possible sign that he
was turned over to the Soviets and executed.

Even while insisting that he was assured by his KGB handlers that
agents he betrayed would come to no harm, Blake was unmoved by
their fates. "The agents whose identities I revealed were not innocent persons," he later said. "Rather they were persons who deliberately set out, more often than not for financial gain, to harm the
interests of their own country and government, knowing the risks
attached to this. In other words, they were in the same position as I
was myself and exposed to the same risks."

LONDON, SPRING AND SUMMER 1959

Blake arrived in London in mid-April 1959 hoping to escape such a
fate. But he was bitterly disappointed to learn that his assignment to
Lebanon was on hold. Superiors at headquarters thought so highly
of his work in Berlin that they assigned him to the British intelligence operational station in London, where his Russian expertise
could assist with espionage against Soviet targets in Britain. He
protested as strenuously as he dared, but had to settle for a promise
that he would be sent to Lebanon in another year's time.

The Blakes, now a family of four following the birth in May of
their second son, James, adjusted to life in England after four years
away, living in suburban Bickley in southeast London. Blake took
the train to work every morning to reach his office at the SIS Directorate of Production at Artillery Mansions on Victoria Street.

Blake's job was to recruit British citizens—businessmen, university dons, students, and scientists—and persuade them to spy on the growing number of Soviets visiting Britain, including trade delegations, scientists, artists, and exchange students. Many of those he approached refused on the grounds that they considered it unethical, which he did not find particularly disappointing. "Of course [I] did not pester them any further," he said.

Blake was more diligent in his work for the Soviets, which involved sabotaging many of the British intelligence operations he learned about. He revealed plans to bug a Russian bank in Moscow, as well as an operation to gather personal information on Soviet officials in Britain in the hopes of blackmailing them. Blake was supposed to encourage British firms working with the Soviets to use an interpreting agency that was staffed by translators secretly working for SIS. Not surprisingly, since he informed the KGB, the scheme was unsuccessful.

Once every three weeks, Blake rendezvoused in a different London suburb with one of his familiar KGB handlers, either the cheerful Vasily Dozhdalev, who had first met Blake in Korea and worked with him in Berlin, or the dour Nikolai Rodin, his first handler, who was again serving as *rezident* in London.

By now, Blake was so confident in both his skills and those of his Soviet handlers that he viewed the danger of being caught in the act of espionage as "virtually nil." What he feared were matters out of his control. In particular, he feared someone like himself—a traitor—who might betray him, someone who "would do for the West what I was doing for the East."

One summer evening, as he and Rodin walked along a quiet street in the London suburb of Croydon, Blake asked what he should do if he was caught. Rodin brusquely refused to even discuss it. "If both of us did everything right, nothing could go wrong," Blake recalled Rodin telling him.

BERLIN, SUMMER 1959

Riding high after six years as Berlin base chief, Bill Harvey prepared in August 1959 for a triumphant return to CIA headquarters.

The tunnel was seen as a wild success. A delighted Allen Dulles had slapped Harvey on the back while awarding him the Distinguished Intelligence Medal for his work on the operation. Berlin was an increasingly coveted posting, one that could make a career. "After the tunnel, an assignment to Berlin became a big deal," said Murphy. "Everyone wanted to go there." Harvey's boys were in high demand for important assignments around the world.

Harvey was cocky, even arrogant, feeling as if his performance in Berlin had put him on a fast track to one of the top spots at the CIA. A prestigious assignment was certainly in hand: He had been chosen to be chief of Division D—the secretive and increasingly important office formerly known as Staff D, overseeing communications intelligence—succeeding Frank Rowlett, who had returned to the NSA in 1958. The senior position was a sign of the high regard and trust Harvey had earned, despite his battles with superiors and reputation for heavy drinking.

Harvey used CIA courier flights to Washington to ship back so many personal weapons—some forty-two revolvers, pistols, rifles, and shotguns—that someone filed an anonymous complaint, sparking an inspector general's investigation. Harvey was unapologetic, explaining that sending that many guns via normal channels, which required documentation, would have made him "stand out like a sore thumb."

Harvey would be leaving Berlin with more than just his arsenal. On the night of August 21, 1958, he and CG went with Dave Murphy and his wife, Marian, to a party thrown by a BOB colleague. Harvey and Murphy departed early to deal with an East German army defector, leaving their wives to get home in CG's car. Arriving at the Murphy home in the Dahlem district, the two women found a brown cardboard shoebox on the doorstep. They spotted a tiny baby inside. Marian Murphy shrieked, attracting the attention of the black-caped neighborhood police watch officer, who came running.

The abandoned baby was wet and cold from an evening rain. Pinned to its clothes was a note in German saying only it had been born ten days earlier. The officer declared that the child should be brought to the police station, but CG refused, insisting the baby needed to be dried off and warmed up. Over the sputtering protests of the officer, the women drove off with the baby, carton and all, to the Harvey home in the nearby Zehlendorf district. Though it was after midnight, CG telephoned and rousted BOB families from their beds, and soon had a crib and a large supply of formula, diapers, and clothing for the infant.

By the time Bill Harvey and Dave Murphy arrived at the house, they found the Berlin police outside the home and chaos inside. "Come in and look what the Lord has sent us," CG told Harvey. "Can we keep it?"

Harvey made a snap decision. "Of course we can," he declared.

The German police thought otherwise and threatened arrests. "Bill was flustered, although he tried to conceal his bubbling excitement," recalled Murphy. "More cops came . . . and Bill told them to get lost." The police reported it as an "unlawful absconding" with an abandoned baby. "This caused a considerable furor in police channels," Harvey acknowledged in a subsequent report to CIA headquarters. Many phone calls were made. Harvey "pulled all the strings he knew how to," recalled Murphy. "He was absolutely determined they were going to keep [the baby], and the hell with what German law said."

All day August 22, there was a continual procession through the house: the mayor of Zehlendorf, police officers, welfare workers, the Army chaplain, doctors, friends, newspapermen, photographers. "It took almost strong-arm methods to maintain a measure of quiet for the child," Harvey's mother, Sara, wrote in a family account of the drama.

The Berlin newspapers were filled with articles about the "cardboard box foundling." Wire service stories carried in American papers reported that the Harveys "went to a friend's party in West Berlin the other night and came home with a baby girl."

Life in Berlin was "seldom dull," Harvey, described as a U.S. diplomat, told the Associated Press. "It's all very, very simple," he added. "My wife found the baby on our friend's doorstep. There was something to be done, and we did it."

Police soon identified and arrested the baby's mother on charges of child abandonment. She was Christa Schmiedgen, an unmarried twenty-six-year-old from the Eastern city of Dresden who had taken refuge in West Berlin in 1956. The child's father still lived in East Germany out of fear for the repercussions his parents would face should he defect to the West. Once the baby was born, Schmiedgen decided to turn the child over to a Western family with the means to raise her. Scoping out the neighborhoods around the Dahlem women's clinic, she settled on the Murphy home. She had not realized the family was American, much less with the CIA, but picked the house because the occupants seemed well-to-do.

In 1950s Berlin, it seemed anyone could be a spy, even a baby. There were jokes around BOB that the infant might be wired or even a KGB plant. Harvey felt obliged to send a three-page memo to headquarters explaining the situation. The facts, he insisted, "reflect that this incident does not involve any possibility of blackmail or pressure and did not involve any compromise of cover or security."

No objections to the Harveys' planned adoption of the girl were raised at headquarters. Equally important, Christa Schmiedgen was on board. After being jailed for three weeks and released pending trial, she asked to see the baby. "She wanted to see where her baby was and to know something of its environment," Sara Harvey later wrote. "Bill arranged for the visit and sent a car for her. . . . Certainly it was for her a very difficult situation. She was much moved. Still, she conducted herself with great composure and dignity."

Schmiedgen signed a waiver agreeing to the child's adoption by the Harveys. "It's painful for me but best for the child," she told a judge. Harvey arranged for an attorney to represent her at her trial, and she was given a six-month suspended sentence, and then American assistance in getting a job.

The adoption of the child, whom the Harveys named Sally, took longer to resolve. "It required practically an act of God to get permission for the Harveys to adopt Sally," recalled Hugh Montgomery, whose language skills were put to use navigating the red tape. Ultimately, the determination of Bill and CG Harvey won out. "Not even German bureaucracy could stop that train from going down the tracks," said Montgomery.

German authorities issued a birth certificate for Sally Josephine Harvey on July 1, 1959. When the Harveys prepared to fly home to Washington the next month, the Berlin papers covered the departure of the cardboard box foundling, now something of a celebrity. Photos showed Bill, CG, and ten-year-old Jimmy laughing delightedly with one-year-old Sally. The smiling family posed on the gangway boarding the Pan American flight that would take the girl from Berlin. There was no hint that the driving force behind the famous Berlin tunnel was leaving town on the same plane.

MOSCOW, FALL 1959

Pyotr Popov arrived at the Aragvi Restaurant on Gorky Street on the evening of September 18 wearing the nicely tailored uniform of a full colonel in the Red Army Transportation Corps. The Aragvi was famous both for its spicy Georgian cuisine and as a rendezvous spot for foreigners and spies. Popov was there to meet his CIA liaison, Russell Langelle. KGB officers stationed in and around the restaurant watched his every move.

After his arrest by the KGB in February, Popov had quickly confessed, but acted remorseful and downplayed the extent of his espionage. He had agreed to cooperate with the KGB, hoping to lessen his punishment. The GRU needed time to arrange the return of the "illegals" Popov had handled, and the KGB decided to double him back against the Americans. In the months that followed, the Soviets carefully controlled his contact with the CIA, trying to learn whether he had accomplices.

Nonetheless, Popov managed to send subtle signals to the CIA that all was not well. His previous messages had been written from back to front, but now the pages were written in conventional order. The CIA's suspicions were further heightened by the pedestrian intelligence included—very unlike the usual wealth of information Popov delivered.

At the restaurant, Popov was carrying two messages. One was a notebook, authored by the KGB, with intelligence of little value. The second was a letter he had written in pencil on eight small pieces of paper and tightly rolled into a cylinder the size of a cigarette. It was wrapped in cloth and suspended with a string inside his pants.

At precisely 8:15, Popov walked into the restroom, where Langelle was washing his hands at a sink. Another man, likely a KGB observer, was inside a toilet stall. Wordlessly, Popov motioned to Langelle that he was wired for sound. He gave the CIA officer the notebook, but as he shook Langelle's hand, he also managed to slip him the cylinder letter.

The letter, still smelling of Popov's shaving lotion, was delivered to George Kisevalter in Berlin. As he deciphered it, Kisevalter began to cry.

Popov warned that he had been arrested in February and was under KGB control, and he gave details about his interrogation. They had questioned him extensively about Zhukov's speech, trying to make sure they had caught the person who gave it to the CIA. Popov laid out what the KGB knew and did not know about his collaboration with the CIA, including what it knew from sources other than his confession.

He theorized that the KGB intended to publicly arrest him soon and use him as a propaganda coup to embarrass the Americans. Khrushchev was at that moment in the midst of the first trip to the United States by a Soviet premier, an attempt to break the continued stalemate over Berlin. He was scheduled to begin talks in a few days with Eisenhower at Camp David in Maryland.

At the end of the message, Popov plaintively asked if there was anything Eisenhower could do on his behalf, or for his family. Reading that, recalled Kisevalter, "I literally bawled." Popov was doomed, Kisevalter realized. "There was nothing that any one of us could do," he said. Harvey also took the news hard, blaming himself for trusting headquarters in the Tairova case.

Though some at the CIA suspected that Popov's secret message was also a KGB production, further analysis of the cylinder letter, including the language and style of writing Popov used and the valuable intelligence it contained, convinced Kisevalter, Murphy, and others that it was genuine. "Above all, it was an extraordinary act of courage and exemplary tradecraft on Popov's part," in Murphy's judgment.

"He was a true Russian patriot," said Kisevalter. "Everything that he did, he did for the Russian peasant, not for himself."

The KGB soon ended the charade. All the GRU illegals whom

Popov might have betrayed had safely returned to the USSR. Popov's next meeting with Langelle was on October 16, 1959, aboard bus 107 in downtown Moscow, where Popov passed along a message as the men brushed by each other. When Langelle alighted from the bus, he was grabbed by five KGB men and hustled by car to a nearby apartment building. For the next two hours, he was pressured to spy for the KGB. When he refused, he was expelled from the country in a blaze of publicity. In East Germany, the Stasi began arresting BOB agents who had worked with Popov, including the East Berlin pensioner known as the Old Man, who was imprisoned for more than two years.

Popov was brought before the Military Collegium of the Soviet Supreme Court on January 6, 1960, and found guilty of treason. In June 1960, the gallant Russian was put before a firing squad and executed.

Oleg Gordievsky, a KGB officer who would defect to Britain, later said, "The demise of this brave man must lie heavy on the conscience of the Anglo-American intelligence community."

CHAPTER 22

Sniper

The letters were typed single-spaced, written in good colloquial German, and simply signed *Heckenschütze*—Sniper.

The notes, which began in April 1958 with a letter sent to the U.S. ambassador to Switzerland, contained enough information to confirm that the writer had access to classified material. They quoted from secret NATO documents and gave details of Soviet and Polish intelligence operations.

The identity of Sniper had become an urgent priority for the CIA. Howard Roman, a gifted German linguist and OSS veteran who was handling the case, had deduced from the syntax and material in the letters that the writer was not a native German speaker, but rather an officer in the Polish intelligence service, the Urząd Bezpieczeństwa, known as the UB.

Sniper was clearly an intelligence professional, setting the rules for when, where, and how he communicated with the CIA. "Questions were put to him, but he pretty much ran us," recalled William Donnelly, then a young CIA officer in the Warsaw station who picked up documents and film from dead drops and left cash for the mysterious agent.

The stakes of the case rose as Sniper began to deliver vague but explosive hints that the KGB had penetrated British intelligence.

The CIA pressed for details. Sniper said the Soviets had two important spies in Britain. One he identified as LAMBDA 1 was in British intelligence; a second he called LAMBDA 2 was in the Royal Navy. Sniper had provided clues to LAMBDA 2's identity, including a rough approximation of his name and the fact that he had been recruited years earlier when he was stationed in Warsaw.

Sniper had less information about LAMBDA 1. But in November 1959, just weeks after Popov's public arrest on a Moscow bus, Sniper gave the CIA detailed information that the KGB had learned from secret British documents it had obtained from LAMBDA 1.

Roman traveled to London to brief a group of senior SIS and MI5 officers about the two spies. After his report, MI5 was soon on the trail of a LAMBDA 2 suspect. As for LAMBDA 1, the British identified three SIS documents the spy must have seen based on the information the KGB had. One was a list of Polish nationals whom the SIS station in Warsaw had identified for possible recruitment as agents. The other two were from annual reports summarizing intelligence that SIS had received. All were close-hold, accessible only to a small number of people in British intelligence at the Berlin or Warsaw stations. SIS drew up a list of ten officers who would have had access to all three documents. Among them was George Blake.

———

The investigation into LAMBDA 1 was led by SIS officer Terrence Lecky, a quiet classicist who served as the chief of British counterintelligence. British intelligence still tended to view their officers as beyond reproach, and Blake was too highly regarded to be seriously considered a suspect. "His behaviour gave no reason for doubting his integrity," according to a subsequent SIS report. The investigators believed he "could not possibly be a spy," recalled Peter Wright. The other nine officers were likewise cleared after their records were examined.

Lecky came up with an alternative explanation for the breach. Two years earlier, there had been an unsolved burglary of a safe in the SIS station in Brussels. While there was no complete record of the contents, there was evidence that at least one of the documents reported by Sniper had been in the safe.

In the spring of 1960, the British informed the CIA that the documents seen by LAMBDA 1 apparently came from the Brussels burglary. The matter came to a rest, for now.

SHEMLAN, LEBANON, FALL 1960

To his immense relief, George Blake was finally freed from duty in London and departed for Lebanon in September 1960. His assignment to the Arabic-language school had almost been derailed. His chief, Robert Dawson, eager to keep him on the job targeting Soviets in Britain, tried to extend his assignment in London by three years. Blake could see his vision of escaping espionage being snuffed out. "I refused to do this and said that if he insisted I would resign from the service," he recalled. The personnel office relented and approved his assignment to Lebanon.

Blake went first, driving the family car stuffed with prams, suitcases, and children's toys to Venice and continuing by ship to Beirut. Gillian flew in with the children two weeks later.

Shemlan was stunning, a village of low, white-terraced homes strung along a winding road on the coastal mountain range above Beirut. Blake rented a stone house that was a short walk from the school and had a large veranda with a view of the sprawling city below and the blue Mediterranean behind it.

The Middle East Centre for Arab Studies, or MECAS, was funded by the British Foreign Office, and featured an intensive language program for about four dozen students. Most of them were foreign service officers, but there were also a handful of intelligence officers as well as a few businessmen from various countries working for oil companies and banks. Blake, under cover as a foreign service officer, was in his element, excelling in his studies with his natural facility for languages and Egyptian background. Louis Wesseling, a thirty-two-year-old Dutch businessman who befriended Blake, considered him "the star of the class." Miles Copeland Jr., a retired CIA officer who lectured at the school, sent a report to the CIA describing Blake as "a gifted language student" who should be an intelligence officer, unaware that he was already working for two services.

Blake, highly regarded because of his record in World War II, Korea, and Berlin, was embraced by the local British intelligence community. Nicholas Elliott, chief of the SIS Beirut station, considered him an officer with potential to go far in SIS, describing him as "a good-looking fellow . . . with excellent manners and universally popular."

One intelligence operative in Beirut whom Blake did not meet was fellow traitor Kim Philby. As of yet, Blake did not know that Philby had worked for SIS and was "like me, a Soviet agent," while Philby had never even heard of Blake. Philby was working as a correspondent for several British periodicals, which provided cover for some work as an agent for SIS arranged by Elliott, his longtime friend, who still believed in Philby's innocence.

Soon after his arrival, Blake made contact with the KGB *rezident* in Beirut, Pavel Nedosekin. Since Blake would have little access to operational information in Lebanon, they agreed that meeting every two months would be enough. Nedosekin gave Blake a telephone number to call in an emergency.

The KGB had been disappointed by Blake's transfer to Lebanon, preferring that he stay in London and continue his rich reporting on SIS operations targeting the Soviet Union. Blake had concealed his own preferences from the KGB. "In reporting my new assignment to the Russians I did not say that it was my own choice that I had been sent to Lebanon but that this was a decision of the Service, which it would be unwise to go against," he said.

For the Blakes, their new life was an idyllic one. "We were frightfully happy there," recalled Gillian, who was pregnant with their third child. They hired a local Lebanese girl named Khadijh as a live-in maid to help with Anthony, then three, and James, one. Blake would go to class in the morning and come home in the afternoon. He romped with the children for a bit, then withdrew to a closed room to study.

There were many outings in the country with the children and the families of other students with whom the Blakes became close. Blake was relaxed with his new friends, making no secret of his leftist views—a surprising political perspective for someone who was supposedly a British foreign service officer. He made clear his distaste for capitalism and his dislike of royal pomp, even predicting to Louis Wesseling that the British royal house was finished.

Recalled Wesseling, "I said to my wife, 'Is that allowed, that he talks that way?'"

BERLIN, SATURDAY, OCTOBER 15, 1960

It was an annual tradition for Horst Eitner and his wife, Brigitte, to celebrate the anniversary of her release from the Soviet camp where she had been imprisoned for spying for the Americans. On the night of October 15, marking her fifth year of freedom, they joined as usual with one of Brigitte's girlfriends, who had been released by the Soviets on the same day.

The Eitners were a hot-tempered, hard-drinking couple, and this evening was no exception. The party consumed ample quantities of liqueur, brandy, and prosecco at dinner and continued with visits to several bars. By midnight, "Mickey" was flirting with his wife's girlfriend at Bierquelle, a drinking establishment on Schlüterstrasse. Brigitte was incensed and demanded he stop. When he ignored her, Brigitte threatened to go to the police and inform them he was spying for the Soviets. Eitner laughed and told her to do what she liked.

Brigitte stormed from the bar and went to a nearby police station. "My husband is a Soviet spy," she announced. The police thought she was simply drunk and tried to send her away. But she persuaded them to come to the nearby Eitner apartment on Wielandstrasse, where she showed the officers two microphones that had been hidden by the Soviets. The police went to Bierquelle, where Eitner was still drunkenly cavorting with Brigitte's girlfriend, and arrested him at 6 a.m.

Under questioning in the days that followed, and confronted with his wife's statements, Eitner admitted to spying for both the British and the Soviets. A week after the arrest, SIS officers questioned him. He told them that after the controller he knew as Max de Vries left Berlin, the Soviets had asked if they could put microphones in his apartment so they could monitor conversations with the new British case officer. This raised a troubling question: Why had the Soviets not bothered to bug the apartment when Eitner was working with Max—or, as SIS knew him, George Blake?

BERLIN, WINTER 1960-61

Sniper had been given an emergency telephone number to call at the Berlin base switchboard should he ever need to make immediate contact. "The operators had been warned that if they missed his call, they would be on the next boat home," according to David Murphy, now the Berlin base chief.

The operators did not miss the call when it came in December 1960. Sniper reported that he was ready to defect to the West, and he would be arriving in Berlin over the New Year holiday. BOB scrambled to put together a plan. No one knew what Sniper looked like, so a clandestine meeting on a street corner was ruled out. In subsequent communications, Sniper was instructed to call once he was in Berlin and report to the American consulate in Dahlem, which was easily accessible to civilians.

At 5:30 p.m. on January 4, 1961, Sniper called and "confirmed delivery of the package in about a half hour," according to a CIA report. He would be accompanied by his wife, for whom he requested "careful and considerate handling."

At 6:06, a West Berlin taxi pulled up in front of the American consulate on Clayallee. A husky, dark-haired man with a large guardsman's mustache climbed out. He and a woman accompanying him were each carrying a small piece of luggage. They looked around nervously before being escorted up the consulate steps and inside the building.

Once the couple was seated in an office, a CIA officer posing as a consular official told Sniper that they were now under the protection of the U.S. government and that a military plane was standing by to fly them to West Germany and then on to the United States, where he and his wife would be granted asylum and U.S. citizenship. The guarantees were contingent, however, on Sniper identifying himself and "making available to the U.S. government all information in his possession deemed of interest—regardless of how long this might take."

At that point, there was a pause, according to the CIA report. "Subject, with obvious embarrassment," explained that his companion was not actually his wife, but his mistress, and asked if she could still be granted asylum, the report said. He was "assured that this made no difference."

Sniper asked the woman to step out of the room, and he then explained to the American that not only did she not know he was an intelligence officer, but she did not know his true name. Listening in from the next room, Murphy and his deputy, John Dimmer, grew anxious as they heard the bizarre conversation. "Who was this guy?" Murphy recalled thinking.

Sniper fumbled through his briefcase and pulled out papers identifying himself as Lieutenant Colonel Michael Goleniewski, the forty-year-old former deputy chief of Polish military counterintelligence and now director of the scientific-technical branch for Polish foreign intelligence. In the next room, there were "great sighs of relief" that Sniper appeared to be a genuine defection, Murphy said. Goleniewski's companion, for her part, was stoic in the face of "what, by any criterion, must have been the most surprising evening of her life," according to the CIA report.

Goleniewski and the woman were flown the next day from Berlin to West Germany, and then on to the United States. "If the KGB knew we were on this plane, they would shoot it down," Goleniewski told the CIA's Howard Roman, who accompanied them on the flight. After landing at Andrews Air Force Base outside Washington, Goleniewski was taken to Ashford Farm, a remote Tudor-style mansion overlooking the Choptank River on Maryland's Eastern Shore that was used as a CIA safe house for defectors.

The debriefings that followed showed Goleniewski to be "an experienced counterintelligence officer of rare sharpness and professionalism," a CIA officer later said. He had an "extraordinary memory," according to an agency report, with an encyclopedic recall for the names, specialties, training, and idiosyncrasies of hundreds of Polish, KGB, and GRU officers.

Goleniewski knew a great deal about KGB intelligence. He had been recruited by the KGB in 1957 to spy on the UB, his own intelligence agency, so the Russians could keep tabs on the Poles. He was liked and trusted by his KGB handlers, which allowed him to pick up a good deal of their shop talk and boasts. But in August 1960, one of the handlers told Goleniewski the KGB suspected that someone in the Polish service was a Western mole. He was asked to help root out the spy, but as he felt the noose tightening, he decided to defect.

In the days that followed his arrival, Goleniewski provided a host of new intelligence, including further clues as to the identity of LAMBDA 1, the Soviet mole within SIS. He was contemptuous of the failure to find the spy, and ridiculed the idea that the documents he had reported to be in the hands of the KGB had been stolen from a safe in Brussels.

LONDON, JANUARY 1961

Goleniewski's defection forced the British to take immediate action against LAMBDA 2. Based on Sniper's letters, he had been identified months earlier as Harry Houghton, a Royal Navy civilian employee assigned to the Underwater Weapons Establishment in Portland.

Houghton had turned out to be just one piece of an astonishing spy ring. He was having an affair with a coworker, Ethel Gee, who had access to secret documents, including material about U.S. nuclear submarines. Surveillance of Houghton on visits to London found him regularly meeting and handing off material to a Canadian named Gordon Lonsdale, who ran a business leasing jukebox machines in London while living the life of a playboy. Further surveillance uncovered the other members of the spy ring, Morris and Lona Cohen, a married American couple wanted by the FBI on suspicion of being accomplices of Julius and Ethel Rosenberg, the atomic bomb spies who had been executed for treason eight years earlier. Posing as convivial New Zealanders who operated a small antiquarian book business on the Strand, the Cohens were using a high-frequency transmitter to send the naval secrets Lonsdale collected from Houghton and Gee to Moscow. Lonsdale—born Konon

Molody in Moscow, raised in California, and groomed by Soviet intelligence from an early age to be an illegal with a false identity—was the ringleader.

Warned on January 4 that Sniper was defecting and fearing this could tip the Soviets that the spy ring had been blown, the British arrested Lonsdale, Houghton, and Gee on January 7 as they exchanged documents and cash on Waterloo Road. Almost simultaneously, the Cohens were arrested at their home.

The Portland spy ring story caused a sensation in England. Inside SIS, the exposure of LAMBDA 2 as a dangerous threat added urgency to the question: Who was LAMBDA 1?

———

Dick White had grown uneasy with the investigation blaming the leak of the documents on the Brussels burglary. White had served as director-general of MI5 for three years prior to being appointed chief of SIS in 1956 to succeed John Sinclair after his resignation in the wake of the frogman episode. He still considered himself a counterintelligence officer at heart, and had assigned a new man to review the clues: the cerebral and unflappable Harry Shergold, a hard-nosed and respected SIS Soviet specialist.

Shergold was "very thoughtful and very honest, which is surprising in this business," recalled Volker Foertsch, a senior West German counterintelligence officer. Perhaps most important, Shergold seemed to have a sixth sense about whether a defector was genuine, or whether an officer was telling the truth. "Shergy had the nose," Nicholas Elliott later told John le Carré.

Working with the Soviet desk at Broadway, Shergold reexamined the clues Goleniewski had provided. A careful study was done of the documents the KGB was known to have acquired, establishing that all had been seen by Blake while he was in Berlin from 1955 to 1959. By spring, after examining the records of all those with access to the documents, Shergold "strongly suspected" that Blake was the Soviet agent, according to an SIS report.

In Berlin, meanwhile, Horst Eitner was telling West German intelligence and SIS everything he knew—and a lot he did not—about his British handler, the man he knew as Max de Vries. Facing trial and prison sentencing, he also passed on gossip he claimed to know from a Russian intelligence officer about a KGB agent in SIS.

For Shergold, the Eitner investigation was the clincher. He homed in on the microphones placed in the apartment only after Blake's departure. The timing suggested that the Soviets had no need to listen to Blake's conversations. "I'm ninety percent sure Blake's our man," Shergold told Dick White in mid-March.

Reviewing Blake's peripatetic background, White was "alarmed and perhaps surprised" at how little SIS internal security procedures had improved since Philby's exposure ten years earlier. The vetting he had been given appeared cursory. Looking at Blake's assignments, White felt a cold shiver as he realized how much he had been in a position to betray for nearly a decade. This, White decided, was "much worse than Philby."

But there was no hard evidence. "We need a confession and an assessment of the damage he's caused," White said. It had to be done fast. He was worried there could be a leak tipping Blake that he was under suspicion. Beirut was not secure enough for an interrogation. White wanted Blake back in London as quickly as possible.

In late March, headquarters sent two letters to Elliott, the SIS Beirut station chief. The first reported that Blake was suspected of being a KGB agent and that he needed to be sent back to London without arousing his suspicion. The second was a letter addressed to Blake, instructing him to return to London for several days of consultations concerning his next posting.

Elliott was shocked, but quickly got to work. His secretary was friends with Gillian Blake, having worked with her at SIS in London. Elliott assigned her to determine the family's whereabouts in the coming days.

SHEMLAN, MARCH 1961

Spring in Shemlan was pastoral. "George and I used to walk a lot too, as it is particularly beautiful at this time, with the olive groves on the way to Beirut now lush and green, and the sea a deep blue, and distant mount peaks still covered in snow," Gillian wrote. "We often talked of the coming summer and made plans for all the different things we would do after the baby, due in May, was born."

In late March, the Blakes had a brief scare when their son Anthony came down with pneumonia after being caught in a sudden downpour during a mountain walk. He had been hospitalized and had recovered nicely, but was being kept in the hospital for several days while his health returned.

All the while, Blake and the other students were buried in books, preparing for end-of-term exams. But there was still time to discuss the latest news from England, including reports about the Portland spy ring, whose members were now on trial.

"This case is not as important as you think," Blake told Louis Wesseling.

"Why not?" Wesseling asked.

"Because these people spied for money," Blake said. "If people spied for their principle, those are the ones who are really dangerous."

By an odd series of coincidences, Blake found himself at the theater Saturday evening, March 25, for a production of *Charley's Aunt,* put on by the local British drama group. Nicholas Elliott's secretary had paid a visit that day to the hospital where George and Gillian were with Anthony. It turned out she had a spare ticket to that evening's performance and suggested that George accompany her. "I was not very keen, but my wife insisted that a break from the books would do me good and I allowed myself to be persuaded," Blake recalled.

The play turned out to be "indeed funny," and Blake was enjoying himself. During the intermission they went for a drink at the bar, where they ran into Nicholas Elliott and his wife, who invited them to join them.

"In the course of the conversation, he drew me aside and said he was glad I happened to be there as this saved him a trip up the mountain to see me," Blake recalled. Elliott nonchalantly passed along word that headquarters had sent a note asking Blake to make a brief visit to London to discuss an upcoming assignment. Broadway suggested that he fly from Beirut in about a week's time, on the Monday after Easter, in order to be available in London the following Tuesday morning.

Elliott's hope was that the casual nature of the staged encounter and the framing of the letter from headquarters as a request rather than a directive would keep Blake's guard down. But Blake was instantly suspicious. After he dropped the secretary at her home following the play, his mind was in turmoil as he drove up the dark mountain road to Shemlan.

"I could not make it out," he later said. "There was something wrong somewhere." Why recall him now, when he was in the midst of exams? Why not wait until July, when he would be home on holiday? By the time he reached home, there was no doubt in his mind.

Blake had a valid visa for Syria, just a few hours drive away. He decided that as soon as his son was released from the hospital, he would drive with the whole family to Damascus, where they could board a flight for Moscow. "There I would explain the situation to [Gillian] exactly as it was, however painful this might be, and leave her to decide whether to accompany me to the Soviet Union or take the car and the children back to Beirut and return to England," he wrote.

But in the morning he reconsidered. Perhaps he was jumping to conclusions. He first arranged an emergency meeting with Pavel Nedosekin, his KGB handler in Lebanon. They met that evening on a deserted beach near Beirut, and Blake described his dilemma. Nedosekin promised to immediately consult with Moscow Center.

Nedosekin soon reported back that headquarters did not see any cause for alarm. In London, Nikolai Rodin saw no problems and approved Agent Diomid's return. Blake felt overwhelming relief. "The moment of truth had been put off," he later reflected. "I did not have to confess to my wife that I was a Soviet agent."

He turned his mind back to his exams. When the results were posted on Thursday, March 30, he had done well, finishing in the top four. That night, students celebrated with a black-tie dinner at one of Beirut's more expensive restaurants, followed by some gambling at the elegant Casino du Liban. "I won; then lost all my gains in a single throw," recalled Blake.

———

On Friday, Blake went to the British embassy to see Elliott and collect money for his airfare. The station chief was spending sleepless nights fearing Blake would defect, but did his best to appear calm. Elliott showed him the letter from headquarters. "It read innocuously enough," Blake recalled. "He could add nothing to it and wished me a pleasant journey with a bland smile."

Seemingly as an afterthought, Elliott offered to make arrangements for Blake to stay at the St. Ermin's Hotel, across the street from the Broadway headquarters—a spot where it would be easy for SIS to keep tabs on him. Blake declined, saying he would be staying with his mother at her home in Radlett, north of London. Elliott persisted, and Blake insisted there was no need. "For a moment the shadow of a doubt again crossed my mind," he recalled. "Strange, this insistence on staying at the St. Ermin's. But it passed away again."

Blake did not give Gillian any indication that he was even "remotely worried" about the trip to London. The Blakes made a lovely Easter Sunday excursion to the ancient city of Byblos, with its beautiful Maronite churches and majestic Greek temples. That night some of Blake's friends held a party for him to celebrate what they assumed would be a plum assignment with the Foreign Office. Everyone in Shemlan had been guessing what it might be. "We had champagne, and we were congratulating George," recalled Trudy Wesseling, Louis's wife. "We said, 'This is going to be wonderful, and we'll have a party when you get back.'"

But she noticed that Blake did not seem as happy about it as they were. "He was certainly in doubt about what would happen to him if he went back," she said.

His flight was on Monday, April 3. "We drove down to the airport on a perfect spring morning and he said goodbye, promising to try and be back before the weekend," Gillian recalled. Anthony's fourth birthday party would be on Saturday and Blake did not want to miss it.

LONDON, TUESDAY, APRIL 4

Shortly after 10 a.m., Blake reported as instructed to the SIS personnel office and was shown to the office of the deputy head of the department. He was surprised to find Harry Shergold also waiting. After a friendly welcome, Shergold suggested that Blake accompany him. "He wanted to discuss certain questions which had arisen in connection with my work in Berlin," Blake said.

Blake expected that they would go to the Head Office, across the street at Broadway, but they instead walked across St. James's Park to a location he knew intimately: his old office at Carlton Gardens. It was where he had met Gillian, and where he had learned of the tunnel. But now he felt a sense of foreboding. They entered the reception room on the ground floor, where Blake found Terrence Lecky and Ben Johnson, a former police officer experienced in interrogating defectors, sitting at a table. It was a grand room, with a nice view of the park, along with space in the adjacent room for equipment to surreptitiously record the conversation.

Dick White was determined to avoid a repeat of the debacle with Philby, who had been able to evade any admission of guilt during his questioning. White was hoping that Shergold's cool, nonconfrontational style coupled with Blake's respect for the Soviet specialist might draw out a confession. Shergold's skill at eliciting answers was well established—during World War II, he had been in charge of British Eighth Army prisoner interrogation at El Alamein and Cassino.

There was some polite conversation, but there was little doubt that Blake was facing an interrogation. Shergold began by describing in detail the arrest of Horst Eitner, and then asking Blake why he thought the Soviets had installed microphones in the apartment only after another officer took over the case. Blake replied that he did not have "the faintest idea."

Since "Mickey" had been a double agent, Shergold continued, it stood to reason that "Boris," the Soviet economic official Blake had recruited to much kudos, was actually a KGB plant. Blake did not dispute this, but again professed to be mystified.

After several hours of this, they broke for lunch. "Nobody suggested, as would normally have been the case, that we should have lunch together," Blake later said. "I thought this was a bad sign." Dining alone at a little Italian restaurant in Soho he had frequented in the old days, he consoled himself with the thought that the evidence thus far presented was circumstantial. If that was all they had, he reasoned, he was safe. The Mickey and Boris episodes were the type of thing that happened all the time in Berlin, where double agents or even triple agents were routine.

His optimism waned in the afternoon when the subject shifted to Poland. Lecky gazed menacingly at a stack of fourteen files ostentatiously piled on the table. Blake was told that they contained sensitive SIS documents that he was among the few to see. How could he account for the fact they had found their way into the hands of the KGB? "I said I couldn't and that their guess was as good as mine," he recalled.

Through the afternoon, his interrogators pressed him, and Blake continued to deny knowledge. By the end of the day, they accused him of being a Soviet spy. "Absolutely untrue!" Blake declared.

The session ended and Blake was told to return the following morning at 10 a.m. Well aware that he was under surveillance, he returned to his mother's place in Radlett. There was no point in calling the Soviets, he realized—there was nothing they could do. At home, he pretended all was well. Catherine Blake, an inveterate organizer, was focused on a shopping list of items Gillian wanted him to bring back to Lebanon, in particular mosquito nets. But inside, Blake was in agony. He realized he was in great danger, and that SIS must have a high-level source in Polish intelligence. Nonetheless, he later said, "I still thought I could save myself."

Throughout the second day of questioning, he steadfastly maintained his innocence. "It wasn't leading anywhere, really," he said. "Because they kept on saying 'We know you're a Soviet spy,' and I kept saying, 'No, I'm not.'" On his lunch break, he dutifully went to Gamages, a London department store, to order Gillian's mosquito nets. When the questioning wrapped up for the evening, he returned to Radlett, told his mother he was exhausted and lay in his room alone with his thoughts.

On the third day, Thursday, April 6, the interrogation continued in the same manner. Shergold was starting to despair, knowing the evidence was purely circumstantial. "As the hours of his interrogation continued, BLAKE showed no indication of weakening," according to a memo Allen Dulles gave to the White House a month later, based on an account from Dick White. "It began to appear that the effort to break him would be unsuccessful. The carefully prepared ammunition had been largely shot away without breaching his defense. The prospect of his getting away with his denials loomed ominously."

After lunch, Shergold tried a line of questioning designed to provoke Blake. "Look, we know that you were working for the Soviets, but we understand why," he said. "While you were their prisoner in Korea, you were tortured and made to confess that you were a British intelligence officer. From then on you were blackmailed. You had no choice but to collaborate with them."

Shergold had hit a nerve. "Suddenly I felt terribly indignant," Blake later said. This offended his ego, his vision of himself as a man above country. "I wanted them to know that I had acted out of conviction, out of a belief in communism and not under duress or for financial gain," he said.

"No, nobody tortured me! No, nobody blackmailed me!" he sputtered at his interrogators. "I myself approached the Soviets and offered my service to them of my own accord!"

His questioners "listened to me in amazed silence," Blake recalled. "Whether by luck or by planning, they hit upon the right psychological approach," he added. "All I can say is that it was a gut reaction."

"After another half hour, Blake might have been free," Shergold later said.

Blake began to describe his espionage in great detail. As he continued, Ben Johnson hurried across St. James's Park to fill in Dick White, who was exhilarated to have a confession. But the SIS senior legal adviser, Bernard Hill, warned that because Blake had not been cautioned on his rights, he could withdraw his confession.

"We need to do it by the book," White said. "We'll have to play him along." Shergold was instructed to maintain a friendly tone and keep Blake talking.

The cat out of the bag, a relieved Blake was happy to cooperate. A chauffeur-driven car took him to Radlett to get some rest before continuing in the morning. He had promised not to reveal anything to his mother, and he told her only that his return to Lebanon had been postponed because he needed to attend an urgent conference outside London for several days.

White telephoned Sir Reginald Manningham-Buller, the attorney general, to discuss the case. SIS wanted to keep Blake over the weekend in the hopes of getting a fuller picture of the extent of the damage, White told him.

"Just make sure you bring him back alive," said Manningham-Buller.

SHERGOLD'S COTTAGE, HAMPSHIRE, WEEKEND OF APRIL 7 TO APRIL 9

On Friday evening, after Blake completed his formal statement to police at Carlton Gardens, the spy and his interlocutors headed off for a weekend in the country. The thought was that a friendly atmosphere would keep him talking. The group included Shergold, Johnson, and John Quine, an old acquaintance who had been Tokyo station chief when Blake was in Korea and was now a senior counterintelligence officer. They headed to Shergold's holiday cottage in a village in Hampshire, south of London, where they were warmly greeted by Shergold's wife and mother-in-law.

The atmosphere was somewhat "surreal," Blake later said, "with everyone pretending that this was just an ordinary weekend party among friends." One difference was that the house was surrounded by police and every time the guests went out for a walk, a police car slowly followed.

"It was a bizarre situation which struck me as very English—I should say endearingly English," Blake said. When it was suggested they have pancakes, he offered to make them. "Here I was a confessed spy . . . in the kitchen with the old grandmother making pancakes, because I was quite good at making pancakes," he recalled.

He shared a bedroom with Quine, and at night they spoke about his motives. "I had a feeling he was trying hard to understand," Blake said. In the relaxed setting, the spy gave more details about the massive scope of his espionage, confessing he had photographed every document that crossed his desk.

Back at Broadway, where frantic work was under way, there was an air of disbelief. "I'm having difficulty persuading some of the staff that he's a spy," White admitted. He was disgusted as reports came in from the cottage describing the extent of Blake's work for the Soviets. "He's like a sponge," White said.

Senior SIS officials debated whether Blake should be charged with a crime. No officer had ever been prosecuted for espionage. Some argued that a public trial would damage the service. But there was no sense in offering him immunity in exchange for cooperation, as he had already been telling all. White was in favor of prosecuting, but only if there were assurances that Blake would not contest his confession. "If he isn't prepared to plead guilty, we'll just put him on a plane to Moscow," he said.

Shergold assured him that Blake showed no signs of recanting.

WASHINGTON

Prime Minister Harold Macmillan had always found espionage unpleasant. With his hooded eyes and mustache, and his penchant for grouse hunting in the moors while dressed smartly in tweed, he had an Old World air that made him look like a figure transported from Edwardian England to 1960s Britain.

Like his predecessor, Anthony Eden, Macmillan had been unhappy to find himself engulfed in an espionage scandal. The exposure of the Portland spy ring, whose members were tried and convicted in March, had caused a sensation. The case revealed major security lapses, including that MI5 had ignored red flags raised about Houghton. Macmillan was being hammered by the opposition, which demanded that heads roll. Awaiting the results of what was expected to be a highly critical formal inquiry, he faced damaging accusations that his government was penetrated by communists.

The Blake matter was hitting at a particularly inopportune time. Macmillan was in the United States for his first meetings with the new American president, John F. Kennedy, who had been inaugurated in January. As Macmillan learned details of the confession, it was becoming clear that this was treachery of a different magnitude.

"The government could fall on this," he reportedly told Dick White. Macmillan's first instinct was to hush it up, perhaps with an offer of immunity to avoid a public trial.

Macmillan preferred to keep these sorts of things quiet. He once scolded the director-general of MI5, Roger Hollis, over publicity about an arrested Soviet spy. "When my gamekeeper shoots a fox, he doesn't go and hang it outside the Master of the Foxhounds drawing room; he buries it out of sight," he told Hollis.

White argued that the credibility of SIS was at stake. "The cost of doing nothing would be enormous, both within the service and with the Americans," he said. Indeed, it was not hard to imagine how the U.S. government was going to react to the news. How could the Americans trust British intelligence if it was riddled with Soviet moles?

Quite apart from the Blake matter, there was already talk that Anglo-American ties might suffer in comparison to the close relationship between Dwight Eisenhower and Macmillan. The two had bonded in North Africa during the war, when Macmillan was in Algiers as resident minister in Churchill's cabinet and Ike was the Allied commander. Macmillan was wary of Kennedy, twenty-three years his junior. Based on what he had heard from Jock Whitney, Eisenhower's ambassador to the United Kingdom, Kennedy "must be a strange character . . . obstinate, sensitive, ruthless and highly sexed," Macmillan wrote in his diary.

But Macmillan was determined to establish good personal relations with Kennedy for the sake of Anglo-American comity. The two broke the ice with a preliminary meeting in Key West, Florida, on March 26. He found Kennedy's frank and freewheeling style quite a change from the more stilted discussions with Ike. "It was really most satisfactory—far better than I could have hoped," Macmillan wrote after arriving in Washington on April 4 for further talks.

Even as Blake poured out his torrential confession on April 6, Kennedy and Macmillan were on the Potomac River enjoying a cruise aboard the ninety-two-foot presidential yacht, *Honey Fitz,* trailed by a press boat struggling to keep up. On the return trip upriver, Kennedy and Macmillan fell so deep into discussions over tensions in Berlin and concerns about South Vietnam that the cruise was extended to give them more time to talk.

The *Times* of London reported after the cruise that while no one expected Macmillan's relationship with Kennedy to be as "old boyish" as with Eisenhower, both sides were pleasantly surprised at the rapport the two leaders had established.

Now, to his great irritation, Macmillan was receiving reports from London about the unfolding Blake disaster. It was a huge embarrassment that risked completely undermining the message he hoped to convey of Britain as a reliable and trustworthy partner. He "thought it right to make a short statement to the president," according to Hollis. He figured it best to break the news to Kennedy in person before his departure from Washington on April 10.

Macmillan adapted a clubby tone with his new friend, casually referring to his SIS chief with the title popularized by the James Bond novels of which Kennedy was a fan, and using British slang for a scoundrel: "C's nabbed a wrong 'un."

But no amount of good cheer between the two leaders could disguise the fact that the news was exceptionally grim. It was clear to Macmillan that if Blake were brought to trial and the penetration made public, he should have the book thrown at him. It was vital that the British public and the American government see his government taking tough and urgent action.

LONDON, SUNDAY, APRIL 9

The weekend at Shergy's cottage—pancake suppers, country walks, and all—had come to an end. The group drove back to London Sunday afternoon, stopping for the night at an SIS safe house in the western suburb of East Sheen.

All weekend, there had been frequent calls back and forth to London, and by Sunday evening a somber mood had fallen. "It became clear that we were all waiting for something, though for what I had no idea," Blake recalled.

What they were waiting for was a decision on what to do with Blake. Even among those on the weekend excursion, there was a divide. Shergold was in favor of prosecution, but Quine was more sympathetic toward Blake, believing that SIS deserved blame for not vetting him more carefully, particularly upon his return from communist captivity.

While the group was eating supper in the safe house kitchen, the telephone rang. "Some decision had evidently been taken and it was not the one they had hoped for," Blake said.

The next morning, as they finished breakfast, two detectives came to arrest Blake. Shaking hands with "my colleagues" from SIS, as he persisted in calling them, he fancied that they "felt some sympathy or perhaps pity for me."

A police car drove Blake to Scotland Yard, where he was charged with violating the Official Secrets Act, fingerprinted, and searched. At a closed hearing at the Bow Street Magistrates' Court, he was remanded into custody, and then taken to Brixton prison.

The CIA station in London was informed. Dick White cabled Peter Lunn, still the station chief in Bonn, informing him of Blake's treachery and asking that he inform West German intelligence. Lunn, who personally decrypted the cable, was devastated by the news. A cable would soon be sent to every SIS station around the world. "The following name is a traitor," the first part read. The second part, when decoded, spelled out "G-E-O-R-G-E-B-L-A-K-E."

CHAPTER 23

The Worst That Can Be Envisaged

SHEMLAN, MONDAY EVENING, APRIL 10, 1961

Gillian Blake had heard nothing from George, but by the weekend she had received a note from the British embassy in Beirut
saying he had been delayed in London.

Monday had been another lovely spring day, and, feeling restless,
Gillian thought about going to Beirut to shop. But then a couple she
knew from the embassy, Christopher and Hilary Everett, stopped by
for tea with some surprising news. Someone from the Foreign Office was in town and would come by that evening to discuss George.

While awaiting the visitor, Gillian and Khadijh, the nanny, put
the children to bed, and Khadijh retired for the evening as well.
With their third child due in six weeks, Gillian tired easily, and she
dozed off in her armchair. Around 8:30 p.m. there was a knock, and
she opened the door to find John Quine. She had never met him, but
had heard George speak of him. "How kind of you to take all this
trouble to come and see me," she told him.

Quine mumbled something in embarrassment. Gillian invited him
to get himself a drink. He poured a whiskey, made a drink for Gillian, and sat down. He asked a few questions, probing to see if she
knew anything. When he realized she did not, Quine began talking.
"I was told the unbelievable news that this man, to whom I have

been so happily married for nearly seven years, was in prison awaiting trial as a Russian spy," Gillian recalled.

She was horror-struck, she later said—"Horror at what had happened to our life, horror at what George had done to my country."
But she had no trouble believing the news.

"I didn't think for a moment they'd made a mistake," she recalled.
"I didn't think 'They must have got hold of the wrong man,' or
'This can't be true' or anything like that. It all fit in and it didn't
seem impossible."

Blake's obvious sympathy with communist ideals had become
only more outspoken in recent years. When Khrushchev had broken off a planned summit with Eisenhower the previous May after
the Soviets shot down a U-2 plane and captured pilot Francis Gary
Powers, Blake had expressed admiration for the way Khrushchev
was handling the whole business.

Gillian could see her husband's turn to the Soviet side as fitting
his personality—the pleasure he took in hidden power and knowing things that others did not. She knew he was capable of being
ruthless and could be "frightfully ambitious" at times. Once he had
determined a course of action, Blake would have seen it as "an act of
cowardice" if he didn't do all in his power to advance the cause, she
said. There was also his rootless youth, his sense of not belonging to
one country, and his resentment of the British class system.

It was not as if he were two different people, she said. "It sort of
goes with him, somehow," she said. "It hasn't been at all difficult for
me to understand."

———

Gillian had to make quick decisions. With the baby due so soon, she
would return with the children to Britain almost immediately. The
Everetts, in the know about Blake's arrest, came back to Shemlan
around 11:15 p.m. to pick up Quine. They were all very solicitous,
promising to come back in the morning to help her pack, and asking
if she wanted company for the night. "Everybody offered to stay,
and I was just longing for them to go," she recalled.

They left her some sleeping pills, which "had a wonderful tran-
quilizing effect and made me feel quite out of this world, though I

felt a bit like that anyway," she said. "But I didn't sleep much." Amid the shock, one thing was clear: "This was the finish of our life."

———

The next day was a blur. The Everetts helped Gillian pack and prepare for the departure. Christopher Everett, who spoke good Arabic, arranged to pay the grocer and other bills, and explained to Khadijh that the Blakes were leaving and not coming back.

Rumors flew around the language school. The school director put out word not to disturb Gillian, but it had the opposite effect. "Practically everybody came round, about eleven wives, one after the other—'Could they help, where was I going, you must be terribly cross with George . . .'—All the most unhelpful things," Gillian recalled. "So we had to deal with all of them, and all the packing of the clothes, and sorting things out, and keeping the children out of the way, in just this one day."

Early on Wednesday morning, April 12, the Everetts collected Gillian and the children and drove them to the airport. Hilary Everett joined the family for the flight to London. The children were terribly excited, running about the airports, unaware how their lives had changed. From Heathrow, they were whisked away in a large car to Sussex in southeast England, where they would stay at a home belonging to friends of Gillian, rather than to her parents' in London. They would be safer from reporters in the country once the story broke.

LONDON AND WASHINGTON, APRIL 1961

Blake's questioning was yielding unpleasant surprises, none bigger than the Berlin tunnel. "The British Intelligence Service did not know or suspect that this operation was known to the Russians until I told them," Blake wrote in a statement for his defense attorneys from Brixton. "In fact they had dated the beginning of my cooperation with the Russians after the tunneling operation had come to light."

Dick White delivered the grim news to Allen Dulles, who in

turn informed the White House. "BLAKE states that he passed to the Soviets all the technical papers bearing on the operation which included the identity of underground cables which were to be attacked, the method to be employed, and the route of the proposed tunnel," Dulles reported to Kennedy.

The CIA was livid at the realization that the tunnel had been betrayed from the start. At headquarters in Washington, Bill Harvey, the man who made the case that Kim Philby was a spy, did not take the news well. "Here we go again," he exploded. "We should never trust the Brits."

As soon as they heard that Blake had been arrested, Harvey and Frank Rowlett feared the worst, recognizing the access the British officer had to the secrets of the tunnel while assigned to Section Y. Rowlett remembered Blake's presence at the meeting in London in December 1953 where the tunnel details were decided. "He was the one who blew it, I'm sure," Rowlett later said.

Among the officers who had worked on the project, Hugh Montgomery was not unique in his reaction. "I would have wrung Blake's neck," he later said. For some, coming five years after the tunnel's discovery, the news was as disconcerting as it was infuriating— "another example of this feeling that the KGB is all around us," said David Murphy.

It immediately raised the question: Was the tunnel intelligence genuine? Had the CIA and SIS been taken in by a massive KGB disinformation campaign? An investigation was launched, along with an urgent CIA review of all operations Blake might have compromised. Every CIA officer who had ever had contact with him was closely questioned.

"An extensive investigation has been underway since the beginning of April to ascertain the extent of BLAKE's compromise to the Soviets of intelligence information," Dulles told Kennedy. British intelligence was also assessing the damage to its intelligence operations. This "analysis is essential if the areas of operational activity believed to have been contaminated by BLAKE's treachery are to be repaired or subject to surgery," Dulles reported. Already it was clear that the case represented "a most serious and damaging compromise of Allied intelligence activity directed against the Soviet," he added.

Nor was the tunnel the only major operation Blake betrayed, Dulles reported. "At an unspecified time in Berlin BLAKE states that he passed to the Soviets information regarding a highly placed Russian agent who was eventually arrested and liquidated in Moscow," he wrote. "It has yet to be established whether the information available to him was sufficient for the Soviets to have taken such counteraction on the basis of his intelligence alone."

The agent was not named in Dulles's report, but the description of the case could be Pyotr Popov. The memo, partly declassified in 2015, is the strongest indication yet linking Blake to the demise of the CIA's spy. The information Blake passed along could have been the bombshell report on Zhukov's speech, or possibly Popov's initial contact with Western intelligence after arriving in East Germany. Whatever it was, it was gut-wrenching.

There were also concerns that Blake might have betrayed a promising new spy—Colonel Oleg Penkovsky, a GRU officer who had approached the Americans in Moscow the previous summer with offers of information. After months of missed messages and hesitation by the CIA, a frustrated Penkovsky had made contact with the British. By the spring of 1961, the CIA and SIS had agreed to work the case together. Penkovsky was due to arrive in London on April 20 for an extended visit escorting a Soviet scientific delegation, providing Western intelligence with its first opportunity to meet and debrief him. The CIA and SIS had each selected top case officers to handle Penkovsky: George Kisevalter and Harry Shergold. They had secured a room in the same hotel where the Soviets would be staying, the Mount Royal near Marble Arch.

Blake's arrest raised new concern at CIA headquarters in Washington about the wisdom of working with the British on the Penkovsky operation. If Blake knew about it and had reported it to the Soviets, it could be a death warrant for Penkovsky. But the Americans respected Shergold's professionalism and analytical prowess, and he was able to calm their fears. A few days before Penkovsky's arrival in London, Shergold invited Kisevalter and Joe Bulik, Kisevalter's branch chief, to dinner at his home in Richmond Park outside London.

Shergold updated them on the Blake case. "You are sitting opposite me just the way George Blake did when he confessed," he told Bulik at the dinner table. He assured the CIA officers that Blake would have had no access to information about Penkovsky and would not have been in a position to betray him.

———

Dick White was also working to reassure the CIA. His candor about the Blake disaster was winning some points with his American counterparts, a welcome change to the reticence felt from then SIS chief Stewart Menzies after Philby's exposure a decade earlier. White told Allen Dulles that he believed the shock of the Polish documents was "the trump card" that had prompted Blake's confession. "It is the view of the Chief of the British Service that it was not only the nature of the material but the timing of the play which achieved the result," Allen Dulles reported to Kennedy. ". . . From that moment on, he began to cooperate with the interrogators and seemingly has answered their questions with a remarkable degree of openness."

White sent the SIS senior liaison officer in Washington, a position once held by Philby, to brief J. Edgar Hoover. The SIS officer was relieved to find the FBI director "genuinely sympathetic and understanding" about the matter. The FBI director told the British officer that the Blake case was a reminder of how alert American and British counterintelligence needed to be "to the dangers which beset us." After all, Hoover added, "Christ Himself found a traitor in His small team of twelve." Hoover was still purring over the British success in breaking up the Portland spy ring, in particular the arrest of the Cohens, the American spies. Moreover, it had not been his tunnel that had been betrayed—perhaps Hoover was celebrating Harvey's comeuppance.

In any event, there was little time for the Americans to lord the Blake fiasco over the British. On April 17, 1961, one week after his arrest, a force of Cuban exiles trained and funded by the CIA landed at the Bay of Pigs on the southern coast of Cuba in an attempt to overthrow Fidel Castro. The botched operation ended in humiliation, and an angry Kennedy demanded changes at the CIA. That included pushing out Allen Dulles, whom he blamed for not being fully frank about the operation. Though the director would remain in office until the end of the year, the Bay of Pigs effectively ended the Dulles reign at the CIA. And it quieted complaints in Washington about the untrustworthiness of the British.

———

The KGB was no less shocked than the CIA by Blake's arrest. Obviously, the green light Nikolai Rodin gave for Blake's return from Beirut had been "a serious mistake," said Viktor Malyavin, then an officer in the London station. Nonetheless, nobody panicked, mainly because the KGB had no idea that Blake had confessed. "In the first stage, we thought we would have to see how the situation developed and how the trial went, because to some extent, we were reassured by the fact that British counterintelligence could have no proof of his cooperation with us," said Sergei Kondrashev.

As of yet, the KGB had not realized that Michael Goleniewski, the Polish defector, would have known about documents Blake had provided. Only later would Moscow Center learn that a KGB adviser had given Polish intelligence the list of SIS recruitment targets in Poland, "apparently with a misplaced desire to help," Kondrashev said. This violated standing orders that any use of information from Agent Diomid had to be personally cleared by Tishkov, the deputy chief of foreign intelligence. Even so, without a confession, "no one could prove that those documents had been handed over by George Blake," Kondrashev believed. Thus, the KGB concluded it would be safest for the moment to do nothing. "They needed proof, so we abstained from any actions which could show our interest in freeing him, because by our actions we would be helping British counterintelligence to prosecute Blake," Kondrashev said.

BRIXTON PRISON, LONDON

In his shabby prison cell at Brixton, Blake spent weeks feeling "nagging regret" for returning to England instead of acting on his initial hunch. Still, he did not blame the KGB. "No, they didn't let me down," he said. "They can't know everything. They too are only human beings."

But he did believe Rodin "made a mistake" by refusing to talk when Blake asked what to do if he was ever caught. "In my case it would have been better if we had discussed this matter soberly and objectively, without being afraid of the possibility, which did exist," he later told an audience of Stasi officers. "That is actually the only criticism that I have about these comrades."

Blake was being represented by two top London attorneys. Bill Cox, a well-known and experienced solicitor with the leading criminal defense firm in London, had been assigned to him by the Legal Aid Agency. To make court arguments, Cox brought in the barrister Jeremy Hutchinson, who had gained renown the previous year defending Penguin Books against obscenity charges for publishing the uncensored version of D. H. Lawrence's novel *Lady Chatterley's Lover*.

The urbane and charismatic Hutchinson was "like one of those fictional heroes who pops up at real-life events," a British newspaper once wrote. His parents were intimates of the Bloomsbury Group and other literary luminaries, including T. S. Eliot; his mother, Mary, a cousin of Lytton Strachey, was the inspiration for the title character in Virginia Woolf's *Mrs. Dalloway*. Hutchinson was married to the famed Shakespearean actress Peggy Ashcroft, an acquaintance from his youth with whom he reconnected by knocking unannounced at her dressing room door. They were wed in London in 1940 at the height of the Battle of Britain, with the celebration cut short by air raid sirens.

A year later, Hutchinson was serving in the Royal Navy on the staff of the illustrious Lord Louis Mountbatten, who was commanding a destroyer flotilla, when their ship HMS *Kelly* was sunk by German Stuka dive bombers off Crete, taking half the crew. Hutchinson and other survivors, including Mountbatten, clung to wreckage in pools of oil, singing vaudeville songs to keep up morale until they were rescued by another destroyer.

Hutchinson worked as a military prosecutor in Italy, and after the war launched a career as a criminal barrister in London, soon making a name for himself. Like his wife, Hutchinson had a commanding stage presence that attracted audiences to hear his arguments. *Lady Chatterley's Lover* was a breakthrough, leading to his being appointed

Queen's Counsel at age forty-six, an honored status in the British judicial system.

At their first meeting at Brixton prison, Blake and Hutchinson hit it off, bonding over their naval service. "Blake was a man who exuded this great and intense charm," Hutchinson later said. "I was immediately taken with him."

At the request of his attorneys, Blake used his time at Brixton to write a detailed life history, including his decision to work for the Soviets. In fourteen tightly scribbled pages, he laid out his story, from his youth in World War II to the moment in North Korea when he decided to betray Britain. He detailed his vast espionage for the Soviets, insisting that he had "no intention to harm this country but [acted] to prevent communist countries from being harmed so that experiment of humanity in communism could go on." He noted that much of his work for SIS involved trying "to induce Soviet officials to do exactly the same of which I stand accused. This was my life work and it is bound to affect the way one looks upon betrayal."

Hutchinson found Blake's story credible. "It's not for me to decide whether a client is genuine or not, but from a personal point of view, now that the case is long over, I was quite convinced that this was a genuine conversion on his part," he recalled more than five decades later.

Nonetheless, it was clear to the attorneys that they had a hard row to hoe. "This is probably one of the gravest cases of its kind that have ever come before a British court," Cox wrote to Hutchinson after reviewing Blake's statement. "It is difficult to conceive that any action could have done more damage than that admitted to by the defendant." Given that the Portland spies had been given sentences ranging from fifteen to twenty-five years, Blake could be facing thirty or more, Cox warned.

There was not much of a defense to be made. Blake would not contest his confession, despite the government's fear that it could be withdrawn at any time with a claim that it had been made under duress. "He didn't want to challenge it," Hutchinson said. "He immediately made it clear to me he made the confession because he wanted to get it off his chest."

Hutchinson's job was to persuade the court to show leniency in the sentencing. The task, Blake said, "seemed to me pretty thankless after the confession I had made."

LONDON, TUESDAY, APRIL 18

The government had decided to try Blake in secret. At a meeting on April 15, officials adapted a strategy to give the press as little information as possible about the case. Accordingly, on April 18, when Blake was brought for a pretrial hearing to the Bow Street Magistrates' Court, where he had been taken after his arrest eight days earlier, it was again closed to the press and public.

Based on the scant details released afterwards by the court, newspapers reported that "a former government official" named George Blake was charged with communicating information that might be "directly or indirectly useful to an enemy power." Blake's address and details of his arrest were kept secret at the order of Sir Robert Blundell, the chief metropolitan magistrate. But reporters dug up the intriguing detail that he was one of the British diplomats held as a prisoner during the Korean War.

The maximum sentence for violating the Official Secrets Act was fourteen years. This was the sentence that had been given to Klaus Fuchs, who had turned over Manhattan Project secrets to the Soviets. But Sir Reginald Manningham-Buller, the attorney general, did not think that was enough for Blake. He proposed to Macmillan that Blake be charged with five separate counts, dividing his offenses into different periods of service. The first count would date to North Korea in November 1951, when Blake made his offer to spy for the Soviets. The second would cover his time at Section Y from September 1953 to April 1955; the third his posting to Berlin from April 1955 to April 1959; and the final two his work in London prior to his departure for Beirut in September 1960. This would allow him to be hit "with the biggest hammer possible," Manningham-Buller believed.

A third hearing on April 24, again closed to the public, set the case for trial May 3 at London's Central Criminal Court, the Old Bailey. The only information released was a notice pinned to the courthouse bulletin board listing three charges against Blake under the Official Secrets Act. Two more charges would soon be added.

Several days before the trial, Hutchinson went to the office of the imposing Manningham-Buller, who would personally prosecute the case. The attorney general's manner was considered so snobbish and disagreeable that a columnist had once dubbed him "Sir Bullying Manner." Manningham-Buller made no effort to disguise his contempt for Hutchinson and the whole left-leaning Bloomsbury Group strata he represented. It certainly did not help that Hutchinson had made fools of his office during the *Lady Chatterley's Lover* trial. (When Manningham-Buller's deputy, Mervyn Griffith-Jones, asked members of the jury whether "you would even wish your wife or your servants to read" the novel, Hutchinson had been unable to resist exchanging mirthful gazes with others in the courtroom.)

Hutchinson told Manningham-Buller that in order to prepare his mitigation speech, he needed to know what kind of damage the prosecution would allege that Blake's espionage had caused. The attorney general replied that the information was so sensitive that no details could be given, either in open court or even to the judge in his chambers. The whole case would be presented in camera.

When Hutchinson protested, Manningham-Buller cut him off. "That is a matter for you and the judge. I have nothing more to say."

———

Predictably, the extraordinary secrecy surrounding the case aroused rather than deflated press attention. The *Daily Mirror* ran a front-page story headlined "A Secret Trial at the Old Bailey," reporting that Blake would be the first defendant since World War II to have a trial entirely closed to the public.

Macmillan fretted that the case was already getting too much publicity. Accordingly, on May 1, the government issued a D-Notice, a formal advisory to news organizations requesting that they not publish or broadcast almost all details of the case, including mention that Blake was an intelligence officer, on grounds that it might endanger national security. "For your personal and confidential information, there is special reason for requesting your co-operation in this case in that the lives of MI6 employees are still in danger," Rear Admiral

Sir George Thomson, the D-Notice secretary, wrote in a notice sent to news organizations.

While the D-Notice was theoretically a voluntary system, news organizations felt obliged to honor it. But the notice also succeeded in fueling even more press interest in the case. Chapman Pincher, a well-known Fleet Street journalist specializing in espionage scoops, suspected that the government notice "had nothing to do with security, only embarrassment."

In any event, the London correspondent for the *New York Herald Tribune* did not receive the notice and wrote a detailed story published in the European edition of the paper on May 2, causing a furor in Britain. On the eve of the trial, the dam had been breached.

BRIXTON PRISON, TUESDAY, MAY 2

Gillian Blake, now nine months pregnant, traveled from Sussex to London to visit her husband at Brixton prison. "It was a sad reunion for us, but my wife never uttered one word of reproach," Blake said.

Gillian's recollection was similar. "It was very emotional and he was heartbroken by it all for my sake," she said. She was determined to be "as undramatic as possible" and saw no reason to ask her husband about what he had done. "There's been very little need for explanation, really," she said. She admitted she resented not being told. "But I couldn't have lived with it for a moment," she added. "Had he told me, we'd have been finished with anyway."

Still, Gillian could never know with certainty what she would have decided had Blake brought the family to Damascus and given her the choice of leaving with him for Moscow or staying behind. "That would have been one hell of a decision," she admitted.

Before leaving Brixton, Gillian brought her husband up to date with his case, and Blake learned to his surprise that his trial was set for the next day. "Nobody had told me anything about this and it all seemed very sudden to me," he said. "In a way, I was quite unprepared. On the other hand, I reflected, what was there to be prepared about?"

He expected to receive the maximum fourteen-year sentence,

which seemed a long time, but survivable. He "hoped against hope" that the judge might shorten it a bit. The possibility that fourteen-year sentences could be piled on top of each other did not seem to occur to him. But he did find himself imagining that prosecutors might "rake up some old law, dating to the Middle Ages, which everyone had forgotten about," and sentence him to death. He spent his last night at Brixton fluctuating between "hope and despondency."

OLD BAILEY, WEDNESDAY, MAY 3

On the morning of the trial, Jeremy Hutchinson worked his way past the heavy police security guarding the courthouse and down a set of steps to meet with Blake in a gloomy basement interview room. They spoke over the din of other prisoners in holding cells awaiting trial. "It was a beautiful spring day, the kind of day when one is inclined to be light-hearted, but as I spoke with George Blake about what was to happen in the courtroom above everything seemed very tense," Hutchinson recalled.

Before heading upstairs, the barrister broached a final topic with Blake. "I asked him whether he wished me to tell the court that he regretted what he had done," Hutchinson recalled. Such a statement "might help a lot."

Blake declined. "In the first place it was untrue," he later said, but beyond that, it struck him as "undignified" for someone who had photographed virtually every document he got his hands on to "suddenly feel sorry for having done this, simply because he had been found out and arrested."

Shortly before Hutchinson entered the courtroom, he was stopped by Manningham-Buller, who told him that the prosecution would present its case in open court. Hutchinson was stunned by the last-minute reversal. If the defense was presented in open court, he would be severely restricted in what could be said. There was no time to construct an argument that did not violate the strict prohibition on revealing anything publicly about Blake's work—even that SIS existed, much less that Blake was an intelligence officer. "The conditions they laid down would have meant I didn't have the freedom to tell George's side of the story," he said. After hurriedly consulting with Blake, he decided it would be better to present the defense in camera.

Hutchinson viewed the maneuver as a ploy to allow the government to release a censored view of Blake without the defense's side, trying to shape the stories coming out in the press. Manningham-Buller "just bullied me, really," he recalled. "If I'd been more senior, maybe I would have stood up to him more than I did. But I was so shocked by the whole thing."

———

Court 1 of the Old Bailey had seen a parade of famous trials over the decades, ranging from notorious criminals such as George Smith, the "Brides in the Bath" serial killer, to more recent dramas such as the *Lady Chatterley* and Portland spy ring cases. Reporters, who had expected to be barred from entry, were delighted to be allowed in for the biggest espionage case in the court's history. Shortly before 10:30 a.m., the mysterious George Blake, wearing a dark gray suit with a checked shirt and blue tie and his dark hair neatly parted, was escorted up a hidden staircase into the criminal dock, which was raised above the courtroom floor.

Lord Parker, the Lord Chief Justice of England and Wales, walked in holding posies, an Old Bailey tradition. Parker, the most senior member of the English judiciary, rarely presided as a trial judge, and his presence marked the case's national significance.

Blake felt oddly detached from the process, his eyes wandering about the imposing wood-paneled courtroom. The red-robed Lord Chief Justice sat high over the court, under a huge carved pediment. Blake thought Parker "looked kindly enough," though he was disappointed with his wig, which was much smaller than he expected. It was pushed so far forward that it almost rested on the gold rim of Parker's spectacles, making him "look slightly old-maidish."

Looking in the public gallery, Blake recognized a white-haired, distinguished gentleman. It was Dick White—"C"—sitting next to Roger Hollis, director-general of MI5, not a particularly reassuring sight. John Quine and other SIS colleagues were nearby.

Blake rose to his feet as the clerk read out the charges. He looked demoralized to observers, standing with his hands resting lightly on the bench. After each count was read, he was asked how he pleaded. "Guilty, sir," he replied in a barely audible tone.

Manningham-Buller rose to explain the gravity of the charges. Blake hardly listened to the presentation from Manningham-Buller, instead focusing on "his wobbling crimson cheeks and . . . apoplectic, bulging eyes of the over-indulgent." The attorney general described Blake only as "employed in the government's service," and spoke in equally general terms of his crimes. Blake "has been working as an agent for the Russians, as a spy for them, and communicating a mass of information to them," Manningham-Buller said. "In short, he has for the past nine and a half years been engaged in betraying his country."

The attorney general said he could not "publicly reveal the nature of the information he has communicated." But he read aloud a sentence from Blake's written confession: "I must freely admit there was not an official document of any importance to which I had access which was not passed to my Soviet contact." Given Blake's confession and accompanying government depositions, Manningham-Buller added, "it is not necessary for me to say anything more." He had finished his case in eight minutes.

The attorney general then asked Parker to close the court on grounds of "national safety" before the defense could proceed. When Parker asked Hutchinson for his view, the barrister made clear that he had been left with little choice. "I am told that much of what I wish to say should not be said in public," Hutchinson said. At Parker's order, the court was cleared of reporters and spectators at 10:40 a.m. The courtroom was locked, and for the first time since World War II, the glass-paneled swing doors and windows were covered with wooden shutters.

"My Lord, whatever else this is, this is not a political trial and it is not a propaganda trial, and it is not a move in a cold war, because all those things are alien to our procedure here," Hutchinson began. ". . . I know your Lordship would take the view that we here in modern days have never had trials in order to give comfort to our allies or bring fear to our enemies."

In fact, Hutchinson believed the opposite of Parker. "He was very much a judge who would support the government through thick and thin," he later said. But the barrister hoped to appeal to Parker's sense of judicial independence.

Hutchinson then laid out Blake's journey through World War II— surviving the bombing of Rotterdam and being separated from his mother; "running the gauntlet, seeing men die in front of him" as a sixteen-year-old courier for the Dutch resistance; making his escape through France and being imprisoned in Spain; arriving in England and serving in the Royal Navy. Blake had lived in the midst of "war, deprivation, murder and suchlike from the age of 16 onwards," Hutchinson said.

He described Blake's transfer to SIS, his work in occupied Germany, and his assignment to Korea. He told of Blake's imprisonment during the war, the horrific march "faced with death . . . pneumonia, dysentery and seeing people dying like flies," as well as the destructive Western bombing campaign he witnessed. All of it, Hutchinson said, led "to that moment in 1951 when George Blake decided to take the course that he took."

It was a decision of conscience, Hutchinson argued, of deciding he was on the wrong side, and not one of greed or selfishness. "He wished to make a positive contribution" to communism, Hutchinson said, and the way he chose to do it was through "the total disruption of the Intelligence Service."

———

Hutchinson finished speaking at 11:30 a.m. Parker adjourned briefly to prepare his sentence. The shutters were removed, and Blake could hear a commotion as the press and public returned to Court 1. After ten minutes, the judge slowly walked back in, and the chamber fell more silent than Hutchinson had ever heard it. Blake rose to face Parker. He allowed himself to think that Hutchinson's eloquence had made an impact on the court. That hope faded as soon as the Lord Chief Justice spoke.

Blake's espionage, Parker said, "has rendered much of this country's efforts completely useless." The judge said he was "perfectly prepared to accept it was not for money that you did this, but because of your conversion to a genuine belief in the communist system."

But instead of resigning, he added, "you retained your employment in positions of trust in order to betray your country."

"It is clear your case is akin to treason. Indeed it is one of the worst that can be envisaged other than in a time of war," Parker continued. "Your conduct in many other countries would undoubtedly carry the death penalty. In our law, however, I have no option but to sentence you to imprisonment, and for your traitorous conduct extending over so many years there must be a very heavy sentence."

Parker imposed a sentence of fourteen years for each count, three of them to run consecutively and two of them concurrently, forty-two years in all. It was the longest sentence imposed in modern British history, going back 150 years. There were audible gasps in the courtroom when the sentence was pronounced.

A guard tapped Blake on the shoulder to lead him back below. When he turned, observers were stunned to see a faint grin on his face. "I couldn't help smiling, because it sounded so unreal to me," he recalled.

———

Hutchinson and Cox saw Blake in his dark and damp cell beneath the courtroom. Newspapers would report that he had collapsed. "Nothing could be further from the truth," Hutchinson said. "Blake was remarkably serene."

Blake made clear his belief that the trial had been purely political. "His attitude throughout was that this was a state trial, and when I went down to see him afterwards, he was quite cool about it," Hutchinson recalled. Blake saw "this enormous sentence" as a Cold War tactic, a gambit meant to gain leverage in a future exchange for a Western spy captured by the Soviets, the barrister added. "He was absolutely convinced it was rubbish and he'd be swapped over for somebody on the other side," said Hutchinson.

Blake also suspected the sentence was meant to placate the U.S. government. A fourteen-year sentence, he later wrote, "had clearly been considered not enough. It would not satisfy the Americans, who were raising hell and calling for my blood. So a way had to be found to make it more."

Later in the afternoon, Blake was handcuffed to two guards and taken in a small van to London's Wormwood Scrubs prison. On the streets, he could see newspaper vendors selling early evening editions with headlines announcing his sentence, along with a photograph showing his return from Korea eight years earlier to a hero's welcome.

———

Blake's trial caused a sensation, both in Britain and around the world. Harold Macmillan's hope of keeping the matter quiet had been completely undercut by the unprecedented sentence. The question was asked: What exactly had George Blake done to deserve it? The trial cast very little light on the matter, but Parker's declaration about the consequences of Blake's actions made clear that whatever he had done, it had been devastating.

"The case of George Blake—a traitor—has shocked the public," Macmillan wrote in his diary. "The [Lord Chief Justice] has passed a savage sentence—42 years in prison!"

Facing stinging criticism, Macmillan made a statement before a raucous House of Commons on May 4. The prime minister tried to downplay the extent of the disaster, conceding that Blake "has done serious damage to the interests of this country," but insisting that it was not "irreparable" and that he had not had access to defense or nuclear secrets. The prime minister's assurances that Blake received "a very thorough security vetting" upon his return from Korea were met with disbelief.

"I had a rather rough passage," Macmillan wrote that night in his diary.

There was more indignation in days that followed, as newspapers reported that Blake had dealt a "crippling blow" to Britain's intelligence networks in East Germany and endangered the lives of many agents. Officers were being recalled for fear that they had been compromised by Blake. The *Telegraph* speculated that the tunnel discovery in Berlin five years earlier might not have been accidental and that Blake could be responsible. Several German newspapers picked up the question, but it was left unanswered.

In Washington, a State Department spokesman told reporters that Blake had apparently not betrayed any U.S. secrets. "In so far as we have been able to determine there were none," the spokesman said—an utterly false statement, whether made from ignorance or as a deliberate ploy.

There were demands in Britain that the government release more information about Blake and his actions. "Naturally we can say nothing," Macmillan wrote. "The public do not know and cannot be told that he belonged to M.I.6—an organization [which] does not theoretically exist."

———

As was the case after Blake's arrest, the KGB was shocked by his trial. Viktor Malyavin and his colleagues at the London residence were "very surprised" to learn that he had confessed. "It goes against the grain," Malyavin said. "Later I realized that he couldn't behave any other way, especially since no one had told him what to do in that situation. He confessed because he is a patently honest man and acted normally even in that situation."

Just as stunning was Blake's forty-two-year punishment. "This came as a shock to all of us, because we hadn't expected such a long sentence," said Kondrashev. The KGB, of course, routinely executed its own traitors, but that did not stop its officers from working themselves into high dudgeon over the harshness of Blake's sentence. "We knew that this was revenge on the part of British intelligence," Kondrashev complained.

The new Soviet spy, Colonel Oleg Penkovsky, in London with his Soviet delegation and meeting almost daily with his American and British handlers at the Mount Royal hotel, knocked on their door the day after the verdict. Blake's sentence had shaken the Soviet embassy, he told Harry Shergold and Joe Bulik. "Their mood right now is very bad," Penkovsky said. "They say this will discourage people from working with us."

———

At the urging of his defense team, Blake filed a notice on May 5 appealing the sentence. Cox told him that there was "not anything to lose by appealing and there is always a faint chance that the Court of Appeal might take a different view."

Hutchinson suspected there had been collusion in the sentencing between Manningham-Buller and Parker. Almost no evidence about the consequences of Blake's espionage had been presented in court, either in closed or open session. Yet Parker had seemed oddly confident in proclaiming that the information Blake gave the Soviets had rendered much of Britain's efforts completely useless.

It was not until decades later Hutchinson learned he was correct. Soon after Blake's trial, Parker attended a dinner party in Manchester with a group of attorneys, including Ben Hytner, then a young barrister. After dinner, Parker discussed the Blake case with some of the attorneys, and told them that "the day before he sentenced, he'd spoken to the prime minister to find out exactly how much damage he had in fact done," Hutchinson said. Parker told the dinner guests that he wanted the information before making his sentence.

Hytner was stunned at the impropriety of Parker using a private conversation with Macmillan outside of the judicial system to make sentencing, leaving the defense no opportunity to respond. But believing that Parker had spoken in confidence, Hytner kept quiet until writing a letter to Hutchinson in 2015.

WORMWOOD SCRUBS, EARLY JUNE

With the baby due in May, Gillian Blake had stayed in Sussex, away from the trial, and was kept apprised of developments by the attorneys and news reports. "It was absolutely ghastly hearing the news of the sentence," she recalled. Cox had warned her that the sentence could be harsh. "Even though I had tried to expect it, it was hard to believe," she wrote Cox. She considered the length of the sentence "worse than death."

But her spirits brightened two weeks after the sentencing when the Blakes' third child, Patrick, was born. "Having the new baby has made me happier and more able to withstand the shock," she said.

In early June, Gillian brought Patrick to meet his father at Wormwood Scrubs. Blake was "delighted" to see him, even though the baby cried throughout the visit. But the joy was fleeting. Such visits "always left a feeling of great sadness at the thought of the happiness that had been destroyed," Blake recalled.

COURT OF CRIMINAL APPEAL, LONDON, MONDAY, JUNE 19

Jeremy Hutchinson's heart sank when he learned that Blake's appeal would be presided over by seventy-seven-year-old Justice Malcolm Hilbery. The lean and ascetic judge, who walked to court each day in his morning coat and tall silk hat, seemed sprung from the pages of a Dickens novel. Hilbery, "an awful acidulated man" in the view of Hutchinson, was a staunch advocate for more flogging. That did not bode well for Blake.

The hearing on Monday, June 19, at the Court of Criminal Appeal was held in secret (like his trial, the first instance since wartime spy cases). Hutchinson came armed with a raft of historical data and arguments that Blake's sentence was unprecedented and unwarranted under British law. "This sentence is so inhumane that it is alien to all the principles on which a civilized country would treat its subjects," he declared.

Blake, he noted, would have been far better off getting a life sentence, which by law required parole—effectively twenty years. By the 1960s, those sentenced to life imprisonment in England, including noncapital murder cases, generally served ten years. But for a determinate sentence such as Blake's, there was no statutory provision for early release. In the past half century, no one had been given a sentence of longer than twenty years except Gordon Lonsdale, the Portland ringleader, who was given twenty-five. "I would ask you to treat Blake as an individual and not as a symbol," Hutchinson said.

Hilbery was scornful of the defense arguments. Nor did he find relevant Hutchinson's contention that Blake was a genuine convert to communism who was following his conscience and had received no material gain. If Blake "had a shred of honesty," Hilbery said, he would have resigned from government service upon his return from Korea. Then he would have been free to go "preach it from the housetops."

The forty-two-year sentence was upheld. "It is of the highest importance, perhaps particularly at the present time, that such conduct should not only stand condemned, should not only be held in utter abhorrence by all ordinary men and women, but should receive, when brought to justice, the severest possible punishment," Hilbery declared.

Serving the sentence, Hutchinson said in his arguments, would leave Blake to either "lose his sanity or gain his freedom." In retrospect, he was quite prescient.

CHAPTER 24

Our James Bond

WORMWOOD SCRUBS, SPRING 1961

Georg Blake fell into a deep depression as his sentence sunk in. But he had convinced himself that the authorities had done him a favor by handing him such a long sentence. "It made me determined to break out of prison, as I truly could say I had nothing to lose but my chains," he later said.

There was little immediate room for optimism at Wormwood Scrubs, the dingy Victorian-era prison in West London, built in an era where inmates were confined to their cells for most of the day. The prison, surrounded by a twenty-foot brick wall, held some sixteen hundred prisoners, including more than a hundred serving life sentences.

The KGB scoped the situation around Wormwood Scrubs to see if an escape was feasible, but was not encouraged. "I must say that we were prepared to spend any amount of money to free Blake, but we could see no practical possibility of doing that," recalled Sergei Kondrashev.

Blake was initially kept on suicide watch in the prison hospital, sleeping on a rubber mattress on the floor, a standard procedure for those given lengthy sentences. After a week, he was released from the hospital but placed on a special watch for inmates deemed an escape risk.

He was housed at first in C Hall, one of four large prisoner barracks, each topped with brick-and-stone Gothic towers on the corners. Like the others, C Hall was a hollow shell with steel staircases and landings on the four floors, each with about a hundred cells. Blake described it as resounding "all day to the tramp of marching feet, the shouting of orders, the ringing of bells, the banging of cell doors, the clatter of steel foodplates and a Babel of voices." As a special watch prisoner, he was allowed out of his cell only for work and exercise and always under close escort. A light was kept burning in his cell all night and he was frequently searched.

Oddly enough, Blake's spirits were soon lifted by another spy serving a lengthy sentence: Gordon Lonsdale, the Soviet illegal who had run the Portland ring. MI5 had directed that the various spies in the British prison system were to be kept strictly apart to keep them from communicating with each other, in particular Blake and the Portland spies. But Lonsdale was also on special watch at Wormwood Scrubs, and by an astonishing bureaucratic oversight, he and Blake were placed in the same daily exercise group with the half dozen other special watch prisoners. They spent thirty minutes every day shuffling in a circle around the prison yard.

Lonsdale was a cheerful, gregarious sort, every bit "the hail-fellow-well-met, hard-living, hard-working, pushing Canadian businessman" role he used for his espionage, Blake recalled. He was full of anecdotes and jokes that kept the two spies chuckling during their walks, puzzling the guards and other prisoners. "They thought, 'Well what have these people to laugh about? One of them has just got twenty-five years and the other forty-two years,'" recalled Blake. "Still that's how it was."

On their daily laps, the two men often chatted about their chances of getting out of Scrubs. In June 1961, after a few weeks together, Lonsdale was suddenly transferred to another prison, but on one of their last walks together, he made a prediction to a skeptical Blake: "You know, George, that on the fiftieth anniversary of the October revolution, which will be in '67, you and I will be in Red Square in Moscow, celebrating.'"

BERLIN, SATURDAY, AUGUST 12, 1961

Around midnight, East German army trucks loaded with coils of barbed wire began moving across East Berlin. At sector borders around the city, troops pulled the rolls from the trucks and began erecting barbed wire barriers. At the same time, the East German government issued orders to stop all S-Bahn and U-Bahn trains from running between East and West Berlin. East German police and military units shut off roads leading into West Berlin, pulling up train tracks and erecting barriers. Three Soviet Red Army divisions moved closer to Berlin to discourage any Western interference and put down any riots. Working methodically, crews created a barrier across the center of the city by the time the sun was rising on Sunday morning. The Berlin Wall was born.

In Hyannis Port, Massachusetts, President Kennedy, on vacation with his family, was boating on his cabin cruiser *Marlin*. His military aide, Brigadier General Chester V. "Ted" Clifton, radioed the boat shortly before 1 p.m. on Sunday. "I've got a top priority message from Washington," Clifton said. "You must turn the president around and come back to shore."

After the *Marlin* pulled into the dock carrying an annoyed-looking Kennedy, Clifton handed the president a yellow, one-paragraph Telex message from the White House Situation Room reporting that Berlin had been split and Soviet forces were on the move around the city.

Kennedy was furious that intelligence had not given him any warning. "How come we didn't know anything about this?" he demanded. "Couldn't a tunnel have found this out?"

———

Whether or not a tunnel might have helped, there was no doubt that the CIA had been caught completely off guard. BOB had long warned that given the continued stream of refugees leaving East Berlin destabilizing the communist regime, the East Germans and Soviets might "seal both the zonal and sector borders without prior warning." But they had missed signs of anything imminent.

The CIA was not the only intelligence agency in the dark. Markus

Wolf heard about it on the radio. "At the risk of damaging my reputation as the man who really knew what was going on in East Germany, I have to confess that the building of the Berlin Wall was as
much a surprise to me as everyone else," the East German spy chief
admitted in his memoir. Even senior KGB officers at Karlshorst and
Moscow Center were not informed until the last minute.

Walter Ulbricht, the driving force behind the wall, had kept information about the operation to a very tight circle of leaders in East
Berlin and Moscow. The exodus of refugees from East Germany had
continued at such a high rate that Khrushchev jokingly told Ulbricht
in the summer of 1961 that he would soon be the only one left in the
country. Ulbricht did not laugh. Instead, he adroitly maneuvered
a reluctant Khrushchev into supporting a barrier by convincing him
that East German political and economic collapse was imminent.

In one fell swoop, Ulbricht had solved the refugee problem. At
great cost, from the smallest family tragedies to the hopes of freedom for millions, the wall brought stability to the confrontation
in Berlin, gradually defusing the crisis that had begun with Khrushchev's ultimatum three years earlier.

The wall also spelled the end of Berlin as the world's espionage capital. Without free access across the border, the conditions that made
the city unique for spying disappeared. By early November, BOB
had managed to reconnect with two dozen agents in the East who
had been trained to use alternative means of communication if access
was cut. But it was a drop in the bucket compared to before the wall.

Bill Graver, who had replaced David Murphy as base chief, was
soon transferring officers out, reducing staff, and consolidating the
separate operations branches Bill Harvey had created. The heady
days of BOB as the tip of the intelligence spear were ending with a
clear tactical victory for the KGB and Stasi. "It pretty well put the
base out of operation," said Hugh Montgomery.

ALTGLIENICKE

The Noack family once again fell victim to Cold War machinations.
Paul Noack had moved with his wife and daughter in the summer

of 1958 into the house he had begun building on the tunnel site, trying to make a go with the orchard that had been replanted in the tortured soil. But his health continued to worsen after his leg amputation, and he died in February 1959 at age forty-six. With his death, the lawsuit for tunnel damages ended. "The home wasn't finished when he died," recalled Dagmar Feick. "There was no money to finish it."

She and her mother struggled to keep the orchard running. But following the wall's construction, East German authorities created a heavily fortified "death strip" on its eastern side, ostensibly for protection against the West, but really to keep East Berliners from escaping. The family gave up a hundred-yard-wide swath of land through the orchard, losing the cherry trees. Guards permitted only Dagmar and her mother to work on the remaining trees. "We couldn't let anybody onto the property, and it wasn't easy for us to have access either, or to tend the orchard," she said. Dagmar recalled her classmates joking that it was too bad the tunnel had been discovered: "We would have had a way to flee."

WORMWOOD SCRUBS, FALL 1961

Since his arrival six months earlier, Blake had presented himself to authorities as a model prisoner, one who had resigned himself to making the best of a long life behind bars. It paid off in October when he was taken off the escape list and moved into D Hall, home to many of the long-term prisoners. But he was still accorded special security, accompanied by an officer whenever he moved around the prison. He was assigned to work in the canvas shop, the most secure of the facility's work stations. Prisoners sat before rows of sewing machines, stitching together mail bags and the like under the watch of guards—screws, as they were known in prison vernacular—on raised platforms.

Blake was surprised to find himself a popular figure among his fellow prisoners. Given his crimes of treachery, he later said, "I didn't think these people would be particularly well disposed to me." Indeed, for some he was simply a traitor who should have been sent to the gallows. But as a police report noted, "despite the offences for which he was convicted, Blake was popular with the inmates of 'D' Wing, most of whom sympathized with him on account of the length of his sentence."

Blake found a certain irony in it. "I must say now, that in a way, I'm grateful to the judge, because it made my position in prison very much easier," he said. "I became a rather unusual person. I think there were a lot of people who felt sorry for me [and] as a result I found people who were willing to help me."

He was also pleased to find Wormwood Scrubs not as harsh as some British prisons, and its criminals not as hardened. "The Scrubs is world-famous as a rest camp," said one of Blake's fellow prisoners, James Poulger. "There aren't any real criminals here. The ones here have just killed people in temper, or done a bit of thieving."

Blake made full use of the prison's robust education program. He resumed his Arabic studies, so abruptly cut off when he was lured away from Lebanon. He also studied English literature with a group including convicted murderers, fraudsters, and bank robbers. They read Chaucer's *Troylus and Cryseyde* in the original Middle English, and listened to a recording of Shakespeare's *The Tempest*. Blake's diligent studies conveyed a sense that he had no intention of going anywhere. Once, the tutor expressed disappointment that Blake was late handing in an essay on Chaucer. "What's the hurry?" the pupil replied. "I've got plenty of time."

He practiced yoga every evening, believing it would keep him physically and mentally fit. One night a guard peered through the spy hole into the cell and, seeing Blake standing on his head, asked with concern if he was all right. Blake assured him that he was. "Well, I suppose that's what you can expect from a man who is doing 42 years," the guard muttered.

Blake's home in cell 8 took on "all the appearance and function of a Cambridge don's tutorial room," complete with sagging bookshelves, a Bokhara rug, and cups of tea for visitors. The curtains his mother made for the barred window gave it a homey look. Friends stopping by might find him standing at a lectern reading the Koran, or lying on his bunk reading a tale from *The Thousand and One Nights* in Arabic. On Sunday mornings after roll call, he would often host a coffee for fellow inmates in his cell to listen to BBC radio discussions of books, plays, and art exhibits.

He made friends with fellow prisoners by always lending a sympathetic ear to their travails, helping them draft letters or petitions seeking parole, and offering counsel. Even some of the screws came to him for advice. Blake befriended all, from a high-class wealthy fraud to an angry Yemeni treated as an outcast by others. He spent an hour a day teaching German to a Caribbean immigrant. A group of working-class East Londoners regularly met in his cell for French lessons. "Sometimes when I go to his cell I am greeted by cockney voices holding an animated conversation in French, or reading to each other from French newspapers or periodicals," said Gerald Lamarque, a war hero serving a life sentence for murder who befriended Blake.

Prison was doing him some good, Blake admitted—it gave "me a new insight into human nature, broadened my horizons and rounded out my personality." He began to see himself "as a monk in a contemplative order," a view that fit nicely in his pious self-conception.

He was also quite obliging to his regular visitors from British intelligence. Even though he was under no obligation to cooperate, he was interrogated by SIS forty-two times and was "entirely free and frank in his replies," according to Dick White. He helped John Quine compile a list of the many SIS officers he had compromised. He also met regularly with MI5 officers who were eager to learn details of how Soviet intelligence operated in Britain. Working from MI5 surveillance photos, he identified three KGB case officers he had worked with in London: Sergei Kondrashev, Nikolai Rodin, and Vasily Dozhdalev. Yet Blake's damage to Western intelligence was not done.

MOSCOW, SATURDAY, DECEMBER 30, 1961

Janet Chisholm, the dark-haired and elegant thirty-one-year-old wife of a diplomat at the British embassy, would often take her three small children out for walks to a park along Tsvetnoy Boulevard, near the family's apartment in Moscow. On her outing December 30,

walking amid Muscovites preparing for the New Year, she casually ducked into a nearby nondescript apartment building, stayed for
several minutes, and then walked out. Shortly afterwards, a man of
medium height, with slightly graying red hair, emerged from the
same doorway.

The encounter had been observed by a KGB surveillance team
who had been following Chisholm since she left her apartment. As
the KGB was well aware, her husband, Rauri, ostensibly the second
secretary at the British embassy, was the SIS station chief in Moscow.
Rauri Chisholm had worked in the Russian section of the SIS station in West Berlin in 1955, where his colleagues included George
Blake.

Blake "had alerted us that Chisholm" was SIS, according to Victor Cherkashin, a KGB counterintelligence officer overseeing the
surveillance. Upon his arrival in Moscow in 1960, Rauri Chisholm
was routinely followed by the KGB, and by the next year, his wife was
as well. After Janet Chisholm's walk on December 30, the KGB was
curious to know more about the man who had been seen coming
out of the building shortly after her.

He was soon spotted a second time and photographed, and it did
not take long to identify him: Colonel Oleg Penkovsky. Cherkashin
was at first skeptical that Penkovsky, with his distinguished record
of service as an intelligence officer and a decorated war veteran,
could be a spy, particularly given the well-connected circles he ran
in, which included Ivan Serov, still heading the GRU. But continued surveillance showed Penkovsky meeting regularly with Janet
Chisholm. "The process took many months because we had to make
absolutely certain of our evidence," wrote Cherkashin. The KGB
wanted to discover the full extent of Penkovsky's espionage and any
accomplices he might have.

SIS had chosen Janet Chisholm to communicate even though
Blake had admitted to betraying Rauri Chisholm. "We . . . knew
from George Blake's prison debriefings that Chisholm's identity as
an MI6 officer was well known to the Russians," recalled MI5's
Peter Wright.

Still, SIS needed someone to communicate with Penkovsky in

Moscow. Poised and smart, Janet Chisholm had studied Russian, had worked for SIS as a secretary after university, and was familiar with security procedures. Harry Shergold thought it would be safe to use her, and she and Penkovsky had been regularly meeting since their first carefully choreographed rendezvous in the Tsvetnoy Boulevard park in July 1961, when the Russian, passing by and seemingly charmed by the children, presented Janet with a box of chocolates in which were hidden notes and film about Soviet missiles in Germany.

Shergold later said that there had been no simple alternative to using Chisholm. "Everyone in the British Embassy was under surveillance," he said. "The name of the game was to avoid surveillance."

But like Pyotr Popov before him, Penkovsky was now a marked man.

WORMWOOD SCRUBS, MAY 1962

Musical Appreciation was one of Blake's favorite classes. Not only did he enjoy listening to classical music, he said, but it "enabled me . . . to meet people with the same tastes of whom one finds relatively few in prison." While he was at it, he always kept an eye out for those who might be willing to help him escape.

Several recent arrivals began attending the class in spring 1962, including Michael Randle and Pat Pottle. They were part of the "Wethersfield Six," antinuclear activists who had been given eighteen-month prison sentences for organizing a December 1961 demonstration intended to disrupt operations at the U.S. Air Force base at Wethersfield in Essex. The attempt had failed, but the government, seeking to quash such demonstrations, convicted them on conspiracy charges.

At their first Musical Appreciation class, Randle and Pottle noticed an inmate of slight build and intelligent brown eyes sitting up front, listening attentively to the music. "That's George Blake," another prisoner whispered. The newcomers chatted afterwards with Blake, who chuckled good-naturedly at their awkward jokes about his forty-two-year sentence. "What struck me—as it struck many who met him in prison—was his apparent composure in face of such a dreadful sentence," Randle recalled.

The serious-minded Randle, twenty-eight, was the secretary of the Committee of 100, a prominent British antiwar group founded by Nobel Prize–winning philosopher Bertrand Russell that had sponsored the Wethersfield demonstration. Pottle, the twenty-three-year-old son of a union organizer and a passionate advocate of civil disobedience, was also in the committee's leadership.

They both felt an immediate rapport with Blake. Randle and Pottle had been prosecuted at the Old Bailey by Manningham-Buller, the attorney general, and defended by Jeremy Hutchinson, whom they had chosen because of his work on the Blake case. As pacifists, they disapproved of espionage, but based on the sentence he had been given, the two activists considered Blake a fellow political prisoner.

Sitting in the back of the classroom one day in May 1962, out of earshot from anyone else, Pottle asked Blake in a whisper if he ever thought about escaping.

"I never think of anything else."

"Well, if you think of any way I can help you get out, let me know," Pottle told Blake.

Days later, when Pottle and Blake were at their stations sewing in the canvas workshop, Blake asked permission to use the lavatory. As he left the room, he signaled with his eyes for Pottle to follow. They stood together at the urinals, which were partly visible to the guards through a glass partition. "We were both aware that the screws could be watching us, so we said nothing," recalled Pottle. As he turned to leave, Blake discreetly pushed something into Pottle's hand, out of view from the guards. Pottle stuck the item into his pocket and later pulled it out to find half a chocolate bar. A note was hidden between the chocolate and the wrapper. After eating the chocolate, Pottle read the note.

"If you feel you can help me on your release, go to the Russian Embassy, introduce yourself and say, 'I bring you greetings from Louise,'" Blake had written. Louise was the code name the KGB had given Blake to use in case of emergency. He asked Pottle to relay a plan to have the Soviets toss a rope ladder over the prison wall near D Hall during the daily prisoner exercise period at 10 a.m., and he included a sketch of the prison showing the spot where the ladder should be thrown. The note continued:

> If this is acceptable to them, put the following ad in the personal column of *The Sunday Times*:
>
> LOUISE LONGING TO SEE YOU
>
> If this ad appears, the break will be the following Sunday. If they cannot help, place this ad:
>
> LOUISE SORRY CAN'T KEEP APPOINTMENT
>
> Thank you for your help. Memorise this note, then destroy it.—G

Pottle was taken aback. He had no interest in getting mixed up with the KGB. He consulted with Randle, who was equally dubious. "Wouldn't the press use it as a stick to beat the peace movement with?" Randle asked.

The idea went nowhere. Pottle was soon transferred to a different prison, and Randle never brought it up with Blake during his remaining year at Scrubs.

"The years passed, but they did not forget me and every year sent me a Christmas card," Blake recalled. "I, in turn, did not forget them and their offer."

WASHINGTON, 1962

Bill Harvey had become the point man for some of the CIA's darkest missions. After the Bay of Pigs debacle, President Kennedy and his brother, Attorney General Robert F. Kennedy, were bent on revenge against Castro. Bobby Kennedy took charge of Operation Mongoose, a top-secret government project aimed at removing Castro from power.

John McCone, Allen Dulles's successor as CIA director, told his new director of clandestine services, Richard Helms, that the president was determined "to be rid of Castro and the Castro regime." Accordingly, in February 1962, Helms appointed Harvey, "the CIA's heaviest hitter," as head of the agency's Cuba task force in support of Mongoose. He had no experience in Latin America, but Helms believed Harvey's energy would drive the project forward. The program demanded as much secrecy as the Berlin tunnel, and no one could keep a secret better than Harvey, Helms knew. Harvey, for his part, had grown restless as head of Division D and was eager for the job.

Harvey had already been assigned by Helms's predecessor, Richard Bissell, to create a CIA assassination capability—euphemistically referred to as "executive action." The highly secret program, called ZR/RIFLE, was developed under the cloak of Division D. Harvey had no particular moral compunctions against assassination, though he was skeptical of its effectiveness, calling it the "last resort beyond last resort and a confession of weakness." Once assigned the job, he was willing to take the heavy responsibility, and ultimately the fall. He assembled a roster of potential assassins, including Corsicans, Italians, and a Belgian. In November 1961, Bissell directed Harvey to use ZR/RIFLE to target Fidel Castro, acting on the wishes of the Kennedy brothers. Harvey was "intricately involved" in the failed assassination plots against Castro.

This included serving as case officer for Johnny Rosselli, one of several mobsters the CIA had recruited in 1960 at the behest of Bissell for "a sensitive mission requiring gangster-type action. The mission target was Fidel Castro," according to a CIA memo. Rosselli, a dapper gangster with a taste for the high life who had emigrated from Italy as a child with his family and started as a rumrunner in the Capone gang, was said to have a patriotic streak and never took a dime for his services, such as they were. Harvey liked that and the two became friends. He supplied Rosselli with poison pills, rifles, explosives, detonators, handguns, and radios.

Harvey puckishly named the CIA's Cuba group Task Force W, after the notorious freebooter William Walker, who launched three expeditions to Central America in the mid-1800s, becoming president of Nicaragua and eventually being executed by a firing squad. Those at headquarters who understood the reference wondered if Harvey meant the name as a comment on the wisdom of the programs the administration was pursuing.

Helms sent a message to CIA stations around the world announcing Harvey's appointment and directing that the information about his assignment be shared with foreign intelligence services. "We wanted the KGB to know that Bill was running the show," Sam Halpern, who served as Harvey's assistant for the task force, later said. "The Sovs knew Bill well. They immediately realized we meant business over Cuba." Helms, feeling intense pressure from the Kennedys to take action against Cuba, meant Harvey's appointment to send the same signal to the White House.

At the senior levels of the CIA, the sickening disclosure that George Blake had betrayed the Berlin tunnel before it was dug had not damaged Harvey's standing. More than a few people at the agency assumed that the tunnel intelligence must have been compromised, and some took grim satisfaction at the idea of Harvey being taken down a notch. But the agency investigation launched after Blake's arrest had concluded that the tunnel intelligence was genuine. "George Blake was aware of it but for some reason the Russians didn't react rapidly to this," Frank Rowlett later mused. "Obviously the entire tunnel product could not be reevaluated, but a study was made of the strategic data," said Helms. "Again, no indication of deception was found."

The CIA could guess why. "Because of the worthwhile information developed from the operation on the Allied side, it is presumed that the Soviets were faced with either stopping a potentially harmful operation and losing a valuable penetration agent in Blake or else in protecting Blake and risking unauthorized disclosure of classified information. They chose the latter course," a CIA report concluded.

Helms wrote, "In retrospect, the tunnel was an operational triumph."

———

The Kennedys were intrigued by what they heard about Harvey, and they were impressed by the aura of the tunnel, which Bobby Kennedy considered "a helluva project."

When Edward Lansdale, chief of operations for Operation Mongoose, told John Kennedy that "the American 007" had been placed in charge of the CIA's Cuba task force, the president asked to meet Harvey. A few days later, Harvey and Lansdale waited outside the Oval Office to be called in to meet JFK. Lansdale suddenly had a worrisome thought. "You're not carrying your gun, are you?" he asked Harvey.

Indeed Harvey was. He pulled a revolver from his shoulder holster and handed it to a Secret Service agent, butt first. Everyone relaxed. Just before they entered the office, as if his memory had been jolted, Harvey reached behind his back and pulled a second gun from under his suit jacket, which he also surrendered.

"So you're our James Bond," Kennedy said. If the president was disappointed that the pear-shaped officer with the bulging eyes did not bear the faintest resemblance to the debonair secret agent imagined by Ian Fleming, he kept it to himself. About the only thing Harvey had in common with Bond was an affection for martinis, and even that was tenuous; Harvey couldn't care less whether they were shaken or stirred, only that they be copious.

Harvey readily acknowledged to the president that he lacked 007's sex appeal. The chat was brief but pleasant, and Kennedy welcomed Harvey to the Cuba task force.

It was all downhill from there.

———

At the heart of the problem was a personality conflict. "If one were to cast about for someone positively calculated to rub against every grain of Bill Harvey's being, the chance of finding anyone who might fit the measure more closely than Robert Kennedy would have been zero," Helms later said. ". . . From his underpants to button-down shirt, Bob was East Coast and Ivy League. Bill had earned his way in life without the benefit of family influence."

Kennedy, thirty-six, operated Mongoose with an air of entitlement, running meetings with his feet on the table, and making clear that anybody who crossed him was crossing his brother. He badgered Harvey with orders, questions, and demands for information. Harvey did not take well to what he regarded as interference from a pip-squeak amateur, or "that fucker," as he called RFK. He was unable to hide his contempt for the attorney general and his coterie of "5th Avenue cowboys," his term for Kennedy's aides.

During a visit in early 1962 to the CIA forward operating base in Miami, the bustling focal point for operations against Cuba, Bobby Kennedy eyed a message that had arrived on the teletype, tore it off to read, and began walking with it toward the door. Harvey brusquely challenged Kennedy and then tore the paper out of his hands. Internal documents were not to leave the room.

When Kennedy demanded to know why teams of anti-Castro exiles had not yet been infiltrated into Cuba, Harvey said they needed training first. "I'll take them out to Hickory Hill and train them myself," Kennedy said, referring to his estate in Northern Virginia. "What will you teach them, sir?" retorted Harvey. "Baby-sitting?"

Bobby Kennedy, for his part, considered Harvey's Cuba performance a "disaster." Harvey's methodical, close-to-the-vest style did not play well at the endless high-level meetings led by Kennedy. When pressed for details and updates on operations, Harvey would launch into long-winded, incomprehensible monologues, essentially saying nothing, probably because he thought it was none of their business. It had worked in Berlin, but not in Washington. The former G-man from Indiana was the antithesis of how the academics making up Kennedy's New Frontier viewed themselves. "Your friend Harvey doesn't inspire much confidence," McGeorge Bundy, the former Harvard University dean serving as national security advisor, told Tom Parrott, a CIA officer assigned to the project.

It did not help that Harvey's drinking had worsened since leaving Berlin. In addition to periodic binges, his daily consumption had increased and he routinely returned from lunch polluted. McCone, a devout Catholic and a bit of a puritan, was appalled when Harvey dozed off at a meeting.

Despite it all, Helms later said, "I doubt that anyone could have done a better job of attempting to run our part of the MONGOOSE project than Harvey did." Harvey was exhausted from drafting plans and options to meet the conflicting orders and abrupt changes directed by Bobby Kennedy and Lansdale, and by the late summer of 1962, he reached the breaking point, according to Helms. "Bill's frustration with trying to carry out a string of next-to-impossible missions while satisfying the two totally different senior people, neither of whom had more than a slight notion of what was involved in agent operations, became impossible for him to hide," Helms said.

In early September, Harvey and Bobby Kennedy had an all-out shouting match, leaving Harvey persona non grata at the White House. Helms assigned Harvey's deputy to deal with Kennedy and decided to remove Harvey from the task force as soon as a replacement was found.

Before that happened, the Cuban Missile Crisis erupted. On October 16, President Kennedy was informed that CIA analysis of U-2 surveillance photographs showed that the Soviets had placed nuclear missiles in Cuba, ninety miles from the American mainland. U.S. forces were placed on maximum alert and a naval quarantine set around Cuba to prevent more ships from reaching the island.

Around October 21, with a U.S. military invasion seen as a distinct possibility, Harvey approved the dispatch of several teams of exiles into Cuba to serve as advance support, something he believed he had the authority and obligation to do.

Robert Kennedy was furious when he learned about it on October 26; he had given orders that nothing be done that might ignite the confrontation. At a meeting of Mongoose principals that afternoon at the Pentagon, Kennedy demanded that the "half-assed operation" be aborted. Three of the teams were beyond recall. "Bill had no way to call the boats back," said Parrott.

When Kennedy suggested that Harvey's actions were a deliberate act of insubordination, Harvey called him a liar. "If you SOBs hadn't screwed up on the Bay of Pigs, we wouldn't be in this mess," he told Kennedy, according to Halpern.

"Harvey has destroyed himself today," McCone told his deputy later that day. "His usefulness has ended." McCone wanted him fired, but Helms managed to save him.

Harvey was immediately removed from Task Force W. He killed

a few months at the Langley headquarters, and then Helms sent him to Rome in July 1963 as station chief. Harvey was a fish out of water; Rome had few operational responsibilities and the position called for someone with diplomatic finesse, which Harvey emphatically lacked.

His health and his career became increasingly incapacitated by alcoholism. "He could no longer stand the liquor," said Hugh Montgomery, the tunnel veteran whom Harvey brought in as operations officer in Rome. "He was six sheets to the wind by noontime on. It was very tragic because he was an extraordinarily talented man."

It was a stunning fall. Friends who visited Harvey in Rome found him pale, defeated, and drunk, a shell of his former self. "It had gone beyond self-immolation," said David Murphy.

MOSCOW, OCTOBER 1962

On October 22, 1962, President Kennedy disclosed the Soviet threat in Cuba during a televised address to an audience of one hundred million Americans. In Moscow the same day, a KGB special forces team stormed Colonel Oleg Penkovsky's apartment on the Moscow River and took him into custody without incident, following months of surveillance of his meetings with Janet Chisholm.

By later assessments, Penkovsky's intelligence played a critical role in enabling President Kennedy to defuse the Cuban Missile Crisis without nuclear war. "Penkovsky had managed to photograph and pass highly sensitive documents that proved invaluable during the crisis," a CIA history states. These included the technical manual for the R-12 missile system the Soviets had deployed to Cuba, which, together with other intelligence he provided, enabled CIA analysts to understand how Soviet missiles forces operated, and to estimate the time they required to achieve different levels of readiness. At a moment when Kennedy was considering a military strike to take out the missile bases, the CIA assessment that it would take three days to launch "gave President Kennedy time to maneuver," Helms later said. "I don't know of any single instance where intelligence was more immediately valuable."

Penkovsky's arrest may have been timed to prevent him from delivering more damaging information to the West at a moment when nuclear war seemed imminently possible. Because of the gravity of the case, KGB chief Vladimir Semichastny personally took charge of the interrogation. Penkovsky was brought to his office on the third floor of the Lubyanka, the building housing the KGB. "Tell me what harm you have inflicted on our country," Semichastny told him. "Describe it all in detail, with the most pertinent facts."

During months of interrogation, Penkovsky was held in a KGB jail on Dzerzhinsky Square until his trial in May 1963, when he was sentenced to death and subsequently shot.

In his jail cell in London, George Blake was biding his time.

CHAPTER 25

Mischief, Thou Art Afoot

WORMWOOD SCRUBS, SEPTEMBER 1965

By 1965, George Blake had come to the realization that if he was to escape from Wormwood Scrubs, he would have to make it happen himself. The KGB, he concluded, was not going to help him break out of prison, both because of the difficulty of the operation and the risk of embarrassment if it failed.

Blake's early confidence that the Soviets would trade him for another spy had likewise faded. The captured American U-2 pilot Francis Gary Powers was traded in February 1962 on the Glienicke Bridge in Berlin not for Blake, but for the Soviet illegal Rudolf Abel. The next most valuable westerner the Soviets held was Greville Wynne, a British businessman serving eight years for helping SIS communicate with Penkovsky. But in April 1964, it was Blake's onetime prison mate, Gordon Lonsdale, who was brought to the bridge and traded for Wynne. Abel and Lonsdale, unlike Blake, were Russians. Moreover, they had refused to talk despite offers to reduce their sentences. Blake's confession likely dimmed his value—since he had already told all, there was less incentive for the Soviets to gain his freedom.

His feeling of hopelessness was doubtless propelled by a new blow. Gillian Blake had recently told him she wanted a divorce, crushing his fervent if unrealistic hope to keep the marriage together. Gillian had faithfully visited once a month, the maximum allowed, always with a prison guard present. It was difficult enough "to keep our marriage going on a few hours together a year without the added strain of these times together being listened into," she told Jeremy Hutchinson. Gillian's continued support for her husband had created a rift with her father, the former SIS officer, who had been close to Blake and felt betrayed. Gillian started seeing another man in the summer of 1965 and told her husband she wanted to begin a new life with him. Blake was devastated but agreed to begin the divorce process. In retrospect, his friend and fellow inmate Gerald Lamarque recognized, this was the turning point. "If I was convinced, as I was, that only George's wife and children kept him in prison, then I should have realized that once the divorce was under way his thoughts must have been directed towards escape," he said.

———

Blake had not given up hope that Michael Randle and Pat Pottle could help him escape, even though they had long since been released from prison. They would be ideal accomplices, he believed, not only because he liked and trusted them, but because they were experienced activists with contacts in left-wing circles. But he needed someone still on the inside, yet due to be released soon, who could serve as the go-between and help pull off the escape.

He had a candidate in mind: Sean Aloyisious Bourke, an Irishman with an antiauthoritarian bent and a literary streak who was serving an eight-year sentence at Scrubs for attempting to kill a police officer.

The thirty-one-year-old Bourke was heavy-boned and dark-haired, with a rugged handsomeness and "typical Irish charm," according to Blake. "This rather stolid exterior hid an intelligent and highly imaginative personality, with a strong sense of the dramatic, an ability to dissemble, an obsessive pride and a deep-rooted hatred of anyone in authority," he added.

Bourke had been born and raised in Limerick, part of an extended family of poets, actors, drunks, and fighters, all holding traits that he shared. His early life as a delinquent culminated at age twelve when he was nabbed for petty theft and sent to the notorious Daingean reformatory. Regular whippings by monks with sticks did little to keep Bourke on the straight and narrow path, and he remained in and out of trouble as an adult. In September 1961, he sent a parcel bomb to a police constable who he claimed had falsely arrested him on a charge of molesting a boy. The bomb, disguised in a tin of coffee on which Bourke had written *Requiescat in Pace,* exploded, but the constable escaped injury by thrusting it away at the last second.

Bourke had arrived at Scrubs not long after Blake, and they met in the English Literature Diploma class. A cousin of the Irish poet Desmond O'Grady, Bourke had a way with words, and before long became editor of the prison magazine, *New Horizon.* This ambitious publication featured articles written by prisoners, among them Blake, weighing in on topics ranging from British foreign policy to profiles of the screws.

With his natural anti-state predilection, Bourke was sympathetic to Blake's plight, viewing him as "a political prisoner" given an inhumane sentence. He was also taken by Blake's role as the prison's comforting shoulder. "I always marveled at the sight of this man-without-hope giving help and advice and comfort to young fellows in their twenties," Bourke recalled. "Blake was one of that all too rare breed of men—a good listener. And in prison such men were in especially high demand."

By the late summer of 1965, Bourke was approaching the end of his parole-shortened sentence. He would soon be eligible for a work-release program, where he would spend nine months working a civilian job in the city and sleeping at night in a hostel attached to the prison. Blake knew he would have to act soon. On Monday, September 6, he approached Bourke in D Hall with a pensive look on his face. "Sean, I've decided the time has come for me to leave this place," he told him. "I had been hoping there might be some chance of an exchange with the Russians or some such thing which might mean my getting out of here earlier, but I now have reason to believe this will not happen and therefore I think I must get out of here on my own initiative. I am asking you to help me escape."

Bourke was surprised. "There had been no warning of this, not the slightest hint in that smiling face over the years," he recalled.

But Blake had read his subject well. Bourke waved off his suggestion that he give the matter some thought. "George, I don't have to think it over," he replied. "I have already made up my mind."

Blake's face clouded. "Oh?" he asked. "What have you decided?"

"I'm your man."

———

Bourke and Blake immediately started planning, tossing out ideas for the next month as they walked around the prison. All were variations involving Bourke tossing a rope ladder over the wall from outside the prison to allow Blake to climb out.

They recruited a fellow prisoner, Philip Anthony Morris, a cool operator serving a six-year term for robbery. Both Blake and Bourke liked and trusted him, and, equally important, Morris was trusted by the authorities, who had made him one of a select group of inmates able to move freely about the prison. Morris had access to the hostel where Bourke would be staying and could relay messages to Blake.

In late November 1965, Bourke began the work-release program, and was given a job at a car accessory factory in Acton, about a mile from the prison. He was much more interested in the escape mission than the job, and spent his free time walking the area around Scrubs. Blending in with other passersby in the busy neighborhood, he studied the prison walls from the outside and got a feel for the streets in the area. The escape would be made over the east wall, the one closest to D Hall. A narrow lane known as Artillery Road ran along the outside of the wall between the prison and its neighbor, Hammersmith Hospital. Bourke studied the parking habits of hospital workers and visitors, getting a feel for the times when Artillery Road was usually empty.

Blake and Bourke calculated that they would need some £700 to finance the escape, including a getaway car and a hideaway apartment. They agreed that Bourke would approach Blake's mother for help. During one of Catherine Blake's visits to the prison, Blake obliquely tipped her to expect a caller. Following instructions Bourke sent her in a letter, she met Bourke outside the Golders Green underground station on a Friday evening in early December. But Catherine Blake was extremely nervous when the stranger outlined her son's request, and she insisted on consulting her daughter Adele. During the early months of 1966, Bourke met with the two women several times. Adele was skeptical of the whole thing, demanding more details on where they would hide her brother and how they would get him out of the country. Before the women would agree to give Bourke any money, Adele told him, "I would . . . have to have confidence in your plans, and I certainly don't have that."

The hot-tempered Bourke was angry at the reticence, taking it as a personal rebuke. After his mother and sister visited him at the prison, Blake feared that their nervousness could endanger the entire operation. "They are obviously very worried about all this, and I have reluctantly come to the conclusion that they should no longer be involved, for their own sakes as well as ours," he wrote Bourke in a note delivered by Morris.

Blake and Bourke agreed that Michael Randle, who had been in their English literature class at Scrubs, should be approached next. Randle was living a hectic life, studying for final exams for an English degree in preparation for a teaching career, and at the same time organizing demonstrations against the Vietnam War. He and his wife, Anne, had two young children. But when Bourke paid a call to their home in Kentish Town in northwest London, the Randles immediately agreed to support the escape by trying to raise money. "We're with you," Michael told Bourke, and they solemnly shook hands.

At Randle's suggestion, Pat Pottle was brought into the plot. Pottle had continued with the peace movement upon his release from prison, working several years as secretary for Bertrand Russell, and was now operating a printing shop. He was similarly willing to help.

———

Pottle and Randle on board, Bourke hit upon the idea of using two-way radios, which thanks to transistor technology were much smaller and cheaper than in the past. At a radio shop in Piccadilly, he found a pair of Japanese walkie-talkies compact enough to fit in his pocket yet able to transmit several miles. With the help of Phil

Morris, he smuggled one of the radios back into the prison for Blake. Conveniently enough, Blake had recently been placed in charge of the Scrubs canteen, where his duties included ordering and taking delivery of supplies sold to prisoners. He had keys to the canteen, which was an ideal spot to hide his walkie-talkie.

A test of the radios was set for the night of May 29. With Bourke's penchant for literary flourishes, the code they had established to confirm their identity on the airwaves was from a poem by Richard Lovelace, a seventeenth-century poet they had studied in English literature class. In his cell on D Hall, Blake lay on his side in his bunk with his back to the door and radio concealed under the blanket in case a guard looked through the spyhole. Bourke, in his room at the hostel, waited until the guards had turned the lights out in D Hall before pushing the transmission button.

"*Stone walls do not a prison make, nor iron bars a cage.* Over," he recited.

After a pause and a humming sound, he heard Blake's unmistakable Dutch-accented voice carefully enunciating the response: "*Minds innocent and quiet take that for a hermitage.* Over."

Both men were delighted. The transmissions were loud and clear. "That first time we talked well into the night," Blake recalled. "Apart from its immense usefulness, it was a wonderful experience to communicate once again completely freely with someone in the outside world."

———

Blake and Bourke spoke once a week, usually on Saturday evenings, refining their escape plan. Blake consulted with Morris, "an expert at breaking and entering," for the best way to exit D Hall. Morris recommended using the tall Gothic-style window that took up much of the exterior wall on the south end of the hall. It held hundreds of thick glass panels set in cast-iron frames, and while each eighteen-by-six-inch panel was too narrow for a man to pass, if the iron bar between two panels was removed, someone Blake's size could squeeze through. Several days in advance of the escape, Morris would use his skills to discreetly break and remove two panes of glass. Enough panes were already missing that two more would not be noticed.

Blake by now was quite familiar with all of Scrubs's security short-comings and knew that some of the guards were a bit lazy. Other prisons outside of London were known to be more secure, and even if he managed to escape from one of them, it would be much more difficult to hide. At Scrubs, by contrast, once he was over the wall he could quickly disappear into a city of eight million people.

Thus Blake was alarmed on June 6 when six prisoners escaped from Scrubs by sawing through the bars on a cell window and using a rope ladder to scale the same east perimeter wall he planned to use. In response, prison authorities decided to install metal grids over the windows in all four halls, a layer of security that could greatly complicate his breakout. Installation would begin with A Hall and continue to D Hall.

Blake also feared that the resulting outcry over lax security at Scrubs would lead to his transfer to another prison. He had good reason to be concerned. Despite his seeming lack of interest in escape, there were always some who feared it could be a ruse. "The one suspicious thing about BLAKE was his apparent contentment with his position," said a November 1966 police report.

"This man must <u>always</u> be under the closest supervision," the Wormwood Scrubs deputy governor wrote in November 1965. "He is a security risk in every sense of the word, caution <u>always</u>."

In January 1966, the prison's new governor named Blake as one of three prisoners who were security risks and should be held else-where. It was the fourth time officials had suggested moving him, but each time bureaucratic inertia set in and no action was taken.

———

By July, Randle had raised £200 to fund the operation, all of it do-nated by an anonymous friend. But getting more money was prov-ing difficult. Randle and Pottle approached several friends, and none wanted anything to do with it, given Blake's notoriety.

Fearing that word of the plan would leak, they stopped asking and tried operating on a shoestring budget. Then, unexpectedly, a young woman who was a family friend of Randle's told him she had come into a modest inheritance. "As a socialist, she did not believe in inherited wealth," Randle recalled. "Could I suggest a suitable project or organization where the money could be put to good use?" Randle, in fact, could, and from that point the money worries were solved.

Bourke, who upon his release from the hostel on July 4 was a free man, rented a room on Perryn Road near the prison. He used the funds to buy a getaway car, a battered two-tone green 1955 Humber Hawk. He practiced various getaway routes, timing how far he could get from the prison in a short time. The car was also handy for communicating with Blake. Bourke would park by the prison wall on Artillery Road, posing as a hospital visitor, and speak into the walkie-talkie concealed in a bouquet of flowers.

In early August, Bourke, Pottle, and the Randles met at the Randle home to review the plan. On the appointed day, Bourke would park his car on Artillery Road along the long wall between the prison and the hospital. The road was usually empty on Saturday evenings until shortly before visiting hours began at 7 p.m. He would pose as someone who had arrived for a visit early. Once in position, he would radio Blake to exit the Gothic window from the second-floor stairway landing.

It was a drop of only three feet to the sloped roof of a covered passageway. From there, Blake could swing down the gutter a short way to reach the ground. The east wall was only about fifty feet from D Hall. He would wait in the building shadows, a short dash from the spot on the wall where Bourke would throw the ladder. Blake would have his radio and signal Bourke when the coast was clear. Foot patrols came by the wall roughly every twenty minutes, leaving plenty of time in between. The closest guard post was more than a hundred yards away, too far to stop Blake from reaching the ladder.

By any measure, they were amateurs. But Pottle and the Randles were impressed with the escape plan Bourke described. The two-way radios and the assistance of Morris were a critical advantage. The peace activists wanted assurances that there would be no violence, and Bourke promised he would use no force if confronted. They were also concerned that Bourke had purchased the Hawk in his own name. That would be an obvious giveaway if the car was found after the escape. Bourke agreed to sell the car and buy a new one under an assumed name.

Pottle was worried that they had no plan for what to do with Blake after the breakout. Where would he be hidden and how would he get out of the country? Pottle was surprised that Blake had not given this more thought. Clearly, he would get only one shot at escaping. "Yet here he was putting his faith completely in Sean, without any clear idea of what would happen once he was over the wall," Pottle later wrote. "Even allowing for his desperation, this would be an enormous gamble."

The group bounced around ideas, proposing that they fly Blake to Ireland with a forged passport on the night of the escape. When Bourke brought the idea to Blake, he was adamant that there be no immediate attempt to get out of the country or anytime soon. It would be safest to lie low in London.

Bourke planned to make the entire ladder out of rope, including the rungs. Randle was worried that this would make for a slow and difficult climb up the twenty-foot wall. "George was not all that fit, yoga or no yoga," he recalled. Wooden rungs would give better support but make the ladder too heavy and noisy. Anne Randle proposed making the rungs with knitting needles. A size 13, made of steel and coated in plastic, would be strong enough to hold a man yet add little weight, she suggested.

Bourke bought nylon clothesline at Woolworths, and then went to a nearby shop to buy the knitting needles. "I'll have thirty," he told the sales clerk.

She raised her eyebrows. "Your wife must be doing a lot of knitting," she said.

———

After Bourke consulted with Blake, the group fixed the date of escape for Saturday, October 22, when the days would be getting shorter. Zero hour was set for 6:15 p.m., as it would be close to dark and most of the prisoners and guards would be away from D Hall, watching the weekly film.

In late September, Bourke quit his job, telling people that he was returning to Ireland for good. He spent a week in Limerick in early October, partly to establish an alibi but mainly to visit family and drink in pubs. Back in London on October 15, he used an assumed name to rent a small, cheap apartment on Highlever Road in North Kensington. The place was a bit dismal, with barely more than a bed, a table, and a stove, but it was only a five-minute drive from the prison. The idea was Blake could be quickly hidden in a spot close to the prison, where the police would never think to look.

Bourke made last-minute preparations, buying a secondhand television they could use to monitor the news, and some clothes that Blake could wear. He tested the homemade ladder to make sure the nylon and knitting needles were taut enough to hold Blake. But despite his assurances to Randle and Pottle, he did not sell the Humber Hawk and intended to use it for the escape.

Blake and Bourke spoke via radio on Tuesday, October 18, to check last-minute details. Blake reported that the crews installing wire mesh over the windows had made it up only to C Hall. "A good thing that, as good bureaucrats, they did the job in alphabetical order," he said.

As they prepared to end the transmission, Blake sounded nervous. "Are you absolutely certain that everything is ready for Saturday, that nothing remains to be done?" he asked.

"I hope in four days time it will be just like the words of the old Irish song," Bourke responded, and then he began singing in a melodious voice:

I'll walk beside you in the world today,
While dreams and songs and flowers bless your way,
I'll look into your eyes and hold your hand,
I'll walk beside you through this golden land.

There was a long silence on the other end. Blake did not quite know how to respond. "I'm looking forward very much to hearing you sing Irish songs very shortly," he finally said. ". . . So come and get it over on Saturday and I hope everything will be all right, because the waiting is getting a little bit nerve racking."

On Thursday, October 20, Catherine Blake came to visit her son, bringing some clothes for an upcoming court hearing on his divorce. She may not have known an escape attempt was imminent, though she certainly was aware of her son's interest. But Blake had not mentioned "even the remotest possibility" of escape to Gillian—she was once again in the dark.

Blake had a nice chat with his mother. The one odd thing the officer monitoring the meeting noticed was that he "appeared far happier than one would have expected for a man with his problems."

LONDON, SATURDAY, OCTOBER 22, 1966

At 1 p.m., Blake and Bourke made a final radio check to confirm that all was ready for the evening. Blake reported that Phil Morris had taken out the glass panes in the window to be used for the escape and that it had gone unnoticed. Morris would knock out the cast-iron bar once Bourke was in position on Artillery Road that evening.

At 4:30, most of the D Hall prisoners filed out to go see the weekly film in the prison's recreation hut. About a hundred stayed behind to enjoy free time under the supervision of two officers. It was always the most peaceful time of the week, when the usual cacophony was replaced by the relative calm of small groups of prisoners tidying up their cells or playing cards and chess.

Blake was restless. He wandered down to the common area, where some prisoners were watching professional wrestling on television, but he could not stomach it for long. The sport was "a farce," he remarked to Officer William Fletcher, who stood watching in the back. Then he wandered off. At some point, he stopped off at the prison canteen and left a note apologizing for failing to add up the outstanding accounts. He was back at his cell at 5:30.

Only a handful of prisoners had the faintest inkling of Blake's plans. He had kept even his closest friends in the dark except for the few involved. "There was an absence of the gossip which normally prevails among the convicts when an escape is in the offing," according to a subsequent police report.

Kenneth de Courcy, serving time for fraud, stopped by Blake's cell to say goodbye. De Courcy, a onetime adviser to Prime Minister Neville Chamberlain's cabinet who held extreme right-wing views, had learned of the escape plan by accident, but kept quiet out of admiration for his communist friend. Blake presented him with his Koran as a parting gift. Then he put a towel around his neck and headed to the bath. "I've got a bit of an ordeal in front of me, and I'm now going down to have a very hot shower," he told de Courcy. "I need it."

Bourke was also having trouble whiling away the final hours. He practiced throwing the ladder in the hideaway flat, tossing it from one corner of the room to the other. In the late afternoon, he drove to a florist to buy a potted chrysanthemum to help him fit in as a hospital visitor. He sat parked near a pub on East Acton Lane, nervously sucking on chocolate sweets before starting the drive to Scrubs at 5:45 p.m. A light rain had begun, and he ran into unexpected traffic at the Western Avenue roundabout, a half mile from the prison. The roads were jammed in all directions. At 6 p.m., when Bourke was supposed to be parked in position on Artillery Road, he was stuck in traffic. He cursed himself for not waiting nearer the prison.

———

Back in his cell after his shower, Blake drank a cup of tea and read the *Times*. Looking out the bars of his cell window, he was delighted to see rain falling and the evening turning dark early. By 6 p.m., it was time to go. He put on his gym shoes, took his walkie-talkie out of its hiding place, and tucked it in the sweater he wore atop his prison-issued striped shirt and gray trousers. He took a final look around cell 8, his home for five years, and stepped out.

He saw that all was peaceful in the hall, with Officer Fletcher still watching television and the second guard off in the pantry. After joining Morris in his cell, Blake radioed Bourke at 6:15. There was no answer at first, but then Bourke came on the air. He had finally broken from the traffic and was parked in position on Artillery Road.

Morris, given the okay to prepare the window, strolled to the stairwell. It was a Saturday ritual for prisoners to hang their blankets over the railing for airing, and several had been conveniently placed to shield the screws' view of the stairwell as Morris did his work. The rusty bar gave way with one kick. Morris was back in his cell in three minutes and told Blake everything was set.

Blake radioed Bourke with the update. "The window has been taken care of," he reported. "I'm ready to make my exit."

"I am ready for you," Bourke replied.

Blake shook hands with Morris and then walked quickly to the second-floor landing. It was now 6:30, and it was just in time, as the film had ended earlier than the plotters anticipated and the first prisoners were already returning. The hall started to fill with their clamor.

Shielded from the officers' view by the draped blankets, Blake slipped out the opening easily and felt with his feet for the roof of the passageway. The tiles were slippery from the steady rain, but he nimbly made his way to the edge of the roof, grabbed the gutter, and dropped to the ground. He pressed himself against the D Hall wall, hiding in a small recess formed by the passageway and the jutting turret at the building corner. With the rain and gathering gloom, he felt well hidden.

He radioed Bourke to say he was ready for the ladder. Bourke sounded agitated. "Hang on just a sec," he replied. "I am up against an unexpected snag."

A security guard in a van was driving down Artillery Road on his way to close the gates leading into a public sports ground behind the hospital for the evening. The guard evidently thought there was something suspicious about Bourke and his car, parked so near the prison wall. After closing the gates, he stopped his van in front of Bourke's car and stepped out, holding a large Alsatian guard dog on a leash. He stood near the Hawk and stared in at Bourke, making no attempt to conceal his suspicions.

Bourke picked up his flowerpot and sniffed the chrysanthemum, glancing at his watch, hoping to convey the impression that he was impatiently waiting for hospital visiting hours. The guard was not impressed and remained standing with his dog, both of them staring at Bourke. Spooked, Bourke drove off. He felt sure that the escape had been blown, and that his departure would be seen as an admission of nefarious intent. But after driving a circuit, he returned to find the van gone.

Now a car was parked where the van had been. Bourke furtively glanced in as he drove by and discovered to his dismay that a young man and his date were sitting in the front seat, necking. It was Bourke's turn to stare. He parked, stood on the road, and peered into the couple's car until they grew uncomfortable and drove off.

Finally, he radioed Blake, who had no idea what had happened. Bourke could hear great anxiety in Blake's voice. "Well, I'm already out of the hall and waiting for that ladder! The men are back from the cinema. The patrol might come along any moment. Hurry!"

Bourke kept hesitating. Another car showed up, this one bearing early arrivals for hospital visiting hours.

Blake, still standing in the recess outside D Hall, called on the walkie-talkie but got no reply. He could hear the bell ringing inside. That was the signal for prisoners to return to their cells for roll call. "There was little time now before they would discover I was missing," he recounted. Hearing still no reply, he concluded that Bourke had been forced to run off. He began folding up the radio antenna, expecting that the guards were likely searching for him. Then suddenly Bourke's voice came clear over the radio.

"Sorry, there was a hitch," Bourke said. "I will throw it soon now." The visitors had parked and walked to the hospital.

"Please hurry," Blake called desperately. "Time is very short."

But Bourke paused again to allow still more visitors to park and walk off. On the other side, Blake was beside himself. "You must throw the ladder now, you simply must!" he radioed. "There's no more time!"

The coast was again clear. Bourke tossed aside his chrysanthemum and resolved to act. He pulled the ladder out of the car trunk. He held the folded rungs in his right hand, started to swing, and then stopped. The wall looked much higher now that he was standing directly below it. He climbed onto the roof of the Hawk. He swung the folded ladder with his right arm three times and then tossed it, holding a rope attached to the ladder in his left hand.

In the dim light of the prison yard's arc lamps, Blake could see the ladder sailing over the top. The rungs writhed momentarily and then the ladder hung motionless on the wall. "It looked incredibly thin and fragile but the moment I saw it I knew nothing now would stop me," he recalled. No patrols were in sight. He pushed the walkie-talkie into his now soaking wet sweater and, bending low, rushed to the wall. He grabbed the ladder and, fueled by adrenaline, scampered up the brick wall in no time.

On the other side, holding the rope attached to the ladder, Bourke could feel the pull of someone ascending the ladder. "But was it Blake who was climbing? Or a screw?" he recalled thinking. He heard a pair of hands slapping on the wet stone coping and saw fingers gripping the top. Then a face appeared. It was Blake.

"He looked down at me, wide-eyed, bewildered," Bourke recalled. Blake seemed to hesitate.

"Come on, man, come on!" Bourke shouted. They were both drenched in rain.

Blake scooted down the wall to avoid falling on the car and then lowered himself until he was hanging by both hands. As he let go, Bourke moved underneath him to break his fall. Blake tried to avoid him and tumbled awkwardly. He hit the ground with a thud, smashing his head on the gravel, and lay still.

Artillery Road exploded with light. Cars were arriving for the 7 p.m. visiting hour, and their turning headlights briefly illuminated the rope dangling from the wall and Blake lying on the ground. Bourke grasped him under the arms. "George! Are you all right? For Christ's sake, what's the matter with you?" Blake could only groan in response.

Bourke dragged him to the car, opened the rear door, and pushed him into the backseat. Bourke jumped in the front, started the car, and lurched forward, driving up Artillery Road past several startled hospital visitors.

Blake was recovering his senses and sat up in the backseat. Blood streamed down his face and he felt a sharp pain in his left arm.

"Are you all right, George?" Bourke asked.

"Not bad, not bad," Blake answered weakly.

Rain was beating down on the car and the windows were fogged up as they drove away from the prison. The car in front of Bourke stopped abruptly to let some hospital visitors cross the road, and he slammed into its bumper with a loud crash. A crowd of onlookers, standing in a queue for a bus, peered quizzically into the two vehicles. The car in front did not budge, leaving the Hawk with no place to go. "For Christ's sake, why doesn't that bastard move!" Bourke shouted.

Blake, wiping blood from his face with a handkerchief, leaned over from the backseat. "Take it easy, Sean. Keep calm," he said. "Whatever happens, we mustn't lose our heads."

Finally, the driver in front pulled his car over to the curb, and signaled for Bourke to do the same. "You've got some bloody hope," Bourke muttered. He floored the accelerator and screeched down the road toward Wood Lane, heading to the hideaway apartment.

The traffic signal ahead was red. "Bollocks to the lights!" Bourke screamed.

"Sean, for heaven's sake, take it easy!" Blake pleaded.

By the time the car reached the intersection, the light was green. Bourke looked in the rearview mirror. No one was following.

WORMWOOD SCRUBS, SATURDAY EVENING, OCTOBER 22

Officer Fletcher had rung the bell at 7 p.m., signaling all inmates to end their free time and return to their cells. Making checks at 7:10, Fletcher noticed that Blake was not yet in cell 8, though the guard did not feel a need yet to raise any alarm. But when he checked back at 7:20 and found Blake still missing, he called the main gate and set the prison escape procedure in motion. Four D Hall officers searched the wing without success. Across the prison, all spare officers scoured the grounds. Officer Buckley, responsible for watching the boundary wall, looked around the outside of D Hall and found nothing. Then he looked over to the east wall and saw a ladder dangling. He yanked it down.

At 7:43 p.m., an officer in the main gate called the nearby Shepherds Bush police station. "A prisoner has escaped over the wall into Artillery Road," the officer reported. "We believe it to be a man called Blake, dressed in prison clothing."

Noel Whittaker, the principal officer at Scrubs, rushed from the prison and made his way around the corner to Artillery Road, which he found deserted. Through the gloom, he spotted something on the ground at the foot of the wall, directly opposite from where the ladder had been found. Walking up to it, he found a potted pink chrysanthemum in green wrapping paper.

———

The Hawk reached the Highlever Road flat in a few minutes. Bourke had a hat and a raincoat for Blake to wear over his prison clothes for the short walk into the apartment, though the street of three-story brick houses was deserted in the rain. They got inside the flat without seeing anyone. Blake's forehead was bleeding, pocked with gravel indentations, and his left wrist was broken and bent at an ugly angle, but he was too elated to feel much pain. "We have done it!" he declared emotionally, and they shook hands.

Bourke left Blake in the apartment while he drove off to ditch the car, abandoning it on a quiet street in Kilburn. After stopping in a pub for four quick double whiskeys, he arrived back at the flat with a bottle of whiskey in one pocket and a bottle of brandy in the other. A bit of first aid was in order. The two tore up Blake's prison shirt to make a sling for his arm, and put cold compresses on his head wound.

Then they settled back for a celebratory drink, Blake sipping brandy and Bourke knocking back whiskey. They turned on the television for the BBC evening news, a broadcast watched by millions.

A photograph of Blake filled the screen. "High drama in West London tonight," newscaster Peter Woods began. "George Blake, the double agent who was serving forty-two years' imprisonment for spying for the Russians, escaped from Wormwood Scrubs Prison in London this evening. Blake was tried at the Central Criminal Court in May 1961. His sentence was the longest ever imposed in a British court of law. . . . A Home Office statement says that Blake was missed from his cell at the seven o'clock roll-call, when all the prisoners were being locked away for the night. A search was made of the prison grounds but no trace of Blake could be found. He is therefore presumed to have escaped. A huge manhunt has been launched under the direction of Scotland Yard's Special Branch. Careful watch is being kept at all airports and harbours, and East European embassies are also being kept under observation. News is still coming in of this dramatic escape, and we will keep you informed."

Sitting a mile from Scrubs, Blake and Bourke chuckled. Bourke refilled their glasses, turned to Blake, and made a toast: *Mischief, thou art afoot; take thou what course thou wilt.*

CHAPTER 26

A Free Man Again

**WORMWOOD SCRUBS, 10 P.M., SATURDAY,
OCTOBER 22, 1966**

I t began as a murmur of sound, prisoners speaking from cell window to cell window. Those with radios tuned to the BBC passed the news to those without.

At first the words were indistinguishable to Gerald Lamarque in his cell, but soon he could hear snippets of conversations. "Blake . . . Blake . . . over the wall . . . George . . . had it away . . . Good old George." Lamarque had been at Wormwood Scrubs during many previous escapes, but had never seen a response like this. "The excitement I hear in the voices is unbelievable," he said.

From one end of the prison, he could hear the faint sound of singing: "For he's a jolly good fellow."

Lamarque's heart pounded as he lay in his bunk. "Think fast, George, don't let them get you back here," he thought. "Be lucky, be lucky." He had been one of Blake's closest friends in prison, despite his own right-wing political views. He had known nothing of the escape in advance, but was ecstatic at the news. Yet his joy for Blake was tempered by a sobering realization: "Within hours he will have become the objective of the greatest manhunt ever organized in this country."

CHEQUERS, SATURDAY NIGHT, OCTOBER 22

The atmosphere was less joyous at Chequers, where Prime Minister Harold Wilson had been enjoying a weekend at his official country home. Wilson had come to power in 1964 at the head of a Labour government, a year after Harold Macmillan resigned in the wake of a string of espionage scandals that followed Blake's 1961 arrest, the last being an affair his secretary of war, John Profumo, carried on with a woman who was also dating a Soviet intelligence officer. Now it was Wilson's turn to suffer his own spy scandal, courtesy of Blake. The prime minister received a note from an aide around 9 p.m. "George Blake, the spy, escaped from Wormwood Scrubs this evening," it read. "This was discovered about one and a half hours ago. He clearly received outside assistance."

Wilson immediately demanded to know whether Blake's escape posed a threat to national security and whether any lives could be endangered. Dick White, the SIS chief, soon reported, rather over-optimistically, that "at first sight there seemed to be no danger of this kind. . . . What Blake knew was now 5 to 6 years out of date; and the SIS felt reasonably satisfied that there was also no danger resulting from what he might reveal about our interrogation procedures."

Embarrassment was a wholly different matter.

LONDON, SATURDAY NIGHT AND SUNDAY MORNING, OCTOBER 22–23

An enormous hunt for Blake was under way, as Lamarque predicted, but not in the right direction. Special Branch, the police force working with the British intelligence services, assumed Blake had been freed by the Soviets or one of their Eastern Bloc allies and that they would immediately try to spirit him out of the country, so they focused on airfields, embassies, and docks.

"We ran around a bit like headless chickens, trying to work out where we should go," recalled Wilf Knight, a Special Branch officer.

They received a tip that Blake was being smuggled out of the country in a harp case being transported by a member of the Czechoslovakian State Orchestra, which had performed that evening in London and was at the airport at 2 a.m. preparing to fly home. "[We] turned them over—men and women, harps, bassoons, cellos, everything," said Knight.

But there was no sign of Blake.

WASHINGTON

Bill Harvey was back in Washington, having been recalled after suffering a heart attack earlier that year during his disastrous tour in Rome. He had continued his destructive drinking, and CIA doctors found him in wretched health. His days at the agency appeared numbered; he had been given a desk job studying countermeasures against electronic surveillance at CIA stations.

Harvey was visiting the home of Will and Anita Potocki, two veterans from the Berlin days, and was in their living room watching the evening news when he learned that Blake had escaped. "There may still be a grease spot on the ceiling where he hit it," recalled Anita Potocki. "He just exploded at the news."

Harvey was not the only one. Dick Helms, now director of the CIA, spoke to Dick White and made it clear that the agency's opinion of SIS had never been lower. "It was a disaster," White recalled.

LONDON, SUNDAY, OCTOBER 23

For his part, White blamed the Home Office, which oversaw the prisons, for not taking SIS warnings seriously that Blake posed a serious escape risk. "I'm livid," he raged to anyone who would listen.

By Sunday morning, Special Branch had created two special squads devoted to recapturing Blake. All the physical evidence, including the ladder, the broken iron bar from the prison window, and the chrysanthemum, was being examined in the police laboratory.

Officers were checking florists around London looking for clues on who might have purchased the chrysanthemum, and they canvassed knitting shops around the country for records of anyone buying an unusual number of size 13 needles.

At Wormwood Scrubs, Blake's cell was minutely searched for clues, and his correspondence carefully examined. Officers began interviewing all 328 D Hall prisoners, most of whom insisted they knew nothing. Investigators picked up hints that Sean Bourke and Phil Morris might have been involved, and that Blake had access to a two-way radio. But Morris gave them nothing when questioned. "I have no ideas," he told questioners. "It's nothing to do with me."

It was impossible not to notice how pleased everyone seemed. "The atmosphere is electric," Lamarque said. "I have never seen so many happy faces in prison. It's like Christmas day, only far more so."

———

George Blake and Sean Bourke had spent a sleepless night reliving the adventure of getting over the wall, both amused and shaken at how close they had come to disaster. The most immediate concern was Blake's wrist, which had swollen overnight. "He was in pain but pretended not to be," recalled Bourke. With Blake's photo on the front page of every paper, going to a hospital did not seem like a good idea. Bourke enlisted the aid of Michael Randle, who spent the day tracking down a doctor willing to help an escaped spy.

Arriving at the apartment with the doctor Sunday evening, Randle was shocked by the sight of Blake, who looked pale and wan and had blood on his scalp, with one eye puffed out and closed. After examining the wrist, the doctor said he needed an emergency bone set. They worked at a small wooden table covered with the day's newspapers, the doctor ignoring the pictures of Blake as well as the news bulletins about the escape on the television. Bourke held Blake steady as the doctor maneuvered the bone back into place. Blake gritted his teeth to stop from crying out, beads of sweat popping up on his forehead. Once the doctor was satisfied with the bone's position, he made a cast using plaster that Randle had obtained from a friend who worked in the BBC wardrobe department. Blake's relief was immediate.

———

After the doctor's departure, the group sat around the Highlever Road apartment pondering their next step. Their giddiness over the escape had been replaced by the harsh reality that they had little idea of what to do with the world's most wanted man. Pat Pottle had joined the gathering and was despondent at the scene. "Looking around the small dingy room, I thought that apart from the police walking in, nothing else could possibly go wrong," he said. He was wrong about that.

Blake posed the question that hung over the group: "What had you in mind for getting me out of the country?" He himself was of little help. "He didn't have any suggestions, really, about how it might progress beyond getting over the prison wall," Randle recalled.

Randle and Pottle did have one idea they had not yet told Blake about, and it was rather outlandish. Randle had recently read about the book *Black Like Me,* by John Howard Griffin, a white American journalist who had darkened the color of his skin by taking the drug Meladinine and exposing himself to ultraviolet light. Griffin's book memorably described the harsh treatment he received during a subsequent journey through the Deep South.

After checking out a copy of the book from the library for guidance, Randle and Pottle bought an ultraviolet light and obtained Meladinine using a prescription they forged at Pottle's printing office. Bourke was confident he could get a counterfeit passport for Blake from his criminal contacts.

Now it was time to tell Blake. "We think you'll like this, George." Pottle grinned. "We plan to turn you black and get you out on a forged passport!"

They all laughed, though Randle noted that Blake did not seem "very keen" about the suggestion. The further they explained it, the more dubious he looked. "Right from the beginning, this plan didn't inspire any confidence in me, though I didn't say so outright," Blake recalled. To his relief, all agreed that he should not begin the drug treatment until he had recovered from his injuries.

Another matter was pressing. It was clear that the Highlever Road flat would not do for a long-term hideout. It offered little anonymity for Blake, who had to use a hallway bathroom that was shared with other tenants. The risk was high that he would be recognized. They needed another place as soon as possible.

The group took some comfort in the widespread news reports that British officials believed the KGB had orchestrated the escape, and that Blake might already be in Moscow. The *Guardian* reported that intelligence officials feared Blake could have reached a vessel on the Thames before the alarm was sounded and was on his way to the Soviet Union. The *Express* speculated that a fishing vessel might have taken Blake to the continent. There were sightings around the world. After getting a tip, police in Australia surrounded a jet that landed in Sydney and vetted passengers for wigs, false beards, or dyed hair, but found no sign of Blake.

London, it seemed, remained the safest place for the time being.

———

Gillian Blake issued a statement through her attorney that news of her husband's escape had come as a shock and she had no knowledge of his whereabouts. A spokesman for Bill Cox, George Blake's attorney, said it was uncertain whether the divorce hearing scheduled for November 18 would proceed. "We have had no further instructions from our client," he said.

Blake's barrister, Jeremy Hutchinson, was openly delighted. "Good God, yes, I was," he recalled. "Flags went up on my house. My prophecy had come true, sooner than I'd thought."

Hutchinson, though, had no inkling of how deep his connections ran with the escape. "Everybody said to me, 'How on earth did the worst spy who's ever been in this country get out of prison? It's unbelievable.' I'd nod my head as if I knew a great deal about things and say, 'Ah, well, mm-hh, something to do with intelligence, it will come out one of these days.' I had no idea it was two of my old clients who got him out." He laughed heartily at the memory.

———

On Tuesday evening, October 25, Randle drove Blake, in his hat and overcoat, to the London home of "Rachel" and "Matthew," friends who had agreed to temporarily harbor the fugitive. But the couple was so nervous about it that they insisted Blake stay in his room. Even when he did, they panicked about his habit of doing yoga in front of the window. They soon told Randle that Blake would have to go.

Finding Blake a safe haven was only one problem. Bourke's behavior was increasingly worrisome to the others. He chafed at his new minor role in the operation and was restless and agitated. He was reckless about going out in public, almost as if he was trying to draw attention to himself. "You've got to try and restrain him," Blake told Pottle.

In prison, Blake had not fully grasped Bourke's predilection for alcohol. "We shuddered to think what remarks he might drop in conversation with a casual pub acquaintance," Blake said, "all the more so as he had no sense of caution and, deep inside him, was burning for everyone to know that it was he who had sprung George Blake from prison."

Pottle suspected that Bourke had lied to them about selling the Humber Hawk before the escape, and Bourke finally acknowledged he had not sold it. That meant the car used for the getaway was registered in Bourke's name. Pottle and Randle decided to retrieve the Hawk before the police found it, and abandon it in a quarry outside the city where it might not be found. Bourke claimed he had thrown away the keys, but finally gave Randle a spare key.

On Friday, October 28, Randle went to Harvist Road in Kilburn, where Bourke had parked the Hawk, and scoured the street up and down, but there was no sign of the car. Walking to a nearby underground station, he saw a headline in the *Evening Standard*: "Blake's Escape Car Found." According to the papers, police found two telltale clues inside linking the car to the crime: fibers from a blue prison uniform, and "the wilting head of a pink chrysanthemum."

Though he was not named, it was clear that police now knew Bourke was involved in the escape. Newspapers reported that police were looking for a thirty-three-year-old Irishman from Limerick, and that the escape had been aided "by a group of sympathizers." The stories were getting "much too close for comfort," Randle said.

"You, my friend, are going to have to lie low from now on," Blake told Bourke.

———

At least Randle had found a new place to hide Blake and Bourke. He had asked a left-wing acquaintance, John Papworth, for help with two people who urgently needed a place to stay out of sight. Papworth, a Church of England priest, agreed that they could stay at his home, a spacious and well-appointed house in Earls Court.

Papworth and his wife were away in the country when Blake and Bourke moved in on Friday, and everything was fine until the couple returned at the end of the weekend. Marcelle Papworth went for a walk with Randle and asked the identity of the two men staying in her home. "Well, one of them is George Blake . . . ," Randle began.

Marcelle Papworth stopped dead in her tracks. "George Blake!" she called in alarm. Randle hushed her, afraid passersby would hear. Back at the house, John Papworth expressed equal shock. "I assumed they were American deserters or something of that kind," he told Randle. "I never dreamt for one moment that you were referring to George Blake."

The Papworths agreed that Blake and Bourke could stay, but for no more than several days. Another plan was needed.

———

Tensions were rising when Randle and Pottle came to the Papworth home on Monday, October 31, to discuss with Blake and Bourke what to do next. "By now, only a week after the escape, all our carefully laid plans for sheltering Blake and organizing his exit from the country were in tatters," Randle recalled.

Randle had a new suggestion: They would smuggle Blake to the Soviet embassy near Kensington Palace Gardens and hoist him over the back wall, thereby "dumping the problem in their lap." The Soviets could fly Blake to Moscow.

Blake stared at Randle in disbelief and jumped up, looking more agitated than the others had ever seen. "I'm the last person the embassy would want dumped on them," he declared. "It would create a major diplomatic incident once the British authorities found out I was inside. The Russians might even be forced to hand me over as a fugitive from British justice." He would rather go back to Scrubs.

The idea was dropped. No one had other suggestions. Blake leaned against the home's elegant marble mantelpiece. "Tell me, what were you planning to do with me?" he asked nonchalantly. "You must have had something in mind when you got me out of prison?"

The mild-mannered Randle flew into a blinding rage. "I felt like hitting him at that moment," he recalled. "You know very well what we planned to do," he shot at Blake. "But things have gone badly wrong." Blake adopted a more conciliatory tone, and tensions subsided.

But that evening, as Randle, Blake, and Bourke sat in the bedroom discussing other options, John Papworth walked in. "There is just one thing I feel I should mention to you," he said. "My wife is undergoing a course of analysis. This requires her to be absolutely frank with her analyst and not to conceal anything from him."

After a pause, Blake spoke, trying to maintain his composure. "Are you saying that she has told him about us?"

"Yes, everything," Papworth said. "There's no point in it if she isn't completely frank. You must understand, of course, that what she says to him is in the strictest confidence."

Blake looked quite pale. When he spoke again, his voice was thin and reedy. "And what did the analyst say when she told him?"

"Oh, he said that she was imagining it, and that it was because there had been so much publicity about the escape of George Blake."

Everyone fell silent for several seconds. Then Blake spoke in a clipped tone: "I think it would be advisable if we left immediately." Bourke dove to the floor, grabbed his suitcase from under the bed, and began piling in his clothing.

After more discussion, Blake agreed to stay one more night. The next day, a new solution had presented itself: He and Bourke would move into Pat Pottle's bachelor apartment.

PRIME MINISTER'S OFFICE, HOUSE OF COMMONS, MONDAY, OCTOBER 31

Harold Wilson, facing opposition demands for more information about Blake's escape, had invited Conservative Party leader Ted Heath and his deputies for a briefing with Dick White. "C" told the group that he was "inclined to doubt whether the Russians had got Blake." Thus far, there was no evidence implicating Soviet intelligence in the escape. Telephone taps indicated that the Soviets were as taken off guard by the escape as everyone else. Nor did the Soviets have much of an incentive to spring him, White noted. "Blake had admitted everything very fully," he said. "There was not therefore any strong Soviet obligation to him. They might conceivably give him some money and leave him to work out his own future."

Moreover, had the Soviets wanted to free any of their spies still held by the British, the Portland spies Morris and Lona Cohen would be a much higher priority, because they had not yet talked. Blake's escape "would make it more difficult" for the Soviets to spring the Cohens because of stringent new security measures, White said.

Wilson told the group that "the latest evidence tended to confirm that Blake had been in contact with an Irishman with a bad criminal record" who had recently been released from Scrubs, and that they may have had radios. MI5 believed that Blake had not been immediately removed from Britain.

Regardless of how Blake had escaped, White warned that the Soviets would try to exploit it "to drive a wedge between us and the Americans on counter-intelligence work." SIS had "very carefully briefed the Americans since Blake's escape in order to minimize any risk of this," he added.

Blake's espionage "had clearly been of considerable danger to us," White told the group. But since he had already told the Russians everything he knew, White said, "we could reasonably say he could not do any more harm in this respect."

———

Pat Pottle lived in Willow Buildings, a former Army barracks on Willow Road in Hampstead that had been converted into working-class tenements. "They looked like something out of Dickens—dark, dreary and damp," Pottle recalled. Indeed, his friends referred to it as "Bleak House." The flat was cramped, with only a kitchen sink for bathing.

Nonetheless, the move of Blake and Bourke into Pottle's apartment on November 1 marked a turning point, an end to the days of panicked movements and desperate flailing. In part, that was a reflection of Pottle's personality—calm, deliberative, and solid. The search for Blake and the public drumbeat about his escape remained incessant, but Anne Randle began to feel as if they were somehow immune. "It just seemed we were floating around in a bit of a balloon," she recalled.

They no longer had to worry about where to hide Blake and could focus on a plan. More than two decades earlier, Blake had traveled across Europe to escape to England. Now he needed to escape out. One idea was to cross the English Channel in a sailboat and deposit him somewhere on the French coast. But there was little to be gained by dropping him in France without a passport. The *Black Like Me* plan was still floated as a possibility, even though Blake had never warmed up to the idea of dyeing his skin. It depended on Bourke using criminal connections to get Blake a forged passport, but now that the Irishman was himself being hunted, that seemed too risky. "To my great relief, the plan had to be abandoned altogether," Blake recalled.

In early November, they began discussing the idea of concealing Blake in some sort of container or compartment and driving him out of England. Constructing a secret compartment big enough to hold a man in the trunk of a car did not seem practical. But a larger vehicle, like a camper van, had possibilities. Randle visited showrooms to scout out different models. Some had bench seats in the back, with cupboard doors that opened up for storage beneath the cushions. But these seemed a likely target for inspection by customs officials. Then it occurred to Randle that the space could be disguised by replacing the cupboard doors with drawers. If the drawers were left pulled out and full of clothes, the space behind them might escape inspection. Everyone liked the idea, including Blake.

The next decision was who would drive. Pottle did not have a license, and neither did Anne Randle. As a wanted man, it was too risky for Bourke to drive across borders. That left Michael Randle. "I'll drive it myself," he said. Anne insisted that she accompany her husband, and she would bring the children, Gavin, four, and Sean, two. It would give the appearance of a family holiday.

Blake was silent. "Don't think," he finally told the Randles, "that

I am unaware of what this decision entails, or that I will ever forget what you and Anne have undertaken."

———

The last big debate was where to go. It was not a simple choice. "Blake had no great desire to go behind the Iron Curtain," Bourke recalled. ". . . He offered no explanation for this, but I suspected that he felt unsure of the sort of reception that might be awaiting him in Russia." Given the confession and full cooperation he had given SIS, he had reason to be doubtful. And despite his stated adoration of communist utopia, he was certainly aware of the reality of life in a police state.

Blake's preference was to go to a neutral country unlikely to turn him over to the British. He had one place in particular in mind: Egypt. It held emotional resonance for him, with his family ties and childhood memories. His Arabic studies, both in Lebanon and Wormwood Scrubs, had only whetted his interest further. But getting to Egypt from England would be a long and complicated journey by land and sea, with risk of discovery. Yugoslavia, which had broken with the Soviet Union, was an option, but getting there would also involve crossing multiple frontiers. He ruled out Switzerland, worried about the close ties between British and Swiss intelligence.

The Randles favored Eastern Europe. Blake did not argue, and it was he who suggested the exact destination. "To me the solution seemed obvious; East Germany," he said. It was the nearest East European country to England. Moreover, he added with understatement, "I knew the situation in and around Berlin extremely well."

They spread a map of Europe on the table. Under the terms of the postwar agreements, the West retained access to West Berlin along defined air, rail, and road transit routes through East Germany, including four autobahn routes from West Germany, and it would not be at all uncommon for a family from England to make the trip. Blake traced out the route they should take, which was the most direct drive, crossing into East German territory at the Helmstedt frontier, and then continuing a hundred miles to the outskirts of Berlin. Blake could be dropped off before the Randles continued into West Berlin. Blake would present himself to the East German border guards, and once he was in East Berlin, the Soviets could fly him to Moscow.

The group calculated that £1,000 would cover the cost of the van, as well as the interior conversion work, ferry tickets, and fuel. Randle approached his friend, the donor, and they received the money on November 10, the day before Blake's forty-fourth birthday.

Randle's friend Matthew, a handy woodworker who would oversee the modifications, accompanied him to a showroom in South London. They picked a two-toned Commer with a light green body and cream-colored roof, and seating for three in the front. The storage bench in the back ran along the driver's side, perpendicular to the front row. Randle liked it because access to the rear was from a set of double doors at the back, which would make the hiding place under the bench awkward for a customs officer to reach.

They brought the van to Matthew's garage for the conversion work, which turned out to be more complicated than anticipated. The space had to be stripped down and rebuilt from scratch, and they needed to match the existing design as much as possible so the alterations did not raise suspicion. After Matthew finished his day job, he and Randle worked feverishly until midnight or beyond almost every night, with the radio in the garage blaring pop music.

As the van conversion continued, the strain of weeks of confinement in Pottle's cramped apartment was showing on Blake and Bourke. Pottle came home from work one evening to find them with their coats on, preparing to leave. "What on earth's going on?" Pottle demanded.

Blake said they were going to the London docks to try to board a Polish freighter. He could not go through with the plan with the Randles. "It is putting them and their children at too great a risk," Blake said. "I have been responsible for the break-up of one family, and I do not want to have another on my conscience." Pottle persuaded them that hopping on a freighter would never work, and nothing would be worse than seeing the two back in prison after months of effort.

They stayed, but Bourke remained restless. It was unclear what to do with him once Blake was smuggled out of the country. Bourke wanted to return to Ireland, confident he could fight British extradition on political grounds. The others were dubious that he would escape prosecution. Bourke reluctantly agreed that he would follow

Blake to the Soviet Union at a later date and stay until the matter died down. How to get him there was another problem. One possibility was to make a second trip with Bourke hidden in the van, but he was much larger than Blake and would have trouble fitting. Instead, they decided to try flying him to Berlin with a forged passport.

In the meantime, there was little for Blake and Bourke to do but follow the news. "Our greatest source of entertainment was to watch television every night and listen to the various theories put forward by the armchair experts," Bourke recalled. Particularly amusing were the assertions that "the whole thing was a highly skilled military operation planned and executed by the KGB." No one knew better than they did what an amateur operation it really was.

Occasionally everyone would gather for a fish pie dinner in Pottle's apartment. After reviewing the latest with the plans, the group would often fall into heated political arguments. Despite their leftist views, Randle and Pottle were critical of Soviet actions, from the Stalinist purges to the ongoing political repression in Eastern Europe. Blake did not explicitly defend them, but would passionately defend Soviet communism, predicting its eventual triumph.

At the same time, it was usually Blake who would speak most favorably of England. "Ironically, he was more Anglophile than any of us," Randle recalled. When Blake spoke of his hope to one day visit England again, it was too much for Randle.

"If you are so attached to this country," he demanded, "why did you spy against it for the Russians?"

———

By December 9, seven weeks after Blake's escape, the camper van was ready. The secret compartment ran down the driver's side of the vehicle, hidden behind the bench seat's two large drawers. As a final touch, they lined it with foam rubber to make it more comfortable for Blake.

The departure was fixed for Saturday, December 17, a date that would fit in well with the story of an English family going on holiday on the continent. Randle bought a ticket for the midnight ferry from Dover to the Belgian port of Ostende.

On the appointed day, Randle packed the van with enough provisions so that they would not need to stop for food before reaching

Berlin. He included a rubber hot water bottle Blake could use as a makeshift urinal if needed inside the compartment.

At 6:30 p.m., everyone met at Pottle's apartment for a final fish pie dinner. All were nervous. The hunt for Blake continued unabated. Newspapers reported that day that vehicles on ferries departing Britain would be subjected to searches. Police had recently stopped a hearse on the highway and searched the coffin, based on a tip that Blake was inside.

Blake offered a thank-you toast, joking about their frequent political arguments. Upon his arrival in Moscow, he told them, "I would have some difficulty in explaining to the Soviet authorities who they were and why they had chosen to help me. It seemed to me that only in England could people like this be found. If all that had happened in my life had been necessary in order to have known such people, even if only for a short time, I considered it all to have been well worth it."

By the time the goodbyes were said and Blake had climbed into his compartment, with the children tucked into their fold-down bed in the rear, it was 8:30 p.m., a good bit later than the Randles had planned to depart to make the midnight ferry. It was another hour before they cleared London for the eighty-mile journey to Dover. "I wish to God we'd set off a bit earlier," Anne told her husband. "We're only just going to make it—if that."

Reaching the open highway, Michael discovered to his dismay that the van could barely reach fifty miles per hour. They were about ten miles from Dover when Anne turned to Michael in alarm. "Listen. I think I can hear something," she said. "I think he's knocking." Michael heard nothing and continued driving. But minutes later Anne heard it again. "Michael, you've got to stop," she shouted. "It's definitely him knocking." This time, there was no mistaking the loud and insistent banging from below.

Randle pulled over. Anne woke the children and brought them up front while Michael opened the drawer. Blake emerged, pale and retching. "I need some air," he gasped. In the confined space, the hot water bottle gave off an odor that made him nauseous. After a few minutes, Blake regained his color and climbed back into the compartment, minus the hot water bottle. The Randles drove on, terrified that with the added delay they would miss the ferry. They made it to the terminal with ten minutes to spare.

From inside his compartment, Blake tried to follow what was happening. He heard a voice asking for passports. After a perfunctory check, Randle inched the van forward toward customs, waiting behind several cars. Everyone's nerves were taut. But a customs officer waved them forward with scarcely a glance.

Blake felt a few bumps and realized they were driving aboard the ferry. He was off the English mainland, but not out of danger. After parking the van where directed, the Randles carried their sleeping children up to the passenger lounge for the journey. Down in the compartment, Blake heard shouted orders as the ship got under way. The sailing was smooth, but as the journey continued, he felt an increasingly urgent need to relieve himself. The hot water bottle was gone. "There was nothing for it but to hold out," he recalled.

At 5:30 a.m., the ferry docked at Ostende. The Randles half expected the camper to be surrounded when they retrieved it, but it was eerily quiet when they climbed in. They drove down a metal ramp off the ferry, and after another cursory check of their papers, they were in Belgium.

Anne moved close to Michael as they drove off. "I don't like it," she whispered. "It's all too quiet. I have this terrible feeling that he's dead—suffocated."

Michael waved it off, but was worried as well. It was an interminable half hour until he found a lonely stretch of road where it was safe to pull over. Outside it was still pitch black. The children were brought up front while Michael pulled out the drawer. Blake emerged from the compartment, stiff but unscathed. "My God, am I glad to see you!" Michael said. "Anne and I were giving you up for dead."

"No, no—I was fine once we got rid of the hot water bottle," Blake assured him, explaining that he had been meditating. He immediately went to the roadside for "what must have been the longest pee in my life."

The group was exhilarated. With no border checks imminent, Blake rode in the backseat as they drove through the gray Belgian morning. The children "took it all in their stride and had shown no surprise when I had suddenly appeared from nowhere," he recalled.

Reaching Brussels, they got lost in the city center. When Michael rolled down the window to ask directions from a passerby, Blake leaned past him and spoke to her in Flemish. They were soon back on the correct route, but Anne was perturbed. "He was meant to keep out of sight the whole journey, but now he's even talking to strangers in the street," she complained to her husband when they stopped for gas.

Around 11 a.m., as they approached the border crossing into West Germany at Aachen, Blake returned to his hiding place. But neither the Belgian nor the German border officials paid much attention to the van, and they were waved through. Blake reemerged and played games of "I spy" with the children as they drove northwest on the autobahn toward Hanover.

The morning's relaxation vanished as the weather worsened and exhaustion set in. The wiper motor gave out in a heavy downpour somewhere past Essen, leaving the windshield awash with rain. They made it to a garage, where Blake once again assumed the role of translator. The mechanics were unable to fix the problem without the proper parts, but rigged the wipers so they could be operated by hand using a small lever on the inside of the windshield. For several hours, Blake and Anne took turns moving the wipers while the van plowed through a continual deluge. It was nearly dark before the rain slowed and then finally stopped.

By 8:30 p.m., they were approaching Helmstedt and the East German frontier, the last border Blake would cross and the one that "might well prove the most difficult," he thought. They stopped a few miles before Helmstedt so that Blake could return to the compartment. At his insistence, he would remain hidden even after crossing into East Germany. "It would be a mistake for me to reveal myself to the East German guards at Helmstedt—the van will still be under observation from the West German side," he told the Randles. "If they see an extra person getting out you will be in difficulties later on. They might even recognize me."

The Randles were shaken by the sight of the fortified border. East German guards with machine guns manned a tall observation tower, with searchlights illuminating a high fence topped with barbed wire. A guard signaled for Randle to stop the van and get out and go inside an office. Randle filled out paperwork and then a guard escorted him back to the van. "Open up," the guard said, nodding at the rear doors. Inside the compartment, Blake could hear the back doors of the van being opened and Germans speaking, and knew they must be looking inside. He held his breath.

The children were lying in the bed in the back, though not asleep. The guard glanced at them. "He nodded again, and the examination was over," said Randle.

———

The Randles felt no elation as they drove into East Germany. "From the moment we had crossed the heavily guarded checkpoint there was a tangible sense of having entered an alien and hostile territory," Michael recalled. It was impossible not to wonder whether they had rescued Blake from one prison and delivered him to another. After the immaculate West German autobahn, the poor condition of the dark and potholed road connecting Helmstedt to Berlin only added to the sense of foreboding. On top of it all, Michael was exhausted after thirty-six hours without sleep, including twelve hours of nearly continuous driving.

After crossing the Elbe River near Magdeburg, Randle stopped to let Blake out of the compartment.

"Well, we made it," Blake said.

"Yes," Michael said flatly. That might be so for Blake, but he wondered about his own family. "It was a bit too good to be true to think we'd get away with it," he recalled. "He would be safe in Moscow with his friends, and we were quite exposed."

Before long, Blake recognized the distant lights of the East German checkpoint at Drewitz, on the southwestern side of Berlin. A mile or so before reaching the checkpoint, he directed Randle to pull over and turn off his lights by a dark stand of pine trees. It was nearly midnight. Blake went over the formalities the Randles would face at the two checkpoints ahead and gave them directions to a hotel on the Kurfürstendamm, an area he knew well.

"Then the time had come to say goodbye," Blake recalled. "With a heavy heart, I took my leave from Michael and Anne, and with them, from England and a whole part of my life," he said. He stood there awkwardly, wearing his trilby hat and long overcoat.

"We should be celebrating in champagne," he told Randle. "I am sure that day will come."

"Good luck, George."

As they drove off, Randle caught a glimpse of Blake in the rear-view mirror, faintly illuminated by the rear lights of the van. "He waved—and almost at once was lost in the darkness," Randle recalled.

Blake watched the lights of the van disappear. He waited to give the Randles plenty of time to get through the checkpoints. He stood in the shadows, among the sighing pine trees, far from the harsh light at the border. "For an instant in time I was free and alone in the dark night, poised between two worlds," he later wrote, "belonging to neither."

DREWITZ CHECKPOINT, EARLY MONDAY MORNING, DECEMBER 19

Since he lacked any identification papers, it took time for the bedraggled Englishman who showed up on foot after midnight to convince the skeptical East German border guards that they needed to call a Soviet army officer to the scene. But with his fluent German, and his knowledge of their security procedures and chain of command, the mysterious arrival eventually persuaded the guards to take his request seriously. When a Soviet officer arrived, the man identified himself. The young officer did not know who George Blake was, but returning to his station, he made a telephone call to Karlshorst.

Sergei Kondrashev, still chief of the KGB's German Department in Moscow, was nearing the end of a visit to East Berlin with KGB deputy chairman Nikolai Zakharov for the annual review of the work of the Karlshorst apparat. After dinner and drinks Sunday night, everyone had gone to bed, and Kondrashev had just fallen asleep when Zakharov walked into his room. "The duty officer reports that some Englishman at the border is asking to meet a Soviet official," Zakharov said. "Maybe it's him."

There was no need to say who "him" was. Blake's whereabouts had been a constant source of wonder for the KGB since his escape two months earlier. They had been able to learn very little of his whereabouts, only that he was somewhere safe.

"Maybe you should go yourself and check," Zakharov suggested.

———

Kondrashev rushed in a KGB car with several other officers to the border crossing. It was close to 4 a.m. by the time they arrived. They were directed to a nearby room where the man was resting on a sofa.

Kondrashev entered the room. It had been years since they had seen each other, and the man on the sofa was unshaven and looking a bit worse for wear. But it was easy to recognize George Blake.

"It's him! It's him!" Kondrashev shouted. Blake rose to his feet, stunned to see his former KGB handler. Kondrashev rushed forward and they embraced. Almost immediately, they were on their way to Karlshorst.

Blake was kept in a KGB villa under tight security, with fears high that Western intelligence agencies might try to kidnap him if they discovered he was in Berlin. Preparations were made to move him quickly to Moscow, where he would be much safer.

In the meantime, agents were sent to West Berlin to buy Blake some quality clothing and boots that would be impossible to find in Moscow. "To my surprise, I was treated somewhat as a hero," Blake recalled. "The KGB officials in Berlin were quite pleased I had chosen their city to surface."

After about a week of celebratory meals and casual debriefing in East Berlin, the Soviets whisked Blake on a KGB jet to a private airfield outside Moscow used by government ministers.

Not long afterwards, British intelligence received a report from an "extremely delicate source" that an unidentified man had shown up in East Berlin shortly before Christmas with nothing more than the clothes on his back, and that he had been important enough to be met by the deputy head of the KGB. "The possibility that this man was BLAKE clearly cannot be discounted," an MI5 report read.

But it was too late—the mole had burrowed his way out of another tunnel. In Moscow, Blake wrote a note to his mother in England, which the KGB posted from Cairo to throw off Western intelligence. "I am a free man again," he said.

Epilogue

In February 2012, Werner Sobolewski, a retired East German army civilian employee, was chopping wood in a forest near his home in Pasewalk, north of Berlin close to the Polish border, when he noticed a depression in the ground amid the birch trees. A forester at the scene thought it was a fox or badger den, but Sobolewski was not so sure. He brushed away leaves with his heavy gloves until he spotted the top edge of the mouth of a large steel pipe, a good six feet wide, filled with dirt.

"Most people wouldn't have known what it was, but I did," Sobolewski recalled. The pipe had been used for military exercises by troops stationed at the nearby army barracks in Pasewalk, where he had worked in the early 1970s. At the time, he heard rumors that the pipe was actually a piece of the once-infamous Berlin spy tunnel. Sobolewski had done research then in a local library and found photographs confirming to his satisfaction that the pipe at the Pasewalk caserne was indeed part of the tunnel.

Forty years later, he had discovered the tunnel in the woods. "I hadn't thought about it at all, but one sight was enough," he recalled. Sobolewski contacted the regional Protestant Church district, which owned the forest. "I told them, 'You have a treasure in your forest,'" he said. "Nothing happened." In the months that followed, Sobolewski began digging out the tunnel by hand, eventually uncovering the top third and removing some of the soil that filled the interior. The steel showed little corrosion. "It was surprising in how good condition it was," he said.

After further calls to church offices resulted still in no action,

Sobolewski called the Allied Museum, established in Berlin at the end of the Cold War to remember the Western occupation of the city. The museum had what were believed to be the only two surviving sections of the Berlin tunnel, both from the old American sector. First, a twenty-foot section was uncovered in 1997 by construction workers building cottages in Rudow. Then, in 2005, road crews constructing an autobahn on the land between Rudow and Altglienicke were surprised when their excavator clanked against a large steel pipe. It was another twenty-foot section, which was also preserved. Unlike other conflicts, the Cold War had left relatively few physical remains, and the surviving tunnel sections served as a reminder of the great fear millions held in those years about what could have happened: a sudden nuclear annihilation.

A survey of the western side after the 2005 discovery found nothing more of the tunnel but a few scraps—everything else had been destroyed by various construction projects. Bernd von Kostka, the museum curator, took Sobolewksi's call, but was skeptical that any more sections of the tunnel existed. The longer stretch of tunnel in the former Soviet sector, dug up from the Noacks' property by East German crews in 1956, had long since disappeared. No trace of its fate was found in the Stasi files. "We assumed it had been melted down because it was made of valuable metal," said Kostka.

Despite his doubts, Kostka drove to Pasewalk the next day and accompanied Sobolewski into the forest to examine the oddity. Kostka was astonished when he saw the pipe. It took barely a minute to confirm that it was from the tunnel, based on the unique bolts holding the steel liner together.

It turned out that the East German army engineers who had overseen the removal in 1956 had recognized that the American-made steel tunnel segments would come in handy. They were cut into manageable sections three or four yards long and shipped out to army engineering units around East Germany. Some were used as shelters, others to store supplies, and others for training. The troops in Pasewalk regularly held military maneuvers in the church forest, and the section Sobolewski found had been used as a command post, with the rotted remains of a wooden door still attached.

Sobolewski told Kostka that there were likely other sections scattered around eastern Germany. After the collapse of the Berlin Wall in 1989 and subsequent reunification of Germany, equipment and supplies at former East German army installations had been sold off, including the tunnel segments. Indeed, not long after Sobolewski's discovery, two more sections were found on an eastern farm, where they were being used as a silo for storing feed and as a makeshift duck pond. Other sections had been sold for scrap.

———

The U.S. government returned the Rudow warehouse site in 1983 to the family of Hermann Massante, the farmer who had rented the land to the Americans. The warehouse and other buildings were still standing, but with no one maintaining them, they soon fell into disrepair.

When British writer Ian McEwan visited the site while researching his 1990 novel *The Innocent,* based on the Berlin tunnel, he found the double perimeter fence and remains of guard shacks still standing, but the buildings inside the compound had been leveled, leaving piles of crumbling concrete. The warehouse basement was a yawning cavity, with the hole leading to the mouth of the tunnel filled with rubble, wiring, and broken pipes.

In *The Innocent,* Leonard Marnham is a British post office technician from Dollis Hill who helps operate the taps, and then returns to the abandoned warehouse compound thirty years after the tunnel's discovery. "He was staring into the old basement, now open to the skies," McEwan wrote. "The great heaps of tunnel workings were all there, thick with weeds." Marnham picks up a piece of cable and kicks at the ground with the toe of his shoe. "What was he expecting to find?" McEwan asked. "Evidence of his own existence?"

After the Massante family sold the land, construction began in 1997 on rows of weekend cottages. The warehouse compound is now covered by fifty-five small, one-story houses with terra-cotta roof tiles, tightly packed next to each other, each hidden behind small hedges and tidy, fenced-off gardens.

———

It was perhaps not surprising that the Berlin tunnel would meet such a mundane fate, given how it had been largely forgotten over the years. After the failed attempt by the Soviets and East Germans to orchestrate a propaganda coup, the East had little reason to celebrate it. And in the West, following the disclosure that George Blake had betrayed the tunnel before it was even built, Operation Gold was labeled a fiasco, and the intelligence gathered assumed to be tainted.

The floodgates of derision opened after the official Soviet newspaper *Izvestia* published a two-part interview with Blake in February 1970, more than three years after his escape, officially confirming for the first time that the spy was in Russia. "Now that the hero of our admiration has long been free and nothing can threaten him, we introduce to our readers: George Blake, Soviet intelligence agent," *Izvestia* declared. In the two-part interview, Blake disclosed that he had told the KGB about the tunnel before it was even dug. It "was doomed to failure before the blueprints were completed," he boasted.

In the years following, many journalists, authors, and historians dismissed the tunnel's value, assuming that the KGB would never have allowed Western intelligence to listen to any information of importance on tapped lines.

The tunnel, the noted British intelligence writer Chapman Pincher wrote in a typical verdict in 1984, "produced nothing but a mass of carefully prepared misinformation." The distinguished intelligence journalist and author Phillip Knightley called the tunnel "a worthless disaster" that left the CIA and MI6 "in somewhat exaggerated terms . . . under the effective control of the KGB." Richard Bennett, in *Espionage: An Encyclopedia of Spies and Secrets,* published in 2002, declares that the CIA and SIS were "victims of a massive and very successful KGB disinformation scam." The tunnel "harvested little information of value," David Wise, one of the preeminent American intelligence writers, wrote in 1992. In *Eclipse: The Last Days of the CIA,* American author Mark Perry called the tunnel "a stark defeat" for the agency, which was "forced to discard many of the secrets it had deciphered because they were useless."

A few authors were more complimentary, including David Martin, who wrote in *Wilderness of Mirrors* in 1980 that the tunnel "had kept a finger on the Soviet pulse." But in general, the Berlin tunnel became a punch line, a symbol of CIA and SIS futility, proof of how the KGB always won in the end. Even at the CIA, memories of the tunnel faded. Hugh Montgomery, whose legendary career at the agency would continue sixty years until his retirement in 2014, would often get only "blank stares" when he mentioned the tunnel to young colleagues. "Of such things are historical verities composed," he noted.

———

Bill Harvey, once among the best American intelligence officers and the man most responsible for the Berlin tunnel, was largely also forgotten. Berlin had been the peak of Harvey's career. After his return to headquarters in 1966 from his ill-fated Rome tour, he had been put under the supervision of Lawrence "Red" White, the CIA's executive director, who told him that he was starting with a clean slate but needed to get his drinking under control. "It wouldn't be long before Bill would show up at some meeting just crocked," White recalled. "I sent for him. He'd come to the door apologizing every time." After three or four times, Harvey told White, "If I ever embarrass you or this agency again, I'll retire."

A month later, following another episode, Harvey reported to White's office. "I made a promise to you and I'm here to live up to it," he told him. On January 6, 1968, he turned in his badge.

Harvey fell back on his law degree, doing some legal work in Washington, but in 1970 he pulled up stakes and moved home to Indiana with CG, his son, Jimmy, and his daughter, Sally, the cardboard box baby. He took a job editing legal interpretations of Indiana Supreme Court decisions for the Bobbs-Merrill Publishing Company. It was sheer drudgery, but it paid the bills. He cut back on his drinking, joined Alcoholics Anonymous, and, according to CG, eventually stopped altogether.

In keeping with a promise to Sally's East German birth mother to raise the child as a Lutheran, Harvey regularly took his daughter to Pleasant View Lutheran Church in Indianapolis, although he made it clear to Reverend David Kahlenberg that he thought "religion to be a bunch of fairy tale stories." But over time, he was baptized in the church and became a deacon. Still, that only went so far. Once, when Kahlenberg roped off the back rows for a service to encourage people to sit up front, Harvey abruptly pulled the ropes down and sat in the last pew, with his back to the brick wall. Afterwards he stormed up to the pastor and flashed open his jacket to reveal the gun in his shoulder holster. "Don't you know the KGB has a price on my head, and I have to sit with my back to the wall in any building?" he declared.

Indeed, the past was never far behind him. "He was always on his guard," Sally recalled. "He felt he was being watched." Harvey lived in relative anonymity in Indianapolis until he was subpoenaed in 1975 to testify about the CIA's assassination program before the Senate Select Committee on Intelligence, chaired by Senator Frank Church.

The committee heard the story about Harvey being described to John Kennedy as America's James Bond. "Given his appearance, demeanor and especially that distinctive voice and the yellow shooter's glasses, he seemed everything but '007,'" recalled former senator Gary Hart, a member of the panel. In a closed hearing, Harvey spoke frankly about his role in the attempts to assassinate Castro, telling the committee that nothing he had done was "unauthorized, freewheeling or in any way outside the framework of my responsibilities and duties as an officer of the agency."

The committee was intrigued by Harvey's continued friendship with mobster Johnny Rosselli. Harvey resisted agency pressure both before and after he left the CIA to cut ties with Rosselli. "We were all struck by the friendship he developed with Rosselli," recalled Hart. "Highly improbable. But then, everything about our investigation, especially involving Cuba, turned out to be highly improbable."

Rosselli's dismembered body would be found in a fifty-five-gallon oil drum in Biscayne Bay in 1976, a year after he gave his own testimony to the Church Committee, naming mobsters Sam Giancana and Santo Trafficante Jr. as also being involved in the Castro assassination attempts.

In later years, as speculation rose over a CIA role in the assassination of President John F. Kennedy, Harvey's name would be floated in JFK conspiracy circles as someone possibly involved. His contempt for the Kennedys, his contacts with assassins and mobsters, and his tough-guy persona made him a "natural suspect," in the view of some. Bay Stockton, the former BOB officer who wrote a biography of Harvey, investigated the morass of murky information and insinuations and found it impossible to make any definitive conclusions. Yet, he added, "No one in the CIA who knew Harvey at his prime believes, or believed, that he possibly could have been involved in the JFK assassination. No one. Not even those who had reason to dislike him." Hugh Montgomery, for one, called the suggestions "absurd and implausible." Yet with many CIA records from the period held from public view, the speculation lingers.

———

Charlie Bray may have been the last of the tunnel veterans to see Harvey, during a visit to Indiana in 1976. "He was still fuming about George Blake, that dirty, no good sack of human debris," Bray recalled.

On June 8, 1976, Harvey woke CG up at 5 a.m. and told her to call the doctor. An ambulance rushed him to the emergency room at Methodist Hospital in Indianapolis, where doctors found that he had suffered a serious heart attack. The cardiologist, Dr. James Hall, told Harvey that surgery to insert a pump gave him a one-in-ten chance of survival. "I've beaten worse odds than that," Harvey replied. "Go ahead." But after thirteen hours of surgery, it was clear that his heart was too badly damaged. CG and Sally were called into the room. "I'll always love you," he told them. Shortly after noon on June 9, Harvey was dead at age sixty-one.

"Bill was simply too honest, too straightforward, and too intelligent for the large collection of bureaucratic hacks who control our destinies," Hugh Montgomery wrote to CG from Rome, where he was then station chief. "The shabby treatment he received from his government was certainly unjust and unfair in every respect."

During its fiftieth anniversary in 1997, the CIA published a list of fifty "trailblazers" who had distinguished themselves over the agency's history. Bray nominated Harvey for the award, but he was left off the list.

———

By contrast, Frank Rowlett, who died in 1998, is a revered figure at the NSA, where he returned in 1958 as special assistant to the director after more than five years with the CIA. He was awarded both the National Security Medal and the President's Award for Distinguished Federal Civilian Service by President Lyndon Johnson, and had a building at NSA headquarters in Maryland named in his honor following his retirement in 1965.

The tunnel he had helped create had been intended to give the CIA its own communications intelligence. The NSA's anger at being excluded from even knowing about the tunnel until its help was needed worsened the already bad relations between the agencies for years. But, ironically, in the long run, the NSA "benefitted immeasurably" from the tunnel, according to an agency history of REGAL. The reliance on the NSA to decrypt coded material gave the fledgling spy agency what it needed above all else—"its acceptance by U.S. intelligence community members as a viable and equal contributor to the intelligence effort."

———

Peter Lunn, the Berlin SIS chief who partnered with Harvey and Rowlett on the tunnel, enjoyed a long and illustrious career with SIS until his retirement in 1986. He never spoke publicly about the tunnel until 2010. "Of course the whole thing was blown by George Blake from the start," Lunn said then. But the KGB decision to stay silent about the tunnel meant "we got plenty of valuable information."

Not only did Lunn survive the devastating Blake confession in April 1961, but less than two years later he played a key role in the Kim Philby saga. Lunn had succeeded Nicholas Elliott as station chief in Beirut. Philby, still living in Beirut, only learned about Blake and his espionage following his arrest, and was badly shaken by the lengthy sentence given his fellow spy. Damning new evidence of Philby's guilt from a KGB defector was so incontrovertible that even Elliott, Philby's staunchest defender at SIS, recognized it. At Dick White's behest, Elliott traveled to Beirut in January 1963 to confront Philby and, according to some accounts, offer him immunity from prosecution in exchange for his cooperation. Philby agreed in principle, and after Elliott returned to London, Lunn was to take over Philby's debriefing.

Lunn had asked Philby to report to the British embassy for further questioning. On the night of January 23, after coordinating with the KGB's Pavel Nedosekin—who had also been Blake's handler in Beirut—Philby apparently boarded a Soviet freighter bound for Odessa. By some accounts, Lunn panicked when he learned that Philby was missing and rushed to the spy's apartment. Philby himself later suggested that he was able to escape thanks to Lunn's incompetence, claiming that a fresh snowfall had blanketed Lebanon's mountains, and Lunn could not resist leaving Beirut to go skiing. But another school of thought holds that SIS wanted Philby to flee to Moscow to avoid another embarrassing espionage trial, which would be hugely damaging to the government coming so soon after Blake's exposure. In this version, Lunn was expecting the news of Philby's flight. Whatever the truth, Lunn's career did not seem to suffer.

Lunn stayed a loyal friend to Harvey until the latter's death. After retirement, Lunn spent every winter skiing in Mürren, Switzerland, where he had first gone down the mountains as a child. When a visitor asked a lift operator where to find him, he was advised to "look for crazy tracks in the deep snow." Lunn was still skiing there a year before his death in 2011 at age ninety-seven.

———

The secrecy that surrounded the tunnel project continued until after the end of the Cold War, leaving many participants in awkward positions.

Keith Comstock, one of the three Army Corps of Engineers captains who oversaw the tunnel construction, learned only in 2007 that the project had been declassified. "All these years, fifty-three years, I'd never said a word to anybody," said Comstock, who retired from the Army as a colonel in 1969. "My kids had always asked me, once in a while, 'What did you do that year that you weren't home?' God, what a relief and a joy to find out that it had been declassified. I sat down and wrote a letter to my kids and gave them the whole thing."

For Eugene Kregg, the Army linguist, the consequences of the secrecy were severe. After leaving Berlin, Kregg earned advanced engineering science degrees and worked as a nuclear materials research scientist. But after he confided to an associate about what he had done in Berlin, he found that work colleagues and even family members doubted his veracity. "Family relationships were shattered and my professional status permanently compromised," he later said.

In 1967, Kregg contacted retired Army colonel James Helgestad, the Rudow installation commander, asking him to vouch for "the credibility of my Berlin activities." Helgestad was sympathetic and wrote a "to whom it may concern" letter attesting that Kregg had been assigned "duties of a highly specialized and important nature" in Berlin, and that his performance had been "of inestimable value to the Government of the United States."

But Helgestad told Kregg he could not go into any details. "I advise you to let sleeping dogs lie," the colonel told him. "I am sure you recall the de-briefing statement you signed before leaving the unit and the penalties described therein for the unauthorized disclosure of classified information. I need not say more."

For Kregg—who after leaving the Army changed his last name to Kovalenko, his father's original name, to honor his Russian roots— the freedom to talk about his experiences in Berlin has been emotional and cathartic. "It has taken a lifetime to rebuild new personal and professional relationships," he said.

———

The fall of the Berlin Wall in 1989, followed soon by the reunification of Germany and the collapse of the Soviet Union, gave, for a time, a sense of triumph to those on the Western side. When BOB was deactivated in a 1994 ceremony attended by former base chiefs, there was confidence that Western liberal values had prevailed and hope that Russia was on a path toward democracy.

A reappraisal of the tunnel became slowly possible after the end of the Cold War. The CIA has gradually declassified records related to the tunnel, including many in recent years. The SIS, on the other hand, has never formally acknowledged its enormous role in the tunnel. For a time, Russia's Foreign Intelligence Service (SVR), the successor to the KGB's First Chief Directorate, cooperated with researchers. Sergei Kondrashev, George Blake's longtime handler, who rose to high ranks in the Soviet intelligence service as deputy chief of clandestine operations worldwide, collaborated after his retirement on a history of the intelligence struggle in Berlin during the Cold War with retired CIA officer David Murphy, who had succeeded Harvey as BOB chief. The SVR gave Kondrashev ready access to his old operational files, including those involving the Berlin tunnel, and he remained close friends with Blake. The resulting 1997 book, *Battleground Berlin,* written with journalist George Bailey, included a wealth of information making the case that the tunnel intelligence was genuine. British intelligence historian David Stafford subsequently reached the same conclusion in his 2002 book, *Spies Beneath Berlin.*

Kondrashev worked on a memoir with the assistance of another retired CIA officer, Tennent "Pete" Bagley. But in 2007, with security tightening and Western relations worsening under Vladimir Putin, the SVR withdrew its clearances, forbidding publication of the material. Kondrashev died of heart disease later that year. But with the permission of his family, Bagley returned to the project. *Spymaster,* published in 2013, included further disclosures about the KGB's decision to protect Blake rather than Soviet communications. As Kondrashev told Bagley, "the value of the source outweighed the value of the secrets."

Together with other revelations in recent years, including declassified papers from the CIA, the NSA, and the Eisenhower and Kennedy presidential libraries, records from Blake's espionage trial in London, letters and papers related to Bill Harvey and the Berlin Operations Base compiled by Stockton, and interviews with key participants, the conclusion is inescapable that the vast majority of the intelligence was both genuine and, taken as a whole, extremely valuable.

East German spy chief Markus Wolf, who had been shocked at the scene of the tunnel on the morning of its discovery in 1956, was stunned once more after the fall of the wall to learn how much the West received from the tunnel. The claims of disinformation, he said, are "a myth."

The common wisdom about the tunnel is "patently false," Hugh Montgomery declared not long before his death in 2017 at age ninety-three. The KGB held knowledge of the tunnel so tightly, and the amount of traffic flowing over the tapped lines was so enormous, that "it would have been impossible to use that as a channel for disinformation," he said.

Notably, to date, not a single example of disinformation connected to the tunnel intelligence has been unearthed.

———

At his dacha in the pinewoods in Kratovo, twenty-five miles southeast of Moscow, George Blake faces his own reappraisal. The vision of a utopian Soviet communist state for which he risked everything is long gone.

The other infamous British Cold War spies of the era who escaped to Russia—Kim Philby, Guy Burgess, and Donald Maclean among them—have long since died, leaving only Blake. He adjusted to life in Russia better than any of them, speaking the language and starting a new family. "Philby had second thoughts, so did Maclean," said Oleg Kalugin, a former KGB officer who oversaw Blake and other British spies in Moscow. "But not George Blake."

Still, after his arrival in Moscow in January 1967, Blake did not take long to recognize that communism in the Soviet Union was an utter failure. "One must be blind or willfully close one's eyes . . . not to see that the noble experiment of building such a society has failed," he later said. He was reunited with Portland spy Gordon Lonsdale in time to celebrate the fiftieth anniversary of the Bolshevik Revolution in 1967, as Lonsdale had predicted while they were at Wormwood Scrubs. But both were disillusioned by what they found. Khrushchev, the last of the true Bolshevik believers in the Soviet leadership, had been expelled from office in October 1964, and replaced by Leonid Brezhnev, who presided over a long Soviet economic stagnation and a system run for the benefit of party elites.

As in prison, Blake did his best to fit into Russian society. The deprivations of Scrubs, he wryly noted, prepared him well for the long lines and endless shortages of life in communist Russia, making "the transition easier and the rough edges less painful." But it was impossible to adjust to everything. His barber smelled of vodka and herring, a combination that "was not only unpleasant but slightly frightening."

Blake stayed at first in a spacious KGB apartment with a house-keeper to prepare his meals. For months he was kept largely out of sight, away from hotels, restaurants, or theaters visited by Western-ers. It was two years before he was allowed to attend the Bolshoi. "God forbid that the West would sniff out early on that he was in Moscow, so he was incognito for some time," recalled Vasily Dozh-dalev, who was initially responsible for his care after his arrival.

Blake spent his days writing long memos for the KGB, compiling every scrap of information he had been unable to pass on before his arrest, as well as details of how the British had investigated and interrogated him. He sat down every evening for two hours with a KGB handler known as Stan, who recorded the conversations and went over the compiled material. Blake helped the KGB identify more SIS officers stationed overseas.

His early months were particularly unhappy. He was anxious about his future and uncertain about his long-term standing with the KGB. On a personal level, he still harbored "secret hopes" that Gil-lian would join him with the children in Moscow. But two months after his arrival, Stan gave him newspaper clippings reporting that their divorce had been granted in his absence. "This news dashed all my hopes of a reunion with my wife and children and caused me a great deal of grief," Blake said.

————

Sean Bourke's time in the Soviet Union was another painful chapter. Bourke arrived two weeks after Blake, flying into West Berlin on a forged passport and crossing into East Berlin, where he was met by the KGB and flown to Moscow.

At Blake's suggestion, Bourke moved into Blake's apartment, which quickly proved a mistake as they were at heart an odd couple— Blake was fussy about neatness and prized equilibrium, while the rambunctious Bourke was given to mercurial mood swings. But a more fundamental problem was that Bourke had not wanted to come to Russia in the first place. He had gone only at the insistence of the others in the escape plot, and from the moment he arrived he felt uncomfortable and was eager to go home to write a book about the adventure.

"I had to make the best of it because there was no going back," Blake recalled. "Whereas Sean wanted to go back, to claim his dues, as it were."

Given Bourke's reckless nature, Blake feared that any book he wrote could lead investigators to the Randles and Pottle. The "ideal solution" would have been for Bourke to remain permanently in the Soviet Union, Blake said, but it was quickly clear that this would be impossible. "Sean was too much of an individualist, not to say anarchist, by nature, too impatient of any form of authority to have settled down happily in a state as authoritarian as the Soviet Union was in those years," Blake later said.

Blake faced what he called "an agonizing choice"—to support Bourke in his wish to go back, or to protect the Randles and Pottle from being exposed as accomplices and possibly facing prison. He chose the Randles and Pottle, earning Bourke's undying enmity.

It was not long before Bourke's discontent turned into angry resentment of Blake. "From the moment I moved into Blake's flat I found myself face to face with a complete stranger," he would write. "Gone was the ever-ready smile, the patient and understanding disposition, the willingness to listen and sympathize. Blake was sullen, intolerant, arrogant and pompous. The George Blake that we had all known in Wormwood Scrubs had never really existed. It had been a deliberately false image, calculatingly projected for his own long-term benefit."

By Bourke's account, one night at the apartment he overheard Blake urging Stan not to allow Bourke to leave for years. "If he gives trouble you will have to give thought to what other steps you might have to take," Blake told Stan, according to Bourke. Paranoid, drinking, and isolated, Bourke believed that Blake was advocating he be eliminated. "I was to be the final sacrifice on the altar of Blake's vanity," Bourke later wrote. Blake has insisted that he never made any such suggestion; if he did, it is a mystery why he would have spoken in English rather than Russian, given that Bourke was in the apartment.

After Bourke had been in Moscow for eight months, the KGB told him he should stay at least five years, since he had been publicly identified as a suspect in the Blake escape and was being hunted by Scotland Yard. Stan dangled promises of a generous stipend, beautiful women, the freedom to live anywhere in the country, and the KGB's help in publishing his book. But Bourke still wanted to go home. "If you want to leave this country, that's your funeral," Blake told him, according to Bourke.

On September 4, 1967, Bourke went to the British embassy in Moscow and identified himself to nonplussed officials, saying he was wanted by Scotland Yard in connection with George Blake's escape, and wanted to return to Britain. But the embassy turned him away; he was not a British citizen. Blake exploded when Bourke told him the news. "You fool! You complete and utter fool! What did you do that for?"

"Because I'm sick and tired of you and the KGB and this cloak-and-dagger life!" Bourke declared.

The KGB, alarmed because Western intelligence now knew that Blake and Bourke were in Moscow, sent the pair out of the city on a monthlong escorted tour of Russia. After they returned, Bourke was given his own place to live, a move that helped calm tensions. The uneasy standoff continued for another year as Bourke pressed to return home. He spent much of his time with his Russian girlfriend, Larissa, and worked on his book. When his brother Kevin visited Moscow in August 1968, Bourke gave him a portion of the manuscript to smuggle home, but the KGB confiscated it at the airport.

In the fall of 1968, Bourke was finally allowed to depart Moscow without his manuscript, and he stepped onto Irish soil on October 22, 1968, the second anniversary of Blake's escape. He successfully fought off being brought to trial in Britain when an Irish judge ruled in 1970 that his reasons for helping Blake escape were to embarrass the British government, and that the charges against him therefore had a political nature barring extradition.

After multiple requests from Bourke, the KGB returned his

confiscated manuscript in the spring of 1969, with large amounts blacked out, apparently by Blake and the KGB, removing details that pointed to the involvement of Anne and Michael Randle and Pat Pottle in the escape. Bourke restored the censored material, and his book, *The Springing of George Blake,* was published in 1970. The Randles and Pottle were horrified when they read an advance copy and discovered that Bourke had given them the pseudonyms "Anne and Michael Reynolds" and "Pat Porter." Said Michael Randle, "An intelligent boy scout could have worked out from the book who we were."

Indeed, based on the book, MI5 and Special Branch quickly concluded that the Randles and Pottle were involved. But police decided not to charge or even interview them. "It was considered that to do so might be persecution—a big fish had got away, so they were taking it out on the little fish," according to a subsequent MI5 report. Left unsaid was the prospect of a hugely embarrassing public trial further exposing how a notorious spy had been freed by rank amateurs.

The Randles, Pottle, and Blake were also stunned to learn from Bourke's book that he had deliberately left clues before and after the escape pointing to his involvement. He had telephoned the police three days after the escape to tell them where they could find the Humber Hawk automobile used in Blake's escape. Just before departing for Moscow, he sent a picture of himself to a British newspaper with his name on the back and the address of the Highlever Road flat where he and Blake had initially hid.

In retrospect, it was clear that Bourke had decided early on to write a book about the escape, and thought he needed to be publicly identified as an accomplice in order for his story to be believed and the book published. This, Randle and Pottle recognized, explained "many of his apparently irrational actions."

Bourke lived large for a time on the proceeds of the book, enjoying a measure of celebrity and drinking heavily, but as the money dwindled he fell on hard times. He was living in a trailer in the seaside resort town of Kilkee in County Clare when he collapsed on a roadside with a massive heart attack in January 1982 at age forty-nine. Two doctors at the scene were unable to revive him. A postmortem at the county hospital found that he had died of "acute pulmonary oedema, left ventricle failure and coronary thombrosis." One of the doctors, knowing of Bourke's notoriety, looked for evidence of "malicious interference" but found none.

"It was a sad end for a gifted, charming, brave, but unpredictable man," Blake later said. "I owe him my freedom, so I cannot think badly of him," he added. "He gave me life."

———

For Blake, life in Russia improved markedly on a Volga riverboat cruise in the spring of 1968 when he met Ida, a Russian woman who worked as a French translator for an economics institution. Blake joined Ida's circle of friends, and his marriage to her in 1969 accelerated his integration into Russian society. Like Gillian, Ida was "a real outdoor girl" who loved swimming, skiing, and long walks in the country, Blake said. She was also honest and given to speaking her mind, another trait that reminded him of Gillian. "It is perhaps a paradox that I, having a less straightforward nature, should twice have married women of this turn of character," he observed.

The KGB had given Blake a "modest sum of money to set myself up" and arranged for him to rent a spacious apartment. After the birth of their son, Mischa, in 1971, the KGB presented him with the dacha in Kratovo.

Blake's residences were bugged, of course. There were two reasons, according to Kalugin, who took over the care of Blake and other traitors in 1971. "One was for security reasons, to make sure no one entered his apartment, for assassination, poisoning, burglary, whatever. That was protection," Kalugin said. "The other was just to make sure he was still loyal to the Soviet system."

Blake had been given a job as a Dutch translator for Progress Publishers, a state-run firm that published Russian works in foreign languages, earning enough to be "financially secure," according to Sergei Kondrashev, who saw Blake frequently. "But we're still supporting him because we are fulfilling our obligation in return for what he did for us," he added. Blake was given privileges and medical benefits similar to a military general, and the KGB helped him cut through the notorious Soviet red tape—he was able, for example, to skip the normal ten-year waiting list to get a car.

Contrary to SIS assurances that Blake could do no more damage, Agent Diomid was still proving useful to the KGB. Rem Krassilnikov, the KGB counterintelligence chief who led the investigations and arrests of the many spies betrayed by the CIA's Aldrich Ames and the FBI's Robert Hanssen, later said that much of what he learned about British intelligence came from spending time in Moscow with Kim Philby and George Blake.

Still, Blake preferred a passive role in his cooperation. When the KGB learned that a British intelligence officer Blake knew was coming to Moscow under diplomatic cover, Kalugin asked him to help recruit the officer. Blake tried to refuse. "Oh no, Oleg," he said. "I'm not a recruiter."

After "much arm-twisting," Blake agreed, and the KGB arranged for him to bump into the officer in a Moscow hotel. But the officer refused to speak to him. "Blake's resistance to the recruitment made some people suspicious, and the electronic eavesdropping in his apartment was continued," Kalugin said.

———

Blake found translation work isolating and dull. With the help of Donald Maclean, his fellow British spy with whom he formed a close friendship, he was given a job at the Institute of World Economy and International Relations, a leading Moscow think tank where Maclean worked. Blake, who specialized in Middle East politics, enjoyed the camaraderie and mental stimulation of the job, remaining at the institute for more than three decades. Colleagues and family referred to him as Georgy Ivanovich.

Maclean, nine years his senior, became something of a father figure to Blake, who saw the elder defector as sharing his Calvinistic character. Blake felt he and Maclean spied out of "a sense of duty," while Kim Philby "spied because he rather liked it."

Indeed, his relations with Philby, whom he met at a KGB luncheon in 1970, were complicated. Their personalities were quite different—Blake was "far shyer" than the suave Philby, said Kalugin.

For a time they were friends—the Blakes even introduced Philby to his fourth and final wife, Rufina, a girlfriend of Ida's. But there was always an underlying tension. Philby considered Blake "a young upstart" who was a less important spy than he was, and was jealous that Blake received the Order of Lenin before he did. Blake had his own resentments, bitter that the British government had treated him far more harshly than the Cambridge spies, especially Philby and Anthony Blunt. Blake believed that Nicholas Elliott, who had sent him back from Beirut to London to face arrest, had allowed Philby to escape. And Blunt, who confessed to being the fourth man in the Cambridge ring in 1964, was given immunity from prosecution and, until his treachery was publicly revealed in 1979, allowed to retain his position as curator to Queen Elizabeth's art collection and even his knighthood. To Blake, it was obvious why. "I was of foreign origin, and I could more easily be made an example of," he said. "They also didn't want yet another spy scandal. They were members of the Establishment and I was not."

Blake's friendship with Philby broke in 1975 when one of Philby's sons took photographs showing the two spies and their families at a gathering at Blake's dacha and gave them to a British magazine. The two colleagues in betrayal never again spoke, though Blake attended Philby's state funeral in 1988. Blake and Maclean stayed very close until the latter's death in 1983. Maclean bequeathed the younger spy his enormous library of political and history books, along with his old, tweed flat cap, which Blake wore for years.

—

After years of pleas, Blake was allowed to leave the Soviet Union under KGB escort for holidays in the Eastern Bloc, usually in East Germany at a Stasi retreat on the Baltic Sea. On the trips, he would generally address officers and trainees at the Stasi headquarters in East Berlin, where posters hailed "Soviet Scout Blake" and his betrayal of the "useless" Berlin tunnel.

Markus Wolf, who hosted the visits, was struck by Blake's habitual understatement. "Even for a former spy, he was more than usually reserved when it came to discussing the more grimy details of the business," Wolf recalled. "Blake suffered terribly under his reputation as a callous agent and wanted to be regarded as an idealist. Despite his commitment to the Soviet cause, I also had the feeling that he refused to accept that he really was the traitor his country considered him to be."

———

In the midst of the dramatic changes that accompanied the perestroika policies of Soviet leader Mikhail Gorbachev, Blake was thrust back into the public eye with the 1990 publication of his autobiography, *No Other Choice,* and accompanying interviews. Blake was frank in admitting his disillusionment with the Soviet experience with communism, saying the lesson was "that Communism cannot be implanted by force, by strict discipline and terror." But he remained committed to the ideology. "I believe the time will come, maybe in many, many generations and not in this country, when humanity will return to this experiment," he told a Moscow press conference with Western journalists a few months after the collapse of the Soviet Union. He refused to admit that he had chosen the wrong side. "The guilt or morality of an action doesn't lie in whether you lose or win but in the morality of the act itself," he said.

In his book, Blake acknowledged revealing the identity of hundreds of agents, but fancifully denied being responsible for the death of a single one. "I challenge anybody . . . to name one who has been executed," he wrote.

Blake has "that innocent mind," said Kalugin, recalling that Blake told him several times that the KGB had promised that none of those he identified had been shot. "He clung naively to that belief, and I didn't have the heart to tell him that his work led directly to the deaths of dozens of agents behind the Iron Curtain," he wrote.

Yet Kondrashev, his longtime handler, claimed that "not a single person" was executed based on Blake's intelligence. Kondrashev, of course, could have had his own reasons to lie—perhaps indulging his friend's delusions. Whatever the truth, Blake remains a "pious traitor," as he was once called.

———

At first, with the fall of the Berlin Wall and the end of the Cold War, Blake seemed to think he would be forgiven. Louis Wesseling, the

Dutch businessman he had befriended in Lebanon, lunched with him in Moscow shortly before the collapse of the Soviet Union. Blake told him he wanted to get a visa to visit the Netherlands, "as if his past was forgiven and forgotten," Wesseling recalled.

"No, it hasn't been forgotten," Wesseling told him.

Eventually, Blake recognized that he could never return to England, the Netherlands, or anywhere else in the West without facing arrest. When his mother died in 1993, he did not attend her funeral in Holland for fear that MI5 might abduct him. Ironically, the collapse of the Iron Curtain shrunk his world further. His occasional visits to East Germany ended with the fall of the wall. "The peculiar sadness of Blake's fate is that he lost his homeland not just once, when he fled England, but twice, when the Soviet Union collapsed and he was left to live out a withdrawn life in an adopted homeland that had abandoned his cause," Wolf observed.

———

On June 25, 1991, George Blake appeared again in Court 1 of the Old Bailey, a full three decades after his conviction and sentencing. This time, he spoke via a video recording at the trial of Michael Randle and Pat Pottle on charges that they had helped him escape from prison and evade arrest.

The matter had been reignited by the 1987 publication of the book *George Blake: Superspy* by Montgomery Hyde, along with subsequent newspaper stories that soon led to Randle and Pottle being identified as Sean Bourke's accomplices in Blake's escape. Concerned about suggestions that peace organizations had collaborated with the KGB to spring Blake, the two decided to write their own account about what they had done, and why. The surrounding publicity led to calls in Parliament for the two men to be prosecuted. Under pressure, Scotland Yard reopened its investigation and the two were charged in May 1988.

In preparation for the trial, the Randles and Pottle traveled to Moscow in February 1990 to get a statement from Blake affirming that there had been no KGB involvement in the escape. The group's first reunion, nearly a quarter century after the escape, "was very emotional," Randle said. Blake brought them to his apartment to meet his wife and son. They drank champagne and picked up conversations where they had left off twenty-four years earlier. Blake seemed jolted awake from the stupor of more than two decades of Soviet life. "For me their visit was an exhilarating experience," he recalled. "I felt I was in the swim again."

At the Old Bailey trial the following year, a packed gallery watched Blake's videotaped statement on three screens set up around the courtroom. Wearing a blue blazer and silk scarf, Blake sat in an armchair in his Moscow apartment and read a statement declaring what had been unsaid thirty years earlier: "I was a member of the British Secret Intelligence Service from August 1944 until the date of my trial in April 1961." He admitted betraying many operatives to the Soviets, but again denied that he was "ever responsible for the death of agents," noting that no such allegation was made at his trial. As for Randle and Pottle, he testified, "There was never any doubt in my mind that they acted as they did out of purely humanitarian concern, and specifically because of the length of my sentence."

Randle and Pottle, who presented their own case in court, admitted to helping Blake escape, but argued that they acted "under duress" because of their outrage over his "cruel and unusual" sentence. "They did it beautifully," barrister Jeremy Hutchinson, who gave the two informal advice during the case, recalled one year before his death in 2017 at age 102. "Much to the fury of the judge, the jury agreed with them." The two were unanimously acquitted of all charges. "I'm absolutely delighted," Blake said upon hearing the news. "It almost makes me cry."

———

At age ninety-six, Blake's eyesight has faded to the point that he is nearly blind, and he now lives with Ida almost entirely in Kratovo. Their dacha is down a narrow, sporadically paved lane that is lined with pine trees and tall fences, which allow only peeks of the homes and gardens behind them. Many former KGB officers have dachas in the area, and neighbors are protective. "I don't know his name, I don't know anything about him," an elderly man said.

Blake's dacha, on a corner lot behind a tall, wood-paneled fence, is watched over by a friendly caretaker with a beret, and a small white schnauzer, Plushka, who curiously sniffs at visitors. The traditional-looking wooden dacha, painted green with a steep gabled roof, has big porches, with tall pines all around the house and a small cottage where the caretaker lives. Inside, the four-bedroom décor is simple and cozy, kept toasty year-round by central oil heating.

By Blake's account, he tried to turn down the dacha when it was offered by the KGB, but now cannot imagine life without it, or death. "I have made arrangements that, after my death, I shall be cremated and the ashes scattered in the woods near our dacha, where I have walked and skied so often with my wife and son, so that it may be said: 'Neither shall his place know him anymore,'" he wrote.

Blake still ventures out for walks with Ida, thirteen years his junior, in the pinewoods around their dacha, hunched over and holding her arm. But the walks now are shorter and less frequent, and he spends most of his time sipping tea in the kitchen. With his eyesight so poor, he can no longer watch the BBC via satellite as he used to, so Ida reads to him—tomes on the Napoleonic Wars and the novels of Gogol and Chekhov, among other things, and he listens to classical music.

By the late 1990s, as Russia descended into a society beset with oligarchs, crime, and a political strongman, Blake's acquaintances detected "a weariness at how some things had turned out." He found some of the big and expensive dachas that had been built around Kratovo in recent years distasteful. His pension was not keeping up with inflation. Still, he considered himself fortunate. "My life has fallen on pleasant lines, perhaps more so than many would say I deserve," he has observed. In addition to his Russian son, Mischa, Blake occasionally sees his three English sons, who with Gillian's blessing began visiting their father in the 1980s and are now close to him. "This is something I could never have hoped for," Blake said.

"George never has any regrets," said Sylvie Braibant, his distant cousin through the Curiel family. "He said it might have been his Jewish origins. When you are Jewish, you can never look back. You never know what might happen to you. So you must always look forward and adapt to wherever you find yourself."

Blake is an honored figure in Russia, decorated with medals for his espionage, including the Order of Friendship medal in 2007 presented by his admirer, President Putin. He is lionized by the Russian press, which calls him the "grave digger of British intelligence," and carries his occasional pronouncements on the state of the world, usually made during annual birthday interviews with official organs. "The American empire will disappear because everyone who lives by the sword dies from the sword," he told *Izvestia* in 2010.

Blake's ninetieth birthday, on November 11, 2012, was a particularly big event, attended by all of his children. "These have been the happiest years of my life, and the most peaceful," he told the official government newspaper.

Blake sipped a bit of vodka and French wine, and nibbled on Camembert and Polish cheesecake. Everyone at the gathering watched some of a special hourlong documentary about him that was aired on government television, but they soon switched it off, as his English sons spoke no Russian. The whole family went for a short walk outside the dacha, with police officers to protect the spy from paparazzi. Blake was blasé about all the attention. "He thought it was normal, but nothing to be proud of," said Braibant, who was among the family members in attendance.

The congratulatory call from Putin came in the afternoon. The Russian president saluted Blake for his "enormous contribution to the preservation of peace," declaring that the spy had earned a place in the "constellation of strong and courageous men."

Blake downplayed the call as nothing important, yet the praise from Putin is a source of discomfort for him. "He doesn't want to talk about Putin," said Braibant. "It's a red line for him." He has told friends that he loathes the Russian president and the cynical and violent authoritarian rule he has imposed. But Blake declines to speak publicly about Putin, dependent as he is at his age on his security services pension. "That I don't want to dwell on at the moment," he told the British film documentarian George Carey.

———

Looking back on his life, Blake has said that sometimes "it all seemed as if it had happened to another person." He embraces his belief in predestination more tightly than ever. "Everything that happened in my life was meant to happen," he said. "There was no other possibility."

He likes to cite the words of Paul from the Book of Romans in the Bible: "The potter uses the clay to form vessels, some to honor, and some to dishonor, and it is not for the clay to ask the potter why he does it," he once said. "And that is my outlook on life. I have been formed in this way, and it is not for me to ask why. And I would say that I have been an unusual vessel, in that I have been fashioned both to shame and to honor."

In describing his espionage, Blake rejects each of the diametrically opposed viewpoints held about him in Russia and the West. "I don't see myself as a hero or a traitor," he said.

When he speaks of the tunnel now, the boastful tone he took in his 1970 *Izvestia* interview is gone. Instead, he acknowledges as true what he privately admitted after his 1961 arrest: "This operation provided the West with more information than a thousand well placed agents could have done," he wrote in the statement he gave his attorneys before the trial.

"All the conversations were real," Blake now says. "There were maybe one or two pieces of information which were not altogether true. But this was very dangerous." Given the enormous volume of monitored conversations, the KGB had no choice but to allow the communications to flow virtually unimpeded, according to Blake. "It was impossible to control that many people," he says.

But the real value of the tunnel, he adds, was not the conversations the West heard, but what was not heard. "During the Cold War, the most important task of all the intelligence services of both sides was to find indications that the one side was mobilizing for a nuclear attack on the other side," he says. "And each side suspected the other one of intending such an attack." The tunnel he betrayed, he now says, kept tensions in check and helped preserve peace. Blake subscribes to the notion that Khrushchev thought that if the West heard what Red Army commanders were actually saying, it would demonstrate that the Soviets had "had no intention to attack." In this telling, leaving the tunnel alone to protect Blake helped protect the peace—a version he finds appealing.

But Blake admits to seeing another reason why the KGB opted to let the tunnel continue. "Probably they thought in the long run, I'd be more valuable to them," he told me.

Were they right? I asked. "I don't know," he said. "That's not for me to say." He laughed.

———

The old Noack farm in Altglienicke is today an open field covered by grass, stone paths, and several small groves of trees, still bordering the peaceful cemetery. An autobahn tunnel bisects the ground where the spy tunnel once crossed from Rudow into East Berlin, carrying traffic rushing to and from the Schönefeld airport. An asphalt path runs along the route where the Berlin Wall once divided the city, and is now busy with bicyclists and families pushing strollers. Occasionally someone stops to look at the information signs put up by the city, describing the tunnel that ran below.

On a recent summer day, Paul Noack's daughter, Dagmar Feick, studied an aerial photograph on one of the signs and pointed to where the family's home once stood. The Cold War in Berlin had been no remote conflict for the Noacks. "For us, it affected the arc of our lives," she said. Her widowed mother had to sell the home and land in 1969. With the security restrictions after the wall was built, "we couldn't keep the orchard going anymore," said Feick, a retired chemist who lives near Altglienicke.

Walking through the field, Feick found a single old pear tree, one of more than a thousand fruit trees her father had planted in 1954, more than sixty years earlier. It had survived the building and excavation of the Berlin tunnel, the construction of the wall and accompanying death strip, the autobahn built after the wall fell, and the booming development of reunified Berlin.

She walked up to the thick-trunked tree, its branches lush with green leaves, and was pleased to see it was bearing fruit. "This is the last one," she said.

Acknowledgments

I was born in Berlin in 1960, too late for the tunnel, but in time for the wall. My father, who was stationed in Berlin as a CIA officer, drew a connection—jokingly, I think—between my birth and the construction of a barrier across the city. We left Berlin in 1962, but the city always held a mystique for me. My visit to Checkpoint Charlie and East Berlin with fellow high school German-language students in 1978 made a strong impression. In September 1989, I arrived in West Germany to work as a freelance journalist, intending to remain only a few months. But when the Berlin Wall fell two months later, my stay turned into five years as I reported on many of the dramatic events that followed, including the unification of Germany, the collapse of the Warsaw Pact, and the intelligence secrets that spilled out with the end of the Cold War.

I knew nothing of my father's work for the CIA until I was nearly an adult. Even then he was unable to discuss almost any aspect of his work, which after Berlin included assignments to Langley, Buenos Aires, Mexico City, and Islamabad. Donald Vogel died in 1986, soon after he was posted to Geneva as station chief, and we never had a chance to hold those conversations. But in subsequent years I would hear bits and pieces from his closest friends, including Ben Pepper and Gardner "Gus" Hathaway, who served in Berlin with my father. When Ben and Gus died in recent years, I realized the window was fast closing on the opportunity to learn about one of the most remarkable places and periods of Cold War history: Berlin and the battle for intelligence before the wall. The story I chose was perhaps the most remarkable of all: the Berlin tunnel.

Many people helped me on this journey. In Berlin, Bernd von Kostka, curator of the Allied Museum, guided me through the museum's tunnel collection and to the site at Altglienicke. Dagmar Feick took me around the field where her father planted fruit trees while the tunnel was dug beneath his feet. Ronald Seiffert shared artifacts, photographs, and articles collected by the Altglienicke museum he helps oversee. Petra Krishok, a *Washington Post* colleague from my time in Germany, helped with research in Berlin. In Russia, Lena Yegorova, a former AP translator and researcher in Moscow, joined me on an adventure to find Blake's dacha in Kratovo.

In the United States, CIA historians David Robarge, Kevin Ruffner, and Don Steury provided helpful information and suggestions, as did Lou Mehrer, a retired officer who has studied the tunnel. Thanks also to Patrick Weadon and Rene Stein at the NSA's National Cryptologic Museum; Kevin Bailey at the Eisenhower Presidential Library; Dana Bronson at the Kennedy Presidential Library; Rich Peuser and Tim Nenninger at the National Archives in College Park, Maryland; Charles Pinck at the OSS Society; Elizabeth Bancroft at the Association of Former Intelligence Officers; Vince Houghton, Peter Earnest, and Amanda Ohlke at the International Spy Museum; Bill Burr at the National Security Archive; Christian Ostermann at the Woodrow Wilson Center; and Professors Eliot Cohen, Bill Allison, and Michael Neiberg.

Peter Snow, veteran British broadcaster and fellow War of 1812 aficionado, hosted me in London during my research. George Carey, who produced the excellent 2015 documentary about George Blake, *Masterspy of Moscow,* graciously shared his knowledge and contacts with me. Thanks also to old pals Dennis Sheehan, John Simonson, and Mark Simon for hosting me in England and Germany.

Ron Jensen, a friend from reporting days in Germany, read the manuscript and checked files for me at the Kennedy Library. Bobbye Pratt, a former *Washington Post* researcher, dug up hard-to-find phone numbers and addresses. Mike Ruane, another *Post* colleague, cast his unerring writer's eye on the draft. Jake Haan, a talented young student of military history, helped with research. Gene Thorp devoted long hours to perfecting the maps.

Deep thanks to my editor, Geoff Shandler, who embraced this

project from the start, and the team at Custom House and Harper-Collins, including Ben Steinberg, Maureen Cole, Vedika Khanna, Molly Gendell, and Roland Ottewell. My agent, Rafe Sagalyn, aided by Brandon Coward, was an invaluable guide as always.

I'm indebted to previous authors and journalists who tackled various aspects of this subject and left valuable road maps, including David Murphy, George Bailey, and Sergei Kondrashev (*Battleground Berlin*); David Martin (*Wilderness of Mirrors*); Bayard Stockton (*Flawed Patriot*); David Stafford (*Spies Beneath Berlin*); Tom Bower ("The Confession"); and Roger Hermiston (*The Greatest Traitor*).

Thanks to the Army participants who told their stories, particularly Keith Comstock, Eugene Kovalenko, Russ Knapp, and Gene Bialas, and to Chris Williamson for sharing the papers of his father, Bob Williamson.

I am grateful to many friends and colleagues of my father who helped and encouraged me in this project. Hugh Montgomery was unfailingly cheerful in answering my questions during many conversations. Special thanks to dear friends Perky Pepper, who shared her memories of Berlin, and Karin Hathaway, who read through the manuscript. My godparents, Tom and Audrey Lamb, hosted me in Switzerland and told me tales of Berlin. Thanks also to Paul Mott, Burton Gerber, Sandy Grimes, Carl Gebhardt, Bill Lonam, Dave Forden, Barry Royden, Jim Fletcher, Dick Montague, John MacGaffin, and Haviland Smith. Most precious to me was learning about the world in which my father operated and the admiration in which he was held by those who worked with him.

It's no small source of sadness that a number of people who helped me over the course of this project have since died, among them Tom and Audrey Lamb, Hugh Montgomery, Dave Murphy, Eddie Kindell, Bill Romey, Bob Williamson, Jeremy Hutchinson, and Peter Montagnon. I was privileged to hear their stories.

Deep love and thanks to my children, Donald, Charlotte, and Thomas, for their love and encouragement. My mother, Joan Vogel, was a rock of support, as were my siblings, Stuart, Peter, and Jenny. Most of all, I would like to remember the undying friendship and devoted service of three happy warriors: Don Vogel, Ben Pepper, and Gus Hathaway.

Note on Sources

References for one or more paragraphs are often grouped in a single note. The order of the citations in each note generally corresponds to the information or quotations referenced. The following abbreviations are used in the endnotes.

AMB—Allied Museum, Berlin

AP—Associated Press

BGB—*Battleground Berlin: CIA vs KGB in the Cold War*

BLH—Blake Life History, IWM

BSP—Bayard Stockton Papers, University of California, Santa Barbara, California

CIA-HRP—CIA Historical Review Program

CSH—*Clandestine Services History: The Berlin Tunnel Operation, 1952–1956*

CWIHP—Cold War International History Project, Woodrow Wilson International Center for Scholars

DDE—Dwight D. Eisenhower Presidential Library and Museum, Abilene, Kansas

GAB—Gillian Allan Blake interview, Churchill Archives Centre, Churchill College, Cambridge

GBD—Gillian Blake draft, IWM

HI—Hoover Institution Library and Archives, Stanford University

int—interview

IWM—Imperial War Museum, London

JFK—John F. Kennedy Presidential Library and Museum, Boston, Massachusetts

LHC—Liddell Hart Centre, King's College London, The Cold War, Television Documentary Archive

NAUK—National Archives of the United Kingdom

ND—Neues Deutschland

*NOC—*George Blake, *No Other Choice*

NYT—New York Times

OFL—On the Front Lines of the Cold War: Documents on the Intelligence War in Berlin

RWP—Robert Williamson Papers

Stasi—Federal Commissioner for the Records of the State Security Service of the Former German Democratic Republic, Berlin

SV int—author interview

WP—Washington Post

Selected Bibliography

This list includes books and articles cited multiple times in the text. All others are listed in the notes.

Books

Aldrich, Richard J. *The Hidden Hand: Britain, America, and Cold War Secret Intelligence.* 2001. New York: Overlook Press, 2002.

Andrew, Christopher. *Defend the Realm: The Authorized History of MI5.* New York: Alfred A. Knopf, 2009.

———. *For the President's Eyes Only: Secret Intelligence and the American Presidency from Washington to Bush.* New York: HarperCollins, 1996.

Andrew, Christopher, and Oleg Gordievsky. *KGB: The Inside Story of Its Foreign Operations from Lenin to Gorbachev.* London: Hodder & Stoughton, 1990.

Andrew, Christopher, and Vasili Mitrokhin. *The Sword and the Shield: The Mitrokhin Archive and the Secret History of the KGB.* New York: Basic Books, 1999.

Ashley, Clarence. *CIA SpyMaster.* Gretna, LA: Pelican Publishing, 2004.

Bagley, Tennent H. *Spy Wars: Moles, Mysteries, and Deadly Games.* New Haven, CT: Yale University Press, 2007.

———. *Spymaster: Startling Cold War Revelations of a Soviet KGB Chief.* New York: Skyhorse Publishing, 2013.

Bamford, James. *Body of Secrets: Anatomy of the Ultra-Secret National Security Agency.* New York: Anchor, 2002.

Beschloss, Michael R. *Mayday: Eisenhower, Khrushchev, and the U-2 Affair.* New York: Harper & Row, 1986.

Blake, George. *No Other Choice: An Autobiography.* New York: Simon & Schuster, 1991.

Bohlen, Charles E. *Witness to History, 1929–1969.* New York: W. W. Norton, 1973.

Bourke, Sean. *The Springing of George Blake.* New York: Viking, 1970.

Bower, Tom. *The Perfect English Spy: Sir Dick White and the Secret War 1935–90.* New York, St. Martin's, 1995.

Catterall, Peter, ed. *The Macmillan Diaries.* Vol. 1, *The Cabinet Years, 1950–1957.* London: Macmillan, 2003.

———. *The Macmillan Diaries.* Vol. 2, *Prime Minister and After, 1957–1966.* London: Macmillan, 2011.

Chavchavadze, David. *Crowns and Trenchcoats: A Russian Prince in the CIA.* New York: Atlantic International, 1990.

Cookridge, E. H. *George Blake: Double Agent.* 1970. New York: Ballantine, 1982.

Crosbie, Philip. *March Till They Die.* 1955. Westminster, MD: Newman, 1956.

Deane, Philip. *I Was a Captive in Korea*. New York: W. W. Norton, 1953.

Dobbs, Michael. *One Minute to Midnight: Kennedy, Khrushchev, and Castro on the Brink of Nuclear War*. New York: Knopf, 2008.

Donovan, Robert J. *Eisenhower: The Inside Story*. New York: Harper & Brothers, 1956.

Dorril, Stephen. *MI6: Inside the Covert World of Her Majesty's Secret Intelligence Service*. London: Fourth Estate, 2000.

Dulles, Allen W. *The Craft of Intelligence*. New York: Harper & Row, 1963.

Eisenhower, Dwight D. *The White House Years: Mandate for Change, 1953–1956*. Garden City, NY: Doubleday, 1963.

———. *The White House Years: Waging Peace, 1956–1961*. Garden City, NY: Doubleday, 1965.

Garthoff, Raymond L. *A Journey Through the Cold War: A Memoir of Containment and Coexistence*. Washington, DC: Brookings Institution, 2001.

Gilbert, Martin. *Churchill: A Life*. New York: Henry Holt, 1991.

Grant, Thomas. *Jeremy Hutchinson's Case Histories*. London: John Murray, 2015.

Grathwol, Robert P., and Donita M. Moorhus. *Berlin and the American Military: A Cold War Chronicle*. New York: New York University Press, 1999.

Grose, Peter. *Gentleman Spy: The Life of Allen Dulles*. New York: Houghton Mifflin, 1994.

Harrison, Hope M. *Driving the Soviets Up the Wall: Soviet–East German Relations, 1953–1961*. Princeton, NJ: Princeton University Press, 2003.

Heefner, Wilson A. *Dogface Soldier: The Life of General Lucian K. Truscott, Jr.* Columbia: University of Missouri Press, 2010.

Helms, Richard, with William Hood. *A Look Over My Shoulder: A Life in the Central Intelligence Agency*. New York: Random House, 2003.

Hermiston, Roger. *The Greatest Traitor: The Secret Lives of Agent George Blake*. London: Aurum Press, 2013.

Hoffman, David E. *The Billion Dollar Spy: A True Story of Cold War Espionage and Betrayal*. New York: Doubleday, 2015.

Höhne, Heinz, and Hermann Zolling. *Network: The Truth About General Gehlen and His Spy Ring*. Translated from the German by Richard Barry. London: Secker & Warburg, 1972.

Hood, William. *Mole: The True Story of the First Russian Intelligence Officer Recruited by the CIA*. New York: W. W. Norton, 1982.

Hyde, H. Montgomery. *George Blake: Superspy*. 1987. London: Futura, 1988.

"Ist ja fantastisch!": The Story of the Berlin Spy Tunnel. Berlin: Allied Museum, 2006.

Johnson, Thomas R. *American Cryptology During the Cold War, 1945–1989; Book 1: The Struggle for Centralization, 1945–1960*. Volume 5 of United States Cryptologic History Series VI, The NSA Period 1952–Present. Fort Meade, MD: Center for Cryptologic History, National Security Agency, 1995.

Kalugin, Oleg. *Spymaster: My Thirty-Two Years in Intelligence and Espionage Against the West*. Philadelphia: Basic Books, 2009. Reprint of *The First Directorate*, 1994.

Kellerhoff, Sven Felix, and Bernd von Kostka. *Haupstadt der Spione: Geheimdienste in Berlin im Kalten Krieg*. Berlin: Berlin Story Verlag, 2012.

Khrushchev, Nikita S. *Khrushchev Remembers*. Introduction and notes by Edward Crankshaw. Translated and edited by Strobe Talbott. Boston: Little, Brown, 1970.

Khrushchev, Sergei N. *Nikita Khrushchev and the Creation of a Superpower*. Translated by Shirley Benson. University Park: Pennsylvania State University Press, 2000.

Lamphere, Robert J., and Tom Shachtman. *The FBI-KGB War: A Special Agent's Story*. 1986. New York: Berkley, 1987.

Macintyre, Ben. *A Spy Among Friends: Kim Philby and the Great Betrayal*. New York: Crown, 2014.

Maddrell, Paul. *Spying on Science: Western Intelligence in Divided Germany 1945–1961.* Oxford: Oxford University Press, 2006.

Mangold, Tom. *Cold Warrior: James Jesus Angleton: The CIA's Master Spy Hunter.* New York: Simon & Schuster, 1991.

Martin, David C. *Wilderness of Mirrors.* New York: Harper & Row, 1980.

Murphy, David E., Sergei A. Kondrashev, and George Bailey. *Battleground Berlin: CIA vs KGB in the Cold War.* New Haven, CT: Yale University Press, 1997.

O'Connor, Kevin. *Blake, Bourke & the End of Empires.* 2003. Dublin: ColourBooks, 2003.

Pincher, Chapman. *Inside Story: A Documentary of the Pursuit of Power.* New York: Stein & Day, 1978.

———. *Their Trade Is Treachery.* London: Sidgwick & Jackson, 1981.

———. *Too Secret Too Long.* New York: St. Martin's Press, 1984.

Powers, Thomas. *The Man Who Kept the Secrets: Richard Helms and the CIA.* New York: Alfred A. Knopf, 1979.

Randle, Michael, and Pat Pottle. *The Blake Escape: How We Freed George Blake and Why.* London: Sphere Books, 1990.

Ranelagh, John. *The Agency: The Rise and Decline of the CIA.* New York: Simon & Schuster, 1986.

Reel, Monte. *A Brotherhood of Spies: The U-2 and the CIA's Secret War.* New York: Doubleday, 2018.

Richart, Wilmer (Bill Romey). *Not to Be a Spy.* Self-published. 1989.

Rositzke, Harry. *The KGB: The Eyes of Russia.* Garden City, NY: Doubleday, 1981.

Schecter, Jerrold L., and Peter S. Deriabin. *The Spy Who Saved the World: How a Soviet Colonel Changed the Course of the Cold War.* New York: Charles Scribner's Sons, 1992.

Shackley, Ted, with Richard A. Finney. *Spymaster: My Life in the CIA.* Dulles, VA: Potomac Books, 2005.

Sichel, Peter M. F. *The Secrets of My Life: Vintner, Prisoner, Soldier, Spy.* Bloomington, IN: Archway, 2016.

Stafford, David. *Spies Beneath Berlin.* New York: Overlook Press, 2003, and ebook edition, London: Thistle, 2013.

Stockton, Bayard. *Flawed Patriot: The Rise and Fall of CIA Legend Bill Harvey.* Washington, DC: Potomac Books, 2006.

Thomas, Evan. *The Very Best Men: Four Who Dared: The Early Years of the CIA.* New York: Touchstone/Simon & Schuster, 1995.

Weiner, Tim. *Legacy of Ashes: The History of the CIA.* New York: Doubleday, 2007.

West, Nigel. *Seven Spies Who Changed the World.* London: Secker & Warburg, 1991.

Wise, David. *Molehunt: The Secret Search for Traitors That Shattered the CIA.* New York: Random House, 1992.

Wise, David, and Thomas B. Ross. *The Espionage Establishment.* 1967. New York: Bantam, 1968.

Wolf, Markus, with Anne McElvoy. *Man Without a Face: The Autobiography of Communism's Greatest Spymaster.* 1997. New York: PublicAffairs, 1999.

Wright, Peter. *Spycatcher: The Candid Autobiography of a Senior Intelligence Officer.* New York: Viking Penguin, 1987.

Wyden, Peter. *Wall: The Inside Story of Divided Berlin.* New York: Simon & Schuster, 1989.

Zellers, Larry. *In Enemy Hands: A Prisoner in North Korea.* Lexington: University Press of Kentucky, 1991.

Zeno (Gerald Lamarque). *Life.* London: Macmillan, 1968.

Articles

Blake, Gillian. "Portrait of a Spy." *Sunday Telegraph,* December 3, 10, and 17, 1961.

Boghardt, Thomas. "Semper Vigilis: The U.S. Army Security Agency in Early Cold War Germany." *Army History,* Winter 2018.

"A Brave, New World." *Studies in Intelligence,* released January 11, 2012.

Cecil, Clem. "How I Became a Lunchtime Spy for Moscow." *Times* (London), May 4, 2003.

Coleman, David G. "Eisenhower and the Berlin Problem, 1953–1954." *Journal of Cold War Studies,* Winter 2000.

Evans, Joseph C. "Berlin Tunnel Intelligence: A Bumbling KGB." *International Journal of Intelligence and Counterintelligence,* Spring 1996.

Feifer, George. "The Berlin Tunnel." *Military History Quarterly,* Winter 1998.

Fellon, Gerald. "Turning a Cold War Scheme into Reality: Engineering the Berlin Tunnel." *Studies in Intelligence,* 2008.

Hart, John L. "Pyotr Semyonovich Popov: The Tribulations of Faith." *Intelligence and National Security,* October 1997.

Heun, Michael, and Dietrich Schier. "Tunnel-Spione." *Berliner Morgenpost,* six-part series, March 6–11, 1994.

Huntington, Thomas. "The Berlin Spy Tunnel Affair." *American Heritage of Invention & Technology,* Spring 1995.

Knightley, Phillip. "George Blake: Confessions of a Traitor." *Sunday Times,* September 9 and 16, 1990.

Maddrell, Paul. "British Intelligence Through the Eyes of the Stasi." *Intelligence and National Security,* February 2012.

Martin, David C. "The CIA's Loaded Gun." *Washington Post,* October 10, 1976.

Merrell, R. M. "The Berlin Spy Tunnel: A Memoir." *The Royal Engineers Journal,* August 2002.

Middleton, Drew. "Now the Russians Turn Charms on Britain." *New York Times,* April 15, 1956.

Peck, Reginald. "Agent's Wife Knew Blake in Berlin." *Sunday Telegraph,* December 3, 1961.

Ruck, Adam. "Thinker, Author, Skier, Spy." *Ski+Board,* 2010.

Sullivan, Walter. "U.S. Investigates Wiretap Tunnel." *New York Times,* April 25, 1956.

Thornton, Jacqui, and Ian Thomas. "Revealed: The Map of Blake's Betrayal." *Sunday Telegraph,* February 23, 1997.

Reports and Document Collections

Browne, Robert T. *Experiences with the CIA 1950's Berlin Spy Tunnel.* Self-published, 2009.

CIA Analysis of the Warsaw Pact Forces: The Importance of Clandestine Reporting. CIA Historical Collections Division, 2012.

A City Torn Apart: Building of the Berlin Wall. CIA Historical Collections Division, 2011.

Clandestine Services History: The Berlin Tunnel Operation 1952–1956. CIA, 1967. 2012 declassified edition.

Hill, T. H. E., ed. *Berlin in Early Cold-War Army Booklets.* 2008.

Operation REGAL: The Berlin Tunnel. United States Cryptologic History, Special Series 4. National Security Agency/Central Security Service, 198. 2012 declassified edition.

Robert Williamson Papers, courtesy Chris Williamson.

Steury, Donald R., ed. *On the Front Lines of the Cold War: Documents on the Intelligence War in Berlin, 1946 to 1961.* CIA History Staff, Center for the Study of Intelligence, 1999.

Tunnel Spione. Nationalen Front des demokratischen Deutschland der Haupstadt Berlin, Spring 1956.

Documentaries and Programs

"Battleground Berlin: CIA vs. KGB." C-SPAN broadcast of book discussion with David Murphy, Sergei Kondrashev, sponsored by Yale University Press and Columbia

University Harriman Institute, September 11, 1997, Yale Club, New York City, www .c-span.org/video/?90860-1/battleground-berlin-cia-vs-kgb.

"The Cold War." Jeremy Isaacs Production for Turner Original Productions. CNN, 1998.

"The Confession." BBC *Inside Story,* Tom Bower, 1990.

"George Blake, agent double et légende de la guerre froide à Berlin." Sylvie Braibant. TV5 Monde, 2012.

"George Blake: Masterspy of Moscow." George Carey. BBC Four *Storyville,* March 23, 2015.

"'Operation Gold': Der Spionagetunnel von Berlin." Christian Klemke and Manfred Köhler. Sender Freies Berlin, 1997.

"The Red Files: Secrets of the Russian Archives Revealed." Invision Production with Abamedia. PBS, 1999. Transcript of interview with George Blake: www.pbs.org /redfiles/kgb/deep/interv/k_int_george_blake.htm.

"Spies Beneath Berlin." ORTV International for Discovery Networks Europe. Discovery Communications Europe, 2011.

"U.S. Postwar Intelligence in Europe." C-SPAN broadcast of conference with the CIA and the Center for the Study of Intelligence, Rosslyn, VA, April 20, 1996. www .c-span.org/video/?71352-1/us-postwar-intelligence-europe.

Archives and Museums

Allied Museum, Berlin. Sergei Kondrashev and David Murphy interview.

Altglienicke Museum, Berlin. Berlin tunnel photographs and documents.

Churchill Archives Centre, Churchill College, Cambridge. Papers of Michael Wolff.

Dwight D. Eisenhower Presidential Library and Museum, Abilene, KS. Dwight D. Eisenhower Papers as President, John Foster Dulles Papers, Eleanor Lansing Dulles Papers, White House Office, Office of the Staff Secretary, Oral History Collection.

Federal Commissioner for the Records of the State Security Service of the Former German Democratic Republic, Berlin. MfS HA PS 10304, MfS ZAIG 25776, MfS Sekr. Neiber 81.

Hoover Institution Library and Archives, Stanford University. R. Harris Smith Papers.

Imperial War Museum, London. George Blake Files.

John F. Kennedy Presidential Library and Museum, Boston, MA. President's Office and National Security files.

Liddell Hart Centre for Military Archives, King's College London, Cold War Television Documentary Archive.

National Archives and Records Administration, College Park, MD. CIA Records Search Tool (CREST).

National Archives of the United Kingdom, Kew, England. Defence, Foreign Office, Cabinet, Prime Minister, Home Office, and Metropolitan Police records.

University of California, Santa Barbara. Bayard Stockton Papers.

Author Interviews

Eugene Bialas, October 2015, November 22, 2015, February 25, 2019; George Blake, December 15, 2014, September 10, 2015; Reiner Bossdorf, August 18, 2015; Sylvie Braibant, August 25, 2014; Keith Comstock, September 15, 2015, October 21, 2015, December 15, 2015, February 27, 2019; William Donnelly, January 2015; Dagmar Feick, August 18, 2015; Volker Foertsch, September 2015; Raymond Garthoff, February 18, 2016; Floyd Hope, July 1, 2015; Jeremy Hutchinson, December 14, 2015, February 5, 2016; Oleg Kalugin, November 3, 2014, November 10, 2014, November 24, 2014; Eddie Kindell, November 4, 2015, December 2015, January 2016; Russ Knapp, January 12, 2015; Bernd von Kostka, August 6, 2015; Eugene Kovalenko (formerly Eugene Kregg),

September 1, 2014, September 15, 2014; Sergei Khrushchev, October 13, 2014, February 8, 2016; Gunther Kuinke, August 17, 2015; Tom and Audrey Lamb, August 24, 2015; Bill Lonam, December 6, 2014; Peter Montagnon, December 16, 2014, March 6, 2015, July 2015, August 23, 2015, December 14, 2015; Dick Montague, November 10, 2015; Paul Hugh Montgomery, May 30, 2014, January 6, 2015, November 17, 2015, December 18, 2015, January 2017; Paul Mott, June 11, 2015, April 7, 2019; David Murphy, May 8, 2014; Helen "Perky" Pepper, February 4, 2014; Larry Plapler, October 2015; John Quirk, October 2015; Michael Randle, November 19, 2015; Bill Romey, October 8, 2014; Walter Schaaf, June 6, 2015; Ed Sheffield, September 8, 2015; Peter Sichel, April 20, 2015; Werner Sobolewski, August 19, 2015; Alice Ojala Sorvo, November 30, 2015; Dorothy Soudakoff, February 2015; John Vacca, October 23, 2018; Joan Vogel, February 4, 2014; Robert Williamson, December 2015.

Notes

Prelude

1   *At midnight, the:* George Blake, "Life History," written by Blake for his attorneys after his arrest in April 1961, in Blake Papers, Department of Documents, IWM (hereafter Blake Life History, abbreviated BLH), 7; Blake, *NOC,* 127.

1   *Herbert Lord, a:* Hermiston, *The Greatest Traitor,* 97.

2   *Unbeknownst to his captors:* BLH, 2–5.

2   *Sitting in the back:* BLH, 7.

3   *"They had been taken":* BLH, 11.

3   *"These ragged, dirty":* Zellers, *In Enemy Hands,* 59; Deane, *I Was a Captive in Korea,* 87, 311.

3   *Blake, like the others:* BLH, 10; Crosbie, *March Till They Die,* 112, 123.

4   *They set out south:* Blake, *NOC,* 128–29.

4   *"I do not want":* Meadmore int, "The Confession," BBC *Inside Story,* Tom Bower.

4   *Alone, Blake crawled:* BLH, 10; Blake, *NOC,* 130–35.

5   *The major was tall:* Crosbie, *March,* 136.

5   *He announced that:* BLH, 10.

5   *"Then let them march":* Zellers, *Enemy,* 85, 89; Crosbie, *March,* 137.

6   *Thornton was blindfolded:* Deane, *Captive,* 113; Zellers, *Enemy,* 99; Crosbie, *March,* 140–41.

6   *When the sun rose:* SV int, Sheffield; Crosbie, *March,* 145.

6   *The march continued:* BLH, 10.

6   *He gave his tunic:* Cookridge, *George Blake: Double Agent,* 87; BLH, 11.

7   *In the morning:* Zellers, *Enemy,* 103–5; BLH, 11.

7   *Each day brought:* Deane, *Captive,* 115; Crosbie, *March,* 151, 158; Zellers, *Enemy,* 113–16.

8   *The Tiger roamed:* SV int, Sheffield.

8   *Blake, though, saw:* Blake, *NOC,* 133; BLH, 11.

8   *On November 8:* Crosbie, *March,* 163, 168; Zellers, *Enemy,* 118, Hermiston, *Greatest,* 115.

9   *Vyvyan Holt and:* BLH, 11; Cookridge, *George Blake: Double Agent,* 93–94.

9   *Their losses were mild:* Deane, *Captive,* 119, 145–51; BLH, 11; Crosbie, *March,* 165; Zellers, *Enemy,* 132, 139.

9   *Blake's own resilience:* Deane, *Captive,* 149; Blake, *NOC,* 133–34.

10   *Blake was "a good":* Cookridge, *George Blake: Double Agent,* 85; Deane, *Captive,* 109; Crosbie, *March,* 85; Zellers, *Enemy,* 73.

11   *The stability brought:* Zellers, *Enemy,* 143; Blake, *NOC,* 135; BLH, 12.

11   *For Blake, the quiet:* Blake int, "The Red Files: Secrets of the Russian Archives Revealed" (hereafter Blake int, Red Files); Blake int, "The Confession."

11   *In the spring:* Blake, *NOC,* 137–38; BLH, 12.

12   *"So there was a vacuum":* Blake int, "The Confession."

12   *One night in November:* Transcript of *Regina v. Blake,* May 3, 1961, George Blake, File 12 A (hereafter Blake trial transcript), IWM; Blake, *NOC,* 143.

Chapter 1: Black Friday

15   *It was known:* David A. Hatch with Robert Louis Benson, *The Korean War: The SIGINT Background* (Washington, DC: Center for Cryptologic History, National Security Agency, 2000), 4; Aldrich, *The Hidden Hand,* 409; Johnson, *American Cryptology,* 166; Helms with Hood, *A Look Over My Shoulder,* 133. The ASA began operation in 1943 as the U.S. Army's Signal Intelligence Service.

15   *U.S. intelligence:* Michael Peterson, "Beyond BOURBON—1948: The Fourth Year of Allied Collaborative COMINT Effort Against the Soviet Union," *Cryptologic Quarterly,* Spring 1995, 24; Johnson, *American Cryptology,* 165; Robert Louis Benson and Michael Warner, eds., *Venona: Soviet Espionage and the American Response 1939–1957* (Washington, DC: National Security Agency and Central Intelligence Agency, 1996), xv.

16   *By some estimates:* Hatch with Benson, *The Korean War,* 4; *CSH,* 1.

16   *The communist aggression:* BGB, 79; Helms with Hood, *Look,* 133, 127.

17   *In 1949, the CIA:* Garthoff, *A Journey Through the Cold War,* 100.

17   *Western intelligence therefore:* CIA Analysis of the Warsaw Pact Forces, 11; Maddrell, *Spying on Science,* 12.

17   *"We were simply blind":* David Murphy int, LHC.

18   *"I don't care what":* Wyden, *Wall,* 95.

18   *Even before Korea:* Stafford, *Spies Beneath Berlin,* 45.

18   *"We considered it":* Sichel, *The Secrets of My Life,* ch. 19.

18   *Some three hundred:* Joint Services Intelligence Group (Germany) report, Apr. 20, 1953, DEFE 41/80, NAUK; Grathwol and Moorhus, *Berlin and the American Military,* 62; Memo from Defence Minister Harold Alexander to Prime Minister, "Relative Strength of the Active Forces of N.A.T.O. and the Soviet Bloc," Nov. 6, 1953, DEFE 13/352, NAUK.

19   *A CIA estimate:* BGB, 91.

19   *Perhaps no one:* BGB, 208; Bamford, *Body of Secrets,* 2; "Frank Rowlett," *Cryptologic Almanac,* 50th Anniversary Series, Center for Cryptologic History, Aug. 2002.

19   *He also led the team:* Author tour, National Cryptologic Museum, Fort Meade, MD, 2015; David Kahn, "The Intelligence Failure of Pearl Harbor," *Foreign Affairs,* Winter 1991–92, 143; Frank Rowlett, *The Story of Magic: Memoirs of an American Cryptologic Pioneer* (Laguna Hills, CA: Aegean Park Press, 1998). The code name PURPLE was used because of the color of the folders that codebreakers used to hold intercepts.

20   *A decade later:* Stafford, *Spies,* 53; Helms with Hood, *Look,* 134; SV int, Hugh Montgomery.

20   *"Our Father":* Stockton, *Flawed Patriot,* 75.

20   *In early 1951:* BGB, 208, 423; SV int, Montgomery; *CSH,* 1; Lyman Kirkpatrick file, Box 10, HI.

21   *Two cities were obvious:* Helms with Hood, *Look,* 135; *CSH,* 4.

21   *The CIA was duly:* Blake int, Red Files; Helms with Hood, *Look,* 135; *CSH,* 4–5; SV int, Montgomery.

21   *Berlin held potential:* BGB, 209; Stafford, *Spies,* 55.

21 *In mid-1951:* BGB, 209; CSH, 2.
22 *Penetrating the ministry:* SV int, Peter Sichel; Stockton, *Flawed,* 76.
22 *The Soviets used two:* OFL, 328; BGB, 208.
22 *The intelligence gathered:* SV int, Sichel; Helms with Hood, *Look,* 133–34.
23 *To learn more:* BGB, 209.
23 *Lacking any engineering:* Fellon, "Turning a Cold War Scheme into Reality," 1.

Chapter 2: To Betray, You First Have to Belong

24 *In the fall of 1951:* Zellers, *Enemy,* 183; Crosbie, *March,* 197.
24 *The next morning:* Blake, *NOC,* 143–45.
25 *Blake, by his later account:* Blake, *NOC,* 144.
25 *The Russian was likely:* Bagley, *Spymaster,* ch. 6; Hermiston, *Greatest,* 132. While Blake's description of the Russian as someone "big and burly" and bald does not match Loenko, Kondrashev said it was Loenko who first interviewed Blake.
25 *"Word by word":* Marcus Warren, "Chocolate Was Soviet Spy's Way to Blake's Heart," *Telegraph,* Apr. 18, 1992.
26 *To divert suspicion:* Blake int, Red Files; Blake, *NOC,* 145; Deane, *Captive,* 183; Cookridge, *George Blake: Double Agent,* 99–100.
26 *"At the beginning":* Malyavin int, "The Confession."
26 *Vasily Dozhdalev:* BGB, 214.
27 *He had been born:* Blake, *NOC,* 27–30.
27 *Behar, a charming:* Gillian Allan Blake interview, WLFF 1/1/1, file 3, Churchill Archives Centre (hereafter GAB); Blake, *NOC,* 31–34.
27 *Albert Behar's health:* Blake, *NOC,* 31.
28 *Behar's death was followed:* Blake, *NOC,* 38.
28 *The family lived:* Blake, *NOC,* 39–45.
29 *"It was a shock":* SV int, Sylvie Braibant.
29 *Henri Curiel—who:* Andrew, *Defend the Realm,* 488; Hermiston, *Greatest,* 11.
29 *In the autumn of 1939:* Blake, *NOC,* 47–53.
30 *In Hummelo:* Hermiston, *Greatest,* 22; Blake int, Red Files; Blake, *NOC,* 55–58.
31 *In the summer of 1942:* BLH, 3; Blake, *NOC,* 60–67.
33 *But his journey:* Blake, *NOC,* 67–72.
35 *The two men were taken:* Blake, *NOC,* 72–77.
36 *The teenage boy:* Gillian Blake draft, file 10, George Blake Papers, IWM (hereafter GBD), 7.
36 *Around this time:* Hermiston, *Greatest,* 47.
36 *In the days after:* Blake, *NOC,* 79.
36 *Blake's commander:* "Background on the Blake Case," n.d., PREM 13/952, NAUK; West, *Seven Spies,* 125.
37 *A week later:* Blake, *NOC,* 85–86.
37 *Sometimes he would accompany:* Blake, *NOC,* 95–96.
38 *Amid all this:* Gillian Blake to Albert Cox, May 1, 1961, file 9a, GBP; Hermiston, *Greatest,* 60.
38 *With the demobilization:* Blake int, Red Files; Cookridge, *George Blake: Double Agent,* 49.
39 *"He smiled a lot":* Wheeler int, "The Confession."
39 *Though colleagues considered him:* Blake, *NOC,* 99–104; Cookridge, *George Blake: Double Agent,* 55.
39 *Shortly before his:* Bower, *The Perfect English Spy,* 260; Hermiston, *Greatest,* 70; Nigel West, *The Friends: Britain's Post-War Secret Intelligence Operations* (London: Weidenfeld & Nicholson, 1990), 135; Cookridge, *George Blake: Double Agent,* 71.
40 *Bicycling along:* GAB, tape II; "The Confession"; BLH, 4.

40   *Cambridge, Blake:* Blake int, "The Confession"; Blake; *NOC,* 106–109; Hermiston, *Greatest,* 77.
41   *Back at SIS headquarters:* Blake, *NOC,* 110.
41   *In late October 1948:* Blake, *NOC,* 111; Blake int, Red Files; "The Confession."
42   *In the spring of 1950:* Bower, *Perfect,* 261.
42   *Blake grew attached:* Blake, *NOC,* 116–18; BLH, 8.
43   *Despite his lost:* Blake, *NOC,* 121–24.
44   *In justifying his betrayal:* Blake int, Red Files; BLH, 14; Blake lecture to Stasi workers, 1976, MfS Sekr. Neiber 81, Stasi, 25.
44   *Yet those reasons:* Wise and Ross, *The Espionage Establishment,* 103; GAB, tape II.
44   *Declaring allegiance:* Hermiston, *Greatest,* 127; Cecil, "How I Became a Lunchtime Spy for Moscow."
45   *He also harbored:* Blake, *NOC,* 187; Knightley, "Confessions of a Traitor," part I; Gillian Blake to Albert Cox, May 1, 1961, file 9a, GBP; Helms with Hood, *Look,* 139.
45   *"To betray, you":* Dominic Kennedy, "The Spy Who Came in for Rough Justice," *Times* (London), Feb. 1, 2016.
45   *Subsequently, some would:* Meadmore int, "The Confession."
46   *Blake's decision that:* BLH, 13–14; Blake, *NOC,* 142; Blake int, "The Confession."
46   *For weeks, the KGB:* Blake, *NOC,* 145–46; "Reporting of Names of Agents to Russia," addendum to BLH.
47   *Eventually, Dozhdalev:* BGB, 214; Malyavin int, "The Confession."
47   *Blake was enormously:* Blake, *NOC,* 146.

Chapter 3: Bill Harvey, of All People

48   *On the surface:* Helms with Hood, *Look,* 152; Stockton, *Flawed,* 25.
48   *Just under six:* Stockton summary of Harvey FBI personnel files, BSP; Martin, *Wilderness of Mirrors,* 38; Norman Mailer, *Harlot's Ghost* (New York: Random House, 1991), 223.
49   *Some suspected that:* BGB, 152–53; Stockton, *Flawed,* 100.
49   *What was not exaggerated:* Martin, "The CIA's Loaded Gun," *WP,* October 10, 1976; Sichel, *Secrets,* ch. 20; Bayard Stockton, "The Bill Harvey I Knew," evaluations file, Box 1, BSP.
49   *Harvey was having:* Stockton, *Flawed,* 26.
49   *Beyond what he carried:* Powers, *The Man Who Kept the Secrets,* 137; BGB, 152.
50   *Regardless, there were:* Wright, *Spycatcher,* 147; Tom Polgar email to Stockton, July 10, 2001, Corr P-R, Box 1, BSP; Martin, *Wilderness,* 38.
50   *Some CIA officers:* Joe Wildmuth letter to David Murphy, July 25, 1993, BSP; BGB, 153.
50   *William King Harvey:* Stockton, *Flawed,* 4–9; Stockton, "The Bill Harvey I Knew," BSP; Martin, *Wilderness,* 25.
51   *Not long after Germany:* Stockton, *Flawed,* 9; Harvey FBI personnel files, BSP.
51   *But Harvey had a streak:* Stockton, *Flawed,* 14.
51   *Despite this misstep:* Stockton, *Flawed,* 15–17; Martin, *Wilderness,* 25; Lamphere and Shachtman, *The FBI-KGB War,* 36; Harvey FBI personnel files, BSP.
52   *But his FBI career:* Harvey FBI personnel files, BSP; Stockton, *Flawed,* 17.
53   *The CIA was only too happy:* Stockton, *Flawed,* 19, 26–28; Polgar email to Stockton, July 10, 2001; SV int, Perky Pepper; SV int, David Murphy.
53   *Hoover was infuriated:* Helms with Hood, *Look,* 152; FBI memo, "William K. Harvey Liaison Relations," Aug. 2, 1950, BSP.
53   *In January 1951:* Kim Philby, *My Silent War* (New York: Grove Press, 1968), 193, 235; Helms with Hood, *Look,* 158; Lamphere and Shachtman, *FBI-KGB,* 240–41;

Stockton, *Flawed*, 30; Martin, *Wilderness*, 46–48; Jefferson Morley, *Our Man in Mexico: Winston Scott and the Hidden History of the CIA* (Lawrence: University Press of Kansas, 2008), ch. 4.

55   *On May 25, 1951:* Macintyre, *A Spy Among Friends*, chs. 10–11; Martin, *Wilderness*, 8, 54; Helms with Hood, *Look*, 159; Philby, *My Silent War*, 193, 235.

57   *Now Bill Harvey:* BGB, 152, 210; Stockton, *Flawed*, 76.

57   *Now that he had:* Sichel, *Secrets*, ch. 20; David Murphy int, Sichel, Corr S–W, Box 1, BSP; SV int, Sichel.

58   *While Harvey's preparations:* BGB, 209; Stockton, *Flawed*, 78.

58   *The one thing Fleetwood:* Osborne letter to Stockton, June 9, 2001, Corr M–O, Box 1, BSP.

58   *Conway had been:* Rowlett int by Murphy, Oct. 21, 1993, Berlin tunnel file, Box 1, BSP; Sichel, *Secrets*, ch. 21.

58   *O'Brien—universally known:* Stafford, *Spies*, 55.

59   *O'Brien was sent:* Stockton, *Flawed*, 78–80; BGB, 209–10; Stafford, *Spies*, 54–55; Michael Burke int, HI; Hugh Montgomery, "Challenges of the Berlin Tunnel," *"Ist ja fantastisch!,"* 46.

59   *Conway's German was:* Osborne email to Stockton, Aug. 16, 2001, Osborne letter to Stockton, Mar. 15, 2001, and Osborne email to Stockton, May 24, 2001, Corr M–O, Box 1, BSP.

60   *By July 1952:* CSH, 1; Wolf with McElvoy, *Man Without a Face*, 98; BGB, 450.

61   *By the late fall of 1952:* Charles Bray int, Veterans Oral History Project, Center for the Study of War and Society, University of Tennessee, October 22, 2004.

61   *Signals intelligence collected:* "A Brave, New World," *Studies in Intelligence*, Jan. 11, 2012.

61   *The CIA decided:* Frank Rowlett oral history, NSA-OH-1976-(1–10), 372–74, NSA; Bamford, *Body of Secrets*, 477; SV int, Montgomery; "Brave, New World," 2.

62   *The three top:* SV int, Montgomery; Stockton, *Flawed*, 104.

Chapter 4: Ground Zero

64   *The Berlin Operations Base:* BGB, 152–53; Stockton, *Flawed*, 37–38.

65   *The base Harvey:* BGB, 8, 153, 456; SV int, Paul Mott; Sichel, *Secrets*, ch. 17; Walter Gorlitz, ed., *The Memoirs of Field Marshal Wilhelm Keitel* (1961; New York: Cooper Square Press, 2000), 196; author visit, Dahlem, Aug. 2015.

65   *Harvey inherited about:* OFL, vii; Chavchavadze, *Crowns and Trenchcoats*, 198; Hood, *Mole*, 195.

66   *All four powers:* BGB, 150; Osborne email to Stockton, May 24, 2001, Corr M–O, Box 1, BSP; Chavchavadze, *Crowns*, 185, 189; "Spies of East, West Never Rest in Berlin," UPI, June 20, 1959; Wyden, *Wall*, 94; Stafford, *Spies*, 7; SV int, Sichel.

66   *Despite its aura:* BGB, 19, 23; Wolf with McElvoy, *Man Without a Face*, 68; Wise, *Molehunt*, 135.

67   *When BOB secretly:* BGB, 113; Martin, *Wilderness*, 66.

67   *The KGB was headquartered:* Bagley, *Spymaster*, ch. 7; "Current Intelligence Summary," May 7, 1959, in OFL, 255–58; author visit, Karlshorst, Aug. 2015.

67   *While Berlin was not:* OFL, vii; Sergei Kondrashev comments, "Battleground Berlin: CIA vs. KGB," C-SPAN.

67   *Harvey was arriving:* BGB, 142–49; Grathwol and Moorhus, *Berlin and the American Military*, 66.

68   *Berlin's isolation:* Osborne email to Stockton, Apr. 25, 2001, Corr M–O, Box 1, BSP; Joint Services Intelligence Group (Germany) report, Apr. 20, 1953, DEFE 41/80, NAUK; Stafford, *Spies*, 56.

68   *In the West:* Hill, ed., Berlin 1953 booklet, in *Berlin in Early Cold-War Army Booklets*,

135–43, 154; Stockton to Norman Mailer, Jan. 31, 2001, Corr M–O, Box 1, BSP; Ian Fleming, *Thrilling Cities* (1963; Las Vegas: Thomas & Mercer, 2013), 156.

69 *In East Berlin:* Cookridge, *George Blake: Double Agent,* 125; Bray to Lions Club, Mar. 6, 1997, Corr A–C, Box 1, BSP.

69 *While Harvey had:* Rick Atkinson, *The Day of Battle: The War in Sicily and Italy, 1943–1944* (New York: Henry Holt, 2007), 83.

69 *CIA director Walter:* Thomas, *The Very Best Men,* 65, 127; Weiner, *Legacy of Ashes,* 64.

70 *Since arriving in:* SV int, Sichel; SV int, Montgomery; Polgar email to Stockton, July 10, 2001, Corr P–R, Box 1, BSP; Stockton, *Flawed,* 77.

70 *Truscott had been:* CG Harvey, int by David Murphy, Nov. 15–16, 1993, Harvey, Bill and family file, Box 2 (hereafter CG Harvey int by Murphy), BSP; Polgar to Stockton email, July 30, 2001, Corr P–R, Box 1, BSP.

71 *The general was usually:* Rick Atkinson, *An Army at Dawn: The War in North Africa, 1942–1943* (New York: Henry Holt, 2002), 141.

71 *The tough-minded:* Dick Cady, "Indianapolis Widow Shares Memories of CIA, but Not Secrets," *Indianapolis Star,* Mar. 7, 1999; CG Harvey int by Murphy, BSP; Polgar email to Stockton, BSP.

72 *Harvey wasted no time:* Stockton, *Flawed,* 100–3; *BGB,* 211.

72 *But the biggest:* SV int, Montgomery.

72 *In January 1953: CSH,* 3; *BGB,* 212.

73 *The nicknames Harvey:* Osborne letter to Stockton, June 9, 2001, Corr M–O, Box 1, BSP; SV int, Dick Montague; Osborne email to Stockton, May 24, 2001, Corr M–O Box 1, BSP; Stockton, *Flawed,* 44, 78; *BGB,* 151; Osborne letter to Stockton, Mar. 12, 2001, Corr M–O, Box 1, BSP.

74 *Even as he moved:* Stockton, *Flawed,* 42.

74 *Harvey did not let:* Osborne email to Stockton, May 24, 2001, Corr M–O, Box 1, BSP; Wise, *Molehunt,* 49; Garbler letter to Stockton, 2001, Corr D–G, Box 1, BSP.

74 *As was the case: BGB,* 309; Hadden letter to Stockton, May 2001, Corr H–L, Box 1, BSP.

75 *The most daunting:* Stockton, *Flawed,* 54.

75 *And indeed, Peter:* Blake, *NOC,* 20; Blake lecture to Stasi workers, 1976, MfS Sekr. Neiber 81, Stasi, 28; SV int, Montgomery; Bray email to Stockton, June 13, 2001, Corr A–C, Box 1, BSP.

76 *Peter Montagnon:* Ranelagh, *The Agency,* 289; SV int, Peter Montagnon.

77 *"We had everything":* Stafford, *Spies,* 83.

77 *In Washington, Helms:* Helms with Hood, *Look,* 135; Stafford, *Spies,* 83.

77 *The CIA called: CSH,* 1; SV int, Montgomery. The PBJOINTLY code name was declassified in February 2007, reclassified in July 2007, and declassified again in 2012. See Steven Aftergood, "CIA Bungles Declassification of Official Histories," Federation of American Scientists, Dec. 6, 2007, https://fas.org/blogs/secrecy /2007/12/cia_bungles_declassification_o/.

77 *The SIS called:* Blake, *NOC,* 21; *BGB,* 218, 449. Stafford suggests Stopwatch may have been chosen because the tunnel was designed to deliver warning of "a count-down to Armageddon." Stafford, *Spies,* 87.

Chapter 5: A Hero's Return

78 *The schoolchildren:* Crosbie, *March,* 216; Blake, *NOC,* 148; Deane, *Captive,* 224.

79 *Stalin's death removed:* Hermiston, *Greatest,* 136–37.

79 *Arriving in Pyongyang:* Deane, *Captive,* 238.

79 *If Blake had any:* Blake, *NOC,* 151; Yuri Modin, *My Five Cambridge Friends: Burgess, Maclean, Philby, Blunt, and Cairncross* (New York: Farrar, Straus & Giroux, 1994), 201; Cookridge, *George Blake: Double Agent,* 111; Wise, *Molehunt,* 271.

80 *Charles Wheeler:* Hermiston, *Greatest,* 141.

80 *Stalin's death on:* Coleman, "Eisenhower and the Berlin Problem," 3; "Russia's Pledge on Nine Britons," *Telegraph,* Mar. 21, 1953.

81 *Churchill, eager:* Gilbert, *Churchill,* 904, 908.

81 *After dinner:* Eisenhower diary, Jan. 6, 1953, DDE Diary, DDE Personal 53–54, Box 9, DDE Papers as President, DDE; Gilbert, *Churchill,* 900.

81 *Churchill had his:* Gilbert, *Churchill,* 908–9.

81 *Eisenhower in fact:* Eisenhower, *Mandate for Change,* 143–44; Beschloss, *Mayday,* 6; Gilbert, *Churchill,* 910.

82 *One subject about which:* Weiner, *Legacy of Ashes,* 73–75; Stafford, *Spies,* 59–60.

82 *Cheers and songs:* "Spies," episode 21 of *Cold War,* CNN documentary series; "Families Greet Freed Britons," *Telegraph,* Apr. 23, 1953; Cookridge, *George Blake: Double Agent,* 114; "Spy for Russia Gets 42 Years," *Telegraph,* May 4, 1961.

83 *A week after his return:* Blake, *NOC,* 5, 154–57; Bower, *Perfect,* 259–61; Easton int, "The Confession"; Cookridge, *George Blake: Double Agent,* 113.

85 *Working the reports:* Osborne email to Stockton, Aug. 7, 2001, Corr M-O, Box 1, BSP.

85 *Already that week:* Hill, ed., "The June 17 Uprising," in Berlin 1954 booklet, *Berlin in Early Cold-War Army Booklets,* 203; Grathwol and Moorhus, *Berlin and the American Military,* 70; *OFL,* 233; "Comment on East Berlin Uprising," CIA Office of Current Intelligence, June 17, 1953, *OFL,* 245.

85 *The East German uprising:* Harrison, *Driving the Soviets Up the Wall,* 23; Sergei Kondrashev int, LHC, 29.

86 *Despite the signs:* Tom Polgar, int by David Murphy, Corr P-R, Box 1, BSP.

86 *But Soviet and East German:* "Probable Effect of Recent Developments in Eastern Germany on Soviet Policy with Respect to Germany," CIA, July 24, 1953, *OFL,* 242; Andrew and Gordievsky, *KGB,* 349; *BGB,* 154, 160, 477; Wolf with McElvoy, *Man Without a Face,* 67.

86 *The American radio station:* Christian Ostermann, "The United States, the East German Uprising of 1953, and the Limits of Rollback," Dec. 1994, CWIHP, 14; "The Berlin Strikes," memo to Foreign Office, July 26, 1953, FO 371/10385, NAUK; *OFL,* 233.

87 *President Eisenhower was certainly:* Eisenhower, *Waging Peace,* 336.

87 *At BOB the night:* Stockton, *Flawed,* 45; Osborne email to Stockton, May 24, 2001, Corr M-O, Box 1, BSP; King Harris, "Bayard Stockton 1930–2006," Aug. 10, 2006, *Santa Barbara Independent*; Osborne email to Stockton, Aug. 6, 2001, Corr M-O, Box 1, BSP.

88 *A klaxon-like buzzer:* Stockton, *Flawed,* 1–4; Stockton letter to CG Harvey, Mar. 15, 1983, Harvey CG file, Box 1, BSP.

88 *At 4:30 a.m.:* "Comment on East Berlin Uprising," CIA Office of Current Intelligence, June 17, 1953, *OFL,* 245; Matthias Uhl, "East Germany in the Sights of the West German Federal Intelligence Service," in Paul Maddrell, ed., *The Image of the Enemy: Intelligence Analysis of Adversaries Since 1945* (Washington, DC: Georgetown University Press, 2015), 133.

89 *BOB was abuzz:* Osborne email to Stockton, Apr. 25, 2001, Corr M-O, Box 1, BSP; Stockton, *Flawed,* 3.

89 *By noon, estimates:* *OFL,* 233; Grathwol and Moorhus, *Berlin and the American Military,* 70; "Comment on the East Berlin Uprising," *OFL,* 246; Eleanor Lansing Dulles Oral History, OH 70, DDE; "Disturbances in East Germany, June 1953," Joint Intelligence Committee, CAB 158/16, NAUK.

90 *Ulbricht and other:* Harrison, *Driving,* 35–36; "After Stalin," episode 7 of *Cold War,* CNN documentary series.

90   *BOB officer David:* Chavchavadze, *Crowns,* 201.

91   *Some demonstrators threw:* "After Stalin," episode 7 of *Cold War,* CNN documentary series; "Comment on the East Berlin Uprising," *OFL,* 246; SV int, Montgomery.

91   *East German Volkspolizei:* Hill, ed., "The June 17 Uprising," in Berlin 1954 booklet, *Berlin in Early Cold-War Army Booklets,* 205; "The Berlin Strikes," memo to Foreign Office, July 26, 1953, FO 371/10385, NAUK.

91   *At midnight, Harvey:* David Chavchavadze letter to Stockton, Jan. 7, 2001, Corr A-C, Box 1, BSP; Chavchavadze, *Crowns,* 202; Osborne email to Stockton, Apr. 25, 2001, Corr M-O, Box 1, BSP; Stockton, *Flawed,* 46–47.

92   *After the meeting:* Stockton, *Flawed,* 46–47.

92   *At a National Security:* Harrison, *Driving,* 38; Coleman, "Eisenhower and the Berlin Problem," 13.

92   *In Moscow, the Berlin:* Khrushchev, *Khrushchev Remembers,* 540, 324, 336; Andrew and Gordievsky, *KGB,* 350.

93   *Despite retaining control:* "National Security Council Progress Report," Sept. 10, 1953, DVD supplement to *A City Torn Apart,* CIA Historical Collections Division; Harrison, *Driving,* 43; Wolf with McElvoy, *Man,* 69; Coleman, "Eisenhower and the Berlin Problem," 3.

93   *To keep better:* Bagley, *Spy Wars,* 131; Bagley, *Spymaster,* ch. 4; *BGB,* 46, 286; *OFL,* 266.

94   *By early July:* Memo to Director CIA, July 2, 1953, NSC Registry Series, Box 4, DDE Papers as President, DDE.

94   *Soon after the uprising:* Osborne email to Stockton, Aug. 7, 2001, Corr M-O, Box 1, BSP.

95   *Such moxie played:* Stockton, *Flawed,* 51–52, 68; SV int, Sichel.

Chapter 6: The Big Prize Was Going to Be Berlin

96   *With the dust:* BGB, 212; CSH, 8.

96   *the East Berlin community of Altglienicke:* At the time of the tunnel project, the community was often referred to as Alt-Glienicke, but the one-word version soon became more common.

96   *Altglienicke was a pleasant:* "Wonderful Tunnel," *Time,* May 7, 1956; SV int, Eugene Bialas; *Ansichten von Altglienicke einst und jetzt* (Berlin: Bürgerverein Altglienicke, 2010), 254; Montgomery, "Challenges of the Berlin Tunnel," *"Ist ja fantastisch!,"* 47–49.

97   *Across the boundary:* CSH, 6–7; Sullivan, "U.S. Investigates Wiretap Tunnel."

97   *Whatever the Americans:* Blake, *NOC,* 20; SV int, Montagnon.

98   *Economic woes:* Maddrell, "British Intelligence Through the Eyes of the Stasi," 827; "Future of the British Intelligence Organisation, Germany," Joint Intelligence Committee, Aug. 13, 1953, CAB 15/16, NAUK; Dorril, *MI6,* 526; Aldrich, *The Hidden Hand,* 417.

98   *Lunn was small:* Blake int, Red Files; Blake, *NOC,* 7; SV int, Volker Foertsch.

98   *The KGB would come:* Andrew and Mitrokhin, *The Sword and the Shield,* 339–40.

99   *Lunn had been born:* "Peter Lunn," *Telegraph,* Dec. 6, 2011; Ruck, "Thinker, Author, Skier, Spy"; Stafford, *Spies,* 16.

99   *When war broke out:* Blake, *NOC,* 7; Andrew and Mitrokhin, *The Sword and the Shield,* 339; SV int, Montagnon.

99   *The following year:* Anthony Cave Brown, *"C": The Secret Life of Sir Stewart Graham Menzies* (New York: Macmillan, 1986), 687; Bagley, *Spymaster,* ch. 9; Hood, *Mole,* 13; Stafford, *Spies,* 21.

99   *Lunn brought to espionage:* SV int, Montagnon; Blake, *NOC,* 8; Dorril, *MI6,* 129; Bower, *Perfect,* 180.

100 *It was relatively simple:* Dorril, *MI6,* 129–31; Brown, *"C,"* 686; Martin, *Wilderness,* 72–74.

100 *A great deal of:* Bower, *Perfect,* 180; Stafford, *Spies,* 31, 41.

100 *Bill Harvey did not ski:* SV int, Montagnon, Montgomery, and Murphy.

101 *Lunn was initially:* Stockton, *Flawed,* 32, 98; Lunn letter to Stockton, Jan. 2001, Corr H-L, Box 1, BSP; SV int, Montagnon.

101 *One of Lunn's first:* Blake, *NOC,* 20–21; Blake lecture to Stasi workers, 1976, MfS Sekr. Neiber 81, Stasi, 113; SV int, Montagnon.

102 *A Berlin project:* SV int, Montagnon; *CSH,* 7; Blake, *NOC,* 8; Helms with Hood, *Look,* 136; Blake, *NOC,* 8–9.

102 *Berlin was known:* Berlin Senate Department for Urban Development and the Environment, 01.17 Geologic Outline (2013 Edition), www.stadtentwicklung.berlin .de/umwelt/umweltatlas/e_text/ek117.pdf; SV int, Comstock; *CSH,* 13; Martin, *Wilderness,* 77.

103 *As the joint planning continued:* Fellon, "Turning a Cold War Scheme into Reality," 3; *CSH,* 13; SV int, Comstock.

104 *Other major questions:* *CSH,* 7–8; "Field Project Outline," Sept. 16, 1953, OFL, 333.

105 *George Blake made:* Blake, *NOC,* 6, 158–60.

107 *By August 1953:* "Field Project Outline," Sept. 16, 1953, OFL, 333–35; "Berlin Operation," Helms memo to Rowlett, Sept. 16, 1953, CIA-HRP.

107 *Not everyone at headquarters:* Bray to Lions, Mar. 6, 1997, Corr A-C, Box 1, BSP; Martin, *Wilderness,* 78.

107 *Allen Dulles had appeared:* Time, Aug. 3, 1953; Grose, *Gentleman Spy,* 340.

108 *Dulles, who had read:* Grose, *Gentleman,* 18, 26–27, 82, 89.

108 *It was no surprise:* Grose, *Gentleman,* 309; Beschloss, *Mayday,* 128; Thomas, *The Very Best Men,* 74.

109 *Peter Sichel:* SV int, Sichel; Sichel, *Secrets,* ch. 21.

109 *Dulles seemed bemused:* Martin, *Wilderness,* 67.

109 *Harvey and Sichel came:* SV int, Sichel; Sichel, int by David Murphy, Corr S-W, Box 1, BSP.

109 *With his love:* SV int, Sichel; Grose, *Gentleman,* 389; Dulles, *The Craft of Intelligence,* 71.

109 *The CIA director informed:* *CSH,* 12; Andrew, *For the President's Eyes Only,* 212–15; Martin, *Wilderness,* 89.

110 *As president, Eisenhower:* Eisenhower, *Waging Peace,* 551; Andrew Goodpaster oral history, OH-477, DDE, 38–39; Dillon Anderson oral history, OH-165, Columbia University Oral History Project, copy at DDE, 110. To his chagrin, Eisenhower would find himself in a position where he felt he had to lie about the U-2 after one of the spy planes was shot down over the Soviet Union in 1960.

110 *On August 12, 1953:* Sergei Khrushchev, *Nikita Khrushchev,* 47; Dorril, *MI6,* 522.

111 *Briefing the president:* Weiner, *Legacy of Ashes,* 74; Beschloss, *Mayday,* 72.

111 *Similar calculations:* David Stafford, "The Berlin Spy Tunnel," *"Ist ja fantastisch!,"* 31; Stafford, *Spies,* 61; Blake, *NOC,* 21.

111 *Lucian Truscott urged:* "Field Project Outline," Sept. 16, 1953, OFL, 335–36; Heefner, *Dogface Soldier,* 276; Fellon, "Turning a Cold War Scheme into Reality," 3.

112 *Truscott also emphasized:* "Special Intelligence," memo from Truscott to Dulles, Sept. 17, 1953, OFL, 332; Helms with Hood, *Look,* 134; *CSH,* i.

Chapter 7: Agent Diomid

113 *On September 1, 1953:* Blake, *NOC,* 6, 13; Dorril, *MI6,* 522.

114 *Section Y's location:* West, *Seven Spies,* 135–36; Blake, *NOC,* 5, 12; Hermiston, *Greatest,* 150.

114 *Section Y chief Tom Gimson:* Blake, *NOC,* 6; Walter Lord, *The Miracle of Dunkirk* (New York: Viking, 1982), 112.

114 *Now Gimson needed:* Hermiston, *Greatest,* 153; SV int, Montagnon.

115 *In an office:* Blake, *NOC,* 15; SV int, Montagnon.

115 *Blake was "in":* GAB, tape II; GBD, V, 1; GAB, tape I; "Masterspy of Moscow," Carey.

115 *He made friends:* GAB, tape I; Blake, *NOC,* 16; Hermiston, *Greatest,* 155.

115 *As the Section Y liaison:* Blake, *NOC,* 12, 16, 162; SV int, Montagnon; "Foreign Office Officials' Disappearance," *Times* (London), Sept. 24, 1955.

116 *As Blake settled into:* BGB, 364; Bagley, *Spymaster,* ch. 5.

116 *Kondrashev proved:* Bagley, *Spymaster,* chs. 1–2; Kondrashev int, LHC, 1, 10; Kondrashev comments, "Battleground Berlin: CIA vs. KGB," C-SPAN.

117 *But Kondrashev's initial:* Kondrashev comments, "Battleground"; Bagley, *Spymaster,* ch. 4.

117 *In the early summer of 1953:* Bagley, *Spymaster,* ch. 6; Stafford, *Spies,* 74; BGB, 215.

118 *Kondrashev was given:* BGB, 215; Andrew and Gordievsky, *KGB,* 363: Kondrashev int, LHC, 11.

119 *One evening in late October:* Blake, *NOC,* 17–18; Kondrashev int, LHC, 11.

120 *At their second meeting:* Bagley, *Spymaster,* ch. 6; Blake, *NOC,* 19–20, 162.

120 *Occasionally, with larger:* Blake, *NOC,* 20; Blake lecture to Stasi workers, 1976, MfS Sekr. Neiber 81, Stasi, 20.

121 *He rendezvoused with Kondrashev:* Bagley, *Spymaster,* ch. 6; Blake int, Red Files; Kondrashev int, LHC, 11–16; Murphy int, LHC, 32.

121 *On December 2, 1953:* Gilbert, *Churchill,* 915, 920.

122 *Upon Eisenhower's arrival:* Eisenhower diary, Dec. 5, 1953, DDE Diary, DDE Personal, 53–54, Box 9, DDE Papers as President, DDE; Gilbert, *Churchill,* 921.

123 *Five days later:* "SIS/CIA Meetings on Stopwatch/Gold held in London of 15th, 16th, 17th & 18th Dec. 1953," appendix 9, Operation Gold, BGB (hereafter "SIS/CIA Meetings on Stopwatch/Gold," BGB), 449; BGB, 217; Hermiston, *Greatest,* 162.

123 *Another participant:* Wolf with McElvoy, *Man Without a Face,* 100; Blake, *NOC,* 22; Blake int, Red Files; SV int, Montagnon.

123 *The broad outlines:* CSH, 10, 15; SV int, Montagnon; Blake, *NOC,* 22; "SIS/CIA Meetings on Stopwatch/Gold," BGB, 450–53.

124 *Based on the survey work:* "SIS/CIA Meetings on Stopwatch/Gold," BGB, 450–53.

124 *Flocks of transcribers:* "SIS/CIA Meetings on Stopwatch/Gold," BGB, 452; Martin, *Wilderness,* 101.

124 *On December 18:* "SIS/CIA Meetings on Stopwatch/Gold," BGB, 449; BGB, 217; Knightley, "Confessions of a Traitor," part I.

Chapter 8: This Was Explosive Material

126 *Sergei Kondrashev:* Bagley, *Spymaster,* ch. 6; Hermiston, *Greatest,* 164; Mark Franchetti, "Revealed: Blake's Bus Ride of Betrayal," *Sunday Times,* Nov. 14, 1999.

126 *A few blocks away:* "Operation 'Gold' und andere," *ND,* Feb. 18, 1970; "'Secret Agent' Jibe Refuted by Whitehall," *Telegraph,* Feb. 17, 1970.

127 *Blake hurriedly told:* "'Operation Gold': Der Spionagetunnel von Berlin"; Heun and Schier, "Tunnel-Spione," *Berliner Morgenpost,* Mar. 6–11, 1994; Blake int, Red Files; Thornton and Thomas, "Revealed: The Map of Blake's Betrayal."

127 *Blake was one of only:* SV int, Blake; Blake, *NOC,* 25; Bagley, *Spymaster,* ch. 6.

127 *Reading Blake's minutes:* Franchetti, "Revealed: Blake's Bus Ride of Betrayal"; BGB, 216.

128 *Two days later:* BGB, 219.

128 *At the same time:* Stafford, *Spies,* 88; Dulles letter to Eisenhower, Jan. 20, 1954, Dulles January 54 file, Box 2, Dulles-Herter Series, DDE Papers as President, DDE.

128 *Arriving in Berlin:* Michael Burke int, HI; Stafford, *Spies,* 50; Heefner, *Dogface Soldier,* 277–78.

129 *For the most part:* Polgar letter to Stockton, May 9, 2001, Corr P-R, Box 1, BSP; Stockton, *Flawed,* 64.

129 *In any event:* Stockton, *Flawed,* 99, 103; Martin, *Wilderness,* 62–63.

129 *Harvey's proposal:* CG Harvey int by Murphy, BSP.

130 *Day in and day out:* Eisenhower, *Mandate for Change,* 344; Catterall, *Macmillan Diaries,* vol. 1, Feb. 6, 1954.

130 *On February 12:* BGB, 216; Stafford, *Spies,* 96; Murphy int, LHC, 32; Kondrashev int, LHC, 13.

130 *In the pantheon:* Dulles, *The Craft of Intelligence,* 86; Andrew and Gordievsky, *KGB,* 353; Hood, *Mole,* 269; OFL, 273; Khrushchev, *Khrushchev Remembers,* 338.

131 *Reviewing Kondrashev's report:* Bagley, *Spymaster,* ch. 6.

131 *But there was another:* Murphy int, LHC, 32–33; Kondrashev int, LHC, 13–14; Kondrashev comments, "Battleground Berlin: CIA vs. KGB," C-SPAN.

132 *In London, Kondrashev:* Blake int, "The Confession"; Blake, *NOC,* 25.

Chapter 9: A Special Assignment

135 *The call came:* SV int, Comstock; Larry Backus, "Keith Comstock," *Crossville* (TN) *Chronicle,* Mar. 7, 2008.

136 *Allen Dulles's request:* CSH, 11–12; BGB, 424.

136 *Les Gross was:* "Col. Leslie M. Gross," *Orlando Sentinel,* Sept. 9, 1988; Browne, *Experiences with the CIA 1950's Berlin Spy Tunnel,* 44; SV int, Eddie Kindell; CSH, 12.

136 *Once assigned to:* Fellon, "Turning a Cold War Scheme into Reality," 3; SV int, Robert Williamson.

137 *Comstock, a graduate:* SV int, Comstock.

137 *Gross's third choice:* SV int, Walter Schaaf; SV int, Williamson; "Special Orders Number 80," Department of the Army, Apr. 27, 1953, RWP.

137 *Following his orders:* SV int, Williamson; "Berlin Tunnel Project," Williamson notes, Jan. 22, 2011, RWP; SV int, Floyd Hope; SV int, Comstock.

138 *Comstock also reported:* SV int, Comstock.

138 *West Berlin farmer:* Kellerhoff and Von Kostka, *Haupstadt der Spione,* 66; Bernd von Kostka, "The Tunnel and Its Aftermath in the American Sector," *"Ist ja fantastisch!,"* 78; Fellon, "Turning a Cold War Scheme into Reality," 4.

139 *The contract for:* SV int, Schaaf.

139 *The CIA's proposed design:* Author visit, Allied Museum, Berlin; Martin, *Wilderness,* 78; "Wonderful Tunnel," *Time.*

140 *Nor was he "the only":* Fellon, "Turning a Cold War Scheme into Reality," 4; CSH, 8; Murphy int, LHC, 22.

140 *Sergei Kondrashev was sick:* Kondrashev int, LHC, 12; Bagley, *Spymaster,* ch. 6.

141 *Indeed, Moscow Center:* BGB, 217–18.

141 *Blake was placated:* Blake int, "'Operation Gold': Der Spionagetunnel von Berlin."

142 *On May 15, 1954:* Department of Army orders, May 10, 1954, RWP; SV int, Comstock.

142 *The team began:* SV int, Kindell, Comstock, and Hope; CSH, 18.

143 *Back home, spouses:* Williamson to Mrs. Marlin D. Keen, June 10, 1954, RWP.

143 *Behind the gates:* Merrell, "The Berlin Spy Tunnel: A Memoir"; Stafford, *Spies* (ebook edition), 103.

144 *Among the few visitors:* Merrell, "The Berlin Spy Tunnel: A Memoir," 106; Fellon, "Turning a Cold War Scheme into Reality," 4.

145 *Such stations were:* Bray to Lions, Mar. 6, 1997, Corr A-C, Box 1, BSP; Sullivan,

"U.S. Investigates Wiretap Tunnel"; Montgomery int by David Murphy, Corr M-O, Box 1, BSP; *CSH,* 9.

145 *By early July:* SV int, Comstock; Williamson, "Berlin Tunnel Project," RWP.

146 *Les Gross had long:* Fellon, "Turning a Cold War Scheme into Reality," 5; SV int, Comstock.

146 *The team packed: CSH,* 17; SV int, Williamson and Comstock.

147 *The 8598th Engineer:* Williamson, "Berlin Tunnel Project," RWP; Fellon, "Turning a Cold War Scheme into Reality," 4–5; "Movement of Unit," order to Commanding Officer 9539th Technical Service Unit, Aug. 11, 1954, RWP; SV int, Williamson.

Chapter 10: It Was Getting So Complicated

148 *Captain Keith Comstock:* Comstock letter to children, circa 2007, courtesy Keith Comstock; SV int, Comstock.

149 *But the most dangerous:* Bray int, University of Tennessee, part II, 17–18; SV int, Comstock; Stockton, *Flawed,* 83; *CSH,* 17.

149 *With the boxcars secure:* SV int, Comstock.

150 *As the equipment: CSH,* 17; (Romey), *Not to Be a Spy,* 31.

151 *The Army installation commander:* SV int, Eugene Kovalenko (formerly known as Eugene Kregg), John Quirk and Larry Plappler; (Romey), *Not to Be a Spy,* 33–34; CG Harvey int by Murphy, BSP.

151 *The same day:* Stafford, "The Berlin Spy Tunnel," *"Ist ja fantastisch!,"* 32; SV int, Comstock and Williamson; "Progress Report 28 August Through 17 October 1954," Chief, Berlin Operations Base to Chief of Mission, Frankfurt, October 18, 1954, *OFL,* 338.

152 *The Rudow compound:* Osborne email to Stockton, Apr. 25, 2001, Corr M-O, Box 1, BSP; Neill Prew, int by David Murphy, Corr P-R, Box 1, BSP; Hill, ed. Berlin 1954 booklet, in *Berlin in Early Cold-War Army Booklets,* 173; Grathwol and Moorhus, *Berlin and the American Military,* 150; author visit, former Clay Headquarters, Aug. 2015.

152 *The Berlin base move:* SV int, Montgomery; Stockton, *Flawed,* 56–57; Montgomery int by Murphy, Corr M-O, Box 1, BSP.

152 *Harvey's feeling of:* Stockton, *Flawed,* 62; SV int, Montgomery; David Murphy, "How I Got to Berlin," May 25, 1994, Corr M-O, Box 1, BSP.

153 *Harvey treated Berlin:* Chavchavadze letter to Stockton, Jan. 7, 2001, Corr A-C, Box 1, BSP; Stockton, *Flawed,* 65; Truscott letter to Frank Wisner, Apr. 20, 1954, Corr S-W, Box 1, BSP.

153 *But when it came:* SV int, Montgomery.

153 *Anyone outside his:* Jack Corris int with David Murphy, Jan. 22, 1994, Corr A-C, Box 1, BCP; Wright, *Spycatcher,* 161; *BGB,* 429.

154 *The Harvey home: BGB,* 153; CG Harvey letter to Stockton, Apr. 10, 1983, Berlin file, Box 1, BSP.

154 *It was not just Harvey:* Murphy int, LHC, 18; Chavchavadze, *Crowns,* 204.

154 *Harvey's drinking:* Garbler letter to Norman Mailer, Dec. 1992, Corr D-G, Box 1, BSP; Stockton, Harvey draft, "Berlin Operations Base," Box 1, BSP; SV int, Montgomery and Pepper; CG Harvey int by Murphy, BSP.

154 *Since her arrival:* CG Harvey int by Murphy, BSP; Corris int by Murphy, Corr A-C, Box 1, BSP; Montgomery letter to Stockton, Apr. 17, 2002, Corr M-O, BSP; Polgar letter to Stockton, May 9, 2001; Stockton, *Flawed,* 104; SV int, Montgomery.

155 *CG was often:* SV int, Montgomery, Pepper, and Audrey Lamb; Stockton, *Flawed,* 101.

155 *Whatever his officers:* Corris int by Murphy, Corr A-C, Box 1, BSP.

156 *Harvey was routinely:* SV int, Montgomery; Montgomery letter to Stockton, Aug. 4, 2011, Corr M-O, Box 1, BSP; Bray email to Stockton, May 14, 2001, Corr A-C, Box 1, BSP; Stockton, *Flawed*, 85; SV int, Murphy; Shackley with Finney, *Spymaster*, 56.

156 *But Harvey decided:* SV int, Montgomery; event program, "Ambassador Hugh Montgomery William J. Donovan Award," Nov. 7, 2015, Washington, DC, OSS Society; "Annemarie J. Montgomery," *WP*, Feb. 8, 2015.

157 *In April 1945:* SV int, Montgomery; Montgomery remarks, OSS Society dinner, Nov. 7, 2015; SV int, Montague.

158 *Harvey brought Montgomery:* SV int, Montgomery; CG Harvey int by Murphy, BSP; *BGB*, 213.

158 *The tunnel team was still:* SV int, Montgomery.

158 *Montgomery recruited:* SV int, Montgomery; Hill, ed., Berlin 1954 booklet, in *Berlin in Early Cold-War Army Booklets*, 199–200; SV int, Murphy; Murphy int, LHC, 16; *BGB*, 211.

160 *For close to a year:* Blake, *NOC*, 165; Hermiston, *Greatest*, 172; GBD, V, 1; Murphy int, LHC, 33.

160 *But the assignment:* Kondrashev int, LHC, 18.

161 *The pending assignment:* GAB, tape I.

161 *Blake had considerable:* BLH, 15; Blake, *NOC*, 164–65.

161 *They announced their:* GAB, tape I; Blake, *NOC*, 164; GBD, V, 1a; Knightley, "Confessions of a Traitor," part II; Cookridge, *George Blake: Double Agent*, 122.

162 *Hurrying the wedding:* GBD, V, 1a; BLH, 15.

Chapter 11: The Dig

163 *With no pomp:* "Progress Report," October 18, 1954, *OFL*, 338–40; SV int, Comstock and Williamson; Williamson int, "Spies Beneath Berlin," Discovery.

164 *Digging a little deeper:* "Progress Report," Oct. 18, 1954, *OFL*, 338–41; SV int, Williamson.

164 *The other option:* "Progress Report," Oct. 18, 1954, *OFL*, 341–42; Stafford, *Spies*, 103; SV int, Williamson.

165 *The long delay:* Comstock letter to children, courtesy Comstock; SV int, Comstock.

166 *The engineers needed:* SV int, Kindell, Montgomery, and Comstock; *CSH*, 20. Although the author of the *Clandestine Services History* is not identified, David Murphy said Leichliter wrote it (see transcript of Montgomery int by Murphy, Berlin Tunnel file, Box 1, BSP). Stockton also said it was likely Leichliter (Stockton, *Flawed*, 82). The report's writer identified himself as the project's field case officer until February 1955; Leichliter served in that position until February 1956 and likely slipped on the date. Rowlett and Harvey assisted in preparing the report (*CSH*, 1).

166 *Another scheme:* SV int, Comstock; Katie McGurl, "Digging Up Soviet Secrets During Cold War," *Bryan County* (GA) *News*, Sept. 7, 2011.

166 *Even now, there was: CSH*, 18.

166 *On October 11:* "Progress Report," Oct. 18, 1954, *OFL*, 342; *CSH*, 18; Stafford, *Spies*, 102; SV int, Williamson.

167 *The engineers assembled:* "Progress Report," Oct. 18, 1954, *OFL*, 342.

167 *The team had:* SV int, Montgomery; Stafford, *Spies*, 107; Fellon, "Turning a Cold War Scheme into Reality," 5; *CSH*, 12.

167 *With the water:* SV int, Comstock; Williamson int, "Spies Beneath Berlin," Discovery.

168 *The soil turned out:* SV int, Comstock and Hope; *CSH*, 19–21; *BGB*, 223. In order

for the steel liner to fit inside the shield, the shield was slightly larger in diameter than the tunnel. That meant that when the shield was moved forward, it left a half-inch void between the exterior of the tunnel and the earth above. This was filled by grout. *CSH*, 13; Fellon, "Turning a Cold War Scheme into Reality," 5; SV int, Comstock.

168 *As they advanced:* CSH, 19; SV int, Comstock; Fellon, "Turning a Cold War Scheme into Reality," 5; Dietmar Linke, "How the Berlin Tunnel Was Excavated and Salvaged 50 Years On," *"Ist ja fantastisch!,"* 103. Leaving sandbags in the tunnel also saved labor—more than 10 percent of the fill lined the tunnel.

168 *The crews had jelled:* SV int, Comstock and Hope.

169 *Bill Harvey liked:* Stockton, *Flawed,* 54; SV int, Comstock.

169 *One thing Harvey noticed:* CG Harvey int by Murphy, BSP; *BGB,* 220.

170 *Mostly, Harvey relied:* SV int, Kovalenko (Kregg), Bill Romey, Montagnon, Montgomery; GG Harvey int by Murphy, BSP; Montgomery int by Murphy, Berlin Tunnel file, Box 1, BSP; Bray email to Stockton, May 14, 2001; Stockton, *Flawed,* 86.

170 *Leichliter was assisted:* SV int, Kindell; Bialis letter to author, Apr. 5, 2019.

172 *As far as most:* SV int, Bialas; "Verzögerungsversuch auf und unter der Erde," *ND,* Apr. 28, 1956; "Progress Report," October 18, 1954, *OFL,* 343.

172 *Paul Noack, a farmer:* SV int, Dagmar Feick; Feick int, *"Ist ja fantastisch!,"* 70; Feick letter to author, Mar. 6, 2019.

173 *In a small dark room:* SV int, Romey, Williamson, Bialas, and Kindell; *CSH,* 10, 19; "Progress Report," October 18, 1954, *OFL,* 343.

174 *KGB chief Ivan:* Bagley, *Spymaster,* ch. 6; Kondrashev int, LHC, 21.

175 *Now that excavation:* Osborne letter to Stockton, May 11, 2001, Corr M-O, Box 1, BSP.

175 *Blake later said:* Blake lecture to Stasi workers, 1976, MfS Sekr. Neiber 81, Stasi, 113.

176 *On September 20:* BGB, 218–19.

176 *The hope was:* Kondrashev int, LHC, 11; Bagley, *Spymaster,* ch. 6; *BGB,* 219; Wolf with McElvoy, *Man Without a Face,* 99.

176 *The KGB likely saw:* Michael Smith, *The Spying Game* (1996; London: Politico's, 2003), 191; Wolf with McElvoy, *Man Without a Face,* 99; Bagley, *Spymaster,* ch. 6. Kondrashev did not specify, but among others he may have been referring to a tunnel with listening devices discovered in June 1978 beneath the U.S. embassy in Moscow ("List of U.S. Moscow Embassy 'Spy' Incidents," UPI, Apr. 18, 1987).

177 *With the excavation approaching:* BGB, 221.

177 *The fear was that:* Murphy int, AMB, 1997; "Memorandum for the Record," Nov. 29, 1954, *OFL,* 347.

177 *Eisenhower, still desperate:* Eisenhower, *Waging Peace,* 544–45; Beschloss, *Mayday,* 74; Weiner, *Legacy of Ashes,* 109; "Meeting the Threat of Surprise Attack," vol. II, Killian Report file, White House Office, Office of the Staff Secretary, DDE, 136.

178 *This was precisely:* Evans, "Berlin Tunnel Intelligence," 45.

179 *It could not come:* Eisenhower, *Mandate for Change,* "Excerpts from a Letter to Winston Churchill," Jan. 23, 1955, Appendix O, 609.

179 *For months, CIA linguist:* (Romey), *Not to Be a Spy,* 25; SV int, Bill Romey.

179 *The number of translators:* CSH, 18.

180 *Romey and the others:* (Romey), *Not to Be a Spy,* 28.

180 *For half a year:* "Orders," Nov. 24, 1954, RWP; SV int, Hope and Comstock; *CSH,* 19.

181 *Still, said Williamson:* Williamson int, "Spies Beneath Berlin," Discovery; Stockton, *Flawed,* 85.

181   *The engineers signed:* "Certification," Mar. 3, 1955, RWP; Travel orders, Mar. 1, 1955, RWP; Stockton, *Flawed,* 85.

181   *With the tapping:* Blake, *NOC,* 21; *BGB,* 217.

Chapter 12: The Baby Was Born

185   *It was the dead:* Merrell, "The Berlin Spy Tunnel"; Stafford, *Spies* (ebook edition), 106.

186   *Running the British operation:* SV int, Montagnon; Stafford, *Spies,* 27–28, 86; Soraya Wilkinson-Wyke, email to author, June 17, 2015; Blake, *NOC,* 10.

186   *Montagnon, a witty:* SV int, Montagnon; "Peter Montagnon, Intelligence Officer and Television Director," *Telegraph,* Dec. 21, 2017.

187   *The Royal Engineers started:* Merrell, "The Berlin Spy Tunnel," 106–7.

187   *On March 10, 1955:* Merrell, "The Berlin Spy Tunnel," 106; Fellon, "Turning a Cold War Scheme into Reality," 6; Stafford, "The Berlin Spy Tunnel," *"Ist ja fantastisch!,"* 34; SV int, Montagnon; Stafford, *Spies* (ebook edition), 107; *CSH,* 14.

188   *By the last week:* Merrell, "The Berlin Spy Tunnel," 107; *CSH,* 15; Martin, *Wilderness,* 83; SV int, Montagnon; Stafford, *Spies* (ebook edition), 108.

189   *As they got closer:* SV int, Kindell; *CSH,* 19; Stafford, *Spies* (ebook edition), 107.

189   *In the days that:* SV int, Montagnon; Wright, *Spycatcher,* 18, 46; Stafford, *Spies,* (ebook edition) 109.

189   *Taylor's planning meetings:* "Masterspy of Moscow," Carey; SV int, Montagnon.

190   *The postal team had:* Phil Harding and Neil Harding emails to author, Jan. 2019.

190   *Upon arrival in Berlin:* Rolf Barnekow, "Tapping Soviet Military Communications," *"Ist ja fantastisch!,"* 61; Stafford, *Spies* (ebook edition), 111; Fellon, "Turning a Cold War Scheme into Reality," 6; author tour, Allied Museum, Berlin.

191   *Meanwhile, a cable:* Barnekow, *"Ist ja fantastisch!,"* 64; SV int, Montagnon; *CSH,* 21–22.

191   *Harding, expert at:* Phil Harding and Neil Harding emails to author; Stafford, *Spies* (ebook edition), 109.

191   *Back at the warehouse:* SV int, Kindell and Bialas; Bialas letter to author, Apr. 4, 2019; Stockton, *Flawed,* 83; Bray email to Stockton, May 14, 2001, Corr A–C, Box 1, BSP; Bruce Mouser, "Social History of the 280th USASA Company," www.280th-usasa-berlin.com.

192   *When the equipment:* CSH, 13; *BGB,* 228; "Memorandum for the record," Nov. 29, 1954, *OFL,* 347; author tour, Altglienicke Museum; Lou Mehrer, "The Berlin Tunnel Operation," presentation at CIA Analysis and Collection conference, U.S. Army Heritage and Education Center, Carlisle, PA, Apr. 22, 2014.

192   *All that remained was:* Barnekow, *"Ist ja fantastisch!,"* 65.

192   *To finish the job:* Stafford, *Spies* (ebook edition), 109.

193   *Blake Rymer:* SV int, Montagnon.

193   *A new officer:* Blake, *NOC,* 178; Andrew, *Defend the Realm,* 490, n 944; GBD, V, 1a; Cookridge, *George Blake: Double Agent,* 126.

193   *Peter Lunn, presiding:* Blake, *NOC,* 169; *BGB,* 225; Stafford, *Spies,* 115; SV int, Montagnon; Bagley, *Spymaster,* ch. 6.

194   *Nor did Blake:* Blake, *NOC,* 10; Bower, *Perfect,* 261; Stafford, *Spies,* 86; SV int, Murphy.

194   *In any event:* Kondrashev int, LHC, 18; *BGB,* 225; Bagley, *Spymaster,* ch. 6.

194   *Yevgeny Pitovranov, chief:* Murphy int, LHC, 34; *BGB,* 219, 226.

195   *By the end of the first week:* (Romey), *Not to Be a Spy,* 33, 36; *CSH,* 21.

195   *Arriving in Berlin:* SV int, Romey and Bialas; (Romey), *Not to Be a Spy,* 30–34.

196   *The waiting on May:* SV int, Montagnon and Romey; Stafford, *Spies* (ebook edition), 109; (Romey), *Not to Be a Spy,* 36, 39; Phil Harding email to author.

196   *The jointers' first:* Barkenow, *"Ist ja fantastisch!,"* 62–64; SV int, Montagnon; Stockton, *Flawed,* 87.

197   *Conditions inside:* SV int, Montagnon; *CSH,* 22.
197   *Back at the warehouse:* (Romey), *Not to Be a Spy,* 38–39; SV int, Romey and Montagnon.
198   *The rank of the callers:* SV int, Montgomery and Montagnon; (Romey), *Not to Be a Spy,* 39.
198   *Sparks and Loomes needed:* Stafford, *Spies* (ebook edition), 110.
198   *There was joy:* Mehrer, "The Berlin Tunnel Operation."

Chapter 13: Striking Gold

199   *A vast amount: Operation REGAL,* NSA, 7; Stockton, *Flawed,* 87; SV int, Romey.
199   *The translator slapped:* SV int, Romey; (Romey), *Not to Be a Spy,* 34, 40–42; Browne, *Experiences,* 57.
200   *Within a few days:* (Romey), *Not to Be a Spy,* 40–44; Martin, *Wilderness,* 83; SV int, Bialas and Romey.
201   *On May 21: CSH,* 21; SV int, Montagnon.
201   *In any event: CSH,* 25; SV int, Russ Knapp; Knapp comments in Browne, *Experiences,* 65.
201   *It fell to Hugh:* SV int, Montgomery, Kovalenko, and Kindell.
202   *Every day, there:* Stockton, *Flawed,* 92; Montgomery int by Murphy, Berlin Tunnel file, Box 1, BSP; *BGB,* 423; SV int, Montgomery and Murphy.
203   *Harvey's deputy:* Murphy, "How I Got to Berlin," May 25, 1994, Corr M-O, Box 1, BSP; SV int, Mott; Bray email to Stockton, May 14, 2001, Corr A-C, Box 1, BSP; Stockton, *Flawed,* 92; Bray int, University of Tennessee, part II, 15.
203   *At CIA headquarter:* Helms with Hood, *Look,* 138; Stockton, *Flawed,* 87.
204   *The tunnel intelligence:* Murphy int, LHC, 28; *Operation REGAL,* NSA, 11; Rowlett int by Murphy, Berlin tunnel file, Box 1, BSP.
204   *After the disaster: BGB,* 236; Murphy int, AMB; *CSH,* b-1.
204   *President Eisenhower, briefed:* Beschloss, *Mayday,* 94, n437; Goodpaster oral history, OH-477, DDE, 37.
204   *The elegant Regency:* (Romey), *Not to Be a Spy,* 28; Murphy int, LHC; *BGB,* 423.
205   *It was clear:* Smith, *Spying Game,* 190; Stafford, *Spies,* 124; *CSH,* 25; (Romey), *Not to Be a Spy,* 50.
205   *"If you listen":* SV int, Montagnon.
206   *A special section:* (Romey), *Not to Be a Spy,* 34; SV int, Montagnon; Browne, *Experiences,* 12.
206   *One of the challenges:* SV int, Romey; (Romey), *Not to Be a Spy,* 50; Stafford, *Spies,* 126–28.
206   *Joe Evans, part of:* Stafford, *Spies,* 125, 128; Wise, *Molehunt,* 214; Evans int, "The Confession"; Evans, "Berlin Tunnel Intelligence," 45.
207   *In contrast to: CSH,* 17; Rowlett int by Murphy, Berlin tunnel, Box 1, BSP.
207   *The heart of the Washington:* SV int, Kindell; Osborne letter to Stockton, June 9, 2001, Corr M-O, Box 1, BSP; Huntington, "The Berlin Spy Tunnel Affair," 50; Martin, *Wilderness,* 84–85; Browne, *Experiences,* 9.
208   *All the teletype:* Browne, *Experiences,* 9–10; SV int, Alice Ojala Sorvo.
208   *As in London:* Browne, *Experiences,* 3–5, 12.
209   *The ubiquitous Peter Montagnon:* SV int, Montagnon; *CSH,* 25; Browne, *Experiences,* 13; SV int, Sorvo.
210   *Much of the teletype:* SV int, Montagnon; Rowlett int by Murphy, Berlin tunnel, Box 1, BSP; "The Berlin Tunnel," Cryptologic Almanac 50th Anniversary Series, parts I and II, 1998, declassified 2012; "A Brave, New World"; Johnson, *American Cryptology,* 106; Ranelagh, *The Agency,* 289.

210 *Despite the tension:* "The Berlin Tunnel," Cryptologic Almanac; *Operation REGAL,* NSA, 25; Rowlett int by Murphy, Berlin Tunnel file, Box 1, BSP.

211 *The NSA had plenty:* SV int, Kindell; Boghardt, "Semper Vigilis," *Army History,* 21; Colin Burke, "The Last Bombe Run, 1955," *Cryptologia,* July 2008. Though the breaking of the Enigma code remained top secret, the Soviets likely knew that it had been cracked. But apparently they did not share this information with the East Germans.

211 *Beyond police reports:* "The Berlin Tunnel," part II, *Cryptologic Almanac.*

211 *Richard Bissell:* John Prados, *The Soviet Estimate: U.S. Intelligence Analysis and Russian Military Strength* (New York: Dial, 1982), 28; Leonard Mosley, *Dulles: A Biography of Eleanor, Allen, and John Foster Dulles and Their Family Network* (New York: Dial, 1978), 372.

212 *"We weren't after":* SV int, Montagnon and Kindell.

Chapter 14: The Penetration of the CIA into Our Midst

213 *Marshal Andrei Grechko:* SV int, Kovalenko (Kregg); Kovalenko letter to David Stafford, Nov. 19, 2005, courtesy Kovalenko; Kovalenko comments, Browne, *Experiences,* 58; SV int, Montagnon.

213 *While lower-level:* Hood, *Mole,* 188; SV int, Montagnon; Helms with Hood, *Look,* 138.

214 *George Blake's assignment:* SV int, George Blake; Murphy int, LHC, 33.

214 *Moscow Center's decision:* Kondrashev int, LHC, 12; Kondrashev int, AMB; John Diamond, "Book Details CIA-KGB Spy Wars in Berlin," AP, Sept. 22, 1997.

215 *"How could anyone":* SV int, Montgomery; Kondrashev int, AMB.

215 *The deception would:* Bagley, *Spymaster,* ch. 6.; Murphy int, LHC, 37; Blake int, "George Blake, agent double et légende de la guerre froide à Berlin," Sylvie Braibant; SV int, Montgomery.

215 *Any significant disinformation:* BGB, 236; Montgomery int by Murphy, Berlin Tunnel file, Box 1, BSP; SV int, Murphy.

216 *The KGB's subtle:* Kondrashev int, LHC, 111; Evans, "Berlin Tunnel Intelligence," 46; "Ein letztes Stück Kalter Krieg," *Berliner Zeitung,* Sept. 23, 1993.

216 *Certainly, the message:* SV int, Montgomery; Browne, *Experiences,* 12; Hood, *Mole,* 188.

216 *Such stories were all:* BGB, 425; "THE GRECHKO FAMILY and their friends," Apr. 17, 1959, CIA-HRP.

217 *The relationship between:* Sergei Khrushchev, *Nikita Khrushchev,* 139; BGB, 162.

217 *Grechko was a powerful:* SV int, Kovalenko; Kovalenko letter to Stafford; "GRECHKO FAMILY," 2.

217 *Not everyone at CIA:* SV int, Montgomery; Stewart comments, "U.S. Postwar Intelligence in Europe," C-SPAN; Murphy int, LHC, 26; SV int, Murphy; BGB, 425.

218 *Still, knowing too much:* Mosley, *Dulles,* 373.

218 *A new Soviet battle:* Nigel West, *The A to Z of British Intelligence* (London: Scarecrow Press, 2009), 44; Bower, *Perfect,* 182; Wolf with McElvoy, *Man Without a Face,* 98; Martin, *Wilderness,* 88.

219 *But other information:* CSH, b-3–4; BGB, 425; "Comments on November 1993 int with CG Harvey," Murphy to Stockton, Harvey, Bill and family file, Box 2, BSP; BGB, 425; "Soviet Interference with Berlin Rail Access," Nov. 24, 1956; DVD supplement to *A City Torn Apart,* CIA.

219 *On May 5, the:* Harrison, *Driving,* 54.

220 *While many viewed:* CSH, b-2–3; "Sovet Bloc's Facsimile NATO," NSC briefing June 7, 1955, DVD supplement to *CIA Analysis of the Warsaw Pact Forces,* CIA.

220 *The tapped circuits: BGB,* 427; "Berlin Tunnel," *OFL,* 396; Murphy int, LHC, 27.

221 *More astonishing:* Murphy comments, "U.S. Postwar Intelligence in Europe"; *BGB,* 236, 426–28; "Soviet Intelligence and Security, Third (Operations) Department, KGB," Sept. 30, 1958, VI, 281, CIA-HRP; Feifer, "The Berlin Tunnel."

221 *"It was unique":* Evans, "Berlin Tunnel Intelligence," 46; Murphy int, LHC, 29.

221 *To a certain extent: BGB,* 208, 236, 427–28; Murphy comments, "U.S. Postwar Intelligence in Europe"; Murphy int, LHC, 28; "Berlin Tunnel," *OFL,* 396.

222 *Though Pitovranov:* "Soviet Intelligence and Security: Lt Gen E.P. Pitovranov," July 23, 1958, CIA-HRP, 3; *BGB,* 428; "Soviet Intelligence and Security: Relationship of the KGB to Wismut SDAG," Aug. 7, 1958, CIA-HRP; Murphy int, LHC, 20.

223 *No American president:* Beschloss, *Mayday,* 94; Gilbert, *Churchill,* 939.

223 *A path had been cleared: CIA Analysis of Warsaw Pact Forces,* 9; Donovan, *Eisenhower: The Inside Story,* 347; Andrew Goodpaster oral history, OH-37, DDE, 66; Harrison, *Driving,* 53.

223 *Soviet premier Nikolai Bulganin:* Beschloss, *Mayday,* 101–3; Khrushchev, *Khrushchev Remembers,* 395, and appendix 3, Crankshaw, "Khrushchev's Kremlin Colleagues," 542–43; Donovan, *Eisenhower,* 343; Bohlen, *Witness to History,* 382.

224 *Khrushchev struck Eisenhower:* Goodpaster oral history, OH-544, DDE, 11; Khrushchev, *Khrushchev Remembers,* 397–98.

224 *With his roots:* Harrison, *Driving,* 61; Beschloss, *Mayday,* 164; Khrushchev, *Khrushchev Remembers,* appendix 3, Crankshaw, "Khrushchev's Kremlin Colleagues," 547.

224 *Certainly, Khrushchev had:* Sergei Khrushchev, *Nikita Khrushchev,* 142.

225 *After two days:* Beschloss, *Mayday,* 102; "Discussion at the 254th Meeting of the NSC," July 7, 1955, box 7, NSC Series, DDE Papers as President, DDE; Eisenhower oral history, OH 14, 43, and OH 11, DDE.

225 *The dramatic offer:* Donovan, *Eisenhower,* 344; Eisenhower oral history, OH 11, DDE.

226 *The conference ended:* Drew Middleton, "Now the Russians Turn Charms on Britain," *NYT,* Apr. 15, 1956; Khrushchev, *Khrushchev Remembers,* 400; Beschloss, *Mayday,* 105.

Chapter 15: The One-Man Tunnel

227 *Even Blake, with:* Blake, *NOC,* 167; author visit, Olympic Stadium, Aug. 2015; Hermiston, *Greatest,* 178.

227 *Once the KGB:* Blake int, "The Confession"; Hermiston, *Greatest,* 180; Blake, *NOC,* 174; Pincher, *Inside Story,* 97.

228 *Every three weeks:* Blake, *NOC,* 166, 173; Hermiston, *Greatest,* 179–80; Memo to Chief, SR/CI, "MYAKOTNYKH, Nikolay Sergeyevich, Col.," Nov. 26, 1962, CIA-HRP; *BGB,* 228.

229 *Dozhdalev was astonished:* Dozhdalev and Blake int, "The Confession"; BLH, 14; Blake, *NOC,* 173.

229 *For the KGB:* Blake int, "The Confession"; Blake int, Red Files.

230 *Of particular interest:* "Hinweise zum Der Sowjetische Kundschafter im britischen Geheimdienst George BLAKE," Dec. 3, 1976, MfS-ZAIG 25776, Stasi; Kondrashev int, LHC, 13.

230 *The numbers are believable:* Maddrell, *Spying on Science,* 144.

230 *Blake professed to:* "Reporting of Names of Agents to Russia," addendum to BLH; Kondrashev int, LHC, 17.

231 *Indeed, a later KGB:* Andrew and Mitrokhin, *The Sword and the Shield,* 438; Maddrell, "British Intelligence," 46.

231 *For the KGB:* Andrew, *Defend the Realm,* 490; Kondrashev int, LHC, 19.

231 *Russian intelligence always:* Helms with Hood, *Look,* 139; Helms int, "The Confes-

sion"; Luke Harding, "Gordievsky: Russia Has as Many Spies in Britain Now as the USSR Ever Did," *Guardian*, Mar. 11, 2013.

232 *Blake was considered:* "Background on the Blake Case," n.d., PREM 13/952, NAUK; Hyde, *George Blake: Superspy,* 46; Stafford, *Spies,* 115–16.

232 *To keep up:* "Reporting of Names of Agents to Russia," addendum to BLH; Blake int, "The Confession"; Blake, *NOC,* 169.

232 *One scheme concocted:* Blake lecture to Stasi workers, 1976, MfS Sekr. Neiber 81, Stasi, 29; Blake, *NOC,* 172.

233 *But Blake had other:* Blake, *NOC,* 174; Peck, "Agent's Wife Knew Blake in Berlin," *Telegraph,* Dec. 3, 1961; Cookridge, *George Blake: Double Agent,* 145.

234 *To boost Agent:* Blake, *NOC,* 175–76; Knightley, "Confessions of a Traitor," part I; Knightley, "The KGB vs. the CIA: The Secret Struggle," Red Files, supplemental article, www.pbs.org/redfiles/kgb/debrief/k_brief_ter_knightley.htm.

235 *All the while:* GBD, V, 2; GAB, tapes I and II; Gillian Blake, "Portrait of a Spy," parts I and II.

236 *The couple mostly:* GAB, tape II; Donald McLachlan, "Lessons of the Blake Case," *Telegraph,* Dec. 17, 1961.

237 *Blake was quite:* Blake int, Red Files; Blake int, "The Confession"; GAB, tapes I and II.

237 *Gillian remained utterly:* GAB, tapes I and II; Gillian Blake, "Portrait of a Spy," part I.

Chapter 16: The Hottest Intelligence Operation on the Face of the Planet

239 *Corporal Eugene Kregg:* SV int, Kovalenko (Kregg); Kovalenko comments, Browne, *Experiences,* 53–54; Kregg travel orders, Sept. 22, 1955, courtesy Kovalenko; Kovalenko, "The Great Berlin Tunnel Mystery," *The Journey Continues* (blog), Sept. 8, 2012, http://eugenesjourneycontinues.blogspot.com/2012/09/kreggra19450328-we-know-who-you-are.html.

241 *The British postal:* CSH, 21; BGB, 423, 450.

241 *Despite Helgestad's concerns:* SV int, Kovalenko; Kovalenko comments, Browne, *Experiences,* 58.

242 *Kregg's fellow linguists:* SV int, Kovalenko; Wolfgang Saxon, "Robert Maguire, 75, Expert on Soviet Literature, Dies," *NYT,* July 31, 2005; "William J. Cockell Jr.," *Los Angeles Times,* June 12, 2000; Kovalenko comments, Browne, *Experiences,* 57.

243 *Inside a station:* SV int, Bialas and Plapler; Bialas letter to author, Apr. 5, 2019.

243 *The countermeasures station:* Russ Knapp, "Berlin Tunnel" memoir, courtesy Russ Knapp; John Quirk comments, Browne, *Experiences,* 46–48; SV int, Montgomery.

243 *John Quirk and Gene Bialas:* SV int, Bialas; "Reflections on SFC Quirk's US Army Service," https://army.togetherweserved.com/bio/John.Quirk.

244 *Helgestad revealed:* SV int, Quirk and Bialas; Quirk comments, Browne, *Experiences,* 47.

245 *Helgestad himself led:* SV int, Quirk and Bialas.

245 *To preserve anonymity:* Browne, *Experiences,* 44; SV int, Bialas and Quirk; Knapp, "Berlin Tunnel"; Knapp comments, Browne, *Experiences,* 63.

246 *In the evenings:* SV int, Bialas, Kovalenko, and Romey; (Romey), *Not to Be a Spy,* 42–43; Knapp, "Berlin Tunnel."

246 *Perhaps the biggest:* SV int, Quirk; Quirk, "Reflections"; Quirk comments, Browne, *Experiences,* 49–50; SV int, Bialas and Romey.

247 *Occasionally the soldiers:* Kovalenko comments, Browne, *Experiences,* 58–59; SV int, Knapp, Bialas, and Quirk; Knapp, "Berlin Tunnel," 11–12.

248 *While no one:* BGB, 222; SV int, Kindell.

249 *Kregg managed to trigger:* SV int, Kovalenko; Kovalenko comments, Browne, *Experiences,* 59.

249 *The first snow:* Helms with Hood, *Look,* 136; Kovalenko, "The Great Berlin Tunnel Mystery"; SV int, Kovalenko.

250 *Eddie Kindell:* SV int, Kindell; Fellon, "Turning a Cold War Scheme into Reality," 6; SV int, Kovalenko.

250 *Something had to be done:* Fellon, "Turning a Cold War Scheme into Reality," 6; Martin, *Wilderness,* 86; Altglienicke Museum photograph collection; SV int, Montgomery; Dulles, *The Craft of Intelligence,* 206–7.

251 *The snow fiasco:* SV int, Quirk; Quirk comments, Browne, *Experiences,* 47–48.

252 *After months of inaction:* Bagley, *Spymaster,* ch. 5; Kondrashev int, LHC, 14; Blake int, "George Blake, agent double."

252 *By late 1955:* BGB, 226; Thornton and Thomas, "Revealed: The Map of Blake's Betrayal"; Heun and Schier, "Tunnel-Spione"; Stafford, *Spies,* 143.

252 *After arriving in Berlin:* BGB, 226.

252 *One afternoon soon:* "GRECHKO FAMILY," CIA-HRP; "'Operation Gold': Der Spionagetunnel von Berlin"; BGB, 226–27.

253 *Despite the disagreement:* SV int, Quirk and Bialas.

253 *Inside the warehouse:* "GRECHKO FAMILY," CIA-HRP.

Chapter 17: Berlin Was on the Top of the World

255 *Vadim Goncharov:* BGB, 226, 428; Murphy int, AMB; Thornton and Thomas, "Revealed: The Map of Blake's Betrayal."

256 *PBJOINTLY was firing:* Bray email to Stockton, May 14, 2001, Corr A-C, Box 1, BSP; CG Harvey int by Murphy, BSP; SV int, Montgomery.

257 *A British military:* Hart, "Pyotr Semyonovich Popov," 66–67; "Popov: The Conformist Who Failed," undated monograph, CIA-HRP; BGB, 269.

258 *The mysterious visitor:* CIA Analysis of the Warsaw Pact, 11; Hood, *Mole,* 108, 138–39, 145; Helms with Hood, *Look,* 129.

258 *Popov took action:* "Popov: The Conformist," 2.

258 *Popov was assigned:* Leonard McCoy, foreword to Ashley, *CIA SpyMaster,* 11; Wise, *Molehunt,* 66; Ashley, *CIA SpyMaster,* 85.

258 *For more than two years:* Hoffman, *Billion Dollar Spy,* 9; Mangold, *Cold Warrior,* 250; "Popov: The Conformist," 3; Ashley, *CIA SpyMaster,* 107.

259 *But the CIA had lost:* BGB, 268; Hood, *Mole,* 190, 204; Ashley, *CIA SpyMaster,* 333.

259 *The British liaison officer:* Hood, *Mole,* 198; BGB, 269; Kondrashev int, LHC, 17; Bagley, *Spymaster,* ch. 6; Hood believed "Blake's report alone could have been enough to undo Popov." See Hood, *Mole,* 298.

260 *Once Lunn was finished:* BGB, 269, 347; Ashley, *CIA SpyMaster,* 111; "Popov: The Conformist," 7.

260 *In his new position:* BGB, 270; Ashley, *CIA SpyMaster,* 95, 113; CIA Analysis of the Warsaw Pact, 11.

260 *Kisevalter, a big:* Ashley, *CIA SpyMaster,* 117–19, 333, n6; BGB, 426.

261 *Between the tunnel:* CIA Analysis of the Warsaw Pact, 11; Murphy int, LHC, 29; BGB, 487, n9; Montgomery int by Murphy, Berlin Tunnel file, Box 1, BSP; Murphy, "How I Got to Berlin," May 25, 1994, Corr M-O, Box 1, BSP; Stockton, *Flawed,* 90.

262 *Klavdiya Grechkova:* "GRECHKO FAMILY," 11. The rival spouse was the wife of Alexei Kirichenko.

262 *There had been no:* Bohlen, *Witness,* 397; "After Stalin," episode 7 of *Cold War,* CNN documentary series.

263 *"How did Father":* Bower, *Perfect,* 182; Stafford, *Spies,* 132–33.

263 *As usual, the tunnel:* BGB, 298; Evans, "Berlin Tunnel Intelligence," 47; Stafford, *Spies,* 133.

263   *A highlight cable:* Hermiston, *Greatest,* 197; *BGB,* 298, 424; Murphy comments, "U.S. Postwar Intelligence in Europe"; Grose, *Gentleman,* 419.

263   *The speech had been:* Sergei Khrushchev, *Nikita Khrushchev,* 163; *BGB,* 298; Ray Cline, *The CIA Under Reagan, Bush and Casey: The Evolution of the Agency from Roosevelt to Reagan* (Washington, DC: Acropolis Books, 2009), 187; Beschloss, *Mayday,* 170; Stafford, *Spies,* 145.

264   *Khrushchev had another:* Beschloss, *Mayday,* 116; Middleton, "Now the Russians Turn Charms on Britain"; NSC Briefing, "Bulganin-Khrushchev Tour of South Asia," Nov. 29, 1955, CIA-HRP; "Complaint from Moscow," *NYT,* Apr. 10, 1956.

264   *Khrushchev was disgruntled:* *BGB,* 227; Stafford, *Spies,* 145; Sergei Khrushchev, *Nikita Khrushchev,* 112.

265   *Beyond the tensions:* Middleton, "Now the Russians Turn Charms on Britain"; SV int, Sergei Khrushchev.

265   *To clear the way:* Cookridge, *George Blake: Double Agent,* 12; BBC, "On This Day, 11 February 1956: 'Cambridge Spies' Surface in Moscow," http://news.bbc .co.uk/onthisday/hi/dates/stories/february/11/newsid_2721000/2721413.stm.

266   *Khrushchev also asked Ivan:* Bagley, *Spymaster,* ch. 11; *BGB,* 227.

266   *Kondrashev's polish:* Bagley, *Spymaster,* ch. 5; Oleg Gordievsky, "No Laughing Boy," *Times Literary Supplement,* Nov. 14, 1997; Wright, *Spycatcher,* 257.

266   *Kondrashev had a ready:* Bagley, *Spymaster,* ch. 11; Kondrashev int, LHC, 15.

266   *Blake was not queried:* Blake int, Red Files.

267   *Serov brought:* Bagley, *Spymaster,* ch. 11; Blake int, "George Blake, agent double"; SV int, Sergei Khrushchev; "Spy Tunnel," *NYT,* Apr. 29, 1956.

267   *Khrushchev understood:* SV int, Sergei Khrushchev; SV int, Foertsch.

267   *Depicting West Berlin:* Stafford, *Spies,* 145; Blake int, "George Blake, agent double."

268   *Besides, Khrushchev was eager:* Kondrashev int, LHC, 15; SV int, Sergei Khrushchev; Kondrashev int, AMB.

Chapter 18: There's a Fast One Coming

269   *Escorted by two:* Sergei Khrushchev, *Nikita Khrushchev,* 115–16.

269   *His presence caused:* Ibid.; "Soviet Visitors Evoke Mixed Greetings in Britain," *NYT,* Mar. 24, 1956; Hood, *Mole,* 270; "Soviets Cut Serov from London Trip," *NYT,* Apr. 7, 1956.

270   *It was a harbinger:* Catterall, *Macmillan Diaries,* vol. 1, Apr. 14, 1956; Sergei Khrushchev, *Nikita Khrushchev,* 122.

270   *It had been an unusually:* Murphy int, LHC, 27; SV int, Montgomery.

270   *For the Soviets:* Knightley, "Confessions of a Traitor," part II; Kondrashev int, LHC, 15; Murphy int, LHC, 25.

271   *In the meantime:* "Soviet Military Intelligence in GSFG: Inspecting Commission from Moscow (28 Mar–21 Apr 56)," Dec. 17, 1956, CIA-HRP; "Soviet Intelligence and Security: Visits of KGB Inspection Commissions to GSFG: 1955–56," Sept. 15, 1958, CIA-HRP; *BGB,* 427.

271   *But on the night:* "'Operation Gold': Der Spionagetunnel von Berlin"; *CSH,* a-1; Berlin Tempelhof precipitation, www.weatheronline.co.uk, April 1956.

271   *The seafaring books:* Sergei Khrushchev, *Nikita Khrushchev,* 122; Drew Middleton, "Russians Greeted Coolly in London," *NYT,* Apr. 19, 1956.

272   *Heads aboard the ship:* Khrushchev, *Khrushchev Remembers,* 403.

272   *As the cruiser glided:* "Visitors in Britain," *NYT,* Apr. 22, 1956; Middleton, "Russians Greeted Coolly."

272   *A cavalcade of cars:* SV int, Sergei Khrushchev; Khrushchev, *Khrushchev Remembers,* 403; Sergei Khrushchev, *Nikita Khrushchev,* 122; Wright, *Spycatcher,* 72.

273   *Red Army communications: CSH,* a-2.

273   *On the morning:* Stafford, *Spies,* 147; *CSH,* a-3.

274   *In the early:* Macintyre, *A Spy Among Friends,* ch. 12; Wright, *Spycatcher,* 73.

274   *But it was nonetheless:* Catterall, *Macmillan Diaries,* vol. 1, May 8, 1956; Peter Day, "How Buster Crabb's Fatal Spy Mission Angered Eden," *Telegraph,* Mar. 8, 2006; Macintyre, *A Spy Among Friends,* ch. 12.

275   *Sergei Kondrashev was breakfasting:* Bagley, *Spymaster,* ch. 5; Khrushchev, *Khrushchev Remembers,* 411.

275   *Lieutenant Colonel Vyunik: CSH,* a-3, 5; Stafford, *Spies,* 147.

276   *The Bulge and Krush road show:* Drew Middleton, "Soviet Chiefs Booed by Oxford Students," *NYT,* Apr. 22, 1956; "Khrushchev and Bulganin in Britain," White House Office, Office of the Staff Secretary, Box 1, CIA file, Vol. 1 (2), DDE; "Visitors in Britain," *NYT,* Apr. 22, 1956.

277   *Khrushchev had sat next to Churchill:* Khrushchev, *Khrushchev Remembers,* 410; Sergei Khrushchev, *Nikita Khrushchev,* 127.

277   *At Chequers:* Khrushchev, *Khrushchev Remembers,* 405.

277   *Gazing through: BGB,* 229–30; *CSH,* a-4.

277   *Bill and CG Harvey:* Murphy int, LHC, 29; SV int, Montgomery; Bray email to Stockton, May 27, 2001, Corr A-C, Box 1, BSP.

278   *Harvey stood by:* SV int, Montgomery; *BGB,* 230.

278   *While the Red Army: BGB,* 227; SV int, Blake; Thornton and Thomas, "Revealed: The Map of Blake's Betrayal."

278   *At 2 a.m.: CSH,* a-4–8; Berlin cable to headquarters, May 10, 1956, CIA-HRP; "Memorandum for the Record," Nov. 29, 1954, *OFL,* 348.

280   *The Army installation:* SV int, Bialas and Knapp; Knapp comments, Browne, *Experiences,* 66; (Romey), *Not to Be a Spy,* 53.

281   *Charlie Bray was deciphering:* Bray email to Stockton, May 27, 2001, Corr A-C, Box 1, BSP; Thomas, *The Very Best Men,* 129.

281   *At Wünsdorf: CSH,* a-8, 11; *BGB,* 228.

282   *Markus Wolf:* Wolf with McElvoy, *Man Without a Face,* 97–99.

283   *The tap was still: CSH,* a-10.

283   *Nikita Khrushchev, up bright and early:* Khrushchev, *Khrushchev Remembers,* 405–7; Drew Middleton, "Russian Leaders Guests of Queen," *NYT,* Apr. 23, 1956; "Khrushchev and Bulganin in Britain," DDE.

284   *The comity at Windsor Castle:* SV int, Montgomery; Montgomery letter to Stockton, Aug. 4, 2001, Corr M-O, Box 1, BSP; Montgomery, *"Ist ja fantastisch!,"* 53; Montgomery int by Murphy, Corr M-O, Box 1, BSP.

285   *Further exploration: CSH,* 11–12; Montgomery int by Murphy, BSP.

286   *Finally, after consultations:* "Soviet Discovery of the Berlin Tunnel," tape transcript, *OFL,* 378; *CSH,* a-14.

286   *Markus Wolf was one:* Wolf with McElvoy, *Man Without a Face,* 99.

287   *The telephone rang:* SV int, Feick; Feick int, *"Ist ja fantastisch!,"* 69; "Operation Gold," *Wochenpost,* May 9, 1986; "USA-Spionage-Tunnel unter DDR-Gebiet," *ND,* Apr. 24, 1956.

288   *A message arrived: BGB,* 232.

288   *Though his hopes:* SV int, Montgomery; Montgomery int by Murphy, BSP; *BGB,* 231.

289   *Before leaving Rudow:* SV int, Montgomery; Bray letter to Stockton, Aug. 21, 2002; Stockton, *Flawed,* 92–93.

289   *Around 3:15 p.m.:* "Soviet Discovery of the Berlin Tunnel," tape transcript, *OFL,* 378; *CSH,* a-15.

Chapter 19: A Sensational Story About American Espionage

293   *CIA director Allen Dulles:* "Telephone call to Allen Dulles," Apr. 23, 1956, file Jan. 3, 1956–Apr. 30, 1956, Box 4, John Foster Dulles Papers, Telephone Conversations Series, DDE; Dulles, *The Craft of Intelligence,* 207; *CSH,* 27.

294   *Inside the tunnel:* SV int, Knapp and Bialas; Knapp comments, Browne, *Experiences,* 67; Knapp, "Berlin Tunnel," 17.

294   *Across the border:* Heun and Schier, "Tunnel-Spione," *Berliner Morgenpost,* part 2, Mar. 7, 1994.

295   *It was early:* Heun and Schier, "Tunnel-Spione"; "Sowjets bewunderten tollkühnes Husarenstück der CIA in Rudow," *Berliner Morgenpost,* May 10, 1992.

295   *To say the invitation:* Nathan J. Margolin, "U.S. Phone Tap Called 'Nonsense,'" *Stars and Stripes,* Apr. 25, 1956.

295   *Following the instructions:* BGB, 232; Telex to Moscow from Grechko, Pushkin, and Pitovranov, Apr. 23, 1956, copy on display at AMB.

296   *Despite having only:* "U.S. Accused of Cable-Tapping," *Times* (London), Apr. 24, 1956; "Wires Tapped by U.S., Berlin Reds Charge," Reuters, in *Chicago Daily Tribune,* Apr. 24, 1956; "Spy Tunnel," *NYT,* Apr. 29, 1956; Höhne and Zolling, *Network,* 307.

296   *With great umbrage:* Heun and Schier, "Tunnel-Spione"; "Wonderful Tunnel," *Time*; Höhne and Zolling, *Network,* 312.

297   *At his direction:* Höhne and Zolling, *Network,* 307; Sullivan, "U.S. Investigates Wiretap Tunnel"; *Neue Berliner Illustrierte,* Nov. 19, 1956.

298   *Reporters explored:* Margolin, "U.S. Phone Tap Called 'Nonsense'"; "USA Spionagetunnel entdeckt," *Das Banner,* Apr. 26, 1956; Walter Sullivan, "Russians Say U.S. Taps Berlin Wire," *NYT,* Apr. 24, 1956.

298   *At 6:01 p.m.:* "Telephone call to Allen Dulles," Apr. 23, 1956, 6:01 p.m., file Jan. 3, 1956–Apr. 30, 1956, Box 4, John Foster Dulles Papers, Telephone Conversations Series, DDE.

298   *It was the first time:* Beschloss, *Mayday,* 114.

299   *He called his brother:* "Telephone call to Allen Dulles," Apr. 24, 1956, 9:01 a.m., file Jan. 3, 1956–Apr. 30, 1956, Box 4, John Foster Dulles Papers, Telephone Conversations Series, DDE.

299   *The tunnel story:* Osborne letter to Stockton, Mar. 15, 2001, Corr M-O, Box 1, BPS; Stockton, *Flawed,* 92.

300   *Still, it was impossible:* SV int, Montgomery; Murphy int, LHC; Mehrer, "The Berlin Tunnel Operation," presentation at U.S. Army Heritage and Education Center, Apr. 22, 2014.

300   *Any Western hope:* Robert Tuckman, "Soviets Make Big Show of Spy Tunnel," AP, in *WP,* Apr. 25, 1956; *CSH,* 21; "Reds Show U.S. 'Spy' Tunnel in Berlin Again," AP, in *Chicago Daily Tribune,* Apr. 25, 1956; Sullivan, "U.S. Investigates Wiretap Tunnel"; "'American Tunnel' on View," *Times* (London), Apr. 25, 1956.

301   *The correspondents crossed:* "Verzögerungsversuch auf und unter der Erde," *ND,* Apr. 28, 1956; *Tunnel Spione* booklet; "Die Ratten im Tunnel sind still," *ND,* Apr. 27, 1956; Sullivan, "U.S. Investigates Wiretap Tunnel."

302   *The Eastern version:* "USA Spionagetunnel entdeckt," *Das Banner;* "Reds Show U.S. 'Spy' Tunnel in Berlin Again"; *CSH,* d-10.

302   *Another fiction:* "From Berlin to Foreign Office," Apr. 26, 1956, FO 371/124647, NAUK; "Ratten," *ND,* Apr. 27, 1956; "'American Tunnel' on View," *Times* (London).

303   *The Eastern version:* Stafford, *Spies,* 212; Sergei Khrushchev, *Nikita Khrushchev,* 133.

303   *Predictions were already:* Drew Middleton, "Russian Leaders End British Talk:

Results Are Few," *NYT,* Apr. 26, 1956; Waldo Drake, "British-Soviet Talks Come to End in Failure," *Los Angeles Times,* Apr. 26, 1956; Drew Middleton, "Stassen Confers with Khrushchev on Arms Dispute," *NYT,* Apr. 25, 1956; Drew Middleton, "Khrushchev Says Soviet Will Make H-Bomb Missile," *NYT,* Apr. 24, 1956; "Memorandum for Colonel Goodpaster," Apr. 27, 1956, file "Apr. 56 Miscellaneous," Box 15, DDE Diary, DDE Papers as President, DDE.

304 *On Tuesday evening:* Charlotte Vogel, "The Leaps of Freedom by Soviet Ballet Dancers," unpublished paper; "Bulganin Calls Dancer 'Wonderful, Wonderful,'" *NYT,* Apr. 26, 1956.

304 *From babes in arms:* Author tour, Altglienicke Museum; "Empörung über USA-Spionagetunnel," *ND,* April 24, 1956; "Berliner aus Ost und West empört den Amerikanischen Spionagetunnel," *Berliner Zeitung,* Apr. 25, 1956; *CSH,* d-5; "Altglienicke ist wachgerüttelt," *ND,* Apr. 24, 1956; SV int, Vacca.

305 *The onslaught:* "Reds Give Berlin Tunnel Their Full Propaganda Run," AP, in *Chicago Daily Tribune,* Apr. 29, 1956; "Reds Play Up 'Tunnel' Case," *Stars and Stripes,* Apr. 30, 1956; "Spy Tunnel," *NYT,* Apr. 29, 1956; *CSH,* 28; C. P. Hope to M. S. Williams, Apr. 28, 1956, FO 371/124647, NAUK.

305 *As requested by:* "'Tap Tunnel' Case Shifted to Capital," *Stars and Stripes,* Apr. 27, 1956; "Army Halts Tunnel Talk," AP, in *Baltimore Sun,* Apr. 26, 1956; "Reds Say Tunnel Probe Is Dodged," AP, Apr. 28, 1956.

305 *Indeed, the reaction:* CSH, 28, c-2-8.

306 *For Peter Lunn:* Blake, NOC, 181; Stafford, *Spies,* 169.

307 *The epic Soviet:* "Failure of a Mission," *NYT,* Apr. 27, 1956; Khrushchev, *Khrushchev Remembers,* 409; SV int, Sergei Khrushchev; Kennett Love, "Scots' Reception to Russians Dour," *NYT,* Apr. 27, 1956.

307 *Despite all the incidents:* Aldrich, *The Hidden Hand,* 524; Sergei Khrushchev, *Nikita Khrushchev,* 143; Drew Middleton, "Moscow Willing to Join a U.N. Ban on Mideast Arms," *NYT,* Apr. 28, 1956; Day, "How Buster Crabb's Fatal Spy Mission Angered Eden."

307 *Speaking to reporters:* Stafford, *Spies,* 163–64; "Visit to the United Kingdom of Bulganin and Khrushchev, 19–27 April 1956," 1956, History and Public Policy Program Digital Archive, FO 371/122836, http://digitalarchive.wilsoncenter.org /document/123798.

308 *In the weeks:* Blake, NOC, 181; Blake int, "Spies," episode 21 of *Cold War,* CNN documentary series.

308 *Despite disappointment:* Helms int, "The Confession."

308 *President Eisenhower felt:* Beschloss, *Mayday,* 115; William Bragg Ewald Jr., *Eisenhower the President: Crucial Days, 1951–1960* (Englewood Cliffs, NJ: Prentice Hall, 1981), 265–66.

308 *Bill Harvey's fury:* CG Harvey int by Murphy, BSP; "Berlin Tunnel," *OFL,* 395–96.

309 *In Washington: Operation REGAL,* NSA, 23; Murphy, "Comments on November 1993 Interview with CG Harvey," Harvey, Bill and family file, Box 2, BSP.

309 *But two of the CIA:* Montgomery letter to Stockton, Aug. 4, 2001, Corr M-O Box 1, *BSP;* Bray to Lions, Mar. 6, 1997 and Bray email to Stockton, May 17, 2001, Corr A-C, Box 1, BSP.

309 *Likewise, in Washington: Operation REGAL,* 19.

309 *However, in the view:* Blake int, Red Files.

309 *There was one:* "Army Halts Tunnel Talk," AP, in *Baltimore Sun,* Apr. 27, 1956.

309 *Blake had kept:* Blake, NOC, 182.

Chapter 20: The Invisible War

310 *In late April 1956:* Stafford, *Spies,* 173; Beschloss, *Mayday,* 112.

310 *Unlike the tunnel:* SV int, Raymond Garthoff; *BGB,* 281; Stafford, *Spies,* 172.

311 *With Soviet leaders:* Aldrich, *The Hidden Hand,* 324–25; Day, "How Buster Crabb's Fatal Spy Mission Angered Eden"; Clarissa Eden, *Clarissa Eden: A Memoir—From Churchill to Eden* (London: Weidenfeld & Nicholson, 2007), diary entry dated May 5, 1956.

311 *Eden addressed:* Aldrich, *The Hidden Hand,* 324–25; Bower, *Perfect,* 162; Macintyre, *A Spy Among Friends,* ch. 12; Richard Alleyne, "I Killed 'Buster' Crabb, Says Russian Diver," *Telegraph,* Nov. 17, 2007.

311 *Coming on the heels:* James Reston, "The Invisible War Rises to the Surface," *NYT,* May 13, 1956.

311 *Adding a spy plane:* Beschloss, *Mayday,* 116–17; Stafford, *Spies,* 173; "Phone calls 5/17/56," May 56 phone calls file, Box 15, DDE Diary, DDE Papers as President, DDE.

312 *Farmer Noack and his family:* Feick int, *"Ist ja fantastisch!,"* 71–72; SV int, Feick.

312 *Early on the morning:* "Der Spionagetunnel wird besichtigt," *ND,* May 4, 1956.

313 *The tunnel soon became:* "East Zone Workers Tour 'Spy Tunnel,' Sign Guest Book," AP, May 3, 1956; SV int, Günther Kuinke.

313 *After exiting the tunnel: Tunnel Spione* booklet, Altglienicke Museum.

313 *Visitors often waited:* "Spy Fever Has Its Fantastic Side," AP, in *Hartford Courant,* May 20, 1956; Blake lecture to Stasi workers, 1976, MfS Sekr. Neiber 81, Stasi, 15; Memo, Political Branch, Berlin, to Chancery, Bonn, May 8, 1956, FO 37/124647, NAUK; Höhne and Zolling, *Network,* 310; *CSH,* c-2.

314 *The favorable reviews:* Edward Burks, "Red Germany Assails U.S. at May Day Show," *Baltimore Sun,* May 2, 1956; "Reds Blame 'Spy Tunnel' on Dulles' Sister," AP, in *Chicago Tribune,* May 11, 1956; "May 11, 1956," file Tel Conv General May 1–June 29, Box 4, John Foster Dulles Papers, Telephone Conversations Series, DDE.

314 *The CIA director:* SV int, Alice Ojala Sorvo; Browne, *Experiences,* 17; *CSH,* 30.

315 *Then it was back: CSH,* 28; Browne, *Experiences,* 18; (Romey), *Not to Be a Spy,* 55.

315 *The magic was gone:* SV int, Knapp.

315 *The U.S. Army engineers:* SV int, Comstock and Hope; Legion of Merit to Captain Robert G. Williamson, RWP. The team performed "arduous labor in an atmosphere of personal danger and mental stress seldom encountered by members of the military services during times of peace," according to the citation.

316 *Despite the tunnel's demise:* SV int, Vacca. The station detected a new radar altimeter used by Russian helicopters.

316 *On July 4, 1956:* Beschloss, *Mayday,* 121; Paul Maddrell, "British-American Scientific Intelligence Collaboration During the Occupation of Germany," in *American-British-Canadian Intelligence Relations 1939–2000* (London: Routledge, 2000), 88; Sergei Khrushchev, *Nikita Khrushchev,* 157; Reel, *Brotherhood,* 117.

317 *With tensions so high:* Stockton, *Flawed,* 96; Martin, *Wilderness,* 89; Stafford, *Spies,* 170; SV int, Montgomery.

317 *With no tunnel:* Blake, *NOC,* 182; Andrew and Mitrokhin, *The Sword and the Shield,* 339, 632–33, n17.

318 *By October:* Kellerhoff and von Kostka, *Haupstadt der Spione,* 82; Feick int, *"Ist ja fantastisch!,"* 72; SV int, Feick.

318 *The American troops:* SV int, Vacca.

318 *Though removing the tunnel:* "A Claim by East Berlin," Reuters, in *NYT,* Dec. 16, 1956; "Bauer Noack verklagt Senat," *ND,* Dec. 24, 1956; SV int, Feick. The amount was 6,500 marks, and the attorney was Friedrich Karl Kaul.

319 *In late March 1957:* CIA teletyped information report, Mar. 29, 1957, CIA-HRP; BGB, 271–72; Ashley, *CIA SpyMaster,* 122; Hart, "Popov," 72.

321 *A week after:* GBD, V, 2a; Blake, *NOC,* 180.

321 *Gillian detected that something:* GBD, VI, 1; GAB, tape II; Hermiston, *Greatest,* 200; Cookridge, *George Blake: Double Agent,* 142; BLH, 15.

Chapter 21: Exit Berlin

325 *Pyotr Popov arrived:* Berlin Dispatch, Nov. 24, 1958, CIA-HRP; *BGB,* 305.

325 *On November 10, 1958:* U.S. Department of State Office of the Historian, "Milestones: 1953–1960; The Berlin Crisis, 1958–1961," https://history.state.gov/milestones/1953-1960/berlin-crises; *CIA Analysis of the Warsaw Pact Forces,* 13; Eisenhower, *Waging Peace,* 329.

325 *"Well, are you preparing":* Berlin Dispatch, Nov. 24, 1958.

326 *Since the tunnel's:* BGB, 273, 281; Hart, "Popov," 67; Hood, *Mole,* 205, 251.

326 *Now Popov filled in:* Berlin Dispatch, Nov. 24, 1958; *BGB,* 305, 492; Eisenhower, *Waging Peace,* 331; Gundula Bavendamm, ed., *Like a Tinderbox: The Berlin Crisis and the Construction of the Wall* (Berlin: Allied Museum, 2011), 14–15.

327 *There were reasons:* Hood, *Mole,* 227; Ashley, *CIA SpyMaster,* 127–30; Stockton notes from John Barron conversation, June 2003, Harvey Corr A–C, Box 1, BSP; Martin, *Wilderness,* 92–93; "Popov: The Conformist Who Failed," CIA-HRP.

327 *Still, as Kisevalter:* BGB, 277; Berlin Dispatch, Nov. 24, 1958, 11; Ashley, *CIA SpyMaster,* 87–88.

328 *George Blake was eager:* GAB, tape II; BLH, 14–16; O'Connor, *Blake, Bourke and the End of Empires,* 142; GBD, V, 2a.

329 *Some 90,000:* CSH, 26; Murphy, "How I Got to Berlin," May 25, 1994, Corr M–O, Box 1, BSP; SV int, Garthoff; Helms with Hood, *Look,* 138.

329 *The CIA put the total:* CSH, 26, 29; Heun and Schier, "Tunnel-Spione"; Martin, *Wilderness,* 89.

329 *More than one thousand:* Helms with Hood, *Look,* 137; Browne, *Experiences,* 18; SV int, Kovalenko (Kregg); Kovalenko comments, Browne, *Experiences,* 59.

330 *On Christmas Day:* BGB, 278; Mangold, *Cold Warrior,* 251. The letter was sent in error by a CIA officer in Moscow.

331 *Khrushchev's formal:* Bavendamm, ed., *Like a Tinderbox,* 16; John Lewis Gaddis, *We Now Know: Rethinking Cold War History* (Oxford: Oxford University Press, 1997), 139–40; Beschloss, *Mayday,* 162.

331 *On New Year's Eve:* BGB, 309, 316, 352, 493, n8; Maddrell, "Western Espionage and Stasi Counter-Intelligence in East Germany, 1953–1961," in *East German Foreign Intelligence: Myth, Reality, and Controversy* (London: Routledge, 2010), 29.

331 *Even as the preparations:* OFL, 410; "Current Status Report Soviet Intelligence Services East Germany," Jan. 16, 1959, and "Bn Sitrep," Feb. 11, 1959, OFL, 440–41, 445; *BGB,* 318.

332 *At CIA headquarters:* Garthoff, *Journey Through the Cold War,* 126; *A City Torn Apart,* 24; "Memorandum of Conference with the President," Mar. 6, 1959, DVD supplement to *A City Torn Apart.*

332 *On May 27:* Beschloss, *Mayday,* 177; Eisenhower, *Waging Peace,* 360.

332 *Popov's arrest:* "KGB Exploitation of Heinz Felfe," Apr. 12, 1978, CIA-HRP; *BGB,* 301, 311.

333 *Disinformation—dezinformatsiya—had:* BGB, 448.

333 *The State Department:* BGB, 325–26; Murry Marder, "Herter Calls East Berlin Nest of Spies," *WP,* June 6, 1959; Murphy int, AMB.

333 *Before leaving Berlin:* Cookridge, *George Blake: Double Agent,* 172; Peck, "Agent's Wife Knew Blake in Berlin"; Hermiston, *Greatest,* 190; Blake, *NOC,* 175; Knightley, "Confessions of a Traitor," part I.

334 *In the late 1950s:* SV int, Paul Mott; Shackley int by David Murphy, Corr S–W, Box 1, BSP; Shackley with Finney, *Spymaster,* 29.

335 *Blake also continued:* "Hinweise zum sowjetische Kundschafter im britischen Geheimdienst, George BLAKE," Dec. 3, 1976, MfS-ZAIG 25776, Stasi; Maddrell, *Spying on Science,* 147; "Masterspy of Moscow," Carey; Tom Parfitt and Justin

Huggler, "Revealed: Grim Fate of the MI6 Agents Betrayed by George Blake," *Telegraph*, March 14, 2015.

336   *Even while insisting:* Blake, *NOC*, 208.

336   *Blake arrived in London:* BLH, 16; "George Blake," memo from Allen Dulles to John F. Kennedy, May 4, 1961, Folder United Kingdom: Security, 1961: May–September, President's Office Files, Presidential Papers, Papers of John F. Kennedy (hereafter "George Blake" from Dulles to Kennedy, JFK); Blake lecture to Stasi workers, 1976, MfS Sekr. Neiber 81, Stasi.

336   *The Blakes, now a family:* GBD, V, 2a; GAB, tape 2; Blake, *NOC*, 183–86.

337   *Blake was more diligent:* Blake int, "The Confession"; Hermiston, *Greatest,* 205–7; Blake lecture to Stasi workers, 1976, MfS Sekr. Neiber 81, Stasi, 119.

337   *By now, Blake:* Blake, *NOC*, 187; Knightley, "Confessions of a Traitor," part II.

337   *Riding high:* Stockton, *Flawed,* 94, 111, 317; David C. Martin, "The American James Bond," *Playboy,* Apr. 1980; SV int, Murphy.

338   *Harvey was cocky:* Stockton, *Flawed,* 311; Bamford, *Body of Secrets,* 477.

338   *Harvey used CIA:* "Shipment of firearms by William K. Harvey from Berlin," Harvey memo to Inspector General, Aug. 15, 1960, Box 2, BSP.

338   *Harvey would be leaving:* Stockton, *Flawed,* 105–7; CG Harvey int with Murphy, BSP.

339   *All day:* Sara Harvey account, Sally papers file, Box 2, BSP.

339   *Life in Berlin:* "U.S. Couple Goes to Berlin Party, Comes Home with Baby Girl," AP, Aug. 23, 1958.

339   *Police soon identified:* "Security/Personnel Identity A," Memo from Chief of Base, Berlin, Sept. 30, 1958, and Sara Harvey account, Sally file, Box 2, BSP; "Ich schämte mich so sehr," *Bild,* Nov. 27, 1958; Stockton, *Flawed,* 105.

340   *The adoption of the child:* SV int, Montgomery; Sally Josephine Harvey birth certificate and newspaper clippings, Sally file, Box 2, BSP; Stockton, *Flawed,* 107–8.

341   *Pyotr Popov arrived:* BGB, 279; "The Popov Case," Sept. 22, 1980, CIA-HRP; Hood, *Mole,* 22.

342   *The letter, still smelling:* "The Popov Case," CIA-HRP; Ashley, *CIA SpyMaster,* 135–36; BGB, 280; "Berlin dispatch Sept. 18, 1959, attachment K, Russian text cylindrical letter," CIA-HRP.

342   *Harvey also took the news:* Stockton, *Flawed,* 50; Stockton notes from John Barron conversation, June 2003, Harvey Corr A-C, Box 1, BSP.

342   *Though some at the CIA:* Mangold, *Cold Warrior,* 252; BGB, 280; Ashley, *CIA SpyMaster,* 136.

342   *The KGB soon ended:* BGB, 281, 348; Gordievsky, "No Laughing Boy," *Times Literary Supplement,* Nov. 14, 1997.

Chapter 22: Sniper

344   *The letters were:* Bagley, *Spy Wars,* 48; Rositzke, *The KGB: The Eyes of Russia,* 242. Although some accounts date Sniper's contact to 1959, his first contact was in April 1958 (CIA Chief Historian David Robarge email to author, Dec. 1, 2016).

344   *The identity of Sniper:* BGB, 343; Shackley with Finney, *Spymaster,* 27; Martin, *Wilderness,* 95.

344   *Sniper was clearly:* SV int, Donnelly.

344   *The CIA pressed:* Rositzke, *The KGB: The Eyes of Russia,* 242; Andrew, *Defend the Realm,* 488.

345   *Roman traveled to London:* Wright, *Spycatcher,* 128; SV int, Donnelly; Bower, *Perfect,* 257.

345   *The investigation into:* Bower, *Perfect,* 259; Pincher, *Their Trade Is Treachery,* 147; "Background on the Blake Case," n.d., PREM 13/952 NAUK; Wright, *Spycatcher,* 129.

346   *To his immense relief:* BLH, 16; GBD, V, 3; Blake, *NOC,* 189–90; GAB, tape 2.

346   *The Middle East Centre:* GAB, tape 2; Hermiston, *Greatest,* 216–17; Miles Copeland, "If Blake Had Been in Baghdad," *Times* (London), Sept. 11, 1990.

347   *Blake, highly regarded:* Anthony Cave Brown, *Treason in the Blood* (Boston: Houghton Mifflin, 1994), 500–1; Macintyre, *A Spy Among Friends,* ch. 12.

347   *Soon after his arrival:* Blake, *NOC,* 190–91; Hermiston, *Greatest,* 217.

347   *The KGB had been:* BLH, 16; GAB, tape 1.

347   *He made clear:* Hermiston, *Greatest,* 216; "Masterspy of Moscow," Carey.

348   *It was an annual:* Knightley, "Confessions of a Traitor," part I; Hermiston, *Greatest,* 212; Blake, *NOC,* 195–96.

349   *Sniper had been given:* BGB, 343; "Activities of 4 and 5 January 1961 and BOB," Feb. 15, 1961, CIA-HRP; Cable from Berlin, Jan. 4, 1961, CIA-HRP.

350   *Sniper fumbled through:* Cable from Berlin, Jan. 4, 1961, CIA-HRP; *BGB,* 346; Murphy int, LHC, 31.

350   *Goleniewski and the woman:* Mary Ellen Reese, *General Reinhard Gehlen: The CIA Connection* (Fairfax, VA: George Mason University Press, 1990), 157.

350   *The debriefings:* Bagley, *Spy Wars,* 49; Operational account of the Goleniewski case, CIA-HRP, 32; "Goleniewski's Work with the Soviets," Jan. 4, 1964, CIA-HRP; SV int, Foertsch; Murphy int, LHC, 41; Pincher, *Their Trade Is Treachery,* 148; Pincher, *Too Secret Too Long,* 258.

351   *Goleniewski's defection forced:* Rositzke, *The KGB: The Eyes of Russia,* 242; Wright, *Spycatcher,* 129, 135; Andrew, *Defend the Realm,* 485; Wise, *Molehunt,* 24.

352   *Who was LAMBDA 1?:* SV int, Donnelly.

352   *Dick White had grown:* Bower, *Perfect,* 259, 262.

352   *Shergold was "very thoughtful":* SV int, Foertsch; John le Carré, afterword in Macintyre, *A Spy Among Friends.*

352   *Working with the Soviet:* Hermiston, *Greatest,* 214, 221; Bower, *Perfect,* 259; "George Blake" Dulles to Kennedy, JFK; "Background on the Blake Case," n.d., PREM 13/952, NAUK.

352   *In Berlin, meanwhile:* "Ein Showman A La James Bond," *Spiegel,* no. 45, 1966, 154; Hermiston, *Greatest,* 213–14.

353   *For Shergold, the Eitner:* Bower, *Perfect,* 259, 263; Hermiston, *Greatest,* 221.

353   *Reviewing Blake's:* Bower, *Perfect,* 259, 262.

353   *But there was no:* Ibid., 263–64.

353   *In late March:* Ibid., 264; Blake, *NOC,* 191–92.

353   *Spring in Shemlan:* GBD, V, 4; Blake, *NOC,* 191.

354   *"This case is not":* "Masterspy of Moscow," Carey.

354   *By an odd series:* Blake, *NOC,* 191; Macintyre, *A Spy Among Friends,* ch. 16.

355   *Blake had a valid visa:* Blake, *NOC,* 192–93; "The Confession."

355   *On Friday, Blake went:* Pincher, *Their Trade Is Treachery,* 149; Blake, *NOC,* 193–94.

356   *Blake did not:* GAB, tape 2; Gillian Blake, "Portrait of a Spy," part III; "Masterspy of Moscow," Carey.

356   *His flight was on:* GBD, V, 4; Blake, *NOC,* 194.

356   *Shortly after 10 a.m.:* Blake, *NOC,* 194; O'Connor, *Blake, Bourke and the End of Empires,* 147; Bower, *Perfect,* 264; "Masterspy of Moscow," Carey.

357   *Dick White was determined:* Bower, *Perfect,* 264; Schecter and Deriabin, *The Spy Who Saved the World,* 35–36; Blake, *NOC,* 194.

357   *There was some:* Blake, *NOC,* 195–96.

358   *His optimism waned:* Blake, *NOC,* 196–97; Pincher, *Their Trade Is Treachery,* 149; Bower, *Perfect,* 265.

358   *The session ended:* Knightley, "Confessions of a Traitor," part II; Blake int, "The Confession"; Blake, *NOC,* 197.

358   *On the third day:* "George Blake," Dulles to Kennedy, JFK.
359   *After lunch, Shergold:* Knightley, "Confessions of a Traitor," part II; Blake, *NOC*, 198.
359   *"After another half hour":* Bower, *Perfect*, 265–66; Blake, *NOC*, 199.
360   *White telephoned:* Bower, *Perfect*, 266.
360   *On Friday evening:* Blake, *NOC*, 199–200; Blake int, "The Confession."
361   *Back at Broadway:* Bower, *Perfect*, 266–68.
361   *Prime Minister Harold Macmillan:* Beschloss, *Mayday*, 173–74.
361   *Like his predecessor:* Grant, *Jeremy Hutchinson's Case Histories*, 55; Knightley, "Confessions of a Traitor," part II; Bower, *Perfect*, 258, 267.
362   *Macmillan preferred:* Bower, *Perfect*, 294.
362   *White argued that:* Bower, *Perfect*, 267.
362   *Quite apart:* Catterall, *Macmillan Diaries*, vol. 2, xxi, 338.
362   *But Macmillan was determined:* "Mr. Macmillan Due in Washington Today," *Times* (London), Apr. 4, 1961; Andrew, *Defend the Realm*, 490; Henry Brandon, "Kennedy Tells Premier: Link Up with 'The Six,'" *Times* (London), Apr. 9, 1961; Catterall, *Macmillan Diaries*, vol. 2, 372.
362   *Even as Blake poured out:* "New Soviet Move on Berlin Foreseen," *Times* (London), Apr. 7, 1961; W. H. Lawrence, "Leaders Discuss Amity as They Sail Past Historic Reminders of Wars Between the U.S. and Britain," *NYT*, Apr. 7, 1961.
363   *Now, to his great irritation:* Andrew, *Defend the Realm*, 944, n32; Hermiston, *Greatest*, 253; Bower, *Perfect*, 267; Knightley, "Confessions of a Traitor," part II.
363   *The weekend at Shergy's:* Hermiston, *Greatest*, 231; Knightley, "Confessions of a Traitor," part II; Bower, *Perfect*, 267.
364   *While the group:* Blake, *NOC*, 200; Hermiston, *Greatest*, 232.
364   *The CIA station in London:* Schecter and Deriabin, *Spy Who Saved*, 44; Stafford, *Spies*, 177; Hermiston, *Greatest*, 236.

Chapter 23: The Worst That Can Be Envisaged

365   *Gillian Blake had:* GAB, tape 2; Gillian Blake, "Portrait of a Spy," part I; GBD, V, 4.
367   *The next day:* GAB, tape 2.
367   *Early on Wednesday:* Hermiston, *Greatest*, 233; Gillian Blake, "Portrait of a Spy," part III.
367   *Blake's questioning was:* "Reporting of Names of Agents to Russia," addendum to BLH.
367   *Dick White delivered:* "George Blake," Dulles to Kennedy, JFK.
368   *The CIA was livid:* Bower, *Perfect*, 269.
368   *As soon as they heard:* Operation REGAL, NSA, 21; Frank Rowlett oral history, NSA-OH-1976-(1–10), 374, NSA.
368   *Among the officers:* Montgomery int, "Spies Beneath Berlin," Discovery; Murphy int, LHC, 32.
368   *It immediately raised:* Operation REGAL, NSA, 22; "George Blake," Dulles to Kennedy, JFK; Shackley int with Murphy, Corr S-W, Box 2, BSP.
369   *There were also concerns:* Schecter and Deriabin, *Spy Who Saved*, ch. 1–2; Ashley, *CIA SpyMaster*, 151.
369   *Blake's arrest raised:* Schecter and Deriabin, *Spy Who Saved*, 44–45.
370   *Dick White was also:* "George Blake," Dulles to Kennedy, JFK.
370   *White sent the SIS:* Andrew, *Defend the Realm*, 489.
370   *The botched operation:* Martin, *Wilderness*, 117; Grose, *Gentleman*, 529, 533.
371   *The KGB was no less shocked:* Malyavin int, "The Confession"; Bagley, *Spymaster*, ch. 6; Kondrashev int, LHC, 29.
371   *In his shabby prison cell:* Blake, *NOC*, 203; Blake int, "The Confession"; Blake lecture to Stasi workers, 1976, MfS Sekr. Neiber 81, Stasi, 120.

372 *Blake was being represented:* Grant, *Jeremy Hutchinson's,* 389; Hermiston, *Greatest,* 236; Blake, *NOC,* 201.

372 *The urbane and charismatic:* Jane Fryer, "Confessions of the Real Rumpole," *Daily Mail,* June 18, 2015; "Jeremy Hutchinson: A Biographical Sketch," in Grant, *Jeremy Hutchinson's,* 14–52.

373 *At their first meeting:* Grant, *Jeremy Hutchinson's,* 64; BLH, 1, 16.

373 *Hutchinson found Blake's:* SV int, Hutchinson.

373 *Nonetheless, it was clear:* "Brief for the defendant," file 12, George Blake Papers, IWM.

373 *There was not much:* SV int, Hutchinson; Pincher, *Their Trade Is Treachery,* 151; Blake, *NOC,* 201.

374 *The government had decided:* Hermiston, *Greatest,* 235; "Ex-British Aide Held on Security Charge," *NYT,* Apr. 19, 1961.

374 *The maximum sentence:* Blake trial transcript, IWM; Bower, *Perfect,* 268.

374 *A third hearing:* Hermiston, *Greatest,* 237.

375 *Several days before:* Grant, *Jeremy Hutchinson's,* 67; Hermiston, *Greatest,* 241.

375 *Predictably, the extraordinary:* Pincher, *Their Trade Is Treachery,* 261; Hermiston, *Greatest,* 234–37; Seth S. King, "Security Inquiry in Britain Set in Wake of Spy Cases," *NYT,* May 12, 1961.

376 *While the D-Notice:* Pincher, *Too Secret Too Long,* 261; Wise and Ross, *The Espionage Establishment,* 108.

376 *Gillian Blake:* Blake, *NOC,* 202; GAB, tape II.

376 *Before leaving Brixton:* Blake int, Red Files; Blake, *NOC,* 202.

377 *On the morning:* Grant, *Jeremy Hutchinson's,* 65; Hermiston, *Greatest,* xviii; Blake, *NOC,* 203.

377 *Shortly before Hutchinson:* Grant, *Jeremy Hutchinson's,* 69; Hermiston, *Greatest,* 241–43.

378 *Hutchinson viewed:* SV int, Hutchinson.

378 *Court 1:* Grant, *Jeremy Hutchinson's,* 65; Cookridge, *George Blake: Double Agent,* 185.

378 *Blake felt oddly:* Blake, *NOC,* 202; Hermiston, *Greatest,* 243; "I Was a Spy for Moscow," *Evening Standard,* May 3, 1961.

379 *Manningham-Buller rose:* Blake trial transcript, IWM, 2; Blake, *NOC,* 203.

379 *The attorney general then asked:* Blake trial transcript, IWM, 3; Seth S. King, "Briton Sentenced as Spy for Soviet," *NYT,* May 4, 1961; Cookridge, *George Blake: Double Agent,* 188.

379 *In fact, Hutchinson:* SV int, Hutchinson.

380 *Hutchinson then laid out:* Blake trial transcript, IWM.

380 *Hutchinson finished speaking:* Blake trial transcript, IWM; Grant, *Jeremy Hutchinson's,* 73; Blake, *NOC,* 203.

381 *Parker imposed a sentence:* Blake trial transcript, IWM; Rebecca West, *The Meaning of Treason* (1949; London: Phoenix Press, 1982), 338; "Spy Gets 42 Years," *Evening News,* May 3, 1961; Blake, *NOC,* 204; Blake int, "The Confession."

381 *Hutchinson and Cox saw:* Grant, *Jeremy Hutchinson's,* 75; SV int, Hutchinson; Blake, *NOC,* 205.

381 *Blake also suspected:* Blake, *NOC,* 207.

382 *Blake's trial caused:* Catterall, *Macmillan Diaries,* vol. 2, 380; Grant, *Jeremy Hutchinson's,* 76; "No Irreparable Damage by Spy, Says Premier," *Telegraph,* May 5, 1961; Hermiston, *Greatest,* 254.

382 *There was more indignation:* "British Spy Net Jeopardised," *Telegraph,* May 8, 1961; Anthony Mann, "Blake's Berlin Life Revealed," *Telegraph,* May 14, 1961; "Blake: Spion," *Bild,* May 15, 1961.

382 *In Washington:* "Spy Had No U.S. Data," AP, in *NYT,* May 6, 1961; Catterall, *Macmillan Diaries,* vol. 2, 380.

383 *As was the case:* Malyavin int, "The Confession"; Kondrashev int, LHC, 20.

383 *The new Soviet spy:* Schecter and Deriabin, *Spy Who Saved,* 161.

383 *At the urging*: Cox letter to Blake, May 6, 1961, file 3, George Blake Papers, IWM.

384 *Hutchinson suspected:* SV int, Hutchinson; Grant, *Jeremy Hutchinson's,* 79; Kennedy, "The Spy Who Came in for Rough Justice," *Times* (London), Feb. 1, 2016.

384 *With the baby:* GAB, tape 2; Gillian Blake letter to Cox, May 13, 1961, file 9, George Blake Papers, IWM; Blake, *NOC,* 217.

385 *Jeremy Hutchinson's heart:* Grant, *Jeremy Hutchinson's,* 77; Hermiston, *Greatest,* 256.

385 *The hearing on Monday:* "Blake Appeal Against 42-Yr Sentence Fails," *Telegraph,* June 20, 1961.

385 *Blake, he noted:* "Law Report, June 19," *Times* (London), June 20, 1961; Grant, *Jeremy Hutchinson's,* 75–77; Home Office to Claude, Hornby & Cox, June 2, 1961, file 12, George Blake Papers, IWM.

Chapter 24: Our James Bond

387 *George Blake fell:* Randle and Pottle, *The Blake Escape,* 25; Blake int, Red Files; Blake, *NOC,* 211.

387 *Wormwood Scrubs, the dingy:* Metropolitan Police Report, Mar. 4, 1967, George Blake file, MEPO, 201736, *NAUK.*

387 *The KGB scoped:* Kondrashev int, LHC, 20.

388 *He was housed:* Blake, *NOC,* 206, 213; Randle and Pottle, *Blake Escape,* 57.

388 *Oddly enough, Blake's:* Blake, *NOC,* 213; Blake int, Red Files; "Prison Security: Escape of George Blake," Home Office Report, HO 391/12, NAUK.

389 *Around midnight, East German:* BGB, 375; *A City Torn Apart,* 18, 22.

389 *In Hyannis Port:* Wyden, *Wall,* 26.

389 *Whether or not a tunnel:* Memorandum for the DDI, "The Berlin Situation," OFL, 537; *A City Torn Apart,* 24; SV int, Bill Lonam.

389 *The CIA was not the only:* Wolf with McElvoy, *Man Without a Face,* 113; BGB, 376–77.

390 *Walter Ulbricht, the driving force:* *A City Torn Apart,* 23; Hope Harrison, "Ulbricht and the Concrete Rose," CWIHP, May 1993, 61; OFL, 533; Garthoff, *Journey Through the Cold War,* 127.

390 *The wall also spelled:* BGB, 385–87, 396; SV int, Montgomery.

390 *The Noack family:* SV int, Feick; Feick int, *"Ist ja fantastisch!,"* 76.

391 *Since his arrival:* Blake, *NOC,* 212, 216–18; Metropolitan Police Report, Nov. 11, 1966, HO 278/7, NAUK; Randle and Pottle, *Blake Escape,* 23–25; Blake int, Red Files.

392 *He was also pleased:* Prisoner statements, Metropolitan Police Report, Mar. 4, 1967, MEPO 201736, NAUK; Metropolitan Police Report, Nov. 11, 1966, HO 278/7, NAUK.

392 *Blake made full use:* "Blake, the Spy, Reads Law in Gaol," *Telegraph,* Sept. 9, 1962; Blake, *NOC,* 221.

392 *Blake's home in cell 8:* Hermiston, *Greatest,* 262; Cookridge, *George Blake: Double Agent,* 211–12; Randle and Pottle, *Blake Escape,* 48; Blake, *NOC,* 218, 220–21; O'Connor, *Blake, Bourke and the End of Empires,* 168; Zeno, *Life,* 145, 161.

393 *He was also quite obliging:* "Note for the Record," Nov. 14, 1966, PREM 13/952, NAUK; "John Quine," *Telegraph,* June 12, 2013; Hermiston, *Greatest,* 262; West, *Seven Spies,* 142.

393 *Janet Chisholm:* Victor Cherkashin and Gregory Feifer, *Spy Handler: Memoir of a KGB Officer* (New York: Basic Books, 2005), 57–60; Schecter and Deriabin, *Spy Who Saved,* 409–11.

394 *SIS had chosen:* Knightley, "The KGB vs. the CIA: The Secret Struggle," Red Files; Pincher, *Their Trade Is Treachery,* 154; Wright, *Spycatcher,* 209.

394 *Still, SIS needed:* Schecter and Deriabin, *Spy Who Saved,* 179, 185, 410; "Janet Chisholm," *Telegraph,* Aug. 6, 2004.

395 *Musical Appreciation was:* Blake, *NOC,* 223; Randle and Pottle, *Blake Escape,* 1; Grant, *Jeremy Hutchinson's,* 256; Hermiston, *Greatest,* 268; "Patrick Pottle," *Telegraph,* Oct. 4, 2000.

396 *They both felt an immediate:* SV int, Randle; Randle and Pottle, *Blake Escape,* 10, 43–44.

396 *Sitting in the back:* Randle and Pottle, *Blake Escape,* 27–29, 33.

397 *The idea went nowhere:* Randle and Pottle, *Blake Escape,* 33, 51; Blake, *NOC,* 223.

397 *Bill Harvey had become:* Stockton, *Flawed,* 121; Helms with Hood, *Look,* 196; Martin, *Wilderness,* 121, 127.

398 *Harvey had already been assigned:* Martin, *Wilderness,* 121; Stockton, *Flawed,* 143, 151, 163–64.

398 *This included serving:* "Roselli, Johnny," memo from CIA Director of Security Howard Osborn to Helms, Dec. 9, 1970, in Roselli, John file, Box 2, BSP; Stockton, *Flawed,* 168–69; Rudy Maxa, "The Calculated Rise and Abrupt Descent of Johnny Roselli," *WP,* Sept. 12, 1976. His name is variously spelled Roselli and Rosselli.

399 *Harvey puckishly named:* Stockton, *Flawed,* 122, 125.

399 *At the senior levels:* Helms with Hood, *Look,* 137–38; SV int, Garthoff; "Berlin Tunnel," *CSH,* 207–8, in *OFL,* 395–96; Frank Rowlett oral history, NSA-OH-1976-(1–10), 374, NSA.

400 *The Kennedys were intrigued:* Martin, *Wilderness,* 136.

400 *When Edward Lansdale:* Gary Hart letter to Stockton, Apr. 16, 2001, Harvey-JFK assas., Box 2, BSP; Stockton, *Flawed,* 120; Martin, *Wilderness,* 129; Martin, "The CIA's Loaded Gun," *WP,* October 10, 1976.

400 *At the heart of the problem:* Helms with Hood, *Look,* 224; Martin, *Wilderness,* 131, 136; CG Harvey int with Murphy, BSP.

401 *During a visit:* Powers, *The Man Who Kept the Secrets,* 141–42; Dobbs, *One Minute to Midnight,* 151; Stockton, *Flawed,* 137.

401 *Bobby Kennedy, for his part:* Martin, *Wilderness,* 134–36.

401 *It did not help:* Stockton, *Flawed,* 128; Powers, *The Man Who Kept the Secrets,* 137.

401 *Despite it all:* Helms with Hood, *Look,* 224.

402 *Around October 21:* Stockton, *Flawed,* 139–40, 235; Martin, *Wilderness,* 144; Shackley with Finney, *Spymaster,* 68.

403 *His health and his career:* SV int, Montgomery; Stockton, *Flawed,* 238–41, 311.

403 *On October 22, 1962:* Cherkashin and Feifer, *Spy Handler,* 61.

403 *By later assessments:* CIA *Analysis of the Warsaw Pact Forces,* 21–22; Schecter and Deriabin, *Spy Who Saved,* 334–35.

404 *Penkovsky's arrest:* Dobbs, *One Minute,* 57; Schecter and Deriabin, *Spy Who Saved,* 415–16. Schecter and Deriabin suggest Penkovsky may have been arrested before October 22.

Chapter 25: Mischief, Thou Art Afoot

405 *By 1965, George Blake:* Blake, *NOC,* 222.

405 *Blake's early confidence:* Martin, *Wilderness,* 180; Catterall, *Macmillan Diaries,* vol. 2, 534.

405 *His feeling of hopelessness:* Grant, *Jeremy Hutchinson's,* 81; SV int, Braibant; GAB, tape 2; Knightley, "Confessions of a Traitor," part II; Blake, *NOC,* 254; Hermis-

ton, *Greatest*, 273; O'Connor, *Blake, Bourke and the End of Empires*, 254; Zeno, *Life*, 165–67.

406 *Blake had not given up:* Blake, *NOC*, 224–25.

406 *Bourke had been born:* Hermiston, *Greatest*, 271; O'Connor, *Blake, Bourke and the End of Empires*, 165; Bourke int, *World in Action*, October 1968, transcript in George Blake file, MEPO 21736, NAUK.

407 *With his natural:* Bourke, *Springing*, 8; Bourke int, *World in Action*.

407 *By the late summer of 1965:* Blake, *NOC*, 224; Bourke int, *World in Action;* Bourke, *Springing*, 10.

408 *Bourke and Blake immediately:* Bourke, *Springing*, 11; Hermiston, *Greatest*, 277.

408 *In late November 1965:* Bourke, *Springing*, 17, 25–27, 40–42, 61.

408 *Blake and Bourke calculated:* Bourke, *Springing*, 42, 62, 65; Randle and Pottle, *Blake Escape*, 54, 62.

409 *Pottle and Randle on board:* Bourke, *Springing*, 49, 54; Metropolitan Police Report, Mar. 4, 1966, MEPO 201736, NAUK; Blake, *NOC*, 225–26.

410 *A test of the radios:* Bourke, *Springing*, 59; Blake, *NOC*, 226.

410 *Blake and Bourke spoke:* Blake, *NOC*, 228; Randle and Pottle, *Blake Escape*, 64; Blake lecture to Stasi workers, 1976, MfS Sekr. Neiber 81, Stasi, 123.

411 *Blake also feared:* Randle and Pottle, *Blake Escape*, 60–61; "Report to Chief Superintendent," Nov. 11, 1956, Police reports, escape of George Blake file, HO 278/7, NAUK; "Prison Security: Escape of George Blake," Home Office Report, HO 391/12, NAUK; Hermiston, *Greatest*, 265; Randle and Pottle, *Blake Escape*, 61.

411 *By July, Randle had raised:* Randle and Pottle, *Blake Escape*, 60, 74–75.

412 *Bourke, who upon:* Randle and Pottle, *Blake Escape*, 60; Blake, *NOC*, 227; Bourke, *Springing*, 99–101; "Police Five," Oct. 23, 1966, transcript in 3/10/B MEPO 2/10736, NAUK.

412 *In early August:* Blake, *NOC*, 228–29; Bourke, *Springing*, 149; Randle and Pottle, *Blake Escape*, 67–69.

413 *Bourke planned to make:* Randle and Pottle, *Blake Escape*, 67–68; Bourke, *Springing*, 108.

413 *After Bourke consulted:* Blake, *NOC*, 228; Bourke, *Springing*, 141–43.

414 *Blake and Bourke spoke:* Blake, *NOC*, 229; Bourke, *Springing*, 143–46; Randle and Pottle, *Blake Escape*, 82.

415 *On Thursday, October 20:* O'Connor, *Blake, Bourke and the End of Empires*, 255; Metropolitan Police Report, Nov. 11, HO 278/7, NAUK.

415 *At 1 p.m., Blake:* Blake, *NOC*, 229; Metropolitan Police Report, Mar. 4, 1966, MEPO 201736, NAUK; Pincher, *Inside Story*, 96.

415 *Only a handful:* Metropolitan Police Report, Nov. 11, 1966, HO 278/7, NAUK; "Kenneth de Courcy," *Telegraph*, Feb. 18, 1999; Hermiston, *Greatest*, 283; de Courcy int, "The Confession."

416 *Bourke was also:* Bourke, *Springing*, 159, 162.

416 *Back in his cell:* Blake, *NOC*, 229–30; Bourke, *Springing*, 162; Metropolitan Police Report, Mar. 4, 1966, MEPO 201736, NAUK.

417 *Shielded from the officers':* Blake, *NOC*, 230–31; Bourke, *Springing*, 166–67.

418 *Blake, still standing:* Blake, *NOC*, 231, Bourke, *Springing*, 167–70.

418 *In the dim light:* Blake, *NOC*, 231–32; Bourke, *Springing*, 170–72.

419 *Rain was beating:* Bourke, *Springing*, 172–73; Blake, *NOC*, 232.

420 *Officer Fletcher had rung:* Metropolitan Police Report, Mar. 4, 1966, MEPO 201736, NAUK.

421 *The Hawk reached:* Bourke, *Springing*, 174; Blake, *NOC*, 233; Blake int, "The Confession."

421   *A photograph of Blake:* Bourke, *Springing,* 178; Bourke int, *World in Action.* Techni-
       cally, Blake was not a double agent but rather an SIS officer and a KGB agent.

Chapter 26: A Free Man Again

423   *It began as a murmur:* Zeno, *Life,* 163–65.

424   *The prime minister:* "Note to Prime Minister," October 22, 1966, and "Note for the
       Record," Nov. 14, 1966, PREM 13/952, NAUK.

424   *An enormous hunt:* Metropolitan Police Report, Mar. 4, 1966, MEPO 201736,
       NAUK; Hermiston, *Greatest,* 292.

425   *Bill Harvey was back:* Stockton, *Flawed,* 241, 295; Martin, *Wilderness,* 188.

425   *Dick Helms, now director:* Bower, *Perfect,* 355.

425   *By Sunday morning:* Metropolitan Police Report, Mar. 4, 1966, MEPO 201736,
       NAUK; Hermiston, *Greatest,* 296; Zeno, *Life,* 168.

426   *George Blake and Sean:* Bourke, *Springing,* 183; Randle and Pottle, *Blake Escape,*
       100–1, 105.

427   *After the doctor's departure:* Randle and Pottle, *Blake Escape,* 104, 107; SV int, Randle.

427   *Randle and Pottle did have:* Randle and Pottle, *Blake Escape,* 76, 107; Blake, *NOC,*
       238, 244; SV int, Randle.

427   *Another matter was:* Randle and Pottle, *Blake Escape,* 106; Blake, *NOC,* 325.

428   *The group took:* Randle and Pottle, *Blake Escape,* 108–9; BBC, "On This Day, 22
       October 1966: Double-Agent Breaks Out of Jail," http://news.bbc.co.uk/onthis
       day/hi/dates/stories/october/22/newsid_3135000/3135206.stm.

428   *Gillian Blake issued:* "Police Seek Source of Knitting Needles as Blake Trail Grows
       Cold," *Financial Times,* Oct. 26, 1966.

428   *Blake's barrister, Jeremy:* SV int, Hutchinson.

428   *On Tuesday evening:* Randle and Pottle, *Blake Escape,* 114–15.

429   *Finding Blake a safe:* Randle and Pottle, *Blake Escape,* 103, 122; Blake, *NOC,* 235–37.

429   *Pottle suspected:* Randle and Pottle, *Blake Escape,* 81, 119.

429   *On Friday, October 28:* Randle and Pottle, *Blake Escape,* 120–22; "Blake's Escape
       Plot Car Found," *Daily Mirror,* October 29, 1966.

430   *At least Randle:* Randle and Pottle, *Blake Escape,* 122–23; Will Bennett, "Priest
       Who Hid Blake Is Banned," *Telegraph,* Mar. 29, 1997; Hermiston, *Greatest,* 298.

430   *Tensions were rising:* Randle and Pottle, *Blake Escape,* 122–25.

431   *The mild-mannered:* SV int, Randle; Randle and Pottle, *Blake Escape,* 126.

431   *But that evening:* Randle and Pottle, *Blake Escape,* 127; Bourke, *Springing,* 206.

431   *Harold Wilson, facing:* Foreign Secretary's brief, "George Blake," Oct. 28, 1966,
       and "Note for the Record," Nov. 14, 1966, PREM 13/952, NAUK; Nigel West,
       The Circus: MI5 Operations, 1945–1972 (New York: Stein & Day, 1983), 156; An-
       drew, *Defend the Realm,* 538.

432   *Pat Pottle lived:* Randle and Pottle, *Blake Escape,* 129–31, 142; "Masterspy of Mos-
       cow," Carey; Blake, *NOC,* 238.

433   *In early November:* Randle and Pottle, *Blake Escape,* 143–44; Blake, *NOC,* 238;
       Bourke, *Springing,* 215.

434   *The last big debate:* Bourke, *Springing,* 214; Blake, *NOC,* 239; Randle and Pottle,
       Blake Escape, 145.

435   *The group calculated:* Randle and Pottle, *Blake Escape,* 145–47.

435   *As the van conversion:* Randle and Pottle, *Blake Escape,* 145, 155, 158.

436   *"Our greatest source":* Bourke int, *World in Action,* October 1968, transcript in George
       Blake file, MEPO 21736, NAUK; Randle and Pottle, *Blake Escape,* 161–62.

436   *By December 9:* Randle and Pottle, *Blake Escape,* 164.

437   *At 6:30 p.m.:* Bourke, *Springing,* 216; Randle and Pottle, *Blake Escape,* 169; Blake,
       NOC, 241.

437 *Randle pulled over:* Randle and Pottle, *Blake Escape,* 171–72, 175; Blake, *NOC,* 242–43.

439 *Reaching Brussels:* Randle and Pottle, *Blake Escape,* 176–77.

439 *By 8:30 p.m.:* Blake, *NOC,* 243; Randle and Pottle, *Blake Escape,* 178–80.

440 *The Randles felt:* Randle and Pottle, *Blake Escape,* 180–81; Blake, *NOC,* 243; SV int, Randle.

440 *Before long, Blake recognized:* Blake lecture to Stasi workers, 1976, MfS Sekr. Neiber 81, Stasi, 40; Randle and Pottle, *Blake Escape,* 183; Blake, *NOC,* 244.

441 *Since he lacked:* Bourke, *Springing,* 250; Bagley, *Spymaster,* ch. 6; O'Connor, *Blake, Bourke and the End of Empires,* 203.

442 *Kondrashev rushed:* Bagley, *Spymaster,* ch. 6; Blake, *NOC,* 245–46; Kondrashev int, LHC, 21; Hermiston, *Greatest,* 314; Blake int, "The Confession."

442 *After about a week:* Bourke, *Springing,* 251, 255; Hermiston, *Greatest,* 314–15.

Epilogue

443 *In February 2012:* SV int, Sobolewski; author visit to site, Aug. 2015; Claus Dieter Steyer, "Spionagetunnel im Wald entdeckt," *Tagesspiegel,* Aug. 16, 2012.

443 *After further calls:* SV int, Kostka, Sobolewski, Bossdorf; Helmut Trotnow, preface, and Stafford, "The Berlin Spy Tunnel," *"Ist ja fantastisch!,"* 16, 44.

444 *Sobolewski told Kostka:* SV int, Kostka and Sobolewski. One of the tunnel sections discovered in eastern Germany was placed on display in 2019 at the International Spy Museum in Washington, DC.

445 *The U.S. government:* Trotnow, *"Ist ja fantastisch!,"* 15; Ian McEwan, *The Innocent* (1989; New York: Anchor, 1999), 260–61; Heun and Schier, "Tunnel-Spione"; Stafford, *Spies,* 184.

445 *After the Massante family:* Kellerhoff and Von Kostka, *Haupstadt der Spione,* 88–89; author visit to Rudow, 2015.

446 *The floodgates of derision:* "Soviet Introduces Its Spy in Izvestia," *NYT,* February 15, 1970; "Wovon man in den CIA-Stäben nichts wußte," *ND,* Apr. 23, 1971; "Spy for Soviet Says He Betrayed Tunnel," UPI, in *NYT,* Feb. 17, 1970. In 1966, following Blake's escape, the German newsmagazine *Spiegel* may have been the first to report that Blake had betrayed the tunnel: "Ein Showman A La James Bond," *Spiegel,* Oct. 31, 1966.

446 *The tunnel, the noted:* Pincher, *Their Trade Is Treachery,* 150; Knightley, "Confessions of a Traitor," part I; Evans, "Berlin Tunnel Intelligence," 48; Wise, *Molehunt,* 25; Stafford, *Spies,* 178; BGB, 207.

446 *A few authors were:* Martin, *Wilderness,* 89; Montgomery letter to Stockton, Apr. 6, 2006, Corr M-O, Box 1, BSP.

447 *Bill Harvey, once:* "An Interview with Former CIA Executive Director Lawrence K. 'Red' White," *CSI Intelligencer,* Winter 1999–2000; Stockton, *Flawed,* 258.

447 *Harvey fell back:* Stockton, *Flawed,* 264, 268; CG Harvey letter to Stockton, Apr. 10, 1983, Berlin file, Box 1, BSP; David Kahlenberg letter to Stockton, Feb. 2, 2001, Corr H-L, Box 1, BSP.

448 *Indeed, the past:* Stockton, *Flawed,* 268.

448 *The committee heard:* Gary Hart letter to Stockton, Apr. 16, 2001, Harvey-JFK assas., Box 2, BSP; Martin, *Wilderness,* 220; David Talbot, *The Devil's Chessboard: Allen Dulles, the CIA, and the Rise of America's Secret Government* (New York: Harper-Collins, 2015), 508; Jack Anderson and Les Whitten, "Smudge Only Clue in Roselli Case," *WP,* Aug. 27, 1976.

448 *In later years:* Jefferson Morley, "Bill Harvey, Armed and Dangerous," July 1, 2017, www.jfkfacts.org/bill-harvey-armed-and-dangerous, David Talbot, "Inside the Plot to Kill JFK," *Salon,* Nov. 22, 2015, www.salon.com/2015/11/22/inside

_the_plot_to_kill_jfk_the_secret_story_of_the_cia_and_what_really_happened_
in_dallas/?source=newsletter; Montgomery letter to Stockton, June 19, 2001,
Corr M-O, Box 1, BSP; Stockton, *Flawed,* 225.

449   *Charlie Bray may:* Bray speech to Lions, Corr A-C, Box 1, BSP.

449   *On June 8, 1976:* "William K. Harvey, Law Editor for Bobbs-Merrill Co., Dies,"
Indianapolis Star, June 10, 1976; CG Harvey letter to Stockton, Berlin file, Box 1,
BSP. CG died at age eighty-six in 2000. "Clara Grace Harvey, 86, Had Distin-
guished CIA, Army Career," *Indianapolis Star,* Oct. 3, 2000.

449   *"Bill was simply":* Montgomery letter to CG and Sally Harvey, June 13, 1976, Harvey death file, Box 2, BSP; Bray letter to Stockton, June 19, 2001, Corr A-C, Box
1, BSP; Stockton, *Flawed,* appendix, 320; CIA press release, Sept. 10, 1997.

450   *By contrast, Frank:* Operation REGAL, NSA, 2; Bamford, *Body of Secrets,* 526;
"Frank Rowlett," *Cryptologic Almanac,* 50th Anniversary Series, Center for Cryptologic History, Aug. 2002.

450   *The tunnel he had helped:* Johnson, *American Cryptology,* 106; *Operation REGAL,*
NSA, 25.

450   *Peter Lunn, the Berlin:* Ruck, "Thinker, Author, Skier, Spy"; Rufina Philby,
Mikhail Lyubimov, and Hayden Peake, *The Private Life of Kim Philby: The Moscow
Years* (New York: Fromm International, 2000), 136; Macintyre, *A Spy Among
Friends,* ch. 18; Tom Carver, "Diary: Philby in Beirut," *London Review of Books,*
Oct. 11, 2012; Andrew and Mitrokhin, *The Sword and the Shield,* 632–33, n17;
Gordon Corea, "Kim Philby, British Double Agent, Reveals All in Secret Video,"
Apr. 4, 2016, BBC News; Bower, *Perfect,* 304.

451   *Lunn stayed a loyal:* CG Harvey with Murphy, BSP; "Peter Lunn," *Telegraph,*
Dec. 6, 2011.

451   *Keith Comstock, one:* SV int, Comstock; Comstock letter to children, courtesy
Comstock.

452   *For Eugene Kregg:* SV int, Kovalenko (Kregg); Kovalenko letter to Stafford,
Nov. 19, 2005; Helgestad letters, Sept. 8, 1967, courtesy Kovalenko.

452   *When BOB was deactivated:* BGB, 397.

452   *For a time, Russia's:* William Drozdiak, "Rival Spies Relive Thrills of Cold War,"
WP, Oct. 21, 1997; SV int, Murphy; Stafford, *Spies,* 179.

453   *Kondrashev worked:* Bagley, *Spymaster,* preface, ch. 11.

453   *East German spy chief:* Markus Wolf and Tennent H. Bagley, "Battleground Berlin," *Los Angeles Times,* Oct. 12, 1997.

454   *The common wisdom:* SV int, Montgomery.

454   *"Philby had second":* SV int, Kalugin.

454   *Still, after his arrival:* Blake, *NOC,* 262, 284; Blake int, Red Files.

454   *Khrushchev, the last of:* Harrison, *Driving,* 60.

454   *As in prison:* Blake, *NOC,* 249, 259.

455   *Blake stayed at first:* Kondrashev int, LHC, 21; Blake, *NOC,* 260; Hermiston,
Greatest, 316.

455   *Blake spent his days:* Bourke, *Springing,* 256; West, *Seven Spies,* 152; Blake, *NOC,* 254.

455   *Sean Bourke's time:* Bourke, *Springing,* 229–33; Bourke int, *World in Action,* Oct.
1968, transcript in George Blake file, MEPO 21736, NAUK; O'Connor, *Blake,
Bourke and the End of Empires,* 212; Blake, *NOC,* 246.

456   *It was not long:* Bourke, *Springing,* 256, 277–78; SV int, Randle; Randle and Pottle,
Blake Escape, 217.

457   *After Bourke had:* Bourke, *Springing,* 269–71, 282.

457   *On September 4:* Bourke, *Springing,* 283–85, 293, 307.

457   *In the fall of 1968:* Bourke, *Springing,* 364; Hyde, *George Blake: Superspy,* 170.

457   *After multiple requests:* Randle and Pottle, *Blake Escape,* 214.

458 *Indeed, based on:* West, *Seven Spies,* 150; Hermiston, *Greatest,* 335; SV int, Randle.

458 *The Randles, Pottle:* Bourke, *Springing,* 196; Randle and Pottle, *Blake Escape,* 215, 223.

458 *Bourke lived large:* Hyde, *George Blake: Superspy,* 172; O'Connor, *Blake, Bourke and the End of Empires,* 305–6. Kalugin wrote that in 1973, when he was named head of foreign counterintelligence, he learned that Aleksandr Sakharovsky, chief of intelligence, feared that Bourke would reveal to British intelligence how he and Blake were smuggled into the USSR and divulge Blake's whereabouts, making him vulnerable to assassination. Before Bourke was allowed to leave, according to Kalugin, Sakharovsky ordered that he be given a drug that would mimic a stroke and cause brain damage, and Bourke returned to England in a debilitated state (Kalugin, *Spymaster,* 275–76). However, Michael Randle, who visited Bourke in Ireland, saw no evidence that Bourke was in a debilitated mental state. "He was no different from when we'd known him—as devil-may-care as ever," Randle said. "I wouldn't give any credence to that" (SV int Randle).

459 *"It was a sad end":* Blake, *NOC,* 248; O'Connor, *Blake, Bourke and the End of Empires,* 328.

459 *For Blake, life:* Hermiston, *Greatest,* 324; Blake, *NOC,* 260.

459 *The KGB had given:* Kondrashev int, LHC, 21; O'Connor, *Blake, Bourke and the End of Empires,* 326–29.

459 *Blake's residences:* SV int, Kalugin.

459 *Blake had been given:* Kondrashev int, LHC, 12; Knightley, "Confessions of a Traitor," part II; Blake, *NOC,* 281.

460 *Contrary to SIS assurances:* James Risen, "Rem Krassilnikov, Russian Bane of C.I.A., Dies at 76," *NYT,* Mar. 24, 2003; Kalugin, *Spymaster,* 160.

460 *Blake found translation:* Blake, *NOC,* 271–72; Cecil, "How I Became a Lunchtime Spy for Moscow"; O'Connor, *Blake, Bourke and the End of Empires,* 257.

460 *Indeed, his relations:* Kalugin, *Spymaster,* 160; Blake, *NOC,* 264; Bower, *Perfect,* 384; Knightley, "Confessions of a Traitor," part I; Blake int, Red Files; Hermiston, *Greatest,* 325.

461 *Blake's friendship with Philby:* Blake, *NOC,* 264–65, 270; Hermiston, *Greatest,* 326.

461 *After years of pleas:* Blake letter to Erich Mielke, Dec. 15, 1981, MfS SdM 879, Stasi, 113; Blake lecture to Stasi workers, 1976, MfS Sekr. Neiber 81, Stasi; Blake poster, MfS—HA PS 10304, Stasi; Wolf with McElvoy, *Man Without a Face,* 100–1.

462 *In the midst:* Blake, *NOC,* 284; John-Thor Dahlburg, "A British Turncoat Superspy Would Still Rather Be Red," *Los Angeles Times,* Jan. 16, 1992. The British government launched a court case that succeeded after ten years in blocking Blake from being paid further royalties for his book, though he had already received £60,000. But the case took so long that the European Court of Human Rights in 2006 ordered the government to pay Blake £5,000 in damages.

462 *In his book:* Blake, *NOC,* 208; Kalugin int, "Spies," episode 21 of *Cold War,* CNN documentary series; Kalugin, *Spymaster,* 160.

462 *Yet Kondrashev:* Kondrashev int, LHC, 16; Simon Kuper, "A Very Cosmopolitan Spy," *Financial Times,* Mar. 20, 2015.

462 *At first, with:* "Masterspy of Moscow," Carey.

463 *Eventually, Blake recognized:* SV int, Braibant; Thornton and Thomas, "Revealed: The Map of Blake's Betrayal"; Blake int, "George Blake, agent double"; Wolf with McElvoy, *Man Without a Face,* 102.

463 *On June 25:* Hermiston, *Greatest,* 332.

463 *The matter had been:* Randle and Pottle, *Blake Escape,* 225, 240; Hermiston, *Greatest,* 336.

463 *In preparation for:* SV int, Randle; Richard Savill, "Champagne Reunion in Moscow with Soviet Spy George Blake," *Telegraph,* June 26, 1991; Blake, *NOC,* 280.

464   *Randle and Pottle, who:* John Steele, "Jury Clears Pair Who Helped Blake Escape," *Telegraph,* June 27, 1991; Grant, *Jeremy Hutchinson's,* 84; SV int, Hutchinson; Hermiston, *Greatest,* 339.

464   *At age ninety-six:* Author visit, Kratovo; SV int, Braibant.

465   *By Blake's account:* Blake, *NOC,* 286.

465   *By the late 1990s:* O'Connor, *Blake, Bourke and the End of Empires,* 335; Blake, *NOC,* 278; SV int, Braibant; "Masterspy of Moscow," Carey.

465   *In addition to:* Cecil, "How I Became a Lunchtime Spy for Moscow"; Andrew Osborn, "British Double Agent George Blake Predicts End of 'American Empire,'" *Telegraph,* Nov. 11, 2010.

466   *Blake's ninetieth birthday:* SV int, Braibant; Ellen Barry, "Double Agent, Turning 90, Says, 'I Am a Happy Person,'" *NYT,* Nov. 12, 2012; Robert Mendick and Tom Parfitt, "Double Agent George Blake Celebrates 90th Birthday," *Telegraph,* Nov. 10, 2012.

466   *Blake downplayed:* SV int, Braibant; "Masterspy of Moscow," Carey.

466   *Looking back:* Knightley, "Confessions of a Traitor," part I; Blake, *NOC,* 108; Blake int, "The Confession." The words are from Romans 9:21.

467   *In describing his espionage:* "Double Agent George Blake Celebrates 90th Birthday," BBC News, Nov. 12, 2012.

467   *When he speaks:* "Reporting of Names of Agents to Russia," addendum to BLH.

467   *"All the conversations":* Blake int, "George Blake, agent double"; SV int, Blake; O'Connor, *Blake, Bourke and the End of Empires,* 152.

468   *"Probably they thought":* SV int, Blake.

468   *The old Noack farm:* Author visit to site with Feick; Feick int, *"Ist ja fantastisch!,"* 76.

468   *She walked up:* SV int, Feick.

Index